ADVANCES IN PSYCHOLOGICAL SCIENCE: SOCIAL, PERSONAL, AND CULTURAL ASPECTS

RÉCENTS DÉVELOPPEMENTS EN PSYCHOLOGIE SCIENTIFIQUE: ASPECTS SOCIAUX, PERSONNELS ET CULTURELS

Advances in Psychological Science
Récents développements en psychologie scientifique

Volume 1

Social, Personal, and Cultural Aspects
Aspects sociaux, personnels et culturels

Congress Proceedings / Actes du Congrès
XXVI International Congress of Psychology
XXVI Congrès international de psychologie

Montréal, 1996

Edited by / Sous la direction de:

John G. Adair
David Bélanger
Kenneth L. Dion

Psychology Press Ltd., Publishers
27 Church Road
Hove
East Sussex, BN3 2FA
UK

British Library Cataloguing in Publication Data

A catalogue record for this book is available from the British Library

ISBN 0–86377–470–9

Typeset by Graphicraft Typesetters Ltd., Hong Kong
Printed and bound in the UK by TJ International Ltd.

Contents

List of contributors   ix

XXVI International Congress of Psychology/XXVI Congrès international de psychologie   xi

Introduction   xiii
John G. Adair, David Bélanger, and Kenneth L. Dion

1. **The psychology of individual differences: The personality puzzle**   1
    Kurt Pawlik

PART ONE: Personality and social psychology   31

2. **Individual differences in temperament: An international perspective**   33
    Jan Strelau

3. **Personal and collective efficacy in human adaptation and change**   51
    Albert Bandura

4. **Intergroup relations: A field with a short history but a long future**   73
    Rupert Brown

5. **Discovering general laws of social motivation**   93
    Bernard Weiner

6. **Contemporary trends in hypnosis research**   111
    Peter W. Sheehan

7. Social psychology across cultures: Two ways forward   137
    Michael Harris Bond

8. An evolutionary-based model integrating research on the characteristics of sexually coercive men   151
    Neil M. Malamuth

9. Attitudes and the processing of attitude-relevant information   185
    Alice H. Eagly

PART TWO: Cross-cultural psychology/national development   203

10. Cadres théoriques en psychologie interculturelle   205
    Pierre R. Dasen

11. Cultural diversity and psychological invariance: Methodological and theoretical dilemmas of (cross-)cultural psychology   229
    Ype H. Poortinga

12. Permanence and modification in national identities   247
    José Miguel Salazar and Miguel A. Salazar

13. China's reform and challenges for psychology   271
    Qicheng Jing and Houcan Zhang

PART THREE: Work and organizational psychology   293

14. Psychology of work and organizations: Scientific inquiry and professional care   295
    P. J. D. Drenth

15. Basic issues in occupational stress research   307
    Anna B. Leonova

16. Work culture in a developing country: The case of India   333
    Jai B. P. Sinha

PART FOUR: Research methods/statistics   351

17. Causal modeling: New interfaces and new statistics   353
    Peter M. Bentler

18. Meta-analysis: Concepts, corollaries and controversies   371
    Robert Rosenthal

PART FIVE: Health psychology   385

19.   Quality of life: Concept and assessment   387
Rocío Fernández-Ballesteros

20.   Alcohol and intentions to engage in risky health-related behaviors: Experimental evidence for a causal relationship   407
Tara K. MacDonald, Mark P. Zanna, and Geoffrey T. Fong

21.   Experimental approaches to the anxiety and mood disorders   429
Susan Mineka and Richard Zinbarg

22.   Sexual and reproductive health education in Latin America: What next?   455
Susan Pick

PART SIX: Social development   473

23.   Human development: Cross-cultural perspectives   475
Çiğdem Kağıtçıbaşı

24.   The person in developmental research   495
David Magnusson

25.   Current perspectives on social and emotional development   513
Carolyn Zahn-Waxler and Angela McBride

Author index   547

Subject index   573

List of contributors

Albert Bandura, Department of Psychology, Stanford University, Building 420, Jordan Hall, Stanford, CA 94305, USA

Peter M. Bentler, Department of Psychology, University of California, Los Angeles, CA 90024-1563, USA

Michael Harris Bond, Department of Psychology, The Chinese University of Hong Kong, Shatin, NT, China

Rupert Brown, Institute of Social and Applied Psychology, University of Kent, Canterbury, Kent CT2 7LZ, England

Pierre R. Dasen, Faculté de Psychologie et des Sciences de l'Éducation, Université de Genève, 9rte de Drize, CH-1227, Carouge, Suisse

P. J. D. Drenth, Vrije Universiteit, De Boelelaan 1081, HV Amsterdam, The Netherlands

Alice H. Eagly, Department of Psychology, Northwestern University, Swift Hall, 2029 Sheridan Road, Evanston, IL 60208-2710, USA

Rocío Fernández-Ballesteros, Facultdad de Psicología, Universidad Autónoma de Madrid, 28049 Madrid, Spain

Geoffrey T. Fong, Department of Psychology, University of Waterloo, Waterloo, Ontario, Canada N2L 3G1

Qicheng Jing, Institute of Psychology, Chinese Academy of Sciences, PO Box 1603, Beijing 10012, China

Çiğdem Kağıtçıbası, Department of Psychology, Koc University, Cayir Cad. 5, 80886 Istanbul, Turkey

Anna B. Leonova, Department of Work and Engineering Psychology, Faculty of Psychology, Moscow State Lomonosov-University, Mokhovaja Str. 8/5, 103009 Moscow, Russia

Tara K. MacDonald, Department of Psychology, University of Lethbridge, 4401 University Drive, Alberta, Canada T1K 3M4

David Magnusson, Department of Psychology, Stockholm University, S-10691, Stockholm, Sweden

Neil M. Malamuth, Departments of Communication Studies and Psychology, 334 Kinsey Hall, University of California, Los Angeles, CA 90095-1538, USA

Angela McBride, National Institute of Mental Health, Bethesda, Maryland, MD 20892, USA

Susan Mineka, Department of Psychology, Northwestern University, Evanston, IL 60208-0001, USA

Kurt Pawlik, Psychologisches Institut 1, University of Hamburg, Von-Melle-Park 11, D-20146 Hamburg, Germany

Susan Pick, Universidad Nacional Autónoma de México and Instituto Mexicano de Investigación de Familia y Población (IMIFAP), Apartado #41-595, Mexico City, DF 11001, Mexico

Ype H. Poortinga, Department of Psychology, Tilburg University, PO Box 90153, 5000 LE Tilburg, The Netherlands, and University of Leuven, Belgium

Robert Rosenthal, Department of Psychology, Wm. James Hall, Harvard University, 33 Kirkland Street, Cambridge, MA 02138, USA

José Miguel Salazar, Departamento de Psicologia, Universidad Central de Venezuela, Apartado 47018, Caracas 1041-A, Venezuela

Miguel A. Salazar, Harvard University, Cambridge, Massachusetts, USA

Peter W. Sheehan, The University of Queensland, St. Lucia, Brisbane, Queensland, Australia

Jai B. P. Sinha, ASSERT Institute of Management Studies, 143/D, S.K. Puri, Patna 800 001, India

Jan Strelau, Faculty of Psychology, University of Warsaw, Stawki 5-7, D00183 Warsaw, Poland

Bernard Weiner, Department of Psychology, University of California, 405 S. Hilgard Avenue, Los Angeles, CA 90024, USA

Carolyn Zahn-Waxler, National Institute of Mental Health, Bethesda, Maryland, MD 20892, USA

Mark P. Zanna, Department of Psychology, University of Waterloo, Waterloo, Ontario, Canada N2L 3G1

Houcan Zhang, Department of Psychology, Beijing Normal University, Beijing 100875, China

Richard Zinbarg, Department of Psychology, University of Oregon, Eugene, OR, USA

XXVI International Congress of Psychology

XXVI Congrès international de psychologie

Montréal, Canada

August 16–21 août 1996

Under the joint sponsorship of/
Sous le parrainage conjoint de:

Canadian Psychological Association
Société canadienne de psychologie

National Research Council Canada
Conseil national de recherches Canada

Under the auspices of / Sous les auspices de

International Union of Psychological Science (IUPsyS)
l'Union internationale de psychologie scientifique (UIPsyS)

President / Président
David Bélanger

Congress Council/Conseil du Congrès

David Bélanger (President), John G. Adair (Scientific Program Committee), Sylvie Fafard, Alain Brissette (Montreal Convention Center), Laurier Forget (Congress Director), Terrence P. Hogan (Finance Committee), Pierre Lamoureux (Congress Manager), Pierre L.-J. Ritchie (Secretary-Treasurer), Mark J. Rosenzweig (IUPsyS Liaison), Michel E. Sabourin (Organizing Committee), John Service (CPA Liaison).

Scientific Program Committee/Comité du programme scientifique

John G. Adair (Chair), John W. Berry, Fergus I. M. Craik, Kenneth L. Dion, Michèle Robert, Gordon Winocur.

Organizing Committee/Comité organisateur

Michel E. Sabourin (Chair), Hélène Cauffopé, Marcelle Cossette-Ricard, François Doré, Jacques Forget, Andrée Fortin, Robert Haccoun, Jacques Lajoie, Luc Lamarche, Jean-Roch Laurence, Jean-Claude Lauzon, Paul Maurice, Stéphane Sabourin, Donald Taylor.

Scientific Advisory Council/Conseil consultatif scientifique

E. W. Ames, K. S. Bowers, A. S. Bregman, M. P. Bryden, C. A. Cameron, J. K. Chadwick-Jones, R. Cloutier, J. B. Conway, K. D. Craig, T. Gouin-Décarie, V. Di Lollo, K. K. Dion, A. R. Dobbs, P. C. Dodwell, V. I. Douglas, L. Dubé, N. S. Endler, R. C. Gardner, M. A. Goodale, J. Grusec, D. N. Jackson, L. Jacoby, D. Kimura, B. E. Kolb, J. De Koninck, W. E. Lambert, F. Lepore, R. S. Lockhart, J. A. McNulty, D. H. Meichenbaum, R. Melzack, P. M. Merikle, B. A. Milner, D. R. Olson, A. U. Paivio, A. Pinard, C. Porac, S. W. Pyke, B. Rusak, S. Shettleworth, L. S. Siegel, J. Stewart, F. Strayer, P. Suedfeld, R. C. Tees, E. Tulving, V. Vikis-Freibergs, T. MacBeth

IUPsyS Executive Committee—1992–1996—Comité exécutif de l'UIPsyS

Kurt Pawlik (President), Mark R. Rosenzweig (Past-President), Qicheng Jing (Vice-President), Lars-Göran Nilsson (Vice-President), Géry d'Ydewalle (Secretary-General), J. Bruce Overmier (Deputy Secretary-General), Michel E. Sabourin (Treasurer), Fouad A.-L.H. Abou-Hatab, Rubén Ardila, Derek Blackman, Michel Denis, Rochel Gelman, Terrence P. Hogan, Hiroshi Imada, Cigdem Kağitçibaşi, Durganand Sinha, Jan Strelau.

Introduction

Under the auspices of the International Union of Psychological Science (IUPsyS) and the joint sponsorship of the National Research Council Canada and the Canadian Psychological Association, the XXVI International Congress of Psychology was held in Montréal, Canada, during the third week of August, 1996. Persons from more than 80 countries attended this session of Psychology's quadrennial international scientific congress, composed of 4200 delegates and students, with another 600 individuals being distinguished guests, accompanying persons, and representatives of the large number (50) of exhibitors. Participants came from all regions of the world including some that have not always been present at the Congress.

Montréal displayed all of the charm for which it is renowned as the second largest French-speaking city in the world and one of North America's most cosmopolitan venues. The colorful Opening Ceremony presented a spectacular display of circus arts in a musical context for which the province of Québec has become famous. Officially opened by the Canadian Minister for International Cooperation, the Honorable Pierre Pettigrew, and the Québec Minister of State for the Métropole de Montréal, the Honorable Serge Ménard, the opening session was also addressed by Madame Francine Fournier, Deputy Director General, Social and Human Sciences, UNESCO.

Altogether more than 400 scientific program items arranged in 24 concurrent sessions for the duration of the Congress provided participants the latest research developments in psychology from around the world. Highlighting the program of invited speakers were 15 Keynote Addresses, 45 State-of-the-Art lectures, and the IUPsyS Presidential address. Covering a range of topics balanced across the entire discipline, 140 invited symposia and 49 submitted, integrated paper sessions contributed to the core of the scientific program. Individually submitted papers arranged into 116 thematic oral sessions and four days of more than 1,700 interactive posters provided an opportunity for individual psychologists from around the world to present and discuss their work with other colleagues.

Following the practice initiated at the 1992 Congress in Brussels, the Congress proceedings volumes present the contributions of the invited speakers. The balanced content of the scientific program has enabled us to arrange these in two equal-sized volumes. Volume 1 covers contributions to the social, personal, and cultural aspects of psychological science. Volume 2 comprises the biological and cognitive aspects of the discipline.

Each volume is divided into sections reflecting the topical foci of the Congress. Featured as Chapter 1 in the first volume is the address of Kurt Pawlik, the President of the International Union of Psychological Science, entitled "The psychology of individual differences: The personality puzzle". There are other impressive chapters on personality and indivdual differences (Jan Strelau on temperament, Neil Malamuth on sexually coercive males, and Albert Bandura on personal efficacy in human adaptation). Chapters chronicling research advances in social psychology range from social motivation (Bernard Weiner) and attitudes (Alice Eagly) to intergroup relations (Rupert Brown). The role of culture in social psychology (Michael Bond) and a review of current developments in hypnosis research (Peter Sheehan) further expanded the range of personal/ social research presented within the Congress.

Undoubtedly due to Canada's multicultural heritage and increasing recognition of its importance in psychology, culture was strongly represented in the Congress program. Chapters on social psychology across cultures (Bond) and national identity (José Miguel Salazar and Miguel A. Salazar) reflect the strong linkage between cross-cultural and social psychology. Chapters focusing on theory (Pierre Dasen) and psychological invariance across cultures (Ype Poortinga) contribute core cross-cultural analyses to the volume. The role of psychology in China's reform (Qicheng Jing and Houcan Zhang) and in understanding work culture in India (Jai Sinha) illustrate the discipline's potential for contributing to national development.

The linkage between basic research and applications was highlighted in a number of contributions within organizational and health psychology. Work and organizations within the Indian culture (Sinha), their linkage with professional care (Peter Drenth), and in occupational stress research (Anna Leonova), illustrate the importance of psychological science and practice to work. The dramatic developments within health psychology are portrayed in chapters illustrating the application of basic research to anxiety and mood disorders (Susan Mineka and Richard Zinbarg), the measurement of the quality of life (Rocio Fernández-Ballesteros), and risky health-related behaviors (Tara Macdonald, Mark Zanna, and Geoffry Fong). Programs addressing sexual and reproductive health in Latin

America (Susan Pick) document the contribution of psychological research to improving health practices internationally.

In the section on Social Development, the full range of contributing factors is illustrated: development across cultures (Cigdem Kağıtçıbaşı), the person in developmental research (David Magnusson), and a review of contemporary research on social and emotional development (Carolyn Zahn-Waxler and Angela McBride). The section on Methods includes chapters by researchers who have developed statistical techniques applied primarily to social, personal, and cultural research, including recent developments and controversies in meta-analysis (Robert Rosenthal) and causal modeling (Peter Bentler).

Although two invited speakers, Paul Baltes and Paul Costa could not, for different reasons, submit chapters to this volume, their contributions to the success of the Congress should be acknowledged. Considering the prominence of all of the contributors, the quality of their chapters, and the range of coverage of the topics, the editors feel that this volume and its companion volume are aptly entitled *Advances in Psychological Science*.

The editors would like to acknowledge several persons and institutions who provided assistance and support in the preparation of this volume. The project was greatly accelerated by the organizational efficiency and editorial skills of Sophia Macrodimitris and by translations by Chantal Arpin, both of whom assisted the senior editor. In addition, we wish to express our appreciation to the Departments of Psychology in our respective universities, the University of Manitoba, Université de Montréal, and the University of Toronto, for the resources and support they provided. We especially want to thank all of the contributing authors, who were so cooperative and prompt in responding to our requests.

The Editors:
John G. Adair
David Bélanger
Kenneth L. Dion

Introduction

Le XXVIe Congrès international de psychologie s'est déroulé à Montréal, au Canada, au cours de la troisième semaine du mois d'août 1996. Cet événement était placé sous les auspices de l'Union internationale de psychologie scientifique (l'UIPsyS) et sous le patronage conjoint du Conseil national de recherches Canada et de la Société canadienne de psychologie. Des participants venus de plus de 80 pays ont assisté à cette session quadriennale qui rassemblait 4200 délégués et étudiants, ainsi que 600 autres personnes, soit des invités d'honneur, des personnes accompagnant les congressistes et des représentants d'un nombre considérable (50) d'exposants. Toutes les parties du monde étaient représentées, y compris certaines n'ayant pas toujours figurer à un tel événement.

Montréal, la deuxième plus grande ville francophone au monde et l'un des sites les plus cosmopolites en Amérique du Nord, a su déployer tout le charme qu'on lui connaît pour accueillir ces invités. Une cérémonie d'ouverture toute en couleur fut marquée d'un spectaculaire assortiment de numéros de cirque artistique avec musique, numéros ayant fait la célébrité du Québec. L'Honorable Pierre Pettigrew, Ministre canadien responsable de la coopération internationale, et l'Honorable Serge Ménard, Ministre d'état québécois pour la métropole montréalaise, ont procédé à l'ouverture officielle du Congrès. Madame Francine Fournier, Directrice générale adjointe (Sciences sociales et humaines) de l'Unesco, a également pris la parole.

Plus de 400 présentations scientifiques, regroupées à l'intérieur de 24 séances simultanées pendant tout le Congrès, ont renseigné les participants sur les progrès les plus récents de la recherche en psychologie à travers le monde. Venaient en tête de ce programme d'éminents chercheurs invités qui ont présenté 15 grandes conférences et 45 exposés-synthèses, ainsi que la conférence présidentielle de l'UIPsyS. Couvrant une variété équilibrée de thèmes, 140 symposiums organisés sur invitation et 49 séances de communications orales intégrées dans des ensembles cohérents formaient le noyau du programme. Des communications individuelles furent présentées oralement au sein de 116 séances thématiques et, durant quatre journées, plus de 1,700 communications affichées donnèrent l'occasion à autant de psychologues provenant de toutes les parties du monde d'exposer leurs travaux à d'autres collègues et d'en discuter avec eux.

Suivant l'initiative lancée par les organisateurs du Congrès de Bruxelles en 1992, les volumes des Actes du Congrès présentent les contributions des conférenciers invités. Le caractère équilibré du contenu du programme scientifique a permis de regrouper ces conférences en deux volumes d'égale ampleur. Le premier inclut les contributions aux aspects sociaux, personnels et culturels de la psychologie et le second, les contributions à ses aspects biologiques et cognitifs.

Chaque volume est divisé en parties reflétant les principaux thèmes abordés durant le Congrès. Le premier chapitre de ce premier volume est consacré à l'allocution intitulée « The psychology of individual differences: The personality puzzle », faite par Kurt Pawlik, le président de l'Union internationale de psychologie scientifique. Suivent d'autres chapitres marquants qui concernent la personnalité et les différences individuelles: Jan Strelau y traite du tempérament, Neil Malamuth de la coercition sexuelle pratiquée par certains hommes et Albert Bandura de l'efficacité personnelle dans l'adaptation humaine. Les chapitres qui retracent les progrès de la recherche en psychologie sociale touchent des thèmes diversifiés, allant de la motivation sociale (Bernard Weiner) et des attitudes (Alice Eagly) aux relations entre groupes (Rupert Brown). Un bilan du rôle de la culture en psychologie sociale (Michael Bond) et des percées récentes dans la recherche sur l'hypnose (Peter Sheehan) a étendu davantage l'éventail des travaux portant sur la personnalité et la psychologie sociale qui ont été présentés à ce Congrès.

Sans doute à cause du patrimoine multiculturel du Canada et de l'appréciation grandissante de son importance en psychologie, la culture s'est vue attribuée une grande place dans le programme. Les chapitres sur la psychologie sociale d'une culture à l'autre (Bond) et sur l'identité nationale (José Miguel Salazar et Miguel A. Salazar) reflètent la force des liens qui rattachent psychologie interculturelle et psychologie sociale. Centrés sur la théorie (Pierre Dasen) et l'invariance psychologique entre cultures (Ype Poortinga), les chapitres suivants ajoutent au contenu de ce volume des analyses interculturelles centrales. Le rôle de la psychologie dans la réforme en cours en Chine (Qicheng Jing et Houcan Zhang) et dans la compréhension de la culture des forces du travail en Indes (Jay Sinha) démontre le potentiel de notre discipline à l'egard du développement national.

Le lien entre la recherche fondamentale et ses applications a été mis en lumière par plusieurs interventions en psychologie des organisations et en psychologie de la santé. Le travail et les entreprises au sein de la culture indienne (Sinha), de même que le rapport entre de telles instances et la prestation de soins professionnels (Peter Drenth) et la recherche sur le stress occupationnel (Anna Leonova) témoignent de l'importance de la science psychologique et de sa pratique dans le domaine du travail. Les progrès dramatiques constatés en psychologie de la santé se trouvent reflétés dans les chapitres qui décrivent l'application de la recherche fondamentale aux problèmes relatifs à l'anxiété et aux troubles de l'humeur (Susan Mineka et Richard Zinbarg), à la mesure de la qualité de vie (Rocio Fernandez-Ballesteros) et aux comportements dangereux quant à la santé (Tara Macdonald, Mark Zanna et Geoffry Fong). Les programmes qui portent sur la santé dans les domaines de la sexualité et de la reproduction en Amérique latine (Susan Pick) attestent de la contribution de la recherche psychologique à l'amélioration des conduites touchant à la santé sur le plan international.

La partie sur le développement social illustre toute la gamme des facteurs qui y participent, qu'il s'agisse du développement d'une culture à l'autre (Cigdem Kagitcibasi), de la place de la personne dans la recherche sur le développement (David Magnusson) ou du développement social et affectif (Carolyn Zahn-Waxler et Angela McBride). La partie intitulée « Méthodes » comprend des chapitres rédigés par des chercheurs qui ont créé des techniques statistiques s'appliquant surtout dans les domaines culturel et social et celui de la personnalité, y compris ceux rendant compte des progrès et des débats récents qui se rapportent à la méta-analyse (Robert Rosenthal) et à la modelisation causale (Peter Bentler).

Deux conférenciers (Paul Baltes et Paul Costa) n'ont pu, pour diverses raisons, produire de chapitre à insérer dans ce volume; nous tenons cependant à leur exprimer notre profonde reconnaissance pour leur contribution au succès de ce Congrès. Etant donné l'éminente compétence de tous les collaborateurs, ainsi que la qualité de leur contribution et l'envergure des questions abordées, nous avons choisi de donner à ces deux volumes le titre approprié de *Récents développements en psychologie scientifique*.

En terminant, nous voulons souligner que la préparation de ce volume a bénéficié de la collaboration de plusieurs personnes et institutions. La réalisation de ce projet a été grandement facilitée par la compétence de Sophia Macrodimitris sur le plan de l'organisation et de la rédaction, et par celle de Chantal Arpin sur le plan de la traduction, ces deux personnes ayant assisté le rédacteur principal de ce volume. De plus, nous tenons à exprimer notre appréciation la plus profonde aux départements de Psychologie de nos universités respectives, l'Université du Manitoba, l'Université de Montréal et l'Université de Toronto, pour les ressources mises à notre disposition et l'appui accordé. En particulier, nous remercions tous les auteurs de ce volume pour leur collaboration soutenue et la promptitude avec laquelle ils ont répondu à nos demandes.

Les rédacteurs:
John G. Adair
David Bélanger
Kenneth L. Dion

CHAPTER ONE

The psychology of individual differences: The personality puzzle

Kurt Pawlik
University of Hamburg, Germany

In the first part, research on individual differences is reviewed with respect to data sources and principal research paradigms (cross-sectional paradigm; criterion-referenced paradigm; nature-nurture paradigm; longitudinal paradigm studying personality as a process; trans-occasion paradigm for the study of consistency). Past consistency research is shown to be widely questionnaire-based and often to employ unrepresentative quasi-orthogonal person-situation designs of data collection. In the second part, a novel computer-based methodology of ambulatory (in-field) assessment of behavior, performance testing, and monitoring of setting characteristics is introduced, which has been developed at the author's laboratory to study consistency under everyday-life conditions and situational variations. Evidence is reviewed on within-occasion and cross-occasion reliability of ambulatory assessments and on consistency across time, settings, and situations. On the basis of these results, a coherence research paradigm of personality study is developed and illustrated from research on mood-alertness coherence. In the concluding section, the nature and utility of trait concepts is discussed for studying individual differences.

Dans la première partie de cette étude, la recherche sur les différences individuelles est passée en revue en fonction des sources de données et des principaux paradigmes de recherche (le paradigme intersectionnel; le paradigme de référence à un critère; le paradigme nature-environnement; le paradigme longitudinal qui étudie la personnalité comme un processus; le paradigme transversal pour l'étude de la cohérence). On démontre que la recherche antérieure sur la cohérence s'appuie largement sur des questionnaires et qu'elle utilise souvent des modèles quasi-orthogonaux, mais non représentatifs, de la personne et de la situation pour la collecte des données. Dans la seconde partie, on présente une méthodologie innovatrice basée sur l'usage de l'ordinateur permettant l'évaluation ambulatoire («in-field») du comportement, le testing de la performance et la surveillance des caractéristiques du milieu; cette méthodologie a été conçue dans le laboratoire de l'auteur afin d'étudier la cohérence dans les conditions de la vie quotidienne et en fonction des variations situationnelles. On examine les données empiriques sur la fidélité des évaluations ambulatoires à l'intérieur d'une même occasion ou d'une occasion à l'autre et leur cohérence à travers le temps, les milieux et les situations. Sur la base de ces résultats, un paradigme de cohérence de la recherche sur l'étude de la personnalité est mis au point et illustré par la recherche sur la cohérence humeur- activation. En conclusion, on discute de la nature et l'utilité des concepts de trait pour l'étude des différences individuelles.

A basic, most striking quality of any form of life—biological, mental or behavioral—is its immense phenomenal diversity, both across and within species. Let me introduce the topic of my address with a quotation from a pioneer of modern psychological science, William James (1907, p. 3):

> I know that you, ladies and gentlemen, have a philosophy, each and all of you, and that the most interesting and important thing about you is the way in which it determines the perspective in your several worlds.

Indeed, individual differences in human behavior, attitude and temperament have been a lasting concern to the reflective human mind, ever since the ancient classics (as in Aristotle's Eudemian ethics; cf. Robinson, 1989), through the high-time of Western philosophy (e.g. in Kant's pragmatic anthropology; Kant, 1798), and up to present-day research on individual psychological differences. In my Presidential Address I shall take you on a focused *tour d'horizon* of the field, highlight basic research paradigms and insights they have provided, and introduce you to recent research innovations, largely from our own work, in the study of individual differences outside the laboratory, in everyday life. For this "guided tour" to differential psychology I have chosen a motto from an author most of us will have cherished since childhood days: Sir Arthur Conan Doyle, whose reminder:

> It is a capital mistake to theorize before one has data. Insensibly one begins to twist facts to suit theories, instead of theories to suit facts (Doyle, 1986, p. 212)

sounds good advice for science and detective stories alike!

Like other fields of psychology, research on individual differences can also celebrate its first centennial: Exactly 100 years ago, in 1896, Binet and Henri published in Volume 2 of *Année Psychologique* their seminal paper entitled "Psychologie individuelle" (Binet & Henri, 1896; see Fig. 1.1), introducing "mental tests" as a key method of "individual psychology". This was ten years after James McKeen Cattell's (1886) classical paper on "Psychometric Investigations", three years after his important article (Cattell, 1893) "Attention and Reaction" (in Volumes 3 and 8, respectively, of Wundt's *Philosophische Studien*), and four years before William Stern was to publish his founding text *On the Psychology of Individual Differences* ("*Über die Psychologie der individuellen Differenzen*": Stern, 1900). Its second edition, entitled *Differential Psychology in its Methodological Foundations* (*Die Differentielle Psychologie in ihren*

TABLE DES MATIÈRES

PREMIÈRE PARTIE

MÉMOIRES DES COLLABORATEURS

Th. Ribot. Les caractères anormaux et morbides.   1
Forel. Un aperçu de psychologie comparée   18
Flournoy. Temps de lecture et d'omission.   45
Bourdon. Sur les phénomènes intellectuels.   54
Gley. Note sur les conditions favorisant l'hypnose   70
Biervliet. Les illusions de poids.   79

TRAVAUX DU LABORATOIRE DE PSYCHOLOGIE
PHYSIOLOGIQUE DE PARIS

Binet et Courtier. La circulation capillaire dans ses rapports
  avec la respiration et les phénomènes psychiques.   87
V. Henri. La localisation des sensations tactiles   168
Xilliez. La continuité des chiffres et des nombres dans la mé-
  moire immédiate   193
Binet et Courtier. Recherches graphiques sur la musique. . .   201
Binet. La peur chez les enfants.   223

REVUES GÉNÉRALES

Azoulay. Psychologie histologique.   255
V. Henri. Revue générale sur le sens du lieu de la peau . . .   295
J. Passy. Revue générale sur les sensations olfactives.   363
A. Binet et V. Henri. Psychologie individuelle   411
V. Henri. Le calcul des probabilités en psychologie.   466

FIG. 1.1   Reproduction of table of contents of Volume 2, 1896, of *Année Psychologique*, with Binet and Henri's paper on *Psychologie individuelle*.

methodischen Grundlagen: Stern, 1911), established the field as a distinct branch of psychology. I was happy to re-edit this classical text recently (Pawlik, 1994), with kind encouragement by Anne Anastasi (1994). Figure 1.2 shows the title-pages of this re-edition and of Stern's original 1911 text.

In the decades to follow, research on systematic individual differences in behavior and experience has seen new paradigms and theoretical perspectives develop, and after some backlashes (notably in the 1970s, from unrealistic demands of prediction; Mischel, 1968) personality psychology, to quote David Funder (1994), "is enjoying a remarkable resurgence characterized by a large

William Stern

Die Differentielle Psychologie

in ihren methodischen Grundlagen

Herausgegeben
von Kurt Pawlik·
Mit einem Geleitwort
von Anne Anastasi

Verlag Hans Huber
Bern · Göttingen · Toronto · Seattle
1994

Die

Differentielle Psychologie

in ihren methodischen Grundlagen.

Von

William Stern.

An Stelle einer zweiten Auflage des Buches:
Über Psychologie der individuellen Differenzen
(Ideen zu einer differentiellen Psychologie).

LEIPZIG.
Verlag von Johann Ambrosius Barth.
1911.

FIG. 1.2   Stern's original 1911 text on differential psychology and a recent re-edition by the present author.

TABLE 1.1
10 data sources and 3 data levels for
assessing individual differences

Data source	Data level		
Biographical and actuarial data	B		
Behavior trace	B		
Behavior observation	B		
Behavior rating		MR	
Expressive behavior	B	MR	
Projective test	B	MR	
Interview	(B)	MR	
Questionnaire		MR	
Objective test	B		
Psychophysiological data	P (B)		

NOTES:

    P   = Physiological
    B   = Behavioral
    MR = Mental representation

(Adapted from Pawlik, 1992)

amount of research activity in numerous advances across a broad front . . . [also] attracting investigators from other subfields" (Funder, 1994, p. 2).[1] To appreciate this development, let us first look at some central questions and paradigms of research in individual differences.

DIFFERENTIAL PSYCHOLOGY: DATA SOURCES AND RESEARCH PARADIGMS

Individual differences in experience and behavior can be studied through a variety of *assessment methods*. Table 1.1 (adapted from Pawlik, 1992) summarizes the ten most prominent *data sources* for individual difference research. They vary in the kind of data sampled and in methods of data acquisition ("data level"), which can be psychophysiological (or other biological), descriptive behavioral, or in terms of mental representations of behavior variations (as in self- and other-ratings). Failure to recognize this multi-modality has been a recurrent source of confusion in the past.

First, data sources differ in their *sensitivity* across attribute domains. For example, differences in intellectual and other aptitudes, i.e. in asymptote or

---

[1] Indeed, recent advances in research on individual differences enable us more and more to fit into place hitherto disconnected pieces of evidence in the "puzzle of personality". And to record a curious coincidence: later in the Montréal Congress and after presentation of my Address, David Funder took me by surprise when he told me of a forthcoming book of his to be entitled *The Personality Puzzle*—the phrase I had chosen before, in summer 1995, as subtitle for my Presidential Address at the 1996 International Congress of Psychology. May completion of the "puzzle" proceed successfully!

maximum behavior (Cronbach, 1970), are better assessed through objective tests, while differences in temperament or interest, i.e. in style or habitual ("typical") behavior, are better assessed through behavior observations, behavior ratings, or questionnaires (Pawlik, 1996a).

Second, as a rule, individual differences correlate higher within than between data sources. This has been known for a long time; special multitrait-multimethod (MTMM) models of analysis have been developed (Campbell & Fiske, 1959; Byrne & Goffin, 1993) to cope with problems which arise from the fact that each assessment method carries (sometimes substantial) variance *unique to that data source*. To quote a well-studied example: it has been known since the 1960s (Hundleby, Pawlik, & Cattell, 1965) that personality trait extraversion-introversion, which ranks highest to second-highest in variance in questionnaire and rating data, has its best-match counterpart in an objective personality test factor (labeled U.I.32 in Cattell's nomenclature) ranking among the lowest in test variance contribution.[2] On the other hand, objective tests outnumber questionnaire and rating data by a ratio of 10 to 100 in number of independent traits identified and replicated (Carroll, 1993).

This calls for a *multi-structure concept of personality* that takes into account the kind of data source sampled or accounted for. Personality as assessed from mental representations in self- or other-report data does not map directly into personality as studied in objective test data, and vice-versa. Different data sources tap different functions and modalities of individual differences, giving rise to different structural representations (Pawlik, 1995; 1996b) which will broaden rather than limit our study of behavioral differences. This complexity need not and should not be deplored but taken into account.

In terms of underlying heuristics, we can distinguish between *five research paradigms* of psychological research on individual differences.

Cross-sectional research paradigm

Up to and through the 1970s, most personality research still adhered exclusively to the cross-sectional paradigm set forth already by W. Stern in 1911. Each person is assessed only once, under equivalent conditions, and in the same set of variables (tests, questionnaires, behavior ratings, etc.). The resulting 2-dimensional summary table of observations (data matrix; rows referring to variables and columns referring to subjects; cf. Table 1.2) can be analyzed by rows (for so-called *nomothetic* assessment of across-persons variations within and covariations between variables) or by columns (for so-called *idiographic* assessment of one person across variables; or for comparisons between two or more persons in a set of variables, so-called *type analysis*). The resulting four designs of cross-sectional research have been explained already by Stern as

---

[2] Similarly, extraversion scores from any of the new Big-Five questionnaire instruments hardly exceed correlations of 0.30 with external behavioral criteria (Costa & Widiger, 1994).

TABLE 1.2
Cross-sectional data matrix

		Person					
		1	2	.	.	.	.
V	1						
a	2						
r	.						
i	.						
a	.						
b	.						
l	.						
e	.						

shown in Fig. 1.3, which is an original copy from p. 18 of his 1911 text. Stern suggested the terms *Variationsforschung, Korrelationsforschung, Psychographie,* and *Komparationsforschung,* in this order, for the four designs of cross-sectional study.

Surely more than 90% of all cross-sectional research on individual differences follows the first two of these four designs. Advanced multivariate statistical methods of data analysis (factor analysis, cluster analysis, and numerous derivatives thereof; see Cattell, 1966; 1978; Harman, 1960; Morrison, 1976; Pawlik, 1968; Royce, 1973; Thurstone, 1931) have been developed for this paradigm of *personality structure research,* which has produced thorough (possibly already exhaustive) knowledge of principle factors (source traits) explaining, in a statistical sense, interindividual variations and covariations in two-dimensional cross-sectional data matrices. This research is particularly indebted to the early work of Ch. Spearman (1927), C. Burt (1949), and L. L. Thurstone (1931; Thurstone & Thurstone, 1941) and, subsequently, to R. B. Cattell (1957; 1966), H. J. Eysenck (1947; 1967), J. P. Guilford (1959) and their students and co-workers. Several dozen primary factors of intelligence (aptitude, ability) and personality (temperament, motivation, interests) have been shown to meet stringent statistical criteria of cross-studies replicability (coefficients of factorial congruence of 0.80 and above; see Carroll, 1993; McCrae & Costa, 1990), giving rise to multi-factor theories of intelligence and personality as developed, for example, by Cattell, Eysenck, and Guilford in their classical texts already referenced.

More recently, and building on earlier work by Digman (1963), Goldberg (1982) and others, a growing international research community, notably under the leadership of McCrae and Costa (1990), has been working towards a cross-reference system of some five broad (second-order) personality dimensions, the so-called *Big Five.* As noted recently by Hofstee (1994), a model of five to six broad second-order (questionnaire and rating) factors of personality evident from meta-analytic studies already by the late 1960s (Pawlik, 1968) translates easily into this new Big Five structure, as summarized in Table 1.3 (from Hofstee, 1994).

Einleitung.

Wir erhalten also folgende Übersichtstabelle über die differentielle Psychologie als empirische Wissenschaft:

Objekt der Forschung   Schema   Disziplin

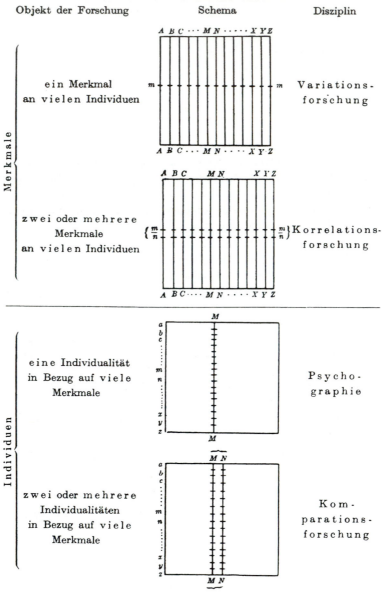

ein Merkmal an vielen Individuen — Variationsforschung

zwei oder mehrere Merkmale an vielen Individuen — Korrelationsforschung

eine Individualität in Bezug auf viele Merkmale — Psychographie

zwei oder mehrere Individualitäten in Bezug auf viele Merkmale — Komparationsforschung

FIG. 1.3 Reproduction, from Stern's original 1911 text on differential psychology, of four basic approaches to cross-sectional personality research.

TABLE 1.3
Second-order factors of personality
and the Big Five

Pawlik (1968)	Big Five
I: Extraversion	E: Extraversion
II: Emotionality	N: Neuroticism
III: Sensitivity/reactivity	O: Openness
IV: Independence of opinion	
V: Cooperativeness	A: Agreeableness
VI: Will-control and persistence	C: Conscientiousness

(after Hofstee, 1994)

Criterion-referenced paradigm

Cross-sectional trait factors, like Thurstone's primary mental abilities or the Big Five, provide a *static* description of individual differences at any one point in time, just as measurements taken from a flashlight photo of people will document on-the-spot differences in physiognomy or stature. So the "discovery" of distinct intelligence factors (of verbal comprehension, word fluency, spatial orientation, semantic flexibility etc.; see Neisser et al., 1996) may still leave us a long way from identifying genuine *process components* of problem solving[3] or personality development. This calls for yet another research approach.

A first such extension was to switch from a purely cross-sectional to a *criterion-referenced paradigm* of research, and study personality structure in different, contrasted groups (for example, adolescents vs. adults, clinical samples vs. non-clinical controls, or populations differing in ethnic or cultural background; see Diaz-Guerrero, 1995) or look into correlations between cross-sectional factors and (antecedent or subsequent) criterion variables (like type of schooling, style of parenting, success in psychotherapy, or educational achievement). A wealth of data has accumulated from this approach, too numerous to be quoted here in detail. Examples would include clinical validities of Big Five personality measures (Costa & Widiger, 1994), personality trait correlates of experimental measures of learning (Eysenck & Eysenck, 1985), or intelligence factor correlates of educational and occupational achievement criteria (Sternberg, 1982; Wolman, 1985). Medium to substantial concurrent and predictive criterion validities (of 0.60 and above for intelligence factors and of 0.50 and above for personality factors; see Guilford, 1959; Neisser et al., 1996) have been ascertained.

A more direct study of causes of individual differences follows a third approach:

---

[3] In this sense and for this reason, current attempts (e.g. by Gardner, 1983; 1993) to employ a multi-factor theory of intelligence as a source for rules of procedure of educational intervention—let alone their current marketing as "multiple intelligences" assessment, training and study kits (for example, Jensen, 1996)—extend way beyond the data base and legitimate interpretation of factor-analytic research results.

Nature–Nurture Analyses of

IQ Tests: Personality Questionnaires:

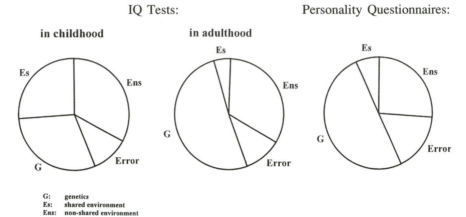

G: genetics
Es: shared environment
Ens: non-shared environment

FIG. 1.4   Nature–nurture analyses of IQ tests and of personality questionnaires (after Plomin, 1990).

Nature–nurture research paradigm

Over the last 10 to 15 years, this paradigm has greatly expanded our understanding of biological (genetic) factors, environmental influences, and their interplay (covariation, interaction) in the development of individual differences. Careful reviews of the field (Loehlin, 1992; Loehlin & Rowe, 1992; Neisser et al., 1996; Plomin, 1990; 1994; 1995) confirm results like those shown in Fig. 1.4 (compiled from Plomin, 1990):[4]

In adults, an average of about 50% of total (cross-sectional interindividual) behavioral variance depend on genetic sources (with, however, significant variations across primary factors of intelligence and personality). In the ability domain, this percentage of genetic variance increases from childhood into adulthood. Contrary to intuitive expectation, non-shared environmental influences (*within-family differences, which act differently on children of the same family*) outweigh shared environmental influences (environmental differences *between* families).

"Hot" issues of current research relate to genotype–environment interaction and covariation (Plomin's "nature of nurture"; Plomin, 1994), to environmental driving forces, and to attempts towards gene identification. Examples of the latter are the recent findings, by Ebstein et al. (1996) and by Benjamin et al. (1996), on the genetic determination of D4-dopamine receptor activity as co-determiner of phenotypical extraversion (especially novelty seeking) or, by Plomin et al. (1994a), on DNA markers associated with phenotypical variations in IQ.

<hr>

[4] See also Bouchard and McGue (1990), Eaves, Eysenck, and Martin (1989), McGue, Bouchard, Iacono, and Lykken (1993), Plomin and Nesselroade (1990), Plomin, Pedersen, Lichtenstein, and McClearn (1994), Vernon (1993, 1994).

While results like these may prove of far-reaching implication, they should also give rise to critical reflexion of what they may mean and need not mean, respectively. (See, for example, the recent excellent summary by Neisser et al., 1996, of intelligence-related results.) While procedures followed in subject sampling seem to guarantee representative estimates of genome variations, this need not hold to an equal degree for available estimates of phenotypical variations due to environment. New forms of *differential* education, of child-rearing or environmental enrichment, if behaviorally effective, can raise the proportion of phenotypical variance due to non-shared environment; conversely, coefficients of heredity can approach those of scale reliability if individual milieus should become more and more identical, so that environment-linked variance will vanish. Therefore, results like those shown in Fig. 1.4 are descriptive also of a given state of society, of social engineering and environmental design for cognitive and personality development.

Still another approach to studying causes of individual differences looks into process characteristics of personality:

Longitudinal research paradigm: Personality process

With few exceptions (like the classical Berkeley and Oakland Growth Studies; see Eichhorn, Clausen, Haan, Honzik, & Mussen, 1981), longitudinal research "studying personality the long way" (Block, 1993) to unravel "the coherences within individuals rather than within variables" (Revelle, 1995) is still fairly recent. (Of 48 longitudinal studies referenced by Pulkkinen (1993), 25 were initiated in the 1960s or later.) Cost of infrastructure may have stood against this powerful design for individual difference research, or as Oscar Wilde has put it so well:

> "The only thing that one really knows about human nature is that it changes. Change is the one quality we can predicate of it." (Wilde, 1891).

Longitudinal research has demonstrated substantial medium-term to long-range stability of trait measures, notably in cognitive abilities (see again, for example, Neisser et al., 1996), assessed through tests given under standardized situational conditions. Recent examples from the personality study include results by Caprara (1996) on the 3-year stability of individual differences in physical and verbal aggression (grades 3 to 8) and by Pulkkinen (1993) on childhood–adulthood stability of measures of lifestyle. As much of this research is still rooted in constructs from cross-sectional designs, studying adult intelligence and personality as a function of *intra*individual consistencies in development over time, as requested and demonstrated successfully by Block (1971), is a goal yet to be broadly fulfilled by research.

This brings me to a fifth and final paradigm of individual difference research:

Trans-occasion research paradigm: The search for consistency

In a cross-sectional study, subjects respond to focal or task stimuli (e.g. questionnaire or test items) while ambient conditions are either held constant or varied according to an experimental design. How will individual differences under these circumstances relate to behavior of the same people in totally different settings, in everyday life? How consistent are these differences across occasions of observation?

Although acknowledged since the 1920s (Hartshorne & May, 1928; Hartshorne, May, & Maller, 1929; see also the recent review by Buse & Pawlik, 1996b), questions of trans-occasion consistency did not get highlighted before Mischel's text (Mischel, 1968) which deplored apparently low *consistency correlations* (of 0.30 and below). Equally modest "personality correlations" were confirmed subsequently in questionnaire-based research (Endler & Hunt, 1968; Endler & Magnusson, 1976; see also Hettema & Kenrick, 1992, for a recent overview). In a typical study, subjects were given verbal descriptions of situations (going to the dentist, facing an examination, etc.) and were asked to indicate for each behavioral variable given (getting wet hands, feeling a dry throat, trembling, etc.), how they would (or might) respond. According to an earlier review by Sarason, Smith, & Diener (1975), the variance due to persons (and consistent across situations) was significant in 31% of the 87 analyses of variance covered, while significant situation effects and significant person × situation interaction effects were obtained in 66 and 60% of the analyses, respectively.

Results like these seemed to cast doubt on the usefulness of cross-sectional, trait-oriented studies of individual differences and to call for what has been referred to as an interactional model of personality (Magnusson & Endler, 1977). Yet the design that typically leads to those results is open to *serious psychological fallacies* (over and above statistical inadequacies in decomposition of variance; see Ozer, 1986). Let me briefly point out some of them:

1. Questionnaires need not (and typically will not) provide semantically valid description of actual behavior and cannot substitute for genuine *"real-life" behavior records* without explicit proof of such validity. Questionnaire responses to verbal descriptions of situations need not lead beyond how people *think* they did, would, or might behave in a situation.

2. Situational descriptions often include *behavioral referents* (i.e. reference to actions, states of feeling, expectations, etc.), which may already explain part of the results.

3. Still more critical: by requesting each subject to respond to the same set of situations, studies followed an *orthogonal person × situation design*. To the extent that people differ in their frequency of attendance in certain situations (also in the way and in the degree to which they take active part in structuring or modifying situational conditions), this design is bound to be highly unrepresentative (Pawlik, 1978). And to the extent that people of different person-

ality structure also differ in how they seek or avoid certain situations or shape their make-up, interindividual differences in behavior "due to situations" can in fact be due to interindividual differences in personality traits in the first place!

4. Finally, a basic distinction of *assessment methodology* comes into play: whether we assess a person's behavior under "laboratory" conditions (in accordance with a research design specifying "standard" assessment conditions) or "out in the field", under conditions as they actually occur in that person's "natural" life space, wherever and whenever he or she will show the behavior in question.[5]

In this sense, most research on individual differences has been *laboratory-based* and followed *quasi-orthogonal person × situation designs* of study, despite being targeted conceptually at behavior in "real-life". This may have affected the study of personality more adversely than other fields of psychological science (see also Tennen, Suls, & Affleck, 1991).

In the second part of this address, I shall introduce an alternative approach to consistency research which we have been developing in my laboratory since the late 1970s: *ambulatory* or *field assessments of individual behavior* under everyday-life conditions, also employing novel methods of ambulatory behavior testing. I shall first introduce basic concepts of assessment development, with some illustrations of assessment hardware and software. After briefly examining evidence on the psychometric reliability of this new assessment technology, I shall present results of studies employing this methodology to re-examine person × situation interactions, cross-occasion consistency, and interindividual consistency of intraindividual personality coherence.

PERSONALITY CONSISTENCY AND COHERENCE IN IN-FIELD ASSESSMENTS

Research questions generate data. Rather than settling for "daily experience" assessment methods as described in the 1991 Special Issue of the *Journal of Personality* (Tennen et al., 1991), our aim was to apply methods and standards of laboratory-based experimental psychology to the study of individual differences in subjects' everyday-life environment.[6] To this end, ambulatory self-protocol assessment methods were developed for these five *target variable domains*:

[5] The distinction between laboratory and field data is essentially orthogonal to the system of data sources in Table 1.1, as most of them can be accessed under either condition (see Pawlik, 1996b, for a more detailed account). In the following, I use the terms "in-field assessment" and "ambulatory assessment" interchangeably to refer to methods of data collection outside laboratory confinements.

[6] This research was carried out in collaboration with Lothar Buse and with the assistance of J. Bünning, J. Drepper, U. Gründemann, U. Kopp, W. Kunde, C. Reitz, R. Schäfer, E. Stern, G. Stürzebecher, and G. Templer. We gratefully acknowledge support by the *Deutsche Forschungsgemeinschaft* (through research grants Pa 108/5, 7, 8/3, 8/4, 8/5, 13/2, 14/1, 14/2, 14/3, 15/1, and 19/1). For detailed description of the ambulatory assessment methodology, of study designs, and of results see Pawlik (1995; 1996a), Pawlik & Buse (1982, 1992, 1996), Buse & Pawlik (1984, 1991, 1994, 1996a).

1. Overt behavior.
2. Covert behavior: emotional variables (moods), motivational states, mental processes.
3. Behavioral performance variables: novel ultra-short objective tests, designed for in-field administration.
4. Peripheral psychophysiological indicators of activation: heart rate and finger temperature (plus ambient temperature).
5. Situational and setting variables.

A *protocol mode* was developed for self-monitoring (self-assessment) of overt and covert behavior and of situational/setting variables. *Automated administration and recording* was set up for assessment of behavioral performance variables and of psychophysiological variables.

Self-monitoring (of behavior and of environmental variations) requires careful prior segmentation of the (essentially continuous) stream of data into suitable units of observation and recording. Successful implementation is dependent on systematic prior observer training of subjects and on control tests for reactivity (i.e. effects of the assessment procedure on the behavior being assessed, affecting concurrent or subsequent behavior of the subject). Available space stands against going into details here; they are covered at length in the reference literature provided (see footnote 6).

Ambulatory assessment may follow different *data acquisition plans* of continuous monitoring or discrete sampling. Research reported here employed time sampling designs, occasionally also mixed time–event sampling. As documented in the reference literature, for our methods of assessment time sampling can be continued over up to 3–5 consecutive weeks, provided that: (1) assessment times **t** at any single occasion will not exceed 3–5 (at most: 8) min. in duration; and (2) (randomly distributed) intervals d_t between any two successive assessment occasions average at least 45–60 min. In this way, ambulatory assessment data can be collected over **n** = 150 – 300 consecutive assessment occasions per subject, without significant reactivity effects in the variables studied here.

In-field research of this type will yield ecologically representative, unbiased estimates of a person's "natural" variability in behavior across the range of settings and situations accessible in that person's daily course of life throughout the assessment period. This method does not request subjects to give retrospective (or predictive) responses; without exception, it involves assessment only of *concurrent* behavior, of *concurrent* moods, and of *concurrent* situational conditions at the time when the acoustic alert signal of the portable data recorder will ask a subject to make the requested input.

The *technical assessment instrumentation* has to be developed for optimal portability. It has to support data acquisition, psychophysiological recording, test administration, and on-line scoring in the field. We settled for a microcomputer-based digital *behavioral data recorder* that a person will have with himself/

FIG. 1.5   Third-generation Behavioral Data Recorder, AMBU, for ambulatory behavior assessments.

herself for the whole assessment period, with weekly visits to the laboratory (for unloading of data and loading of next week's assessment program). We are currently working with our third-generation behavioral data recorder called AMBU (for "ambulatory assessment") which employs a miniaturized PC 286-technology (see Fig. 1.5).

From the second recorder generation onwards, we began implementing also ultra-short in-field *behavioral performance tests* (to measure functions of perception, immediate (visual) memory, spatial reasoning and, more recently, of phasic vs. tonic alertness, continuous compensatory tracking, receiver operating characteristic parameters in a Go-No-Go reaction task, immediate memory performance in a modified Sternberg design, etc.). All tests are designed for field administration. Our so-called Rota-Test of perceptual speed may serve as an example: 14 circles are presented in the display, each one showing a radial pointer. In 13 circles the pointer is in identical position; in the remaining one circle it is displaced ("advanced") by 45°. All circles rotate (at the same speed), and the subject's task is to identify (by cursor response) the one circle with the "advanced" pointer. Test duration: 60 seconds; for adaptive testing, the speed of circle rotation can be varied dependent on a subject's performance.

Self-monitoring of overt behavior, of moods and other covert behavior, and of environmental conditions employed item lists employing multiple-choice selective-response formats, with adaptive item presentation according to hierarchical item clustering.

TABLE 1.4
Psychometric reliability

Within-Occasion	(n = 149)
Heart Rate	r = .71
Finger Temp.	r = .88
Mood List	r = .71
Rota Test-Score	r = .75
Cubes Test—Time	r = .71
Mazes Test—Error	r = .43
6 Days odd-even	(n = 135)
Setting List	r = .57
Behavior List	r = .62
Mood List	r = .76
Motive List	r = .80

TABLE 1.5
Temporal stability

5 × 6 Days Retest	(5 weeks; n = 40)
Behavior List	r = .51
Mood List	r = .66
2 × 6 Days Retest	(6 mos re-test interval; n = 104)
Behavior List	r = .42
Mood List	r = .57
EPI: E-I	r = .32
EPI: Neu	r = .31

Reliability of in-field assessments

How reliable and sensitive can assessment data be if collected in this way? Table 1.4 summarizes results of two tests of *psychometric reliability*: (1) averaged *within-occasion* reliability correlations (psychophysiology: averaged retest correlations of 3 20-sec. measurement intervals per occasion; Rota Test, Cubes Test (of spatial reasoning) and Mazes Test (of immediate visuo-spatial memory): internal consistency reliabilities); and (2) averaged Spearman-Brown-corrected *6 days odd-even* reliabilities. With one exception (Mazes Test: error score) all values equal 0.70 or above. It should be noted that these are reliabilities at *item level* for each of the four lists (settings, overt behavior, moods, motives) and from ultra-short measurement periods (1 min. or less) in the physiological and behavioral performance variables.

Table 1.5 looks into a second aspect of reliability: *temporal stability*. Over a 5-week assessment program, between-week *item* reliabilities average 0.51 for the Behavior List and 0.66 for the Mood List (upper section of Table 1.5). When comparing 2 weeks of assessment 6 months apart, average between-week reli-

TABLE 1.6
Trans-occasion stability
(Consistency I) (n = 149)

Heart Rate	r = .25
Finger Temp.	r = .27
Mood List	r = .38
Rota Test—Score	r = .40
Cubes Test—Time	r = .34
Mazes Test—Error	r = .35

ability correlations drop to 0.42 and 0.56 (lower section of Table 1.5), again at single item level. For the sake of comparison, corresponding average *item* level half-year retest reliabilities are also shown for the Extraversion–Introversion and Neuroticism scale of the German-language edition of the Eysenck Personality Inventory (EPI; Eysenck & Eysenck, 1968); they average in the lower 0.30s, i.e. 0.10–0.15 *below* average half-year item reliabilities of ambulatory assessment measurements.

By psychometric standards and following proper training of subjects, in-field behavior assessments do meet or even exceed levels of reliability familiar from stationary, laboratory-based testing.

Consistency across occasions and settings

A first—and naive—test of consistency would compare assessment data across any two in-field occasions of testing. Table 1.6 shows such average between-occasion correlations for two psychophysiological measures, the Mood List (again at item level) and three in-field performance tests. Correlations run low, in the upper 0.20s to mid-0.30s—and indeed resemble those meager "personality coefficients" criticized by Mischel (1968). Yet they are misleading: why should individual differences correlate substantially between *any two* occasions of observation, totally irrespective of (internal and external) situational conditions? High correlations of this kind would be contradictory to everything known about stimulus-dependent control of behavior. Furthermore, they would even stand against a basic premise of cross-sectional personality research, which describes individual differences (as in the specification equation of the factor-analytic model; see Cattell, 1978) as a joint function of stimulus (or task) parameters (given by the factor loadings) and person parameters (given by the factor scores as trait measures).[7]

---

[7] Expecting high average correlations between *any* two occasions of assessment is as unfounded an expectation as one looking for high average correlations between *any* two items of personality or performance testing, irrespective of item content and make-up. Obviously, this would not stand verification from factor-analytic or other trait research, which tells us that different personality scales or different tests of performance functions will, as a rule, differ in trait-composition (pattern of factor loadings) (cf. Pawlik, 1968; Carroll, 1993).

TABLE 1.7
Trans-setting stability (Consistency II)

Pos. Moods	r = .83 (.67–.96)
Neg. Moods	r = .71 (.52–.86)
Behavior List, soc.	r = .54 (.27–.86)
Behavior List, not-soc.	r = .69 (.46–.88)

NOTE:
n = 149; 7 setting classes

In a second—more advanced—step one would better look at consistency correlations between *settings* (or setting classes), where "setting" refers to an objective social, time, and place address of a given occasion of assessment.[8] Table 1.7 shows such average trans-setting consistency correlations, again at item level, for moods and overt behavior (differentiating between behaviors requiring or not requiring social partners), with ranges of correlations given in brackets. Obviously, these figures look much different: in-field assessments of concurrent mood states and of overt behavior *do* show substantial cross-setting consistency, provided correlations are calculated between internally homogeneous setting classes.

This is amplified even further in Table 1.8 which summarizes average consistencies with respect to three different *consistency criteria*: within and between setting classes, within and between days of assessment, and within and between situations, the latter referring to prototypical combinations of a setting class with an overt core or "lead" activity (provided the activity is not limited to this and only this one setting class).[9] The upper part of Table 1.8 shows average consistency correlations of assessment data *aggregated* over one day, one setting class, or one situational class, while figures in the lower section show corresponding correlations for de-aggregated assessment data from a single occasion on *one* day, in *one* setting or *one* situational class.

These results seem noteworthy:

1. With one exception (finger temperature, between days), consistency correlations tend to *average above 0.60*.
2. Without exception, consistencies "between" are lower than respective consistencies "within". This is easily understood: assessment variables sensitive to changes in time, setting and situation characteristics *must* yield higher within than between consistency. The difference between the two can serve as a measure of *sensitivity* of a variable to temporal, setting, and situational change. In the 149 individual 3-week assessment records underlying

---

[8] In this sense, "being together with others in a public place" or "in the evening at a friend's place" are examples of setting addresses. It should be noted that this setting definition does *not* include activity descriptors.

[9] In this sense, "being together with others at a friend's place and watching television" would constitute a prototypical situation.

TABLE 1.8
Trans-situational stability (Consistency III) and sensitivity

	Days		Settings		Situations	
$\bar{r}$	w	b	w	b	w	b
Moods	.90	.68	.87	.68	.85	.75
Bodily Complaints	.86	.47	.76	.67	.70	.63
Heart Rate	.79	.49	.75	.51	.74	.59
Finger Temp.	.59	.14	.59	.47	.56	.50
Rota Score	.88	.78	.87	.77	.85	.70

	Days		Settings		Situations	
De-aggregated $\bar{r}$	w	b	w	b	w	b
Moods	.56	.43	.55	.48	.50	.44
Bodily Complaints	.51	.27	.34	.29	.30	.27
Heart Rate	.39	.24	.40	.27	.28	.20
Finger Temp.			.19	.25	.17	.15
Rota Score	.52	.46	.51	.45	.50	.45

NOTES:

n = 149

w = within

b = between

Table 1.8, assessment results prove more sensitive to changes in setting and situational characteristics than to lapse of time.

3. Finally, differences between aggregated and de-aggregated consistency correlations allow to adjust the *level of aggregation* (also in the sense of Epstein, 1990) to a desired and satisfactory (predictive) consistency of assessment within or between different points in time, different setting classes, or different situations, respectively.

Rather than following some authors and deploring situational co-determination of individual differences, we should open up for the positive message in these findings: behavioral prediction can and must pay attention to changing levels of aggregation which will be mandatory for sufficient trans-occasion consistency, depending on the consistency criterion chosen (temporal, setting, situational, or other), the nature of the assessment variable and, most likely, personal moderators.

Results like these also encourage the use of in-field assessments to approach old questions on a novel data base.

Person × setting interactions in ambulatory assessment data

In one study (Buse & Pawlik, 1984), decomposition-of-variance analyses were conducted to study personality × setting interactions in real-life behavior records.

TABLE 1.9
Analyses of variance in 74 ambulatory assessment variables

Variable domain	p	Main effects			Interactions			
		A settings	B neurot.	C extrav.	AB	AC	BC	ABC
mood items	.01	3	1					
(negative)	.05	2	1		1			
m = 15	.10	1	2	1				
	.15	2	1	1	1	1	3	2
mood items	.01	6						
(positive)	.05	3						
m = 15	.10	2	1	1			1	
	.15	1	1	1	1			
Behavior List	.01	11	2			1	1	
(non-soc. b.s.)	.05	4		3	2		1	1
m = 24	.10		1	1			2	
	.15	2	1	2				
Behavior List	.01	14						2
(soc. b.s.)	.05	3	1		1	1	1	
m = 20	.10	1	1					2
	.15	3	2	1	2		1	

NOTE:
  n = 104; 2 weeks of assessment

Table 1.9 summarizes results in 74 assessment variables (n = 104 male adolescents, aged 16–18 years; 2 weeks of ambulatory assessments). Entries shown are the number of F-ratios significant at each p-level in each group of assessment variables (negatively vs. positively toned mood items; behavior items not requiring vs. items requiring a social partner) for main effects due to settings (setting classes), personality factors neuroticism and extraversion (measured by the EPI prior to in-field data collection), and for setting × personality-factor interaction effects.

As expected, many assessment variables yield significant main effects due to setting conditions (particularly for overt behavior) and the two personality factors, whereas the number of significant personality × setting interactions (AB, AC) remains at chance level: only 7 out of 74 analyses of variance yielded AB or AC interactions significant at the 5% level or better.

The message to be learnt seems clear: for situational variations that typically occur in subjects' everyday life, in-field self-protocol assessments of concurrent behavior do not give rise to personality × situation interaction effects as found in retrospective (or predictive) questionnaire data. Such interaction effects may rather relate to the way in which persons build up *mental representations* of their behavior, or simply constitute an artifact from unrepresentative quasi-orthogonal person-situation research designs.

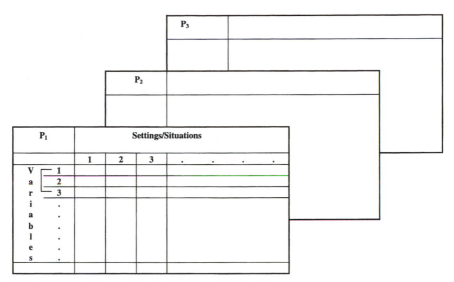

FIG. 1.6   The coherence paradigm of personality research.

From consistency to coherence: The study of within-person situation × behavior covariance

Longitudinal consistency research makes it all too clear: Cross-sectional study of individual differences has missed out on a critical *"third dimension" of personality* in real life: patterns of behavior that characterize a person *across* occasions, *across* time, settings and situations. I use the term *coherence*[10] to refer to systematic (statistically significant and stable) covariations in a person's behavior *across* naturalistic occasions of observation. Ambulatory assessment techniques constitute a powerful methodology of choice to study within-person patterns of coherence, to extend cross-sectional research into the third dimension.

A schematic representation of this *coherence paradigm of personality research* is sketched in Fig. 1.6. Assume we collect ambulatory assessment records (over suitable lengths of time and representative samples of settings and situations) in m assessment variables from persons P_1, P_2, etc. The data obtained for each person P can be arranged in such 2-way tables ("data cards"), with rows denoting assessment variables and columns representing the occasions (or classes of settings or situations) as found in a person's record.[11] In this scheme, row means

---

[10] For earlier reference to aspects of coherence see Revelle (1995) and literature referenced there.

[11] If occasions are grouped into settings or situations, "data cards" of different persons can differ considerably in the number and kind of settings or situations represented as columns, as well as in the numbers of entries per cell (assessments per variable and setting/situation), as persons differ in their setting/situation frequency-of-attendance profile over the total assessment period.

are estimates of (aggregated) trait measures, while "coherence" refers to statistically significant and stable *intra-individual* covariation between assessment variables (rows) across occasions, settings, or situations (indicated by the square bracket correlating variables 1 and 3 for person P_1).

The coherence paradigm of personality research involves the search for within-person regularities in covariations of behaviors across occasions (*patterns of coherence*) and for *interindividual differences* in such coherence pattern[12], possibly to be followed by search for *trait markers* to predict individual patterns of coherence from cross-sectional trait data. Extent and degree to which this may be possible will tell us more about the usefulness of traits than most past discussions ever could.

Coherence-oriented personality research will introduce into psychology a taxonomic paradigm which is well established already in at least one other science: climate research. A classificatory distinction between, say, continental and oceanic climate in Europe, is *not* only or primarily one in terms of cross-sectional weather data, but is rooted in longitudinal (seasonal and other time-series) data on region-specific mean-variance-covariance structures in salient meteorological variables. To learn their lesson from the "climate model", students of personality need to genuinely combine cross-sectional and longitudinal research designs. The coherence paradigm is basically different also from older "data box" models of personality (as proposed by Cattell, 1978, pp. 321–376), in that "data cards" for different subjects P can differ in some or many or even all of the columns listed (i.e. occasions, settings or situations as represented and identifiable in a person's ambulatory assessment protocol). Coherence-oriented personality research no longer imposes unrealistic "data box" restrictions of quasi-orthogonality of persons and situations/settings.

How can this be accomplished? How can one identify systematic, statistically significant and stable within-person patterns of coherence between assessment variables across occasions, settings or situations?

The following last two results from current research in our laboratory are to provide examples. The first one (from Pawlik, 1995) illustrates stable *psychophysiological coherence patterns*. Subjects participated in two 3-week assessment programs in the same variables, 3 years apart. Assessment records were analyzed for significant within-person cross-occasion correlations between variables, that proved stable over the 3-year retest interval. Figure 1.7 shows sample *coherence functions* between heart rate (HR; average number of beats per minute)[13] and the

---

[12] This approach is different from Mischel's recent proposal (Mischel & Shoda, 1995) to study interindividual differences in *situation-specific* behavior profiles *across* variables, which would look at profiles *within columns* rather than correspondence between rows of an intraindividual data table. This proposal should also meet scaling problems of the kind typical in Q-factor analysis.

[13] Three blocks of 15 artifact-free consecutive beat-to-beat interval measurements per occasion, with approximately 2 min. interval between blocks. Heart rate data shown are within-person within-occasion averages, expressed in number of beats per minute.

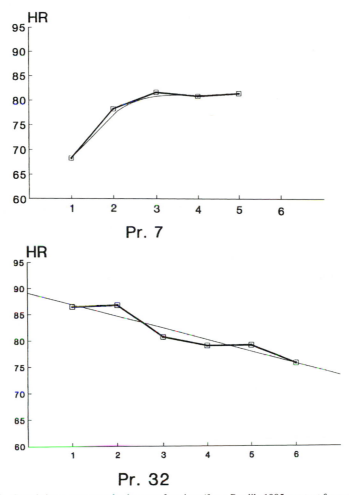

FIG. 1.7   Sample heart-rate–mood coherence functions (from: Pawlik, 1995; see text for explanation).

subject's response, at the same assessment occasion, to the scaled Mood List item "relaxed" (data base: 362 [Subject 7] and 238 [Subject 32] assessment occasions). Both within-person coherence functions are highly stable and significant (repeated-measurement analyses of variance), yet the two coherence functions differ markedly. Subject 32 behaves "in accordance" with experimental psychology textbooks: his heart rate decreases with increasing relaxation. By contrast, Subject 7 shows an equally significant and stable relationship the other way round: his heart rate decreases with increasing experience of tension. This difference in heart rate–mood coherence is not the only difference between the two subjects, however. Maximum heart rates obtained for Subject 7 come close to minimum heart rates obtained for Subject 32. And, not shown in Fig. 1.7, the

TABLE 1.10
Patterns of coherence: alertness—moods

	Subject 57	Subject 18
No. Occasions:	161	147
Age:	57 y.	41 y.
Alertness:		
mean RT:	339.9 ms	391.1 ms
SD:	55.1	52.9
Rel.:	.91	.74
Mood List:		
Av. Rel.:	.86	.81
Canonical R:	n.s.	$R^2 = .92$; $p < .009$
Correlated Moods:	5/28; $\bar{r} = .09$	15/28; $\bar{r} = 0.20$

two persons differ in their marginal frequency distributions for the Mood List item "relaxed": Subject 7 produced a unimodal, slightly left-skewed distribution, Subject 32 a clearly bimodal distribution. This (plus results of pre-assessment trait tests) may lead to the *interpretation* that Subject 7 shows (compensatory?) vagotonic response to experienced tension, while reactions of the emotionally less stable Subject 32 follow a sympathicotone response function.

Results like these let us appreciate why a naive trait-state approach that seeks to predict a person's current emotional state on the basis of that person's current heart rate is to fail. Without knowing a person's individual heart rate–mood coherence function, such predictions are bound to be of low validity (see also Fahrenberg & Myrtek, 1996).

Systematic coherence analyses reveal that persons differ widely in the number and type of significant within-person coherence functions underlying their in-field assessments of heart rate and moods. This may give rise to fruitful new hypotheses about the nature of emotional stability and of emotional control functions in everyday-life behavior.

My other example comes from ongoing research on *coherence patterns* in *activation*, functions of *attention*, and *moods* (data base: 3-week ambulatory performance test records; yet unpublished.) I shall restrict myself again to an illustrative comparison between two persons, this time looking at linear coherence functions relating scaled Mood List item responses to variations (across occasions) in ambulatory attention test performance. The two (female) subjects, whose results are shown in Table 1.10, differ profoundly in attention–mood coherence: for subject 57, variations in alertness are largely unrelated to mood variations; and the same variables yield a highly significant first canonical root ($R^2 = .92$) for Subject 18—despite good comparability of both assessment records in descriptive statistical and psychometric terms. Only 5 (out of 28) Mood List items correlate significantly with variations of Subject 57 in alertness, while performance of Subject 18 is a valid linear function of 15 of the same 28 Mood items. Assessment data describe Subject 18 as more composed and self-confident, and she scored higher than Subject 57 on pre-assessment tests of introversion and emotional stability. In current research we are looking closely into individual differences in such coherence functions and how they relate to trait measures of aptitudes and personality.

On the theoretical side, significant coherence functions can give rise to new insights into the genesis of individual behavioral consistency. For example, they may reflect patterns of individual (social or other) behavioral learning, including individually characteristic patterns of behavior elicitation and/or reinforcement that affect different variables in a person's behavior in the same way (Pawlik, 1974). Coherence functions like those described in Fig. 1.7 may also point at individual differences in biological bases of behavior control and may prove useful for testing theories of development of individual differences.

TRAIT CONCEPTS AND INDIVIDUAL DIFFERENCES

Coherence analysis can help understanding trait concepts of personality in a new perspective. The following conclusions seem warranted:

1. Trait concepts can differ in *behavioral variance targeted*, in *behavioral breadth* (item aggregation; first- vs. second-order factor concepts), and in *situational generality*. Success in proceeding from taxonomic-descriptive to explanatory or predictive trait concepts will depend on better understanding of relationships between cross-sectional traits and within-person patterns of coherence. Ambulatory assessment techniques should prove instrumental in this pursuit.
2. As a rule, traits are construed to account for observed (co)variations in behavior.[14] Unless assumptions of stationarity will be met, such trait concepts need not prove valid for predictions. If traits were to be conceived primarily for purposes of prediction, cross-sectional procedures of trait definition should have been replaced a long time ago by longitudinal, coherence-type procedures of trait extraction!
3. We should not allow personality research to be narrowed down and rendered unproductive by overcommitting it to issues of behavioral prediction at too low levels of aggregation (see Table 1.8 earlier). No serious physicist would

---

[14] For example, in factor analysis, observed test scores are expressed as (linear) functions of latent factors (traits). As factor analysts will appreciate, the loading vectors of tests (rows of the factor matrix) do not, however, define the factors as (linear) combinations of tests (Harman, 1960). Yet authors invariably interpret factors by reading the factor matrix column-wise, although proper description of factors (traits) on the basis of (correlated) tests would require solving for the regression of factors onto tests (coefficients for factor score estimation; Pawlik, 1968). Ensuing implications for conceptualizing psychological traits from factor-analytic studies are frequently overlooked.

accept as a task of science to predict the result of a single throw of dice. Yet differential psychologists have allowed themselves to get caught in such "chaos traps"—and even take the blame for being unable to predict the unpredictable: the behavior of a single person under singular circumstances. This cannot be a viable goal; instead, science should procure knowledge for proper aggregation of data, at the predictor and at the criterion side, so as to provide for acceptable accuracies of possible predictions. Here again coherence analysis should prove a good safeguard against attempting the impossible.

4. In an open society, human behavior is an open system in itself. Students of personality should not deplore problems of predictions at too low a level of aggregation, but value individual and collective freedom that contribute to such behavioral entropy. Here psychology of personality needs to play a key function in bringing behavioral science knowledge to bear on the study of individual persons in their natural behavioral habitat.

To return to my opening remarks: In classical times, in the writings of Aristotle, individual differences in behavior and experience were treated in the context of ethics and of state philosophy. The human mind has kept aware of this ever since, as a quotation from the writings of the German novelist Hermann Hesse (1930, p. 43) expresses so nicely:

> An jedem Menschen die Merkmale finden, die ihn von andern unterscheiden, heißt ihn erkennen. [Finding in each person the qualities that make him or her differ from others means recognizing the person.]

Individual differences are a necessary condition for individuality, of personal identity. How else could we recognize and identify each other as individually distinct? Personal identity presupposes inter-individual variability. A prerequisite to the development of personal individuality, it is individual differences that enrich our social and cultural life. So they deserve our fullest attention, as scientists and in the pursuit of personal freedom. Through their research, students of personality can contribute to these goals—and let come true by way of science what André Gide (quoted from Robert, 1973, p. 480) has put in these fine words:

> Si nous n'étions si différents, nous n'aurions pas si grand plaisir à nous entendre. (If we weren't so different, we wouldn't have the great pleasure in understanding each other.)

REFERENCES

Anastasi, A. (1994). Differential psychology: origin and sources. In K. Pawlik (Ed.), *William Stern: Die Differentielle Psychologie in ihren methodischen Grundlagen* (pp. ix–xi). Bern: Huber.

Benjamin, J., Li, L., Patterson, C., Greenberg, B. D., Murphy, D. L., & Hamer, D. H. (1996). Population and familial association between the D4 dopamine receptor gene and measures of Novelty Seeking. *Nature Genetics, 12*, 81–84.

Binet, A., & Henri, V. (1896). Psychologie individuelle [Individual psychology]. *Année psychologique, 2*, 411–465.

Block, J. (1971). *Lives through time.* Berkeley, CA: Bencroft.

Block, J. (1993). Studying personality the long way. In D. C. Funder, R. D. Parke, C. Tomlinson-Keasey, & K. Widman (Eds.), *Studying lives through time: Personality and development* (pp. 9–41). Washington, DC: American Psychological Association.

Bouchard, T. J. Jr., & McGue, M. (1990). Genetic and environmental influences on adult personality: An analysis of adopted twins reared apart. *Journal of Personality, 58*, 263–292.

Burt, C. (1949). The two-factor theory. *British Journal of Psychology-Statistical Section, 2*, 151–178.

Buse, L., & Pawlik, K. (1984). Inter-Setting-Korrelationen und Setting-Persönlichkeits-Wechselwirkungen: Ergebnisse einer Felduntersuchung zur Konsistenz von Verhalten und Erleben [Intersetting-consistencies and setting personality interactions: Results of a field study of consistency of behavior and experience]. *Zeitschrift für Sozialpsychologie, 15*, 44–59.

Buse, L., & Pawlik, K. (1991). Zur State-Trait-Charakteristik verschiedener Meßvariablen der psychophysiologischen Aktivierung, der kognitiven Leistung und der Stimmung in Alltagssituationen [On the state-trait characteristic of different measurement variables of psychophysiological activation, of cognitive performance, and of moods in everyday-life situations]. *Zeitschrift für experimentelle und angewandte Psychologie, 38*, 521–538.

Buse, L., & Pawlik, K. (1994). Differenzierung zwischen Tages-, Setting- und Situationskonsistenz ausgewählter Verhaltensmerkmale, Maßen der Aktivierung, des Befinden und der Stimmung in Alltagssituationen [Differentiating between day, setting, and situation consistency of selected measures of behavior, of activation, of feeling, and moods in everyday-life situations]. *Diagnostica, 40*, 2–26.

Buse, L., & Pawlik, K. (1996a). Ambulatory behavioral assessment and in-field performance testing. In J. Fahrenberg & M. Myrtek (Eds.), *Ambulatory assessment* (pp. 29–50). Göttingen: Hogrefe.

Buse, L., & Pawlik, K. (1996b). Konsistenz, Kohärenz und Situationsspezifität individueller Unterschiede [Consistency, coherence, and situation-specificity of individual differences]. In K. Pawlik (Ed.) *Grundlagen und Methoden der Differentiellen Psychologie. Enzyklopädie der Psychologie*, Vol. C/VIII/1 (pp. 269–300). Göttingen: Hogrefe.

Byrne, B. M., & Goffin, R. D. (1993). Modelling MTMM data from additive and multiplicative covariance structures: An audit of construct validity research. *Multivariate Behavioral Research, 28*, 67–96.

Campbell, D. T., & Fiske, D. W. (1959). Convergent and discriminant validation by the Multitrait-Multimethod Matrix. *Psychological Bulletin, 103*, 276–279.

Caprara, G.-V. (1996). Structures and processes in personality psychology. *European Psychologist, 1*, 14–26.

Carroll, J. B. (1993). *Human cognitive abilities.* Cambridge: Cambridge University Press.

Cattell, J. McK. (1886). Psychometrische Untersuchungen [Psychometric investigations]. *Philosophische Studien, 3*, 305–335; 452–492.

Cattell, J. McK. (1893). Aufmerksamkeit und Reaktion [Attention and reaction]. *Philosophische Studien, 8*, 403–406.

Cattell, R. B. (1957). *Personality and motivation structure and measurement.* Yonkers-on-Hudson, NY: World Book Company.

Cattell, R. B. (Ed.). (1966). *Handbook of multivariate experimental psychology.* Chicago: Rand McNally.

Cattell, R. B. (1978). *The scientific use of factor analysis in behavioral and life sciences.* New York: Plenum.

Costa, P. T. Jr., & Widiger, T. (Eds.). (1994). *Personality disorders and the five-factor model of personality*. Washington, DC: American Psychological Association.

Cronbach, L. J. (1970). *Essentials of psychological testing* (3rd ed.). New York: Harper & Row.

Diaz-Guerrero, R. (1995). Origins and development of Mexican ethnopsychology. *World Psychology, 1*, 49–67.

Digman, J. M. (1963). Principal dimensions of child personality as seen in teacher's judgments. *Child Development, 34*, 43–60.

Digman, J. M. (1990). Personality structure: Emergence of the five-factor model. *Annual Review of Psychology, 50*, 116–123.

Doyle, A. C. (1986). Adventures of Sherlock Holmes: A scandal in Bohemia. In A. C. Doyle: *Sherlock Holmes: The complete novels and stories* (Vol. 1). New York: Bantam. (First published: 1891)

Eaves, L. J., Eysenck, H. J., & Martin, N. G. (1989). *Genes, culture, and personality*. London: Academic.

Ebstein, R. P. Novick, O., Umansky, R., Priel, B., Osher, Y., Blaine, D., Bennett, E. R., Nemanov, L., Katz, M. Q., & Belmaker, R. K. (1996). Dopamine D4 receptor (D4DR) exon III polymorphism associated with human personality trait of Novelty Seeking. *Nature Genetics, 12*, 78–80.

Eichhorn, D. H., Clausen, J. A., Haan, N., Honzik, M., & Mussen, P. H. (Eds.). (1981). *Present and past in middle life*. New York: Academic.

Endler, N. S., & Hunt, J. McV. (1968). S-R inventories of hostility and comparisons of the proportions of variance from persons, responses, and situations for hostility and anxiousness. *Journal of Personality and Social Psychology, 9*, 309–315.

Endler, N. S., & Magnusson, D. (1976). Toward an interactional psychology of personality. *Psychological Bulletin, 83*, 956–974.

Epstein, S. (1990). Comment on the effects of aggregation across and within occasions on consistency, specificity, and reliability. *Methodika, 1*, 95–100.

Eysenck, H. J. (1947). *Dimensions of personality*. London: Kegan Paul.

Eysenck, H. J. (1967). *The biological basis of personality*. Springfield, Ill.: Thomas.

Eysenck, H. J., & Eysenck, M. W. (1985). *Personality and individual differences. A natural science approach*. New York: Plenum.

Eysenck, H. J., & Eysenck, S. B. G. (1968). *The manual to the Eysenck Personality Inventory*. San Diego: Educational and Industrial Testing Service.

Fahrenberg, J., & Myrtek, M. (Eds.). (1996). *Ambulatory assessment*. Göttingen: Hogrefe.

Funder, D. (1994). Editorial. *Journal of Research in Personality, 28*, 1–3.

Gardner, H. (1983). *Frames of mind: The theory of multiple intelligences*. New York: Basic Books.

Gardner, H. (1993). *The theory of multiple intelligences: From theory into practice*. New York: Basic Books.

Goldberg, L. R. (1982). From aze to zombie: Some explorations in the language of personality. In C. D. Spielberger & J. N. Butcher (Eds.), *Advances in personality assessment* (Vol. 1, pp. 203–234). Hillsdale, NJ: Erlbaum.

Guilford, J. P. (1959). *Personality*. New York: McGraw Hill.

Harman, H. H. (1960). *Modern factor analysis*. Chicago: University of Chicago Press.

Hartshorne, K., & May, M. A. (1928). *Studies in the nature of character: Studies in deceit* (Vol. 1). New York: Macmillan.

Hartshorne, K., May, M. A., & Maller, J. B. (1929). *Studies in the nature of character: II. Studies in service and self-control*. New York: Macmillan.

Hesse, H. (1930). *Narziss und Goldmund*. Berlin: Fischer.

Hettema, J., & Kenrick, D. T. (1992). Models of person-situation interactions. In G.-V. Caprara & G. L. Van Heck (Eds.), *Modern personality psychology* (pp. 393–417). New York: Harvester Wheatsheaf.

Hofstee, W. K. B. (1994). Personality and factor analysis: Bind or Bond? *Zeitschrift für Differentielle und Diagnostische Psychologie, 15*, 173–183.

Hundleby, J. D., Pawlik, K., & Cattell, R. B. (1965). *Personality factors in objective test devices.* San Diego: Knapp.

James, W. (1907). The present dilemma in philosophy. Lecture I in W. James, *Pragmatism: A new name for some old ways of thinking* (pp. 3–40). New York: Longmans, Green.

Jensen, E. (1996). *Multiple intelligences. How you can better understand, teach and assess.* San Diego: Turning Point.

Kant, I. (1798). *Anthropologie in pragmatischer Hinsicht* [Anthropology in pragmatic regard]. Königsberg: Nicolovius.

Loehlin, J. C. (1992). *Genes and environment in personality development.* Newbury Park, CA: Sage.

Loehlin, J. C., & Rowe, D. C. (1992). Genes, environment, and personality. In G.-V. Caprara & G. L. Van Heck (Eds.), *Modern personality psychology* (pp. 352–370). New York: Harvester Wheatsheaf.

Magnusson, D., & Endler, N. S. (1977), Interactional psychology: Present status and future prospects. In D. Magnusson & N. S. Endler (Eds.), *Personality at the crossroads: Current issues in interactional psychology* (pp. 3–36). Hillsdale, NJ: Erlbaum.

McCrae, R. R., & Costa, P. T. Jr. (1990), *Personality in adulthood.* New York: Guilford.

McGue, M., Bouchard, T. J., Iacono, W. G., & Lykken, D. T. (1993). Behavioral genetics of cognitive ability: A life-span perspective. In R. Plomin & G. E. McClearn (Eds.), *Nature, nurture, and psychology* (pp. 59–76). Washington, DC: American Psychological Association.

Mischel, W. (1968). *Personality and assessment.* New York: Wiley.

Mischel, W., & Shoda, Y. (1995). A cognitive-affective system theory of personality: Reconceptualizing situations, dispositions, dynamics, and invariance in personality. *Psychological Review, 102,* 246–268.

Morrison, D. F. (1976). *Multivariate statistical methods* (2nd ed.). New York: McGraw-Hill.

Neisser, U., Boodoo, G., Bouchard, T. J. Jr., Boykin, A. W., Brody, N., Ceci, S. J., Halpern, D. F., Loehlin, J. C., Perloff, R., Sternberg, R. J., & Urbina, S. (1996). Intelligence: Knowns and unknowns. *American Psychologist, 51,* 77–101.

Ozer, D. J. (1986). *Consistency in personality.* Berlin: Springer.

Pawlik, K. (1968). *Dimensionen des Verhaltens.* [Dimensions of behavior]. Bern: Huber.

Pawlik, K. (1974). Ansätze für eine eigenschaftsfreie Interpretation von Persönlichkeitsfaktoren [Attempts towards a trait-free interpretation of personality factors]. In L. Eckensberger & U. S. Eckensberger (Eds.), *Bericht über den 28. Kongress der Deutschen Gesellschaft für Psychologie 1972 in Saarbrücken* (pp. 248–256). Göttingen: Hogrefe.

Pawlik, K. (1978). Umwelt und Persönlichkeit [Environment and behavior]. In C. F. Graumann (Ed.), *Ökologische Perspektiven in der Psychologie* (pp. 112–138). Bern: Huber.

Pawlik, K. (1992). Psychological assessment. In M. R. Rosenzweig (Ed.), *International psychological science* (pp. 253–287). Washington, DC: American Psychological Association.

Pawlik, K. (Ed.). (1994). *William Stern: Die Differentielle Psychologie in ihren methodischen Grundlagen* [William Stern: Differential Psychology in its methodological foundations]. Bern: Huber.

Pawlik, K. (1995). Persönlichkeit und Verhalten: Zur Standortbestimmung von Differentieller Psychologie [Personality and behavior: Reviewing the state of differential psychology]. In K. Pawlik (Ed.), *Bericht über den 39. Kongress der Deutschen Gesellschaft für Psychologie in Hamburg 1994* (pp. 31–49). Göttingen: Hogrefe.

Pawlik, K. (Ed.) (1996a). *Grundlagen und Methoden der Differentiellen Psychologie.* [Foundations and Methods of Differential Psychology]. *Enzyklopädie der Psychologie* (Vol. C/VIII/1). Göttingen: Hogrefe.

Pawlik, K. (1996b). Differentielle Psychologie und Persönlichkeitsforschung: Grundbegriffe, Fragestellungen, Systematik [Differential psychology and personality research: Basic concepts, problems, systematics]. In K. Pawlik (Ed.), *Grundlagen und Methoden der Differentiellen Psychologie. Enzyklopädie der Psychologie* (Vol. C/VIII/1, pp. 3–30). Göttingen: Hogrefe.

Pawlik, K., & Buse, L. (1982). Rechnergestützte Verhaltensregistrierung im Feld: Beschreibung und erste psychometrische Überprüfung einer neuen Erhebungsmethode [Computer-assisted field records of behavior: Description and first psychometric evaluation of a new assessment method]. *Zeitschrift für Differentielle und Diagnostische Psychologie, 3*, 101–118.

Pawlik, K., & Buse, L. (1992). Felduntersuchungen zur transsituativen Konsistenz individueller Unterschiede im Erleben und Verhalten [Field studies of trans-situational consistency of individual differences in experience and behavior]. In K. Pawlik & K. H. Stapf (Eds.). *Umwelt und Verhalten* (pp. 25–69). Bern: Huber.

Pawlik, K., & Buse, L. (1996). Verhaltensbeobachtung in Labor und Feld [Behavior Observation in the laboratory and in the field]. In K. Pawlik (Ed.) *Grundlagen und Methoden der Differentiellen Psychologie. Enzyklopädie der Psychologie* (Vol. C/VII/1, pp. 359–394). Göttingen: Hogrefe.

Plomin, R. (1990). *Nature and nurture. An introduction to behavioral genetics.* Belmont, CA: Brooks-Cole.

Plomin, R. (1994). *Genetics and experience.* Thousand Oaks, CA: Sage.

Plomin, R. (1995). Nature, nurture and psychology. In K. Pawlik (Ed.), *Bericht über den 39. Kongress der Deutschen Gesellschaft für Psychologie in Hamburg 1994* (pp. 114–127). Göttingen: Hogrefe.

Plomin, R., McClearn, G. E., Smith, D. L., Vignetti, S., Chorney, M. J., Chorney, K., Venditti, C. P., Kasarda, S., Thompson, L. A., Detterman, D. K., Daniels, J., Owen, M., & McGuffin, P. (1994a). DNA markers associated with high versus low IQ: The IQ Quantitative Trait Loci (QTL) Project. *Behavior Genetics, 24*, 107–118.

Plomin, R., & Nesselroade, J. R. (1990). Behavioral genetics and personality change. *Journal of Personality, 58*, 191–220.

Plomin, R., Pedersen, N. L., Lichtenstein, P., & McClearn, G. E. (1994b). Variability and stability in cognitive abilities are largely genetic later in life. *Behavior Genetics, 24*, 207–215.

Pulkkinen, L. (1993). Longitudinal approaches to adult lifestyles. *Acta Psychologica Fennica, 13*, 13–37.

Revelle, W. (1995). Personality processes. *Annual Review of Psychology, 46*, 295–328.

Robert, P. (1973). *Le Petit Robert.* Paris: Société du Nouveau Littré.

Robinson, D. N. (1989). *Aristotle's psychology.* New York: Columbia University Press.

Royce, J. R. (Ed.). (1973). *Multivariate analysis and psychological theory.* London and New York: Academic.

Sarason, I. G., Smith, R. E., & Diener, E. (1975). Personality research: Components of variance attributable to the person and the situation. *Journal of Personality and Social Psychology, 32*, 199–204.

Spearman, C. (1927). *The abilities of man.* London: Macmillan.

Stern, W. (1900). *Über die Psychologie der individuellen Differenzen* [On the psychology of individual differences]. Leipzig: Barth.

Stern, W. (1911). *Die Differentielle Psychologie in ihren methodischen Grundlagen* (2nd Auflage) [Differential Psychology in its methodological foundations (2nd ed.)]. Leipzig: Barth.

Sternberg, R. J. (Ed.). (1982). *Handbook of human intelligence.* Cambridge: Cambridge University Press.

Tennen, H., Suls, J., & Affleck, G. (Eds.). (1991). Personality and daily experiences. *Journal of Personality, 59*, 313–662.

Thurstone, L. L. (1931). Multiple factor analysis. *Psychological Review, 38*, 406–427.

Thurstone, L. L., & Thurstone, T. G. (1941). Factorial studies of intelligence. *Psychometric Monographs, 2*.

Vernon, P. A. (Ed.). (1993). *Biological approaches to the study of human intelligence.* Norwood, NJ: Ablex.

Vernon, P. A. (Ed.). (1994). *The neuropsychology of individual differences.* San Diego: Academic.

Wilde, O. (1891). The soul of man under socialism. *Fortnightly Review, XLIX*, 292–319.

Wolman, B. B. (Ed.). (1985). *Handbook of intelligence.* New York: Wiley.

PART ONE

Personality and Social Psychology

CHAPTER TWO

Individual differences in temperament: An international perspective

Jan Strelau
University of Warsaw & Silesian University, Poland

Recent decades have witnessed increasing psychological research on temperament. This research is integrated by classifying theories from four following perspectives: child vs. adult, descriptive vs. causal, unidimensional vs. multidimensional, and emotion vs. behavior of the whole person. The taxonomy of temperament theories illustrates the links and divergences among different approaches, which have also stimulated development of an increasing number of assessment techniques, especially inventory measures. Methodological issues relating to self-report and report by others (parents, teachers, and peers) are discussed with regard to assessing child and adult temperament. Attempts to reduce the proliferating number of temperamental traits by relating them to the Big Five personality factors is noted. Biological roots of temperament are illustrated by behavior-genetic studies and research on physiological and biochemical markers of temperamental traits. The functional significance of temperament, illustrated by concepts such as difficult temperament, goodness of fit, and temperament risk factors, is also discussed.

Les récentes décennies ont été les témoins d'un accroissement de la recherche psychologique sur le tempérament. On classifie les théories du tempérament selon quatre perspectives: enfance—âge adulte; descriptive—causale; unidimensionelle—multidimensionelle; émotivité—comportement global. Cette taxonomie fait ressortir les liens et divergences qui caractérisent les diverses approches théoriques et qui ont également stimulé la conception des techniques d'évaluation, tout particulièrement les mesures basées sur des questionnaires. L'auteur traite des problèmes métrologiques associés aux témoignages sur soi et sur les autres (parents, enseignants, pairs) dans l'évaluation du tempérament des enfants et des adultes. Il parle des tentatives qu'on a faites pour réduire le nombre croissant des traits de tempérament en les associant aux "cinq grands" facteurs de personnalité. Les études sur la genèse du comportement et la recherche sur les marqueurs physiologiques et biochimiques des traits de tempérament font ressortir les racines biologiques du tempérament. L'auteur discute également de la signification fonctionnelle du tempérament, reflétée dans des concepts, comme ceux de tempérament difficile, caractère de bonne adaptation et facteurs tempéramentaux de risque.

After several decades of being dominated by behavioristic-oriented theories, it has become clear in psychology that environment by itself cannot explain the variety of behaviors and behavioral disorders, a lesson especially evident to professionals such as psychiatrists, pediatricians, teachers, and educators. Ample evidence has emerged demonstrating that medical treatments and educational procedures based on the behavioristic approach were unsuccessful in clinics, schools, and in the home.

The failure of environmentalists to explain human behavior has created an opportunity for developing theories based on an individual differences paradigm. Behavior-genetic methods applied to studies of human behavior have provided strong evidence that phenotypic variance in intelligence, special abilities, temperament, and some other personality characteristics can be explained only when environment and genetic factors are both taken into account.

The roots of contemporary temperament research are traceable to the 1950s. The theories and empirical studies of Hans Eysenck in England, Alexander Thomas and Stella Chess in the USA, and Boris Teplov in Russia have made possible the development of new ideas and approaches in the psychological study of temperament. Although scientists disagree as to what temperament is, this theoretical construct has to be defined in order to achieve progress. In spite of differences in conceptualizing this phenomenon, most temperament researchers agree with the following definition: temperament refers to basic, relatively stable personality traits that are present from early childhood, occur in human beings, but also have their counterpart in animals. Being primarily determined by inborn neurobiochemical mechanisms, temperament is subject to slow changes caused by maturation and individual-specific, genotype–environment interactions.

Criteria for classifying a trait as temperamental include determinants of development, developmental stages in which the specific characteristic occurs, the population to which it refers, and whether the behavior under study is content saturated or not. We may say that a given trait is *not* temperamental, and belongs instead to other domains of personality, if: (1) there is no evidence for biological determination; (2) the behavioral expression of the trait cannot be observed in childhood; (3) it does not have an equivalent or analogue in animal behavior; and (4) it is strongly content saturated in the sense of reflecting the individual's personality rather than her or his style or manner of expression. Using these criteria, one may question whether some of the Big Five factors considered as basic personality characteristics, such as agreeableness, conscientiousness, and culture (intellect), can be considered as being temperamental in nature, as some authors suggest.

THEORIES OF TEMPERAMENT

The three theoretical approaches to temperament of Eysenck (1970), Thomas and Chess (1977), and Teplov (1964) developed independently and also in isolation from one another. These approaches stimulated many researchers in different parts of the world to evolve their own ideas and conceptualizations of temperament that has led to the development of many micro-theories during the two last decades. I have proposed three criteria in order for a conceptualization to qualify as a theory of temperament: (1) it suggests new views and solutions to problems in the domain of temperament; (2) the conceptual problems are susceptible to verification by means of adequate measures; and (3) empirical evidence exists to support the theory. These additional criteria have allowed me to distinguish Eysenck's biological theory of PEN, Thomas and Chess's interactional theory of child temperament, and Teplov's neo-Pavlovian typology, from nine other conceptualizations of temperament, each of which has the status of a micro-theory. These micro-theories include:

1. Buss and Plomin's behavior-genetic theory of temperament.
2. The developmental model of temperament by Rothbart and Derryberry.
3. The emotion-centered theory of temperament developed by Goldsmith and Campos.
4. Kagan's inhibited and uninhibited types of temperament.
5. Mehrabian's pleasure-arousability-dominance temperament model.
6. The neuropsychological model of temperament developed by Gray.
7. The biological theory of sensation seeking developed by Zuckerman.
8. Rusalov's theory of temperament based on a functional systems approach.
9. Strelau's regulative theory of temperament.

A clear-cut taxonomy of the combined twelve theories of temperament is hardly possible because these theories can be viewed from different perspectives. To show the links as well as the differences between theories of temperament, four additional criteria must be taken into account. These additional criteria are the following:

1. Child (developmental)-oriented versus adult (non-developmental)-oriented.
2. Descriptive versus causal (behavior-genetic or arousal-oriented).
3. Unidimensional versus multidimensional.
4. Emotion versus oriented to the behavior of the whole person.

As can be seen in Table 2.1, the same theory can be classified into several different categories, depending on which criterion is taken into account. For example, Thomas and Chess's interactional theory of temperament can be characterized as child-oriented, multidimensional, descriptive, and centered not only on emotions but on a person's total behavior. In these terms, my own

TABLE 2.1
Classification of temperament theories

Criterion	Author
(1) *Child vs. Adult*	
(a) Child	Buss & Plomin, Goldsmith & Campos, Kagan, Rothbart & Derryberry, Thomas & Chess.
(b) Adult	Eysenck, Gray, Mehrabian, Rusalov, Strelau, Teplov & Nebylitsyn, Zuckerman.
(2) *Descriptive vs. Causal*	
(a) Descriptive	Goldsmith & Campos, Mehrabian, Thomas & Chess.
(b) Causal	Buss & Plomin, Eysenck, Gray, Kagan, Rothbart & Derryberry, Rusalov, Strelau, Teplov & Nebylitsyn, Zuckerman.
(3) *Unidimensional vs. Multidimensional*	
(a) Unidimensional	Kagan, Zuckerman.
(b) Multidimensional	Buss & Plomin, Eysenck, Goldsmith & Campos, Gray, Mehrabian, Rothbart & Derryberry, Rusalov, Strelau, Teplov & Nebylitsyn, Thomas & Chess.
(4) *Emotion vs. Behavior of the whole person*	
(a) Emotion	Goldsmith & Campos, Gray, Mehrabian, Kagan.
(b) Behavior of the Whole Person	Buss & Plomin, Eysenck, Rothbart & Derryberry, Rusalov, Strelau, Teplov & Nebylitsyn, Thomas & Chess, Zuckerman.

theory of temperament would be described as adult-oriented, causal, multidimensional, and comprising temperament characteristics which refer to the behavior of the whole person.

The numerous temperament theories reflect the diversity of views, the richness of temperament approaches, and the range of problems being attacked. On the other hand, they also illustrate that temperament research is not well integrated, which does not facilitate the accumulation of empirical evidence or allow a reasonable synthesis regarding the nature of child and adult temperament. My belief is that taxonomies of temperament theories, as exemplified by the classification proposed in Table 2.1, may be one step toward showing how many temperament theories relate to one another, and where the links and divergences are.

SELECTED ISSUES RELATED TO ASSESSING TEMPERAMENT

The diversity in temperament approaches is even more evident if we take into account the measurement instruments employed in temperament research. Let me limit consideration only to temperament inventories. At first glance, it seems paradoxical that temperament, as a biological phenomenon present in human infants and animals, can be studied by means of "paper and pencil" measures.

It is generally accepted that temperament, whatever mechanisms underlie it, reveals itself in behavioral and emotional reactions. If so, it is reasonable to ask participants to answer questions about matters presumed to be indicators of temperamental expressions present in behaviors and reactions that have occurred in the recent past (last week, month, or year). This retrospective procedure has become popular in studying both child and adult temperament.

There are perhaps 50 child temperament inventories at present. Hubert, Wachs, Peters-Martin, and Gandour (1982), in their analysis of psychometric properties of instruments for infants and children, listed 26 inventories. Seven new questionnaires have since been added in a more recent review (Slabach, Morrow, & Wachs, 1991). I was able to identify 25 English-language temperament inventories for adults (Strelau, 1991a), a list that does not comprise all of the many "paper-pencil" instruments used in different countries. Table 2.2 illustrates this diversity by presenting 17 selected temperament questionnaires for adults, constructed or adapted for English-speaking populations, and which, in my judgment, are currently among the most popular.

One of the issues relevant in the contemporary assessment of child and adult temperament is the preference for self-ratings versus rating by others. Since, with infants and children, only rating by others (parents, teachers, educators) can be employed, it has led some to ask whether inventory ratings are measures of the child's actual temperament (Thomas, Chess, & Korn, 1982) or merely the child's perceived temperament (Bates, 1983; 1989). Without denying that temperament can be measured in infants and children by inventories, several authors (Goldsmith & Rieser-Danner, 1990; Lerner & Lerner, 1987; Rothbart & Mauro, 1990) postulate that the assessment of temperament is an outcome of interactions between the assessed child and the rater, including the social context, the actual situation, accumulated experience, and the rater's own personality-temperament characteristics. The influence of these factors has been confirmed by only moderate interrater agreement when temperament rating is performed by different persons in different relationships to the child, with different views on what kind of behavior is important, and interacting in different situations in which behavior is assessed.

Many studies have aimed at relating temperament scores for children obtained from their mothers and fathers, or their mothers (sometimes both parents) and teachers. These studies have shown that interparent agreement varies from zero to about 0.60, depending on the kind of scale and age of children being compared (e.g. Goldsmith & Campos, 1986; Martin & Halverson, 1991; Pfeffer & Martin, 1983; Rothbart & Derryberry, 1981). A recent meta-analysis of the temperament literature (Strelau, in press) led me to conclude that interparent agreement averages between 0.40 and 0.50; and for mother (parents)–teacher rating, interrater agreement rarely exceeds a correlation of 0.40.

From the beginning of the 1990s, rating by others also entered the domain of adult temperament, which has been traditionally assessed by self-rating. The

TABLE 2.2
Questionnaires aimed at assessing temperament in adolescents and adults

Inventory & References	Scale	Format
Affect Intensity Measure (AIM) Larsen & Diener, 1987[1]	Affect intensity	40 items 6-point scale
Arousal Predisposition Scale (APS) Coren, 1988; 1990	Arousability	12 items 5-point scale
Barratt Impulsiveness Scale (BIS–10) Barratt, 1985	Motor impulsiveness Cognitive impulsiveness Non-planning impulsiveness	34 items 4-point scale
Early Adult Temperament Questionnaire (EATQ) Thomas et al., 1982	Activity level Rhythmicity Adaptability Approach/Withdrawal Intensity Sensory threshold Mood quality Distractibility Persistence/Attention span	140 items 7-point scale
EAS Temperament Survey (EAS–TS)—for adults Buss & Plomin, 1984	Distress Fearfulness Anger Activity Sociability	20 items 5-point scale
Eysenck Personality Questionnaire—Revised (EPQ–R) Eysenck et al., 1985a; for EPQ see Eysenck & Eysenck, 1975	Psychoticism Extraversion Neuroticism Lie scale	100 items short scale: 48 items Yes/No format
Formal Characteristics of Behavior—Temperament Inventory (FCB–TI) Strelau & Zawadzki, 1993; 1995	Briskness Perseverance Sensory sensitivity Emotional reactivity Endurance Activity	120 items Yes/No format
I7 Impulsiveness Questionnaire (I7) Eysenck et al., 1985b	Impulsiveness Venturesomeness Empathy	54 items Yes/No format
Mehrabian Temperament Scale (MTS) Mehrabian, 1978a	Trait-pleasure Trait-arousal Trait-dominance	47 pairs of adjectives 9-point scale
Pavlovian Temperament Survey (PTS) Strelau & Angleitner, 1994; Newberry et al., in press	Strength of excitation Strength of inhibition Mobility of nervous processes	66 items 4-point scale

(continued)

TABLE 2.2
(continued)

Inventory & References	Scale	Format
Reactivity Scale (RS) Kohn, 1985	Reactivity	24 items 5-point scale
Reducer—Augmenter Scale (RAS) Barnes, 1985; Kohn et al., 1986; for revised RAS (RRAS) see Clapper, 1990	Reducing—Augmenting	54 items RRAS: 34 items Forced choice items (A & B)
Revised Dimensions of Temperament Survey (DOTS–R) Windle & Lerner, 1986; for DOTS see Lerner et al., 1982	Activity level—general Activity level—sleep Approach—Withdrawal Flexibility—rigidity Mood Rhythmicity—sleep Rhythmicity—eating Rhythmicity—daily habits Distractibility Persistence	54 items 4-point scale
Sensation Seeking Scale (SSS)—Form IV & V Zuckerman, 1979; 1994	Thrill and adventure seeking Experience seeking Disinhibition Boredom Susceptibility Sensation seeking (general—IV, total—V)	SSS-IV: 72 items SSS-V: 40 items Forced choice items (A & B)
Structure of Temperament Questionnaire (STQ) Rusalov, 1989	Ergonicity, object-related Ergonicity, social Plasticity, object-related Plasticity, social Tempo, object-related Tempo, social Emotionality, object-related Emotionality, social	105 items Yes/No format
Thurstone Temperament Schedule (TTS)	Active Vigorous Impulsive Dominant Emotionally stable Sociable Reflective	140 items 3-point scale
Trait Arousability Scale (TAS) Mehrabian, 1977a; 1977b)	Stimulus screening— Arousability	40 items 9-point scale

[1] For reasons of space, many of the citations in this Table are not listed in the Reference section.

largest study in which both self- and peer-rating of temperament were compared with each other is the Bielefeld-Warsaw Twin Project (BWTP) (Angleitner et al. 1995; Strelau, Oniszczenko, Zawadzki, Bodunov, & Angleitner, 1995). Data were collected from over 3,000 twins (with only one twin from each pair) and more than 6,000 peers (each twin assessed by two peers). In this study, five

TABLE 2.3
Means of reliability scores and rater agreement on temperament inventories:
Self(S)- and Peer(P)-Rating Data from German (G) and Polish (P) Samples

	Cronbach α S-report		P-report[1]		Agreement betw. raters[2]		S-P reports[3]	
	G	P	G	P	G	P	G	P
PTS	.85	.79	.86	.81	.57	.50	.48	.43
G: n = 2087								
P: n = 1092								
FCB–TI	.80	.81	.82	.83	.56	.60	.49	.51
G: n = 2087								
P: n = 1092								
EAS-TS	.70	.64	.71	.68	.58	.55	.49	.49
G: n = 1303								
P: n = 1092								
DOTS–R	.79	.68	.77	.69	.45	.45	.41	.39
G: n = 1303								
P: n = 1092								
EPQ–R	.74	.79	.77	.84	.60	.59	.53	.55
G: n = 1303								
P: n = 1092								
Mean	.78	.74	.79	.77	.55	.54	.48	.47

NOTES:

[1] For peer-report the number of subjects is double because each twin was rated by two peers.

[2] Intraclass-correlations (ICC 1.2 including Spearman–Brown correction for 2 raters) for rater agreement (rater 1 and rater 2 per target).

[3] Correlations between self-report and averaged peer-report.

temperament inventories were employed: The Pavlovian Temperament Survey, (PTS; Strelau, Angleitner, Bantelmann, & Ruch, 1990), the Formal Characteristics of Behavior—Temperament Inventory (FCB–TI; Strelau & Zawadzki, 1993), the EAS Temperament Survey (EAS–TS; Buss & Plomin, 1984), the Revised Dimensions of Temperament Survey (DOTS–R; Windle & Lerner 1986) and the Eysenck Personality Questionnaire—Revised (EPQ–R; Eysenck, Eysenck, & Barrett, 1985). For peer-rating, the items were phrased in the third person.

Results from this study, depicted in Table 2.3, permit several conclusions. First, the cross-cultural comparisons are very consistent and striking regarding agreement between raters. Second, average agreement between raters across the five inventories is over 0.50 (0.55 and 0.54), and only a little lower than 0.50 between self-report and average peer-report. Third, internal consistency reliability of the five temperament inventories applied in the BWTP, as assessed by Cronbach's α, is also consistent across countries and type of rating. On average, the reliability scores for self- and peer-rating are close to the 0.80s (0.78 and 0.77 for self-report, and 0.79 and 0.77 for peer-report in the German and Polish study, respectively).

THE NUMBER OF BASIC
TEMPERAMENTAL TRAITS

From the 17 questionnaires listed in Table 2.2 for adults and the 21 inventories for assessing temperament in infants and children (Strelau, in press), the number of temperament traits (characteristics) assessed by these various instruments is 71. These traits range from very narrow constructs (for example, activity level–sleep or rhythmicity–eating) to very broad ones (such as extraversion or general activity), reflecting different levels of behavioral organization.

The trend to reduce basic personality traits to a small number of factors, as exemplified by the Big Five approach, has led temperament researchers to revise the number of basic temperament traits. This tendency has been most clearly shown in the recent volume edited by Halverson, Kohnstamm, and Martin (1994). Studies by Angleitner and Ostendorf (1994) as well as Strelau and Zawadzki (1996) showed that when over two dozen scales from popular temperament inventories for adults are factor analyzed, five or six factors result. These factors, however, only replicate the Extraversion and Neuroticism factors of the Big Five, as measured by the NEO inventories.

A study by Strelau and Zawadzki (1996) on 527 subjects aged from 20 to 77 years (259 males and 268 females), in which four temperament inventories representing four different approaches to temperament were factor analyzed, suggests that only extraversion and neuroticism should be regarded as being temperamental in nature. As shown in Table 2.4, the first factor, identified as Emotionality, had the highest correlation with Neuroticism measured by the NEO–FFI. The second factor, labeled Extraversion, has its highest correlation with the NEO Extraversion scale. Factor III, Rhythmicity, has only low, although significant, correlations with three NEO–FFI scales (Costa & McCrae, 1992). Factor IV, called Activity/Attentional Focus, shows a moderate correlation with Conscientiousness and a rather low correlation with the Extraversion scale. The last factor, labeled Sensory Sensitivity, shows only low correlations with the O, A, and C scales of the NEO. If a temperament inventory other than the DOTS–R had been included, the Rhythmicity factor would not emerge.

At least two general conclusions may be drawn from the preceding study, which was also replicated by Strelau, Zawadzki, and Oniszczenko (1996) on twins. First, when about two dozen or more temperamental scales are factor analyzed, only two of the resulting factors—Extraversion and Neuroticism (Emotionality) —are directly related to corresponding factors from the Big Five and Giant Three. The other factors are temperament-specific and relate only loosely to the remaining three factors from the Big Five. Conscientiousness, Agreeableness, and Openness (Culture, Intellect) should be considered as belonging to the domain of character (Strelau & Zawadzki, 1996). However, character does not develop in isolation from temperament, which explains some links between temperament factors and the NEO C, A, and O factors of the Big Five.

TABLE 2.4
Temperamental traits related to the Big Five
personality factors

	Factor				
Scale	*I*	*II*	*III*	*IV*	*V*
PTS					
SE	−.69			.31	
SI	−.52				.42
MO	−.51	.56			
FCB–TI					
BR	−.48			.52	
PE	.76				
SS					.79
ER	.84				
EN	−.72				
AC		.71			
EAS–TS					
SOC		.68			
ACT		.33		.71	
EMO	.71				
DOTS–R					
A–G		.33		.69	
A–S	.32				
A–W	−.30	.67			
F–R	−.54	.42			
MQ		.71			
R–S			.73		
R–E			.78		
R–H			.79		
DIS				.56	
PER			.36	.51	.40

Correlations of the factors with the NEO–FFI scales

N	.59	−.26	−.14		
E		.70		.31	
O		.23	−.20		.29
A		.14			.20
C	−.12		.27	.43	.22

NOTE:
    Factor loadings <.30 are omitted. Only statistically significant
correlations are listed.

Second, the results of factor analysis depend on which temperament scales
are included. The more scales aimed at measuring a similar trait, the higher the
probability they will emerge as a separate factor, as exemplified by rhythmicity.
In a factor analysis that takes into account several inventories, scales specific

to a given theory rarely emerge as an independent factor. This fact cannot be used, however, to argue that traits measured by theory-specific scales should be regarded as marginal.

THE BIOLOGICAL NATURE OF TEMPERAMENT

The definition of temperament presented at the outset implies a biological co-determination of temperament. One may assume that genes are responsible for the physiological and biochemical mechanisms underlying temperament (Zuckerman, 1995). If so, the genetic factor should essentially contribute to individual differences in temperament. During the last two decades, numerous studies have been conducted with children and adults showing that the genetic factor contributes considerably to individual differences in temperament, although not as highly as expected in the earlier stage of behavior–genetic research (Buss & Plomin, 1975; Eysenck, 1970). Studies of infants and children suggest that heritability accounts for approximately 50% of the phenotypic variance of temperament characteristics (e.g. Braungart, Plomin, DeFries, & Fulker, 1992; Goldsmith, 1989). Somewhat lower heritability scores have arisen from recent meta-analyses of adult temperament data. For example, Loehlin (1992) stated that genes account for 35% to 39% of the variance in individual differences in extraversion; and broad-sense heritability for neuroticism (emotionality) is about 0.42. Close to these findings are data collected from a sample of 2680 adult participants by Heath, Cloninger, and Martin (1994). A robust finding, consistently replicated in these studies, is that nonshared environment is an essential factor contributing to individual differences in temperament.

Behavior–genetic data from the BWTP project, in which five temperament inventories (EPQ–R, EAS–TS, DOTS–R, PTS and FCB–TI) were employed, strongly correspond with recent findings regarding the contribution of genes and nonshared environment to the phenotypic variance of temperament characteristics. Table 2.5 presents results obtained in self-rating scores based on the Polish sample composed of 546 adolescent and adult twin pairs (229 MZ and 317 DZ pairs). Taking ratings from five temperament inventories, including 27 scales altogether, the average contribution of the genetic factor is estimated to be 36% of the variance, similar to that stated by Loehlin with respect to extraversion and neuroticism. This study also supports the importance of nonshared environment in molding individual differences in temperament. If we consider that the average reliability of the temperament scales is slightly less than 0.80, then one may conclude that about 40% of the phenotypic variance of temperament can be explained by nonshared environment.

Behavior–genetic studies in the domain of temperament are almost exclusively based on parent or teacher ratings of children and on self-ratings in adolescents and adults. I know of no research in which the contribution of heredity and environment to individual differences in temperament was derived from two

TABLE 2.5

Estimates of genetic and environmental variance components under the best-fitting models with respect to 27 temperamental traits

Temperament scale	Variance estimate			
	A	D	C	E
FCB–TI				
BR	50			50
PE	43			57
SS	42			58
ER	34		19	46
EN	46			54
AC	54			46
Mean		45		52
PTS				
SE	42			58
SI		38		62
MO			32	68
Mean		27		63
EAS–TS				
SOC		32		68
ACT		33		67
FE	47			53
DS	43			57
AN	27			73
Mean		36		64
DOTS–R				
A–G		36		64
A–S		27		73
A–W	25			75
F–R	24		15	61
MQ	31			69
R–S	42			58
R–E			33	67
R–H		45		55
DIS	29			71
PER	21			79
Mean		28		67
EPQ–R				
P		46		54
E		36		64
N	49			51
Mean		44		56
Mean for 5 invent.		36		60

NOTE:

A = additive genetic variance; D = nonadditive genetic variance; C = shared environment; E = nonshared environment. The means of the genetic variance are taken from the sum of A and D. No average score was calculated for C which contributes only to four temperament traits.

independent measures. Such a study, however, was recently conducted within the BWTP project (Angleitner et al., 1995; Strelau et al., 1995) in which each twin was rated with respect to 27 temperament characteristics by two peers, who differed for each twin. Preliminary findings in regard to peers suggest that the contribution of both genes and nonshared environment is similar to that for self-ratings. These results will be very supportive of findings regarding the impact of genes and nonshared environment to individual differences in temperament.

More studies are now being undertaken in which data from different neuro-physiological and behavioral levels are compared with each other, mostly with the aim of validating one measure by comparing it against another one, or in order to assess both the behavioral and physiological components of tempera-ment characteristics, as exemplified in Kagan's (1994) approach to inhibited temperament. The combination of psychometric or behavioral measures with neurophysiological markers seems to be the most adequate way for studying the nature of temperament. Researchers who advocate this approach are confronted, however, with serious difficulties that arise frequently: viz. the lack of consist-ency between physiological measures and behavioral ones, as well as between physiological and inventory (i.e. self-report) data. In particular, temperament characteristics reflecting the construct of arousal or arousability are frequently inconsistent between these classes of measures. Findings showing a lack of agreement between psychophysiological or psychophysical markers of tempera-ment, as well as a lack of correlation between these markers and psychometric assessments of temperamental traits, have been recorded with regard to extraver-sion (Eysenck & Levey, 1972; Amelang & Ullwer, 1991), sensation seeking (Zuckerman, Simons, & Como, 1988), and strength of excitation (Kohn, 1987; Strelau, 1972) and most evident with respect to neuroticism. For many years, Fahrenberg (1987; Fahrenberg, Walschburger, Foerster, Myrtek, & Mueller, 1983) and his co-workers have studied the physiological markers of psychometrically measured neuroticism (emotionality) and have shown that neuroticism does not correlate with any of the many markers employed, whether the physiological measures are taken under rest or when performing tasks. In this research, the following physiological characteristics were taken into account: heart rate, pulse volume, electrodermal activity, EEG alpha characteristics, respiratory irregular-ity, eye-blink activity and electromyographic changes.

Studies of the relationship between neurotransmitters, their enzymes and tem-perament characteristics, especially sensation seeking (Ballenger et al., 1983), emo-tionality (Depue, Luciana, Abisi, Collins, & Leon, 1994), impulsivity (Schalling, Edman, Asberg, & Oreland, 1988), and extraversion (Netter & Rammsayer, 1991) have recently gained increasing popularity. The hope that CNS biochemistry will shed some light on the biological background of temperament is based on several premises that, in general, concern the possibility of identifying neuro-transmitter systems in the brain regarded as essential sources of individual dif-ferences in temperamental traits. Results from these studies are, however, far from being unequivocal (see Strelau, in press; Zuckerman, 1995). It may be concluded that trait-specific neurotransmitters will probably not be found in the domain of temperament, and that an essential part of the variance of these traits is a complex interaction between different kinds of neurotransmitters and their enzymes.

Although some inconsistencies between physiological (biochemical) markers and psychometric assessments of temperament are due to methodological shortcomings or theoretical defects of the measures compared (Gale & Edwards, 1983), it also has to be borne in mind that fundamental differences exist between self- or peer-rating measures based on retrospective reports and measures of physiological and biochemical processes that are qualitatively different phenomena and not necessarily related directly to psychometric measures (Strelau, 1991b). When studying the physiological or biochemical markers of temperament, we are confronted with qualitatively different levels of behavioral organization, although both physiological (biochemical) processes and macro-behavior refer to the same phenomenon (i.e. temperament), but from different perspectives.

THE FUNCTIONAL SIGNIFICANCE OF TEMPERAMENT

One of the main features of contemporary research on temperament is increasing concentration on issues relating to the functional significance of temperament. Studies examining the role temperament plays in human functioning under different circumstances and in different environments are age-specific. For example, in children, the functional significance of temperament is mainly expressed in social interactions with parents and other caretakers and in scholastic behavior from nursery to college level. In adults, the role of temperament is evident in professional activity, leisure-time activity, and social interaction or partner relationships. Independently of age-specific activity and situations, many researchers (e.g. Chess & Thomas, 1989; Kagan, 1983; Nebylitsyn, 1972; Strelau, 1983; Thomas & Chess, 1977; Zuckerman, 1994) agree that the functional significance of temperamental traits arises when the individual is confronted with difficult situations and extreme demands.

One must distinguish whether these situations and demands refer to children or adults. In children, specific concepts, such as "difficult temperament" (Carey, 1986; Thomas, Chess, & Birch, 1968) and "goodness of fit" (Chess & Thomas, 1991; Lerner, 1984) have been developed; whereas in studies of adults, concepts referring to different aspects of stress have gained widest popularity (Eysenck, 1983; Strelau, 1995). In both approaches, temperament is regarded as a risk factor, which, in interaction with other persistent or recurrent factors, heightens the probability of developing behavioral disorders and pathology, or favors development of a maladjusted personality.

Over a hundred studies have been conducted during recent decades to demonstrate the functional significance of temperament (for a review, see Strelau, in press). In general, one may say that the results are positive and very promising.

Also, our own studies (Eliasz, 1981; Klonowicz, 1992; Strelau, 1983) examining the "temperament–stress" relationship have shown that temperament, being a moderator variable, affects the intensity of stressors and states of stress, thus influencing outcomes such as level of performance or ways of coping. Our findings also accord with many findings reported in the literature, showing that temperament contributes to the consequences of stress in terms of behavioral disorders and pathology (see Carey & McDevitt, 1989; Chess & Thomas, 1984; Garrison & Earls, 1987; Grossarth-Maticek & Eysenck, 1995; Maziade et al., 1990; Windle, 1991). In most of these studies, the "temperament–stress" relationship emerges as a complex one, where temperament, only when in interaction with other external or internal factors, co-determines the state of stress as well as its consequences in terms of physiological and biochemical costs or disorders and pathology.

CONCLUSION

Research on temperament conducted during the last few decades of this century has made an essential step forward in the attempt to understand this phenomenon. In spite of diverse viewpoints regarding the nature of temperament, its structure, and the ways of assessing temperamental traits, an opportunity to integrate the variety of different approaches seems to be present in contemporary research. Although many issues remain unresolved (e.g. the biological bases of temperament and the number of primary or fundamental, temperamental traits), the findings to date justify further research aimed at discovering the complex nature of temperament. Of special importance are studies that explore the functional significance of temperament in children and adults. Such constructs as difficult temperament, goodness of fit, and temperament risk factor have been shown to be powerful concepts in explaining causes of behavioral disorders and pathology.

ACKNOWLEDGEMENTS

Part of the research reported in this paper was supported by the Polish Research Foundation KBN, Grant 1H01F06609.

REFERENCES

Amelang, M., & Ullwer, U. (1991). Correlations between psychometric measures and psychophysiological as well as experimental variables in studies on extraversion and neuroticism. In J. Strelau & A. Angleitner (Eds.), *Explorations in temperament: International perspectives on theory and measurement* (pp. 287–315). New York: Plenum.

Angleitner, A., & Ostendorf, F. (1994). Temperament and the Big Five factors of personality. In C. F. Halverson, Jr., G. A. Kohnstamm, & R. P. Martin (Eds.), *The developing structure of temperament and personality from infancy to adulthood* (pp. 69–90). Hillsdale, NJ: Erlbaum.

Angleitner, A., Riemann, R. Spinath. F. M., Hempel, S., Thiel, W., & Strelau, J. (1995). *The Bielefeld–Warsaw Twin Project: First report on the Bielefeld samples.* Pultusk, Poland: Workshop on Genetic Studies on Temperament and Personality.

Ballenger, J. C., Post, R. M., Jimerson, D. C., Lake, C. R., Murphy, D., Zuckerman, M., & Cronin, C. (1983). Biochemical correlates of personality traits in normals: An exploratory study. *Personality and Individual Differences, 4,* 615–625.

Bates, J. E. (1983). Issues in the assessment of difficult temperament: A reply to Thomas, Chess, and Korn. *Merrill-Palmer Quarterly, 29,* 89–97.

Bates, J. E. (1989). Concepts and measures of temperament. In G. A. Kohnstamm, J. E. Bates, & M. K. Rothbart (Eds.), *Temperament in childhood* (pp. 3–26). Chichester, UK: Wiley.

Braungart, J. M., Plomin, R., DeFries, J. C., & Fulker, D. W. (1992). Genetic influence on tester-rated infant temperament as assessed by Bayley's Infant Behavior Record: Nonadoptive and adoptive siblings and twins. *Developmental Psychology, 28,* 40–47.

Buss, A. H., & Plomin, R. (1975). *A temperament theory of personality development.* New York: Wiley.

Buss, A. H., & Plomin, R. (1984). *Temperament: Early developing personality traits.* Hillsdale, NJ: Erlbaum.

Carey, W. B. (1986). The difficult child. *Pediatrics in Review, 8,* 39–45.

Carey, W. B., & McDevitt, S. C. (Eds.). (1989). *Clinical and educational applications of tempera-ment research.* Lisse: Swets & Zeitlinger.

Chess, S., & Thomas, A. (1984). *Origins and evolution of behavior disorders: From infancy to early adult life.* New York: Brunner/Mazel.

Chess, S., & Thomas, A. (1989). Temperament and its functional significance. In S. I. Greenspan & G. H. Pollock (Eds.), *The course of life* (Vol. 2, pp. 163–227). Madison, CT: International Universities Press.

Chess, S., & Thomas, A. (1991). Temperament and the concept of goodness of fit. In J. Strelau & A. Angleitner (Eds.), *Explorations in temperament: International perspectives on theory and measurement* (pp. 15–28). New York: Plenum.

Costa, P. T., Jr., & McCrae, R. R. (1992). *Revised NEO Personality Inventory (NEO-PI-R) and NEO Five Factor Inventory (NEO-FFI): Professional manual.* Odessa, FL: Psychological Assessment Resources.

Depue, R. A., Luciana, M., Arbisi, P., Collins, P., & Leon, A. (1994). Dopamine and the structure of personality: Relationship of agonist-induced dopamine activity to positive emotionality. *Journal of Personality and Social Psychology, 67,* 485–498.

Eliasz, A. (1981). *Temperament a system regulacji stymulacji* [Temperament and system of regu-lation of stimulation]. Warszawa: Państwowe Wydawnictwo Naukowe.

Eysenck, H. J. (1970). *The structure of human personality* (3rd ed.). London: Methuen.

Eysenck, H. J. (1983). Stress, disease, and personality: The "inoculation effect". In C. L. Cooper (Ed.), *Stress research* (pp. 121–131). London: Wiley.

Eysenck, H. J., & Levey, A. (1972). Conditioning, introversion–extraversion and the strength of the nervous system. In V. D. Nebylitsyn & J. A. Gray (Eds.), *Biological bases of individual behavior* (pp. 206–220). Orlando, FL: Academic.

Eysenck, S. B. G., Eysenck, H. J., & Barrett, P. (1985). A revised version of the Psychoticism scale. *Personality and Individual Differences, 6,* 21–29.

Fahrenberg, J. (1987). Concepts of activation and arousal in the theory of emotionality (neuroticism): A multivariate conceptualization. In J. Strelau & H. J. Eysenck (Eds.), *Personality dimensions and arousal* (pp. 99–120). New York: Plenum.

Fahrenberg, J., Walschburger, P, Foerster, F., Myrtek, M., & Muller, W. (1983). An evaluation of trait, state, and reaction aspects of activation processes. *Psychophysiology, 20,* 188–195.

Gale, A., & Edwards, J. A. (1983). Psychophysiology and individual differences: Theory, research procedures, and the interpretation of data. *Autralian Journal of Psychology, 35,* 361–379.

Garrison, W. T., & Earls, F. J. (1987). *Temperament and child psychopathology.* Thousand Oaks, CA: Sage.

Goldsmith, H. H. (1989). Behavior–genetic approaches to temperament. In G. A. Kohnstamm, J. E. Bates, & M. K. Rothbart (Eds.), *Temperament in childhood* (pp. 111–132). Chichester, UK: Wiley.

Goldsmith, H. H., & Campos, J. J. (1986). Fundamental issues in the study of early temperament: The Denver Twin Temperamental Study. In M. E. Lamb, A. L. Brown, & B. Rogoff (Eds.), *Advances in developmental psychology* (Vol. 4, pp. 231–283). Hillsdale, NJ: Erlbaum.

Goldsmith, H. H., & Rieser–Danner, L. A. (1990). Assessing early temperament. In C. R. Reynolds & R. W. Kamphaus (Eds.), *Handbook of psychological and educational assessment of children: Personality, behavior, and context* (pp. 245–278). New York: Guilford.

Grossarth-Maticek, R., & Eysenck, H. J. (1995). Self-regulation and mortality from cancer, coronary heart disease, and other causes: A prospective study. *Personality and Individual Differences, 19*, 781–795.

Halverson, C. F., Jr., Kohnstamm, G. A., & Martin R. P. (Eds.). (1994). *The developing structure of temperament and personality from infancy to adulthood.* Hillsdale, NJ: Erlbaum.

Heath, A. C., Cloninger, C. R., & Martin, N. G. (1994). Testing a model for the genetic structure of personality: A comparison of the personality systems of Cloninger and Eysenck. *Journal of Personality and Social Psychology 66*, 762–775.

Hubert, N. C., Wachs, T. D., Peters-Martin, P., & Gandour, M. J. (1982). The study of early temperament: Measurement and conceptual issues. *Child Development, 53*, 571–600.

Kagan, J. (1983). Stress and coping in early development. In N. Garmezy & M. Rutter (Eds.), *Stress, coping and development in children* (pp. 191–216). New York: McGraw-Hill.

Kagan, J. (1994). *Galen's prophecy: Temperament in human nature.* New York: Basic Books.

Klonowicz, T. (1992). *Stres w Wieiy Babel: Róinice indywidualne a wysiłek inwestowany w trudni pracę umysłową* [Stress in the Tower of Babel: Individual differences and allocation of effort during difficult mental work]. Wrocław: Ossolineum.

Kohn, P. M. (1987). Issues in the measurement of arousability. In J. Strelau & H. J. Eysenck (Eds.), *Personality dimensions and arousal* (pp. 233–250). New York: Plenum.

Lerner, J. V. (1984). The import of temperament for psychosocial functioning: Tests of a "goodness of fit" model. *Merrill-Palmer Quarterly, 30*, 177–188.

Lerner, R. M., & Lerner, J. V. (1987). Children in their contexts: A goodness of fit model. In J. B. Lancaster, J. Altmann, A. S. Rossi, & L. R. Sherrod (Eds.), *Parenting across the life span: Biosocial dimensions* (pp. 377–404). Chicago: Aldine.

Loehlin, J. C. (1992). *Genes and environment in personality development.* Thousand Oaks, CA: Sage.

Martin, R. P., & Halverson, C. F., Jr. (1991). Mother–father agreement in temperament ratings: A preliminary investigation. In J. Strelau & A. Angleitner (Eds.), *Explorations in temperament: International perspectives on theory and measurement* (pp. 235–248). New York: Plenum.

Maziade, M., Caron, C., Coté, R., Merette, C., Bernier, H., Laplante, B., Boutin, P., & Thivierge, J. (1990). Psychiatric status of adolescents who had extreme temperaments at age 7. *American Journal of Psychiatry, 147*, 1531–1536.

Nebylitsyn, V. D. (1972). *Fundamental properties of the human nervous system.* New York: Plenum.

Netter, P., & Rammsayer, T. (1991). Reactivity to dopaminergic drugs and aggression related personality traits. *Personality and Individual Differences, 12*, 1009–1017.

Pfeffer, J., & Martin, R. P. (1983). Comparison of mothers' and fathers' temperament ratings of referred and nonreferred preschool children. *Journal of Clinical Psychology, 39*, 1013–1020.

Rothbart, M. K., & Derryberry, D. (1981). Development of individual differences in temperament. In M. E. Lamb & A. L. Brown (Eds.), *Advances in developmental psychology* (Vol. 1, pp. 37–86). Hillsdale, NJ: Erlbaum.

Rothbart, M. K., & Mauro, J. A. (1990). Questionnaire approaches to the study of infant temperament. In J. Colombo & J. Fagen (Eds.), *Individual differences in infancy: Reliability, stability, prediction* (pp.411–429). Hillsdale, NJ: Erlbaum.

Schalling, D., Edman, G., Asberg, M., & Oreland, L. (1988). Platelet MAO activity associated with impulsivity and aggressivity. *Personality and Individual Differences, 9*, 597–605.

Slabach, E. H., Morrow, J., & Wachs, T. (1991). Questionnaire measurement of infant and child temperament. In J. Strelau & A. Angleitner (Eds.), *Explorations in temperament: International perspectives on theory and measurement* (pp. 205–234). New York: Plenum.

Strelau, J. (1972). The general and partial nervous system types: Data and theory. In V. D. Nebylitsyn & J. A. Gray (Eds.), *Biological bases of individual behavior* (pp. 62–73). London: Academic.

Strelau, J. (1983). *Temperament, personality, activity.* London: Academic.

Strelau, J. (1991a). Renaissance in research on temperament: Where to? In J. Strelau & A. Angleitner (Eds.), *Explorations in temperament: International perspectives on theory and measurement* (pp. 337–358). New York: Plenum.

Strelau, J. (1991b). Are psychophysiological/psychophysical scores good candidates for diagnosing temperament/personality traits and for a demonstration of the construct validity of psychometrically measured traits? *European Journal of Personality, 5,* 323–342.

Strelau, J. (1995). Temperament and stress: Temperament as a moderator of stressors, emotional states, coping, and costs. In C. D. Spielberger & I. G. Sarason (Eds.), *Stress and emotion: Anxiety, anger, and curiosity* (Vol. 15, pp. 215–254). Washington: Hemisphere.

Strelau, J. (in press). *Temperament: A psychological perspective.* New York: Plenum.

Strelau, J. Angleitner, A., Bantelmann, J., & Ruch, W. (1990). The Strelau Temperament Inventory—Revised (STI–R): Theoretical considerations and scale development. *European Journal of Personality, 4,* 209–235.

Strelau, J., & Zawadzki, B. (1993). The Formal Characteristics of Behavior—Temperament Inventory (FCB–TI): Theoretical assumptions and scale construction. *European Journal of Personality, 7,* 313–336.

Strelau, J., & Zawadzki, B. (1996). Temperament dimensions as related to the Giant Three and the Big Five factors: A psychometric approach [in English]. In A. V. Brushlinsky & T. N. Ushakova (Eds.), *V. D. Nebylitsyn: Life and scientific creativity* (pp. 260–281). Moscow: Ladomir [in Russian].

Strelau, J., Oniszczenko, W., Zawadzki, B., Bodunov, M., & Angleitner, A. (1995). *Genetic determination and the structure of temperament and personality in adults: Cross-cultural study based on German and Polish samples: Report from the Polish part of the German-Polish project.* Pultusk, Poland:Workshop on Genetic Studies on Temperament and Personality.

Strelau, J., Zawadzki, B., & Oniszczenko, W. (1996, August). Where is the place of temperament: Among the Giant Three, the Big Five or anywhere else? In N. S. Endler (Chair), *Personality: Biological, psychological, and social models.* Symposium conducted at the XXVI International Congress of Psychology, Montreal, Canada.

Teplov, B. M. (1964). Problems in the study of general types of higher nervous activity in man and animals. In J. A. Gray (Ed.), *Pavlov's typology: Recent theoretical and experimental developments from the Laboratory of B. M. Teplov* (pp. 3–153). Oxford: Pergamon.

Thomas, A., & Chess, S. (1977). *Temperament and development.* New York: Brunner/Mazel.

Thomas, A., Chess, S., & Birch, H. G. (1968). *Temperament and behavior disorders in children.* New York: New York University Press.

Thomas, A., Chess, S., & Korn, S. J. (1982). The reality of difficult temperament. *Merrill-Palmer Quarterly, 28,* 1–20.

Windle, M. (1991). The difficult temperament in adolescence: Associations with substance use, family support, and problem behaviors. *Journal of Clinical Psychology, 47,* 310–315.

Windle, M., & Lerner, R. M. (1986). Reassessing the dimensions of temperamental individuality across the life-span: The Revised Dimensions of Temperament Survey (DOTS–R). *Journal of Adolescent Research, 1,* 213–230.

Zuckerman, M. (1994). *Behavioral expressions and biosocial bases of sensation seeking.* New York: Cambridge University Press.

Zuckerman, M. (1995). Good and bad humors: Biochemical bases of personality and its disorders. *Psychological Science, 6,* 325–332.

Zuckerman, M., Simons, R. F., & Como, P. G. (1988). Sensation seeking and stimulus intensity as modulators of cortical, cardiovascular, and electrodermal resonse: A cross-modality study. *Personality and Individual Differences, 9,* 361–372.

CHAPTER THREE

Personal and collective efficacy in human adaptation and change

Albert Bandura
Stanford University, California, USA

Perceived self-efficacy operates as a central self-regulatory mechanism of human agency. People's beliefs that they can produce desired effects by their actions influence the choices they make, their aspirations, level of effort and perseverance, resilience to adversity, and vulnerability to stress and depression. This chapter addresses the origins of efficacy beliefs, the processes through which they operate, their diverse effects, and the modes by which they can be modified. Human adaptation and change are rooted in social systems. Personal agency through efficacy belief operates within a broad network of sociostructural influences. In these agentic transactions, people are producers as well as products of social systems. People often have to work together to shape their social future. Self-efficacy theory, therefore, extends the conception of agent causality to people's beliefs in their collective efficacy to produce desired outcomes. With growing transnational interdependencies, life in the societies of today is now shaped by events in distant places. The globalization of human interconnectedness presents new challenges for people to exercise some control over their personal destinies and national life.

La perception qu'un individu a de sa propre efficacité agit comme un mécanisme autorégulateur de l'action humaine. La croyance qu'ont les gens de pouvoir produire des effets désirés par l'entremise de leurs actions exerce une influence sur les choix qu'ils font, sur leurs aspirations, sur leur niveau d'effort et de persévérance, sur leur résistance dans l'adversité et sur leur vulnérabilité face au stress et à la dépression. Ce chapitre traite des origines des croyances dans l'efficacité personnelle, du processus de leur action, de leurs effets variés et des façons dont elles peuvent être modifiées. L'adaptation et le changement de l'être humain sont ancrés dans les systèmes sociaux. Par l'intermédiaire de la croyance en l'efficacité, l'action personnelle agit à l'intérieur d'un vaste réseau d'influences socio-structurelles. Dans ces transactions, les individus sont des producteurs ainsi que des produits des systèmes sociaux. Les gens doivent souvent travailler ensemble pour forger leur avenir social. Par conséquent, la théorie de l'efficacité personnelle étend la conception d'un lien causal entre agents, aux croyances des individus dans leur

efficacité collective pour la production des résultats désirés. Avec l'accroissement d'interdépendances entre nations, la vie dans les sociétés d'aujourd'hui est
maintenant moulée par des évènements dans des endroits lointains. La globalisation
des liens entre humains présente aux gens de nouveaux défis les obligeant à exercer
un certain contrôle sur leur destin personnel et leur vie nationale.

People have always striven to control events that affect their lives. Control is
sought because it provides countless personal and social benefits. By influencing events over which they have some control, people are better able to realize
desired futures and to forestall undesired ones. Growth of knowledge has greatly
increased people's ability to predict events and to control them. By applying this
knowledge, people built physical technologies that transformed how they live
their lives. They developed biological technologies to alter the genetic makeup
of plants and animals. They created medical and psychosocial technologies to
improve the quality of their physical and psychosocial lives. They devised social
systems with entitlements and institutional protections against tyrannical control
that expanded freedom of belief and action.

The enhanced human power to transform the environment is not an unmixed
blessing. Control wielded for short-run benefits can have pervasive harmful consequences on current life and on how future generations live their lives. There
is growing public concern over where some of the technologies we are creating
are leading us.

The accelerated pace of informational, social and technological evolution has
placed a premium on people's capabilities to exert a strong hand in their own
development throughout the life course. Under rapidly changing environments,
skills that were functional are quickly outmoded requiring continual self-renewal.

SELF-EFFICACY IN THE EXERCISE OF
HUMAN AGENCY

Because of the centrality of control in people's lives many theories about it have
been proposed. Much of this research is tied to general measures of perceived control and search for their correlates. In social cognitive theory, perceived efficacy is
embedded in a theory of human agency. People make causal contribution to their
lives through mechanisms of personal agency. Among the mechanisms of agency,
none is more central or pervasive than people's judgments of their efficacy.
Unless people believe they can produce desired effects by their actions they
have little incentive to act. Efficacy belief is, therefore, the foundation of action.

Theorizing and research address each of the various facets of this self-
regulative mechanism. These include: the nature and structure of efficacy beliefs;
their origins; the diverse ways in which they affect psychosocial functioning; the
intervening processes through which they exert their effects; and the modes by
which they can be instilled and strengthened to enhance human functioning. The
vast literature and wide-ranging applications of self-efficacy theory to different

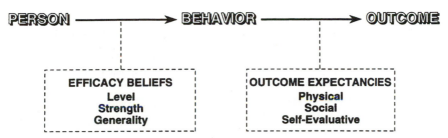

FIG. 3.1   Diagrammatic representation of the conditional relations between efficacy beliefs and outcome expectancies. In given domains of functioning, efficacy beliefs vary in level, strength and generality. The outcomes that flow from a given course of action can take the form of positive or negative physical, social, and self-evaluative effects.

spheres of life are reviewed in *Self-Efficacy: The Exercise of Control* (Bandura, 1997).

Perceived efficacy refers to beliefs in one's capabilities to organize and execute the courses of action required to produce given levels of attainments. The events over which influence is exercised vary widely, however. They may entail regulating of one's own motivation, thought processes, affective states and actions or changing environmental conditions, depending on what one seeks to manage.

People's judgments of how well they will be able to perform largely determine what outcomes they expect their actions to produce. The causal relation between efficacy beliefs and outcome expectations is shown in Fig. 3.1. Perceived self-efficacy is a judgment of one's capabilities. An outcome expectation is what people expect their actions to produce. The outcomes may be physical, social or self-evaluative.

NATURE AND STRUCTURE OF EFFICACY BELIEFS

Human competencies are developed and expressed in many different forms. Thus, the efficacy belief system is not an omnibus trait. It is a differentiated set of self-beliefs linked to distinct realms of functioning. Comparative studies show that domain-linked measures of perceived efficacy are good predictors of motivation and action (Bandura, 1997). General measures of perceived control are weak predictors or are nonpredictive. Global all-purpose tests are measures of convenience rather than of explanatory and predictive power.

SOURCES OF PERCEIVED SELF-EFFICACY

People's beliefs in their efficacy can be enhanced in four principal ways. The most effective way of instilling a strong sense of efficacy is through *mastery experiences*. Successes build a robust sense of efficacy. Failures undermine it, especially if failures occur before a sense of efficacy is firmly established. If people experience only easy successes, they come to expect quick results and are easily discouraged by failure. A resilient sense of efficacy requires experience in overcoming obstacles through perseverant effort. By sticking it out through tough times people emerge more able and stronger from adversity.

The second way of creating, and strengthening self-efficacy is by social *modeling*. Models are a source of aspiration, competencies, and motivation. Seeing people similar to oneself succeed by perseverant effort raises observers' beliefs in their own abilities. The failures of others instill self-doubts about one's own ability to master similar activities.

Social persuasion is the third mode of influence. Realistic boosts in efficacy can lead people to exert greater effort. This increases their chances of success. But effective efficacy builders do more than convey positive appraisals. They structure situations for others in ways that bring success and avoid placing them, prematurely, in situations where they are likely to fail. They measure success by self-improvement rather than by triumphs over others.

People also rely partly on their *physical and emotional states* in judging their capabilities. They read their emotional arousal and tension as signs of vulnerability to poor performance. In activities involving strength and stamina, people interpret their fatigue, aches and pains as indicators of low physical efficacy. Mood also affects how people judge their efficacy. Positive mood enhances a sense of efficacy; depressed mood diminishes it. The fourth way of modifying efficacy beliefs is to reduce people's stress and depression, build their physical strength and change misinterpretations of their physical states. Mastery experiences produce stronger and more generalized efficacy beliefs than the other modes of influence.

COGNITIVE PROCESSING OF EFFICACY INFORMATION

Information for judging self-efficacy, whether conveyed enactively, vicariously, persuasively or somatically is not inherently informative. It is only raw data. Experiences become instructive through cognitive processing of efficacy information and reflective thought. One must distinguish between information conveyed by events and information as selected and integrated into self-efficacy judgments.

The cognitive processing of efficacy information involves two separate functions. The first is the types of information people attend to and use as indicators of personal efficacy. The theory specifies the set of efficacy indicators that are distinctive for each of the four major modes of influence. These are summarized in Table 3.1. For example, judgments of efficacy based on performance attainments may vary depending on people's interpretive biases, the difficulty of the task, how hard they worked at it, how much help they received, the conditions under which they performed, their emotional and physical state at the time, their rate of improvement over time, and biases in how they monitor and recall their attainments.

TABLE 3.1
The distinctive sets of factors within each of the four modes of influence
that can affect the construction of efficacy beliefs

Enactive efficacy information	*Vicarious efficacy information*
Interpretive biases	Model attribute similarity
Perceived task difficulty and diagnosticity	Model performance similarity
Effort expenditure	Model historical similarity
Amount of external aid received	Multiplicity and diversity of modeling
Situational circumstances of performance	Mastery or coping modeling
Transient affective and physical states	Exemplification of coping strategies
Temporal pattern of successes and failures	Portrayal of task demands
Selective bias in self-monitoring of performance	
Selective bias in memory for performance attainments	

Persuasory efficacy information	*Somatic and affective efficacy information*
Credibility	Degree of attentional focus on somatic states
Expertness	Interpretive biases regarding somatic states
Consensus	Perceived source of affective arousal
Degree of appraisal disparity	Level of arousal
Familiarity with task demands	Situational circumstances of arousal

The indicators people single out provide the information base on which the self-appraisal process operates. The second function in efficacy judgment involves the combination rules or heuristics people use to integrate efficacy information from different sources. There is much work to be done in the integrative aspect of the efficacy judgment process.

VERIFICATION OF CAUSATION

A central question in any theory of cognitive regulation of motivation and action concerns the issue of causality. Do efficacy beliefs operate as causal factors in human functioning? This issue has been examined by a variety of experimental strategies. In some studies perceived self-efficacy is raised to differential levels through vicarious modes of influence (Bandura, Reese, & Adams, 1982). In others, perceived efficacy is altered by comparison of personal attainments with those presented in bogus peer norms (Bouffard-Bouchard, 1990; Jacobs, Prentice-Dunn, & Rogers, 1984; Litt, 1988). Some studies bias self-efficacy judgment with anchoring influences using arbitrary reference points (Cervone & Peake, 1986; Peake & Cervone, 1989). Still other approaches to the verification of causality employ a contravening design in which a procedure that can impair functioning is applied but in ways that raise beliefs of personal efficacy (Holroyd et al., 1984). In each case, perceived self-efficacy is systematically varied by non-performance influences and the effects of efficacy on performance are measured.

These divergent experimental procedures provide convergent evidence that perceived self-efficacy contributes independently to motivation and performance accomplishments regardless of the activity in both children and adults alike (Bandura, 1997).

Numerous multivariate investigations have been conducted using panel designs in which efficacy beliefs, along with other possible determinants and performance attainments, are measured on two or more occasions. In some of these studies, efficacy beliefs are altered by naturally occurring influences during the intervening period. More often, efficacy beliefs are modified experimentally. The temporal ordering and systematic variation of efficacy beliefs antecedently to the predicted behavior helps to remove ambiguities about the source and direction of causality. In addition to controlled induction and temporal priority of efficacy change, multiple controls are applied for other potentially influential factors. The results of such studies reveal that efficacy beliefs make substantial independent contribution to variations in motivation and performance attainments (Bandura & Jourden, 1991; Dzewaltowski, 1989; Locke, Frederick, Lee, & Bobko, 1984; Ozer & Bandura, 1990; Wood & Bandura, 1989). The causal contribution of efficacy beliefs to human functioning is further documented in comparative tests of the predictive power of social cognitive theory and alternative conceptual models (Dzewaltowski, Noble, & Shaw, 1990; Lent, Brown, & Larkin, 1987; McCaul, O'Neill, & Glasgow, 1988; Siegel, Galassi, & Ware, 1985; Wheeler, 1983).

BENEFITS OF OPTIMISTIC
SELF-EFFICACY BELIEF

It is widely believed that misjudgment breeds dysfunction. Certainly, gross misjudgments can get one into trouble, but optimistic appraisals of efficacy can be advantageous. Veridical judgments can be self-limiting. When people err in their self-appraisal they tend to overestimate their abilities.

The realities of everyday life are strewn with difficulties. They are full of disappointments, impediments, adversities, failures, setbacks, frustrations and inequities. Optimistic self-efficacy is, therefore, an adaptive judgmental bias not a cognitive failing to be eliminated. Evidence shows that human accomplishments and positive well-being require an optimistic sense of personal efficacy to override the numerous impediments to success. Indeed, the striking characteristic of people who have achieved success in their fields is an inextinguishable sense of efficacy and a firm belief in the worth of what they are doing (Shepherd, 1995; White, 1982).

Early rejection is the rule, rather than the exception, in virtually all innovative and creative endeavors. A resilient self-belief enables people to override repeated early rejections of their work. People who are successful, innovative, sociable, nonanxious, nondepressed, and effective social reformers take an optimistic view of their efficacy to influence events that affect their lives. If not unrealistically exaggerated, such self-beliefs raise aspirations, and enhance and sustain the level of motivation needed for personal and social accomplishments.

There is a controversy in the literature over whether people are better served by veridical or by optimistic self-belief. These debates fail to make important distinctions that specify when optimistic judgment of capabilities is beneficial. Tenacious strivers should be differentiated from wistful dreamers. Wistful optimists lack the efficacy strength to put up with the uncertainties, disappointments and drudgery that are required for high accomplishments. Tenacious strivers believe so strongly in themselves, that they are willing to exert extraordinary effort and suffer countless reversals in pursuit of their vision. They abide by objective realism about the normative reality but subjective optimism about their chances of success. They do not delude themselves about the tough odds of high attainments but they believe they have what it takes to beat those odds.

The functional value of veridical self-appraisal also depends on the nature of the activity. In activities where the margins of error are narrow and missteps can produce costly or injurious consequences, people had better be accurate in judging their efficacy. It is a different matter where difficult accomplishments can produce substantial personal or social benefits. The personal costs involve time, effort and resources. Individuals have to decide for themselves which abilities to cultivate, whether to invest their efforts in ventures that are difficult to fulfill, and how much hardship they are willing to endure in pursuits strewn with obstacles and uncertainties. Societies enjoy the considerable benefits of the accomplishments in the arts, sciences and technologies of its persisters and risk takers. To paraphrase the astute observation of George Bernard Shaw: since reasonable people adapt to the world and unreasonable ones try to alter it, human progress depends on the unreasonable ones.

We study extensively the costs of mistaken actions that are taken, but we ignore the costs of promising actions not taken because of underconfidence. Yet, people have greater regrets about the career opportunities not pursued, personal relationships not cultivated and risks not taken than regrets about the actions they have taken. Preoccupation with the risks of optimistic efficacy reflects a pervasive conservative bias in psychology.

EFFICACY-ACTIVATED PROCESSES

Efficacy beliefs regulate human functioning through four major processes. They include cognitive, motivational, emotional and selection processes.

Cognitive processes

Efficacy beliefs affect thought patterns that can enhance or undermine performance. These cognitive effects take various forms. People who have a high sense of efficacy take a future time perspective in structuring their lives. Much human behavior is regulated by forethought in the form of goals. The stronger the perceived efficacy, the higher the goals people set for themselves and the firmer their commitment to them (Bandura, 1991). Challenging goals raise motivation and performance attainments (Locke & Latham, 1990).

People's beliefs in their efficacy also influence the anticipatory scenarios and visualized futures they construct and rehearse. Those of high efficacy visualize success scenarios that provide positive guides for performance. Those who doubt their efficacy visualize failure scenarios that undermine performance by dwelling on how things will go wrong.

A major function of thought is to enable people to predict events and to exercise control over those that are important to them. People of high efficacy show greater cognitive resourcefulness and strategic flexibility. Rapid discovery of predictive and operative rules enables them to manage their environment more effectively and productively (Wood & Bandura, 1989).

Motivational processes

Efficacy beliefs play a central role in the self-regulation of motivation. Most human motivation is cognitively generated. One can distinguish three forms of cognitive motivators around which different theories have been built. These include *causal attributions*, *outcome expectancies* and *cognized goals*. The corresponding theories are attribution theory, expectancy-value theory and goal theory. Figure 3.2 summarizes these theories of cognitive motivation.

Much human motivation and behavior is regulated anticipatorily by the outcomes expected for given actions. The capacity to exercise self-influence by personal challenge through goal setting and evaluative reaction to one's own performances provides another major cognitive mechanism of motivation and self-directedness. Once people commit themselves to valued goals, they seek self-satisfaction from fulfilling them and intensify their efforts by discontent with substandard performances. The causal attributions people make for their performances also affect their motivation.

The effects of goals, outcome expectations and causal attributions on motivation are partly governed by beliefs of personal efficacy. There are many activities

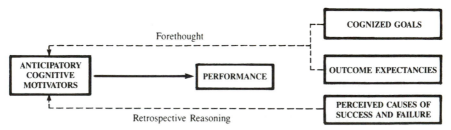

FIG. 3.2   Schematic representation of conceptions of cognitive motivation based on cognized goals, outcome expectancies and causal attributions.

which, if done well, produce valued outcomes, but they are not pursued by people who doubt they can do what it takes to succeed. They do not regard options in domains of low perceived efficacy worth considering whatever benefits they may hold. Such exclusions of large classes of options are made rapidly on efficacy grounds with little thought of costs and benefits. Rational models of decision making that exclude efficacy judgment sacrifice explanatory and predictive power.

It is partly on the basis of efficacy beliefs that people choose what goal challenges to undertake, how much effort to invest and how long to persevere in the face of difficulties (Bandura, 1997; Locke & Latham, 1990). When faced with obstacles, setbacks and failures, those who doubt their abilities slacken their efforts, give up or settle for mediocre solutions. Those who have strong belief in their abilities exert greater effort to master the challenges.

Efficacy beliefs also influence causal attributions. The influence of efficacy beliefs on causal attributions is highly reproducible across cognitive attainments (Matsui et al., 1988; Silver, Mitchell, & Gist, 1995), interpersonal transactions (Alden, 1986), physical performances (Courneya & McAuley, 1993; McAuley, Duncan, & McElnoy, 1989), and management of health habits (Grove, 1993). People who regard themselves as highly efficacious ascribe their failures to insufficient effort, inadequate strategies or unfavorable circumstances. Those of low efficacy attribute their failures to low ability. The effects of causal attributions on achievement strivings are mediated almost entirely through efficacy beliefs (Relich, Debus, & Walker, 1986; Schunk & Gunn, 1986; Schunk & Rice, 1986).

Affective processes

People's beliefs in their coping capabilities also affect how much stress and depression they experience in threatening or difficult situations. There are four major ways in which efficacy beliefs regulate emotional states (Bandura, 1997). They do so through cognitive processing of threats, transformational actions, exercise of thought control, and regulation of affective states.

Efficacy beliefs influence how threats are perceived and cognitively processed. If people believe they can manage threats they are not distressed by them; but if they believe they cannot control them they experience high anxiety, dwell on their coping deficiencies, view many aspects of their environment as fraught with danger, magnify possible risks and worry about perils that rarely happen. By such thinking they distress themselves and impair their functioning.

People who have a high sense of coping efficacy adopt strategies that change threatening environments into safe ones. In this mode of emotion regulation, efficacy beliefs reduce stress and anxiety through their impact on coping behavior. The stronger the sense of efficacy the bolder people are in tackling the problems that breed stress and anxiety, and the greater is their success in shaping the environment to their liking (Bandura, 1988).

People have to live with a psychic environment that is largely of their own making. Many human distresses result from failures to control disturbing thoughts. Control of one's thought processes is, therefore, a key factor in self-regulation of emotional states. The process of efficacious thought control is summed up well in the proverb: *You cannot prevent the birds of worry and care from flying over your head, but you can stop them from building a nest in your hair.* Research shows that it is not the sheer frequency of disturbing thoughts but the perceived helplessness to turn them off that is the major source of distress (Kent, 1987; Kent & Gibbons, 1987). Hence, the frequency of aversive cognitions is unrelated to anxiety level when the influence of perceived thought control efficacy is removed, whereas perceived thought control efficacy is strongly related to anxiety level when extent of aversive cognitions is removed.

In addition, people can exercise control over their affective states in palliative ways without altering the causes of their emotional arousal. Self-relaxation, engrossment in diversionary reactional activities, calming self-talk and seeking the solace of social support are examples of palliative ways for reducing stress and anxiety. Belief that one can relieve unpleasant emotional states when they arise makes them less aversive (Arch, 1992a; 1992b). These alternative paths of affect regulation must be considered in analyzing the role of perceived coping efficacy in human stress and anxiety.

Efficacy and depression   Perceived inefficacy to control things one values also produces depression. A theory must specify when perceived inefficacy will generate anxiety or depression. The nature of the outcomes over which personal control is sought is an important differentiating factor. Attenuation or control of injurious events is central to anxiety. Irreparable loss and perceived inefficacy to gain highly valued outcomes figures prominently in despondency. Human distress does not come packaged in neatly separable forms, however. When losses of what one values highly produce aversive outcomes, as when loss of a job jeopardizes one's livelihood, a sense of powerlessness to control vital aspects of one's life is both distressing and depressing.

As in the case of anxiety arousal, perceived inefficacy contributes to depression in varied ways. One route is through unfulfilled aspirations. People who impose on themselves standards of self-worth which they judge they cannot attain drive themselves to depression (Bandura, 1991; Kanfer & Zeiss, 1983). Depression, in turn, weakens people's beliefs in their efficacy, creating a downward cycle (Kavanagh & Bower, 1985).

A second route to depression is through a low sense of social efficacy to develop social relationships that bring satisfaction to one's lives and cushion the adverse effects of chronic stressors. A low sense of social efficacy contributes to depression both directly and by curtailing development of social support. Perceived efficacy and social support operate bidirectionally in human adaptation and change. Social support is not a self-forming entity waiting around to buffer harried people against stressors. Rather, people have to go out and find or create supportive relationships for themselves. Individuals of high perceived social efficacy create more supportive environments for themselves than those who have a low opinion of their social capabilities (Holahan & Holahan, 1987a; 1987b). Supportive relationships, in turn, can enhance personal efficacy (Cutrona & Troutman, 1986; Major, Mueller, & Hildebrandt, 1985). Supporters can raise efficacy in others in several ways. They can model effective coping attitudes and strategies for managing problem situations, demonstrate the value of perseverance, and provide positive incentives and resources for efficacious coping. Mediational analyses reveal that social support has beneficial effects to the extent that it raises perceived coping efficacy.

The third route to depression is through thought control efficacy. Much human depression is cognitively generated by dejecting ruminative thought (Nolen-Hoeksema, 1991). A low sense of efficacy to control ruminative thought contributes to the occurrence, duration, and recurrence of depressive episodes (Kavanagh & Wilson, 1989).

Selection processes

The preceding discussion documents how efficacy beliefs enable people to create beneficial environments and to control them. People are partly the product of their environment. By choosing their environments they can have a hand in what they become. Efficacy beliefs can, therefore, play a key role in shaping the courses lives take by influencing the types of activities and environments people choose to get into. In self-development through choice processes, destinies are shaped by selection of environments known to cultivate valued potentialities and lifestyles.

The power of efficacy beliefs to affect life paths through selection processes is most clearly revealed in studies of career choice and development (Lent, Brown, & Hackett, 1994). The stronger people believe in their efficacy, the more career options they consider possible, the greater the interest they show in them, the better they prepare themselves educationally for different occupational careers, and the greater their staying power in the chosen pursuits.

The diverse effects of perceived self-efficacy on human well-being and functioning can be summarized as follows:

People who have a low sense of efficacy in a given domain of life: shy away from difficult tasks which they perceive as personal threats; have low aspirations and weak commitment to the goals they choose; maintain a self-diagnostic focus rather than concentrate on how to perform successfully; dwell on personal deficiencies, obstacles and adverse outcomes; attribute failures to deficient capability; slacken their efforts or give up quickly in the face of difficulties; are slow to recover their sense of efficacy after failures or setbacks; and are prone to stress and depression.

People who have a strong sense of efficacy: approach difficult tasks as challenges rather than as threats; set challenging goals and sustain strong commitment to their goals; maintain a task-diagnostic focus that guides effective performance; attribute failures to insufficient effort; heighten effort in the face of difficulties; display low vulnerability to stress and depression; and quickly recover their sense of efficacy after failures or setbacks. Success usually comes through renewed effort after failed attempts. It is resiliency of personal efficacy that counts.

INTERDEPENDENCE OF PERSONAL AGENCY AND SOCIAL STRUCTURE

In social cognitive theory (Bandura, 1986), human agency operates in an interdependent causal structure involving triadic reciprocal causation (see Fig. 3.3). In this transactional view of self and society, personal factors in the form of cognitive, affective and biological events, behavior, and environmental influences all operate as interacting determinants that influence each other bidirectionally.

Human adaptation and change are rooted in social systems. Personal agency, therefore, exerts its effects within a broad network of sociostructural influences. In these agentic transactions, people are producers as well as products of social systems. Social structures are created by human activity to organize, guide and regulate human affairs in given domains by authorized rules and sanctions. The structural practices, in turn, impose constraints and provide resources and opportunity structures for personal development and functioning. Given this bidirectionality of influence, social cognitive theory rejects a dualism between social structure and personal agency.

Sociostructural theories and psychological theories are often regarded as rival conceptions of human behavior or as representing different levels of causation. Human behavior cannot be fully understood solely in terms of sociostructural factors or psychological factors. A full understanding requires an integrated

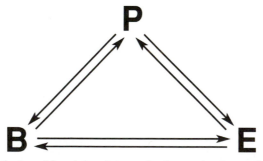

FIG. 3.3   Schematization of the relations between the three major classes of determinants in triadic reciprocal causation. *B* represents behavior; *P* the internal personal factors in the form of cognitive, affective and biological events; and *E* the external environment (Bandura, 1986).

perspective in which social influences operate through psychological mechanisms to produce behavioral effects. However, the self-system is not merely a conduit for external influences. The self is socially constituted; but by exercising self-influence human agency operates generatively and proactively rather than just reactively. Thus, in the theory of triadic reciprocal causation, sociostructural and personal determinants are treated as cofactors within a unified causal structure.

Different lines of research lend support to this interdependent multicausality. Consider some examples. Elder and Ardelt (1992) have shown that economic hardship by itself has no direct influence on parental efficacy. Rather, financial hardship creates subjective strain (see Fig. 3.4). In intact households, subjective strain impairs parental efficacy by creating marital discord. A supportive marital relationship enables parents to withstand poverty without its undermining belief in their ability to guide their children's development. For single parents, financial strain weakens parents' efficacy both directly and by instilling depression. Regardless of family structure, parents who have a high sense of efficacy are active in promoting their children's competencies.

The study of children's academic development provides further evidence that psychosocial processes mediate the influence of sociostructural conditions. Our discipline went through a period of austere, insulated cognitivism in which the

INTACT FAMILY

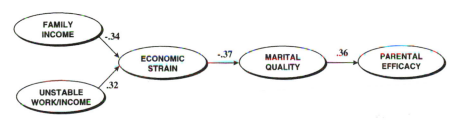

SINGLE-PARENT FAMILY

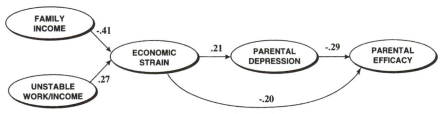

FIG. 3.4   Path analysis showing that the effect of objective economic hardship on parents' sense of efficacy to guide their children's development operates through psychosocial processes rather than directly. Marital discord is the mediator in intact households, and depression is the mediator in single parent households (Elder & Ardelt, 1992).

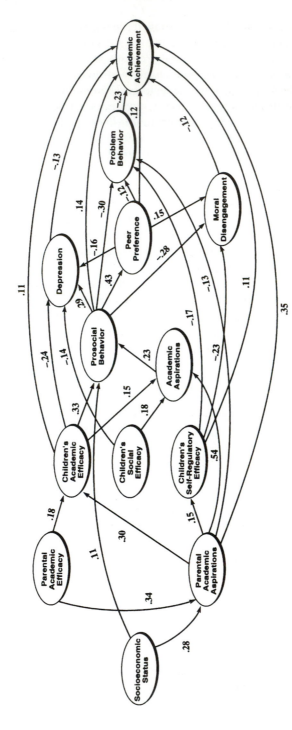

FIG. 3.5 Path analysis of the pattern of influence through which parental and children's efficacy beliefs and academic aspirations promote children's academic achievement. All of the path coefficients are significant beyond the $p < .05$ level (Bandura, Barbaranelli, Caprara, & Pastorelli, 1996).

mechanics of how the mind works in processing, representing, organizing and retrieving information was intensively studied but the social nature of cognitive development was largely ignored. Children's intellectual development cannot be isolated from the social relations within which it is imbedded and from its inter-personal effects: it must be analyzed from a social perspective. A secure sense of intellectual and self-regulatory efficacy not only promotes academic successes, but supportive social relationships and positive emotional development that are conducive to learning. Social cognitive theory adopts an ecological perspective to the contribution of efficacy beliefs to cognitive and social development. Socio-economic, familial, peer and self-processes operate in concert to shape the course of academic development. Figure 3.5 summarizes the intricate causal structure.

The impact of the socioeconomic status of the families on children's aca-demic achievement is entirely mediated through parental academic aspirations and children's prosocial behavior. The higher the families' socioeconomic status, the higher the academic and occupational aspirations parents have for their children and the greater is their children's prosocialness. In this network of influences, parents' beliefs in their efficacy to promote their children's intellectual develop-ment and the educational aspirations they hold for them raise children's beliefs in their efficacy and academic aspirations. Children's perceived efficacy, in turn, affects their academic achievement both directly and by its effects on their social behavior and emotional well-being.

PERCEIVED EFFICACY IN COLLECTIVE AGENCY

Conceptions of human agency have been confined to individual agency. How-ever, people do not live their lives as isolates. They work together to produce the results they desire. Social cognitive theory extends the analysis of mechan-isms of human agency to collective agency. People's shared beliefs in their collective power to produce desired outcomes is a crucial ingredient of collect-ive agency. Group performance is the product of interactive and coordinative dynamics of its members. Therefore, perceived collective efficacy is not simply the sum of the efficacy beliefs of individual members. It is an emergent group-level attribute.

Personal and collective efficacy differ in the unit of agency, but in both forms efficacy beliefs serve similar functions and operate through similar processes. People's beliefs in their collective efficacy influence the type of futures they seek to achieve; how well they use their resources; how much effort they put into their group endeavor; their staying power when collective efforts fail to produce quick results or meet forcible opposition; and their vulnerability to discouragement.

Some writers inappropriately equate self-efficacy with individualism and pit it against collectivism (Schooler, 1990). In fact, a high sense of personal efficacy contributes just as importantly to group-directedness as to self-directedness. To

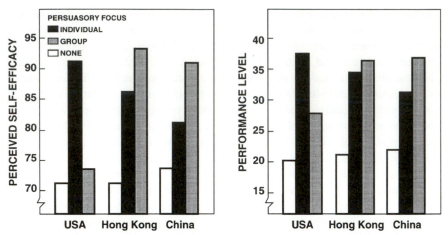

FIG. 3.6   The differential effect of efficacy-boosting influences on the perceived efficacy and productivity of managers in individualistic and collectivistic cultures depending on whether the social influence was individually oriented or group oriented (plotted from data of Earley, 1994).

work together successfully members have to perform their roles with a high sense of efficacy. Chronic self-doubters are not easily formed into a collective efficacious force. Personal efficacy is valued, not because of reverence for individualism, but because a strong sense of efficacy is vital for successful functioning regardless of whether it is achieved individually or by group members working together.

Group achievements and social change are rooted in self-efficacy. The cross-cultural research conducted by Earley (1993; 1994) on organizational functioning confirms the universal functional value of efficacy beliefs. In these cross-cultural studies, efficacy beliefs contribute to productivity by members of collectivist cultures just as they do by those raised in individualistic cultures. But cultural values shape how efficacy beliefs are developed, the purposes to which they are put, and the social arrangements through which they are best expressed. As shown in Fig. 3.6, people from the United States, an individualistic culture, feel most efficacious and perform best under an individually oriented system, whilst those from collectivistic cultures, namely Hong Kong and China, judge themselves most efficacious and work most productively under a group-oriented system. However, the critical factor is not collectivism *per se*. Collectivists display lower personal and group efficacy and low productivity when they have to perform in a culturally mixed group.

Cultures are not as homogeneous as the stereotypic portrayals would lead one to believe. Collectivistic systems, such as East Asian ones founded on Confucianism or Buddism, favor a communal ethic. But they differ from each other in the values, meanings and customs they promote (Kim et al., 1994). Nor are so-called individualistic cultures a uniform lot. Americans, Italians, Germans, and the British differ in their particular brands of individualism. Even within the individualistically oriented culture of the United States, the New England brand of individualism is quite different from the Californian version or that of the Southern region of the nation.

There are collectivists in individualistic cultures and individualists in collectivistic cultures. Regardless of cultural background, people achieve the greatest personal efficacy and productivity when their personal orientation is congruent with the social system. For example, American collectivists do better under a group-oriented system and Chinese individualists do better under an individually-oriented system. The personal orientation rather than the cultural orientation is a major carrier of the effects. Both at the societal and individual level of analysis, strong efficacy fosters high group effort and performance.

UNDERMINERS OF COLLECTIVE EFFICACY IN CHANGING SOCIETIES

The growing interdependence of social and economic life requires effective collective action at both local and transnational levels. As the need for efficacious collective effort grows, so does the sense of collective powerlessness. Many of the contemporary conditions of life undermine the development of collective efficacy. Life in the societies of today is increasingly shaped by transnational interdependencies. What happens economically and politically in one part of the world can affect the welfare of vast populations elsewhere. The transnational forces, which are hard to disentangle let alone control, challenge the efficacy of governmental systems to exert a determining influence on their own economic and national life.

Global market forces are restructuring national economies and shaping the social life of societies. There are no handy social mechanisms or global agencies through which people can shape transnational practices that affect their lives. As nations wrestle with the loss of control, the public expresses disillusionment and cynicism over whether their leaders and institutions can work for them to improve their lives. The crisis of leadership and governmental efficacy affects most nations nowadays. People strive to regain some control over their lives by seeking to shape their local circumstances over which they have some influence. The retreat to localism, fueled by public disillusionment with its national systems, ironically comes at a time calling for strong national leadership to manage powerful influences from abroad to shape their nation's own destiny.

Under the new realities of growing transnational control, nation states increase their controlling leverage by merging into larger regional units such as the European Union. Other regional nation states will be forced to merge into larger blocks, otherwise they will have little bargaining power in transnational relations. These regional marriages do not come without a price. Paradoxically, to gain international control, nations have to negotiate reciprocal pacts that require some loss of national autonomy and changes in traditional ways of life. Some members of the society gain from the agreements others lose. This creates disputes within nations between the winners and losers. The major challenge to leadership is to build a national sense of efficacy to take advantage of the opportunities of globalization while minimizing the price that the changes extract from local cultures.

Modern life is increasingly regulated by complex technologies that most people neither understand nor believe they can do much to influence. The very technologies that people create to control their life environment can become a constraining force that, in turn, controls how they think and behave. As an example of such paradoxical consequences, the citizens of nations that are heavily dependent on deteriorating atomic plants for their energy feel powerless to remove this catastrophic hazard from their lives even though they acknowledge the grave danger. The devastating consequences of mishaps do not respect national borders.

The social machinery of society is no less challenging. Bureaucracies thwart effective social action. Many of the bureaucratic practices are designed more to benefit the people who run the social systems than to serve the public. Long delays between action and noticeable results discourage efforts at change. Most people relinquish control in the face of bureaucratic obstacles.

Social efforts to change lives for the better require merging diverse self-interests in support of common core values and goals. Disagreements among different constituencies create additional obstacles to successful collective action. The voices for parochial interests are usually much stronger than those for collective responsibility. It requires efficacious, inspiring leadership to create unity within diversity.

The recent years have witnessed growing social fragmentation into separate interest groups, each exercising its own power. Pluralism is taking the form of antagonistic factionalism. In the more extreme forms of social fragmentation, countries are being dismantled with a vengeance along racial, religious, and ethnic lines. While some forces are creating social fragmentation, others are breaking down national identities. Advanced telecommunications technologies are spreading ideas, values and styles of behavior transnationally at an unprecedented rate. The symbolic environment feeding off communication satellites is supplanting national cultures and homogenizing collective consciousness. With further development of the computerized Web world, people will be heavily embedded in global symbolic environments. In addition, mass migration of people fleeing tyranny or seeking a better life is changing cultural landscapes. As migration changes the ethnic composition of populations, societies are becoming less distinctive. Cultures are no longer insular. These new realities will transform the agendas of cross-cultural research.

The magnitude of human problems also undermines perceived efficacy to find effective solutions for them. Profound global changes are destroying the ecosystems that sustain life. These changes are creating new realities requiring transnational remedies. Worldwide problems of growing magnitude instill a sense of paralysis that there is little people can do to reduce such problems. Global effects are the products of local actions. The strategy of *Think globally, act locally* is an effort to restore in people a sense of efficacy that they can make a difference.

The psychological barriers created by beliefs of collective powerlessness are more demoralizing, and debilitating than are external impediments. The less people bring their influence to bear on conditions that affect their lives the more control they relinquish to others. People who have high collective efficacy will mobilize their efforts and resources to surmount the obstacles to the changes they seek. But those convinced of their collective powerlessness will cease trying, even though changes are attainable through perseverant collective effort. As a society, we enjoy the benefits left by those before us who collectively fought inhumanities and worked for social reforms that permit a better life. Our own collective efficacy will, in turn, shape how future generations will live their lives. The times call for social initiatives that build people's sense of collective efficacy to influence conditions that shape their lives and that of future generations.

ACKNOWLEDGEMENTS

Preparation of this chapter and some of cited research were supported by grants from the Spencer Foundation and the Johann Jacobs Foundation. Some sections of this chapter include revised and expanded material from the book, *Self-Efficacy: The Exercise of Control*, Freeman, 1997.

REFERENCES

Alden, L. (1986). Self-efficacy and causal attributions for social feedback. *Journal of Research in Personality, 20,* 460–473.

Arch, E. C. (1992a). Sex differences in the effect of self-efficacy on willingness to participate in a performance situation. *Psychological Reports, 70,* 3–9.

Arch, E. C. (1992b). Affective control efficacy as a factor in willingness to participate in a public performance situation. *Psychological Reports, 71,* 1247–1250.

Bandura, A. (1986). *Social foundations of thought and action: A social cognitive theory.* Englewood Cliffs, NJ: Prentice Hall.

Bandura, A. (1988). Perceived self-efficacy: Exercise of control through self-belief. In J. P. Dauwalder, M. Perrez, & V. Hobi (Eds.), *Annual series of European research in behavior therapy* (Vol. 2, pp. 27–59). Amsterdam/Lisse, Netherlands: Swets & Zeitlinger.

Bandura, A. (1991). Self-regulation of motivation through anticipatory and self-regulatory mechanisms. In R. A. Dienstbier (Ed.), *Perspectives on motivation: Nebraska symposium on motivation* (Vol. 38, pp. 69–164). Lincoln: University of Nebraska Press.

Bandura, A. (1997). *Self-efficacy: The exercise of control.* New York: Freeman.

Bandura, A., Barbaranelli, C., Caprara, G. V., & Pastorelli, C. (1996). Multifaceted impact of self-efficacy beliefs on academic functioning. *Child Development, 67,* 1206–1222.

Bandura, A., & Jourden, F. J. (1991). Self-regulatory mechanisms governing the impact of social comparison on complex decision making. *Journal of Personality and Social Psychology, 60,* 941–951.

Bandura, A., Reese, L., & Adams, N. E. (1982). Microanalysis of action and fear arousal as a function of differential levels of perceived self-efficacy. *Journal of Personality and Social Psychology, 43,* 5–21.

Bouffard-Bouchard, T. (1990). Influence of self-efficacy on performance in a cognitive task. *Journal of Social Psychology, 130,* 353–363.

Cervone, D., & Peake, P. K. (1986). Anchoring, efficacy, and action: The influence of judgmental heuristics on self- efficacy judgments and behavior. *Journal of Personality and Social Psychology, 50,* 492–501.

Courneya, K. S., & McAuley, E. (1993). Efficacy, attributional, affective responses of older adults following an acute bout of exercise. *Journal of Social Behavior and Personality, 8,* 729–742.

Cutrona, C. E., & Troutman, B. R. (1986). Social support, infant temperament, and parenting self-efficacy: A mediational model of postpartum depression. *Child Development, 57,* 1507–1518.

Dzewaltowski, D. A. (1989). Towards a model of exercise motivation. *Journal of Sport and Exercise Psychology, 11,* 251–269.

Dzewaltowski, D. A., Noble, J. M., & Shaw, J. M. (1990). Physical activity participation: Social cognitive theory versus the theories of reasoned action and planned behavior. *Journal of Sport and Exercise Psychology, 12,* 388–405.

Earley, P. C. (1993). East meets West meets Mideast: Further explorations of collectivistic and individualistic work groups. *Academy of Management Journal, 36,* 319–348.

Earley, P. C. (1994). Self or group? Cultural effects of training on self-efficacy and performance. *Administrative Science Quarterly, 39,* 89–117.

Elder, G. H., & Ardelt, M. (1992, March). *Families adapting to economic pressure: Some consequences for parents and adolescents.* Paper presented at the Society for Research on Adolescence, Washington, DC.

Grove, J. R. (1993). Attributional correlates of cessation self-efficacy among smokers. *Addictive Behaviors, 18,* 311–320.

Holahan, C. K., & Holahan, C. J. (1987a). Self-efficacy, social support, and depression in aging: A longitudinal analysis. *Journal of Gerontology, 42,* 65–68.

Holahan, C. K., & Holahan, C. J. (1987b). Life stress, hassles, and self-efficacy in aging: A replication and extension. *Journal of Applied Social Psychology, 17,* 574–592.

Holroyd, K. A., Penzien, D. B., Hursey, K. G., Tobin, D. L., Rogers, L., Holm, J. E., Marcille, P. J., Hall, J. R., & Chila, A. G. (1984). Change mechanisms in EMG biofeedback training: Cognitive changes underlying improvements in tension headache. *Journal of Consulting and Clinical Psychology, 52,* 1039–1053.

Jacobs, B., Prentice-Dunn, S., & Rogers, R. W. (1984). Understanding persistence: An interface of control theory and self-efficacy theory. *Basic and Applied Social Psychology, 5,* 333–347.

Kanfer, R., & Zeiss, A. M. (1983). Depression, interpersonal standard-setting, and judgments of self-efficacy. *Journal of Abnormal Psychology, 92,* 319–329.

Kavanagh, D. J., & Bower, G. H. (1985). Mood and self-efficacy: Impact of joy and sadness on perceived capabilities. *Cognitive Therapy and Research, 9,* 507–525.

Kavanagh, D. J., & Wilson, P. H. (1989). Prediction of outcome with a group version of cognitive therapy for depression. *Behaviour Research and Therapy, 27,* 333–347.

Kent, G. (1987). Self-efficacious control over reported physiological, cognitive and behavioural symptoms of dental anxiety. *Behaviour Research and Therapy, 25,* 341–347.

Kent, G., & Gibbons, R. (1987). Self-efficacy and the control of anxious cognitions. *Journal of Behavior Therapy and Experimental Psychiatry, 18,* 33–40.

Kim, U., Triandis, H. D., Kağıtçıbaşı, C., Choi, S., & Yoon, G. (1994). *Individualism and collectivism: Theory, method, and applications.* Thousand Oaks, CA: Sage.

Lent, R. W., Brown, S. D., & Hackett, G. (1994). Toward a unifying social cognitive theory of career and academic interest, choice, and performance. *Journal of Vocational Behavior, 45*, 79–122.

Lent, R. W., Brown, S. D., & Larkin, K. C. (1987). Comparison of three theoretically derived variables in predicting career and academic behavior: Self-efficacy, interest congruence, and consequence thinking. *Journal of Counseling Psychology, 34*, 293–298.

Litt, M. D. (1988). Self-efficacy and perceived control: Cognitive mediators of pain tolerance. *Journal of Personality and Social Psychology, 54*, 149–160.

Locke, E. A., Frederick, E., Lee, C., & Bobko, P. (1984). Effect of self-efficacy, goals, and task strategies on task performance. *Journal of Applied Psychology, 69*, 241–251.

Locke, E. A., & Latham, G. P. (1990). *A theory of goal setting and task performance.* Englewood Cliffs, NJ: Prentice Hall.

Major, B., Mueller, P., & Hildebrandt, K. (1985). Attributions, expectations, and coping with abortion. *Journal of Personality and Social Psychology, 48*, 585–599.

Matsui, T., Konishi, H., Onglatco, M. L. U., Matsuda, Y., & Ohnishi, R. (1988). Self-efficacy and perceived exerted effort as potential cues for success–failure attributions. *Surugadai University Studies, 1*, 89–98.

McAuley, E., Duncan, T. E., & McElroy, M. (1989). Self-efficacy cognitions and causal attributions for children's motor performance: An exploratory investigation. *The Journal of Genetic Psychology, 150*, 65–73.

McCaul, K. D., O'Neill, K., & Glasgow, R. E. (1988). Predicting the performance of dental hygiene behaviors: An examination of the Fishbein and Ajzen model and self-efficacy expectations. *Journal of Applied Social Psychology, 18*, 114–128.

Nolen-Hoeksema, S. (1991). Responses to depression and their effects on the duration of depressive episodes. *Journal of Abnormal Psychology, 100*, 569–582.

Ozer, E. M., & Bandura, A. (1990). Mechanisms governing empowerment effects: A self-efficacy analysis. *Journal of Personality and Social Psychology, 58*, 472–486.

Peake, P. K., & Cervone, D. (1989). Sequence anchoring and self-efficacy: Primacy effects in the consideration of possibilities. *Social Cognition, 7*, 31–50.

Relich, J. D., Debus, R. L., & Walker, R. (1986). The mediating role of attribution and self-efficacy variables for treatment effects on achievement outcomes. *Contemporary Educational Psychology, 11*, 195–216.

Schooler, C. (1990). Individualism and the historical and social-structural determinants of people's concerns over self-directedness and efficacy. In J. Rodin, C. Schooler, & K. W. Schaie (Eds.), *Self-directedness: Cause and effects throughout the life course* (pp. 19–58). Hillsdale, NJ: Erlbaum.

Schunk, D. H., & Gunn, T. P. (1986). Self-efficacy and skill development: Influence of task strategies and attributions. *Journal of Educational Research, 79*, 238–244.

Schunk, D. H., & Rice, J. M. (1986). Extended attributional feedback: Sequence effects during remedial reading instruction. *Journal of Early Adolescence, 6*, 55–66.

Shepherd, G. (Ed.). (1995). *Rejected: Leading economists ponder the publication process.* Sun Lakes, AZ: Horton.

Siegel, R. G., Galassi, J. P., & Ware, W. B. (1985). A comparison of two models for predicting mathematics performance: Social learning versus math aptitude-anxiety. *Journal of Counseling Psychology, 32*, 531–538.

Silver, W. S., Mitchell, T. R., & Gist, M. E. (1995). Responses to successful and unsuccessful performance: The moderating effect of self-efficacy on the relationship between performance and attributions. *Organizational Behavior and Human Decision Processes, 62*, 286–299.

Wheeler, K. G. (1983). Comparisons of self-efficacy and expectancy models of occupational preferences for college males and females. *Journal of Occupational Psychology, 56*, 73–78.

White, J. (1982). *Rejection.* Reading, MA: Addison-Wesley.

Wood, R., & Bandura, A. (1989). Social cognitive theory of organizational management. *Academy of Management Review, 14*, 361–384.

CHAPTER FOUR

Intergroup relations: A field with a short history but a long future

Rupert Brown
University of Kent, Canterbury, UK

The past 50 years have seen the steady growth of intergroup relations as a field of study to the point where it is now a major focus of research interest on both sides of the Atlantic. A central issue has been to understand the origins of intergroup discrimination with a view to designing interventions for its reduction. A review of contemporary theory and research reveals at least three sources of discrimination: ingroup enhancement, intergroup differentiation, and outgroup derogation. The major theoretical models relevant to each of these are discussed, together with the research they have inspired. The paper concludes with a review of current research aimed at the diminution of intergroup discrimination.

La croissance soutenue, au cours des 50 dernières années, du champ d'études portant sur les relations entre groupes a été telle que ce thème de recherche est devenu un centre d'intérêt important des deux côtés de l'Atlantique. L'une des questions majeures a porté sur la compréhension des origines de la discrimination entre les groupes, dans la perspective d'élaborer des moyens d'intervention en vue de sa diminution. L'examen des théories et recherches contemporaines révèle au moins trois sources de discrimination: l'auto-protection des groupes, la différenciation entre les groupes et la dépréciation des autres groupes. Cet article considère les principaux modèles théoriques se rapportant à chacune de ces sources, de même que les travaux de recherche qu'ils ont suscités. On conclut en faisant le bilan des travaux de recherche courants visant à la réduction de la discrimination entre groupes.

It is sometimes said that Social Psychology is a young discipline. If that is so, then the social psychological study of intergroup relations must really be regarded as still being in its infancy. A search of some of the earliest textbooks of the discipline reveals that "intergroup relations" seldom appears in their indices and contents pages (e.g. Allport, 1924; McDougall, 1908; Ross, 1908; although, see Sumner (1906) for an exception). Even in the first edition of the *Handbook of Social Psychology* there is hardly a mention of intergroup prejudice in Allport's

(1935) classic chapter on attitudes. It is not until the post-Second World War era that intergroup relations emerged as a significant field of enquiry, very much stimulated by two classic publications, *Groups in Harmony and Tension* (Sherif & Sherif, 1953) and, of course, *The Nature of Prejudice* (Allport, 1954) which appeared one year later. These two books mark the real starting point of intergroup relations as a recognizable field in our discipline. In short, we have a field of study which has a relatively brief history. In this paper I begin by defining "intergroup behavior". I then concentrate on two broad issues: (1) social psychological approaches and research on intergroup prejudice, discrimination and conflict; and (2) the implications of that work for the reduction of prejudice.

DEFINING INTERGROUP BEHAVIOR

As 1996 is the thirtieth anniversary of the publication of Sherif's (1966) last book on intergroup relations, it is fitting to take a definition of intergroup behavior from that book: "Whenever individuals belonging to one group interact, collectively or individually, with another group or its members in terms of their group identification we have an instance of intergroup behavior" (Sherif, 1966, p. 12). This definition is now widely accepted by researchers in the field. Note that it is not, in fact, necessary to have many people in a situation to call it an instance of intergroup behavior. One could have just two individuals. If they were acting in terms of their group identification, then this would be an example of intergroup behavior according to this definition.

THREE VARIETIES OF INTERGROUP FAVORITISM

When we talk about various phenomena associated with intergroup relations—for example, identification, ethnocentrism, ingroup favoritism, bias, prejudice, outgroup derogation and hostility—we often conflate these terms together and consider them as similar entities. However, a closer inspection reveals they are recognizably different empirically, and they have different theoretical traditions associated with them.

Consider, first, three common kinds of ingroup favoritism (see Fig. 4.1). On the left (a) is a form of preference which can be summarised as "we are good." The ingroup is overevaluated but the outgroup is regarded rather neutrally. The other end of the continuum (c) is a form of ingroup preference which could be characterised as "they are bad." Here the ingroup is more or less neutrally valued, but there is clear evidence of outgroup derogation. And then, of course, there is a combination of the two (b) which can be called intergroup differentiation: ingroup enhancement and some mild outgroup derogation.

It is important to distinguish these because, first of all, it is not at all clear that these different forms are empirically related to one another. For example, ratings of ingroup and outgroup are not usually, as one might expect, negatively

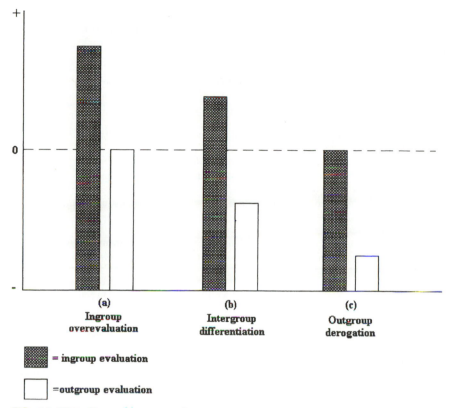

FIG. 4.1   Three forms of ingroup preference.

correlated (Brewer, 1979; Turner, 1978). If anything, they are usually positively correlated. Moreover, strength of ingroup identification and attachment is not always very reliably correlated with different forms of ingroup differentiation (Hinkle & Brown, 1990). Finally, overt and direct expressions of outgroup hostility and aggression are seldom, if ever, correlated very well with various forms of evaluative ingroup bias (Struch & Schwartz, 1989). So, these are distinct phenomena and associated with them are some distinct theoretical traditions. It will therefore be convenient to organize the discussion of ingroup favoritism under these three headings.

INGROUP OVEREVALUATION

Some empirical findings

As Sumner (1906) noted in his discussion of "ethnocentrism," it is a commonplace to observe that group members overestimate the worth of the ingroup, its products, and achievements. In a more formal documentation of this tendency

TABLE 4.1
The empirical reality of ingroup bias and its moderators

1. Ingroup bias
In 103/137 tests positive ingroup bias was observed.
Fisher $z = 0.36$, $p = 6.9$ E^{-77}; failsafe $N = > 45000$.

2. Moderators
(a) relative size
  ingroup bias was stronger when the ingroup is proportionately smaller than the outgroup
  $r = .11$ $p < .006$
(b) status
  ingroup bias was stronger in high status groups than in low status groups
  $r = .34$ $p = 9.1$ E^{-13}
  especially in artificial laboratory groups ($r = .60$ $p = 1.7$ E^{-18}), and not in real-life groups
  ($r = -.04$, n.s.)
(c) dimensional relevance (real-life groups only)
  ingroup bias is stronger on less "relevant" dimensions amongst low status groups ($r = .28$,
  $p = 3.1$ E^{-9}), but on more "relevant" dimensions for high status groups ($r = .16$, $p < .005$)

NOTE:
  A meta-analysis of 42 studies conducted between 1960–1990 yielded 137 hypothesis tests: N of participants = 5746 (from Mullen et al., 1992).

toward "ingroup bias" (as it is called), we carried out a meta-analysis of some 42 studies of intergroup evaluations conducted between 1960 and 1990 (Mullen, Brown, & Smith, 1992; see Table 4.1). The first outcome of this analysis was to confirm that ingroup bias is, indeed, quite pervasive: it was observed in 75% of the 137 independent hypothesis tests that were performed, resulting in a statistically highly reliable, if moderate, effect size.

More interestingly, though, are the various moderators of that ingroup bias. First, the size of the group is important. In general, smaller groups evince more ingroup favoritism than relatively larger groups. Status, too, is a significant moderator: higher status groups show more bias than lower status groups, particularly in the relatively clear cut and artificial confines of the laboratory; in real-life settings that effect dwindles virtually to non-existence. The status effect is itself moderated by another variable, the relevance of the rating dimension to the ingroup (particularly for real-life groups). Ingroup bias is stronger on the less relevant dimensions for subordinate groups but tends to be more focused on the relevant dimensions for the superior or dominant groups.

All these studies used fairly straightforward overt measures of ingroup favoritism (usually pencil-and-paper ratings) at a very controlled level of responding. There is emerging evidence, though, that ingroup favoritism may actually have some automatic and unconscious aspects to it (Perdue, Dovidio, Gurtman, & Tyler, 1990). Perdue et al. presented various trait words that were overtly positive or negative and the respondent had to make a quick judgement,

"Is this a positive word or a negative word?." The dependent measure was response time. Prior to that presentation, however, there was a subliminal prime which was a symbolic associate either of the ingroup or the outgroup (e.g. "we" or "us," or "them"). They observed a clear effect of these primes on the latencies with which the evaluative judgement was made: responses to negative words preceded by an ingroup prime were inhibited; responses to positive words preceded by an ingroup prime were facilitated. There was little corresponding effect for the outgroup primes. This evidence, then, suggests some kind of unconscious and automatic ingroup favoritism, an effect driven, as we see, by ingroup associations and dissociations rather than any outgroup devaluation.

Social Identity Theory and related developments

There is thus no doubt that ingroup preference exists. I want to turn now to what I regard as the major theoretical explanation for this ingroup favoritism effect. This is the theory of social identity, first proposed by Tajfel and Turner in the late 1970s and the focus of sustained research programs in Europe and elsewhere over the last 15 or 20 years (Abrams & Hogg, 1990; Tajfel, 1978; 1982; Tajfel & Turner, 1986). Social Identity Theory is based on a very simple idea. It says that underlying most forms of ingroup favoritism is the need for a positive self-concept. Because the "self" is often, sometimes exclusively, defined by our membership in various groups, the standing of those ingroups in relation to various other groups becomes psychologically important. In effect, then, the theory proposes that we are motivated to seek out and to maintain some kind of positive distinctiveness from outgroups in the service of a satisfactory identity.

There is one other theoretical development worthy of note here. As just seen, at the heart of Social Identity Theory is the concept of distinctiveness. Brewer (1991) has proposed an interesting development of this idea by suggesting that in addition to this need for differentiation, which is so emphasised by Social Identity Theory, there is also a need for inclusion, a need to assimilate the self into collectivities. She suggests, plausibly enough, that these two needs are somewhat countervailing: the need for differentiation is maximal in very large groups but there the need for assimilation is best satisfied; in very small groups the need for differentiation is least but the desire for assimilation is strongest. Because these two needs run in opposite directions, there should be some sort of balance point, an optimal level of group size, which would be likely to elicit the highest levels of satisfaction and identification. This optimal size is probably for relatively small rather than large groups. This theory is beginning to attract a good deal of empirical support. Recall from the meta-analysis presented earlier that there was a moderating effect of group size such that, in general, we find smaller groups showing more ingroup bias, perhaps as a reflection of this greater identification. This same pattern has been found consistently with both laboratory and natural groups in various research centers around the world (e.g. Brewer,

Manzi, & Shaw, 1993; Sachdev & Bourhis, 1991; Simon & Brown, 1987; Simon, Glassner-Boyerl, & Stratenworth, 1991).

An unresolved problem within Social Identity Theory

There is no doubt that Social Identity Theory and its offshoots have been successful in making sense of a number of different intergroup phenomena. Later in the paper further examples will be presented. However, at this point it is worth identifying one problematic issue for the theory. This concerns the relationship between the strength of group identification and the amount of ingroup bias. It is a reasonable prediction that the more someone identifies with the group the more we should find attempts to achieve positive group distinctiveness or, in other words, higher levels of ingroup favoritism. That hypothesis has been the subject of repeated tests over the past decade (Hinkle & Brown, 1990). What emerges from that research is that the predicted correlation between strength of group identification and ingroup bias is not always observed. The median correlation is positive but is typically rather weak (of the order of .2), and there is considerable variation both in the magnitude and direction of the relationship in different kinds of groups (Hinkle & Brown, 1990).

In an attempt to make sense of that diversity, Hinkle and Brown (1990) suggested that it would be useful to classify groups or group situations according to a simple two-dimensional taxonomy. The first dimension was borrowed from Triandis and his colleagues (e.g. Triandis, Bontempo, Villareal, Asai, & Lucca, 1988). Their Individualism–Collectivism dimension denotes the extent to which people define themselves, their activities and their achievements in terms of the collectivity or more individually. The second dimension, which we labeled Autonomous–Relational Orientation, concerns the way people evaluate their groups. One pole is the familiar form of evaluation involving comparisons between the ingroup and other groups. The other pole refers to the many kinds of groups or group situations in which evaluations are made autonomously— perhaps in relation to the group's past history or in relation to some abstract standard. We predicted that the kind of processes posited by Social Identity Theory would typically be found only in the combination of circumstances when groups had a strongly *collectivist* orientation and were either structurally or motivationally concerned with *relational* types of comparisons, although a similar link between identity and bias would be much less evident, if not completely absent, in the autonomous–individualist combination.

The initial evidence for this model was quite encouraging (Brown, Hinkle, Ely, Fox-Cardamone, Maras, & Taylor, 1992). Members of both laboratory and natural groups were classified according to their position on the two dimensions. Those who were collectivist and relational showed on average a higher correlation between identification and bias (.55) than those who were individualist

and autonomous (.05). Subsequent research has yielded a mixed set of find-
ings with supportive (Feather, 1994; Grant, 1996), ambiguous (Torres, 1996;
Van Knippenberg & Coolen, 1993), and contradictory results (Brown, Capozza,
Paladino, & Volpato, 1996). Thus, there are grounds for caution in endorsing the
Hinkle and Brown model unequivocally.

Nevertheless, the important issue may be less the complex patterns of results
than the recognition that groups are different, that they may serve different kinds
of identity functions for their members, and that not all of these identity functions are driven by the need for positive distinctiveness proposed by Social
Identity Theory. There is some particularly interesting work by Deaux and her
colleagues which is providing the first pointers in mapping this group diversity.
She shows that there are distinguishable clusters of social identities and that we
can indeed link these different clusters of social identities with different social
psychological processes (Deaux, Reid, Mizrahi, & Ethier, 1995). For example,
some identities could be clearly described by such constructs as Expressive–
Agentic, others better by individualism–collectivism.

INTERGROUP ORIENTATION

Let me now consider the second major orientation, one that focuses on the
intergroup relationship. There are three major issues I should like to deal with
here: Realistic Group Conflict Theory, Self-Categorization Theory, and Status
and Power Relations.

Realistic Group Conflict Theory

An approach of continuing significance to the field of intergroup relations is the
Realistic Group Conflict perspective, given most prominence by the Sherifs
(e.g. Sherif & Sherif, 1953; Sherif, Harvey, White, Hood, & Sherif, 1961), but
also contributed to by Campbell (1965) and Coser (1956). As is well known,
the major determinants of intergroup attitudes and behavior in this account are
presumed to be the real interests of the groups, the goals that they are striving
towards. Where these are negatively interdependent or conflictual, one expects
a stronger hostility, bias and so on; where complementary, one predicts amicable
relations and cooperation. Over the years this theory has received continuous
empirical support (Turner, 1981), so much so that little current work tends to
be addressed to it. Nevertheless, there is one interesting development initiated
by Struch and Schwartz (1989) which suggested an important link between the
Realistic Group Conflict approach and the Social Identity perspectives discussed
earlier. In their study, they were concerned with attitudes towards an ultra-
orthodox religious group in Israel. A key independent variable was the perceived
conflict between the person's own group and that orthodox religious group.
Consistent with Realistic Group Conflict theory, they observed a clear-cut positive correlation between perceived conflict and intergroup aggression. However,

that correlation was moderated by level of group identification: those who were particularly strongly identified with their ingroup showed an even stronger relationship between perceived conflict and intergroup aggression (.6); for the lower identifiers that correlation was substantially weaker (.3). Two other results from this study reinforce some points made earlier: intergroup aggression was not correlated at all with the normal kind of evaluative ingroup bias; and strength of identification (which moderated the conflict–aggression relationship) was itself uncorrelated with the amount of ingroup bias.

Self-Categorization Theory

Another approach which places much emphasis on the nature of the intergroup context, and one which is attracting a growing body of research attention, is Self-Categorization Theory (Turner, Hogg, Oakes, Reicher, & Wetherell, 1987). The emphasis in Self-Categorization Theory is very much on the social and psychological importance for people of finding the appropriate level of categorization by which to construe any given social situation. The theory postulates a simple ratio—a meta-contrast ratio—which, it proposes, is maximized in most social situations. The meta-contrast ratio compares average perceived differences between categories with the average perceived differences within the ingroup category. Maximizing this contrast is thought to lend optimal cognitive clarity to people's interpretation of any situation and is also associated with the process known as depersonalization and self-stereotyping (Turner et al., 1987). These concepts have been used most productively to explain such diverse phenomena as social influence, group polarization, cohesion and, especially, stereotyping and stereotype change (Hogg, 1992; Hogg, Turner, & Davidson, 1990; Oakes, Haslam, & Turner, 1994; Turner, 1991).

A recurring theme of the studies on stereotyping within this tradition has been to demonstrate the importance of the comparative intergroup context in which stereotypic judgements are made, rather than any inherent features of the stimulus situation itself (e.g. Haslam et al., 1992). This finding is an interesting development because it contrasts rather starkly with the emphasis in much North American social cognition research which tends to focus either on the stimuli themselves or the perceiver, sometimes on the interaction between these; but it rarely takes much account of the intergroup context in which these stimuli and perceivers are located (Hamilton, 1981; Mackie & Hamilton, 1993).

Status and power relations

The third area under this rubric is concerned with status and power because, of course, in most naturally occurring social situations, groups are not all equal. What can we expect in terms of intergroup differentiation from high or low status groups? On the one hand, one might expect that high status groups will show greater discrimination in order to maintain or justify their position against the lower status group on grounds of equity, self-esteem maintenance, or some such mechanism (Brown, 1995). Indeed, there is evidence of more bias from higher status groups as we saw in the meta-analysis presented earlier (Mullen et al., 1992). High status groups, particularly in relatively straightforward, stratified contexts in the laboratory, do show substantially more ingroup favoritism than lower status groups. On the other hand, one could read Social Identity Theory as implying that low status groups should need to show greater bias because they are the ones whose identity is somewhat under threat by being in a subordinate position. Hence, they should have to work harder to restore their positive self-concept (Brown, 1995). In its earliest formulations, Social Identity Theory proposed a number of circumstances in which, indeed, one might expect to find such additional favoritism from subordinate status groups (Tajfel, 1978; Turner & Brown, 1978). One of these might be where alternative kinds of dimensions for making evaluations are available. Studies by Van Knippenberg and Van Oers (1984) as well as by Mummendey and Schreiber (1984) have demonstrated exactly this point. They showed that you can find alternative or, as we might say, less relevant dimensions that the lower status groups will use to achieve some kind of positive distinctiveness. Recall from the Mullen et al. (1992) meta-analysis that there was a moderating effect of dimensional relevance.

However, another condition in which subordinate status might give rise to increased ingroup favoritism will be when the nature of the intergroup status relationship is somehow under threat because it is directly perceived to be unstable, or the status positions of the groups are somehow unfair or based on arbitrary criteria (Tajfel & Turner, 1986). In these circumstances, Social Identity Theory argues, one might find some sort of insecurity of group identity, which then leads to renewed attempts to establish positive distinctiveness even, or especially, from subordinate status groups. On the other hand, any conditions which make movement between the groups possible, perhaps because the boundaries of the groups are somewhat permeable, are more likely to lead to a decrease in group identification and bias from those low status groups because they have some kind of individual mobility option available to them to deal with their "negative" identity (Tajfel & Turner, 1986). There have been some sustained research programs which have shown the importance of variables like group permeability, perceived illegitimacy, and instability in changing subordinate group members' identification with their group and their propensity to try to change the status quo (Brown, & Ross, 1982; Caddick, 1982; Ellemers, 1993; Turner & Brown, 1978; Van Knippenberg & Ellemers, 1993; Wright, Taylor, & Moghaddam, 1990).

OUTGROUP DEROGATION AND PREJUDICE

There are three topics of interest here: negative treatment of outgroups in minimal group settings, the role of affect, and automatic components of prejudice.

Negative treatment of outgroups in minimal group settings

It is now well established that the merest psychological presence of a social categorization is enough to trigger intergroup discrimination (Rabbie & Horwitz, 1969; Tajfel, Billig, Bundy, & Flament, 1971). In this paradigm very minimal kinds of group memberships—for example, an arbitrary classification into two meaningless categories—are associated with various kinds of ingroup favoritism, usually in the form of differential reward allocations to ingroup and outgroup members, or sometimes in the form of biased evaluations (Brewer, 1979; Turner, 1981). The vast majority of that early work using the minimal group paradigm tended to use allocations or evaluations along positively valued dimensions. In other words, the ingroup received more points, or more money, or a higher evaluation than the outgroup. Recently, however, it has emerged that in minimal group settings, we may not observe so easily the same kind of bias if negatively valued entities are used (Mummendey et al., 1992). For example, if group members have to allocate different amounts of aversive stimuli (e.g. durations of exposure to unpleasant "white noise"), or are asked to make evaluations along negative rating scales (e.g. undesirable traits), then the "usual" ingroup bias is eliminated. It takes the addition of some "aggravating conditions"—for example, being in a minority or low status group—to restore the "normal" minimal intergroup discrimination effect in this negative domain (Mummendey et al., 1992).

Mummendey (1996) has argued that in these kinds of experimental situations, where only negative treatments of others are possible, the experimental participants become, as it were, "welded together" by some sort of common unpleasant fate. This common fate "experience" seems to create a new superordinate category which subsumes the minimal categories that they were originally allocated to, and hence eliminates the usual intergroup discrimination. It is not until additional factors are present (e.g. being in a minority group or having particularly high levels of identification), that re-categorization into that superordinate group becomes more difficult and the "normal" intergroup discrimination reappears.

The role of affect

A second line of work, for too long neglected in the intergroup domain, concerns the role of affect. In the 1970s a number of researchers were interested in studying arousal levels in interethnic interaction, nonverbal indicators of emotions, and other unobtrusive indicators of intergroup prejudice (Crosby, Bromley, & Saxe, 1980). This strand of work seemed to go out of fashion in the 1980s with the social cognitive revolution. However, now a number of different lines of work are converging on the importance of negative affect, either interacting with, or in some cases, completely superseding the kinds of cognitive processes that the social cognitive revolution was so concerned to spell out (e.g. Haddock,

Zanna, & Esses, 1993; Jussim, Nelson, Manis, & Soffin, 1995; Mackie & Hamilton, 1993; Monteith, 1993; Stephan & Stephan, 1985). To give just one example, consider the studies reported by Jussim et al. (1995). Jussim and his colleagues were concerned with the classic labeling effect in social judgement tasks (e.g. Darley & Gross, 1983). As is usual in this paradigm, they presented some ambiguous information associated with some target person who was labeled as a member of a positively or negatively valued category. Not surprisingly, attaching a negative or a positive category label had a substantial effect on the subsequent social judgements (between 15 and 30% variance accounted for). However, further analyses revealed that this labeling effect virtually disappeared when an affective variable—how much the two categories were liked—was included as a covariate. The same analysis of covariance including various cognitive measures (e.g. beliefs about the categories) reduced, but did not eliminate, the categorical effect. What Jussim et al. conclude is that, in this particular instance, the category labeling effect is almost entirely mediated by an affective rather than by a cognitive variable.

Automatic components of prejudice

Over the past decade, there has been some debate about whether various elementary forms of prejudice can operate at an automatic level outside of our conscious control. (e.g. Devine, 1989; Dovidio & Gaertner, 1993; Perdue et al., 1990). In a seminal paper, Devine (1989) argued that, at an automatic level, high and low scorers on a modern prejudice scale could not be distinguished. She used a subliminal priming paradigm in which she primed with various category labels—in her case, it was black people—and some stereotypic material, and then measured the judgement of a target person. She observed a priming effect on social judgements but that effect was just as strong for high- and low-prejudice people. The conclusion she drew from this study was that, at an automatic level, prejudice is more or less inevitable and equally evident for all. For low-prejudice people, she argued, it is only when they have time and sufficient cognitive resources to suppress that automatic prejudice that they will emerge with manifestly differently responses from the so-called high-prejudiced people.

There are now a number of lines of research beginning to suggest that this conclusion may not be valid and that one can find differences at an automatic level, even between high- and low-prejudice people (Lepore & Brown, 1997; Locke, Macleod & Walker, 1994; Wittenbrink, Judd, & Park, 1997). In our own laboratory, we have carried out a replication of Devine's experiment, but with one important modification (Lepore & Brown, 1997). We did not include in our subliminal prime any stereotypical material; we believe that was the reason she got the null effect across high- and low-prejudice people. Instead, we primed only the category label. With this procedure we do indeed observe differences in social judgement as a function of that subliminal prime. On negative judgement

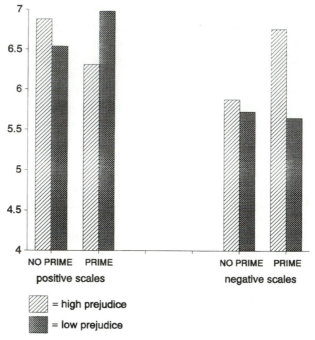

FIG. 4.2   Effects of subliminal priming on social judgements.

scales, the high-prejudice people showed a substantial effect of the prime, which was not evident in the low-prejudice people. On the positive rating scales, the effect was in exactly the opposite direction (see Fig. 4.2).[1] The reason we believe this happens is that a long history of endorsement of positive and negative stereotypic beliefs by low- and high-prejudice people leads to a different pattern of activation of those stereotypic beliefs. Other work suggests that repeated activation of particular cognitive constructs eventually causes an automatic activation of those constructs (Bargh, 1984; Higgins & King, 1981).

Reducing prejudice

In the short history of social psychology that I referred to earlier, perhaps one of the most familiar—and, I would say, most successful—ideas has been the Contact Hypothesis (Allport, 1954). Allport proposed that if groups are brought together under the appropriate conditions—equal status, cooperative contact, and so on—one will observe a reduction in the hostility and prejudice between them. In the 40 years since Allport's book was published, there has been extensive

---

[1] Parenthetically it should be noted that Devine's (1989) result (of an absence of difference between high- and low-prejudice people) is replicable provided one primes both categorical and stereotypical material (Lepore & Brown, 1997).

support for this idea from both field and laboratory work (Amir, 1976; Hewstone & Brown, 1986). However, there has been one area which has caused researchers something of a problem: the issue of generalization (Cook, 1978). It is relatively straightforward to obtain positive attitude change toward the particular outgroup members with whom one has had the contact. It is a much tougher job to get that attitude change to generalize to the other members of outgroup category who have not yet been encountered. This generalization issue has been addressed by three different models of contact that have been the focus of research efforts in this area since the mid 1980s (Brewer & Miller, 1984; Gaertner, Dovidio, Anastasio, Bachevan, & Rust, 1993; Hewstone & Brown, 1986; Vivian, Hewstone, & Brown, 1997).

First, there is the decategorization model proposed by Brewer and Miller (1984). They have argued that if category salience leads so quickly to ingroup favoritism and bias (Brewer, 1979), then the goal of successful contact should be to make categories less salient and the interaction more interpersonal. In this way relations between the different group members should become more positive.

A slightly different approach has been suggested by Gaertner et al. (1993). They suggest that while categorization is potentially problematic for intergroup relations, it can be harnessed to beneficial ends. They propose that the goal of the contact experience should be to "recategorize" the situation, so that the two former subgroups—the ingroup and outgroup—can become seen as members of the same superordinate category. Hence, the normal kind of intergroup discrimination should diminish or evaporate altogether. However, with both of these models, there may be a problem: to the extent that one is successful in "decategorizing" or "recategorizing" a situation, then the members of the two groups are psychologically no longer associated with the original categories. So, when it comes to generalization—i.e. when the participants meet members of those categories outside the immediate contact situation—there is no way to connect the positive attitude and stereotype change generated in the contact situation to those unfamiliar outgroup members. For this reason, Hewstone and Brown (1986) suggest that instead of completely eradicating these subgroup categories, there are advantages in maintaining some minimal level of salience, while at the same time maximizing all the other Allport conditions specified. The interaction remains at an intergroup level—in some sense the participants are dealing with each other as group members—so that any attitude change is associated with the category as a whole. The hope is that in the external situation the positive change will generalize.

Let me now briefly review the different studies which have been associated with these three models, all of which have attracted support in various forms. Bettencourt, Brewer, Croak, and Miller (1992) found clear evidence for the decategorization model. Using artificially created categories, they formed cooperative groups containing members of both categories. Depending on experimental condition, they instructed participants either to focus on each other's personal characteristics in an effort to get to know one another, or to focus on the task. This procedure was designed to make the situation more (or less) personal and hence reduce (or maintain) category salience. The participants' subsequent ratings and reward allocations were less biased in the former as compared to the latter condition, both towards those with whom they had interacted and towards others whom they had not met but who were shown in a brief video extract (see also Miller, Brewer, & Edwards, 1985). Significantly, though, the people portrayed in the video sequence were clearly identified by their category labels, thus ensuring that some minimal level of category salience had been retained, even in the "personal focus" conditions.

Likewise, Gaertner and his colleagues, in a series of laboratory and field studies, have demonstrated the value of recategorizing the social situation (Gaertner et al., 1989; 1990; in press). Typically, these researchers create a context in which members of two (artificial) categories interact, either as members of a superordinate group in which the original category differences are subsumed, or as members of the two groups, or as separate individuals. Their results indicate that the most favorable intergroup attitudes are observed in the first condition, least favorable in the second, with the third condition being somewhat intermediate.

There is also evidence for maintaining some category salience. Van Oudenhoven, Groenewoud, and Hewstone (1996) employed the real-life categories of Dutch and Turkish in a cooperative learning group setting. During this cooperative encounter the salience of the Turkish outgroup was varied so as to be maximal, moderate, or minimal. Subsequently, the real Dutch participants were asked to rate both the individual Turkish person with whom they had interacted and Turkish people as a whole. The ratings of the individual outgroup member were uniformly positive across conditions. However, the generalized ratings of the outgroup were reliably more favorable in the two conditions which had enhanced category salience than in the "interpersonal" minimal salience condition. This suggests that the latter condition did not facilitate the possibility of generalizing from the particular to the general (see also Maras & Brown, 1996; Vivian et al., 1994; 1997).

So, all three models show that it is possible to reduce intergroup discrimination if the social situation is arranged in appropriate ways. One way of reconciling these different approaches is to adopt some kind of trade-off policy in which one seeks the benefits of reducing category salience, either by decategorizing or recategorizing, but not below some minimal level, in order to retain the possibility of generalization. However, the story is even more complicated because when categories are made salient, it may increase the anxiety of the participants (Islam & Hewstone, 1993; Greenland & Brown, 1996). Note, again, the introduction of affective variables. We know from other research that heightened anxiety tends to be antithetical to positive intergroup attitudes (Stephan & Stephan, 1985;

Wilder & Shapiro, 1989a; 1989b). The reasons for this are either because there are fewer cognitive resources to deal with the situation—and hence a greater propensity to stereotype—or because of the negative affect associated with anxiety, which then spills over onto the outgroup target (Stephan & Stephan, 1985). So, again, a delicate balancing act seems to be called for between maintaining some level of intergroup salience, but not so much as to heighten the anxiety to detrimental levels.

CONCLUSION

At the beginning of this paper, I noted the short history of the field. However, it is clear from the range of different theories and research covered here, and the many outstanding issues still to be addressed, that the future of the field will be long and fruitful. It only remains to add that the continuing and—it has to be said—in many cases tragic sagas of problematic intergroup relations around the world—in Quebec, in Ireland, in Rwanda, and in the former Yugoslavia—make it obvious that the outcome of that future work will have very much more than purely academic significance.

ACKNOWLEDGEMENTS

I should like to acknowledge the contribution of Marilynn Brewer to this paper. Some of it draws on a recent chapter which she and I have just completed for the forthcoming *Handbook of Social Psychology* (Brewer & Brown, in press).

REFERENCES

Abrams, D., & Hogg, M. (Eds.). (1990). *Social identity theory: Constructive and critical advances.* Hemel Hempstead, UK: Harvester Wheatsheaf.

Allport, F. H. (1924). *Social psychology.* New York: Houghton Mifflin.

Allport, G. W. (1935). Attitudes. In C. Murchison (Ed.), *Handbook of social psychology* (pp. 798–844). Worcester, MA: Clark University Press.

Allport, G. W. (1954). *The nature of prejudice.* Reading, MA: Addison-Wesley.

Amir, Y. (1976). The role of intergroup contact in change of prejudice and ethnic relations. In P. Katz (Ed.), *Towards the elimination of racism.* New York: Pergamon.

Bargh, J. (1984). Automatic and conscious processing of social information. In R. S. Wyer & T. K. Srull (Eds.), *Handbook of social cognition* (Vol. 3). Hillsdale, NJ: Erlbaum.

Bettencourt, B. A., Brewer, M. B., Croak, M. R., & Miller, N. (1992). Cooperation and the reduction of intergroup bias: The role of reward structure and social orientation. *Journal of Experimental Social Psychology, 28,* 301–309.

Brewer, M. B. (1979). Ingroup bias in the minimal intergroup situation: A cognitive motivational analysis. *Psychological Bulletin, 86,* 307–324.

Brewer, M. B. (1991). The social self: On being the same and different at the same time. *Personality and Social Psychology Bulletin, 17,* 475–482.

Brewer, M. B. & Brown, R. J. (in press). Intergroup relations. In D. Gilbert, S. Fiske, & G. Lindzey (Eds.), *Handbook of social psychology* (4th ed.). New York: McGraw Hill.

Brewer, M. B., Manzi, J. M., & Shaw, J. S. (1993). In-group identification as a function of depersonalization, distinctiveness, and status. *Psychological Science, 4,* 88–92.

Brewer, M. B., & Miller, N. (1984). Beyond the contact hypothesis: Theoretical perspectives on desegregation. In N. Miller & M. B. Brewer (Eds.), *Groups in contact: The psychology of desegregation*. Orlando, FL: Academic.

Brown, R., Hinkle, S., Ely, P. G., Fox-Cardamone, L., Maras, P., & Taylor, L. A. (1992). Recognising group diversity: Individualist–collectivist and autonomous–relational social orientations and their implications for intergroup processes. *British Journal of Social Psychology, 31*, 327–342.

Brown, R. J. (1995). *Prejudice: Its social psychology*. Oxford: Blackwell.

Brown, R., Capozza, D., Paladino, M. P., & Volpato, C. (1996). Identificazione e favoritismo per il proprio gruppo: Verifica del modello di Hinkle e Brown [Identification and ingroup favoritism: A test of the Hinkle & Brown model]. In P. Boscolo, F. Cristante, A. Dellantonio, & S. Soresi (Eds.), *Aspetti Qualitativi e Quantitativi Nella Ricerca Psicologica*. Padova, Italy: Il Poligrafo.

Brown, R. J., & Ross, G. R. (1982). The battle for acceptance: An exploration into the dynamics of intergroup behaviour. In H. Tajfel (Ed.), *Social identity and intergroup relations*, Cambridge: Cambridge University Press.

Caddick, B. (1982). Perceived illegitimacy and intergroup relations. In H. Tajfel (Ed.), *Social identity and intergroup relations*. Cambridge: Cambridge University Press.

Campbell, D. T. (1965). Ethnocentric and other altruistic motives. In D. Levine (Ed.), *Nebraska Symposium on Motivation*. Lincoln, NB: University of Nebraska Press.

Cook, S. W. (1978). Interpersonal and attitudinal outcomes in cooperating interracial groups. *Journal of Research and Development in Education, 12*, 97–113.

Coser, L. (1956). *Functions of social conflict*. New York: Free Press.

Crosby, F., Bromley, S., & Saxe, L. (1980). Recent unobtrusive studies of Black and White discrimination and prejudice. *Psychological Bulletin, 87*, 546–563.

Darley, J. M., & Gross, P. H. (1983). A hypothesis-confirming bias in labeling effects. *Journal of Personality and Social Psychology, 44*, 20–33.

Deaux, K., Reid, A., Mizrahi, K., & Ethier, K. A. (1995). Parameters of social identity. *Journal of Personality and Social Psychology, 68*, 280–291.

Devine, P. (1989). Stereotypes and prejudice: Their automatic and controled components. *Journal of Personality and Social Psychology, 56*, 5–18.

Dovidio, J., & Gaertner, S. (1993). Stereotypes and evaluative intergroup bias. In D. Mackie & D. Hamilton (Eds.), *Affect, cognition and stereotyping*. Orlando, FL: Academic.

Ellemers, N. (1993). The influence of socio-structural variables on identity management strategies. *European Review of Social Psychology, 4*, 27–58.

Ellemers, N., Wilke, H. & Van Knippenberg, A. (1993). Effects of the legitimacy of low group or individual status as individual and collective status-enhancement strategies. *Journal of Personality and Social Psychology, 64*, 766–778.

Feather, N. T. (1994). Values, national identification and favouritism towards the ingroup. *British Journal of Social Psychology, 33*, 467–476.

Gaertner, S. L., Mann, J., Dovidio, J. F., Murrell, A. J., & Ponere, M. (1990). How does cooperation reduce intergroup bias? *Journal of Personality and Social Psychology, 59*, 692–704.

Gaertner, S. L., Dovidio, J. F., Anastasio, P. A., Bachevan, B. A., & Rust, M. C. (1993). The common ingroup identity model: Recategorisation and the reduction of intergroup bias. In W. Stroebe & M. Hewstone (Eds.), *European Review of Social Psychology* (Vol. 4, pp. 1–26). Chichester, UK: Wiley.

Gaertner, S. L., Mann, J., Murrell, A., & Dovidio, J. F. (1989). Reducing intergroup bias: The benefits of recategorization. *Journal of Personality and Social Psychology, 57*, 239–249.

Gaertner, S. L., Rust, M., Dovidio, J. F., Bachman, B., & Anastasio, P. (in press). The contact hypothesis: The role of a common ingroup identity on reducing intergroup bias. *Small Group Research*.

Grant, P. (1996). *Enhancing collective and personal self-esteem through differentiation: Further exploration of Hinkle and Brown's taxonomy*. Unpublished manuscript, Department of Psychology, University of Saskatchewan, Canada.

Greenland, K., & Brown, R. (1996, August). *The role of anxiety in intergroup contact*. Paper presented at the XXVI International Congress of Psychology, Montreal, Canada.

Haddock, G., Zanna, M. P., & Esses, V. M. (1993) Assessing the structure of prejudicial attitudes: The case of attitudes towards homosexuals. *Journal of Personality and Social Psychology, 65*, 1105–1118.

Hamilton, D. L. (Ed.). (1981). *Cognitive processes in stereotyping and intergroup behaviour*. Hillsdale, NJ: Erlbaum.

Haslam, S. A., Turner, J. C., Oakes, P. J., & McGarty, C. (1992). Context-dependent variation in social stereotyping: I The effects of intergroup relations as mediated by social change and frame of reference. *European Journal of Social Psychology, 22*, 3–20.

Hewstone, M., & Brown, R. J. (1986). Contact is not enough: An intergroup perspective on the contact hypothesis. In M. Hewstone & R. Brown (Eds.), *Contact and conflict in intergroup encounters*. Oxford: Blackwell.

Higgins, E. T., & King, G. (1981). Accessibility of social constructs: Information-processing consequences of individual and contextual variability. In N. Cantor & J. F. Kihlstrom (Eds.), *Personality and social interaction* (pp. 69–121). Hillsdale, NJ: Erlbaum.

Hinkle, S. & Brown, R. (1990). Intergroup comparisons and social identity: Some links and lacunae. In D. Abrams & M. Hogg (Eds.), *Social identity theory: Constructive and critical advances* (pp. 48–70). Hemel Hempstead, UK: Harvester Wheatsheaf.

Hogg, M. A. (1992). *The social psychology of group cohesiveness: From attraction to social identity*. Hemel Hempstead: Harvester Wheatsheaf.

Hogg, M., Turner. J., & Davidson, B. (1990). Polarized norms and social frames of reference: A test of the self-categorization theory of group polarization. *Basic and Applied Social Psychology, 11*, 77–100.

Islam, M. R., & Hewstone, M. (1993). Dimensions of contact as predictors of intergroup anxiety, perceived outgroup variability and outgroup attitude: An integrated model. *Personality and Social Psychology Bulletin, 19*, 700–710.

Jussim, L., Nelson, T. E., Manis, M., & Soffin, S. (1995). Prejudice, stereotypes, and labelling effects: Sources of bias in person perception. *Journal of Personality and Social Psychology, 68*, 228–246.

Lepore, L., & Brown, R. (1997). Category and stereotype activation: Is prejudice inevitable? *Journal of Personality and Social Psychology, 72*, 275–287.

Locke, V., Macleod, C., & Walker, I. (1994). Automatic and controled activation of stereotypes: Individual differences associated with prejudice. *British Journal of Social Psychology, 33*, 29–46.

Mackie, D. M., & Hamilton, D. L. (Eds.). (1993). *Affect, cognition and stereotyping: Interactive processes in group perception*. Orlando, FA: Academic.

Maras, P., & Brown, R. (1996). Effects of contact on children's attitudes towards disability: A longitudinal study. *Journal of Applied Social Psychology, 26*, 2113–2134.

McDougall, W. (1908). *An introduction to social psychology*. London: Methuen.

Miller, N., Brewer, M. B., & Edwards, K. (1985). Cooperative interaction in a desegregated setting: A laboratory analogue. *Journal of Social Issues, 41* (3), 63–79.

Monteith, M. (1993). Self-regulation of prejudiced responses: Implications for progress in prejudice-reduction efforts. *Journal of Personality and Social Psychology, 65*, 469–485.

Mullen, B., Brown, R., & Smith, C. (1992). Ingroup bias as a function of salience, relevance and status: An integration. *European Journal of Social Psychology, 22*, 103–122.

Mummendey, A. (1996, August). *The positive–negative assymmetry of social discrimination: A challenge to Social Identity Theory?* Symposium conducted at the XXVI International Congress of Psychology, Montreal, Canada.

Mummendey, A., & Schreiber, H-J. (1984). "Different" just means "better": Some obvious and some hidden pathways to ingroup favouritism. *British Journal of Social Psychology, 23*, 363–7.

Mummendey, A., Simon, B., Dietze, C., Grunert, M., Haeger, G., Kessler, S., Lettgen, S., & Schaferhoff, S. (1992). Categorization is not enough: Intergroup discrimination in negative outcome allocations. *Journal of Experimental Social Psychology, 28*, 125–144.

Oakes, P. Haslam, S., & Turner, J. (1994). *Stereotyping and social reality* Oxford: Blackwell.

Perdue, C. W., Dovidio, J. F., Gurtman, M. B., & Tyler, R. B. (1990). "Us" and "Them": Social categorization and the process of intergroup bias. *Journal of Personality and Social Psychology, 59*, 475–486.

Rabbie, J. M., & Horwitz, M. (1969). Arousal of ingroup–outgroup bias by a chance win or loss. *Journal of Personality and Social Psychology, 13*, 269–277.

Ross, E. A. (1908). *Social psychology: An outline and sourcebook.* New York: Macmillan.

Sachdev, I., & Bourhis, R. Y. (1991). Power and status differentials in minority and majority group relations. *European Journal of Social Psychology, 21*, 1–24.

Sherif, M. (1966). *Group conflict and co-operation: Their social psychology.* London: Routledge & Kegan Paul.

Sherif, M., Harvey, O. J., White, B. J., Hood, W. R., & Sherif, C. W. (1961). *Intergroup conflict and co-operation: The Robber's Cave experiment.* Norman, OK: University of Oklahoma.

Sherif, M., & Sherif C. W. (1953). *Groups in harmony and tension: An integration of studies on intergroup relations.* New York: Octagon.

Simon, B., & Brown, R. J. (1987). Perceived intragroup homogeneity in minority–majority contexts. *Journal of Personality and Social Psychology, 53*, 703–711.

Simon, B., Glassner-Boyerl, B., & Stratenworth, I. (1991). Stereotyping and self-stereotyping in a natural intergroup context: The case of heterosexual and homosexual men. *Social Psychology Quarterly, 54*, 252–266.

Stephan, W. G., & Stephan, C. W. (1985). Intergroup anxiety. *Journal of Social Issues, 41* (3), 157–175.

Struch, N., & Schwartz, S. H. (1989). Intergroup aggression: Its predictors and distinctness from ingroup bias. *Journal of Personality and Social Psychology, 56*, 364–373.

Sumner, W. (1906). *Folkways.* New York: Ginn.

Tajfel, H. (Ed.). (1978). *Differentiation between social groups.* London: Academic.

Tajfel, H. (Ed.). (1982). *Social Identity and intergroup relations.* Cambridge: Cambridge University Press.

Tajfel, H., Billig, M. G., Bundy, R. P., & Flament, C. (1971). Social categorization and intergroup behavior. *European Journal of Social Psychology, 1*, 149–178.

Tajfel, H., & Turner, J. (1986). The social identity theory of intergroup behavior. In S. Worchel & W. G. Austin (Eds.), *Psychology of intergroup relations* (pp. 7–24). Chicago, IL: Nelson.

Torres, A. (1996). *Exploring group diversity.* Unpublished doctoral dissertation, University of Kent, England.

Triandis, H., Bontempo, R., Villareal, M. J., Asai, M., & Lucca, N. (1988). Individualism and collectivism: Cross-cultural perspectives on self–ingroup relationships. *Journal of Personality and Social Psychology, 54*, 323–338.

Turner, J. C. (1978). Social categorization and social discrimination in the minimal group paradigm. In H. Tajfel (Ed.), *Differentiation between social groups: Studies in the social psychology of intergroup relations* (pp. 235–250). London: Academic.

Turner, J. C. (1981) The experimental social psychology of intergroup behaviour. In J. Turner & H. Giles (Ed.), *Intergroup behaviour.* Oxford: Blackwell.

Turner, J. C. (1991). *Social influence,* Milton Keynes, UK: Open University Press.

Turner, J. C., & Brown, R. J. (1978). Social status, cognitive alternatives, and intergroup relations. In H. Tajfel (Ed.), *Differentiation between social groups: Studies in the social psychology of intergroup relations* (pp. 201–234). London: Academic.

Turner, J. C., Hogg, M. A., Oakes, P. J., Reicher, S. D., & Wethrell, M. S. (1987). *Rediscovering the social group: A self-categorization theory.* Oxford: Blackwell.

Van Knippenberg, A., & Coolen, P. (1993, September). *Social identification, intergroup differentiation and self-esteem.* Paper presented at the Congress of the European Association of Experimental Social Psychology, Lisbon, Portugal.

Van Knippenberg, A., & Ellemers, N. (1993). Strategies in intergroup relations. In M. Hogg & D. Abrams (Eds.), *Group motivation: Social psychological perspectives* (pp. 17–32). Hemel Hempstead, UK: Harvester Wheatsheaf.

Van Knippenberg, A., & Van Oers, H. (1984). Social identity and equity concerns in intergroup perceptions. *British Journal of Social Psychology, 23,* 351–361.

Van Oudenhoven, J. P., Groenewoud, J. T., & Hewstone, M. (1996). Cooperation, ethnic salience, and generalization of interethnic attitudes. *European Journal of Social Psychology, 26,* 649–662.

Vivian, J., Brown, R. J., & Hewstone, M. (1994). *Changing attitudes through intergroup contact: The effects of membership salience.* Unpublished manuscript, University of Kent, England.

Vivian, J., Hewstone, M., & Brown, R. (1997). Intergroup contact: Theoretical and empirical developments. In R. Ben-Ari & Y. Rich (Eds.), *Understanding and enhancing education for diverse students: An international perspective.* Ramat Gan, Israel: University of Bar Ilan Press.

Wilder, D. A., & Shapiro, P. N. (1989a). Role of competition-induced anxiety in limiting the beneficial impact of positive behavior by an outgroup member. *Journal of Personality and Social Psychology, 56,* 60–69.

Wilder, D. A., & Shapiro, P. N. (1989b). Effects of anxiety on impression formation in a group context: An anxiety assimilation hypothesis. *Journal of Experimental Social Psychology, 25,* 481–499.

Wittenbrink, B., Judd, C. M., & Park, B. (1997). Evidence for racial prejudice at the implicit level and its relationship with questionnaire measures. *Journal of Personality and Social Psychology, 72,* 262–274.

Wright, S. C., Taylor, D. M., & Moghaddam, F. M. (1990). Responding to membership in a disadvantaged group: From acceptance to collective protest. *Journal of Personality and Social Psychology, 58,* 994–1003.

CHAPTER FIVE

Discovering general laws of social motivation

Bernard Weiner
University of California, Los Angeles, USA

Regularities in social motivation are derived from a causal analysis of the ability–effort distinction, which has implications for perceptions of personal responsibility. A responsibility analysis is then extended and applied to reactions to the stigmatized, to help-giving, and to aggression. A general theory of motivation is proposed in which responsibility judgments give rise to the affects of anger and sympathy, which then direct social conduct.

L'analyse causale de la distinction aptitude–effort révèle l'existence de régularités dans la motivation sociale qui ont des implications par rapport aux perceptions de responsabilité personnelle. Cette étude se poursuit par une analyse de responsabilité et son application aux réactions des individus stigmatisés, au comportement d'aide à autrui, et à l'aggressivité. On propose enfin une théorie générale de la motivation dans laquelle des jugements de responsabilité donnent lieu à des sentiments de colère et de sympathie, qui orientent ensuite le comportement social.

When seeking to discover general laws of social motivation, the daunting task one must first face is where to look? How can one narrow the field? After all, the number of observations related to social motivation is virtually endless.

To start this task, I decided to have my search guided by the classroom, which is a microcosm of the total social universe. What observations in the classroom might be pertinent to social motivation? First, we know that teachers appraise and evaluate their students. This is certainly a social act. What else of a social nature happens in the classroom? Among other things, students form peer groups; some children are accepted while others are neglected or rejected. Some students are stigmatized and labeled as "dumb" or "braggarts." This is a social perception with motivational implications. In addition, teachers help the students and the students help one another. Help-giving surely is a part of social motivation, both within and outside of the classroom. And of course there is much aggression—from peers to one another, from students toward the teacher, and even from the teacher toward the students.

Of course, there are many other instances of social behavior in the classroom, but let us ask for a moment: can student evaluation, stigmatization, help-giving, and aggression be brought within one conceptual framework? If so, then this certainly would be an important advancement. And that will be my goal in the present chapter—to bring these disparate phenomena within one over-riding conceptual network. I shall not confine my observations to the classroom, but shall always come back to that setting. Let me start, then, with achievement evaluation.

ACHIEVEMENT EVALUATION

The prototypical investigation concerning judgments of others in achievement contexts was conducted by Weiner and Kukla (1970). Students were depicted as succeeding or failing on an exam. This outcome information was factorially combined with accounts of each student's ability level and effort expenditure, the dominant causes of achievement performance. Thus, for example, in one condition a student was characterized as high in ability, low in effort, and failing an exam, whereas in a contrasting condition the student was described as low in ability, high in effort, and succeeding. The respondents were asked to evaluate (provide feedback to) each of these hypothetical students.

The data from one investigation reported by Weiner and Kukla (1970) are shown in Fig. 5.1. In Fig. 5.1 the outcomes ranged from excellent through fair, borderline, moderate failure and clear failure. Furthermore, evaluations ranged from maximum reward (+ 5) to maximum punishment (−5). Figure 5.1 reveals, as would be expected, that positive outcomes are rewarded more (punished less) than are negative outcomes. Of greater importance in the present context, higher effort or motivation (M) is rewarded more for success and punished less, given failure, than is lack of motivation or effort (−M). Conversely, low ability is associated with somewhat greater reward and less punishment than is high ability. That is in part because, given this set of information, low ability accompanied by high effort and success is particularly valued, whereas high ability in conjunction with low effort and failure is especially admonished.

If for now we concentrate on just the failure outcomes, and on the conditions in which the cause of failure is unambiguous, that is, the low ability–high effort condition in which failure must be due to lack of ability, and the high ability–low effort condition in which the failure must be due to lack of effort, then we can conclude the following:

1. Failure → lack of effort → high punishment.
2. Failure → lack of ability → low (or no) punishment.

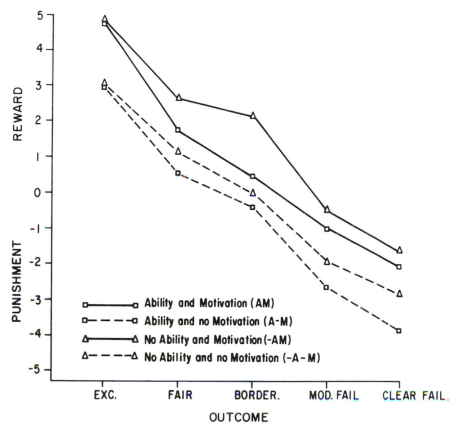

FIG. 5.1   Evaluation as a function of outcome, effort, and ability (from Weiner & Kukla, 1970).

These relations between causality and achievement evaluation have been often reported, replicated in numerous cultures, and can be accepted as empirical facts (see review in Weiner, 1986). Now then, let us turn to another aspect of social behavior, found outside of as well as within the classroom, that of stigmatization.

JUDGMENTS OF THE STIGMATIZED

Let me start with some studies outside of the classroom, and then return to the school setting. In one pair of illustrative investigations, Weiner, Perry, and Magnusson (1988) examined the relations between stigmas and a number of attitudinal and affective variables including liking, anger, and sympathy. In these studies, we selected ten very prominent stigmas (e.g. AIDS, Alzheimer's disease, obesity, paraplegia) to be rated. The data, shown in Table 5.1, reveal that individuals with somatically-originated problems, such as Alzheimer's disease and blindness, elicited less negative reactions than did persons with behavioral

TABLE 5.1
Mean ratings of stigmatized others

Stigma	Responsibility	Blame	Like	Pity	Anger
Alzheimer's disease	0.8	0.5	6.5	7.9	1.4
Blindness	0.9	0.5	7.5	7.4	1.7
Cancer	1.6	1.3	7.6	8.0	1.6
Heart disease	2.5	1.6	7.5	7.4	1.6
Paraplegia	1.6	0.9	7.0	7.6	1.4
Vietnam War syndrome	1.7	1.5	5.7	7.1	2.1
Acquired immune deficiency syndrome (AIDS)	4.4	4.8	4.8	6.2	4.0
Child abuser	5.2	6.0	2.0	3.3	7.9
Drug abuse	6.5	6.7	3.0	4.0	6.4
Obesity	5.3	5.2	5.7	5.1	3.3

NOTE:

Ratings were made on 9-point scales with higher values reflecting higher ratings (from Weiner, Perry, & Magnusson, 1988). Copyright 1988 by the American Psychological Association. Adapted with permission.

TABLE 5.2
Typical stigma evaluation, considering
relative reprimand

Stigma	Classification	Reprimand
Alcohoism	Behavioral	High
Obesity	Behavioral	High
AIDS	Behavioral	High
Blindness	Somatic, Genetic	Low
Alzheimer's	Somatic, Genetic	Low
Heart disease	Somatic, Genetic	Low

or mental-originated problems such as being a child abuser or using drugs. The negativity of responses toward others with behavioral-based stigmas including AIDS, obesity, and drug addiction has been reported many times in many investigations, and can be taken as empirical fact. To compare these findings with achievement evaluation, and with the focus on behavioral reactions of reprimand or not, one can observe in Table 5.2 that alcoholism and obesity, for example, contrast with blindness and Alzheimer's disease in the reactions that are elicited.

Returning to the classroom, it has been documented that children generally do not accept peers who have non-normative characteristics such as being socially withdrawn, unattractive, handicapped, and so on (see, for example, review in Hartup, 1983). However, peer reactions differ according to the type of deviance. Children who exhibit aggressive, anti-social, or hyperactive behavior typically are rated as least liked, whereas the mentally and physically handicapped are most "preferred" among the deviant groups (see Juvonen, 1991; Sigelman & Begley, 1987). These data are summarized in Table 5.3.

TABLE 5.3
Evaluation of school-related stigmas (Reprimand)

Stigma	Classification	Reprimand
Hyperactivity	Behavioral	High
Braggart	Behavioral	High
Aggressive	Behavioral	High
Physical handicap	Somatic, Genetic	Low
Mental handicap	Somatic, Genetic	Low
Unattractive	Somatic, Genetic	Low

I now have presented two phenotypically disparate sets of relations (low effort is punished more for achievement failure than is lack of ability; mental and behavioral stigmas are reacted to with more reproachment than are somatic stigmas). These should be kept in mind as I turn from these empirical generalities towards classification, a necessary step in the formulation of general laws.

CLASSIFICATION OF CAUSES

Classification in psychology takes many forms, from the grouping of external stimuli to the categorization of internal mechanisms and behavioral reactions. The taxonomic system of importance here bears on the differences between ability and effort as the causes of achievement success and failure, and a corresponding distinction between biology and behavior as the causes of stigmatization.

There are, of course, many causes of achievement outcomes. Failure, for example, may be due to lack of effort or ability, as already documented, but also due to poor strategy, bad luck, the bias of teachers, hindrance from peers, illness, and on and on. In a similar manner, and now considering the affiliative domain, a social rejection might be due to poor interpersonal skills, the desired partner already has plans, the other regards you as "sloppy," and so on.

These diverse and manifestly different causes have common characteristics or properties and therefore they may be genotypically similar in spite of phenotypic disparities. To start with, ability, effort, social skills, and being sloppy all describe (are internal to) the person, whereas teacher bias, hindrance from peers, and the desired partner being busy all place causality external to the person. It has been found repeatedly that locus is a fundamental property of phenomenal causality (see Heider, 1958; Rotter, 1966). It therefore may be stated that lack of math ability and being sloppy are, at least in one feature, similar respective causes of achievement failure and affiliative rejection in that they are internal to the actor. In a similar manner, teacher bias and the desired date having already made plans share the property of external causality.

A second causal property that will prove to be of great centrality in this context is controllability, or the degree to which a cause is volitionally alterable. Lack of effort is perceived as controllable or personally changeable. In addition,

TABLE 5.4
Causal properties of ability and effort

Causal properties	Ability	Effort
Locus	Internal	Internal
Controllability	Uncontrollable	Controllable
Stability	Stable	Unstable

personal characteristics including "sloppiness" are often judged by others as alterable—the causal agent can be better dressed. Lack of effort as a cause of achievement failure and being viewed as untidy as a cause of social rejection therefore are in some sense alike in regards to their causal properties—both are internal as well as controllable. Furthermore, low aptitude as a cause of math failure and the desired partner already having prior commitments as a cause of affiliative rejection are also alike in that they would be construed as not controllable by the causal agent. Just like causal locus, controllability again and again has been identified as a basic dimension or property of phenomenal causality (see review in Weiner, 1986).

There is most likely one additional underlying property of causality. This relates to the generality of causal explanations over time (causal stability). For example, low general intelligence as a cause of math failure tends to be considered stable over time, whereas affiliative rejection due to the desired partner having a prior engagement is likely to be construed as unstable. There is a vast array of evidence supporting the position that locus, controllability, and stability are the only replicable properties of phenomenal causality (see review in Weiner, 1986).

Now let us return to the distinction between ability and effort introduced earlier. Ability and effort would be classified as internal to the causal agent. On the other hand, ability tends to be considered uncontrollable and stable (using ability here as akin to aptitude), whereas effort is controllable and unstable. These two causes, therefore, are similar in one basic attribute, but differ in two others (see Table 5.4).

Given this analysis, differences in reprimand for failure associated with ability versus effort ascriptions cannot be traced to the locus dimension of causality (considering this a dichotomous classification of internal versus external). On the other hand, inequities in the reactions elicited, given failure, can be ascribed to either of the two remaining causal properties. It is known, however, that if one is perceived as either "lazy" or just not exerting effort on this occasion, then reprimand is voiced for failure. Conversely, if one lacks general intelligence or just the ability at this point in time, then reprimand is relatively withheld, given nonattainment of a goal. Hence, only the controllability dimension of causality covaries with punishment for achievement failure. Given this conclusion, the prior findings reported by Weiner and Kukla (1970) may be represented as:

1. Failure → lack of effort / controllable causality → punishment.

2. Failure → lack of ability / uncontrollable causality → no punishment.

TAXONOMIC SIGNIFICANCE

A specific fact in and of itself is of less interest than what that evidence more broadly represents. It is of great importance that lack of effort is punished more than lack of ability, given failure. However, it is of greater significance to realize that causal controllability, which is substantiated or materialized by lack of effort, generates greater punishment than does causal uncontrollability, which is embodied within low aptitude. This importance becomes apparent when it is recognized that the causes of mental and behavioral stigmas generally are considered controllable (e.g. sexual behavior as a cause of AIDS; overeating as a cause of obesity), and thus they differ from the causes of somatic stigmas, which are often construed as personally uncontrollable (e.g. a genetic defect as a cause of Alzheimer's disease). Hence, the two sets of phenomena presented earlier related to achievement evaluation and reactions to the stigmatized can now be embraced within the same conceptual analysis or framework:

1. Achievement failure due to lack of effort
   Mental / behavioral-based stigmas → controllable causality → reprimand.

2. Achievement failure due to low ability
   Somatic-based stigmas → uncontrollable causality → no reprimand.

Note that two empirical laws have been joined and that the causal dimensionality makes possible explanatory generalization.

These sequences should be stated more generally, however, to capture the observation that what typically are labeled as behavioral and mental stigmas on occasion are perceived as due to uncontrollable causes (e.g. obesity caused by a thyroid problem), whereas at times somatic-based stigmas may be construed as due to controllable causes (e.g. cancer because of smoking). Thus, a more adequate representation of the data is:

Achievement failure; stigma → controllable causality → reprimand.
uncontrollable causality → no reprimand.

Now two social phenomena are embraced under one rubric. However, achievement appraisal and reactions to the stigmatized do not represent the core of social behavior. When considering social motivation and research related to causal controllability, two other areas of study are of special significance in that they form the very heart of social psychology. They are helping (altruism), or going toward others, and aggression, or going against others. I next turn to these two motivational domains, guided by and essentially repeating the interpretations of achievement evaluations and reactions to the stigmatized. However, it will be seen that new theoretical obstacles are faced.

HELP-GIVING

Let me again start with two earlier investigations, the first from outside of the classroom and the second more pertinent to educational contexts. In an early investigation conducted by Piliavin, Rodin, and Piliavin (1969), a confederate fell to the floor on a subway train while other experimenters observed the spontaneous tendencies of the riders to help the needy individual. In one condition, "the victim smelled of liquor and carried a liquor bottle wrapped tightly in a brown bag," whereas in a second condition he "carried a black cane" (p. 219). Thus, there were two causes of the need for aid. It was found that the person with the cane was helped on about 95% of the occasions in which he fell, whereas the drunk was aided on only about 50% of the incidents. Furthermore, the assistance was given sooner to the cane-carrying person.

Ten years later, Barnes, Ickes, and Kidd (1979) examined help-giving in an academic context. They had experimenters pretend to be classmates of other students, whom they called to borrow class notes. Two experimental conditions conveyed the reason for the need, which corresponded to the ability–effort distinction in the study of achievement evaluation. In one condition, the experimenter communicated that the notes were needed because "I just don't seem to have the ability to take good notes," whereas in a second condition the confederate stated: "I just don't seem to have the motivation to take good notes" (p. 369). Barnes et al. reported a much higher rate of agreement to help the student in the low ability rather than the low motivation condition.

The experimental findings by Piliavin et al. (1969) and Barnes et al. (1979) have been replicated many times (see review in Schmidt & Weiner, 1988). These data may be descriptively represented as:

1. (a) Falling in subway → illness
                              → help given.
   (b) No class notes → low ability

2. (a) Falling in subway → drinking
                              → help withheld.
   (b) No class notes → lack of motivation

It has been documented in the prior pages that alcoholism and lack of motivation to take notes are perceived as personally controllable, whereas illness as the cause of falling and lack of ability to take notes both are not subject to volitional alteration. Hence, these data may be more broadly depicted as follows:

1. Need for help → uncontrollable causality → help given.
2. Need for help → controllable causality → help withheld.

Note, therefore, that help-giving in these contexts can be conceptualized with the same structure as was imposed on achievement evaluation and reactions to the stigmatized. In all cases, perceptions of causal controllability are the key mediating variable between an event or state and the elicited reaction.

AGGRESSION

Prior to turning from help-giving to aggression, I want to make it clear that much of aggressive behavior, as well as much of helping behavior, is not subject to a causal or attributional analysis. One might help one's mother, for example, without considering the controllability of her need state, for kin relationships certainly influence prosocial conduct. In a similar manner, when a bully takes the toy of another, or when a robber threatens harm, it is unlikely that the doer of these deeds has engaged in an attributional search and is concerned about causal controllability for an act that the other has committed. The aggression considered here is retaliatory or reactive rather than proactive, and even given this restriction, it certainly is acknowledged that there are many determinants of aggression other than causal perceptions. However, this should not be taken to mean that aggression instigated by a causal understanding of a negative act committed by another can be ignored.

In this area again I shall first turn to studies conducted outside of classroom contexts, and then return to issues of direct educational relevance. One set of investigations bearing on an attributional approach to aggression adhered to a deception paradigm. In these experiments, a subject received an aversive stimulus (e.g. shock, a loud noise) from an experimental partner (who may have been a confederate or did not "actually" exist but was thought to be in an adjoining room). Information was then conveyed that the partner did or did not know the effects of her action, was or was not aware of the level of aversive stimulation that she had administered, and the like. After undergoing this negative experience, in conjunction with the additional information, the subject was provided with the opportunity to respond aggressively toward this person (see Dyck & Rule, 1978; Epstein & Taylor, 1967; Nickel, 1974). In this manner, the experimentally manipulated inferences of personal accountability were related to behavioral aggression (retaliation).

This research consistently has found that subjects' overt aggression matches the intensity of the aversive stimulation that they believe the partner intended to administer, rather than the level of shock or noise that had actually been experienced (see Ferguson & Rule, 1983). Thus, for example, given high aversive stimulation, the data can be depicted as:

intended → retaliation.

High aversive stimulation →

not intended → no retaliation.

A second literature more pertinent to the classroom contains an individual difference or correlational component as well as some experimental manipulations. Here, the attention of attributional research is on the beliefs held by aggressive children that others provoked them "on purpose," which justifies their own retaliation. Indeed, even among nonaggressive individuals the person who believes that another acted with malicious intent feels justified in the endorsement of aggressive behavior. It therefore follows that persons who tend to be aggressive may be prone to perceive that others acted with such intent.

In one of the original studies guided by this line of research, Dodge (1980) first identified aggressive and nonaggressive boys based on teacher and peer ratings. The children, who were tested individually, were given a puzzle-assembly task to complete with the possibility of winning a prize. During the middle of the task, they were interrupted and taken into an adjoining room where they could view a puzzle supposedly being worked on by another child. At that time, they "overheard" a bogus intercom system conveying that this other child was examining their own partially completed puzzle. The child was then heard destroying the puzzle. Three experimental conditions conveyed that the damage was either done on purpose, or accidentally, or that the cause of the damage was unknown. After receiving this information, the subject was left alone in that room to observe whether he would retaliate by damaging the other child's puzzle.

In the hostile intent condition, both aggressive and nonaggressive children responded with retaliatory aggression, whereas in the accidental damage condition they acted with restraint. But in the ambiguous condition, the aggressive children behaved more aggressively than did the nonaggressives. Similar findings have been reported by Graham, Hudley, & Williams (1993), Nasby, Hayden, & dePaulo (1980), and others (see review in Crick & Dodge, 1994).

In sum, the laboratory research making use of a retaliatory shock paradigm, and the individual difference research assessing the tendency to attribute hostile intent to others, is consistent in documenting strong intent–retaliation linkages. Recall that when examining achievement evaluation, reactions to the stigmatized, and help-giving, the relations included the concept of controllability, not that of intentionality. Thus, the question now becomes can aggression be included within the same framework as these other phenomena? That is, is there a connection between judgments of controllability and inferences of intent?

ARE CAUSAL CONTROLLABILITY AND
INTENTIONALITY EQUIVALENT?

There are many reasons to contend that controllability and intentionality are quite distinct concepts. Among their differences is that controllability, in this context, refers to a property of a cause; e.g. effort is considered a controllable cause of failure, whereas aptitude is not. On the other hand, intention refers to the motives or goals of a person. One did or did not intend to (desire to, want to) harm another.

However, close inspection of the two concepts reveals that they share the attribute that both are antecedents to or components of a more encompassing inference, that of personal responsibility. Inferences of responsibility require that the causal agent have freedom of choice, or free will (see Fincham & Jaspars, 1980; Shaver, 1985). Hence, a person failing because of lack of effort is deemed to be personally responsible inasmuch as one can choose to expend effort or not. On the other hand, one does not make a decision about aptitude. For this reason, failure because of lack of aptitude does not result in a judgment of responsibility (see Weiner, 1995).

In a similar manner, intention is also a crucial antecedent or determinant of perceptions of responsibility. It has been clearly established that one is held more responsible for an intentional rather than an accidental occurrence, as exemplified in the distinction between murder and manslaughter, and that greater punishment is given for intended rather than unintended consequences.

Given a distinction between controllability and responsibility, it also follows that there may be instances in which causal controllability is not accompanied by judgments of responsibility and reprimand for failure. For example, one is not reprimanded for failure to put forth school-related effort if there was a need to take care of one's sick parent. This justification (the act serves a higher moral goal) is viewed as a mitigating circumstance that frees the person from responsibility (see Weiner, 1995). In a similar manner, an intended aggressive action carried out by an individual who could not distinguish right from wrong by virtue of age, mental state, culture, and so on would result in the absence (or relative absence) of a judgment of responsibility, as well as no (or diminished) punishment, despite the presence of controllability.

The foregoing pages provide the material for a general (but, as will be soon argued, incomplete) theory of social motivation. The general format of the theory is:

event $\rightarrow$ attribution of control $\rightarrow$ inference of responsibility $\rightarrow$ action,

and incorporates the disparate social phenomena of achievement evaluation, reactions to the stigmatized, help-giving, and aggression.

THE ROLE OF EMOTIONS

The shortcoming to the theory outlined above is that it is very "cold." There are no feelings, no emotions playing a part of motivated behavior. Imagine, for example, your feelings when your child is doing poorly in school because of a refusal to do homework, or when an athlete on your favorite team is loafing. Not only are there thoughts about controllability and responsibility, but there are feelings of anger. You are mad at the rebellious child and at the lackadaisical athlete. Anger is an accusation or a value judgment that follows from the belief that another person "could and should have done otherwise" (see Averill, 1982; 1983; Frijda, 1986; Reisenzein & Hoffman, 1990; Roseman, 1991).

There is an array of research supporting this position. Averill (1983), for example, asked persons to report about recent events that made them angry. In his research, more than 50% of the incidents were considered "voluntary"; that is, the harmdoer was fully aware of the consequences of the action, and the act was perceived by the victim as unjustified. The next largest category of situations that gave rise to anger (30%) was associated with an avoidable harm that was not necessarily intended, but the act was perceived as subject to personal control, such as an injury resulting from another's negligence or carelessness. Hence, nearly 80% of the contexts eliciting anger involved ascriptions to negative prior actions for which the other person would be held responsible (see Weiner, Graham, & Chandler, 1982, for a replication of these findings).

In contrast to the linkage between responsibility and anger, the absence of responsibility given the personal plight of another is associated with sympathy and the related emotions of pity and compassion. Thus, a person confined to a totalitarian state (situational causality), athletic failure because of a physical handicap (internal, uncontrollable causality) and school failure because of the need to care for a sick mother (a mitigating circumstance or justification) are typical predicaments that elicit sympathy inasmuch as the person is not held responsible for his or her negative plight.

There has been relatively little research on this emotion. In one investigation, Weiner et al. (1982) asked college students to recall instances in their lives when pity or sympathy was experienced. The most frequently recalled contexts were when observing others with handicaps and personal interactions with the very aged. More broadly conceived, Wispé (1991, p. 134) summarized that "one will sympathize more with a brave sufferer, in a good cause, in which one's afflictions are beyond one's control".

Now, in addition to being consequences about thoughts of responsibility or nonresponsibility, both anger and sympathy also are considered as stimuli for subsequent action (see Averill, 1983; Frijda, 1986). That is, they provide bridges between thinking and conduct. Anger directs the person experiencing this emotion to "eliminate" the wrongdoer, to go toward that person and retaliate with some form of aggressive action, or to go away from that person to withhold some positive good. Anger therefore is viewed here as an emotion that "pushes" or incites the person to undertake self-protective and/or retaliatory actions. Sympathy, on the other hand, directs the person to increase prosocial behaviors such as help-giving, and decreases antisocial conduct including punishment (see Eisenberg, 1986). That is, like anger, sympathy is a motivator, but unlike anger, the motivation is prosocial in nature rather than antisocial.

THE COMPLETE THEORY

When emotional reactions to responsibility appraisals are included within the motivational sequence, the conceptual system for social motivation may be represented as follows:

Event (e.g. achievement failure)   Response (punish).
↓   ↑
Cause   → Causal property → Responsibility inference → Affect
(Lack of Effort)   (Controllable)   (Responsible)   (Anger)

This contrasts with the following exemplar:

Stigmatized state (e.g. Alzheimer's disease)   Response (not punish).
↓   ↑
Cause   → Causal property → Responsibility inference → Affect
(genetics)   (Uncontrollable)   (Not responsible)   (Sympathy)

The full theory which includes these two exemplar sequences is shown in Fig. 5.2. The theory includes the fundamental assumption that the motivational process progresses from thinking, to feeling, to action, or more specifically, from causal understanding and responsibility inferences to the emotions of anger and sympathy, which then give rise to social reactions that involve reprimand, help, aggression, and so forth. Of course, other motivational orders are conceivable. One possibility is that thinking gives rise to both feelings and actions, so that emotions have a noncausal status. And many more complex conceptions readily come to mind.

TESTING THE THEORY

The most extensive data putting these motivational sequences to test, which then also examine the component processes regarding the effects of cognitive appraisal on emotions and the effects of emotions on action, have been in the helping domain. Within this context, a number of investigations have assessed responsibility and/or controllability, the emotions of sympathy and/or anger, and some indicator of helping, typically a judgment of aid rather than an actual behavioral observation.

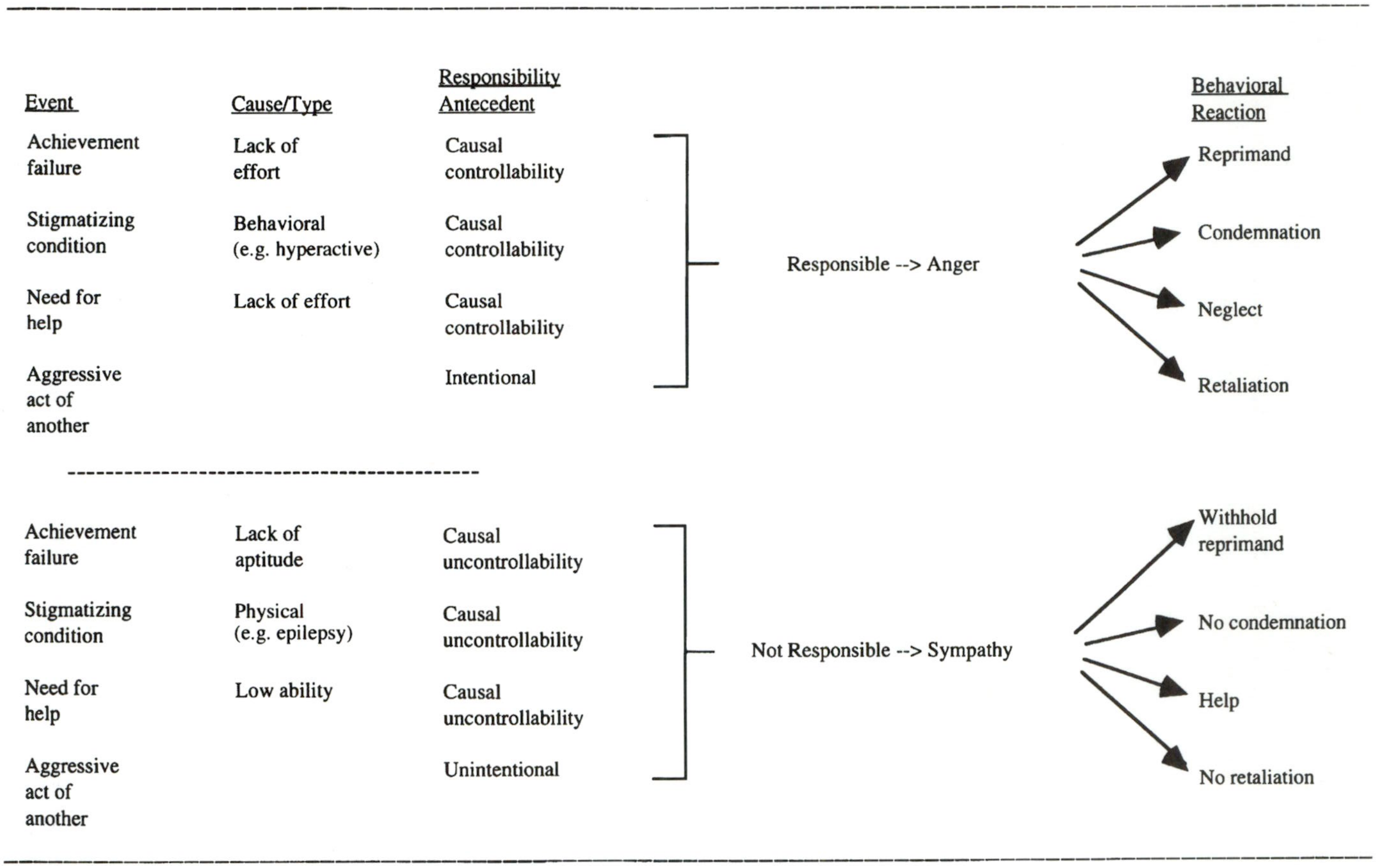

Event	Cause/Type	Responsibility Antecedent		Behavioral Reaction
Achievement failure	Lack of effort	Causal controllability		Reprimand
Stigmatizing condition	Behavioral (e.g. hyperactive)	Causal controllability	Responsible --> Anger	Condemnation
Need for help	Lack of effort	Causal controllability		Neglect
Aggressive act of another		Intentional		Retaliation
Achievement failure	Lack of aptitude	Causal uncontrollability		Withhold reprimand
Stigmatizing condition	Physical (e.g. epilepsy)	Causal uncontrollability	Not Responsible --> Sympathy	No condemnation
Need for help	Low ability	Causal uncontrollability		Help
Aggressive act of another		Unintentional		No retaliation

FIG. 5.2   A responsibility-based theory of social conduct, with affects as the proximal determinants of action.

TABLE 5.5
Averaged analysis of help-giving of subjects (N > 2,000)
from 15 investigations that included attributional, affect,
and helping reports

Raw correlations	Regression values
Controllability × Sympathy = −.52	
Controllability × Anger = .48	
Controllability × Help = −.38	Controllability × Help = −.11
Sympathy × Help = .51	Sympathy × Help = .49
Anger × Help = −.51	Anger × Help = −.43

I have examined 15 studies in detail in an earlier publication (Weiner, 1995). They involve over 2,000 subjects, both children and adults, a variety of need conditions, and various indicators of help giving. Table 5.5 summarizes the raw correlations between thinking, feeling, and acting. Table 5.5 shows that there are negative associations between controllability/responsibility and sympathy (average $r = -.52$) and positive associations between controllability/responsibility and anger (average $r = .48$). These data strongly support the postulations regarding appraisal–emotion linkages. Turning next to the correlations between thought and feelings with judgments of helping, it can be seen that control and help are negatively related (average $r = -.38$), while the correlations between emotions and helping are negative for anger and positive for sympathy, both with an average $r = .51$. These correlations also are in the anticipated direction and encourage the belief that affects may be more significant determinants of helping than are thoughts.

More sophisticated analyses involving partial correlations, regression, and/ or path analyses provide more exacting tests of the hypothesized motivational sequence shown in the theory. As shown in Table 5.5, control has a small but significant direct effect on helping. Of greater significance, the emotions are strongly related to aid-giving in the predicted direction. That is, affects are the more proximal and more important determinants of help than are thoughts, although there is some scattered evidence that attributions of control (responsibility) have a direct influence on help-giving. As suggested by Weiner (1993) and by Zucker and Weiner (1993), it may be that the more personally involving the situation, the greater the relative importance of emotions in guiding behavior. Thus, "cold" thoughts could prove to be especially predictive when considering, for example, welfare from the government rather than personal help-giving.

SOME CONCLUDING REMARKS

What conclusions, then, can be reached about the determinants of social motivation? I have contended that:

1. The causes of events or states are crucial determinants of action.
2. The causes can be classified into basic properties, or characteristics, with locus and controllability having special social significance.
3. This causal assessment, along with other information related to, for example, mitigating circumstances, results in responsibility inferences about the person.
4. Cognitive appraisals of personal responsibility are linked with the affects of anger and sympathy.
5. These affects have motivational significance, with anger giving rise to anti-social responses and sympathy giving rise to prosocial responses.
6. Affects are the primary determinants of responding; attributions may or may not have an independent contribution to doing. The relative effects of feeling and thinking on behavior may depend on the personal importance or personal involvement of the actor.

ACKNOWLEDGEMENTS

The research reported in this article and the writing of this article was supported by Grant DBS-9211982 from the National Science Foundation.

REFERENCES

Averill, J. R. (1982). *Anger and aggression: An essay on emotion.* New York: Springer-Verlag.
Averill, J. R. (1983). Studies on anger and aggression. *American Psychologist, 38,* 1145–1160.
Barnes, R. D., Ickes, W. J., & Kidd, R. (1979). Effects of perceived intentionality and stability of another's dependency on helping behavior. *Personality and Social Psychology Bulletin, 5,* 367–372.
Crick, N. R., & Dodge, K. A. (1994). A review and reformulation of social information-processing mechanisms in children's social adjustment. *Psychological Bulletin, 115,* 74–101.
Dodge, K. A. (1980). Social cognition and children's aggressive behavior. *Child Development, 51,* 162–170.
Dyck, R. J., & Rule, B. G. (1978). Effect on retaliation of causal attributions concerning attack. *Journal of Personality and Social Psychology, 36,* 521–529.
Eisenberg, N. (1986). *Altruistic emotion, cognition, and behavior.* Hillsdale, NJ: Lawrence Erlbaum Associates Inc.
Epstein, S., & Taylor, S. P. (1967). Instigation to aggression as a function of degree of defeat and perceived aggressive intent of the opponent. *Journal of Personality, 35,* 265–289.
Ferguson, T., & Rule, B. (1983). An attributional perspective on anger and aggression. In R. Geen & E. Donnerstein (Eds.), *Aggression: Theoretical and empirical reviews: Vol. 1. Theoretical and methodological issues* (pp. 41–74). San Diego, CA: Academic.
Fincham, F. D., & Jaspars, J. M. (1980). Attribution of responsibility: From man the scientist to man as lawyer. In L. Berkowitz (Ed.), *Advances in experimental social psychology* (Vol. 13, pp. 82–139). San Diego, CA: Academic.
Frijda, N. (1986). *The emotions.* Cambridge: Cambridge University Press.
Graham, S., Hudley, C., & Williams, E. (1993). Attributional and emotional determinants of aggression among African-American and Latino young adolescents. *Developmental Psychology, 28,* 731–740.
Hartup, W. W. (1983). Peer relations. In E. W. Hetherington (Ed.), *Handbook of child psychology: Socialization, personality, and development* (Vol. 4, pp. 103–196). New York: Wiley.

Heider, F. (1958). *The psychology of interpersonal relations.* New York: Wiley.

Juvonen, J. (1991). Deviance, perceived responsibility, and negative peer reactions. *Developmental Psychology, 27,* 672–681.

Nasby, W., Hayden, B., & dePaulo, B. M. (1980). Attributional bias among aggressive boys to interpret unambiguous social stimuli as displays of hostility. *Journal of Abnormal Psychology, 89,* 459–468.

Nickel, T. W. (1974). The attribution of intention as a critical factor in the relation between frustration and aggression. *Journal of Personality, 42,* 482–492.

Piliavin, I. M., Rodin, J., & Piliavin, J. A. (1969). Good Samaritanism: An underground phenomenon? *Journal of Personality and Social Psychology, 13,* 289–299.

Reisenzein, R., & Hoffman, T. (1990). An investigation of the dimensions of cognitive appraisal in emotion using the repertory grid technique. *Motivation and Emotion, 14,* 1–26.

Roseman, I. (1991). Appraisal determinants of discrete emotions. *Cognition and Emotion, 5,* 161–200.

Rotter, J. B. (1966). Generalized expectancies for internal versus external control of reinforcement. *Psychological Monographs, 80* (1, Serial No. 609).

Schmidt, G., & Weiner, B. (1988). An attribution-affect-action theory of behavior: Replications of judgments of help-giving. *Personality and Social Psychology Bulletin, 14,* 610–621.

Shaver, K. (1985). *The attribution of blame: Causality, responsibility, and blameworthiness.* New York: Springer-Verlag.

Sigelman, C. K., & Begley, N. L. (1987). The early development of reactions to peers with controllable and uncontrollable problems. *Journal of Pediatric Psychology, 12,* 99–115.

Weiner, B. (1986). *An attributional theory of motivation and emotion.* New York: Springer-Verlag.

Weiner, B. (1993). On sin versus sickness: A theory of perceived responsibility and social motivation. *American Psychologist, 48,* 957–965.

Weiner, B. (1995). *Judgments of responsibility: A foundation for a theory of social conduct.* New York: Guilford.

Weiner, B., Graham, S., & Chandler, C. (1982). Causal antecedents of pity, anger, and guilt. *Personality and Social Psychology Bulletin, 8,* 226–232.

Weiner, B., & Kukla, A. (1970). An attributional analysis of achievement motivation. *Journal of Personality and Social Psychology, 15,* 1–20.

Weiner, B., Perry, R., & Magnusson, J. (1988). An attributional analysis of reactions to stigmas. *Journal of Personality and Social Psychology, 55,* 738–748.

Wispé, L. (1991). *The psychology of sympathy.* New York: Plenum.

Zucker, G. S., & Weiner, B. (1993). Conservatism and perceptions of poverty: An attributional analysis. *Journal of Applied Social Psychology, 23,* 925–943.

CHAPTER SIX

Contemporary trends in hypnosis research

Peter W. Sheehan
The University of Queensland, Australia

This paper reviews contemporary trends in hypnosis research, the term "contemporary" being defined in terms of major themes in research occurring since the 1985 review of the field of hypnosis in the *Annual Review of Psychology*. Focus will be placed on theoretical, empirical, methodological, and pragmatic developments in the field, this choice of classification reflecting in part the need for an adequate taxonomy for the domain of suggestion and suggestibility. An example of a major theoretical development is the recent shifts that have occurred in theorizing about the process of dissociation. Methodological developments inevitably cut across major content concerns. Pragmatic developments relate clearly to major content concerns expressed in the laboratory literature. One such area is the extent to which memories reported in hypnosis are distorted in their accuracy. This clearly relates, for example, to the evidenced need for sensitive and ethical professional guidelines covering such potentially complex fields of inquiry as forensic hypnosis, and the clinical expression of repressed memories. Finally, the last decade, more than the one before, has been characterised by strong links between laboratory and clinical concerns. The way ahead, however, points to the fact that much greater rapprochement is actually required.

Cet article passe en revue les tendances contemporaines dans la recherche sur l'hypnose, le terme «contemporain» étant défini en termes des principaux thèmes de recherche rencontrés depuis la recension de 1985 du domaine de l'hypnose publiée dans l'*Annual Review of Psychology*. L'accent est placé sur les développements théoriques, empiriques, méthodologiques et pragmatiques dans ce champ d'étude, ce choix de classification reposant en partie sur le besoin d'une taxonomie valable pour le domaine de la suggestion et de la suggestibilité. On trouve un exemple de développement théorique majeur dans les récents changements qui se sont produits dans les théories sur le processus de dissociation. Les développements méthodologiques recoupent inévitablement les principales préoccupations quant au contenu. Les développements pragmatiques sont clairement associés aux principales préoccupations de contenu exprimées dans les rapports de recherche. L'un de ces domaines concerne le degré suivant lequel l'exactitude des souvenirs rapportés sous hypnose serait faussée. Ceci est clairement relié, par exemple, au besoin évident de directives professionnelles à la fois sensibles et conformes à l'éthique qui recouvrent des domaines de recherche potentiellement aussi complexes que l'hypnose légale et l'expression clinique des souvenirs réprimés. Enfin, la dernière décennie, plus que celle qui l'a précédée, a été caractérisée par l'établissement de liens étroits entre les préoccupations cliniques et la recherche. Il est évident, toutefois, qu'un beaucoup plus grand rapprochement s'impose dans l'avenir.

This paper attempts to review contemporary trends in hypnosis research. I choose to define the term "contemporary" in terms of major themes in research occurring since the 1985 review of the field of hypnosis by John Kihlstrom in the *Annual Review of Psychology*.

Borrowing from Oxman and Guyati's (1994, p. 131) recent article on the science of reviewing research, I want to present to you an address that acknowledges the "issue of . . . recognizing subtle, but important clues that science without expertise might overlook while, at the same time, appreciating the risks of blind faith in the subjective thought processes of experts." Additionally, I am attracted by the ancient quote of Chalmers (1903) "Teach thy tongue to say 'I do not know' and thou shalt progress."

Before moving to key domains of study, I want to comment comparatively at the outset on research in hypnosis viewed internationally over the last decade. I shall return in the concluding sections of the paper to overview these trends and the themes abstracted.

COMPARATIVE ANALYSIS OF THE FIELD SINCE 1985

From Kihlstrom's review (which covers publications up to 1983), one acquires a significant understanding of some of the shifts in fields of interest and controversy over time. His original review (Kihlstrom, 1985) was divided into discussion of assessment of hypnotizability, investigations of specific phenomena such as age regression, perceptual effects and the hidden observer, clinical applications focusing on the utilization of hypnotic phenomena, and significant theoretical developments such as controversy over state, the neodissociation theory of divided consciousness, and hypnosis viewed as strategic social behavior.

Table 6.1 gives the major content areas in hypnosis journals for the period 1986–1995. The journals analyzed are: The *American Journal of Clinical Hypnosis*, the *Australian Journal of Clinical and Experimental Hypnosis*, the *International Journal of Clinical and Experimental Hypnosis (IJCEH)* and *Contemporary Hypnosis* (previously known as the *British Journal of Experimental and Clinical Hypnosis*). An overwhelming number of publications classified under Health and Mental Health treatment have been excluded. The classification shown in Table 6.1 is quite similar to the content area covered in Kihlstrom's

TABLE 6.1
Content categories drawn from the literature
in the last decade

	1	ABSORPTION
	2	AMNESIA
	3	ANALGESIA
*	4	BRAIN MECHANISMS
	5	DEVELOPMENT OF HYPNOTIZABILITY
*	6	ETHICAL/PROFESSIONAL ISSUES
*	7	EXPECTANCY EFFECTS
*	8	FORENSIC ISSUES
	9	HISTORICAL ASPECTS
*	10	HYPNOTIC COMMUNICATIONS
*	11	HYPNOTIC RELATIONSHIP
	12	HYPNOTIC TYPES
	13	HYPERMNESIA
	14	IMAGERY
*	15	IMMUNE FUNCTIONING
	16	MPD
	17	MEMORY
*	18	MODIFYING HYPNOTIZABILITY
	19	OTHER HYPNOTIC PHENOMENA
	20	PERSONALITY CORRELATES
*	21	PHENOMENOLOGY/EAT
*	22	PHYSIOLOGICAL LINKS
	23	PTSD
	24	SCALES OF HYPNOTIZABILITY
	25	SELF-HYPNOSIS
*	26	SPORTS HYPNOSIS
	27	STATISTICS/PSYCHOMETRICS

NOTE:
* Rapidly expanding/new categories in the decade
since Kihlstrom's review article (1985).

review; only 11 of the categories are actually distinct. Figure 6.1 shows the distribution of content areas in the *IJCEH* (the most international of the journals). The modal themes illustrated in this figure are physiological linkages (17 articles), historical aspects and memory (15 in each category), and hypnotic communications, other hypnotic phenomena and forensic issues (12 in each category).

Table 6.2 takes the PsycLIT classification scheme and applies it to the field of hypnosis. Immediately it is obvious how much research in hypnosis really interrelates to major domains in the study of psychology as a whole. The significant size of the category excluded (33; Health/Mental Health: Treatment and prevention) tells us immediately that there is an enormous emphasis in our literature on the practical uses of hypnosis, the importance of this category of literature being documented by Frankel (1987). And, worldwide, the field of forensic

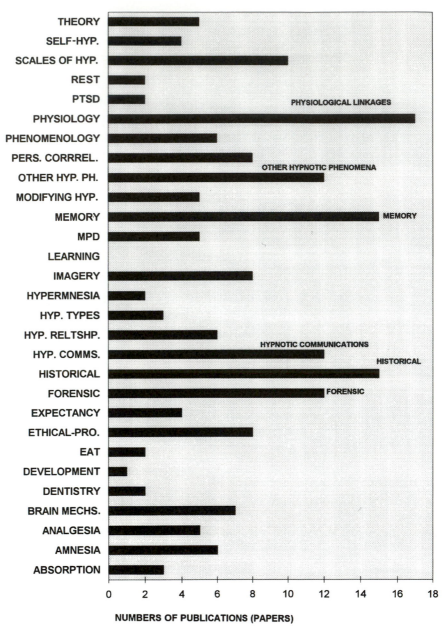

FIG. 6.1 Analysis of contents of *International Journal of Clinical & Experimental Hypnosis* 1986–1995.

TABLE 6.2
The PsycLIT Classification Scheme* as applied to the major areas
of Hypnosis literature

21	**General Psychology**
	Historical aspects and debate on underlying nature of hypnosis
22	**Psychometrics, Statistics, Methodology**
	Scales of hypnotizability, absorption, imagery; experimental methods
23	**Human Experimental Psychology**
	Experimental work on hypnotic phenomena: analgesia, memory effects, perceptual distortions
25	**Physiological Psychology, Neuroscience**
	Brain processes—EEG rhythms and diurnal rhythms
26	**Communication systems**
	Hypnotic communications; induction types
28	**Developmental Psychology**
	Development of "high" hypnotizability; aging and hypnotizability
29	**Social Processes, Social Issues**
	The hypnotic relationship
30	**Social Psychology**
	Beliefs, attitudes and expectancy effects; experimental demand effects
31	**Personality Psychology**
	Individual differences in hypnotizability; hypnotizability correlates
32	**Psychological/Physical Disorders**
	Mental/physical disorders and hypnosis
33	**Health/Mental Health Treatment and Prevention**
	Medical, dental hypnosis; hypnotherapy; hypnotic interventions
34	**Professional Psychology/Health Personnel Issues**
	Professional and ethical issues in use of hypnosis by professionals
35	**Educational Psychology**
	Modifications of hypnotizability; learning enhancement
37	**Sport Psychology and Leisure**
	Hypnosis in sport
42	**Forensic Psychology and Legal Issues**
	Forensic hypnosis, hypnosis and the law

NOTE:
  * Numbered and in bold

psychology is clearly on the increase. Figure 6.2 analyses three of the major hypnosis journals for their contents over the last decade (1986–1995) based on the PsycLIT classification scheme.

There are differences in the reporting patterns of journals and some obvious arbitrariness on my part in the choice of classification categories, but certain major themes nevertheless emerge from the data.[1]

---

[1] Interpretation of the classification data is somewhat tentative. Eleven per cent of the journal articles classified were genuinely multidisciplinary and could not be segregated into single content areas. These 11% were classified into two content areas for the purposes of the analysis.

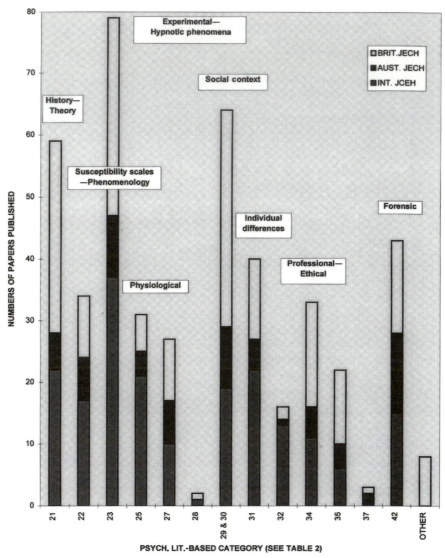

FIG. 6.2   Analysis of the combined contents of three major hypnosis journals over the decade 1986–1995, based on the PsycLIT classification scheme.

The major trends in research hypnosis (reflected in Figs. 6.1 and 6.2) are: the history and nature of hypnosis, individual differences in susceptibility, experiments on hypnotic phenomena, social influences on hypnosis, and forensic issues and legal concerns. Table 6.3 lists in summary form those emerging issues as important in the comparison of Kihlstrom's 1985 review with the content analysis conducted of the three main hypnosis journals (listed in Fig. 6.2).

TABLE 6.3
Issues arising from the comparison of Kihlstrom's 1985 review with the
content of 3 main hypnosis journals, 1986–1995

1. The rise in the use of phenomenological data.
2. The increased acceptance of the importance of social and contextual influences in the production of hypnotic responses.
3. The inclusion of consciousness and self-consciousness as legitimate topics for study amongst "mainstream" experimental psychologists.
4. The rise in the use of hypnosis and corresponding professional and ethical dilemmas in all applied (legal, medical and clinical) areas.
5. The increase in numbers of professional and legal guidelines for the use of hypnosis.
6. New areas of application of hypnosis in the sports and health fields.
7. The emergence of cross-disciplinary studies on topics in hypnosis—in particular, attention, memory and analgesia.
8. The increasing numbers of experimental studies linking physiological systems functioning and hypnosis.
9. Continuing controversy over the validity of the concept of susceptibility, and the nature of the hypnotic response.

Comparison of these data on hypnosis with trends reflected in the number of psychology publications in the world show that hypnosis is idiosyncratic with its continuing emphasis on its history and debate about the underlying nature of the construct of hypnosis, issues concerning individual differences in susceptibility, and forensic hypnosis. According to this broad comparison there appears to be an under-representation also of hypnosis papers on developmental, educational and psychological aspects of hypnosis.

This address moves now to pass particular comment on specific issues in the field, most of which are highlighted in some way by the comparisons noted in Table 6.3.

THE CONSTRUCT: THEORETICAL
DEVELOPMENTS AND CRITICAL ASSUMPTIONS

Wider theories of hypnosis seem now to be developing. In 1991, the comment was made in addendum to a review of current theories of hypnosis that there appeared to be increasing numbers of different explanations of hypnotic phenomena, but "bitter controversy" with no resolution in sight (Kirsch, 1991). The reviewer added that he hoped that empirical work would eventually save the day (Kirsch, 1991, p. 107). Two years later, in 1993, the same reviewer—Irving Kirsch—was majorly responsible for a move towards a definition of hypnosis for the public with input from 14 notable researchers in the field with very different theoretical positions (Kirsch, 1993).

Some researchers still think descriptive materials useful but explanations of one's own behavior is unreliable, depending on such factors as self-knowledge and prior information. However, as gaps in our understanding of various aspects and phenomena of hypnosis have become apparent, researchers in the last decade have been turning increasingly to a wider range of measures to gain more insight. Collaborative inquiries such as the Experiential Analysis Technique (EAT: Bányai, 1991; Sheehan & McConkey, 1982) have used retrospective memory guides, while others have employed paper-and-pencil inventories of personal experiences during hypnosis, such as the Phenomenology of Consciousness Inventory (PCI: Pekala & Kumar, 1989; Pekala & Nagler, 1989; Spinhoven, Vanderlinden, TerKuile, & Linssen, 1993), and the Hypnotic Experience Questionnaire (HEQ: Matheson, Shue, & Bart, 1989).

Hilgard was at pains in 1988 (Hilgard, 1988) to point out that much of the apparent theoretical disputes arise from the historical overlap of psychological disciplines. Hypnosis, he argued, is of interest to social psychologists, because it is an interpersonal process and therefore subject to influences in the social context. It is of interest to personality and developmental psychologists because of the findings of age and individual differences in responding. It lies within the domain of the cognitive psychologists and studies of perception because of the altered perceptions, thoughts and images during hypnosis. Finally, it is of interest to all those who make the study of brain mechanisms their business. Each discipline has its own viewpoint, its own paradigms and its own terminology. Consequently, theories about the same phenomenon can be viewed from the perspective of personal construct theory (Kirmayer, 1992), personality trait theory (Tellegen & Atkinson, 1974), socio-psychological perspectives (Sarbin, 1991; Spanos & Chaves, 1989), dissociation theory (Bowers, 1992; Hilgard, 1977) or some combination of these (Nadon, Laurence, & Perry, 1989). This is seen by Hilgard (1987) to be a necessary phase in the developmental process of theory, somewhat akin to the development of Psychology's sophisticated theorizing about the construct of intelligence.

Fellows sees the goalposts of hypnosis research as having shifted (Fellows, 1993). No longer is the prime objective of modern hypnosis research to account for the "hypnotic state" but rather how to explain responses to "hypnotic-type" suggestions. Different types of suggestion probably require different types of explanation. As some have put it, there has also been a movement from important theories to important questions.

Some of the critical assumptions for examination are: (1) subjects are active agents; (2) hypnotic susceptibility is a trait; and (3) subjective experience is the most reliable focus of study. According to Fellows (1994, p. 28), concepts drawn from role theory such as "keeping secrets" and "self-deception" need now to be developed in a "fresh empirical context". And the extent of cognitive effort manifest in hypnotic responses is likely to be a key theoretical concern for the future.

Digging deeper into the cognitive and social construction of experiences is seen by some to be a necessity (e.g. Kirmayer, 1992) for distinguishing between constructs which have been used to explain behavior. For example, "involuntary" is yet to be clearly distinguished from "self-deceiving" and "self-authored" from "socially constructed". Such a debate, however, brings into question the role of consciousness and a need to further differentiate between different aspects of consciousness and the cognitive effect for tasks that divide or control it.

In the last decade there has been a definite move away from the claim that hypnosis is a specific state in itself, with recent psychophysiological evidence supporting that move. However, the cry of "What is special about hypnosis?" (especially from the cognitive–behavioral, social–psychological camp) still haunts the field.

Clearly some accommodation has taken place where theorists are talking now in terms of interactions of influences and multifaceted situations, with competing variables. As Hilgard (1987, p. 261) says: "We are not dealing with some one thing (hypnosis) that can be defined as a limited state of consciousness with clear boundaries, physiological specificity, and independent of the many interacting processes of interest to psychologists".

The next content area to which I turn is Methodology and Measurement. This is a complex area, and I want to make only a few brief points, less about the variations in particular methodologies that have taken place (e.g. Erdelyi's recent development of a paradigm to investigate repressed memories (Erdelyi, 1994; in press), or, Bányai and her associates' (Bányai, Gosi-Gerguss, Vago, Varga, & Horvath, 1990; Bányai, 1991) modification of the Experiential Analysis Technique, than about the assessment of salient parameters of hypnotic responsiveness.

METHODOLOGY AND MEASUREMENT

There is discontent clearly emerging about the traditional ways of assessing hypnotic responding. The motivation for new scales has been more to advance knowledge and use of hypnosis by using measurement to test facets in detail (e.g. subjective experience: Kirsch, Council, & Wickless, 1990; Kihlstrom, 1989; Pekala & Kumar, 1987).

A second factor promoting broad change in the measurement of hypnotic responsiveness has been the wider acceptance of the influence of the social and situational contexts of hypnotic responding and some experimental researchers (see Spanos & Chaves, 1989) have wanted explicitly to move away from standard inductions where the influence of the hypnotist was unduly enhanced. However, research using new instruments does pose a problem for the comparison of results with research using other measures, and it behoves authors of articles in the literature to make sure that their reporting of what they have done contains enough detail to ensure that methods are actually replicable in order to distinguish artifact from essence.

The rapprochement of clinicians and experimentalists as an emerging issue for the field is a major one, there being quite different needs and different uses of tests by researchers in clinics and laboratories. Clinicians have different professional needs and values from experimentalists (Coe, 1992) and have been concerned for many years with making use of the hypnotic relationship as a desirable adjunct in therapy. Their concerns have been rather distinctive: they wish to assess a client's abilities to make use of hypnotism, preferably without changing positive expectations concerning the use of hypnosis. But also, there is a desire to tap the experiential component in hypnosis to see whether an individual has really experienced alterations in subjective experience during a hypnotic session (Spinhoven et al., 1993). This concern has reproduced in the experimental literature radically new methodologies for investigating the phenomenology of hypnosis.

In clinical practice, therapists are more concerned with dissociative, imagery and absorption abilities (Diamond, 1989) than a probabilistic estimate of susceptibility (Barber, 1993). Whether this will lead the field to adopting new, empirically derived scales which can be incorporated into an induction procedure or using separate tests for each ability, or even avoiding testing seems to depend not only on the strength of conviction of the clinician concerned, but also on how they view the role of clinicians in the advancement of scientific research in hypnosis. For example, some (Frankel, 1989; Mott, 1989; Spiegel, 1989) emphasize the importance of standard measurement in assessing the contribution of hypnosis to different types of client problems, while others regard the therapeutic relationship as the main variable in therapy, therapy being more art than science.

Recently, there has been a call from various theorists (Lynn & Rhue, 1991; Perry, 1992; see also, Balthazard, 1993) for scales with more differentiation in the measuring of the hypnotic response. This requires firm acknowledgement of the complex nature of hypnotic responses which do not clearly fit into any simple category. Hypnotic susceptibility scales can neither be described as a hierarchy of responses scored dichotomously, nor labeled simply as either voluntary or involuntary. Lynn likens the situation to other social behavior such as conversational behavior, the responses being neither clearly premeditated, nor undertaken in the service of goals clearly defined in advance (Lynn & Rhue, 1991). Accordingly, to disentangle the complex situation of hypnotic experience, the plea has been made by some for more "fine-grained analysis" (e.g. Kirmayer, 1992, p. 280), of the interaction of state, trait and social context.

In nearly all of the major work that has been done since Kihlstrom's 1985 review, the relevance and importance of hypnotizability (or the individual's level of "imaginative suggestibility" to hypnotic treatment) has emerged consistently. Such is the continuity of emphasis that it merits separate discussion.

FACTORS UNDERLYING HYPNOTIZABILITY

A veritable plethora of studies has investigated hypnotizability in relation to mechanisms underlying hypnotic responsiveness (e.g. Crawford, 1994). Much work has gone on to produce physiological evidence of changes during hypnosis (e.g. DeBenedittis, Cigada, Bianchi, Signorini, & Cerutti, 1994; Kirmayer, 1992; Sturgis & Coe, 1990) and study of individual reactions (Glisky & Kihlstrom, 1993; and Wallace, Allen, & Weber, 1994). The multiplicity of factors associated with hypnotizability is perhaps well captured by one of the researchers who dramatically pinpoints its relevance. Kirmayer (1992, p. 290) conceptualises a *"general factor of ability to change state* which, in combination with other specific processes, results in a capacity to become intensely absorbed in imagery, empty the mind, inhibit self-consciousness, respond automatically, and dissociate memories and motor control". Intense imagery, change in volition and verbal suggestibility may be correlated, says Kirmayer, because they all depend on some general underlying process, a viewpoint that can be seen as not inconsistent with neodissociative theory (Hilgard, 1977; also, Hilgard, 1991).

The field as a whole continues to bear in convergent fashion on major theoretical issues, some of them relatively new in their emphasis, while others represent continuing work on important but historically traditional themes. I shall sample only some of these briefly. Those related to forensic hypnosis are most new in their emphasis and this review taps them as the more emergent issues.

HYPNOTIC PHENOMENA: CURRENT ISSUES

Amnesia

In the past, work has highlighted errors in memory in hypnosis that clearly depend on a combination of social psychological variables, such as beliefs, attitudes, sets/expectations, and person attributes (like imagery, imagination, absorption, automaticity, and dissociation ability). However, although posthypnotic amnesia clearly relates to subjects' abilities, beliefs may also be involved (Perry, 1992, p. 247), and amnesia has been found to be "highly responsive to suggestions, enhancement and cancellation" (Hilgard, 1987, p. 253). The specific thrust of recent research has, however, clearly focused on particular hypnotially influenced memories, questioning their legal status.

Hypnotically influenced memories

The phenomenon of hypnotic hypermnesia, or enhanced memory accessibility under hypnosis, is of special interest both clinically and forensically. It has been investigated in the laboratory setting with inconsistent results. Research has attempted to unravel the effects of different variables, such as the type of material remembered and the process of recall. Using a methodology which eliminated reported hypermnesic effects of repeated recall, and "response bias" of highly susceptible subjects (Whitehouse, Dinges, E. Orne, & M. Orne, 1988), investigators (Dinges et al., 1992; Erdelyi, 1994) have concluded that hypnosis *per se* does not improve memory for recent events.

It has been demonstrated, however, that whole memories (pseudomemories) can be implanted into a person's real-life autobiographically and even non-experienced events into the minds of pre-schoolers (Loftus, 1993). It is intriguing that one important feature of successful "implantations" is the type of relationship between the subject in the experiment and the source of the pseudomemory: ". . . false memories can be created by a small suggestion from a trusted family member, by hearing someone lie, by suggestion from a psychologist, or by incorporation of the experience of others (who were present at the real event) into one's own autobiography" (Loftus, 1993, p. 533). One might conjecture that the special relationships of trust between person and source of the pseudomemory are also significantly involved in cases of false criminal confessions (Ofshe, 1992), the so-called "false-memory syndrome" and some cases of Multiple Personality Disorder. Belief in the authenticity of the information received may be a critical factor in the creation of the pseudomemory, supplementary to the suggestibility of the recipient of the information, or it may be inextricably involved in the phenomenon of suggestibility itself.

Research evidence tends to suggest, therefore, not only that false memories can be implanted, but that actual memories can be readily distorted under hypnosis. It also implicates the major influence of social–contextual factors in the shaping of pseudomemories.

Some combination of the greater hypnotizability of some people with other factors is most likely responsible for facilitating the production of pseudomemories. The literature warns that the variables involved in pseudomemory creation are complex, involving some combination of what is measured by inventories assessing "absorption", those assessing some preference for imagining, and some interaction between the two (Labelle, Laurence, Nadon, & Perry, 1990) as well as other contextual factors in relation to the pseudomemory suggestion itself (Sheehan, Statham, & Jamieson, 1991). However, hypnotizability, rather than other factors, remains the most probable single indicator of whether a pseudomemory will be accepted (Labelle et al., 1990; McConkey, 1992, Weekes, Lynn, Green, & Brentar, 1992), and confidence in the memory is clearly affected (Dinges et al., 1992; Pettinati, 1988).

Recovered memories

A special category of hypnotically influenced memories is recovered memories, representing memories of events that may or may not have occurred and that are typically distant in time. McConkey (1995), and others (e.g. Ofshe, 1992) have observed the explosion in literature on this controversial issue which has become a minefield of emotional issues, litigation and passionately felt testimonials of people who have suffered in the process.

The development of any tools which can differentiate between real and constructed memory may not be possible if it is proven that original memories are overlaid by recent imaginings and remembering.[2] If however, original memory is still intact after being recalled as suggested in some research (McCann & Sheehan, 1987), there may be a way in some cases (e.g. Johnson, Foley, Suengas, & Raye, 1988; Steller & Koehnken, 1989; Spence, 1994) of making the important distinction between fact and fantasy or differentiating "the signal of true repressed memories from the noise of false ones" (Loftus, 1993, p. 534). Research into memory systems and how they function is of crucial importance in establishing how best to investigate the extremely controversial and emotive area of "truth in memory."

The limitations imposed by the content of memories pose difficulty for researchers when the results of pseudomemory studies are extrapolated into the clinic or courtroom (Greene, Wilson, & Loftus, 1989). Laboratory experiments do not relate well to situations such as cases of suspected child abuse, or criminal events where the memories may have strongly emotional overtones. As Yuille and Cutshall (1986) comment in relation to eyewitness reports of traumatic events, subjects can behave and remember very differently when they are true participants, and not passive observers.

One of the major lessons of the last decade is that much more research is required on issues which have such important outcomes for experimental clinical and forensic hypnosis. These are especially the issues of distinguishing the influence of suggestion from deception, and the confusion of fact with fantasy (Scheflin, 1994); whether central or peripheral details of memories are both subject to modification during hypnosis or interrogation (Lynn & Nash, 1994); the individual variability in susceptibility to pseudomemory creation, both in the waking state and in hypnosis; and the obvious relevance of situational demands and contextual features (see the work of Lynn, Rhue, Myers, & Weekes, 1994).

Analgesia, the hidden observer, and trance logic

The phenomena of analgesia, hidden observer (HO) and trance logic represent traditional concerns that still occupy researchers' attention. The heart of the problem, according to Hilgard (1987, p. 260), is "not whether to speak of a 'hidden observer', but to recognize that there may be cognitive distortions in hypnosis even while some more realistic information is being processed in parallel, so that everything is not *reportable* by the subject". The significance of the Hidden Observer (HO), however, is now enhanced as a key phenomenon in currently differentiating rival, competing theories of dissociation (Bowers, 1992; Hilgard, 1994).

---

[2] Researchers in the field suggest that the original level of processing of the memory (Shields & Knox, 1986; Kunzendorf, Lacourse, & Lynch, 1987) and the level of trauma for the individual (Watkins, 1989; Hammond, 1993; Kirsch, 1993; Loftus, 1993) are critical in the phenomena of enhanced recall of events under hypnosis.

As to trance logic—a widely held concept of theoretical significance—". . . hypnosis can be descriptively viewed as a situation in which a person is asked to set aside critical judgment, without abandoning it completely, and is further asked to engage in make-believe and fantasy" (Perry, 1992, p. 245). This description of trance logic is generally supported by others previously in the field (Gill & Brenman, 1959; Hilgard, 1977) and is dramatically illustrated in cases of hallucination, for example, by the person who "tolerates the inconsistency which would not be expected if the experiences were judged according to familiar experiences outside hypnosis" (Hilgard, 1987, p. 254).

ISSUES FACING PROFESSIONAL GROUPS

Professional issues have emerged as salient in the last decade. A major reason for this, as foreshadowed in my opening remarks (see Table 6.1), is the growth of research in forensic hypnosis. A second reason is the increased emphasis now being placed on the responsibilities of practitioners.

Forensic hypnosis

An important conclusion that has emerged from the literature is that memory contamination is a function of memory and influence, and not a danger specific to the use of hypnosis (Beahrs, 1987; Loftus, 1993; McConkey & Sheehan, 1995). Beahrs (1987) makes a valid point that there is a larger unresolved issue of how courts and clinical practice deal with altered volition, cognition, perception and recall that occur unconnected to a deliberate procedure of hypnosis. Cases of spontaneous trance (Gudjonsson, 1992) and false confession cases (Ofshe, 1992) raise the larger problem of the role of suggestion in general. Confabulations are an inevitable fact of life in the normal course of events, and increased in the ordinary forensic situation by frequent, inept questioning (Wells & Loftus, 1984).

A number of researchers have highlighted a range of issues in applying hypnosis in the professional forensic setting which still remain. Hypnotic memory reports depend on: (1) the type of person who is being hypnotized (victim or defendant); (2) the role emotions play in hypnotic recall; (3) the possibility of faking hypnosis; (4) the problem of defining unambiguous procedures for collecting hypnotic testimony; and (5) the need to protect the civil rights of the person reporting in hypnosis (Sheehan, 1988). The consensus of opinion (Scheflin, 1994; Sadoff & Dubin, 1990; McConkey & Sheehan, 1995) appears to be that, "the courts must decide on a case by case basis the admissibility of hypnotically recalled material" (Scheflin, 1994, p. 36).

The debate so far on hypnotically refreshed testimony, and appropriate guidelines has also surfaced another important and major concern, namely the competency of the person required to conduct the hypnotic interview. The result is that the professional literature has generally drawn attention to the combined clinical and investigative qualifications which should be required for the person in this position.

Responsibilities of practitioners: Ethics and regulations

The last decade has been particularly marked by the issuing of guidelines for the conducting of hypnotic procedures both in gaining testimony for court cases (see Gibson, 1989) and in the clinical context, particularly with regard to the issue of recovering memories (American Medical Association, 1994; American Psychiatric Association Board of Trustees, 1994; American Psychological Association, 1994; Bloom, 1994; McConkey & Sheehan, 1995). Yapko's important work on a survey of the beliefs of 869 psychotherapists in the United States (Yapko, 1994) points us also to the fact that misinformed views of memory and hypnosis are prevalent and likely to cause problems. Having guidelines is a necessary first step in the business of educating practising professionals. But changing their beliefs will take more time and require active efforts by professional associations which understandably have a vested interest in guarding the reputations of their Members.

McConkey and Sheehan (1995; see also, McConkey, 1995) and others (e.g. Scheflin, 1994; Yapko, 1994) have raised a host of forensic and clinical issues associated with recovered memories and the uncertainties they pose for practising professionals. Part of the solution seems to be the emergence of specific guidelines for assisting professionals not only to understand all the issues involved, but to help them base their therapeutic approaches on appropriate scientific evidence and on proper professional standards.

The next section of this paper draws on a sample of trends in research that illustrate broad and major themes. The list of trends, of course, is not exhaustive and is illustrative only.

SOME CONTEMPORARY TRENDS IN HYPNOSIS RESEARCH

Collaborative ventures

The growth of collaborative ventures in the field in the last decade has been enormous. There is increasing pressure for researchers to solve practitioner problems such as the veracity of memories of child abuse, the responsibility of diagnosed Multiple Personality Disorder (MPD) clients in court cases, and the treatment of phobias. This has resulted in an increasing amount of interdisciplinary research on common issues (e.g. Spiegel & Scheflin, 1994) as well as transdisciplinary papers, where research from different disciplines is combined to resolve a particular issue (e.g. Kihlstrom, 1992; Kirsch, 1993; Watkins, 1989). These studies from people of recognized scholarship not only link and stimulate research in different disciplines, but provide a source of reliable information to people having to make decisions in an area where there is ambiguous and sometimes inaccurate information.

Related areas

Looking at research in related areas reveals that the findings of many studies implicate processes in hypnosis.

Psychophysiology Sturgis and Coe (1990) found that the only parasympathetic measure which distinguished highs from lows was responsiveness of heart rate, the changes in heart rates of highs being significantly greater on some items than those of lows. They explain their results as being in correspondence with the imagined content of hypnotic suggestions used and also refer to Hughes and Bowers' (1987) claim that heart rate is the physiological measure most sensitive to imaging. However, as DeBenedittis et al. (1994) point out the autonomic nervous system has proved to be rather elusive for study in dynamic conditions because of the inadequate sensitivity of the tools usually used, and the difficulties of sorting out the various interactions of the efferent systems. The comparison between hypnosis and other states involving relaxation and imagery has not yet been made and the "unique" biomarkers still elude the search. Recent work at Penn State University is providing intriguing new evidence of possible differences in patterns of brain activity between highs and lows (Ray, 1996; Sabourin, Cutcomb, Crawford, & Pribram, 1990).

Neurology Some theorists are already couching theory in terms of brain functioning (e.g. Kunzendorf, 1987–88; DePascalis, 1994). Kunzendorf (1987–88, p. 3) and his associates, for instance, view the brain in hypnosis as ceasing "to monitor whether conscious sensations are peripherally innervated percepts or centrally innervated images". However, it will be some time before psychophysiological or neurological research is able to provide us with a full understanding of the mechanisms of consciousness involved.

Self-consciousness One's tacit knowledge that one is perceiving an image, as opposed to imaging a sensation is at the root of distinguishing fact from fantasy, or reality from hallucination or dream. Important work has been going on in this area of self-consciousness, and research has proposed a theory that the brain might tell the difference between centrally innervated images and peripherally innervated percepts by monitoring cognitive states or not (Kunzendorf, Lacourse, & Lynch, 1987). Hallucinations are seen as "unmonitored images", images which are not accompanied by an awareness that one is imaging them nor by an illusory self-consciousness that one is perceiving them. Data suggest that in sleep, hypnosis and psychosis there is a lack of monitoring and that imaged sensations are not distinguished from hallucinations.

Conflict and consensus in experimental hypnosis

Researchers have personal views on the state of agreement and conflict amongst research workers in the same field. Significantly, Tellegen commenting on theories about the nature of hypnosis, in the foreword to Lynn and Rhue's edited work (Lynn & Rhue, 1991), remarks that he anticipates a closer agreement between the various camps. Fellows (1994) on the other hand, reviewing the same book sees deep, complex and varied divisions still remaining.

Though Fellows' (1993) comments on the clash between the "state" and "non-state" positions as essentially causing the blossoming of hypnosis research, Perry and associates see such conflict in the literature as being counterproductive and unnecessary (Perry, 1992; Nadon, Laurence, & Perry, 1989). There is energy in conflict, and conflict can be productive, but there is a danger of the debate becoming more important than the issue.

One theoretical construct which has caused unexpected conflict of late in the experimental literature is that of "hypnotic susceptibility," "hypnotizability," or "hypnotic capacity." Arguments have reflected those in the history of the construct of intelligence in personality theory: is there a trait, based on genetic influences on brain mechanisms which underlies a potential ability, or a propensity for experiencing "hypnotic" behavior? And if this trait exists, is it validly measured by the various tests of susceptibility? A considerable amount of research time and effort has been spent on trying to measure susceptibility and, particularly in the last decade, to increase a person's susceptibility (Bates, 1992; Bates & Brigham, 1990; Bates & Kraft, 1991; see also the work of Spanos and his associates—e.g. Spanos & Chaves, 1989). A recent challenge goes to the heart of the question when Irving Kirsch provocatively claims that we are measuring "imaginative suggestibility" and not hypnotizability with our standard scales.

There is now considerable agreement from all perspectives about the general nature of hypnosis in so far as it concerns imagery—multi-sensory, free-flowing, and effortless. In some cases, the imagination is so intense and compulsive as to be thought of by the imaginer ("fantasy addicts," Wilson & Barber, 1983; or "fantasy prone people" Lynn & Rhue, 1991) as indistinguishable from external reality. The defining construct, however, still eludes us. This kind of imagining in hypnosis is described variously as "imaginative involvement" (Hilgard, 1970), "delusion" (Sutcliffe, 1961), and "believed-in imaginings" (Sarbin & Coe, 1979).

Experimental and applied hypnosis: A symbiotic relationship   Above all, in the last decade there is emerging something of what I would call a symbiotic relationship between experimental and applied concerns—a developing theme throughout this paper. The fusion is fueled, I think, not only by the applied concerns of "forensic hypnosis," but by the stimulation of the particular controversies currently captured in the field, and especially by the ongoing debate on "recovered memories."

SUMMARY OVERVIEW OF THEMES, TRENDS AND ISSUES

Ten years down the track, the issues and themes I have canvassed tell us that there are still marked differences in conceptualisations about the underlying nature of hypnotic experience—whether the procedure of hypnosis directly affects brain processes of imagery, learning, pain, attention and memory, whether hypnotic phenomena are mediated indirectly through social influences via expectations, beliefs and attitudes, or whether the processes of dissociation control or divide consciousness. One decade ahead, the convergence of theoretical viewpoints is not about to happen. What Kihlstrom did not perhaps anticipate in 1985 was a landmark event in the history of hypnosis 8 years later. In 1993, a definition of hypnosis was produced for the public by Division 30 of the APA. It was contributed to by 14 hypnotists of international reputation and from a wide variety of theoretical persuasions and endorsed by the executive committee (Kirsch, 1993). Criticism of the "definition" followed, chiefly that it was neither a rigorous definition nor description of hypnosis, but it did not detract substantially from the field's achievements, especially its clinical usefulness. It also provided a working statement which could be refined and improved.

There has been a move away from the claim that hypnosis is a special state which has a characteristic neurophysiological identity. But there is a growing interest (Kihlstrom, 1992; Bowers, 1993; Kirmayer, 1992) in incorporating some construct of consciousness into contemporary theorizing about hypnosis to help clarify the relevance of the term "dissociation," and to clarify the labels of "involuntary" or "self-deceiving," which are all descriptions used by competing theories aiming to explain behavior in terms of other constructs.

The influence of the social processes in the form of interpersonal factors, experimental demands, and expectancies based on attitude and beliefs has been ably and ingeniously demonstrated in the many experiments and topics of the social-psychological movement spearheaded by the recently deceased Nicholas Spanos. No mention of the changes in the hypnosis literature can be complete without some tribute to both Kenneth Bowers and Nicholas Spanos as exceptional researchers who have profoundly influenced the course of hypnosis research (see, for example, Bowers, 1992; 1993; Spanos et al., 1989; 1991; 1992).

The reporting of professional issues has been the effect of the increased practice of hypnosis, fueling subsequent debate and pronouncements over the guidelines for its proper and ethical use. Main areas of interest concern the possible dangers of hypnosis, and the proper relationship between hypnotist and client, though the issue of lay hypnotists is still both contentious and troubling to the profession. Problems of trust and control are not unique to the hypnosis profession, but the influence of the hypnotist on highly hypnotizable people is a topic of special concern and in need of further clarification. The matter reappears in the literature, and professional attitudes are still in conflict.

Forensic hypnosis is a significant area which has come to the fore in the last decade (see Figs. 6.1 & 6.2) and was not foreshadowed by Kihlstrom's 1985 review. The literature now abounds with statements on the proper conduct of therapy and the position of the profession on "recovered" memories. This has been a stimulus in turn to much work in the area of hypnosis and memory. Increases in litigation, not only in the United States and other western countries, have been accompanied by a resurgence of interest in the veracity, or otherwise, of memories under hypnosis and a clear interest in potential influence on juries and courts in the form of the confidence of witnesses in their memories. The use and misuse of hypnosis in the courts in the last decade has been the impetus for papers not only classified under Forensic (42), but also specific experimental studies (23) on pseudomemories and the influence of interrogation and its interaction with hypnotic susceptibility.

Since the time of Kihlstrom's review there has been a gradual increase in the numbers of papers which make use of phenomenological data in order to gather more "in depth" data on personal differences in hypnotic responding and style of response. These publications come under the phenomenology heading (category 21) in Table 6.1. Some researchers, notably Pekala and associates (see Pekala, 1991; Pekala & Nagler, 1989) make use of inventories (Pekala & Kumar, 1987) and questionnaires (Matheson, Shue, & Bart, 1989) of personal experiences. Sheehan and McConkey (1982) pioneered use of the Experiential Analysis Technique (EAT) as a guide to eliciting subjects' data-rich retrospective memories of hypnosis. This technique is now being extended and investigated intensively by Eva Bányai and her associates in Hungary.

A continuing trend in hypnosis studies is that of individual differences—the primary construct that lies behind the centrality of "hypnotic susceptibility." The search for unique correlates of hypnotic ability has subtly given way to studies on the abilities of individuals and their individual experiences of hypnosis. There is still continued interest, however, in the concept of hypnotizability, its etiology, assessment and the many pathways into hypnosis via induction procedures and different types of suggestions.

Strong evidence of growing discussion and consensus between practitioner and experimenter orientations comes from the 1993 *Bulletin* of the APA Division 30 which contained its definition of hypnosis for the public. An interesting feature of the definition is that it refers to hypnosis as a "procedure." The definition corresponds more accurately with the range of client experiences described by the label "hypnosis." "Altered states of consciousness" are mentioned as "a way in which some people describe their experiences;" and "changes in sensations, perceptions, thoughts or behaviors" describe the outcomes of suggestions. In such a manner, loaded terms (like "hallucinations," "age-regression," and "delusions") and some negative associations of the past come to be avoided. However, the definition may be one which appeals more to practitioners and those of the social-cognitive-behavioral persuasion, those who regard the "thought-process" and "contextual-cue" variables as being of paramount importance.

The most sophisticated theoretical perspective to emerge over the last 10 years clearly lies in current modifications of the term "dissociation," recognized most recently by the late Kenneth Bowers' (1993) modification of Hilgard's (1977; 1994) neodissociation theory of divided consciousness. The theories essentially differ from each other in the way they theorize about the distribution of attention among competing tasks.

FUTURE CONCERNS

In conclusion, I want to say something about future issues facing the field beyond the here-and-now. One way of approaching this is to summarize briefly theoretical and methodological issues relating to a sample of forthcoming research.

Research anticipations

Analyses of planned research has been attempted for a group of 12 invited key researchers (personal communication) who have just come together in a conference sponsored by Brock University in August of this year (in memory of Kenneth Bowers). Their talk about the future of hypnosis tempts me to make the following predictions.

Theoretically, work ahead seems likely to continue some of the major themes that have already been outlined. The notion of "state" will continue to be debated, but it must be recognized that conceptions of the nature of the hypnotic state have changed with untenable versions of state theory now abandoned. The simple dichotomies of past theory are reflected currently as points on a continuum. Focus will be much more on critical variables that interact to shape hypnotic phenomena. Methodologies should be further attuned to investigate, and control for context effects, reflecting additionally the influence of work outside the traditional domain of hypnosis. What has previously been observed as divergent findings will occupy the attention of researchers who seek to reconcile (what Jean-Roch Laurence calls "synergise") experimental and clinical findings.

I believe the most dominant theoretical perspective demanding the attention of future researchers will continue to be the dissociation perspective on events in hypnosis, and the improvement of memory will continue to be a relevant focal point in this theoretical debate. The notion of dissociation will incorporate systematic study of ongoing experiences and thought as well as action with the apparent automaticity of that action being emphasized and related to the executive mode of functioning. Reduced executive control may prove to be a reliably differentiated feature of the production of hypnotic response. The push towards greater rapprochement of experimental and clinical findings has emerged as salient in this debate, as it has in the recovered memory one, and is likely to be further manifest in the future—the continued exploration, for example, of Bowers' (1992) dissociated control theory linked analogously at least to a clinical disorder, and of memory processing characteristics of clinically relevant trauma.

Despite these measured guesses about some of the future directions, I predict continuing tensions will remain. One of these tensions relates to the ongoing difficulty of integrating hypnosis research into the main stream of personality theory and theories of psychological functioning. No extant theory, for example, is really explicit about the trait-situation (theoretical and methodological) mix. Relatedly, in their data analysis, hypnosis researchers will continue to use inadequate data analysis strategies not optimally geared to the interactive mix. Part of this tendency, as one of the group (Nadon) has observed, is due to the predilection of hypnosis researchers to preoccupy themselves with competing models as opposed to systematic exploration of a particular point of view.

The core phenomenon among the applied issues which are most likely to occupy our attention in the future is that of recovered memory. Are such memories real and/or fabricated? There is also the unanswered and vexed questions, in particular, of what law courts can do with uncorroborated information and whether research can isolate when, in fact, hypnosis is being faked. The implications that these issues have for the legal status of hypnotically produced testimony are major. The special relevance of the faking issue is already emerging in the recent experimental literature of Kinnunen, Zamansky, and Block's work (1994) "Is the hypnotized subject lying?" Analysis of recovered memories tied perhaps to contemporary theorizing about dissociation will be, I predict, hypnosis' test case for the rapprochement of its clinical and laboratory concerns.

Predicting the future requires one also to consider where the researchers of tomorrow are going. Strong indications of this trend are given by Barton, Strauss, and Reilley (1995) in their survey of doctoral dissertations on hypnosis for the period 1980–1989. Results from their study show a substantial rise in the number of doctoral dissertations concerned with hypnosis. Not surprisingly, there is a strong move toward investigating issues relating to utility rather than validation of an entity, and evidence of a growth in cross-disciplinary work (especially relating to medicine). Susceptibility retains its high profile and there is a fresh emergence of the relevance of post-hypnotic suggestion and physiological responsiveness. Collectively, these data on training reinforce the same trends that I have abstracted elsewhere in this Address from the standard publication literature.

CONCLUSION

This paper has reviewed contemporary trends in hypnosis research. Focus has been placed on theoretical, empirical, methodological, and pragmatic developments in the field. An example of a major theoretical development is the recent shifts that have occurred in theorizing about the process of dissociation. Methodological developments inevitably cut across major content concerns and pragmatic developments relate clearly to major content concerns expressed in the laboratory literature. As to the latter development, one such area is the extent to which memories reported in hypnosis are distorted in their accuracy. This clearly relates, for example, to the evidenced need for sensitive and ethical professional guidelines covering such potentially complex fields of inquiry as forensic hypnosis, and the clinical expression of repressed memories. Finally, the last decade, more than the one before has been characterized by strong links between laboratory and clinical concerns. The way ahead points to the fact that even greater rapprochement is now actually required. The rapprochement issue is of increasing importance and demands our urgent attention.

ACKNOWLEDGEMENTS

The author wishes to thank especially Rosemary Robertson for her help in the preparation of this paper.

REFERENCES

American Medical Association. (1994, June 16). *Report of the Council on Scientific Affairs: Memories of childhood abuse* (CSA Report 5-A-94).

American Psychiatric Association Board of Trustees. (1994). Statement on memories of sexual abuse. *International Journal of Clinical and Experimental Hypnosis, 42*, 261–264.

American Psychological Association. (1994). *Interim report of the APA working group on investigation of memory of childhood abuse.* Washington, DC: APA Public Affairs Office.

Balthazard, C. G. (1993). The hypnosis scales at their centenary: Some fundamental issues still unresolved. *International Journal of Clinical and Experimental Hypnosis, 41*, 47–73.

Bányai, É. I. (1991). Toward a social-psychobiological model of hypnosis. In S. J. Lynn & J. W. Rhue (Eds.), *Theories of hypnosis: Current models and perspectives* (pp. 564–598). New York: Guilford.

Bányai, É. I., Gosi-Gerguss, A. C., Vago, P., Varga, K., & Horvath, R. (1990). Interactional approach to the understanding of hypnosis: Theoretical background and main findings. In R.Van Dyck, P. H. Spinhoven, A. J. W. Vander Does, Y. R. Van Rood, & W. De Moor (Eds.), *Hypnosis: Current theory, research and practice* (pp. 53–69). Amsterdam: Elsevier University Press.

Barber, J. (1993). The clinical role of responsivity tests: A master class commentary. *International Journal of Clinical and Experimental Hypnosis, 41*, 165–168.

Barton, D. A., Strauss, B., & Reilley, R. R. (1995). Doctoral dissertations on hypnosis: 1980–1989. *American Journal of Clinical Hypnosis, 37*, 267–270.

Bates, B. L. (1992). The effect of demands for honesty on the efficacy of the Carleton Skills-Training Program. *International Journal of Clinical and Experimental Hypnosis, 40*, 88–102.

Bates, B. L. & Brigham, T. A., (1990). Modifying hypnotizability with the Carleton Skills Training Program: A partial replication and analysis of components. *International Journal of Clinical and Experimental Hypnosis, 38*, 183–195.

Bates, B. L. & Kraft, P. M., (1991). The nature of hypnotic performance following administration of the Carleton Skills Training Program. *International Journal of Clinical and Experimental Hypnosis, 39*, 227–242.

Beahrs, J. O. (1987). Hypnosis can not be fully nor reliably excluded from the courtroom. *American Journal of Clinical Hypnosis, 31*, 18–27.

Bloom, P. B. (1994). Clinical guidelines in using hypnosis in uncovering memories of sexual abuse: A master class commentary. *International Journal of Clinical and Experimental Hypnosis, 42,* 173–178.

Bowers, K. S. (1992). Imagination and dissociative control in hypnotic responding. *International Journal of Clinical and Experimental Hypnosis, 40,* 253–275.

Bowers, K. S. (1993). The Waterloo-Stanford Group C (WSCG) Scale of Hypnotic Susceptibility: Normative and comparative data. *International Journal of Clinical and Experimental Hypnosis, 41,* 35–46.

Chalmers, L. (1903). Scientific enquiry and authoritarianism in perinatal care and education. *Birth, 10,* 151–162.

Coe, W. C. (1992). Hypnosis: Wherefore art thou? *International Journal of Clinical and Experimental Hypnosis, 40,* 219–237.

Crawford, H. J. (1994). Brain dynamics and hypnosis: Attentional and disattentional processes. *International Journal of Clinical and Experimental Hypnosis, 42,* 204–232.

DeBenedittis, G., Cigada, M., Bianchi, A., Signorini, M. G., & Cerutti, S. (1994). Autonomic changes during hypnosis: A heart rate variability power spectrum analysis as a marker of sympatho–vagal balance. *International Journal of Clinical and Experimental Hypnosis, 42,* 140–152.

DePascalis, V. (1994). Event-related potentials during hypnotic hallucination. *International Journal of Clinical and Experimental Hypnosis, 42,* 39–55.

Diamond, M. (1989). Invited discussion: Clinical uses of measures of hypnotizability. *American Journal of Clinical Hypnosis, 32,* 11–12.

Dinges, D. F., Whitehouse, W. G., Orne, E. C., Powell, J. W., Orne, M. T., & Erdelyi, M. H. (1992). Evaluating hypnotic memory enhancement (hypermnesia and reminiscence) using multitrial forced recall. *Journal of Experimental Psychology: Learning, Memory and Cognition, 18,* 1139–1147.

Erdelyi, M. H. (1994). Hypnotic hypermnesia: The empty set of hypermnesia. *International Journal of Clinical and Experimental Hypnosis, 42,* 379–390.

Erdelyi, M. H. (in press). *The recovery of unconscious memories: Hypermnesia and reminiscence.* Chicago. University of Chicago Press.

Fellows, B. (1993). Whither hypnosis?: Editorial comment. *Contemporary Hypnosis, 10* (1), ii–iii.

Fellows, B. (1994). Book review: Theories of hypnosis, current models and perspectives. *Contemporary Hypnosis, 11,* 26–31.

Frankel, F. H. (1987). Significant developments in medical hypnosis during the past 25 years. *International Journal of Clinical and Experimental Hypnosis, 35,* 231–247.

Frankel, F. H. (1989). Invited discussion: Clinical uses of measures of hypnotizability. *American Journal of Clinical Hypnosis, 32,* 13–14.

Gibson, H. R. (1989). Commentary on the 1988 Home Office Circular No. 66: The Home Office attitude to forensic hypnosis: A victory for scientific evidence or for medical conservatism? *British Journal of Experimental and Clinical Hypnosis, 6,* 25–27.

Gill, M. M., & Brenman, M. (1959). *Hypnosis and related states: Psychoanalytic studies in regression.* New York: International Universities Press.

Glisky, M. L., & Kihlstrom, J. F. (1993). Hypnotizability and facets of openness. *International Journal of Clinical and Experimental Hypnosis, 42,* 112–123.

Greene, E., Wilson, L., & Loftus, E. F. (1989). Impact of hypnotic testimony on the jury. *Law and Human Behavior, 13,* 61–78.

Gudjonsson, G. (1992). *The psychology of interrogations, confessions and testimony.* Chichester, UK: Wiley.

Hammond, D. C. (1993). False memories, misrepresentations and ritual abuse. *Psychological Hypnosis: Bulletin of APA Division 30,* 2 (3), 2–3, 9–11.

Hilgard, E. R. (1977). *Divided consciousness: Multiple controls in human thought and action.* New York: Wiley.

Hilgard, E. R. (1987). Research advances in hypnosis: Issues and methods. *International Journal of Clinical and Experimental Hypnosis*, *35*, 248–264.

Hilgard, E. R. (1988). Response to contextual demands an insufficient account of hypnotic phenomena. *British Journal of Experimental and Clinical Hypnosis*, *5*, 13.

Hilgard, E. R. (1991). A neodissociative interpretation of hypnosis. In S. J. Lynn & J. W. Rhue (Eds.), *Theories of hypnosis: Current models and perspectives* (pp. 83–104). New York: Guilford.

Hilgard, E. R. (1994). Neodissociation theory. In S. J. Lynn & J. W. Rhue (Eds.), *Dissociation: Clinical, theoretical and research perspectives* (pp. 32–51). New York: Guilford.

Hilgard, J. (1970). *Personality and hypnosis: A study of imaginative involvement*. Chicago: University Chicago Press.

Hughes, D. E., & Bowers, K. S. (1987, October). *Hypnotic ability as a mediator of heart rate responsiveness to imagery*. Paper presented at the 38th Annual Meeting of the Society for Clinical and Experimental Hypnosis, Los Angeles, CA.

Johnson, M. K., Foley, M. A., Suengas, A. G., & Raye, C. L. (1988). Phenomenal characteristics for perceived and imagined autobiographical events. *Journal of Experimental Psychology: General*, *117*, 371–376.

Kihlstrom, J. F. (1985). Hypnosis. *Annual Review of Psychology*, *36*, 385–418.

Kihlstrom, J. F. (1989). Dispositional correlates of hypnosis: A phenomenological approach. *International Journal of Clinical and Experimental Hypnosis*, *37*, 249–263.

Kihlstrom, J. F. (1992). Hypnosis: A sesquicentennial essay: Comment. *International Journal of Clinical and Experimental Hypnosis*, *40*, 301–314.

Kinnunen, T., Zamansky, H. S., & Block, M. L. (1994). Is the hypnotized subject lying? *Journal of Abnormal Psychology*, *103*, 184–191.

Kirmayer, L. J. (1992). Social constructions of hypnosis. *International Journal of Clinical and Experimental Hypnosis*, *40*, 276–300.

Kirsch, I. (1991). Current theories of hypnosis: An addendum. *Contemporary Hypnosis*, *8*, 105–108.

Kirsch, I. (1993). Defining hypnosis for the public. *Psychological Hypnosis: Bulletin of APA Division 30*, *2* (3), 15.

Kirsch, I., Council, J. R., & Wickless, C. (1990). Subjective scoring for the Harvard Group Scale of Hypnotic Susceptibility, Form A. *International Journal of Clinical and Experimental Hypnosis*, *38*, 112–124.

Kunzendorf, R. G. (1987–88). Self-consciousness as the monitoring of cognitive states: A theoretical perspective. *Imagination, Cognition and Personality*, *7*, 3–22.

Kunzendorf, R. G., Lacourse, P., & Lynch, B. (1987). Hypnotic hypermnesia for subliminally encoded stimuli: State-dependent memory for "unmonitored" sensations. *Imagination, Cognition and Personality*, *6*, 365–377.

Labelle, L., Laurence, J-R., Nadon, R., & Perry, C. (1990). Hypnotizability, preference for an imagic cognitive style and memory creation in hypnosis. *Journal of Abnormal Psychology*, *99*, 222–228.

Loftus, E. F. (1993). The reality of repressed memories. *American Psychologist*, *48*, 518–537.

Lynn, S. J., & Nash, M. R. (1994). Truth in memory: Ramifications for psychotherapy and hypnotherapy. *American Journal of Clinical Hypnosis*, *36*, 194–208.

Lynn, S. J., & Rhue, J. W. (Eds.), (1991). *Theories of hypnosis: Current models and perspectives*. New York: Guilford.

Lynn, S. J., Rhue, J. W., Myers, B. P., & Weekes, J. R. (1994). Pseudomemory in hypnotized and simulating subjects. *International Journal of Clinical and Experimental Hypnosis*, *42*, 118–129.

Matheson, G., Shue, K. L., & Bart, C. (1989). A validation study of a short-form hypnotic experience questionnaire and its relationship to hypnotizability. *American Journal of Clinical Hypnosis*, *32*, 17–26.

McCann, T., & Sheehan, P. W. (1987). The breaching of pseudomemory under hypnotic instruction: Implications for original memory retrieval. *British Journal of Experimental and Clinical Hypnosis*, *4*, 101–108.

McConkey, K. M. (1992). The effects of hypnotic procedures on remembering: The experimental findings and their implications for forensic hypnosis. In E. Fromm and M. Nash (Eds.), *Contemporary hypnosis research* (pp. 405–426). New York: Guilford.

McConkey, K. M. (1995). Hypnosis, memory, and the ethics of uncertainty. *Australian Psychologist, 30*, 1–10.

McConkey, K. M., & Sheehan, P. W. (1995). *Hypnosis, memory, and behavior in criminal investigation.* New York: Guilford.

Mott, T. Jnr. (1989). Hypnotizability testing and clinical hypnosis. *American Journal of Clinical Hypnosis, 32*, 2–3.

Nadon, R., Laurence, J-R., & Perry, C. (1989). Interactionism: Cognition and context in hypnosis. *British Journal of Experimental Clinical Hypnosis, 6*, 141–150.

Ofshe, R. J. (1992). Inadvertent hypnosis during interrogation: False confession due to dissociative state, misidentified multiple personality and the satanic cult hypothesis. *International Journal of Clinical and Experimental Hypnosis, 40*, 125–156.

Oxman, A. D., & Guyati, G. H. (1994). The science of reviewing research. *Annals of New York Academy of Sciences.*

Pekala, R. J. (1991). Hypnotic types: Evidence from a cluster analysis of phenomenal experience. *Contemporary Hypnosis, 8*, 95–104.

Pekala, R. J., & Kumar, V. K. (1987). Predicting hypnotic susceptibility via a self-report instrument: A replication. *American Journal of Clinical Hypnosis, 30*, 57–65.

Pekala, R. J., & Kumar, V. K. (1989). Phenomenological patterns of consciousness during hypnosis: Relevance to cognition and individual differences. *Australian Journal of Clinical and Experimental Hypnosis, 17*, 1–20.

Pekala, R. J., & Nagler, R. (1989). The assessment of hypnoidal states: Rationale and clinical applications. *American Journal of Clinical and Experimental Hypnosis, 31*, 231–236.

Perry, C. (1992). Theorizing about hypnosis in either/or terms. *International Journal of Clinical and Experimental Hypnosis, 40*, 238–252.

Pettinati, H. M. (Ed.), (1988). *Hypnosis and memory.* New York: Guilford.

Ray, W. J. (1996, August). *It's the person, not the state: But who is the person, and what is the state it's not?* Paper presented at Niagara-on-the-Lake Hypnosis Conference, Niagara-on-the-Lake, Ontario, Canada.

Sabourin, M., Cutcomb, S. D., Crawford, H. J., & Pribram, K. H. (1990). EEG correlates of hypnotic susceptibility and hypnotic trance: Spectral analysis and coherence. *International Journal of Psychophysiology, 10*, 125–142.

Sadoff, R. L., & Dubin, L. L. (1990). The use of hypnosis as a pretrial discovery tool in civil and criminal lawsuits. In C. H. Wecht (Ed.), *Legal medicine* (pp. 105–124). Salem, NH: Butterworth.

Sarbin, T. R. (1991). Hypnosis: A fifty year perspective. *Contemporary Hypnosis, 8*, 1–16.

Sarbin, T. R., & Coe, W. C. (1979). *Hypnosis: A social psychological analysis of influence communication.* New York: Holt, Rinehart & Winston.

Scheflin, A. W. (1994). Forensic hypnosis: Unanswered questions. *Australian Journal of Clinical and Experimental Hypnosis, 22*, 25–27.

Sheehan, P. W. (1988). Issues in the forensic application of hypnosis. *Australian Journal of Clinical and Experimental Hypnosis, 16*, 103–111.

Sheehan, P. W., & McConkey, K. M. (1982). *Hypnosis and experience: The exploration of phenomena and process.* Hillsdale, NJ: Erlbaum.

Sheehan, P. W., Statham, D., & Jamieson, G. A. (1991). Pseudomemory effects occurring over time in the hypnotic setting. *Journal of Abnormal Psychology, 100*, 39–44.

Shields, I. W., & Knox, V. J. (1986). Level of processing as a determinant of hypnotic hypermnesia. *Journal of Abnormal Psychology, 95*, 358–364.

Spanos, N. P., & Chaves, J. F. (1989). *Hypnosis: The cognitive behavioral perspective.* Buffalo, NY: Prometheus Books.

Spanos, N. R., Gwynn, M. I., Comer, S. L., Baltruweit, W. J., & de Groh, M. (1989). Are hypnotically induced pseudomemories resistant to cross-examination? *Law and Human Behavior, 13,* 271–289.

Spanos, N. P., Quigley, C. A., Gwynn, M. I., Glatt, R. L., & Perline, A. H. (1991). Hypnotic interrogation, pretrial preparation and witness testimony during direct and cross-examination. *Law and Human Behavior, 15,* 639–653.

Spanos, N. P., Myers, B., DuBreuil, S. C., & Pawlak, A. E. (1992). The effects of polygraph evidence and eyewitness testimony on the beliefs and decisions of mock jurors. *Imagination, Cognition and Personality, 12,* 103–113.

Spence, D. P. (1994). Narrative truth and putative child abuse. *International Journal of Clinical and Experimental Hypnosis, 42,* 289–303.

Spiegel, D., & Scheflin, A. W. (1994). Dissociated or fabricated?: Psychiatric aspects of repressed memory in criminal and civil cases. *International Journal of Clinical and Experimental Hypnosis, 42,* 411–432.

Spiegel, H. (1989). Invited discussion: Clinical uses of measures of hypnotizability. *American Journal of Clinical Hypnosis, 32,* 15–16.

Spinhoven, P., Vanderlinden, J., TerKuile, M. M., & Linssen, A. C. G. (1993). Assessment of hypnotic processes and responsiveness in a clinical context. *International Journal of Clinical and Experimental Hypnosis, 41,* 210–224.

Steller, M., & Koehnken, G. (1989). Criteria-based statement analysis. In D. C. Raskin (Ed.), *Psychological methods in criminal investigation and evidence* (pp. 217–245). New York: Springer.

Sturgis, L. M., & Coe, W. C. (1990). Physiological responsiveness during hypnosis. *International Journal of Clinical and Experimental Hypnosis, 38,* 196–207.

Sutcliffe, J. P. (1961). "Credulous" and "sceptical" views of hypnotic phenomena: Experiments in aesthesia, hallucination, and delusion. *Journal of Abnormal and Social Psychology, 62,* 189–200.

Tellegen, A., & Atkinson, G. (1974). Openness to absorbing and self-altering experiences ("absorption"), a trait related to hypnotic susceptibility. *Journal of Abnormal Psychology, 83,* 268–277.

Wallace, B., Allen, P. A., & Weber, T. A. (1994). Hypnotic susceptibility, imaging ability, and the detection of embedded words within letters. *International Journal of Clinical and Experimental Hypnosis, 42,* 20–38.

Watkins, J. G. (1989). Hypnotic hypermnesia and forensic hypnosis: A cross-examination. *American Journal of Clinical Hypnosis, 32,* 71–83.

Weekes, J. R., Lynn, S. J., Green, J. P., & Brentar, J. T. (1992). Pseudomemory in hypnotized and task-motivated subjects. *Journal of Abnormal Psychology, 101,* 356–360.

Wells, G. L., & Loftus, E. F. (1984). *Eyewitness testimony.* Cambridge: Cambridge University Press.

Whitehouse, W. G., Dinges, D. F., Orne, E. C., & Orne, M. T. (1988). Hypnotic hyperamnesia: Enhanced memory accessibility or report bias? *Journal of Abnormal Psychology, 97,* 289–295.

Wilson, S. C., & Barber, T. X., (1983). *The inventory of childhood memories and imaginings.* (ICMI). Framington, MA: Cushing Hospital.

Yapko, M. D. (1994). Suggestibility and repressed memories of abuse: A survey of psychotherapists' beliefs. *American Journal of Clinical Hypnosis, 36,* 163–171.

Yuille, J. C., & Cutshall, J. L. (1986). A case study of eyewitness memory of a crime. *Journal of Applied Psychology, 71,* 291–301.

CHAPTER SEVEN

Social psychology across cultures: Two ways forward

Michael Harris Bond
Chinese University of Hong Kong, China

This paper addresses two key issues which its author judges to be important in enhancing the credibility of cross-cultural social psychology. The first is the need to unpackage at the psychological level the effects of culture on behavior. Such efforts will help the discipline to develop universal theories of social behavior. Secondly, a wider diversity of cultural groups must be included in our studies than has previously been attempted. This enlargement will test the robustness of our hypotheses, help to uncover new constructs, and strengthen our claims to universality. An energetic focus on these two concerns will bring cross-cultural social psychology greater scientific attention and respect.

L'auteur de cet article aborde deux questions fondamentales qu'il juge importantes pour l'accroissement de la crédibilité de la psychologie sociale interculturelle. La première est le besoin de déballer, au niveau psychologique, les effets de la culture sur le comportement; de tels efforts aideront cette discipline à concevoir des théories universelles du comportement social. Il faut, en second lieu, que nos études incluent une plus grande variété de groupes culturels qu'on n'a tenté de le faire jusqu'à présent. Cet élargissement éprouvera la solidité de nos hypothèses, aidera à découvrir de nouveaux concepts et renforcera nos prétentions à l'universalité. La concentration énergique sur ces deux préoccupations vaudra à la psychologie sociale une attention et un respect scientifiques plus grands.

Now the general who wins a battle makes many calculations in his temple ere the battle is fought. The general who loses a battle makes but few calculations beforehand. Thus do many calculations lead to victory, and few calculations to defeat: how much more no calculation at all! It is by attention to this point that I can foresee who is likely to win or lose.

—Sun Tzu, *The art of war* (1, 26)

When could one date the beginning of cross-cultural social psychology? Certainly a noteworthy call-to-arms was the 1954 attempted replication and extension by Schachter and his colleagues (1954) of his earlier study on opinion deviates in a small group in seven European countries. If so, then social psychologists with an interest in culture have been toiling in the trenches for over 40 years. In recent years that activity has been increasing, fueled by the diversity initiative in North America, the specter of vicious ethnic conflicts around the globe, and the internationalization of trade, the internet, and travel. The educated public at large is now much more interested in what social psychologists know about culture's effects on behavior and is increasingly willing to support our attempts at contributing insights (Featherman, 1993).

The consequence of this scientific enterprise in cross-cultural social psychology is a recent efflorescence of textbooks on the topic (Berry, Segall, & Kağıtçıbaşı, 1997; Moghaddam, Taylor, & Wright, 1993; Smith & Bond, 1993; Triandis, 1994). These textbooks, combined with triennial surveys in the *Annual Review of Psychology* (e.g. Bond & Smith, 1996) can provide a panoramic view of our current knowledge base.

By reading such sources, we can learn what topics have been studied, and by whom; how culture has been conceptualized and its effects translated into psychologica variables. With some imagination, we could use this information to anticipate where our future energies might be deployed—on what topics and in which cultures and by whom.

Given some judicious reflection at this stage, however, we might shape those future extensions of our discipline so that we use our resources more efficiently and thereby honor the goodwill that social developments have accorded our discipline. It is these reflections that I wish to share in this paper. I focus on two fronts: (1) psychologizing culture scientifically, and (2) expanding our net of cultures studied. I acknowledge that these are my assessments of emergent needs for the discipline of cross-cultural social psychology, and that other professionals might make a different selection or give the same issues a different twist. Of course, in cross-cultural studies we encourage such varied, "emic" (i.e. culture-specific) inputs. If this presentation stimulates you to contribute your insights to the conversation, then a synergistic view of diversity would predict both our separate and joint benefit!

May I also add that we are all learning from experience, our own and others'. If I now suggest that we could profitably proceed in a different way and use the work of others to demonstrate why, then I hope that you will forgive me any resulting offense. Nothing succeeds like failure carefully considered; in fact, so-called "failure" may be an essential antecedent to eventual success for those many of us who grow through a steady diet of experiments. So, I thank all of those I cite in this presentation for their contributions to my intellectual growth as a cross-cultural social psychologist and hope that we may continue to assist one another as we stumble out of darkness towards the dawn.

It is only one who is thoroughly acquainted with the evils of war
that can thoroughly understand the profitable way of carrying it on.

Sun Tzu, *The art of war* (2, 7)

PSYCHOLOGIZING CULTURE SCIENTIFICALLY

Spies are a most important element in war,
because on them depends an army's ability to move.

Sun Tzu, *The art of war* (13, 27)

In 1984, Kwok Leung and I published a study on resource allocation. It was rather sophisticated for cross-cultural studies of the time, as it hypothesized and confirmed a three-way interaction among culture, amount of work input, and type of relationship between the resource allocator and recipient. This interaction was found for both allocation behavior and judgments of the allocations as fair.

In explaining these outcomes, we wrote that "... the results are entirely consistent with the notion that collectivists are oriented toward harmony in well-defined in-groups and behave in a sharply different way toward outgroup members" (Leung & Bond, 1984, p. 803). Despite the crisp prose, a sensitive reader will have noted a certain tentativeness in the phrases "consistent with" and "oriented towards." For, the two key psychological terms in our explanation were "collectivists" and "harmony," but we had not measured either of these constructs in our research participants.

Instead, we had presumed that Hong Kong Chinese were collectivists and Americans were individualists because Hofstede's (1980) work had identified Hong Kong as a collective culture and the United States as an individualistic culture. Based on his illuminating discussion of the cultural dynamics in collectivist cultures, we had likewise argued that the pressure for interpersonal harmony within the group would be greater in collectivist cultures. However, we had not measured these constructs at the level of the individuals who were producing the behaviors our models were attempting to predict. We had "unpackaged" culture (Whiting, 1976) only at the level of culture and then had "laddered" ourselves down to the individual level verbally.

As T. S. Eliot warns us in *Four Quartets*, "Words strain, Crack and sometimes break, Under the tension, slip, slide, perish, Decay with imprecision, will not stay in place, Will not stay still." Many of us had become adept at taking a broad cultural construct like individualism and using our experience in contrasting cultural systems to paint a persuasive word-picture about how their comparative dynamics played out at the psychological level (Bond, 1994). Cross-cultural social psychology was in danger of becoming a branch of creative writing, some of it remarkably elegant and persuasive (e.g. Miller, 1984).

However, was it fiction or non-fiction? Given the distance of the laddering and the looseness of the rungs, many competent mainstreamers were skeptical (e.g. Messick, 1988). He points out (p. 46) that, "When cultural variables are implemented as individual difference variables, research outcomes are subject to all the ambiguities that plague research on individual differences within a culture". So, even if we had unpackaged culture *at the cultural level* by invoking Hofstede (or Chinese Culture Connection, 1987; Schwartz, 1994; Smith, Dugan, & Trompenaars, 1996), we had not yet unpackaged it scientifically *at the individual level* (see also Clark, 1987). However informed and sensible our linkage of culture was to personality (or social context), we still had to anchor that reasoning with direct measures of the putative psychological processes involved.

A seductive shortcut

> Thus one who is skillful at keeping the enemy on the move
> maintains deceitful appearances,
> according to which the enemy will act.
> He sacrifices something that the enemy may snatch at it.
>
> Sun Tzu, *The art of war* (5, 19)

One can of course finesse the need to "ladder" down from the culture level to the individual level—one simply commits the ecological fallacy (Hofstede, 1980, pp. 28–31). That is, one interprets a relationship at the culture (or country) level as being a correlation at the individual level. So, for example, one could rework the Smith and Peterson (1995) finding about organizational event management that across 30 countries a country's score on individualism is correlated with that country managers' *average* reported reliance on their own experience and training. The fallacious recreation of this result asserts that the more individualistic the manager, the more likely he or she is to use personal experience or training in event management. This claim may, in fact, be true. It is, however, not warranted—Smith and Peterson (1995) did not measure individualism at the individual level, nor did they correlate individualism with event management across individuals in their 30 countries. Nor did they claim to have done so.

The problem for cross-cultural social psychology is that many will naively or perversely commit the ecological fallacy in their rush to collect cross-cultural findings that psychologists can use in training, teaching, and theorizing. The problem is that the outcome of the ecological fallacy is often wrong (Hofstede, Bond, & Luk, 1993; Shweder, 1973). That is, the results *and* the constructs themselves are typically not reproduced across levels.

Those of us who fashion constructs at the cultural level could discourage such wrongheadedness by using less psychological sounding labels. Terms like "individualism" or "uncertainty avoidance" (Hofstede, 1980), "human heartedness" and "moral discipline" (Chinese Culture Connection, 1987), or "mastery" and "egalitarian commitment" (Schwartz, 1994) encourage the ecological fallacy by over-psychologizing the labels for cultural constructs. Such restraint in labeling will of course be difficult, given the origin of these constructs from psychological measures! However, the coinage of such nonpsychological terms as "power distance" (Hofstede), Confucian work dynamism (Chinese Culture Connection), and harmony (Schwartz) suggests that appropriate sounding cultural terms can be created. At the very least, we should begin by routinely adding the words "culture-level" or "societal" to constructs developed at that level to discourage their unwarranted application to the individual level. For example, Dion and Dion (1996) routinely distinguish between *societal* individualism–collectivism and *psychological* individualism–collectivism, perhaps the clearest designation and differentiation of cultural and individual level for the I-C construct. Labels hold a seductive lure and must be made our allies, not our quislings.

Using culturally relevant psychological measures

For the men of Wu and the men of Yueh are enemies;
yet if they are crossing a river in the same boat and are caught by a storm,
they will come to each other's assistance just as the left hand helps the right.

Sun Tzu, *The art of war* (11, 30)

The basic steps involved in developing such measures are straightforward: (1) develop a theory which relates the behavior of interest to psychological variables hypothesized to be associated with that behavior and also to differ across cultures; (2) measure that psychological variable in all participants along with the behavior of interest; (3) regress that behavior against the psychological predictor in the pooled sample; and (4) regress the residuals from Step 3 against the culture term and the interaction between culture and the psychological variable (see also Smith & Bond, 1993, pp. 221–223).

If Step 3 shows significance, then the effects of culture have been scientifically unpackaged at the individual level. If the culture effect from Step 4 is significant, then one still has to undertake further theorizing and instrumentation to explain the persisting cultural difference. If the interaction between culture and the psychological variable is significant, then the psychological processes involved vary across cultures (see e.g. Diener & Diener, 1995) and further variables will be needed to try and account for such variation.

Fortunately, we now have many culturally relevant measures of psychological variables available: of values (e.g. Schwartz, 1992); of independent and interdependent self-construals (e.g. Gudykunst et al., 1994); of horizontal and vertical collectivism (Singelis, Triandis, Bhawuk, & Gelfand, 1995); of social axioms (Leung & Bond, 1993); and of personality itself (e.g. Costa & McCrae, 1992). Of course, each of these measures must be used only after first having its linguistic and metric equivalence established in the cultural groups concerned (e.g. McCrae & Costa, 1997); and this process may require considerable cultural decentering of the instrument's original content and language (Wierzbicka, 1993).

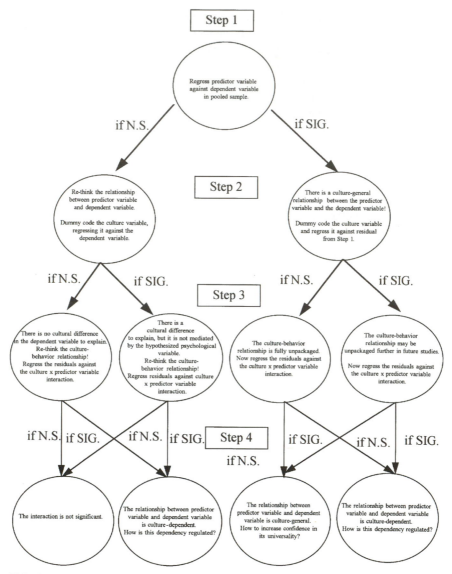

FIG. 7.1   Proposed flow-chart in unpackaging culture's effects on individual behavior.

Useful cross-cultural work, however, requires more time and care than equivalent monocultural research (Gabrenya, 1988; Malpass, 1988), so researchers without tenure should reflect carefully before committing themselves to this venture. The potential yield, however, from all this theorizing, instrumentation, and analysis is the discovery of universal, psychological models of social behavior (Triandis, 1978; 1988). This goal is worthy of our efforts!

Failures to unpackage?

By means of [attack by] water, an enemy may be intercepted,
but not robbed of all his belongings.

Sun Tzu, *The art of war* (12, 14)

There is, of course, no guarantee that psychological keys will unlock the doors
of cultural difference. The weight of history, religion, and ecology confer stability and consistency on behavior that may resist psychological unpackaging.
Levine and Norenzayan's (1996) data on pace of life in 31 countries may provide an interesting test case. They have unpackaged their country averages *at
the culture level* via GNP per capita, which accounted for 60% of the variance
in country pace measures.

Suppose, however, one were to try making this a cross-cultural study of
individual rather than of country pace. First, one would need to take individual
measures of the construct(s) believed to relate to individual pace and to vary
across cultures. Given the country-level finding for GNP per capita, one might
choose some psychological measure like internal locus of control or individual modernity (or both!). Even if one followed the steps outlined above for
psychological-level unpackaging, however, I doubt that cultural differences
would be eliminated. Reduced, yes, but not eliminated.

Despite our diligence and creativity, we may then be confronted with some
cultural irreducibles; no psychological instrument can unpackage them. Enthalpy
(i.e. a combination of heat and humidity—see Robbins, DeWalt, & Pelto, 1972)
may be such a cultural irreducible. In such cases, cross-cultural social psychology may itself be forced into the very "decentering" it has long advocated. Only
this time, it will be a disciplinary rather than a cultural decentering; we shall be
forced to develop theories which synthesize influences from geography, political
science, the arts, and so forth, rather than simply unpackaging these influences
psychologically. I believe, however, that ultimately we shall need to integrate
such multidisciplinary, "foreign" influences in developing universal theories of
human behavior.

The different measures suited to the nine varieties of ground
. . . and the fundamental laws of human nature:
these are things that must most certainly be studied.

Sun Tzu, *The art of war* (11, 14)

EXPANDING OUR NET OF CULTURES

Ground which forms the key to three contiguous states,
so that he who occupies it first has most of the empire at his command,
is ground of intersecting highways.

Sun Tzu, *The art of war* (11, 6)

Our choice of ground in cross-cultural social psychology has too often been opportunistic rather than strategic. In consequence, our theorizing has been limited and, I suspect, occasionally wrong. Our choices of where to do battle are understandable, usually following the laws of least effort and the need for tenure. However, our disciplinary environment is changing, and we can do better by being more resourceful and courageous. Let me illustrate both themes and then suggest the obvious solutions.

Resourcefulness and its theoretical consequences

> According as circumstances are favorable,
> one should modify one's plan.
>
> Sun Tzu, *The art of war* (1, 17)

Like Hofstede (1980) before him, Smith has advanced our enterprise by exploiting an emerging affordance (Gibson, 1979)—the data set of values collected by Trompenaars during his cross-cultural management training in many countries. Those countries included some from the former Soviet bloc not previously included in multicultural studies of values. Smith, Dugan, and Trompenaars (1996) ran a multidimensional scaling of the responses of managers in 43 countries to Trompenaar's value items tapping universalism—particularism, achievement—ascription, and individualism—collectivism. The first two dimensions they found were labeled utilitarian vs. loyal involvement and conservatism vs. egalitarian commitment.

These two dimensions bear a striking resemblance to Hofstede's power distance and individualism, respectively. However, Hofstede (1980) found these two dimensions to be empirically conflated in this data set, and separated them in his book only for conceptual purposes. If one covers the lower left quadrant of Fig. 7.2 containing mostly the former Communist countries, that same conflation re-appears. It is, however, disentangled when one adds these novel country samples to the array. This is an arresting demonstration, I believe, of the possibilities for construct elaboration when our set of sampled countries is enlarged.

Bond and Smith (1996) have lamented the paucity of data from South America and Africa in our cross-cultural work. Countries with a Muslim tradition are also under-represented. Research collaboration does not occur by cultural accident, of course—a similarity principle may be operating. If so, then it may well be that informants from these missing cultural traditions have much to tell the mainstream of cross-cultural psychology about our conceptual blindspots!

Already, for example, work in the formerly inaccessible People's Republic of China has suggested a sixth factor to supplement the Big Five (Cheung, Leung, & Zhang, 1996). Who knows what theoretical landfalls might lie before us in such uncharted cultures? Accessing informants from these distant settings will require considerable skill, creativity, and resourcefulness, of course. Surely,

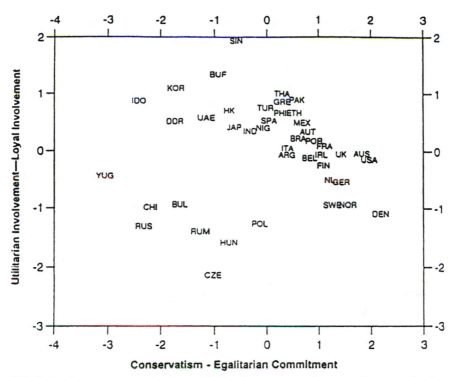

FIG. 7.2   Country scores on loyal vs. utilitarian involvement and conservatism vs. egalitarian commitment. Reproduced with permission from Smith et al. "National culture and the values of organizational employees" in *Journal of Cross-Cultural Psychology*, 27, 248, Sage Publications, 1996.
NOTE:
    ARG = Argentina; AUS = Australia; AUT = Austria; BEL = Belgium; BRA = Brazil; BUF = Burkina Faso; BUL = Bulgaria; CHI = China; CZE = Ex-Czechoslovakia; DDR = Ex-East Germany; DEN = Denmark; ETH = Ethiopia; FIN = Finland; FRA = France; GER = Ex-West Germany; GRE = Greece; HK = Hong Kong; HUN = Hungary; IDO = Indonesia; IND = India; IRL = Ireland; ITA = Italy; JAP = Japan; KOR = South Korea; MEX = Mexico; NIG = Nigeria; NL = Netherlands; NOR = Norway; PAK = Pakistan; PHI = Philippines; POL = Poland; POR = Portugal; RUM = Rumania; RUS = Ex-U.S.S.R.; SIN = Singapore; SPA = Spain; SWE = Sweden; THA = Thailand; TUR = Turkey; UAE = United Arab Emirates; UK = United Kingdom; USA = United States; YUG = Ex-Yugoslavia.

however, cross-cultural psychology is precisely the discipline to yield up such contemporary Magellans!

Courage and pattern detection

At the critical moment, the leader of an army acts like one
who has climbed up a height and then kicks away the ladder behind him.
He carries his men deep into hostile territory before he shows his hand.

Sun Tzu, *The art of war* (11, 38)

In the "flora and fauna" stage of cross-cultural psychology, we busied ourselves carving out a discipline by demonstrating differences in behavior between pairs of cultural groups. This necessary first step was initially subjected to methodological critiques by creative spirits skilled at identifying "plausible rival hypotheses" (Brislin, Lonner, & Thorndike, 1973) to account for these differences.

In time, our methodological sophistication improved. Then we were confronted with the "So what?" challenge from the mainstream. Wheeler and Reis (1988, p. 38) were "spot on" when they averred:

> So what *does* the mainstream want? It seems to us that the mainstream is not interested in studies of culture; that is, in studies that describe the peculiarities of Bahumphia and Xoma. Rather, we are interested in studies that utilize known differences between two (or more) cultures to demonstrate the impact of those known differences on social behavior. Findings derived from the former kind of research are limited: they tell me only about Bahumphia and Xoma. The latter kind of research is more broadly generalizable; it tells one about the process by which cultural practices and characteristics influence behavior.

Confronted with this "so what-ing," we pushed ourselves towards theorizing with the available data and Hofstede's (1980) dimensions of culture. The watershed in this development was, of course, Markus and Kitayama's (1991) landmark review entitled "Culture and the self: Implications for cognition, motivation, and emotion." This *tour de force* provided a theoretical structure focused on the cultural construct of collectivism and integrated much of the available cross-cultural data in these three important topic areas.

The mainstream was impressed—Markus and Kitayama's (1991) paper has become one of the most frequently cited articles in contemporary psychology. Cross-culturalists were vindicated: our trench warfare had been recognized back at headquarters and we could use the Markus and Kitayama beachhead to gain a hearing in mainstream journals. Of course, the timing was right: the diversity movement was in full swing, and intellectual appreciations of culture's influence on behavior were essential contributions to this social movement.

Were we, however, premature in our rush to print? Markus and Kitayama (1991) linked collectivism/individualism at the cultural level to self-construals at the individual level theoretically, and then used the results of many Japanese-American comparisons at the individual level to support their arguments.

As pointed out elsewhere (e.g. Bond, 1994), a two-culture comparison is not decisive in testing a cultural hypothesis; one needs multiple cultural groups in order to disentangle the influences of various possible dimensions of culture which may be responsible for the differences observed (e.g. Leung et al., 1990). The inclusion of additional cultural groups enables us to discard many plausible rival hypotheses.

Regrettably, however, such multicultural studies often refute our cherished hypotheses. A study by Watkins et al. (1995) on category usage for the self-concept as measured by the Twenty Statements Test (TST) is a case in point. Markus and Kitayama (1991) had linked socialization of an independent self-construal to the use of "abstract, situation-free self-descriptions"; an interdependent self-construal to the use of "more concrete and role-specific" self-descriptions. Using categories developed from these considerations, Watkins et al. scored the TST protocols from comparable samples in five collectivist and four individualist countries. Their courageous use of so many collectivist and individualistic cultural groups enabled Watkins et al. to put Markus and Kitayama's speculations to an unambiguous test. After analyzing the data, however, they concluded (p. 14), ". . . individual subjects from what are considered to be examples of Individualistic and Collectivist cultures do not tend to report Idiocentric, Large and Small Group, or Allocentric self-descriptions as might be expected from the theorizing of Triandis (1989) and Markus & Kitayama (1991)." This sobering conclusion by Watkins et al. should sound a tocsin to us all about premature theoretical foreclosure. How many of our cherished cultural nostrums would survive such multicultural assays, I wonder?

Of course, some multicultural studies do confirm such theorizing (Bochner, 1994); some do not (Bond & Cheung, 1983). My point is that we cannot be sure what are the operative cultural constructs, if any, until we cast a much wider cultural net. This is no easy task, however. The energy, time, patience, persistence, enthusiasm, and discipline required to orchestrate such multicultural studies are Herculean—and risky for the untenured (Gabrenya, 1988). Without the courage to show such enterprise, however, we are doomed to sew patchwork quilts into questionable patterns out of scattered bicultural contrasts (Bond, 1993).

Furthermore, given the history of cross-cultural social psychology, most of these bicultural contrasts have involved an Oriental culture in opposition to that of the United States. However, Oriental collectivism may be a distinctive type of collectivism, just as America may socialize a distinctive variant of individualism (Schwartz & Ros, 1995). Furthermore, Oriental cultures are typically high in power distance; American, low (Hofstede, 1980). We now know, however, from the work of Smith et al. (1996) that power distance and individualism can be *independent* cultural dimensions if a sufficiently broad array of cultures is sampled. So, continued reliance on bicultural Oriental-American contrasts is likely to skew and distort our conclusions seriously by confounding the operative cultural dimensions. Our discipline needs other cultural groups, especially those from Africa and South America and the Middle East, to join the banquet (Bond & Smith, 1996). It also needs cooperative, enthusiastic team players to serve up their local cuisine!

We shall be unable to turn natural advantages to account
unless we make use of local guides.

Sun Tzu, *The art of war* (11, 52)

A POSSIBLE FUTURE

The art of war is of vital importance to the state.
It is a matter of life and death. A road to either safety or ruin.
Hence it is a subject which can on no account be neglected.

Sun Tzu, The art of war (1, 1–2)

We have been indulged long enough. We have been accorded license because of the enchanting exotica we were exploring or the admiration some felt for our risk-taking and pioneering spirit. However, the time has come for cross-cultural social psychologists to repay their loans.

I have argued that the way forward requires: (1) psychologizing the concept of culture; and (2) broadening the range of cultures examined in our work. The goal of both these strategies is to develop theories of individual social behavior with greater claim to universality. These theories will become universal when we have comprehensive maps of cultural variation, when these dimensions of variation are linked to social practices, when these social practices are linked to universal psychological constructs where possible, and when these psychological constructs unpackage functionally equivalent social behaviors of individual actors.

This is a tall order, I know. Nevertheless, cross-cultural social psychologists can undertake no less. Otherwise, I believe that we are at risk of being swept away as historical curiosities, as crusty cataloguers of precious peculiarities. Our litmus test is skeptical mainstreamers, worthy opponents who will heed our clamor only if we continue creating more defensible, more comprehensive theory.

While heeding the profit of my counsel,
avail yourself of any helpful circumstances
over and beyond the ordinary rules.

Sun Tzu, The art of war (1, 16)

ACKNOWLEDG MENTS

The author wishes to express his thanks to Peter B. Smith for his helpful comments on an earlier draft and for his continuing colleagueship. Kenneth Dion improved the clarity of my presentation with his characteristic empathy and attention to detail.

REFERENCES

Berry, J. W., Segall, M. H., & Kağıtçıbaşı, C. (Eds.) (1997). *Handbook of cross-cultural psychology*: *Vol. 3. Social behavior and applications* (2nd ed.). Boston: Allyn & Bacon.

Bochner, S. (1994). Cross-cultural differences in the self concept: A test of Hofstede's individualism/collectivism distinction. *Journal of Cross-Cultural Psychology*, *25*, 273–283.

Bond, M. H. (1993). Emotions and their expression in Chinese culture. *Journal of Nonverbal Behavior*, *17*, 245–262.

Bond, M. H. (1994). Into the heart of collectivism: A personal and scientific journey. In U. Kim, H. C. Triandis, C. Kāgıtçıbaşı, S. C. Choi, & G. Yoon (Eds.), *Individualism and collectivism: Theory, method, and applications* (pp. 66–76). Thousand Oaks, CA: Sage.

Bond, M. H., & Cheung, T. S. (1983). The spontaneous self-concept of college students in Hong Kong, Japan, and the United States. *Journal of Cross-Cultural Psychology, 14,* 153–171.

Bond, M. H., & Smith, P. B. (1996). Cross-cultural social and organizational psychology. *Annual Review of Psychology, 47,* 205–235.

Brislin, R. W., Lonner, W. J., & Thorndike, R. M. (1973). *Cross-cultural research methods.* New York: Wiley.

Cheung, F. M. C., Leung, K., & Zhang, J. X. (1996). *A joint factor analysis of personality facets from the NEO PI-R and the Chinese Personality Assessment Inventory (CPAI): A six factor model?* Manuscript in preparation, Chinese University of Hong Kong.

Chinese Culture Connection. (1987). Chinese values and the search for culture-free dimensions of culture. *Journal of Cross-Cultural Psychology, 18,* 143–164.

Clark, L. A. (1987). Mutual relevance of mainstream and cross-cultural psychology. *Journal of Consulting and Clinical Psychology, 55,* 461–470.

Costa, P. T., Jr., & McCrae, R. R. (1992). *Revised NEO Personality Inventory (NEO-PI-R) and NEO Five-Factor Inventory (NEO-FFI) Professional Manual.* Odessa, FL: Psychological Assessment Resources.

Diener, E., & Diener, M. (1995). Cross-cultural correlates of life satisfaction and self-esteem. *Journal of Personality and Social Psychology, 68,* 653–663.

Dion, K. K., & Dion, K. L. (1996). Cultural perspectives on romantic love. *Personal Relationships, 3,* 5–17.

Featherman, D. L. (1993). What does society need from higher education? *Items, 47* (2/3), 38–43.

Gabrenya, W. K., Jr. (1988). Social science and social psychology: The cross-cultural link. In M. H. Bond (Ed.), *The cross-cultural challenge to social psychology* (pp. 48–66). Thousand Oaks, CA: Sage.

Gibson, J. J. (1979). *The ecological approach to visual perception.* Boston: Houghton Mifflin.

Gudykunst, W. B., Matsumoto, Y., Ting-Toomey, S., Nishida, T., & Karimi, H. (1994, June). *Measuring self-construals across cultures: A derived-etic analysis.* Paper presented at the International Communication Association, Sydney, Australia.

Hofstede, G. (1980). *Culture's consequences: International differences in work-related values.* Thousand Oaks, CA: Sage.

Hofstede, G., Bond, M. H., & Luk, C. L. (1993). Individual perceptions of organizational cultures: A methodological treatise on levels of analysis. *Organization Studies, 14,* 483–583.

Leung, K., & Bond, M. H. (1984). The impact of cultural collectivism on reward allocation. *Journal of Personality and Social Psychology, 47,* 793–804.

Leung, K., & Bond, M. H. (1993). *Invitation to participate in a multicultural study of social axioms.* Unpublished manuscript.

Leung, K., Bond, M. H., Carment, D. W., Krishnan, L., & Liebrand, W. B. C. (1990). Effects of cultural femininity on preference for methods of conflict resolution: A cross-cultural study. *Journal of Experimental Social Psychology, 26,* 373–388.

Levine, R., & Norenzayan, A. (1996). *The pace of life in 31 countries.* Manuscript submitted for publication. California State University, Fresno.

Malpass, R. S. (1988). Why not cross-cultural psychology? A characterization of some mainstream views. In M. H. Bond (Ed.), *The cross-cultural challenge to social psychology* (pp. 29–35). Thousand Oaks, CA: Sage.

Markus, H., & Kitayama, S. (1991). Culture and the self: Implications for cognition, motivation, and emotion. *Psychological Review, 98,* 224–253.

McCrae, R. R., & Costa, P. T., Jr. (1997). Personality trait structure as a human universal. *American Psychologist, 52,* 509–516.

Messick, D. M. (1988). On the limitations of cross-cultural research in social psychology. In M. H. Bond (Ed.), *The cross-cultural challenge to social psychology* (pp. 41–47). Thousand Oaks, CA: Sage.

Miller, J. G. (1984). Culture and the development of everyday social explanation. *Journal of Personality and Social Psychology, 46,* 961–978.

Moghaddam, F. M., Taylor, D. M., & Wright, S. C. (1993). *Social psychology in cross-cultural perspective.* New York: Freeman.

Robbins, M. C., DeWalt, B. R., & Pelto, P. J. (1972). Climate and behavior: A bicultural study. *Journal of Cross-Cultural Psychology, 3,* 331–344.

Schachter, S., Nuttin, J., De Monchaux, C., Maucorps, P. H., Osmer, D., Duijker, H., Rommetveit, R., & Isreal, J. (1954). Cross-cultural experiments on threats and rejection. *Human Relations, 7,* 403–439.

Schwartz, S. H. (1992). Universals in the content and structure of values: Theoretical advances and empirical tests in 20 countries. In M. P. Zanna (Ed.), *Advances in experimental social psychology* (Vol. 25, pp. 1–65). Orlando, FL: Academic.

Schwartz, S. H. (1994). Beyond individualism/collectivism: New cultural dimensions of values. In U. Kim, H. C. Triandis, C. Kağıtçıbaşı, S. C. Choi, & G. Yoon (Eds.), *Individualism and collectivism: Theory, method, and applications* (pp. 85–119). Thousand Oaks, CA: Sage.

Schwartz, S. H., & Ros, M. (1995). Values in the West: A theoretical and empirical challenge to the individualism–collectivism cultural dimension. *World Psychology, 1,* 1–22.

Shweder, R. A. (1973). The between and within of cross-cultural research. *Ethos, 1,* 521–545.

Singelis, T. M., Triandis, H. C., Bhawuk, D. S., & Gelfand, M. J. (1995). Horizontal and vertical dimensions of individualism and collectivism: A theoretical and measurement refinement. *Cross-Cultural Research, 29,* 240–275.

Smith, P. B., & Bond, M. H. (1993). *Social psychology across cultures: Analysis and perspectives.* Hemel Hempstead, UK: Harvester Wheatsheaf.

Smith, P. B., Dugan, S., & Trompenaars, F. (1996). National culture and the values of organizational employees. *Journal of Cross-Cultural Psychology, 27,* 231–264.

Smith, P. B., & Peterson, M. F. (1995, August). *Beyond value comparisons: Sources used to give meaning to management work events in thirty countries. International comparisons of work meanings and values.* Paper presented at a symposium conducted at the Academy of Management annual meeting, Vancouver, BC, Canada.

Sun, T. (1981). *The art of war* (L. Giles, Trans.). London: Hodder & Stoughton. (Original work published in English 1910).

Triandis, H. C. (1978). Some universals of social behavior. *Personality and Social Psychology Bulletin, 4,* 1–16.

Triandis, H. C. (1988). Cross-cultural contributions to theory in social psychology. In M. H. Bond (Ed.), *The cross-cultural challenge to social psychology* (pp. 122–140). Thousand Oaks, CA: Sage.

Triandis, H. C. (1989). Self and social behavior in differing cultural contexts. *Psychological Review, 96,* 269–289.

Triandis, H. C. (1994). *Culture and social behavior.* New York: McGraw-Hill.

Watkins, D., Adair, J., Akande, A., Gerong, A., McInerney, D., Sunar, D., Watson, S., Wen, Q. F., & Wondimu, H. (1995). *Individualism–collectivism, gender, and the self-concept: A nine-country study.* Manuscript submitted for publication, University of Hong Kong.

Wheeler, L., & Reis, H. (1988). On titles, citations, and outlets: What do mainstreamers want? In M. H. Bond (Ed.), *The cross-cultural challenge to social psychology* (pp. 36–40). Thousand Oaks, CA: Sage.

Whiting, B. B. (1976). The problem of the packaged variable. In K. F. Riegel & J. A. Meacham (Eds.), *The developing individual in a changing world* (pp. 303–309). The Hague: Mouton.

Wierzbicka, A. (1993). A conceptual basis for cultural psychology. *Ethos, 21,* 205–231.

CHAPTER EIGHT

An evolutionary-based model integrating research on the characteristics of sexually coercive men

Neil M. Malamuth
Communication Studies and Psychology, University of California, Los Angeles, USA

In ancestral environments in which the human mind evolved, males could achieve reproductive success by engaging in strategies that involved "converging" or "diverging" interests with those of females. Psychological mechanisms evolved designed to increase effectiveness in each of these types of strategy, with early life experiences calibrating relevant mechanisms to prepare the individual for later interactions. Using this conceptual framework, a model of the characteristics of men who use sexually coercive tactics is presented. It integrates many seemingly independent correlates of sexual aggressors within three major constellations of characteristics: (1) a general personality orientation to assert one's own interests at the expense of others; (2) a short-term mating orientation likely to create a conflict of interests with females; and (3) a constellation of emotions and attitudes priming coercive tactics for dealing with strategic interference or conflict. While each of these three constellations makes a unique contribution to the likelihood that a man will use sexual coercion, it is argued that their confluence is particularly likely to characterize sexual aggressors. A series of interrelated hypotheses derived from this model is described and supporting data are presented.

Dans les environnements ancestraux dans lesquels l'esprit humain a évolué, les mâles pouvaient atteindre le succès reproductif en adoptant des stratégies qui comportaient des intérêts "convergents" ou "divergents" par rapport à ceux des femelles. Des mécanismes psychologiques se développèrent afin d'accroître l'efficacité de chacun de ces types de stratégies, alors que les premières expériences de la vie servaient à étalonner des mécanismes pertinents préparant l'individu à des interactions futures. A partir de ce cadre conceptuel, l'auteur présente un modèle des caractéristiques des hommes qui utilisent des tactiques sexuellement coercitives. Il intègre plusieurs corrélats apparemment indépendants d'aggresseurs sexuels dans trois constellations majeures de caractéristiques: (1) une orientation générale de la personnalité vers la revendication de ses propres intérêts aux dépens des autres; (2) une orientation de l'accouplement à court-terme susceptible de créer un conflit d'intérêts avec les femelles; et (3) une constellation d'émotions et d'attitudes amorçant des tactiques coercitives pour se charger des interférences stratégiques ou des conflits. Bien que chacune de ces trois constellations apporte une contribution unique à la probabilité qu'un homme ait recours à la coercition sexuelle, l'auteur soutient que leur confluence est particulièrement apte à caractériser les aggresseurs sexuels. Il élabore une série d'hypothèses intimement reliées qui sont dérivées de ce modèle et présente des données à leur appui.

INTRODUCTION

The causes and consequences of violence against women are topics of international concern. Some studies indicate that about 25% of women have experienced an attempted or completed rape (Koss, Gidycz, & Wisniewski, 1987; Russell, 1984). Research with cohabiting and married couples suggests that about 20% of all women will experience physical violence at the hands of their male partner (Hotaling & Sugarman, 1986; Straus & Gelles, 1986). There are also indications that battered women may be particularly likely to be victims of marital rape (e.g. Hanneke, Shields, & McCall, 1986).

Research has documented the occurrence of serious long-term consequences of aggression against women. Studies indicate similar effects on victims of both stranger and acquaintance rape (Koss, Dinero, Seibel, & Cox, 1988). Physical abuse among co-habitants is known to have serious consequences not only for the participants and their children but it appears to be an important factor in the transmission of violence from one generation to the next (Straus, 1987).

It is essential to understand the etiology of these behaviors and to develop strategies to predict and prevent them. Research suggests that the characteristics of male perpetrators of aggression against women provide an important basis for understanding such aggression (e.g. Hotaling & Sugarman, 1986; Markman, Floyd, Stanley, & Storaasli, 1988). While the primary focus of this chapter is on the characteristics of men from the general population who commit sexual aggression[1] against women, the theory and data are also relevant to understanding the causes of other forms of male aggression against women (e.g. Malamuth, Sackloskie, Koss, & Tanaka, 1991).

Much of the research in this area has consisted of independent lines of investigation focusing on a correlate or small group of correlates of sexual aggression. The factor(s) chosen by investigators has reflected their disciplinary and theoretical orientation. Criminologists often focused on variables contributing to various kinds of antisocial behavior, viewing sexual coercion as just one of

---

[1] For the purposes of this article I interchangeably use terms such as *sexual aggression*, *sexually coercive tactics* and *coercive sex* to refer to non-consensual sex. The term *rape* similarly refers to non-consensual intercourse. Although I recognize that finer distinctions can be made among such terms, these are not particularly relevant to the focus here.

many manifestations of delinquent acts. The variables studied within this frame-work included abusive home environments and delinquent adolescence (Ageton, 1983). Feminists and cultural anthropologists primarily focused on factors such as dominance motives (Sanday, 1981a; 1981b), attitudes condoning violence (Burt, 1980) and hostility towards women (Check, Malamuth, Elias, & Barton, 1985). Sociologists considered the role of sexual experiences, norms and expec-tations (Kanin, 1985). Psychiatrists and clinical psychologists focused on sexual arousal in response to aggression (Abel, Barlow, Blanchard, & Guild, 1977) and fantasy patterns (Greendlinger & Byrne, 1987). Personality psychologists identified the role of general personality traits (Rapaport & Burkhart, 1984), including lack of empathy or sympathy for others (Hanson, 1997; Gold, Fultz, Burke, Prisco, & Willett, 1992). Each of the groups of investigators from these diverse traditions found support for the particular characteristics they focusd on as correlates of sexual aggression. Although these studies have been valuable in identifying correlates of sexually aggressive behavior, these findings need to be integrated within a unified framework. The present chapter attempts such an integration within a unified theoretical and empirical model.

AN EVOLUTIONARY-BASED MODEL

The evolutionary framework

Overview.   Evolutionary psychology applies knowledge of evolutionary pro-cesses to understanding the human mind and behavior (Buss, 1995; Tooby & Cosmides, 1990). The psychological mechanisms that constitute the human mind were designed in response to the recurrent adaptive problems faced by our ancestors over many generations, with the "bottom line" for selection being reproductive success (Dawkins, 1986). To understand emotions, thoughts and behaviors in contemporary environments, therefore, it is essential to analyze the *function* of the psychological mechanisms that evolved in ancestral environ-ments. The mechanisms and the type of environmental input they can process are not two separable causal processes, but elements of the same evolved pack-age (Tooby & Cosmides, 1990). The function of psychological mechanisms cannot be understood solely in terms of current environments which in mod-ern technological societies are radically different in many respects from the types of environment that were a relatively stable feature during most of human evolutionary development. Although evolutionary processes continue, of course, in current environments, the processes of natural selection typically take many generations to significantly change features of the human mind. Therefore, evo-lutionary psychology contends that it is important to contextualize the develop-ment of the mind within ancestral environments because the mind's mechanisms developed to their present form in those environments and have undergone only minor changes since then (Cosmides & Tooby, 1987).

Psychological mechanisms which are adaptations were naturally selected in the evolutionary history of our species. Human responses may be the result either of adaptations, by-products of adaptations or "noise" (e.g. mutations, genetic drift, etc.). Just because a behavior was adaptive in evolutionary environments in the sense that it contributed to reproductive success does not mean that such a behavior contributes to reproductive success in current environments nor that it is desirable, moral or inevitable. One of the fallacies about this approach is that it suggests that humans are "hard-wired" or do not make choices. On the contrary, evolutionary approaches focus on the interaction between organisms and their environments and under what conditions organisms change their behavior in different environments (Crawford & Anderson, 1989).

There are two interrelated aspects of evolutionary psychology's conceptualization of behavior that are particularly relevant to the model presented later of the characteristics of sexual aggressors. The first pertains to variability in human behavior and the second to gender differences.

Variability in human behavior.   Some critics erroneously assume that evolutionary approaches do not allow for variability. It is correct that evolutionary psychologists have generally assumed that selective pressures are essentially the same for all humans in most domains where problem-solving adaptations occurred (e.g. how to regulate heat, how to detect cheaters, etc.). These mechanisms are therefore considered human universals (i.e. species-typical; Tooby and Cosmides, 1990). Although the mechanisms are fundamentally the same, there are variations in degrees and their calibration levels (e.g. all humans have anger-producing mechanisms, but these differ in threshold for elicitation and range of expression). These differences can result from genetic variability within the species as well as environmental differences, both developmentally and contemporarily.

There is often confusion in equating evolutionary psychology with some form of genetic determinism. Although genes obviously play a role in enabling and limiting the range of all human behaviors, the algorithms underlying human development in different domains differ in the extent to which they are open to influence by enviromental conditions. A *facultative developmental algorithm* is a relatively open mental program that directs development via interaction with particular features of the environment whereas an *obligative developmental algorithm* is a mental program that is minimally affected by variations in environmental conditions (Alcock, 1984). The degree of genetic contribution to individual differences in various domains is a function of the extent to which the mental programs are facultative or obligative.

Facultative developmental programs may also differ in the extent to which certain environmental influences, particularly during critical periods, may "fix" mechanisms at certain levels as compared to those that remain more flexible to changes throughout the lifespan. The evolutionary paradigm provides insights into the reasons that varied mechanisms have differing periods of neurological plasticity and degrees of flexibility in response to environmental input (e.g. Gazzaniga. 1992). Additionally, it is noteworthy that inherited and developmental–experiential differences may systematically affect how people select their environments (Loehlin, 1992). For example, children of differing physical size or strength may be differentially reinforced for choosing differing strategies for dealing with conflict (e.g. compromise or aggression). These early experiences may help shape life-long patterns.

Gender differences.   Evolutionary metatheory provides a framework for predicting when gender differences are or are not expected, the direction of the differences, and why these differences are predicted—a set of testable predictions typically not made in advance by other gender differences theories (Buss, 1995). Males and females are expected to have the same psychological mechanisms in those domains where natural selection has favored the same solutions to adaptive problems for all humans regardless of their gender. Correspondingly, in some domains the problems faced in evolutionary history by males have not been identical to those faced by females. In this case, mechanisms are expected to have evolved differently, because the identical solution for the different genders would not have been optimal for dissimilar problems.

One cannot consider either gender's mechanisms superior or inferior to the other (Buss, 1995). Rather they form a co-evolved strategy, each representing the *evolutionary-based interests* (i.e. costs vs. benefits affecting reproductive success) of those engaging in such strategies, which sometimes complement and sometimes compete with others' strategies of the same or of the opposite gender (i.e. *convergent or divergent interests*). Although considerable individual differences would be expected in some aspects of female versus male sexual strategies, they should be considered gender-linked differences (such as height), rather than gender-absolute (such as the ability to give birth). These gender-linked differences may be best described as differences in threshold levels (Money, 1986).

The study of aggression within an evolutionary framework

Before turning to specifically focus on the topic of sexual aggression, it is important to briefly consider an evolutionary-based perspective on aggression generally (Daly & Wilson, 1987; 1994). Other models have often conceptualized aggression as a form of pathology because of the terrible harm and suffering that it can cause. From an evolutionary perspective, pathological behavior involves the failure of a set of mechanisms to function in the way they were designed by evolutionary forces, owing to such factors as decay or subversion by competitive forms of life (e.g. viruses). Although some aggressive acts may result from such pathology, aggressive behavior generally does not reveal such characteristics or those that might be associated with other possibilities, such as by-products of other adaptations. Instead, aggression shows characteristics of functional design revealing an evolved adaptation which resulted in fitness-promoting consequences for the aggressing individuals, at least in some recurring ancestral environments (see Daly & Wilson, 1994, p. 269):

> The relationship-specificity of human violence bespeaks its functionality: circumstances eliciting it are threats to fitness, and the targets of violence are generally not merely those available but those with whom assailants have substantive conflict . . . and hence have something to gain by subduing them. Threats to fitness as a result of others' actions depend not only on the nature of the threats but also on the relationship and the reproductive value of the parties, and on the alternative avenues to fitness of each. The utility of using violence to protect, defend or promote fitness in past environments can be discerned by an analysis of the complex functionality of morphology and psychology.

It is worth emphasizing that, although the capacity to aggress may reflect the workings of adaptive mechanisms, this does not imply that aggressive behavior is justified or inevitable. The recognition of such a capacity is no more "biological pessimism" than the recognition that the mechanisms underlying the capacity for empathy, attachment and cooperation are "biological optimism". Such recognition in no way minimizes the importance given to factors such as culture, individual experience, and situational variables in the development, nurturance and activation of such mechanisms. The existence of evolved mechanisms potentiating such behaviors may be a necessary condition for their occurrence under some conditions, but they are clearly not a sufficient condition. As Lore and Schultz (1993, p. 16) note, "Even in so-called violence-prone animals, aggression is always an optional strategy . . . All organisms have coevolved equally potent inhibitory mechanisms that enable them to use an aggressive strategy selectively or to suppress aggression when it is in their interest to do so".

An evolutionary-based model of the characteristics of sexual aggressors

The frequency of sexual coercion.   An issue relevant to an evolutionary-based model of sexual coercion is its frequency in human history. As Wrangham & Peterson (1996, p. 138) note, "evolutionary theory suggests that any behavior occurring regularly or consistently has a logic embedded in the dynamics of natural selection for reproductive success". Various data suggest that sexual coercion has not been rare in human evolutionary history and that there continues to be some propensity to rape in the psychology of many men. First, it appears that male abduction of females from neighboring groups was quite common in our species' evolutionary history (Chagnon, 1994). Such acts were probably accompanied by sexual coercion. Second, there are several sources of data (see Brownmiller, 1970; Stiglmayer, 1994) suggesting that when fear of punishment is reduced, many men do rape and this is particularly evident in times of war. Noteworthy examples include the 1937 case where Japanese men raped 20,000 women in a single month in the city of Nanking (Friedmann, 1972); the rape of hundreds of thousands of German women, including victims of Nazi concentration camps, by the Allied troops during the 1945 liberation of Berlin (Stiglmayer, 1994); and the recent rapes in Bosnia-Herzegovina and Croatia (Allen, 1996). Further, cross-cultural surveys reveal that male attack and rape of women occurs with considerable frequency in most societies today (Broude & Greene, 1978; Levinson, 1989; Sanday, 1981b). Moreover, it is interesting to note that even relatively rape-free societies described in such surveys (e.g. Sanday, 1981b) have various mixes of high internal and external mechanisms counteracting male tendencies for sexual aggression, suggesting that there may be a universal "risk" for such behavior. In addition, research indicates that approximately one-third of the male population says that they would coerce a woman into sexual acts if they could be assured that they would not suffer any negative consequences and that they would find such acts sexually arousing whereas a much smaller percentage of women indicate such a potential (e.g. Malamuth, 1981; 1989a; 1989b; Young & Thiessen, 1991). Related to these data are findings that fantasies involving the use of sexal coercion are quite common among men (Greendlinger & Byrne, 1987), and that such fantasies and other forms of imagined sexual aggression are associated with risk factors predictive of actual sexual aggression (Dean & Malamuth, 1997; Malamuth, 1981; 1988a; Seto & Kuban, 1996). Imagined aggression may reveal important information regarding evolved mechanisms of the mind (Ellis & Symons, 1989; Kenrick & Sheets, 1993). Finally, although great caution must be exercised in generalizing from one species to another, it may be instructive to consider the data for other primates. Although clearly not universal in primates, Smuts (1992) concludes that male use of aggression toward females in a sexual context is common in primates, particularly in some of our closest relatives (e.g. chimpanzees and orangutans).[2]

---

[2] The characteristics of male orangutans more likely to use sexual coercion provides an example in another species of how studying the characteristics of sexual aggressors can provide insight into motivations for such behavior. Wrangham and Peterson (1996) describe two distinct classes of orangutan males, large compared to small ones. Rape of females in this species is common (accounting for about one-third to one-half of all copulations), but it is virtually exclusively perpetrated by the small males. Wrangham and Peterson propose that size is a critical feature here because small size results in a relative failure to succeed in mutually consensual sex but is an advantage in using sexually coercive tactics. Specifically, in this species females do not appear to be attracted to the small males who therefore have little opportunity to mate based on mutual attraction with females. However, their size gives these small males a distinct advantage in implementing coercive sex. Females can easily escape from the large males, if they choose, because, the big males can't move quickly in the rainforest trees. But the small males, about the same size as the females, can travel as fast as them, and are, therefore, much more successful than the large males in catching the females and using coercive sex.

As noted earlier, it appears that sexual coercion has not been a rare act, particularly if used in a strategic way that takes potential punishment and other contingencies into consideration. The capacity to engage in such acts under some circumstances may have contributed to male reproductive success with sufficient frequency to have played a role in natural selection for certain characteristics associated with such acts. Granted, there may be some important differences among the characteristics that lead to such coercive behavior in varied situations (e.g. dating relations, in non-acquaintance rape, in times of war, etc.). Unfortunately, comparisons between the characteristics of rapists during war and peacetime conditions are not available. However, comparisons of the characteristics of men who imagine aggressing, commit sexual aggression in dating relations and convicted rapists (who typically coerce non-acquaintances) reveal considerable similarities (Dean & Malamuth, 1997; Malamuth, 1981; 1988a).

The mate deprivation model.   As Quinsey & Lalumiere (1995) note, evolutionary approaches to sexual offending may be conceptualized in terms of either (1) psychological mechanisms contributing to reproductive success in ancestral environments; or (2) pathology caused by psychological mechanisms gone awry. In keeping with the evolutionary approach to aggression already summarized, the models of the characteristics of sexual aggressors that have appeared in the literature have typically used the first of these conceptualizations. Perhaps the most well known is the mate deprivation model (Thornhill & Thornhill, 1983; 1992). This model essentially argues that all males have the potential to use sexual coercion. Experiencing lack of success in competition for the resources and status necessary to attract desirable mates activates this potential by triggering, via specialized psychological mechanisms for such behavior, the use of sexually coercive tactics. This mate deprivation model is similar in some respects to clinical theories describing rapists as lacking in the heterosocial and intimacy skills necessary to form successful relationships (e.g. Marshall, Hudson, & Hodkinson, 1993; Stermac & Quinsey, 1986).

There have been some data offered in support of the mate deprivation model. In particular, it has been reported that arrested rapists generally come from lower social strata (Thornhill & Thornhill, 1983) and that some rapists lack relationship skills (Marshall et al., 1993). However, there also have been considerable data inconsistent with this model, particularly in studies focusing on non-incarcerated sexual aggressors. For example, sexually coercive men often report having more sexual partners than their non-coercive counterparts (Kanin, 1985; Malamuth et al., 1991). In a particularly direct test of the mate deprivation model, Lalumiere, Chalmers, Quinsey, and Seto (1996) found considerable contradictory data: sexual aggressors had higher self-perceived mating success, significantly more extensive sexual histories, and did not report lower relative earning potential.

The confluence model. From the perspective of evolutionary psychology, conflict between individuals is related to the degree to which their reproductive interests are at odds (e.g. Alexander, 1979; Hamilton, 1964) and male aggression against females often reflects male reproductive striving (Smuts, 1992). Using this framework, the confluence model described here suggest that the use of sexually coercive tactics can be understood within the larger context of reproductive strategies and varied tactics used to implement those strategies.[3] The mating of two individuals may involve convergence of their reproductive interests (e.g. mating with each other and raising common offspring reflects their best reproductive alternative) or in situations where their mating may reflect a divergence of interests (e.g. such mating may represent a net reproductive gain for one person but a reproductive loss for the other; Crawford & Galdikas, 1986).

Psychological mechanisms are presumed to have evolved that are relevant to the implementation of divergent vs. convergent interests strategies. These mechanisms are presumed to be species-wide characteristics that for varied individuals become calibrated at different levels or thresholds as a function of such factors as genetic differences and environmental experiences. Here I shall focus only on environmental factors as setting the threshold or calibrating these mechanisms. Calibration of psychological mechanisms for success using a convergent interests strategy creates more effective evaluation of the needs of others. This enables a better fit for the convergence of interests and for increasing what Buss (1996) has labeled "strategic facilitation." For example, emotions such as sympathy function to enhance processing of the other's feelings and difficulties, which can serve to inform and better respond to the other's interests.[4] In contrast, calibration of psychological mechanisms for a relatively divergent interests strategy mobilizes or energizes behaviors that reduce strategic interference by others so as to override or circumvent such interference (Buss, 1989). For example, anger can "energize" aggressive behavior and can communicate threat in a way that may reduce victim resistance. Similarly, sexual arousal to force can provide a pleasurable cue associated with the imposition of one's own will

---

[3] The importance of male sexual coercion as a means of limiting female choice and thereby her "reproductive success" has been emphasized by evolutionary theorists Barbara Smuts (1992) and by Sarah Blaffer Hrdy (1997). In this view, sexual coercion should be considered in Darwinian theory as one of the three major processes of "sexual selection" (with equal importance as male–male competition and female choice). Hypotheses regarding the possibility that coercive sex is related to reproductive success include those suggesting direct reproductive benefits for some males (e.g. Thornhill & Thornhill, 1992) and indirect reproductive benefits by increasing the general ability of a male to dominate a female (Smuts & Smuts, 1993).

[4] Buss (1988) found that both men and women rated a man's "showing sympathy to a female's troubles" as one of the ten most effective mating tactics. Also, while it may be useful to distinguish between such concepts as sympathy and empathy (Wispe, 1986), I consider them here as interrelated constructs that involve both heightened awareness and feeling for another's plight.

at the expense of the other's. At least in some aspects, calibration of the psychological mechanisms to effectively implement one of these two strategies may be in opposition to the effective implementation of the other (e.g. greater feelings of sympathy for another person may subvert ignoring their interests).[5]

At its current stage of development, the confluence model suggests that there are *three constellations of characteristics* that when calibrated in particular directions create divergent interests conditions likely to result in the use of sexually coercive tactics. These three constellations are encompassed within a hierarchical approach that includes both general personality characteristics relevant to divergent and convergent strategies as well as more specific characteristics directly relevant to sexual coercion:

1. A reproductive interests perspective suggests that there may be some general personality characteristics reflecting the extent to which a person solves adaptive problems by focusing exclusively on his own interests as contrasted with incorporating the interests of others. For this purpose, we have relied on what are considered by many theorists as the two most basic or pure dimensions of personality (Wiggins & Trapnell, 1996). They have been referred to by various names: surgency and agreeableness; agency and communion; and dominance and nurturance. Wiggins (1991, p. 89) defined the first dimension as a concern for "mastery and power which enhance and protect (the self)", and the second as a concern for "intimacy, union and solidarity with (other people)".

The first constellation of characteristics included in this confluence model uses these two personality dimensions of dominance vs. nurturance to reflect

---

[5] In the development of species over the evolutionary landscape, mechanisms promoting divergent interests' behavior (e.g. aggression elicited by competitive struggle over a resource) evolved millions of years earlier from those promoting convergent behavior (e.g. sharing a resource elicited by love; Eibl-Eibesfeldt, 1971, 1990). As Lorenz (1966, p. 217) notes, "intra-specific aggression can certainly exist without its counterpart, love, but conversely there is no love without aggression". Parental care that evolved in certain fishes, birds and mammals is viewed by these ethologists as the major source of the development of bonding mechanisms which inhibit aggression against offspring and foster their nurturance. A second source of long-term bonding mechanisms in humans and a few other primates that evolved to reinforce the parental bond is borrowed from the sexual repertoire for appeasement (Eibl-Eibesfeldt, 1971). These bonding mechanisms can therefore be particularly useful in inhibiting aggression against long-term sexual mates and facilitating cooperation among them in the nurturant rearing of their young. These mechanisms later generalized, at least to some degree, to encompass individuals other than one's offspring or mates. Data supporting the inverse relationship between mechanisms associated with aggressiveness and parental care are illustrated by the findings of Wingield, Hegner, Dufty, and Ball (1990). These investigators concluded that among males of socially monogamous species, there are only temporary surges (a few minutes to hours) of circulating testosterone. These surges are designed to meet antagonistic challenges but a major cost of high levels of this hormone was an interruption of male ability in parental care. In contrast, they found that males of socially polygynous species tend not to engage in parental care but maintain high levels of circulating testosterone for long periods (days to weeks).

the degree to which a person is oriented to assert his own interests at the expense of others. It is reasoned that if a person's mechanisms are calibrated in a way that his dominance characteristics are relatively high compared with his nurturance characteristics, his general personality mechanisms are more aligned with a divergent interests strategy and he is more at risk for using sexually aggressive tactics. As elaborated on later, we believe that this constellation may be particularly relevant to whether aggressive potential is actually carried out in behavior or remains at the level of imagined aggression.

To reiterate: the first of the three constellations of characteristics included in the confluence model is a general personality assessment of the calibration of a man's mechanisms along the *dominance vs. nurturance* dimensions. Although this constellation is a relatively recent addition to our model (for an earlier version see Malamuth, 1996; Malamuth & Heilmann, in press), it is presented first because conceptually it is considered as a relatively general framework for understanding the workings of the more specific mechanisms.

2. While this general personality constellation is viewed as having some relevance to the likelihood that a man uses sexually coercive tactics, the next two constellations are seen as having even more direct bearing. One is what has been referred to in the literature as mating strategies (Buss & Schmitt, 1993) and sociosexuality (Gangestad & Simpson, 1990; Simpson & Gangestad, 1991), which we have referred to in the context of the development of the confluence model as *impersonal vs. personal sexuality* (e.g. Malamuth et al., 1991).

    As various evolutionary writers have noted and as described in greater detail below, a man who is oriented to a short-term sexual strategy as compared to a long-term strategy would be more likely to be in conflict with a woman's reproductive interests. In adopting a long-term mating strategy, a male is more likely to take into consideration the intersection of the male and female fitness interests and find ways of compromising with each other's interests. Here both individuals are given the opportunity to evaluate and choose each other as mates (Hirsch & Paul , 1996). In contrast, male attempts to pursue a short-term mating strategy are likely to contribute to a situation of divergent interests. Therefore, the calibration of mating mechanisms in the direction favoring a short-term mating strategy is the second constellation increasing risk for sexual aggression.

3. The calibration of a third constellation of characteristics is also important as to whether sexually coercive tactics are likely to be used. We describe this as an associative network of emotions (e.g. hostility toward women) and attitudes (e.g. acceptance of the appropriateness of aggression against women) and motor tendencies (e.g. impulsivity) that directly "mobilize" or prime the use of coercive tactics for dealing with strategic interference or conflict. When calibrated in the direction of increasing the likelihood of such coercion, this

network has been labeled as *hostile masculinity*. It contains two interrelated components: (1) an insecure, defensive, hypersensitive and hostile orientation, particularly toward women; and (2) gratification from controlling or dominating women (Malamuth, Heavey, & Linz, 1993).[6]

Antecedents of mechanisms calibration.   The next question that is important to consider is how do these three constellations of mechanisms become calibrated at various levels? The approach taken here is in keeping with a common evolutionary analysis that humans share the same basic underlying mechanisms or a common evolved psychology. As suggested by various theorists (Belsky, Steinberg, & Draper, 1991; Draper & Harpending, 1982; Trivers, 1972), part of this evolved psychology is an adaptation to permit the individual to "identify" the relevant aspects of the environment early on and choose the strategy most suited to his attributes and the local conditions. Particularly relevant to the constellations of characteristics described here may be the "harshness" or "exploitativeness" of early social environments in the home and among peers that may calibrate the relevant mechanisms to anticipate and deal with relatively more exploitative or cooperative interactions, particularly with women. Identifying early on whether one is likely to succeed in using the tactics associated with convergent or divergent strategies and calibrating mechanisms accordingly would make particular sense if the calibration most suited for the mechanisms associated with one of these strategies generally undermine effectiveness with the other one.

These early experiences may "lock" a person into one reproductive strategy to the exclusion of others that could have developed if environmental inputs had been different. More specific to the current analysis, it is suggested that in harsh early environments in which exploitation occurs frequently, mechanisms may be calibrated in line with divergent strategies, including a general self-centered personality, a short-term mating strategy, and hostile masculinity. However, there may be different elements of those environments that provide the particularly relevant information to specific constellations of mechanisms. For example, perceived strategic interference from women, such as a history of rejection, may be particularly likely to affect the calibration of the hostile masculinity characteristics. A more specific analysis of the particular features of early environments relevant to each of the three constellations of characteristics should be undertaken in future research.

Figure 8.1 provides a visual display of some of the ideas just described. It suggests that in differing ecological conditions natural selection may affect the frequency of certain genetic characteristics and cultural norms. These interact

---

[6] An evolutionary model of rapists that also focuses on the role of three somewhat similar dimensions has been presented by Ellis (1989). There are, however, many central differences between the present model and Ellis' conceptualization of these dimensions.

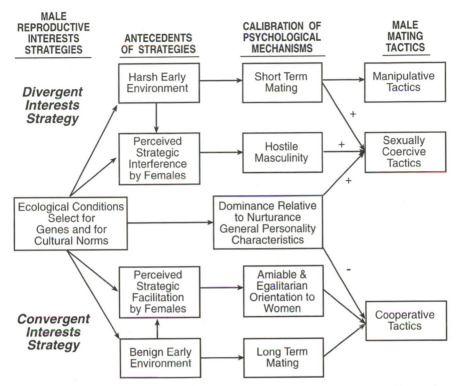

FIG. 8.1 Hypothesized confluence model of the characteristics of men who use sexually coercive tactics shown within the framework of divergent vs. convergent interests strategies. *Plus signs* indicate the paths of the three major constellations of characteristics hypothesized to synergistically contribute to sexual coercion, whereas the *minus sign* indicates hypothesized reverse association with the use of cooperative tactics.

with the environmental effects on the calibration of characteristics relevant to the use of sexually coercive tactics. At the center of the figure, the relevance of the general personality constellation of dominant relative to nurturant personality characteristics is shown: Relatively high dominance and low nurturance contributing to sexual coercive tactics and having the opposite effect on cooperative tactics. This figure also displays (at the top vs. bottom parts) the opposite patterns of mechanism calibration shunting men into relatively divergent or convergent interests strategies with women. Although not all of the hypothesized connections are shown here, the major ones are indicated by arrows. Plus signs at the right side of the graph leading into sexually coercive tactics show the confluence or synergistic impact of the three major constellations. On the bottom of the figure, the calibration in the direction of a convergent interests strategy—high nurturant personality, long-term mating, and an amiable and egalitarian orientation to women—is expected to increase the use of cooperative tactics, such as open and honest communication, allowing ample opportunity for mutual evaluation and choice before sexual intimacy, etc. (see Hirsch & Paul, 1996 for further examples). Finally, at the very top of the graph it is suggested that a short-term mating orientation alone may increase the use of manipulative tactics.

RESEARCH ON SEXUAL AGGRESSORS' CHARACTERISTICS

Testing interrelated hypotheses about sexual aggressors

Several interrelated hypotheses are subsequently described which focus on particular elements of the confluence model just presented and summarized in Fig. 8.1. These are not intended as a full list of the testable hypotheses that can be derived from the ideas presented but as an analysis of the major components of the model presented and amplification on some of the assertions made. They are organized into three sets of two related hypotheses, totaling six hypotheses. Each set includes a hypothesis relevant to the connection between the calibration of the three constellations of characteristics and the use of sexually coercive tactics (i.e. where the three *plus signs* appear in Fig. 8.1) and a hypothesis focusing on antecedents of such calibration. In a later section, analyses are presented that simultaneously test several aspects of the full model.

An evolutionary-based understanding of the environmental antecedents contributing to the three constellations of characteristics focused on in this chapter would benefit from attention to both variations between groups of people (i.e. culture) and within such groups (i.e. individual experiences). Due to limits of space, discussion of the role of cultural factors will only be included in discussion of the antecedents of general personality characteristics affecting convergent vs. divergent strategies, whereas the discussion of antecedents of the other two constellations will focus primarily on individual experiences.

Hypothesis 1a: Men whose general personality characteristics are calibrated as high in dominance and low in nurturance are more likely to use sexually coercive tactics.

Explication of hypothesis.   Another way of describing the characteristics typically included in these two personality dimensions is self-directed (dominance) as compared with other-oriented (nurturance; Ballard-Reisch & Elton, 1992). Examples of self-descriptors encompassed in the dominance dimension are "dominant" and "self-sufficient." Examples of items assessing the nurturance dimension are "sympathetic," "compassionate," and "sensitive to the needs of others." As suggested earlier, the actual use of coercive tactics that cause pain or suffering is likely to be inhibited by relatively high feelings of compassion and sensitivity to others' feelings and needs. In contrast, individuals low in nurturance but high on the dominance dimension would be expected to have a self-centered personality with little concern for the negative consequences of their actions on others.

Relevant data.　Wiggins & Holzmuller (1981) concluded that Bem's (1974) masculinity and femininity scales are some of the best measures of the broad personality dimensions of dominance and nurturance. Using these scales, Dean & Malamuth (1997) recently created a single score assessing the extent to which men were relatively high on dominance relative to nurturance. They found that this measure—which directly taps personality characteristics bearing on the extent to which a person's general personality is oriented to imposing his own needs only (i.e. divergent interests) as compared with also incorporating others' needs (i.e. convergent interests)—correlated significantly with sexual aggressivity. Similarly, men's sexual aggressivity has been shown to inversely correlate with nurturant characteristics such as empathy levels (e.g. Lisak & Ivan, 1995; Rice, Chaplin, Harris, & Coutts, 1994; Seto & Barbaree, 1993). In keeping with the hierarchical approach advocated in our research program (e.g. Malamuth, 1988b), recent research indicates some differences in general empathy measures but even stronger differences in rape empathy among men with differing proclivities to engage in sexual aggression (Osland, Fitch, & Willis, 1996). Also relevant are studies showing that sexual aggressors score lower on measures of relationship intimacy than non-aggressors. Some of these indicate that sexual offenders are even lower on intimacy measures than other offender groups such as incest offenders or wife batterers (e.g. Seidman, Marshall, Hudson, & Robertson, 1994). Other studies reveal differences with nonviolent offenders but similar reductions in measures of intimacy and empathy as other violent nonsexual offenders (Ward, McCormack, & Hudson, 1997).

The most comprehensive study of variations in sexual aggression across cultures has been conducted by Sanday (1981a; 1981b). Two general hypotheses guided the research: (1) the incidence of rape varies cross-culturally; and (2) a high incidence of rape is embedded in a distinguishably different cultural configuration than a low incidence of rape. Using the anthropological record, this research coded a representative sample of the world's known and well-described societies. The complete sample consists of 156 societies, ranging in time from 1750 BC to the late 1960s. Sanday found that the societies' rates of rape related strongly to the overall ideologies pertaining to dominance of and aggression towards others and to dominance of women. A common feature of rape-prone societies was the need for a man to prove his status and worthiness by displaying dominant qualities such as the ability to be aggressive and not displaying nurturant qualities, such as compassion and tenderness, which were often perceived as weaknesses in those cultures.

Hypothesis 1b: The antecedents influencing dominance and nurturance include cultural and individual socialization.

Explication of hypothesis. Cultures that developed in ecological conditions where male destructive capacities created a competitive advantage are likely to have norms socializing boys to accentuate traditionally masculine characteristics (i.e. dominance) and to inhibit traditionally feminine or nurturant qualities, such as compassion and tenderness (Sanday, 1981a; 1981b). An example of such an environment is one where competition for resources may be relatively high and where dominance, aggressiveness and risk taking in the face of danger may have aided survival and reproductive success. In contrast, environments where resources were relatively abundant, and where dominance, aggressiveness and risk taking in dangerous situations do not provide survival advantage, are far less likely to result in cultures with a high degree of gender dimorphism and associated dominating values (Gilmore, 1990; Sanday, 1981a; 1981b). As well, socialization within cultures (e.g. parental modeling and reinforcement) is expected to influence the development of these personality characteristics.

Relevant data. Hall and Barongan (1997) provide an extensive discussion and relevant findings of the importance of "feminine socialization" in current cultures as a possible factor protecting against the development of sexually aggressive proclivities. Further, in a recent analysis of cooperation and competition in the world's nonviolent societies, Bonta (1997) concluded that while they raise their children with a strong emphasis on nurturant, affiliative qualities they also emphasize the lack of dominant, competitive, achievement oriented and aggressive characteristics. To the extent that one may generalize from such cultural practices to the individual level, these studies suggest that it is the relative balance of nurturant to competitive/dominant personality characteristics that may be most relevant to the display of aggressive behaviors. Similarly, there are studies showing that individual differences in the development and display of traditionally masculine or feminine characteristics are shaped by the social environment's (e.g. parents, peers, etc.) reinforcement and modeling of these characteristics (e.g. Kelly & Worell, 1976; Radke-Yarrow & Zahn-Waxler, 1984;).

Hypothesis 2a: In comparison to a long-term mating strategy, a short-term mating strategy is more likely to be associated with the use of sexually coercive tactics.

Explication of hypothesis. The psychological mechanisms governing male sexuality are not the same as those guiding female sexuality due to the different reproductive consequences of sexual behavior for the two genders, in ancestral environments. Gender differences in orientation to mating strategies in humans can be traced to the minimum obligatory parental investment (i.e. 9 months of internal gestation for women vs. one sex act for men; Trivers, 1972). Given that females can produce a maximum of about 20 offspring in a lifetime, having sex with a relatively large number of males is unlikely to have adaptive advantages. It is generally far better to invest more in each offspring by carefully selecting a mate with successful characteristics, who will participate in the raising of the offspring. For males, having intercourse with a larger number of fertile females is likely to be correlated with reproductive success, since in ancestral environments contraceptive devices were not available, and the upper limit for siring offspring is in the thousands. Even totally uninvested sex may therefore have favorable reproductive consequences (Buss, 1995). Although females are clearly capable of taking advantage of short-term mating opportunities and in some environmental conditions are particularly likely to do so (Thiessen, 1994), their psychological mechanisms are relatively more consonant with a long-term sexual strategy or personal sex involving some relationship context, emotional bonds or potential ties. Therefore, the goals of a man oriented to a short-term mating strategy are likely to differ from those of a woman oriented to a long-term strategy and are more likely to result in a conflict of interests that might lead to the use of sexually coercive tactics (also see Hirsch & Paul, 1996)[7].

Relevant data. Hirsch and Paul (1996) and Paul and Hirsch (1996) conducted a series of studies in which people rated their perceptions of and reactions to various tactics that might be used by quality (long-term) and quantity (short-term) mating strategists. Their findings generally supported their predictions that short-term mating is more likely to be perceived as associated with exploitative and coercive mating tactics. While these data show that people believe that there are associations between a short-term mating strategy and the use of coercive tactics, there are considerable data based on men's actual reports of their behaviors and desires which show that those using sexually coercive tactics are more likely to be oriented to a short-term strategy. These data show that sexual aggressors report starting to engage in sexual acts earlier; having more sexual partners over the lifetime; reporting a greater preference for partner variety and casual sex; foreseeing having larger number of sex partners in the future; having less of a need to feel attached to someone to have sex with them; having more extramarital relationships; and being more attracted to and fantasizing more about women with whom they are not personally acquainted (Kanin, 1957; 1984; 1985; Kanin & Parcell, 1977; Lalumiere, Chalmers et al.,

---

[7] One important difference between models such as those described by Hirsch & Paul (1996) and the ideas presented here is that only the confluence model specifies the additional characteristics differentiating among short-term mating strategists who are unlikely to use coercive tactics (the majority of such strategists) and those at high risk for such coercion (e.g. those also high in hostile masculinity).

1996; Lalumiere, Seto et al., 1996; Malamuth et al., 1991; Malamuth et al., 1995; Sarwer et al., 1993). Although some investigators (e.g. Ellis, 1989; Kanin, 1984; Kanin & Parcell, 1977) asserted that these data may be due to differences in sex drive (i.e. wanting more sex of any kind), the data appear more consistent with a short-term mating strategy or an impersonal sexual orientation (e.g. desiring more variety of sex partners) rather than differences in sex drive (e.g. Lalumiere, Seto et al., 1996; Malamuth et al., 1995; Tang, Critelli, & Porter, 1993).

Hypothesis 2b: The antecedents of a short-term sexual strategy include relatively harsh home social environments and "acting out" or delinquent acts during adolescence.

Explication of hypothesis. Belsky et al. (1991) presented a developmental model of reproductive strategies. They suggest that early experience may serve as a "switch" or "trigger" at a critical formative period (i.e. the first 5 to 7 years of life) which will shape an enduring reproductive strategy (also see Draper & Harpending, 1982). The environmental input at this critical stage informs the developing child (unconsciously, of course) of the extent to which the social environment (e.g. the trustworthiness of others and the enduringness of close personal relationships) is relatively benign or harsh. Evolutionary pressures would be expected to select for differing reproductive strategies in different ecological conditions. More benign environments are likely to favor a long-term "quality" strategy that involves high investment in relatively few offspring. Harsh environments are more likely to favor a short term sexual strategy; that is, a high "quantity" of offspring with relatively little investment in each. Particularly relevant to the present focus on the calibration of the mechanisms in the direction of a short-term mating strategy (labeled in this research as a promiscuous/impersonal sexual orientation) are "harsh" familial stressors such as marital discord and rejecting, violent or abusive parenting behaviors.

Belsky et al. (1991) also propose that such "harsh" early childhood environments may lead to "problem" behavior patterns involving nonconformity, impulsivity, and antisocial behaviors. They suggest that this oppositional behavior, via some yet unspecified biological mechanism that may involve androgenic activity, stimulates earlier biological maturation that also fosters among boys indiscriminate and opportunistic sexuality, increasing the likelihood of becoming fathers before other men. Belsky et al. (1991) noted that in "harsh" environments such a high quantity orientation would make "biological sense" since it would be more likely to result in successful reproduction than a strategy involving "quality" long-term investment.

Relevant data. Belsky et al. (1991) summarize a large body of cross-sectional and longitudinal data consistent with the configuration of factors just described that I shall not repeat here. In a recent replication and extension of this work with secondary school students in Italy, Kim, Smith, & Palermiti (1997) found that factors such as more parental marital conflict in early childhood and less emotional closeness to parents in childhood were associated with earlier physical sexual maturation for boys (e.g. spermarche), which in turn was associated with more unruliness/aggressiveness, earlier dating, more opposite sex partners, greater likelihood of having intercourse, and more intercourse partners. In addition, various other recent studies (e.g. Dean & Malamuth, 1997; Lalumiere & Quinsey, 1996; Lisak, 1994; Malamuth et al., 1991; 1995) show that a reliable constellation of factors exists consistent with this hypothesis. The constellation of factors consist of harsh home social environments associated with delinquent tendencies in adolescence, and with a short-term mating orientation or what we have labeled an impersonal sexual orientation. These data are described in greater detail later in this chapter.

The findings summarized above are presented as supporting a conditional strategy model or a facultative developmental algorithm (i.e. inherited mental mechanisms that enable individuals reared in differing environments to adjust their strategies in response to information about those environments). However, the data could instead be interpreted as supporting an alternate strategy or an obligative developmental algorithm model (see earlier). Such a model argues that genetic factors alone are responsible for the differences in the various factors incorporated within the "short-term" mating constellation of characteristics (e.g. the genes that make some parents more likely to abuse their children or to have conflict in the home are inherited by these children and it is these genes that cause their children's problem behaviors, early biological development, association with delinquent peers, and promiscuous sexual behavior; Hunt & McNeill, 1997; Rowe & Jacobson, 1997). While it may be premature at this stage of research to conclude in favor of the alternate or conditional strategy models (Cleveland, 1997), it is noteworthy that the confluence model presented here would require relatively little modification to accommodate the alternate rather than the conditional strategy model.[8]

Hypothesis 3a: Men high in hostile masculinity are more likely to use sexually coercive tactics.

Explication of hypothesis. From an evolutionary perspective, characteristics such as emotions are adaptations which function to alert the person to threats

---

[8] Although the degree of contribution of genes to individual variation may differ somewhat for the three constellations of characteristics emphasized here (e.g. Rushton et al., 1986; Waller & Shaver, 1994), virtually all individual differences in psychological characteristics are clearly a function of both genetic and environmental factors (i.e. the degree to which inherited developmental programs are obligative vs. facultative). As noted earlier, in this chapter I am largely focusing on the role of environmental factors while recognizing the potential importance of genetic factors as well.

and opportunities and to prepare the organism for strategic behaviors (Tooby & Cosmides, 1990). Emotions are not organized into one general emotional system but each type of emotion (e.g. anger, affection, etc.) is designed to respond to a particular set of delimited conditions (or adaptive problems) as input, and to transform that input into physiological and behavioral output specifically addressing that type of condition (Ellis & Malamuth, 1997; LeDoux, 1996). For example, inputs perceived as strategic interference elicit anger that produces output changes in information processing (e.g. increased sensitivity to cost-inflicting behaviors), the release of certain hormones (e.g. testosterone), and increased arousal (heightened autonomic activity) which prepares the organism to respond with quick "fight or flight" actions that reduce interference (e.g. energizing action such as aggression toward sources of provocation) (Buss, 1989; Ellis & Malamuth, 1997; Malamuth, 1996).

Understanding the role of emotions may be facilitated by a concept similar to that of associative networks (e.g. Berkowitz, 1993), which may be thought of as psychological mechanisms forming interconnected emotions, perceptions, cognitions, memories and motor tendencies designed to increase the likelihood of certain actions (i.e. output) consistent with a strategy. These involve "spreading activation" so that individual elements (e.g. emotions) become linked with and can lower the threshold for "turning on" other corresponding psychological mechanisms (e.g. attitudes, sexual arousal patterns, etc.) that collectively facilitate the strategic acts, such as aggression. The "associative network" of perceptions, attitudes and emotions of sexually aggressive men has been set to threshold levels that more easily activate other elements in such networks in a way that potentiates a more effective implementation of coercive behavior in the context of a "diverging interests" strategy. We have labeled this pattern of the "associative network" the *hostile masculinity* pattern.

Relevant data.   The above hypothesis may be divided into two components. First, are there a set of perceptual, emotional, and other related responses that are sufficiently interrelated to constitute an "associative network"? Second, do the characteristics comprising such a network affect sexually coercive acts? The existence of a "hostile associative network" of characteristics relevant to sexual aggression is supported by considerable data revealing interrelationships among factors such as hostility toward women, anger proneness, dominance as a sexual motive, sexually coercive fantasies and various ideological beliefs and attitudes condoning aggression against women (e.g. Burt, 1980; Malamuth, Check, & Briere, 1986; Malamuth et al., 1995). These interrelated factors have also been found to be quite strongly linked with other responses such as a distrusting "mental set" of social perceptions of women (Malamuth & Brown, 1994); an "automatic" mental association between power over someone and sexual attraction to them (Bargh, Raymond, Pryor, & Strack, 1995); and sexual arousal in response to aggression (Barbaree & Marshall, 1991;

Malamuth, 1983; Malamuth & Check, 1983; Yates, Barbaree, & Marshall, 1984).[9] Additional evidence relevant to the existence of an associative network with "spreading activation" (i.e. lower threshold for eliciting related responses) is found in a recent study by Vass and Gold (1995). These investigators used an inventory developed by Mosher and Sirkin (1984) to classify men on their degree of "hypermasculinity" which they and other investigators have found to correlate with sexual aggressivity. This inventory includes some of the components of the hostile masculinity network of characteristics described here. Vass and Gold (1995) randomly assigned men who scored in the upper and lower thirds of the hypermasculinity measure to receive imagined negative, neutral or positive feedback from a woman in guided imagery of an imagined date. In the positive feedback condition, the participant was asked to imagine the woman telling him he was a "great lover" and that she was interested in having a sexual relationship with him in the future. In the negative feedback condition, the participant was asked to imagine the woman telling him he was not a "real man" and that he probably did not know how to "satisfy" a woman. No feedback was imagined in the neutral feedback condition. As expected, the results showed that, in comparison to their lower hypermasculine counterparts, high hypermasculine men reacted with more anger and less empathy to the woman in the negative feedback condition. Interestingly, they also reacted with more anger to her in the neutral condition. The data therefore suggest that men whose mechanisms are calibrated in the hostile masculinity direction have a lower threshold for activating responses such as anger to women.

The assertion that calibration of mechanisms as anger and hostility to women (and the other elements of the hostile masculinity associative network) actually facilitate sexual coercion would be ideally tested by randomly assigning men to have different calibration levels of these characteristics and observing their likelihood of using sexual coercion. Clearly, such methodologies are ethically impossible. There are, however, quite a few cross-sectional and longitudinal studies indicating that various elements of the hostile masculinity calibration predict greater use of sexually coercive tactics in naturalistic settings (e.g. Christopher, Owens, & Stecker, 1993; Malamuth, 1986; Malamuth et al., 1991; 1995; Muehlenhard & Linton, 1987; Spence, Losoff, & Robbins, 1991; Spaccarelli, Bowden, Coatsworth, & Kim, 1997). Additional supportive evidence is provided by laboratory studies showing that some of these characteristics (e.g. dominance as a sexual motive; attitudes supporting violence against women; sexual arousal to aggression) predict men's aggression against women but not necessarily aggression against male targets (Malamuth, 1983; 1988b).

---

[9] In the current model, sexual arousal to aggression is considered as part of the hostile masculinity constellation, although it may well be that it should be considered a strong correlate of this constellation but one with separate direct influence on sexually coercive behavior.

Hypothesis 3b: The antecedents of the hostile masculinity pattern include perceptions of relatively frequent rejections by women.

Explication of hypothesis.   In the current context focusing on sexual coercion, strategic interference may include classes of behavior performed by women (e.g. sexual rejection, delay of sexual access, attempt to extract resources, perceived deception, etc.) that in our natural selective history regularly interfered with the pursuit of a short-term mating strategy. It is therefore predicted that men who perceive that they have relatively often had such strategic interference from women (e.g. feelings of rejection, betrayal, hurt by women) will be more likely to have characteristics such as anger and hostility to women, gratification from controlling women, and attitudes accepting of aggression against women which can mobilize and energize coercive acts against such targets, thereby functioning to reduce "strategic interference." Although it is difficult to disentangle whether more coercive men have actually experienced more rejection or whether they are more sensitive to such rejections, they are expected to react more strongly (or to have a lower threshold to respond) to such rejections.

Relevant data.   Several of the items on the Hostility Toward Women scale (Check, 1984; Check et al., 1985), one of the key measures assessing hostile masculinity, refer to earlier experiences of having been rejected and deceived by women. Lisak & Roth (1988) compared sexually aggressive and non-aggressive college students and focused on the factors underlying their anger and power motivations. They concluded that sexually aggressive men were more likely to perceive themselves as having been hurt by women, including perceptions of being deceived, betrayed and manipulated. They also found that variables assessing such hurt correlated highly with items assessing anger towards women and a desire to dominate them. Similar findings have also been reported by Christopher et al. (1993) who used a more formal path analytic statistical framework to test the role of a variable specifically measuring perceived negative experiences in relationships with women.

Research integrating two constellations of characteristics

Although the aforementioned data provide important support for the hypothesized relationship between sexual aggression and each of the three constellations, it is essential to test the viability of the proposed confluence of these dimensions. The various "risk factors" comprising the constellations discussed earlier may reveal alternative "routes" leading to the same behavior, a possibility not ruled out in our model. Various typology models of this sort have been emphasized by some investigators (e.g. Hall, 1996; Prentky & Knight, 1991). However, our model emphasizes that the three sets of characteristics constitute elements of the "package" within the same persons contributing to sexual aggression. Our model may be described as similar to the type labeled a "cumulative-conditional-probability" type (Belsky et al., 1991). It suggests that the extent to which the same person has more of these interrelated risk factors determines how likely he is to be sexually aggressive.

In more formal terms, such a model suggests three aspects:

1. The probability of the occurrence of certain characteristics within a constellation is affected by the presence or absence of antecedent factors. However, each antecedent does not constitute a necessary condition for the characteristics in a hypothesized sequence (e.g. other antecedents in addition to abusive home environments may contribute to a short-term mating strategy) nor are any of characteristics identified always necessary for the final outcome (sexual aggression) to occur.
2. When there is a combination of "risk" characteristics, the probability of sexual aggression is greater than when a smaller subset of these characteristics is present.
3. While each constellation of characteristics contributes to a higher probability of sexual aggression, a synergistic effect is also predicted such that a combination of the constellations results in more than a simple additive effect of each on sexual aggression.

The research presented next provides data relevant to these predictions.

Initial testing of the confluence model.   Using structural equation modeling, Malamuth et al. (1991) considered the role of both the short-term mating strategy constellation (labeled sexual promiscuity/impersonal sex) and the hostile masculinity constellation. In effect, this research integrates several of the individual hypotheses presented earlier within the same statistical model. These investigators hypothesized that more sexually aggressive men would often show characteristics reflecting the confluence of both constellations. Data were gathered from a nationwide representative sample of about 3000 males enrolled in any form of post-high school education (e.g. trade schools, colleges, universities, etc.). The data consisted of subjects' responses to self-report measures and recollections of earlier experiences. The model was tested by using half of the sample for analysis and the second half for cross-validation purposes. The results produced by both "half" samples generally fit the proposed model well.

An example of the findings is shown in Fig. 8.2. They showed that coming from a home with parental violence and/or child abuse was associated with a higher rate of delinquency in adolescence, which in turn was strongly predictive of greater sexual promiscuity (i.e. a short-term mating strategy). This path (labeled the *Sexual Promiscuity/Impersonal Sex* path) contributed to coerciveness against women, as did the other major constellation, which consisted of *Attitudes*

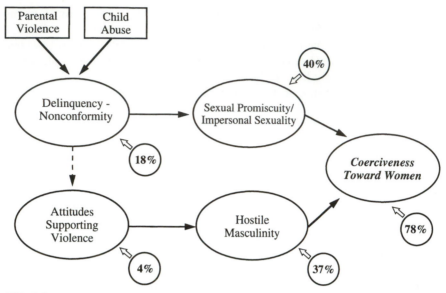

FIG. 8.2   Model of the characteristics of coercive men tested with a national randomly selected sample (based on Malamuth et al., 1991). *Percentages* indicate amount of latent variance that was successfully accounted for. *Solid lines* indicate strong paths whereas *broken lines* indicate weak paths.

Supporting Violence and *Hostile Masculinity* (both elements of the Hostile Masculinity path). Together, these two paths accounted for 78% of the latent variance of *Coerciveness Toward Women*, which was indicated by scales measuring sexual and non-sexual aggression against women.[10]

Additional analyses presented by these investigators were designed to show the mean differences between nonaggressive men and those displaying sexual and/or nonsexual aggression on the Hostile Masculinity and Sexual Promiscuity/ Impersonal Sex dimensions. Their sample consisted of 1713 men for whom data were available for both aggression measures. Subjects were divided into two levels on the dimensions of sexual and of nonsexual aggression, thereby creating four groups: (1) Low on both sexual and nonsexual aggression (n = 1076); (2) High on nonsexual aggression only (n = 414); (3) High on sexual aggression only (n = 120); and (4) High on both types of coercion (n = 103).

A 2 × 2 MANOVA was performed using the sexual and nonsexual aggression groups as the independent variables. and scores on Sexual Promiscuity and Hostile Masculinity as dependent variables. The results revealed very strong multivariate and univariate main effects, except for the effect of nonsexual

---

[10] A recent meta-analytic review of studies focusing on attitudes toward rape (Anderson, Cooper, & Okamura, 1997) supported a number of elements of the confluence model, particularly the relationship between such attitudes and sexually aggressive behavior as well as the independence of the sexual promiscuity and hostile masculinity constellations.

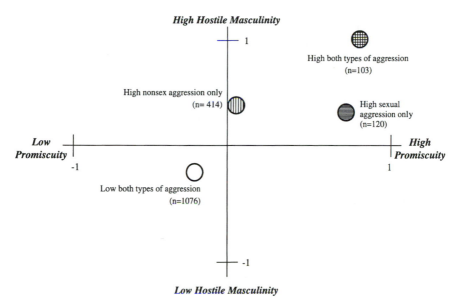

FIG. 8.3   Means of Hostile Masculinity and Sexual Promiscuity (i.e. short-term mating) dimensions for subjects classified as scoring high or low on sexual aggression and on nonsexual aggression (from Malamuth et al., 1991).

aggression on Sexual Promiscuity, which was much weaker. As indicated in Fig. 8.3, men high on both types of aggression also were high on both Hostile Masculinity and Sexual Promiscuity. Those high only on nonsexual aggression showed moderately elevated levels of Hostile Masculinity and were close to the average on the Sexual Promiscuity dimension. In contrast, men high only on sexual aggression were also relatively high on Sexual Promiscuity and moderately high on Hostile Masculinity. Finally, those low on both types of aggression were also relatively low on both the Sexual Promiscuity and Hostile Masculinity dimensions. Taken together, these data are consistent with the prediction that sexual aggression is associated with the confluence of both a short-term sexual strategy (i.e. Sexual Promiscuity) and Hostile Masculinity, whereas elevated Hostile Masculinity scores alone are associated with the use of coercive tactics in non-sexual conflicts.

Replicating and extending the confluence model. Efforts to refine and extend the confluence model presented earlier were undertaken by Malamuth et al. (1995). In a longitudinal study, the model was used to predict difficulties in men's relationships with women. About 160 men were assessed twice, with an intervening period of about 10 years. The latter assessment focused on four behaviors that might have occurred during the ten years since initial participation: (1) sexual aggression; (2) nonsexual physical aggression; (3) nonsexual verbal aggression; and (4) general relationship quality and distress. The researchers were able to secure, in many cases, collateral information from the men's partners and to videotape some of the couples, thus lending further validity to the self-report measures. Using cross-sectional data, Malamuth et al. (1995) replicated the findings that were obtained in the 1991 study. More importantly, in extending the model to make longitudinal predictions, it was argued that the two-path "causal structure" would be a useful predictor of sexual aggression assessed 10 years later. The results were indeed in accord with this prediction: information about Hostile Masculinity and Sexual Promiscuity/Impersonal Sex orientation enabled prediction of later aggression above and beyond that achieved based on knowing earlier sexual aggression only. Finally, Malamuth et al. (1995) used the data to successfully test a hierarchical model. It indicated that some of the factors contributing to sexual aggression (e.g. proneness to general hostility) underlie various types of conflict and aggression in intimate relations, whereas other factors (e.g. hostility to women, sexual dominance) are more specific to sexual aggression itself.

Research integrating three constellations of characteristics

Dean and Malamuth (1997) recently extended testing of the confluence model of individual differences by incorporating the third constellation of characteristics described above—they used Bem's (1974) scales to compute for each subject the relative balance of dominance (masculinity) vs. nurturance (femininity). They predicted that calibration of the mechanisms along the first two constellations (Sexual Promiscuity/Impersonal Sex and Hostile Masculinity) was sufficient to create considerable risk for sexually aggressing. However, the characteristics of this third constellation would moderate the actual carrying out of sexually coercive behavior. This research therefore integrated within the same analyses all of the hypotheses described earlier regarding the characteristics of sexual aggressors.

Dean and Malamuth (1997) conducted their analyses in the following way: First, the two-path model developed by Malamuth et al. (1991) of the risk constellations of characteristics predicting sexual coercion was successfully replicated; second, analyses were conducted dividing this sample into two levels on the basis of the relative balance of nurturance to dominance characteristics. In both groups, the basic two-path structure on the "predictor" side of the model remained essentially the same. However, in men with high dominance relative to nurturance, the linkages between the risk characteristics and actual aggressive behavior were strong. In contrast, when the personality profile reflected higher levels of nurturance relative to dominance, the relationship between the risk characteristics and actual aggression was weak or not significant. However, these investigators also demonstrated that even when aggressive behavior may be inhibited, the risk created by the first two constellations (Sexual Promiscuity/Impersonal Sex and

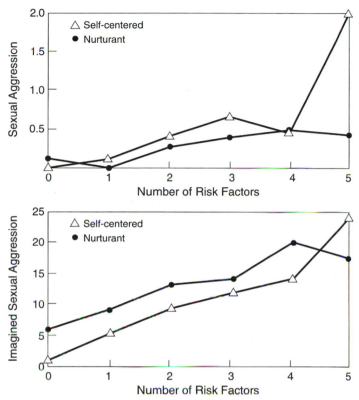

FIG. 8.4   Mean levels of sexual aggression and of imagined sexual aggression as a function of a self-centered versus a nurturant personality and the number of risk factors present (from Dean & Malamuth, 1997).

Hostile Masculinity) is still likely to be revealed in such areas as fantasized sexual aggressivity where actual victim suffering does not occur.

Figure 8.4 presents an illustration of these findings. The authors classified subjects into two types of personalities. Those relatively high on dominance relative to nurturance personality characteristics were labeled *self-centered*, whereas those with the opposite pattern were classified as *nurturant*. A risk analysis was then performed using five predictor variables associated with the Hostile Masculinity and Impersonal Sex (short-term strategy) constellations. Subjects were classified as "having" a particular risk factor if they scored above the median on that factor (e.g. a person scoring above the median on all variables was considered to have all the listed characteristics). As indicated in Fig. 8.4, imagined sexual aggression increased in both the self-centered and nurturant groups with increased number of risk factors. However, actual aggressive behavior showed marked increases only in the self-centered personality group. This is consistent with the prediction that it is the confluence of all three constellations (short-term sexual strategy, hostile masculinity, and low nurturance relative to dominance) that is the configuration most likely to characterize men who use sexually coercive tactics.

SUMMARY

Using a conceptual framework that distinguishes between converging and diverging interests and focuses on the calibration of psychological mechanisms at varying levels, a model of the characteristics of men who use sexually coercive tactics was presented. It integrates many seemingly independent correlates of sexual aggressors within three major constellations of characteristics: (1) a general personality orientation to assert one's own interests at the expense of the other's (i.e. personality characteristics emphasizing dominance and not nurturance); (2) a mating orientation likely to create a conflict of interests with females (i.e. a short-term mating strategy); and (3) a constellation of emotions and attitudes that prime the use of coercive tactics to deal with conflicts (i.e. hostile masculinity).

The data supported the model's hypotheses regarding the three constellations in showing that sexually aggressive men are more likely to be high on dominance relative to nurturance, pursue a short-term sexual strategy, and have hostile masculinity characteristics. Consistent with a functional analysis of the antecedents of these characteristics, data were described indicating that: (1) differences in socialization in cultural and individual environments affect the extent to which a man's personality accentuates nurturant or dominant characteristics; (2) a short-term sexual strategy is associated with relatively harsh early environments; and (3) hostile masculinity characteristics are associated with high perceived rejections by women. It was also shown that the combination of a short-term mating orientation and hostile masculinity is sufficient to create the proclivity to use sexually coercive tactics (as revealed in imagined sexual aggression) but that the degree to which a person has dominant vs. nurturant personality characteristics moderates whether such proclivity is expressed in actual aggressive behavior.

ACKNOWLEDGEMENTS

The author expresses his deep appreciation to David Buss, Bruce Ellis, Daniel Linz and Jeff Valle for their comments on earlier drafts of this chapter. The writing of this article was facilitated by a Lady Davis Fellowship at the Hebrew University in Jerusalem, Israel. Much of our research reported here was funded by a grant from the National Institute of Mental Health.

REFERENCES

Abel, G. G., Barlow, D. H., Blanchard, E., & Guild, D. (1977). The components of rapists' sexual arousal. *Archives of General Psychiatry, 34*, 895–903.

Alcock, J. (1984). *Animal Behaviour: An evolutionary approach*. Sunderland, MA: Sinauer.

Alexander, R. D. (1979). *Darwinism and human affairs*. Seattle, WA: University of Washington Press.

Allen, B. (1996). *Rape warfare: The hidden genocide in Bosnia-Herzegovina and Croatia*. Minneapolis, MN: University of Minnesota Press.

Ageton, S. S. (1983). *Sexual assault among adolescents*. Lexington, MA: Lexington Books.

Anderson, K. B., Cooper, H., & Okamura, L. (1997). Individual differences and attitudes toward rape: A meta-analytic review. *Personality and Social Psychology Bulletin, 23*, 295–315.

Ballard-Reisch, D., & Elton, M. (1992). Gender orientation and the Bem Sex Role Inventory: A psychological construct revisited. *Sex Roles, 27*, 291–306.

Barbaree, H. E., & Marshall, W. L. (1991). The role of male sexual arousal in rape: Six models. *Journal of Consulting and Clinical Psychology, 59*, 621–630.

Bargh, J. A., Raymond, P., Pryor, J. B., & Strack, F. (1995). Attractiveness of the underling: An automatic power-sex association and its consequences for sexual harassment and aggression. *Journal of Personality and Social Psychology, 68*, 768–781.

Belsky, J., Steinberg, L., Draper, P. (1991). Childhood experience, interpersonal development, and reproductive strategy: An evolutionary theory of socialization. *Child Development, 62*, 647–670.

Bem, S. L. (1974). The measurement of psychological androgyny. *Journal of Consulting and Clinical Psychology, 42*, 155–162.

Berkowitz, L. (1993). Towards a general theory of anger and emotional aggression: Implications of the cognitive-neoassociationistic perspective for the analysis of anger and other emotions. In R. S. Wyer & T. K. Srull (Eds.), *Advances in social cognition: Vol. 6. Perspectives on anger and emotion* (pp. 1–46). Hillsdale, NJ: Erlbaum.

Bonta, B. D. (1997). Cooperation and competition in peaceful societies. *Psychological Bulletin, 121*, 299–320.

Broude, G. J., & Greene, S. J. (1978). Cross-cultural codes on 20 sexual attitudes and practices. *Ethnology, 15*, 409–430.

Brownmiller, S. (1975). *Against our will: Men, women, and rape*. New York: Simon & Schuster.

Burt, M. R. (1980). Cultural myths and supports for rape. *Journal of Personality and Social Psychology, 38*, 217–230.

Buss, D. M. (1988). The evolution of human intrasexual competition: Tactics of mate attraction. *Journal of Personality and Social Psychology, 54*, 616–628.

Buss, D. M. (1989). Conflict between the sexes: Strategic interference and the evocation of anger and upset. *Journal of Personality and Social Psychology, 56*, 735–747.

Buss, D. M. (1995). Evolutionary psychology. *Psychological Inquiry, 6*, 1–30.

Buss, D. M. (1996). Social adaptation and five major factors of personality. In J. S. Wiggins (Ed.), *The five-factor model of personality: Theoretical perspectives*. (pp. 180–207). New York: Guilford.

Buss, D. M., & Schmitt, D. P. (1993). Sexual strategies theory: An evolutionary perspective on human mating. *Psychological Review, 100*, 204–232.

Chagnon, N. A. (August, 1994). How important was "marriage by capture" as a mating strategy in the EEA? *Human Behavior and Evolution Society Newsletter, 3*, 1–2.

Check, J. V. P. (1984). *The hostility toward women scale*. Unpublished doctoral dissertation, University of Manitoba, Canada.

Check, J. V. P., Malamuth, N. M., Elias, B., & Barton, S. (1985). On hostile ground. *Psychology Today, 19*, 56–61.

Christopher, F. S., Owens, L. A., & Stecker, H. L. (1993). Exploring the dark side of courtship: A test of a model of premarital sexual aggressiveness. *Journal of Marriage and the Family, 55*, 469–479.

Cleveland, H. H. (1997, June). *Environmental and genetic contributions to behavior problems of children of single parents: Support for a biological theory of self-selection into family structures.* Paper presented at the Annual Meetings of the Human Behavior and Evolution Society, Tuscon, Arizona.

Cosmides, L., & Tooby, J. (1987). From evolution to behavior: Evolutionary psychology as the missing link. In J. Dupre (Ed.), *The latest on the best: Essays on evolution and optimality* (pp. 277–306). Cambridge, MA: MIT Press.

Crawford, C. B., & Anderson, J. L. (1989). Sociobiology: An environmentalist discipline? *American Psychologist, 44,* 1449–1459.

Crawford, C. B., & Galdikas, B. (1986). Rape in non-human animals. *Canadian Psychology, 27,* 215–230.

Daly, M., & Wilson, M (1987). *Homicide.* New York: Aldine.

Daly, M., & Wilson, M. (1994). Evolutionary psychology of male violence. In J. Archer (Ed.), *Male violence* (pp. 253–288). London: Routledge.

Dawkins, R. (1986). *The blind watchmaker.* Burnt Hill: Longman Scientific.

Dean, K., & Malamuth, N. M. (1997). Characteristics of men who aggress sexually and of men who imagine aggressing: Risk and moderating variables. *Journal of Personality and Social Psychology, 72,* 449–455.

Draper, P., & Harpending, H. (1982). Father absence and reproductive strategy: An evolutionary perspective. *Journal of Anthropological Research, 38,* 255–273.

Eibl-Eibesfeldt, I. (1971). *Love and hate: The natural history of behavior patterns.* New York: Holt, Rinehart & Winston.

Eibl-Eibesfeldt, I. (1990). Dominance, submission, and love: Sexual pathologies from the perspective of ethology. In R. Jay (Ed.), *Pedophilia–biosocial dimensions* (pp. 150–175). New York: Springer.

Ellis, L. (1989). *Theories of rape.* New York: Hemisphere.

Ellis, B., & Malamuth, N. M. (1997, June). *Love and anger in romantic relationships: An independence model.* Paper presented at the Annual Meetings of the Human Behavior and Evolution Society, Tucson, Arizona.

Ellis, B., & Symons, D. (1989). Sex differences in sexual fantasy. *Journal of Sex Research, 27,* 527–555.

Friedmann, L. (1972). *The law of war.* New York: Random House.

Gangestad, S. W., & Simpson, J. A. (1990). Toward an evolutionary history of female sociosexual variation. *Journal of Personality, 58,* 69–96.

Gazzaniga, M. S. (1992). *Nature's mind: The biological roots of thinking, emotions, sexuality.* New York: Basic Books.

Gilmore, D. D. (1990). *Manhood in the making: Cultural concepts of masculinity.* New Haven, CT: Yale University Press.

Gold, S. R., Fultz, J., Burke, C. H., Prisco, A. G., & Willett, J. A. (1992). Vicarious emotional responses of macho college males. *Journal of Interpersonal Violence, 7,* 165–174.

Greendlinger, V., & Byrne, D. (1987). Coercive sexual fantasies of college men as predictors of self-reported likelihood to rape and overt sexual aggression. *Journal of Sex Research, 23,* 1–11.

Hall, N. G. C. (1996). *A theory of sexual aggression.* New York: Oxford University Press.

Hall, N. G. C., & Barongan, C. (1997). Prevention of sexual aggression: Sociocultural risk and protective factors. *American Psychologist, 52,* 5–14.

Hamilton, W. D. (1964). The genetical evolution of social behaviour, I and II. *Journal of Theoretical Biology, 7,* 1–52.

Hanneke, C. R., Shields, N., & McCall, G. (1986). Assessing the prevalence of marital rape. *Journal of Interpersonal Violence, 1,* 350–362.

Hanson, R. K. (1997). Invoking sympathy: Assessment and treatment of empathy deficits among sexual offenders. In B. K. Schwartz & H. R. Cellni (Eds.), *The sex offender: New insights, treatment innovations and legal developments* (Vol. 2) (pp. 1–12). Kingston, NJ: Civic Research Institute.

Hirsch, L. R., & Paul, L. (1996). Human male mating strategies: I. Courtship tactics of the "quality" and "quantity" alternatives. *Ethology and Sociobiology, 17*, 55–70.

Hotaling, G. T., & Sugarman, D. B. (1986). An analysis of risk markers in husband to wife violence: The current state of knowledge. *Violence and Victims, 1*, 101–124.

Hrdy, S. B. (1977). Raising Darwin's consciousness: Female sexuality and the prehominid origins of patriarchy. *Human Nature, 8*, 1–49.

Hunt, C. B., & McNeill, P. L. (1997, June). *Does environment condition the heritability of menarche?* Paper presented at the Annual Meetings of the Human Behavior and Evolution Society, Tuscon, Arizona.

Kanin, E. J. (1957). Male aggression in dating–courtship relations. *American Journal of Sociology, 63*, 197–204.

Kanin, E. J. (1984). Date rape: Unofficial criminals and victims. *Victimology: An international Journal, 9*, 95–108.

Kanin, E. J. (1985). Date rapists: Differential sexual socialization and relative deprivation. *Archives of Sexual Behavior, 14*, 219–231.

Kanin, E. J., & Parcell, S. R. (1977). Sexual aggression: A second look at the offended female. *Archives of Sexual Behavior, 6*, 67–76.

Kelly, J. A., & Worell, L. (1976). Parent behaviors related to masculine, feminine, and androgynous sex role orientations. *Journal of Consulting and Clinical Psychology, 44*, 843–851.

Kenrick, D. T., & Sheets, V. (1993). Homicidal fantasies. *Ethology and sociobiology, 14*, 231–246.

Kim, K., Smith, P. K., & Palermiti, A. (1997). Conflict in childhood and reproductive development. *Evolution and Human Behavior, 18*, 109–142.

Koss, M. P., Gidycz, C. A., & Wisniewski, N. (1987). The scope of rape: Incidence and prevalence of sexual aggression and victimization in a national sample of higher education students. *Journal of Consulting and Clinical Psychology, 55*, 162–170.

Koss, M. P., Dinero, T., Seibel, C., & Cox, S. (1988). Stranger and acquaintance rape: Are there differences in the victim's experience? *Psychology of Women Quarterly, 12*, 1–24.

Lalumiere, M. L., & Quinsey, V. L. (1994). The discriminability of rapists from non-sex offenders using phallometric measures: A meta-analysis. *Criminal Justice and Behavior, 21*, 150–175.

Lalumiere, M. L., & Quinsey, V. L. (1996). Sexual deviance, antisociality, mating effort, and the use of sexually coercive behaviors. *Personality and Individual Differences, 21*, 33–48.

Lalumiere, M. L., Chalmers, L. J., Quinsey, V. L., & Seto, M. C. (1996). A test of the mate deprivation hypothesis of sexual coercion. *Ethology and Sociobiology, 17*, 299–318.

Lalumiere, M., Seto, M. C., & Quinsey, V. L. (1996). Self-perceived mating success and the mating choices of human males and females. Unpublished manuscript, Clarke Institute, Toronto, Canada.

LeDoux, J. (1996). *The emotional brain: The mysterious underpinnings of emotional life.* New York: Simon & Schuster.

Levinson, D. (1989). *Family violence in cross-cultural perspective.* Thousand Oaks, CA: Sage.

Lisak, D. (1994). Subjective assessment of relationship with parents by sexually aggressive and nonaggressive men. *Journal of Interpersonal Violence, 9*, 399–411.

Lisak, D., & Ivan, C. (1995). Deficits in intimacy and empathy in sexually aggressive men. *Journal of Interpersonal Violence, 10*, 296–308.

Lisak, D., & Roth, S. (1988). Motivational factors in nonincarcerated sexually aggressive men. *Journal of Personality and Social Psychology, 55*, 795–802.

Loehlin, J. C. (1992). *Genes and environment in personality development.* Thousand Oaks, CA: Sage.

Lore, R. S., & Schultz, L. (1993). Control of human aggression: A comparative perspective. *American Psychologist, 48*, 16–25.

Lorenz, K. (1966). *On aggression.* New York: Harcourt.

Malamuth, N. M. (1981). Rape proclivity among males. *Journal of Social Issues, 37*, 138–157.

Malamuth, N. M. (1983). Factors associated with rape as predictors of laboratory aggression against females. *Journal of Personality and Social Psychology, 45*, 432–442.

Malamuth, N. M. (1986). Predictors of naturalistic sexual aggression. *Journal of Personality and Social Psychology, 50,* 953–962.

Malamuth, N. M. (1988a). A multidimensional approach to sexual aggression: Combining measures of past behavior and present likelihood. In R. Prentky & V. Quinsey (Eds.), *Human sexual aggression: Current perspectives. Annals of the New York Academy of Sciences.* (Vol. 528, pp. 123–132). New York: The New York Academy of Sciences.

Malamuth, N. M. (1988b). Predicting laboratory aggression against female and male targets: Implications for sexual aggression. *Journal of Research in Personality, 22,* 474–495.

Malamuth, N. M. (1989a). The attraction to sexual aggression scale: Part one. *Journal of Sex Research, 26,* 26–49.

Malamuth, N. M. (1989b). The attraction to sexual aggression scale: Part two. *Journal of Sex Research, 26,* 324–354.

Malamuth, N. M. (1996). The confluence model of sexual aggression: Feminist and evolutionary perspectives. In D. Buss & N. Malamuth (Eds.), *Sex, power and conflict: Evolutionary and feminist perspectives* (pp. 269–295). Oxford: Oxford University Press.

Malamuth, N. M., & Brown, L. (1994). Sexually aggressive men's perceptions of women's communications: Testing three explanations. *Journal of Personality and Social Psychology, 67,* 699–712.

Malamuth, N. M., & Check, J. (1983). Sexual arousal to rape depictions: Individual differences. *Journal of Abnormal Psychology, 92,* 55–67.

Malamuth, N. M., Check, J. V. P., & Briere, J. (1986). Sexual arousal in response to aggression: Ideological, aggressive and sexual correlates. *Journal of Personality and Social Psychology, 50,* 330–340.

Malamuth, N. M., Heavey, C., Linz, D. (1993). Predicting men's antisocial behavior against women: The "interaction model" of sexual aggression. In G. N. Hall, R. Hirschmann, J. R, Graham & M. S. Zaragoza, (Eds.), *Sexual aggression: Issues in Etiology and Assessment, and Treatment* (pp. 63–97). New York: Hemisphere.

Malamuth, N. M., & Heilmann, M. (in press). Evolutionary psychology and sexual aggression. In C. B. Crawford, & D. Krebs (Eds.), *Handbook of Evolutionary Psychology: Ideas, issues and applications.* Hillsdale, NJ: Erlbaum.

Malamuth, N. M., Linz, D., Heavey, C. L., Barnes, G., & Acker, M. (1995). Using the confluence model of sexual aggression to predict men's conflict with women: A ten-year follow-up study. *Journal of Personality and Social Psychology, 69,* 353–369.

Malamuth, N. M., Sackloskie, R., Koss, M. P., & Tanaka, J. (1991). The characteristics of aggressors against women: Testing a model using a national sample of college students. *Journal of Consulting and Clinical Psychology, 59,* 670–681.

Markman, H. J., Floyd, F. J., Stanley, S. M., & Storaasli, R. D. (1988). Prevention of marital distress: A longitudinal investigation. *Journal of Consulting and Clinical Psychology, 56,* 210–217.

Marshall, W. L., Hudson, S. M., & Hodkinson, S. (1993). The importance of attachment bonds in the development of juvenile sex offending. In H. E. Barbaree, W. L. Marshall, & S. M. Hudson (Eds.), *The juvenile sex offender* (pp. 164–181). New York: Guilford.

Money, J. (1986). *Lovemaps.* New York: Irvington.

Mosher, D. L., & Sirkin, M. (1984). Measuring a macho personality constellation. *Journal of Research in Personality, 18,* 150–163.

Muehlenhard, C. L., & Linton, M. A. (1987). Date rape and sexual aggression in dating situations: Incidence and risk factors. *Journal of Counseling Psychology, 34,* 186–196.

Osland, J. A., Fitch, M., & Willis, E. E. (1996). Likelihood to rape in college males. *Sex Roles, 35,* 171–183.

Paul, L., & Hirsch, L. R. (1996). Human male mating strategies: II. Moral codes of "quality" and "quantity" strategies. *Ethology and Sociobiology, 17,* 71–86..

Prentky, R. A., & Knight, R. A. (1991). Dimensional and categorical discrimination among rapists. *Journal of Consulting and Clinical Psychology, 59,* 643–661.

Quinsey, V. L., & Lalumiere, M. L. (1995). Evolutionary perspectives on sexual offending. *Sexual Abuse, 7*, 301–315.

Radke-Yarrow, M., & Zahn-Waxler, C. (1984). Roots, motives and patterns in children's prosocial behavior. In E. Staub et al., (Eds.), *Development and maintenance of prosocial behavior*. New York: Plenum

Rapaport, K., & Burkhart, B. R. (1984). Personality and attitudinal characteristics of sexually coercive males. *Journal of Abnormal Psychology, 93*, 216–221.

Rice, M. E., Chaplin, T. C., Harris, G. T. & Coutts, J. (1994). Empathy for the victim and sexual assault among rapists and nonrapists. *Journal of Interpersonal Violence, 10*, 435–449.

Rowe, D. C., & Jacobson, K. (1997, June). *Testing the conditional strategy hypothesis for self-reported aggression*. Paper presented at the Annual Meetings of the Human Behavior and Evolution Society, Tuscon, Arizona.

Rushton, J. P., Fulker, D. W., Neale, M. C., Nias, D. K. B., & Eysenck, H. J. (1986). Altruism and aggression: The heritability of individual differences. *Journal of Personality and Social Psychology, 50*, 1192–1198.

Russell, D. E. H. (1984). *Sexual exploitation: Rape, child sexual abuse and workplace harassment*. Thousand Oaks, CA: Sage.

Sanday, P. R. (1981a). *Female power and male dominance: On the origins of sexual inequality*. Cambridge: Cambridge University Press.

Sanday, P. R. (1981b). The sociocultural context of rape: A cross-cultural study. *Journal of Social Issues, 37*, 5–27.

Sarwer, D. B., Kalichman, S. C., Johnson, J. R., Early, J., & Akram, A. S. (1993). Sexual aggression and love styles: An exploratory study. *Archives of Sexual Behavior, 22*, 265–275.

Seidman, B. T., Marshall, W. L., Hudson, S. M., & Robertson, P. J. (1994). An examination of intimacy and loneliness in sex offenders. *Journal of Interpersonal Violence, 9*, 518–534.

Seto, M. C., & Barbaree, H. E. (1993). Victim blame and sexual arousal to rape cues in rapists and nonoffenders. *Annals of Sex Research, 6*, 167–183.

Seto, M. C., & Kuban, M. (1996). Criterion-related validity of a phallometric test for paraphilic rape and sadism. *Behaviour Research and Therapy, 34*, 175–183.

Simpson, J. A., & Gangestad, S. W. (1991). Individual differences in sociosexuality: Evidence for convergent and discriminant validity. *Journal of Personality and Social Psychology, 60*, 870–883.

Smuts, B. (1992). Male aggression against women: An evolutionary perspective. *Human Nature, 3*, 1–44.

Smuts, B., & Smuts, R. (1993). Male aggression and sexual coercion of females in nonhuman primates and other animals: Evidence and theoretical implications. *Advances in the Study of Behavior, 22*, 1–63.

Spaccarelli, S., Bowden, B., Coatsworth, J. D., & Kim, S. (1997). Psychological correlates of male sexual aggression in a chronic delinquent sample. *Criminal Justice and Behavior, 24*, 71–95.

Spence, J. T., Losoff, M., & Robbins, A. S. (1991). Sexually aggressive tactics in dating relationships: Personality and attitudinal correlates. *Journal of Social and Clinical Psychology, 10*, 289–304.

Stermac, L. E., & Quinsey, V. L. (1986). Social competence among rapists. *Behavioral Assessment, 8*, 171–185.

Stiglmayer, A. (Ed.). (1994). *Mass rape*. Arkansas, NE: University of Nebraska Press.

Straus, M. (1987, August). *Family patterns and research on primary prevention of family violence*. Paper presented at the 1987 meeting of the American Psychological Association, New York.

Straus, M. A., & Gelles, R. J. (1986). Societal change and change in family violence from 1975 to 1985 as revealed by two national surveys. *Journal of Marriage and the Family, 48*, 465–479.

Tang, C. S., Critelli, J. W., & Porter, J. F. (1993). Motives in sexual aggression: The Chinese context. *Journal of Interpersonal Violence, 8*, 435–445.

Thiessen, D. (1994). Environmental tracking by females: Sexual lability. *Human Nature, 5,* 167–202.

Thornhill, R., & Thornhill, N. W. (1983). Human rape: An evolutionary analysis. *Ethology and Sociobiology, 4,* 137–173.

Thornhill, R., & Thornhill, N. W. (1992). The evolutionary psychology of men's coercive sexuality. *Behavior and Brain Sciences, 15,* 363–421.

Tooby, J., & Cosmides, L. (1990). On the universality of human nature and the uniqueness of the individual: The role of genetics and adaptation. *Journal of Personality, 58,* 17–68.

Trivers, R. L. (1972). Parental investment and sexual selection. In B. Campbell (Ed.), *Sexual selection and the descent of man.* (pp. 1871–1971). Chicago: Aldine.

Vass, J. S., & Gold, S. R. (1995). Effects of feedback on emotion in hypermasculine males. *Violence and Victims, 10,* 217–226.

Waller, N. G., & Shaver, P. R. (1994). The importance of nongenetic influences on romantic love styles: A twin-family study. *Psychological Science, 5,* 268–274.

Ward, T., McCormack, J., & Hudson, S. M. (1997). Sexual offenders' perceptions of their intimate relationships. *Sexual Abuse: A Journal of Research and Treatment, 9,* 57–74.

Wiggins, J. S. (1991). Agency and communion as conceptual coordinates for the understanding and measurement of interpersonal behavior. In W. M. Grave & D. Cichetti (Eds.), *Thinking clearly about psychology: Vol. 2. Personality and psychology* (pp. 89–113). Minneapolis: University of Minnesota Press.

Wiggins, J. S., & Holzmuller, A. (1981). Further evidence on androgyny and interpersonal flexibility. *Journal of Research in Personality, 15,* 67–80.

Wiggins, J. S., & Trapnell, P. D. (1996). A dyadic-interactional perspective on the five-factor model. In J. S. Wiggins (Ed.), *The five-factor model of personality: Theoretical perspectives* (pp. 88–162). New York: Guilford.

Wingield, J. C., Hegner, R. E., Dufty, A. M. Jr., & Ball, G. F. (1990). The "challenge hypothesis": Theoretical implications for patterns of testosterone secretion, mating systems, and breeding strategies. *American Nature, 136,* 829–846.

Wispe, L. (1986). The distinction between sympathy and empathy: To call forth a concept, a word is needed. *Journal of Personality and Social Psychology, 50,* 314–321.

Wrangham, R., & Peterson, D. (1996). *Demonic males: Apes and the origins of human violence.* New York: Houghton Mifflin.

Yates, E., Barbaree, H. E., & Marshall, W. L. (1984). Anger and deviant sexual arousal. *Behavior Therapy, 15,* 287–294.

Young, R. K., & Thiessen, D. (1991). The Texas rape scale. *Ethology and Sociobiology, 13,* 19–33.

CHAPTER NINE

Attitudes and the processing of attitude-relevant information

Alice H. Eagly
Northwestern University, Evanston, Illinois, USA

The study of attitudinal selectivity in information processing was one of the first research areas identified by social psychologists, who typically hypothesized that attitudes bias information processing in favor of attitudinally congenial material. Despite this early interest, clear understanding of attitudinal selectivity has eluded researchers. To clarify attitudes' effects on memory for attitude-relevant information, Eagly and her colleagues have completed a quantitative synthesis of attitude–memory research. This meta-analysis found only very weak overall evidence for the congeniality hypothesis, although experimental findings were quite heterogeneous. The synthesis produced considerable evidence that measurement artifacts may have biased early studies toward congeniality effects. Also reported is new primary research on attitude–memory suggesting that message recipients invoke different processes to encode and remember attitude-relevant information, depending on whether it is proattitudinal or counterattitudinal. Although memory for counterattitudinal information and proattitudinal information proved to be equally good, counterattitudinal information was remembered by a more effortful process involving counterarguing.

L'étude de la sélectivité des attitudes dans le traitement de l'information a été l'un des premiers domaines de recherche identifié par les psychologues sociaux; ils faisaient habituellement l'hypothèse que les attitudes prédisposent le traitement de l'information en faveur de matériel de même nature que les attitudes. Malgré cet intérêt qui s'est manifesté depuis le tout début, la nette compréhension de la sélectivité d'attitudes a échappée aux chercheurs. Afin d'élucider l'influence des attitudes sur le souvenir de toute information ayant rapport aux attitudes, Eagly et ses collègues ont fait une synthèse quantitative de la recherche portant sur la relation attitude–mémoire. Cette méta-analyse n'a décelé qu'une évidence globale très faible pour appuyer l'hypothèse d'affinité, alors que les données expérimentales étaient assez hétérogènes. La synthèse a produit beaucoup de faits qui suggèrent que des artefacts de mesure auraient pu faire dévier les résultats d'études antérieures en faveur des effets d'affinité. On fait état également de nouvelles données de recherche fondamentale sur la relation attitude–mémoire. Celles-ci portent à croire que les récepteurs de messages font appel à divers procédés pour l'encodage et le rappel de l'information pertinente à l'attitude, selon que celle-ci s'avère favorable ou défavorable à l'attitude. Bien que le souvenir de l'information favorable ou défavorable se soit révélé aussi bon dans l'un ou l'autre cas, l'information défavorable à l'attitude a exigé un effort plus grand faisant intervenir la contre-argumentation.

A good starting point for understanding social psychologists' analyses of attitudes' effects on information processing is a statement published in 1962 that purported to summarize scientific knowledge about this research area. This statement was contained in the behavioral sciences report of the President's Science Advisory Committee, a group of eminent behavioral scientists who were charged with summarizing the important principles of human behavior. Their clear-cut statement (Behavioral Sciences Subpanel, 1962, p. 277) suggested that psychologists knew a lot about the selective effects of attitudes on information processing:

> Individuals engage in selective exposure and selective perception. Those least predisposed to change are least likely to allow themselves to be exposed to a persuasive communication, and if they are exposed, are most likely to engage in misperception, a kind of motivated missing-the-point. If a new piece of information would weaken the existing structure of their ideas and emotions, it will be shunned, rejected, or quickly forgotten; if it reinforces the structure, it will be sought out, quickly accepted, and remembered.

This very interesting statement, which was presented within a discussion of attitudes, summarizes the classic ideas about attitudinal selectivity. Appearing in various guises in this statement is one overarching principle, which is now generally labeled the *congeniality hypothesis*. According to this hypothesis, attitudes bias information processing in favor of attitudinally congenial, or congruent, material—that is, in favor of information that supports one's attitudes (see Eagly, 1992; Eagly & Chaiken, 1993; in press).

The underlying rationale for this proposition is that people are motivated to defend their attitudes from challenges. According to the traditional logic, people screen out uncongenial information: in other words, they get rid of it in one way or the other. This screening could occur at more than one stage of information processing. People might not expose themselves to uncongenial information at all; if exposed to it, they might not pay attention to it; they could distort it perceptually in a way that blunts its impact; they could evaluate it negatively; and they might not remember it. The overall theme in much early theory about attitudes' impact on information processing was that people are profoundly closed-minded in the sense that they are reluctant to encode or remember information that challenges their attitudes (e.g. Festinger, 1957).

Are these assumptions about attitudinal selectivity reasonable? Attitudes certainly should affect information processing to the extent that they are important psychological structures. Consistent with claims about attitudes' importance, many theorists have maintained that attitudes organize people's knowledge, direct and motivate individual behavior, are linked to the self and core values, and are synonymous with prejudice in intergroup contexts, making them the root cause of discrimination and social conflict (e.g. Allport, 1935; Katz, 1960; Smith, Bruner, & White, 1956). Given such assumptions (and considerable evidence supporting these assumptions; see Eagly & Chaiken, 1993), attitudes certainly should exert some sort of selective effects on information processing. Moreover, it seems reasonable that people would arrange their subjective realities in ways that favor their attitudes, at least to the extent that attitudes are strong or important.

However reasonable it is to think that attitudes affect information processing, it does not necessarily follow that congeniality effects would prevail. In fact, in so far as the empirical history of congeniality effects is concerned, there is a somewhat complicated tale to tell. The 1962 statement from the President's Science Advisory Committee actually represented the zenith of belief in the congeniality hypothesis, and the nadir appeared only a few years later. By the late 1960s some reviewers had taken a closer look at selectivity research. They invoked the process that we now call narrative reviewing, and for the most part they did not endorse what had been written a few years earlier by the President's Science Advisory Committee (e.g. Freedman & Sears, 1965; Greenwald, 1975; McGuire, 1969). Instead, the reviewers either affirmed the null hypothesis by claiming that the congeniality hypothesis failed, or they cautiously advocated interaction hypotheses by maintaining that congeniality is confirmed only under some circumstances. Since these negative verdicts, progress in understanding attitudes' effects on information processing has been generally slow. It has been difficult to come to a clear theoretical understanding of how attitudes should affect information processing, and it has been difficult to document expected phenomena empirically.

To provide some background, I shall briefly sketch the somewhat troubled history of research on attitudinal selectivity. Then I shall present some of the findings of a newly completed meta-analysis of the studies that examined the effects of attitudes on memory. Finally, I shall summarize new primary research that reveals some of the reasons for the elusiveness of the congeniality effects that have long been postulated by social psychologists.

STATE OF THE EVIDENCE ON ATTITUDINAL SELECTIVITY

Selective exposure and attention

Psychologists expected that attitudes would affect exposure to information and the attention paid to it. These are the *selective exposure* and *selective attention* hypotheses. Festinger (1957; 1964) was the first to subject this idea to serious empirical scrutiny. He promoted a somewhat specialized version of the attitudinal selectivity principle by mainly investigating bias in favor of information that supports a decision that an individual has made. He maintained that people are willing to expose themselves to information in a relatively unbiased manner before they commit themselves to a decision, whereas following commitment they are selective in the sense that they seek out information supportive of their decision and avoid nonsupportive information.

Belief in selective exposure and attention was challenged by Freedman and Sears' (1965) review of the early studies that tested the hypothesis. They argued that there was, in fact, little evidence for selective exposure or attention when other causes of selectivity were controlled. According to Freedman and Sears, people are indeed exposed to a greater amount of supportive than nonsupportive information in their natural environments, but for reasons other than their attitudinal preferences. For example, supportive information may merely be more frequent in many settings or more useful. Freedman and Sears argued that once these causes of *de facto selectivity* were experimentally controlled, there was no evidence for attitudinal selectivity.

Considerably more positive conclusions were offered by Frey (1986) in a later narrative review. Frey argued that preference for attitudinally congenial information is present some of the time and can be detected in a pattern of interactions that are consistent with many of Festinger's hypotheses. For example, selectivity is more likely when people have freely chosen to perform an attitude-relevant behavior or have committed themselves to a particular attitude or course of action. It would be desirable to determine whether Frey's conclusions would be substantiated by a quantitative synthesis that takes all of the studies in this extensive research literature into account. Still, a tentative conclusion about selective exposure and attention is that attitudinal selectivity is present only under defined circumstances. Also, Freedman and Sears' (1965) lesson is worth heeding: the impact of attitudes on exposure and attention must be carefully disentangled from the effects of other causal variables that are correlated with attitudes and can also produce selectivity effects.

Selective perception and judgment

Another form of the selectivity hypothesis pertains to biased perception and judgment of attitude-relevant information. Such biases could dampen the persuasive impact of whatever counterattitudinal information has been encoded. Sherif's social judgment theory embodied one form of this claim—specifically, that people assimilate information that is relatively close to their own attitudes, whereas they contrast information that is relatively distant (Sherif & Hovland, 1961). Moreover, these perceptual distortions were assumed to influence judgment so that statements that are assimilated are evaluated relatively positively (i.e. judged as fair and unbiased), and statements that are contrasted are evaluated relatively negatively (i.e. judged as unfair and biased).

The extent of support for these assimilation and contrast effects remains somewhat unclear. Early research provided some support, but the status of these effects as true perceptual effects was called into question by methodological criticisms (e.g. Upshaw, 1969). Although subsequent research suggested that assimilation and contrast may to some extent survive these criticisms, the theoretical understanding of these effects remains a matter of some debate (Eiser, 1990; Schwarz & Bless, 1992).

In contrast, the principle that people unfavorably evaluate information that challenges their attitudes has received consistent support. For example, on thought-listing tasks participants list more counterarguments for counterattitudinal messages than proattitudinal messages (Cacioppo & Petty, 1979; Edwards & Smith, 1996). People rate counterattitudinal information as less convincing and less valid (Lord, Ross, & Lepper, 1979). Television viewers bias their judgments of who won presidential debates in favor of the candidate they preferred prior to the debate (Bothwell & Brigham, 1983). Also, partisans on issues often judge that the media are hostile to their views (Vallone, Ross, & Lepper, 1985). Thus, several lines of evidence converge in their support for selective evaluation—the most commonsensical of the selectivity postulates. Ordinarily people do not like or enjoy attitudinally uncongenial information, and they generally find such information relatively unconvincing and invalid.

Selective memory

The hypothesis that proattitudinal information is more memorable than counterattitudinal information was the heart of the original selectivity hypothesis. This idea was very popular in the earliest period of systematic research on attitudes. Some of the early studies of attitudinal selectivity in memory yielded support for this congeniality bias. However, the very first systematic study, by Watson and Hartmann (1939), produced only somewhat weak evidence for the congeniality effect. In this experiment 10 atheists and 10 theists (i.e. participants from a theological seminary) received statements that were pro and con the existence of God. Far stronger findings were presented by Levine and Murphy (1943). In their study 5 Communists and 5 anti-Communists received messages that were favorable or unfavorable to the Soviet Union. The findings were stunning: the congeniality bias appeared to be very strong. Figure 9.1 shows their data for the anti-Soviet Union passage: the anti-Communist participants showed better memory than the pro-Communist participants.

A substantial amount of research on attitude memory followed in the 1940s through the 1960s, and the picture became murkier (see Eagly & Chaiken, 1993; in press). Findings were often weak and not entirely consistent within studies.

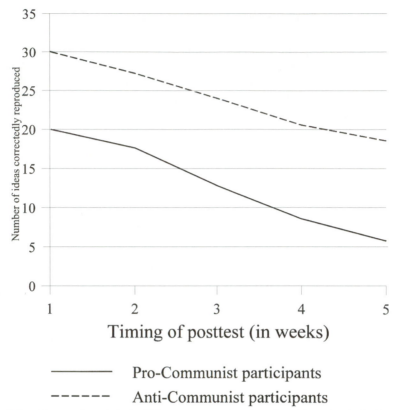

FIG. 9.1   Memory for anti-Soviet Union passage as a function of participants' attitudinal position and the timing of the recall posttest (data graphed from Table 2, Levine & Murphy, 1943).

Some of these studies featured interaction predictions by which congeniality was hypothesized to be present under specific circumstances. For example, Jones and Aneshansel (1956) showed that the congeniality effect could reverse when uncongenial information would be useful in a subsequent counterarguing task.

Researchers' ability to produce congeniality appeared to erode almost entirely in the 1960s. Several researchers produced stunningly null effects. Greenwald and Sakumura's (1967) research was probably the best known of these studies; these findings seemed to suggest that the null hypothesis was valid (Greenwald, 1975). Although there were some hints of possible methodological failings in early research, the disappearing congeniality effect remained essentially mysterious. It was not clear why early investigators such as Levine and Murphy (1943) were successful in producing the congeniality effect and many subsequent investigators were not successful. Despite these ambiguities and puzzles, by the 1970s some social psychologists seemed willing to believe that attitudes exert little, if any, impact on memory for attitude-relevant information.

META-ANALYSIS OF ATTITUDE–MEMORY RESEARCH

The obvious inconsistencies of this attitude–memory literature make it a particularly inviting site for quantitative synthesis. Some of the uncertainties in interpretations of this research area may stem from the well-known limitations of narrative reviewing (see Cooper, 1989; Johnson & Eagly, in press), especially from reviewers' use of statistical significance as a criterion for evaluating and comparing studies. As contemporary researchers realize, an effect that is nonsignificant may actually be moderately large in magnitude if the study has little power because of its small participant sample, unreliable measures, and other weaknesses. Conversely, an effect that is significant may be extremely small in magnitude if the study has a large amount of power because of its large participant sample, reliable measures, and other strengths. To circumvent these problems and to explicate this very interesting literature, I undertook a meta-analysis of attitude memory studies, with collaborators Serena Chen, Shelly Chaiken, and Kelly Shaw-Barnes (Eagly, Chen, Chaiken, & Shaw-Barnes, 1997). This project considerably extends a quantitative synthesis by Roberts (1985), which included only a portion of the available studies and analyzed relatively few of the potential moderators of the congeniality effect.

We searched thoroughly for studies and implemented somewhat stringent selection criteria to narrow the sample to studies that examined the impact of the attitudinal congeniality of verbal attitude-relevant information on memory for the information. Eliminated from the sample were studies that provided weak tests of the hypothesis—for example, studies which assessed attitude only as a post-measure, rendering the attitude measure vulnerable to the persuasive effects of the information. The final sample consisted of 60 documents reporting 70 studies that had appropriate designs. We coded these studies with respect to many study characteristics and computed effect sizes.

The studies in this literature mainly consist of laboratory experiments, with the classic design of Watson and Hartmann (1939) and Levine and Murphy (1943) being the most common. Specifically, the typical experiment presented participants with information on their own side versus the opposite side of an issue by varying both participant attitude (pro vs. con on the issue) and the position of the information (pro vs. con). These stimuli usually pertained to controversial social issues that were moderately or highly familiar to the participants, issues such as communism in the 1940s, racial integration in the 1950s, the war in Viet Nam in the 1960s, and abortion in the 1980s and 1990s. The messages were generally written, but other modes of presentation were not uncommon. These stimuli were usually presented in the form of passages but sometimes as sentences or even as words. In the typical procedure, the attitude was assessed in a prior session, the stimuli were presented in the experimental session, and then memory was measured, often along with other responses.

Sometimes the experiment included a delayed measure in a later session. Memory was most commonly assessed by free recall, although recognition measures were also used. Most of the studies were conducted in the United States, but several other nations were represented, including Canada, Germany, India, and Japan.

The overall congeniality effect in this literature was small. The mean weighted effect size was 0.23 in the d metric of standardized differences, based on the 65 studies for which we could compute effect sizes. Because the 95% confidence interval around this mean extended from 0.19 to 0.27, the effect can be considered significant. The hypothesis of homogeneity of the effect sizes was rejected. When outlying effect sizes were removed to produce a homogeneous data set, the mean effect size receded to only 0.08. This operation required the removal of 18 studies, or 28% of the total; this proportion is relatively large, confirming the heterogeneity of the effect sizes. Finally, 60% of the studies had findings that went in the congeniality direction, and 40% went in the opposite direction. Most effect sizes clustered around zero, with 31 of the 65 falling in the range from 0.20 to −0.20, but there was a somewhat larger number of positive than negative effect sizes.

The sample of studies included one very extreme outlier, a Japanese study that yielded an effect size of 8.74 (Kitano, 1970). Because this study appeared to be classic in its design and typical in its measures, we regarded it as anomalous and deleted it from further analyses. The next largest effect size, a value of 2.20, is from the Levine and Murphy (1943) citation classic. Thus, the study that initially attracted attention and focused research on attitude memory produced a value that can be considered extreme, in the context of subsequent research.

Reviewers of this literature should be wary about a variety of methodological issues, especially in relation to the measurement of memory. Most assessments of memory were by free recall measures that demanded coding. Provocative with respect to these measurement issues was the finding that, in more than half of the studies that used recall measures which required coding, there was no indication that the coders were blind to the participants' attitudes. Also worrisome was the finding that, among the recognition measures, there were only a few recognition sensitivity measures, which are controlled for bias—that is, the type of measure generally known as d-prime (Srull, 1984). The majority of recognition measures were various other less controlled types, usually hit rate, or some variant of a multiple choice or forced choice measure.

The type of memory measure made a major difference in studies' findings, and these trends raised serious questions about the presence of artifacts in early experiments that required coding of participants' responses. Specifically, effect sizes were considerably elevated in the studies using recall measures requiring coding which were published prior to 1960 and for which coding was not known to be blind (e.g. Jones & Kohler, 1958; Levine & Murphy, 1943). In the absence of evidence that coding of free recall responses in these early studies was blind to participants' attitudes, it is possible that coders were aware of participants' attitudinal positions and of the researchers' prediction of congeniality. In contrast, classifying the post-1960 studies according to whether blind coding was explicitly mentioned in the primary report did not produce a significant model. Presumably in the later studies, the omission of information about the blindness of coding of free recall usually reflected incomplete reporting of the method, not a failure to implement blind coding.

For the recognition measures, the size of the congeniality effect depended on whether studies assessed memory by recognition sensitivity, which is corrected for bias, or by measures that are not corrected for bias. The uncorrected recognition measures produced a larger mean effect size, a finding consistent with the interpretation that participants in attitude–memory experiments made guesses consistent with their own attitudes in responding to the recognition task. Guessing of this type could be due to the tendency of participants to use their own attitudes and beliefs as retrieval cues in responding to the recognition task. Recognition sensitivity measures would remove these and other biases by subtracting the false alarm rate from the hit rate.

The meta-analysis also revealed a very strong tendency for the congeniality effect to have eroded over time, as many attitude researchers suspected. Regression analyses were consistent with the conclusion that this erosion was due in large part to improvements in the assessment of memory—that is, blind coding of recall measures and the use of recognition sensitivity measures rather than potentially biased measures of recognition. The more stringent measurement procedures that were prevalent at a later point evidently removed the biases that had allowed earlier studies to appear to produce congeniality.

One of the other potential methodological problems in attitude–memory research is that participants might have been more familiar with information on their own side of the issue and therefore displayed better memory for congenial information, especially in early studies in which familiarity may not have been controlled. However, coding of the likelihood that participants were more familiar with information on their own side of the issue failed to support this hypothesis. Of course, with the kinds of controversial social issues typically used in this research, there would generally be at least some familiarity with arguments on both sides of the issue.

The meta-analysis produced evidence of several other interesting moderators of congeniality. Specifically, the congeniality effect was larger when the attitudinal issue was high in value-relevance compared with low in value-relevance, and the effect was weaker when the issue was high in outcome-relevance compared with low in outcome-relevance (see Johnson & Eagly, 1989). The congeniality effect was larger when it was tested with a within-subjects error term compared with a between-subjects error term; it was also larger in the published literature than the unpublished literature. The congeniality effect was also larger in studies conducted in countries other than the United States. Although these several moderator variables are important theoretically and methodologically (see Eagly et al., 1997), the most striking outcome of the meta-analysis is its demonstration of the general weakness of the congeniality effect in studies that have more controlled memory measures that render the results less vulnerable to artifact.

Given these findings, it would be tempting to conclude that attitudes have little, if any, impact on information processing after all. This conclusion would actually be wrong and would reflect the narrow focus of many of the earlier researchers. Their logic was that people would screen out information that challenges their attitudes, in an effort to defend these attitudes. They assumed a profoundly closed-minded information processor, an individual who does not give counterattitudinal information much of a chance at any stage of information processing. These assumptions are much too extreme. Our meta-analysis and other evidence suggests that people are often moderately willing to expose themselves to challenging information, to attend to it and encode it accurately, and to remember it, even though they do not like the information.

Earlier attitude theorists were correct in one of their underlying assumptions—namely, that people are generally motivated to defend their attitudes. People are so motivated, especially with the highly controversial issues used in attitude–memory research, but do not necessarily follow the defensive strategy that was initially assumed by social psychologists. Early theorists assumed a defensive approach that can be called *passive*, whereby people would selectively screen out challenging information (see Eagly & Chaiken, 1995).

What these researchers neglected to consider is perhaps fairly obvious from a contemporary perspective: they failed to consider the possibility of an active defense that would enhance rather than reduce memory for uncongenial information. Thus, instead of passively screening out incongruent information, recipients who are active defenders would attend to it and process such information systematically, in order to refute it through counterarguing. Even though challenging information would become memorable, it would pose little threat to existing attitudes, to the extent that the challenge was successfully met through counterarguing.

Counterarguing challenging information is especially feasible if a person is familiar with the potential attack and thus has defenses already worked out. Recognizing this point, Pratkanis (1989) has drawn attention to attitudes' bipolar or unipolar structure. Pratkanis's point is that, to the extent that people's attitudes are unipolar (i.e. they possess predominantly knowledge that is congruent with their own position), they may find it difficult to encode incongruent information or to counterargue it to the extent that they have encoded it. They may thus show the congeniality effect. Conversely, to the extent that people are bipolar (i.e. familiar with both supporting and opposing viewpoints), uncongenial information may be as strongly linked to stored knowledge as is congenial information. Bipolarity is probably the usual situation in attitude–memory studies. Under such circumstances, congenial and uncongenial information should be encoded equally well. Given sufficient motivation to defend attitudes, uncongenial information should be extensively counterargued and therefore recalled at least as well as congenial information. We have begun to test these ideas in new research.

PRIMARY RESEARCH ON ATTITUDES' EFFECTS ON MEMORY

To enable the new research to illuminate prior attitude–memory research, the experiments are in the classic paradigm of Watson and Hartmann (1939) and Levine and Murphy (1943). Therefore, we first sought strong attitudes that maximally polarized our population of students. Pretesting yielded two especially promising issues—gays in the military and abortion; and most of our research has used the abortion issue. We tested whether attitudes were bipolar on these issues by asking our participants to list arguments that they had "heard people make on both sides of the issue." Coders judged the position of these arguments. Particularly on the abortion issue, the participants wrote down as many statements opposing as supporting their own attitudinal position. In other words, they appeared to be bipolar—that is, knowledgeable about both sides of the issue.

Participants were selected as prochoice or prolife and came from an introductory psychology subject pool or from abortion activist organizations. There was a pretest session assessing abortion attitudes and other variables. Two weeks later, participants attended the main experimental session, which included an audiotaped message, followed by memory measures and other measures. Memory was assessed by recall and by a recognition measure which yielded recognition sensitivity or d-prime. In one study, there was a delayed session two weeks after the main session.

The congeniality effects proved to be null for recall and recognition, thus confirming the verdict of the meta-analysis. For example, one study involved 141 psychology students and 33 abortion activists. The effect sizes for the congeniality effect were 0.05 for recall and −0.11 for recognition, comparable to the overall effects that we obtained in the meta-analysis with the more controlled memory measures. In fact, the congeniality effect was everywhere null in this research. The effect was null regardless of whether participants were exposed to only one side of the issue, in a between-subjects test of the congeniality hypothesis, or whether participants were exposed to both sides of the issue, in a within-subjects test of the congeniality hypothesis. The congeniality effect was null for the activists as well as for the psychology students; it was null at the delayed session and the immediate session. Not surprisingly, activists had better memory than psychology students, and memory had declined by the delayed session. However, these effects were similar for the proattitudinal and counterattitudinal messages and therefore congeniality did not emerge under any of these circumstances.

Measures assessing information processing showed that participants engaged in more effortful processing of the counterattitudinal messages. Thus, participants

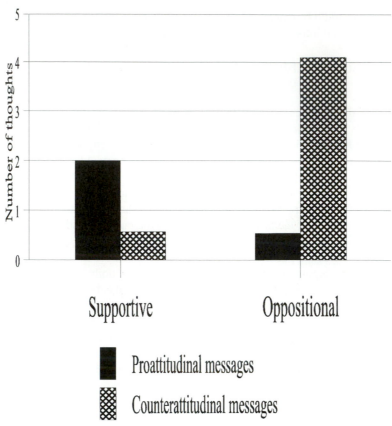

FIG. 9.2   Number of supportive and oppositional differentiated thoughts as a function of the attitudinal congeniality of the messages (data graphed from Table 1, Eagly, Kulesa et al., 1997).

rated themselves as giving more thought and attention to the counterattitudinal message. Also, participants who received a counterattitudinal message generated more thoughts that were relevant to the message or issue. These message- and issue-relevant thoughts were divided into those that were supportive or opposi-tional in relation to the message. The thoughts were also divided into those that were global (that is, very general statements) and those that were differentiated (or more elaborated). As Fig. 9.2 shows, the counterattitudinal message elicited a lot of differentiated thoughts that opposed the message. The global thoughts were fewer, as Fig. 9.3 shows, and were somewhat concentrated among parti-cipants who received a proattitudinal message. Thus, participants not only thought more when contending with a counterattitudinal message, but they also thought more deeply and systematically.

Consistent with the commonsensical selective evaluation effect discussed earlier, participants showed dislike and disapproval of the counterattitudinal

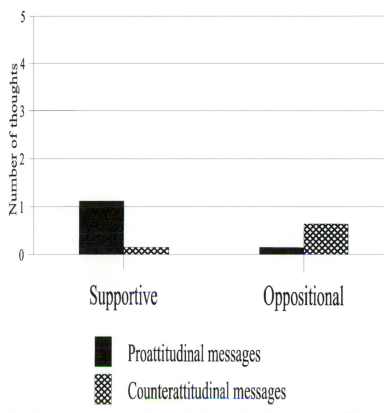

FIG. 9.3   Number of supportive and oppositional global thoughts as a function of the attitudinal congeniality of the messages (data graphed from Table 1, Eagly, Kulesa et al., 1997).

message. This effect was shown on a *general approval* measure, which combined items assessing evaluation of the message and its communicator. However, there was no evidence of selective perception in the form of assimilation of proattitudinal messages or of contrast of counterattitudinal messages.

In view of the findings indicating more thorough processing of the counterattitudinal messages, it may be puzzling that the congeniality effect did not reverse. After all, the processing of the proattitudinal messages appeared to be lazier and less thorough. If systematic processing improved memory, a measure of this type of processing should be correlated with memory in the counterattitudinal condition. Such relationships were obtained. Supporting the idea that engaging in detailed oppositional thinking enhanced memory for the counterattitudinal messages, we obtained a negative relationship between the supportiveness of differentiated thinking and recall of the message arguments. To the extent that participants engaged in detailed thinking opposed to the counterattitudinal message, they remembered it better.

In contrast, with the proattitudinal messages, measures of systematic processing were unrelated to memory. The best predictor of memory was general approval of the message. Participants remembered the message to the extent that they liked it, especially on the recall measure. With a proattitudinal message, which resonates with one's own attitudes, there is no need to engage in systematic, elaborative cognitive processing to remember the message. Recipients can more simply use their own attitude as a retrieval cue or heuristic, tagging in some fashion the message arguments, based on the beliefs that they personally endorse. A person could easily store arguments (for example, as the "adoption" argument or the argument that "back-alley abortions are dangerous") without elaborative processing. This simple retrieval process, guided by one's own attitude and beliefs, would be more critical for recall than recognition, accounting for the stronger relationships of our general approval variable to recall.

This research has also given a role to attitude strength, a variable that was neglected in most earlier research on selectivity (see Eagly & Chaiken, in press; Petty & Krosnick, 1995). To test the hypothesis that attitudinal selectivity operates more powerfully to the extent that attitudes are strong, the research used a straightforward self-report measure of attitude strength that averaged responses over five items (such as how important is the issue, and how sure the respondent is of his or her position). The congeniality effect did not emerge for participants with strong attitudes. Instead, attitude strength was associated with better memory for *both* counterattitudinal and proattitudinal messages. Path analyses suggested that these effects occurred because both of the mediating processes operated more strongly to the extent that attitudes were strong. Thus, to the extent that attitudes were stronger, systematic processing was more vigorous, and evaluative reactions were more extreme. Therefore, in the counterattitudinal condition, participants with strong attitudes had good memory because they counterargued so vigorously. In the proattitudinal condition, participants with strong attitudes had good memory because their evaluative reactions were more extreme. Because the message resonated so strongly with their own attitudes, they may have used their own attitudes and beliefs more effectively to help them remember (see Eagly, Kulesa et al., 1997).

The evidence for this interpretation is still being developed in our primary research. Current efforts involve using experimental manipulations that impact on the mediating processes I have described. The overall aim is to show that attitudes impact on memory by quite different processes, depending on the congeniality of the information.

In conclusion, attitudes do affect information processing, especially if these attitudes are strong. Attitude researchers failed to discern these effects because they were forever looking for the congeniality effect, which is the wrong place to look. What was neglected in earlier research is the possibility of active processes by which people enthusiastically engage attitudinally incongruent information, in order to counter its persuasive impact. Of course, the idea that defense of one's attitudes can be active or passive is in harmony with contemporary dual-process theories of social judgment such as the heuristic–systematic model and the elaboration likelihood model (see Chaiken, Wood, & Eagly, 1996; Eagly & Chaiken, 1993). Consistent with these theories, whether recipients of messages use a cognitively demanding, active approach or an avoidant, passive approach to defending their attitudes from attack would depend on their motivation and ability to use the more effortful, active approach. In the absence of motivation or ability, the easier, passive route to defense would be chosen; in the presence of both motivation and ability, the more effortful route of attacking counterattitudinal material would be more likely. In the typical attitude–memory study, both motivation and ability have been generally present. The threat from a counterattitudinal message on a highly involving issue is motivating, and the familiarity of the issue makes people highly able to defend themselves.

Research on attitudinal selectivity should thrive once more, despite its troubled history. Although early researchers may have led us astray into a search for congeniality effects, the elements for progress are now in place: (1) improved understanding of the cognitive processes that mediate outcomes such as memory; (2) improved measurement of memory so that researchers do not become sidetracked by effects that may be artifactual; and (3) improved knowledge of attitude structure and attitude strength and their role in relation to information processing.

REFERENCES

Allport, G. W. (1935). Attitudes. In C. Murchison (Ed.), *Handbook of social psychology* (pp. 798–844). Worcester, MA: Clark University Press.

Behavioral Science Subpanel of President's Science Advisory Committee (1962). Strengthening the behavioral sciences. *Behavioral Science, 7*, 275–288.

Bothwell, R. K., & Brigham, J. C. (1983). Selective evaluation and recall during the 1980 Reagan–Carter debate. *Journal of Applied Social Psychology, 13*, 427–442.

Cacioppo, J. T., & Petty, R. E. (1979). Effects of message repetition and position on cognitive response, recall, and persuasion. *Journal of Personality and Social Psychology, 37*, 97–109.

Chaiken, S., Wood, W. L., & Eagly, A. H. (1996). Principles of persuasion. In E. T. Higgins & A. Kruglanski (Eds.), *Social psychology: Handbook of basic principles* (pp. 702–742). New York: Guilford Press.

Cooper, H. M. (1989). *Integrating research: A guide for literature reviews* (2nd ed.). Thousand Oaks, CA: Sage.

Eagly, A. H. (1992). Uneven progress: Social psychology and the study of attitudes. *Journal of Personality and Social Psychology, 63*, 693–710.

Eagly, A. H., & Chaiken, S. (1993). *The psychology of attitudes.* Fort Worth, TX: Harcourt Brace Jovanovich.

Eagly, A. H., & Chaiken, S. (1995). Attitude strength, attitude structure, and resistance to change. In R. E. Petty & J. A. Krosnick (Eds.), *Attitude strength: Antecedents and consequences* (pp. 413–432). Mahwah, NJ: Erlbaum.

Eagly, A. H., & Chaiken, S. (in press). Attitude structure and function. In D. Gilbert, S. Fiske, & G. Lindzey (Eds.), *The handbook of social psychology* (4th ed.). New York: McGraw-Hill.

Eagly, A. H., Chen, S., Chaiken, S., & Shaw-Barnes, K. (1997). *The impact of attitudes on memory: An affair to remember*. Manuscript under review.

Eagly, A. H., Kulesa, P., Brannon, L., Shaw-Barnes, K., & Hutson-Comeaux, S. (1997). *Message congeniality determines the processes by which attitudes influence memory*. Unpublished manuscript.

Edwards, K., & Smith, E. E. (1996). A disconfirmation bias in the evaluation of arguments. *Journal of Personality and Social Psychology, 71*, 5–24.

Eiser, J. R. (1990). *Social judgment*. Pacific Grove, CA: Brooks/Cole.

Festinger, L. (1957). *A theory of cognitive dissonance*. Evanston, IL: Row, Peterson.

Festinger, L. (1964). *Conflict, decision, and dissonance*. Stanford, CA: Stanford University Press.

Freedman, J. L., & Sears, D. O. (1965). Selective exposure. In L. Berkowitz (Ed.), *Advances in experimental social psychology* (Vol. 2, pp. 57–97). New York: Academic Press.

Frey, D. (1986). Recent research on selective exposure to information. In L. Berkowitz (Ed.), *Advances in experimental social psychology* (Vol. 19, pp. 41–80). New York: Academic Press.

Greenwald, A. G. (1975). Consequences of prejudice against the null hypothesis. *Psychological Bulletin, 82*, 1–20.

Greenwald, A. G., & Sakumura, J. S. (1967). Attitude and selective learning: Where are the phenomena of yesteryear? *Journal of Personality and Social Psychology, 7*, 387–397.

Johnson, B. T., & Eagly, A. H. (1989). The effects of involvement on persuasion: A meta-analysis. *Psychological Bulletin, 106*, 290–314.

Johnson, B. T., & Eagly, A. H. (in press). Quantitative synthesis of social psychological research. In H. T. Reis & C. M. Judd (Eds.), *Handbook of research methods in social psychology*. London: Cambridge University Press.

Jones, E. E., & Aneshansel, J. (1956). The learning and utilization of contravaluant material. *Journal of Abnormal and Social Psychology, 53*, 27–33.

Jones, E. E., & Kohler, R. (1958). The effects of plausibility on the learning of controversial statements. *Journal of Abnormal and Social Psychology, 57*, 315–320.

Katz, D. (1960). The functional approach to the study of attitudes. *Public Opinion Quarterly, 24*, 163–204.

Kitano, E. (1970). A socio-psychological study on memory trace: The effect of attitude upon memory and its transformation. *Japanese Journal of Psychology, 40*, 310–318.

Levine, J. M., & Murphy, G. (1943). The learning and forgetting of controversial material. *Journal of Abnormal and Social Psychology, 38*, 507–517.

Lord, C. G., Ross, L., & Lepper, M. R. (1979). Biased assimilation and attitude polarization: The effects of prior theories on subsequently considered evidence. *Journal of Personality and Social Psychology, 37*, 2098–2109.

McGuire, W. J. (1969). The nature of attitudes and attitude change. In G. Lindzey & E. Aronson (Eds.), *Handbook of social psychology* (2nd ed., Vol. 3, pp. 136–314). Reading, MA: Addison-Wesley.

Petty, R. E., & Krosnick, J. A. (Eds.). (1995). *Attitude strength: Antecedents and consequences*. Mahwah, NJ: Erlbaum.

Pratkanis, A. R. (1989). The cognitive representation of attitudes. In A. R. Pratkanis, S. J. Breckler, & A. G. Greenwald (Eds.), *Attitude structure and function* (pp. 71–98). Hillsdale, NJ: Erlbaum.

Roberts, J. V. (1985). The attitude–memory relationship after 40 years: A meta-analysis of the literature. *Basic and Applied Social Psychology, 6*, 221–241.

Schwarz, N., & Bless, H. (1992). Constructing reality and its alternatives: An inclusion/exclusion model of assimilation and contrast effects in social judgment. In L. L. Martin & A. Tesser (Eds.), *The construction of social judgments* (pp. 217–245). Hillsdale, NJ: Erlbaum.

Sherif, M., & Hovland, C. I. (1961). *Social judgment: Assimilation and contrast effects in communication and attitude change*. New Haven, CT: Yale University Press.

Smith, M. B., Bruner, J. S., & White, R. W. (1956). *Opinions and personality*. New York: Wiley.

Srull, T. K. (1984). Methodological techniques for the study of person memory and social cognition. In R. S. Wyer & T. K. Srull (Eds.), *Handbook of social cognition* (pp. 73–150). Hillsdale, NJ: Erlbaum.

Upshaw, H. S. (1969). The personal reference scale: An approach to social judgment. In L. Berkowitz (Ed.), *Advances in experimental social psychology* (Vol. 4, pp. 315–371). New York: Academic Press.

Vallone, R. P., Ross, L., & Lepper, M. R. (1985). The hostile media phenomenon: Biased perception and perceptions of media bias in coverage of the Beirut massacre. *Journal of Personality and Social Psychology, 49*, 577–585.

Watson, W. S., & Hartmann, G. W. (1939). The rigidity of a basic attitudinal frame. *Journal of Abnormal and Social Psychology, 34*, 314–335.

PART TWO

Cross-cultural Psychology/ National Development

CHAPTER TEN

Cadres théoriques en psychologie interculturelle

Pierre R. Dasen
Faculté de Psychologie et des Sciences de l'Éducation,
Université de Genève, Suisse

L'auteur retrace les grandes lignes de sa carrière de recherche, en partant des études cherchant à vérifier la théorie de Piaget dans des contextes culturels différents, en passant par la description fine des contextes physiques et sociaux dans lesquels se développe l'enfant, ainsi que des pratiques éducatives et des ethnothéories parentales, et jusqu'au domaine des "savoirs quotidiens". Il aboutit à une combinaison de méthodes psychologiques et anthropologiques, illustrée sur le terrain par une recherche portant sur le système d'orientation spatiale à Bali et son influence sur les représentations de l'espace. Les différentes étapes de ce programme de recherche sont situées par rapport aux deux cadres théoriques principaux de la psychologie développementale interculturelle (comparative), le cadre écoculturel et la niche développementale. L'auteur défend une position médiane entre positivisme et constructivisme social, entre absolutisme et relativisme total, position qui revient à faire la part de ce qui est universel et de ce qui est particulier à chaque culture.

The author reviews the main phases of his research career, starting with studies aiming at testing Piaget's theory in various cultures, through the detailed description of the physical and social contexts in which human development takes place, including child-rearing practices and parental ethnotheories, up to the field of "everyday cognition". He ends up using a combination of psychological and anthropological methods, illustrated by a recent study of the Balinese spatial orientation system and its influence on spatial encoding. The various steps in this research program are presented in reference to the two main theoretical frameworks used in cross-cultural developmental psychology, the eco-cultural framework and the developmental niche. The author advocates an intermediate position between positivism and social constructivism, between absolutism and complete relativism, a position that amounts to taking into account both universality and cultural diversity.

Quels sont les cadres théoriques spécifiques de la psychologie interculturelle comparative? Au moment où j'avais reçu l'invitation de préparer cette conférence, mon intention première avait été de partir d'un article de Gustav Jahoda (1995), paru dans le premier numéro de la revue «Culture & Psychology» et portant sur les antécédents du cadre théorique "écoculturel" de John Berry (1976; 1987), que nous avons utilisé comme cadre général de référence pour nos manuels de psychologie interculturelle (Berry, Poortinga, Segall, & Dasen, 1992; Segall, Dasen, Berry, & Poortinga, 1990). Malgré le respect que je dois à l'un des pionniers de la psychologie interculturelle comparative, j'avais été un peu déçu par cet article de Jahoda qui retraçait l'histoire menant à ce cadre théorique mais s'arrêtait dans les années '40 et ne disait rien de plus actuel, et surtout ne le mettait pas en rapport avec d'autres cadres théoriques utilisés en psychologie interculturelle.

Berry (1995) ayant eu l'occasion de répondre lui-même à l'article de Jahoda, et puisqu'il s'agit ici d'une conférence sur invitation, j'ai décidé de me centrer davantage sur mes propres travaux, en essayant néanmoins de les relier à deux cadres théoriques, en particulier au cadre théorique écoculturel susmentionné et à celui de la niche développementale (Harkness & Super, 1995; Super & Harkness, 1986; 1997). L'exposé est donc structuré en trois parties. Je retournerai d'abord très brièvement à des recherches maintenant anciennes qui étaient directement inspirées par le cadre théorique écoculturel; la seconde partie reflète le moment de ma carrière où j'ai commencé à faire des recherches qui seraient maintenant illustrées par le modèle de la niche développementale. Finalement, j'expliquerai mon intérêt pour les *savoirs quotidiens* avec, en particulier, des recherches que j'effectue avec un collègue anthropologue, et qui essaient de marier les méthodes de l'anthropologie cognitive et celles de la psychologie interculturelle. Cette troisième partie sera illustrée par une recherche assez récente que nous avons effectuée ensemble à Bali, sur le système d'orientation spatiale et l'utilisation de référents absolus ou relatifs dans les conceptions de l'espace chez l'enfant.

LE CADRE THÉORIQUE ÉCOCULTUREL

Revenons tout d'abord en arrière, au début des années '70. Le cadre théorique qui inspirait alors mes travaux était en train d'être élaboré par John Berry (1966; 1971), avec qui j'ai eu le plaisir de collaborer occasionnellement dès cette époque (p. ex. Berry & Dasen, 1974). L'idée générale du cadre théorique écoculturel de Berry (voir la Fig. 10.1) est que la culture est une réponse fonctionnelle, une adaptation aux contextes écologique et sociopolitique, et qu'elle influence le comportement par l'intermédiaire des processus de transmission culturelle et d'acculturation. Dans la deuxième partie de ce texte, on verra que la niche développementale de Super et Harkness (1986; 1997) va préciser surtout ces processus de transmission culturelle. Le cadre théorique tient également compte de l'adaptation biologique et de la transmission génétique.

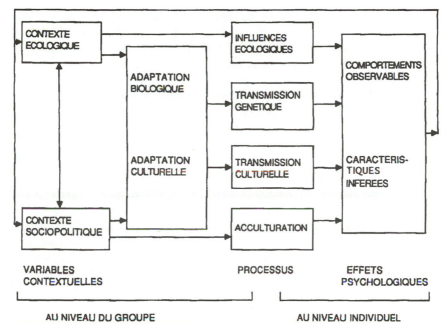

FIG. 10.1   Cadre théorique écoculturel de Berry.
NOTE:

D'après *Human behavior in global perspective: An introduction to cross-cultural psychology* (p. 19) par M. H. Segall, P. R. Dasen, J. W. Berry, & Y. H. Poortinga, 1990, Boston: Allyn & Bacon. Copyright 1990 par Allyn & Bacon. Adapté avec la permission de l'éditeur.

Le développement des opérations concrètes selon Piaget

Un exemple de mes recherches inspirées par ce cadre théorique porte sur le développement des opérations concrètes selon Piaget, avec l'hypothèse que les contextes écologiques et culturels vont favoriser le développement de certaines notions plutôt que d'autres, selon ce qui est adaptatif, et donc valorisé. Il s'agit, par exemple, des notions spatiales dans les populations de nomades, chasseurs-cueilleurs, qui ont besoin d'une bonne orientation spatiale. Leur survie en dépend, alors qu'ils n'ont pas besoin ou ont moins besoin de notions quantitatives, telles que les notions de conservation de la quantité, du poids ou du volume selon Piaget. Les populations sédentaires d'agriculteurs, qui cultivent et échangent des produits, ont au contraire besoin de notions quantitatives beaucoup plus que de notions spatiales.

Une étude comparative avec tout d'abord trois groupes, des enfants Inuit au Canada, Aborigènes en Australie et Ebrié en Côte d'Ivoire (Dasen, 1975a), complétée par la suite par des études avec des enfants Baoulé en Côte d'Ivoire et Kikuyu au Kenya, a permis de constater un développement rapide de la notion de conservation des quantités continues chez les enfants de sédentaires agriculteurs (Baoulé et Kikuyu), un peu moins rapide chez des sédentaires agriculteurs et pêcheurs (Ebrié) et nettement moins rapide chez des enfants de chasseurs-cueilleurs, Aborigènes australiens et Inuit.

Dans le domaine de l'espace, en prenant l'exemple de l'épreuve piagétienne de l'horizontalité (une notion qui est relativement difficile et acquise tardivement), on voit que l'ordre de développement est exactement inverse. On constate un développement très rapide de cette notion chez les enfants Inuit, un peu moins rapide chez les enfants Aborigènes et beaucoup plus lente dans les trois populations sédentaires.

L'occasion de commenter ces résultats m'a été donnée plusieurs fois, quoique peut-être moins souvent en français (Dasen, 1983a; 1988a) qu'en anglais (p. ex. Dasen, 1993a; 1994; Dasen & Heron, 1981). Un des problèmes que j'ai rencontrés dans leur interprétation était de décider si, avec la transposition et l'adaptation d'épreuves de ce type, qui ont leur origine dans la société occidentale, des enfants peu familiarisés avec ce genre de situations ont réellement l'occasion de donner des réponses qui reflètent leur compétence cognitive, ou s'il se produit un décalage entre leurs réponses spontanées (ce qu'on pourrait appeler leur performance) et leur compétence réelle. Nous avons essayé d'élucider ce problème en utilisant des situations d'apprentissage opératoire. Dans la recherche sur la conservation des liquides avec des enfants Inuit (Dasen, 1975b), effectuée dans l'année que j'ai passée à l'Université de Montréal, entre 10% et 30% des enfants de 10 à 14 ans avaient donné, dans un premier temps, des réponses de non-conservation. A une seconde présentation de la même épreuve, à la fin de quelques semaines de familiarisation avec le chercheur et ses jeux bizarres, les enfants de 12 à 14 ans ont donné des réponses intermédiaires ou de conservation, alors que les réponses des enfants de 10 et 11 ans n'ont pas changé. Deux à trois séances d'apprentissage opératoire, selon la méthode de Lefebvre et Pinard (1972), ont suffi pour déclencher des réponses systématiques de conservation chez les enfants de 12 à 14 ans, alors qu'elles ont fait passer les enfants de 10 et 11 ans au stade intermédiaire.

Un apprentissage aussi rapide chez ces enfants Inuit de 12 ans et plus indique qu'ils devaient avoir la compétence associée à cette notion de conservation des quantités, mais ne parvenaient pas à l'exprimer spontanément, probablement parce qu'il s'agit d'un concept qui n'est pas valorisé dans leur milieu culturel. Il a donc fallu un "coup de pouce" pour leur permettre d'actualiser la compétence en performance. Le fait que cette notion ne soit pas valorisée dans cette culture est reflété dans l'apprentissage beaucoup plus lent chez les enfants de 10 et 11 ans. En résumé, dans ce cas particulier, la courbe de développement de la performance est asymptotique, alors que celle de la compétence atteint le 100%, mais présente un décalage d'environ trois ans dans l'âge d'accession aux différents stades par rapport aux résultats d'enfants africains (ou européens). D'autres recherches en Côte d'Ivoire et au Kenya, utilisant des techniques d'apprentissage

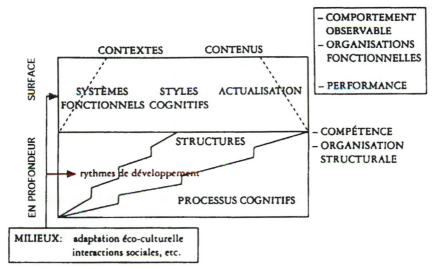

FIG. 10.2   Représentation schématique des résultats des recherches interculturelles sur le développement cognitif.

NOTE:

D'après "Schlusswort. Les sciences cognitives: Do they shake hands in the middle?" par P. R. Dasen, 1993c. In J. Wassmann & P. R. Dasen (Eds.), *Savoirs quotidiens. Les sciences cognitives dans le dialogue interdisciplinaire* (pp. 331–349). Fribourg, Suisse: Presses de l'Université de Fribourg. Copyright 1993 par Universitätsverlag Freiburg. Adapté avec la permission de l'éditeur.

opératoire (Inhelder, Sinclair, & Bovet, 1974) pour d'autres notions telles que l'inclusion de classes ou l'horizontalité ont permis de généraliser ce type de résultats (Dasen, Lavallée, & Retschitzki, 1979; Dasen, Ngini, & Lavallée, 1979; Lavallée & Dasen, 1980).

Culture et cognition

La Fig. 10.2 présente un résumé des conclusions tirées de l'ensemble des recherches interculturelles sur le développement cognitif, que ce soit les miennes ou d'autres (pour une revue de question récente, voir Mishra, 1997).

Une distinction primordiale, nous venons de le voir, est celle entre les structures profondes et la surface, c'est-à-dire entre la compétence et la performance ou comportement observable. A noter que cette distinction figure de façon saillante dans le cadre théorique écoculturel. Tous les résultats montrent que le développement cognitif au niveau compétence, c'est-à-dire au niveau structurel, est universel, en tout cas pour les processus cognitifs de base comme les opérations concrètes de Piaget. Je maintiens par ailleurs, contrairement à certaines affirmations néo-piagétiennes (voir Dasen & de Ribaupierre, 1987), que le développement se passe de façon constructive, sinon nécessairement par stades homogènes. Les résultats nous font penser que l'influence du milieu (culturel, social) s'exerce à la fois dans le rythme de développement au niveau de la compétence et dans l'actualisation de cette dernière.

Les phénomènes d'actualisation, tels que celui illustré par un apprentissage très rapide, sont certainement particulièrement importants quand la situation expérimentale est inhabituelle, ou quand il s'agit de concepts qui ne sont pas d'emblée valorisés dans la culture. Dans le même ordre d'idées, on peut dire qu'il n'y a pas de différence culturelle dans les processus cognitifs de base, mais qu'il y a des différences dans les contextes dans lesquels ces processus sont utilisés. Ce serait là la formulation de Cole et de son équipe (Cole, Gay, Glick, & Sharp, 1971; Cole & Scribner, 1974). On pourrait encore dire qu'il y a diversité dans la façon dont les différentes composantes de base se regroupent, ce qu'on pourrait appeler des styles cognitifs (Mishra, 1997). C'est également de cette manière que j'interprète les résultats de Tapé (1994) qui démontrent une préférence dans la culture africaine pour un raisonnement symbolique ou global plutôt qu'analytique, expériencé plutôt qu'expérimental, analogique plutôt que conceptuel, visant l'explication finale plutôt que causale. Mais pour Tapé, ces deux formes de pensée coexistent, elles "fonctionnent de façon autonome et s'élèvent à des niveaux d'abstraction variables suivant la nature de l'objet de connaissance" (p. 222). La préférence pour une forme de pensée n'exclut pas la compétence pour l'autre, mais pour être actualisée, cette dernière doit faire l'objet de sollicitations du milieu, notamment par la scolarisation.

Ce schéma n'exclut pas, a priori, la possibilité de l'existence de logiques totalement différentes, mais les preuves nous manquent encore. Troadec (1996) cherche à expliquer ainsi l'échec presque total d'enfants tahitiens de tous âges à l'épreuve piagétienne de l'inclusion des classes. Il fait l'hypothèse que ces enfants utiliseraient une logique intensionnelle, appelée *méréologie* à la place de la logique propositionnelle et ensembliste de Piaget. Cette logique serait plus "concrète", ou plus "naturelle", postulant l'existence d'objets aux significations discrètes, qui ne peuvent logiquement appartenir en même temps à deux ensembles différents.

Si je n'exclus pas la possibilité de logiques différentes, j'ai par contre une certaine méfiance à l'encontre des théories du "grand partage" (Segall et al., 1990, p. 99), celles qui opposent de façon binaire le concret et l'abstrait, le prélogique et le logique, le bricoleur et le scientifique, l'illettré et l'alphabétisé et donc, de façon au moins implicite, le non-occidental et l'occidental. Je me méfie des théories trop simples, qui sont souvent simplistes.

LA NICHE DÉVELOPPEMENTALE

Même si ces recherches reviennent à faire un lien entre des variables au niveau de la population et des comportements au niveau individuel, l'approche reste un peu monodisciplinaire. On étudie des processus internes du sujet et la façon dont ils se développent avec, finalement, relativement peu d'attention au contexte culturel dans lequel cela se déroule. A l'époque où j'ai effectué ces recherches, je lisais bien entendu les écrits des ethnologues, mais les considérais seulement comme une information de base indispensable pour pouvoir travailler et non pas comme mon propre sujet d'étude. Ainsi, les processus de transmission culturelle restaient implicites, n'étant pas observés directement par le chercheur.

Lors des deux années que j'ai passées à l'Université de Nairobi, où un Centre de recherche sur le développement de l'enfant avait été mis en place par Beatrice et John Whiting et leur équipe de Harvard, j'ai été intéressé par des méthodologies beaucoup plus inspirées de l'anthropologie. Selon cette approche, en même temps qu'on étudie le développement de l'enfant, par exemple au niveau cognitif, on essaie de décrire toute une série de variables portant sur l'environnement de l'enfant, sa famille, son contexte socioéconomique, sa vie quotidienne, les pratiques éducatives, bref, l'enculturation et la socialisation de l'enfant, et l'on peut alors chercher un lien entre toutes ces données. C'est donc à partir de la fin des années '70 que j'ai commencé à essayer des méthodologies du type observation de comportement de l'enfant dans la vie quotidienne, telles que développées, par exemple, par Ruth et Lee Munroe (Munroe & Munroe, 1971; 1980; Munroe, Munroe, & Michelson, 1983; Munroe & Munroe, 1997).

Le cadre théorique qui a été élaboré par Charles Super et Sara Harkness (1986; 1997), celui de la niche développementale, reflète parfaitement ce type d'intérêt. Ces collègues avaient d'ailleurs passé plusieurs années dans l'équipe des Whiting à Harvard, et avaient travaillé dans le même centre de recherches au Kenya un peu avant ma venue. Dans cette approche, l'objet d'études n'est pas seulement l'enfant en lui-même, comme le verraient les psychologues, ni seulement le contexte, étudié par les anthropologues, mais l'enfant dans son contexte. Même si le cadre théorique n'a été développé et formalisé que plus tard, je peux maintenant y situer mes travaux.

Le cadre théorique de la niche développementale est d'ailleurs parfaitement compatible avec le cadre théorique écoculturel, dont il précise les processus de transmission culturelle (enculturation et socialisation). L'organisme (avec ses données biologiques, dont le tempérament) est situé au milieu d'un système ouvert où trois composantes du contexte sont en interaction: les contextes physiques et sociaux dans lesquels se trouve l'enfant; les pratiques éducatives; et ce que Super et Harkness (1986; 1997) appellent la psychologie des parents (ou des personnes qui s'occupent de l'enfant) et que je préfère appeler représentations sociales, ou encore, en suivant Bril et Lehalle (1988), ethnothéories parentales. Tout comme dans le cadre théorique de Bronfenbrenner (1979; 1989), où le microsystème est entouré d'un exosystème, qui fait lui-même partie d'un macrosystème, celui de la niche développementale est un système ouvert, entouré des contextes culturels, écologiques, et sociohistoriques.

Ce cadre théorique est illustré à la Fig. 10.3 et les composantes des différentes parties énumérées au Tableau 10.1.

Les ethnothéories parentales sont donc les représentations dites naïves ou de sens commun, autrement dit les idées que se font les adultes (le plus souvent

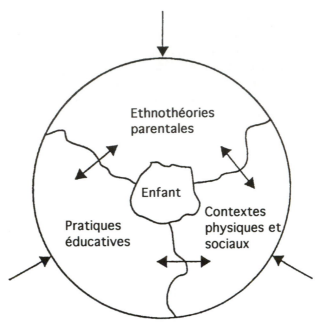

FIG. 10.3   Représentation schématique du cadre théorique de la niche développementale.
NOTE:

D'après "The cultural structuring of child development" par C. Super et S. Harkness, 1997. In J. W. Berry, P. R. Dasen, & T. S. Saraswathi (Eds.), *Handbook of cross-cultural psychology: Vol. 2. Basic processes and human development* (2nd ed., pp. 1–40). Boston: Allyn & Bacon. Copyright 1997 par Allyn & Bacon. Adapté avec la permission des auteurs et de l'éditeur.

les parents) sur ce que sont le développement de l'enfant, les étapes attendues, l'âge d'acquisition de telle ou telle aptitude, le type d'aptitudes et de connaissances exigées de l'enfant, en somme tout ce qui est considéré comme important dans la société par rapport au développement et à l'éducation de l'enfant. Ces représentations sociales déterminent en partie les pratiques éducatives et interagissent avec les contextes physiques et sociaux, et cet ensemble interagit à son tour avec les caractéristiques de l'individu, qui participe activement à sa propre socialisation (Camilleri, 1989; Camilleri & Malewska-Peyre, 1997). Il s'agit bien d'un système, mais comme Blandine Bril et Colette Sabatier (Bril, Dasen, Krewer, & Sabatier, sous presse; Sabatier & Bril, 1996) le soulignent, les liens entre les différentes parties sont complexes: il y a parfois des incohérences, par exemple, entre ce que les parents disent et ce qu'ils font.

Les activités quotidiennes

Mes propres travaux qui illustrent ce cadre théorique ont tout d'abord utilisé des observations dites ponctuelles: on fait un grand nombre d'observations (environ 30 par enfant) de ce que fait l'enfant dans des situations quotidiennes, avec un

TABLEAU 10.1
Composantes de la niche développementale

CONTEXTES

PHYSIQUES	SOCIAUX
— climat	— type de famille
— nutrition	— groupe de pairs
— écologie visuelle	— générations
— objets, dessins, livres	— mères multiples
etc.	— enfants gardiens
	— présence père/mère
	etc.

PRATIQUES EDUCATIVES
- soins
- postures
- stimulations
- jeu
- travaux
etc.

REPRÉSENTATIONS SOCIALES
- psychologie des parents
- ethnothéories parentales
- théories indigènes, naïves
    - facteurs du développement
    - âges d'acquisition
    - types de compétences
    - niveau de maîtrise
    - évaluation
    - valeurs, stade final
etc.

échantillonnage de toutes les heures de la journée, ce qui permet de quantifier le temps consacré à chaque activité. Je me suis intéressé en particulier aux jeux et travaux dans deux contextes africains (Dasen, 1983b; 1984b; 1985; 1988b). Comme c'est aussi le cas ailleurs en Afrique (Munroe, R. H. et al. 1983; Whiting & Whiting, 1975), les enfants Baoulé en Côte d'Ivoire et les enfants Kikuyu du Kenya effectuent beaucoup de travaux au service de la famille, et nous pensons qu'il s'agit là d'un contexte de socialisation très important, y compris pour leurs apprentissages cognitifs, à distinguer nettement de l'exploitation des enfants par le travail dénoncée par l'UNICEF et l'Organisation Internationale du Travail.

En regardant combien de temps ces enfants passent à jouer ou à travailler, on voit que, dès l'âge de 5 à 7 ans, ces jeunes enfants africains consacrent environ la moitié de leur temps à rendre des services à la famille. Ce pourcentage augmente avec l'âge, jusqu'à atteindre 80 % entre 12 et 16 ans pour les filles, un peu moins pour les garçons. Effectuer des tâches pour la famille est extrêmement important dans la vie quotidienne de ces enfants.

Une ethnothéorie parentale: les définitions de l'intelligence

Les ethnothéories parentales que nous avons relevées sont cohérentes avec ces observations. Dans une recherche sur le concept d'intelligence chez les Baoulé de Côte d'Ivoire (Dasen, 1984a; Dasen et al., 1985), les parents nous ont dit qu'on peut observer l'enfant pour prédire s'il aura plus ou moins de *n'glouèlê* en tant qu'adulte. *N'glouèlê* est la traduction la plus proche de ce que nous appelons *intelligence* en français. Et qu'est-ce que les parents Baoulé regardent? Ils observent en particulier si l'enfant est serviable, s'il assume des responsabilités, mais aussi s'il prend des initiatives. Ils disent, par exemple: "Une fille (de 9 ans environ) rentre à la maison et trouve que la vaisselle n'a pas été lavée; alors spontanément elle la lave, et comme la maman n'est toujours pas rentrée des champs, elle commence à préparer le repas". Des observations tout à fait similaires ont été rapportées par Super (1983) qui a travaillé chez les Kipsigis du Kenya, et par Serpell (1989; 1993) en Zambie.

Les Baoulé disent aussi qu'un enfant qui aura du *n'glouèlê* est un enfant respectueux, obéissant, qui sait bien parler, et se comporte un peu comme un adulte; d'autre part, il est attentif, "voit tout", apprend vite, a une bonne mémoire, réussit bien à l'école et porte chance. Selon la terminologie introduite par Mundy-Castle (1975), il y a là des éléments d'une intelligence sociale qui prédominent (deux réponses sur trois dans l'analyse de contenu), mais aussi des éléments technologiques. Dans un jargon plus actuel, on parlerait d'éléments collectivistes et individualistes (Kaḡıtçıbaşı, 1997). Pour les Baoulé, ces aspects plus technologiques, plus cognitifs et scolaires, ne font partie du *n'glouèlê* que s'ils sont mis au service du groupe social, et non pas s'ils sont mis au profit d'une promotion personnelle. On voit la cohérence, dans une telle société collectiviste, entre ces ethnothéories, les pratiques éducatives et les activités quotidiennes des enfants.

Nous avons demandé à des adultes Baoulé d'évaluer un groupe d'enfants selon les différentes composantes du *n'glouèlê*. Les coefficients de corrélation entre ces évaluations et les performances à des épreuves piagétiennes étaient dans l'ensemble proches de zéro; elles étaient même négatives (de façon statistiquement significative) avec la réussite dans les épreuves spatiales, ce qui illustre bien la valorisation culturelle différente de ces domaines.

Lorsque j'ai présenté cette recherche à des collègues, certains m'ont dit: «Tu prétends que c'est une définition africaine de l'intelligence. Qu'en sais-tu? En Suisse, si l'on questionnait des parents dans un contexte rural, par exemple dans une vallée des Alpes où il y a encore des fermes familiales, où les enfants peuvent aider les parents, ne trouverait-on pas la même chose?». Kaḡıtçıbaşı (dans ce volume) pose un peu la même question. Effectivement, il s'agit peut-être d'une conception commune à toutes les sociétés collectivistes. A vérifier!

Quand nous avons interrogé des parents dans un village resté traditionnel dans une vallée des Alpes (Schurmans & Dasen, 1992; Schurmans, Dasen, &

TABLEAU 10.2
Pourcentages des thèmes évoqués dans chacune des catégories
(composantes sociales; composantes technologiques) dans les entretiens
semi-directifs et le tri de descripteurs, en Côte d'Ivoire et en Suisse (Evolène),
en Baoulé, français et patois.

Lieu	Kpouebo Côte d'Ivoire		Evolène Suisse		Evolène Suisse	
Langue	Baoulé		Français		Patois	
Groupe d'âge (ans)	< 68	< 68	< 68	> 75	< 68	> 75
Occupation*	A	NA	A	A	A + NA	A
Entretiens Composantes sociales:	63	24	27	21	33	65
Composantes technologiques:	37	76	73	79	67	35
Tri de descripteurs Composantes sociales:	—	32	44	52	—	—
Composantes technologiques:	—	68	56	48	—	—
Nombre de couples interrrogés	42	17	17	32	8	12

* Occupation: A = agriculteurs, NA = non-agriculteurs

Vouilloz, 1990/91), leurs réponses spontanées étaient à environ 70% à 80% des définitions technologiques, comme on le voit au Tableau 10.2.

En utilisant, comme nous l'avions fait en Côte d'Ivoire, l'entretien semi-directif puis une analyse de contenu, les définitions que nous avons obtenues chez ces parents suisses, qu'ils soient agriculteurs ou non, jeunes ou vieux, étaient donc des définitions très technologiques. Mais nous ne nous sommes pas arrêtés là. Nous avons tout d'abord utilisé une deuxième technique, un tri de cartes avec des descripteurs sociaux et technologiques, à parts égales, tirés des entretiens. Avec cette technique, les personnes âgées, et de façon marginale aussi les jeunes agriculteurs, changeaient partiellement leur type de réponse, en choisissant plus de descripteurs sociaux, alors que pour les jeunes dans le secteur moderne (non-agriculteurs), cela ne faisait aucune différence. Dans cette recherche, les "jeunes" étaient des personnes entre 23 et 68 ans, alors que les personnes âgées avaient plus de 75 ans, et avaient donc vraiment passé leur jeunesse et élevé leurs propres enfants à un moment où la société, dans cette partie de la Suisse, était effectivement encore très collectiviste. On peut penser que le tri de cartes, en montrant que des descripteurs sociaux pouvaient être choisis, les autorisait, en somme, à faire valoir des représentations sociales groupales, là où les entretiens avec des chercheurs universitaires les incitaient à se cantonner dans une conception sociétale, dominante et exogène, véhiculée par les médias et l'école.

Une autre occasion d'arriver à mettre en évidence une conception beaucoup plus sociale de l'intelligence, qui se rattache à la vie traditionnelle dans cette vallée, nous a été donnée quand une de nos étudiantes, qui venait de cette vallée et qui en parlait le patois, a pu répéter l'étude dans cette langue (Fournier, Schurmans, & Dasen, 1994). On voit que dans ce contexte, les personnes âgées donnent des réponses avant tout sociales plutôt que technologiques, alors que ce n'est pas le cas des jeunes. L'utilisation du patois local par une enquêtrice qui appartient au lieu permet l'émergence d'une conception endogène dans le sous-groupe le plus attaché à la tradition.

Voilà donc, en résumé, quelques travaux qui forment le deuxième volet de ma carrière de chercheur, et qui illustrent le modèle de la niche développementale. Du point de vue méthodologique, ces recherches utilisent avant tout l'observation directe, dans les contextes quotidiens, et l'entretien de recherche. Même si l'on peut utiliser les épreuves piagétiennes dans des contextes culturels divers (en les adaptant et en introduisant toutes sortes de contrôles sur la communication entre sujet et chercheur), en trouvant une structure factorielle qui correspond bien à la théorie (Dasen, 1984a), l'emploi d'épreuves et de tests transposés dans une autre culture ne montre qu'un aspect de la réalité. Peu à peu je me suis plutôt intéressé à ce qu'on peut dire sur le fonctionnement ou le développement cognitif en observant simplement ce que font les gens dans la vie quotidienne.

LES SAVOIRS QUOTIDIENS

Le domaine de recherche relativement récent, appelé *everyday cognition*, ou *savoirs quotidiens* (Dasen & Bossel-Lagos, 1989; Rogoff & Lave, 1984; Schliemann, Carraher, & Ceci, 1997; Segall et al., 1990), correspond pour moi et certains de mes collaborateurs et étudiants à un désir d'étudier certains savoirs dits traditionnels, par exemple dans l'agriculture en Afrique (Akkari, 1993; Tshingeji, 1989; 1993). En imposant des savoirs extérieurs, industriels et marchands, on néglige tout un savoir qui existe sur place, risque de disparaître et mérite peut-être d'être revalorisé (Verhelst & Sizoo, 1994).

Mon intérêt pour les savoirs quotidiens m'a amené à collaborer avec Jürg Wassmann, un collègue ethnologue de l'Université de Bâle, qui a aussi travaillé à l'Institut Max Planck de Nijmegen, et qui est maintenant professeur à Heidelberg. Wassmann est un spécialiste de l'anthropologie cognitive (Wassmann, 1993) et s'intéresse à la psychologie et en particulier à la théorie de Piaget (Wassmann, 1988). En travaillant ensemble sur le terrain, nous nous sommes mis à réfléchir à la collaboration entre l'ethnologue et le psychologue et avons défini une méthodologie en trois étapes. La première, qui est celle de l'ethnologue, est de bien décrire la culture de la société étudiée, en tant que système global. Anciennement, l'ethnologue se contentait de son observation participante et interrogeait quelques informateurs privilégiés qu'il considérait particulièrement bien informés sur l'ensemble du système culturel. Sans doute sous l'influence de la sociologie et de la psychologie, les ethnologues se sont mis à interroger beaucoup plus de personnes et à décrire aussi la variation à l'intérieur de la société. Il s'agit donc d'interroger ce qu'on a appelé les *jpfs* (*just plain folks*), autrement dit «l'homme de la rue», et pas seulement les "experts".

Deuxièmement, ce que les gens disent ne correspond pas toujours à ce qu'ils font. Il faut donc aussi procéder à l'observation des pratiques de la vie quotidienne. Finalement, si l'on cherche à étudier un processus particulier, on risque d'attendre très longtemps qu'il se produise spontanément. Il faut donc mettre les personnes dans des situations qui permettent de le provoquer. Il peut s'agir d'un test, d'une épreuve piagétienne, en fait de n'importe quelle situation organisée spécifiquement pour observer le comportement qui nous intéresse, plutôt que de l'observer uniquement dans la vie quotidienne. Pour cette troisième étape de situations provoquées, l'ethnologue devient généralement très prudent, sinon réticent, alors que le psychologue a moins d'hésitations.

Wassmann et moi avons travaillé ensemble sur le terrain en Papouasie-Nouvelle-Guinée chez les Yupno, en particulier sur les classifications (Wassmann & Dasen, 1994a) et sur le concept du nombre et le système numérique (Wassmann & Dasen, 1994b). Les Yupno comptent avec les parties du corps. J'avais été fasciné par les recherches de Geoffrey Saxe sur le système de comptage sur le corps chez les Oksapmin, également en Papouasie-Nouvelle-Guinée (Saxe, 1981; 1983). Ces recherches représentent, pour moi, ce qui a été fait de plus intéressant dans le domaine de la psychologie interculturelle piagétienne, et nous voulions nous en inspirer. Mais chez les Yupno, le système numérique traditionnel n'est utilisé que par les hommes, et les enfants Yupno ne l'apprennent plus, si bien que nous n'avons pas pu en faire une étude développementale. Par contre, nous avons observé des variations individuelles étonnantes dans l'utilisation de ce système: sur huit hommes interrogés, quatre, y compris l'informateur principal de l'ethnologue, utilisaient un système aboutissant à l'équivalent de 33, mais quatre autres utilisaient un système légèrement différent, aboutissant à 30, 32 ou 37. Il se pourrait que cela soit dû à des erreurs, du fait que le système n'est plus d'usage très courant, mais il est aussi possible qu'il en ait toujours été ainsi. En effet, un décompte se fait toujours en public, et on ne désigne jamais un nombre—c'est-à-dire une partie du corps—sans démontrer également toute la séquence de parties du corps pour y parvenir. On peut donc dire "C'est tel chiffre tel que compté par untel".

Orientation spatiale et relativité linguistique

Plus récemment, j'ai eu l'occasion de travailler avec Wassmann sur une recherche à Bali (Wassmann & Dasen, 1996). Dans cette île, tout est structuré selon un système d'orientation spatiale particulier: l'organisation du village, celle des

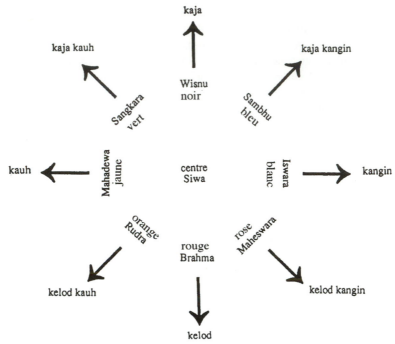

FIG. 10.4   Le système d'orientation spatiale balinais avec ses huit directions et les dieux et couleurs qui leur sont associés.

temples, l'architecture de la maison, l'endroit où chacun dort selon la hiérarchie sociale et la direction dans laquelle on place un enfant pour dormir. Tout est organisé selon ce système où il y a toujours le haut de la montagne, l'amont, appelé *kaja*, et le bas, l'aval, la direction de la mer, *kelod*. *Kaja* c'est le sacré, *kelod* le profane. Par rapport à cet axe principal, la dimension transversale comporte les directions *kauh* et *kangin*. Toute la vie balinaise est réglée selon ce système d'orientation, et il n'est pas difficile d'en constater l'ubiquité. Ce système est illustré à la Fig. 10.4, qui comporte également les noms des dieux du panthéon hindouiste associés à chaque direction et les couleurs symboliques qui y correspondent.

En balinais, on localise les objets avec ce même système d'orientation, c'est-à-dire par rapport à un référent extérieur au corps, "absolu" ou géocentrique, plutôt que d'utiliser des référents relatifs au corps propre, comme gauche et droite. Au lieu de dire que tel objet est à ma droite, je dirais qu'il est *kangin* (du moins si je suis orienté vers *Kaja* et que je me trouve au sud de l'île). Les termes *gauche* et *droite* existent dans la langue balinaise, mais ne sont utilisés que pour des parties du corps; si je tiens un objet, je peux dire "je l'ai dans ma main droite", mais à partir du moment où je le pose et que je ne le touche plus, je dirai qu'il est, par exemple, *kauh* si je suis moi-même orienté *kelod*.

Un tel système géocentré existe également dans d'autres langues, par exemple en Australie et en Amérique centrale, et a fait l'objet d'études menées par un groupe de chercheurs en anthropologie cognitive à l'Institut Max Planck de psycholinguistique à Nijmegen (p. ex. Brown & Levinson, 1993b; Levinson, 1992a; 1992b; 1996). Dans certains cas, ces langues ne comportent aucun équivalent pour *gauche* et *droite*.

Pour déterminer, dans un premier temps, comment les Balinais utilisent dans les faits ce genre de système d'orientation, nous avons fait le tour, non pas de toute l'île de Bali, mais d'une péninsule située dans la partie orientale qui comporte un massif montagneux central. A différents endroits de la péninsule, nous avons demandé aux gens comment ils s'orientaient dans l'espace. Nous avons ainsi pu constater une impressionnante diversité, géographique plutôt qu'individuelle, dans l'utilisation du système. En suivant la côte, l'amont (*kaja*) reste orienté vers le centre, alors que l'aval (*kelod*) tourne tout autour de l'île. Et qu'arrive-t-il à la dimension transversale? Elle tourne aussi, mais à un moment donné, d'un village à l'autre, se renverse; si des habitants de ces deux villages voisins se rencontrent, ils doivent préciser à quel système ils se réfèrent. A l'intérieur des terres, l'amont peut se référer à un col plutôt qu'à la montagne centrale. Le système d'orientation, tout en gardant la même structure, s'adapte donc à la topographie; il s'agit, en somme, d'un système absolu assez relatif!

Quel est l'influence d'un tel système symbolique et linguistique sur la représentation de l'espace? Il serait difficile de répondre à cette question à partir de l'observation directe ou d'entretiens de recherche, et nous avons donc eu recours à des situations provoquées. Nous avons utilisé deux situations mises au point par l'équipe de Nijmegen (Danziger, 1993) qui nous permettent de dire si la personne, qu'il s'agisse d'un enfant ou d'un adulte, utilise un encodage absolu de l'espace ou un encodage relatif. On dispose sur une table trois figurines d'animaux, qui sont alignées et orientées d'une certaine façon; on demande au sujet de bien regarder le dispositif afin de se souvenir de l'ordre de ces animaux. Le sujet effectue ensuite une rotation de 180° vers une deuxième table et, après une pause, on lui demande de replacer les animaux dans le même ordre. Si le sujet adopte des référents relatifs à son corps et que sur la première table les animaux regardaient à sa gauche, il va également les orienter vers la gauche sur la seconde table. Si le sujet adopte un référent extérieur ou absolu, il gardera le même référent absolu malgré sa rotation; donc si les animaux regardaient par exemple en amont, sur la seconde table ils regarderont aussi en amont.

Une deuxième tâche utilisait la même procédure avec des schémas d'un paysage sur lequel il faut compléter le tracé d'un chemin. Là encore, on peut encoder cette situation de façon absolue ou relative. Chaque tâche comporte cinq essais. Les résultats obtenus figurent au Tableau 10.3. Les enfants les plus jeunes, ceux de 4 et 5 ans, donnent des réponses totalement absolues à la première

TABLEAU 10.3

Fréquences des réactions systématiquement (4 ou 5 réponses) absolues (A) ou
relatives (R) et partiellement (3 réponses) absolues (A-) ou relatives (R-),
aux deux épreuves utilisées, selon les groupes d'âge.

Age (années)	Animaux				Chemins				N
	A	A-	R-	R	A	A-	R-	R	
4–5	10	0	0	0	—	—	—	—	10
7–9	8	0	0	0	2	2	3	1	8
11–15	5	1	2	0	2	2	3	1	8
Adultes	9	3	0	0	3	4	0	5	12
Total	32	4	2	0	7	8	6	7	38/28

épreuve, la seule qui leur soit accessible. Cela est également vrai des enfants de
7 à 9 ans, alors que, vers les âges de 11 à 15 ans, quelques réponses relatives
commencent à surgir. En comparaison, les personnes qui parlent une langue
indo-européenne, comme le hollandais, utilisent exclusivement un encodage relatif
(Brown & Levinson, 1993a).

Dans l'épreuve des paysages, des encodages relatifs sont un peu plus fréquents,
mais l'encodage absolu prédomine aussi. Il s'agit donc du mode fondamental
d'encodage de l'espace pour les balinais. Mais les sujets ont-ils une possibilité
de changer leur type de réponse? Pour répondre à cette question, nous avons
répété les épreuves après un certain temps en essayant d'induire une modification du type d'encodage par des changements du dispositif et des consignes.
Alors que les jeunes enfants continuent à donner des réponses totalement absolues,
les enfants plus âgés et les adultes se montrent capables de passer d'un encodage
absolu à un encodage relatif. Ces résultats nous amènent à prendre une position de relativisme linguistique modéré: la langue et la culture déterminent non
pas l'existence d'un processus cognitif ou d'un autre, mais la séquence de leur
apparition.

Les psychologues du développement dans leur ensemble, et Piaget en particulier (voir, p. ex. Acredolo, 1988; Pick, 1993), nous disent que l'enfant commence par coder l'espace de façon relative, égocentrée, centrée sur le corps
propre, et que ce n'est que plus tard qu'il arrive à se décentrer et à utiliser
les référents extérieurs. Certains pensent que ces deux types de représentations
apparaissent en même temps, mais personne n'a encore suggéré qu'il était possible de commencer la séquence ontogénétique par un encodage absolu pour
n'arriver au relatif que plus tard. Si nos résultats balinais devaient être confirmés
par une recherche avec un échantillon plus grand, et en utilisant également d'autres
épreuves (p. ex. la célèbre épreuve des trois montagnes ou "coordination des
perspectives" de Piaget), on aurait le premier exemple de renversement d'une
séquence de développement.

Situation de cette étude par rapport aux cadres théoriques

Comment situer cette étude, qui provient de mon travail sur le terrain le plus récent, par rapport aux deux cadres théoriques que j'ai évoqués? L'étude n'a pas été directement inspirée par le cadre théorique écoculturel, mais n'est pas incompatible avec lui. Le contexte écologique (une île avec un massif montagneux central) est effectivement un des points de départ, ainsi que le contexte sociopolitique particulier de cette microculture hindouiste dans l'univers musulman indonésien; le système d'orientation est totalement cohérent avec l'ensemble de la culture balinaise, vue comme un système, avec ses différents aspects, symbolique, social, linguistique et comportemental. Différents aspects de la transmission culturelle ont été étudiés, dont je n'ai pas pu rapporter tous les détails, en relation avec la niche développementale, en particulier les pratiques éducatives. Les moyens nous ont manqué, par contre, pour faire une étude développementale de l'acquisition du langage, qui formerait un complément indispensable. A partir de ces données, nous évoquons l'influence de ce système écoculturel sur les comportements observables et sur des caractéristiques inférées, dans ce cas particulier, l'encodage spatial.

Une partie de l'étude pourrait être décrite comme "émique": Il s'agit d'étudier ce système particulier d'orientation spatiale dans son contexte culturel particulier. Mais assez rapidement, la comparaison intervient, intraculturelle d'abord: comment ce système est-il mis en pratique dans différents lieux? Il n'y a pas, en soi, de comparaison interculturelle, mais elle est implicite à cause du choix des situations provoquées, deux épreuves standardisées de manière à pouvoir être utilisées par des équipes différentes aux quatre coins du monde. Néanmoins, nous ne recherchons pas uniquement des processus universels, et sommes mêmes prêts à envisager l'hypothèse d'une inversion de la séquence développementale considérée jusqu'à présent comme "naturelle".

LE DIALOGUE DES PARADIGMES

Par rapport à l'opposition que font Guba (1990) et Lincoln (1990), dans leur "dialogue des paradigmes", entre positivisme, postpositivisme et constructivisme, je me situe sans doute au milieu. Pour rappel, le positivisme considère qu'il existe une réalité objective mue par des lois naturelles, que le chercheur peut mettre en évidence par des expériences bien contrôlées, analysées avec des méthodes quantitatives destinées à prouver un lien causal (Lonner & Adamopoulos, 1997; van de Vijver & Leung, 1997). A l'opposé, le constructivisme cherche à décrire qualitativement, et sans craindre la subjectivité, des réalités multiples, considérées comme des constructions sociales locales et spécifiques (Miller, 1997). Les méthodes relèvent de l'herméneutique et visent la pertinence culturelle plus que la rigueur psychométrique. Entre ces deux extrêmes, le postpositivisme considère qu'il y a effectivement une réalité à étudier, mais qu'il est difficile de l'atteindre de façon totalement objective; ses adhérents prônent la triangulation par la multiplication des méthodes (Greenfield, 1997; Pourtois & Desmet, 1988). La pertinence culturelle est considérée comme importante, ce qui amène à avoir surtout recours à l'étude de situations naturelles.

Aux trois paradigmes mentionnés plus haut correspondent plus ou moins les trois approches décrites par Berry et al. (1992), l'absolutiste, l'universaliste et la relativiste. Là encore, nous choisissons très clairement la solution médiane. Le terme *universaliste* n'est sans doute pas optimal, car il pourrait faire penser qu'on ne poursuit que ce qui est universel, alors qu'il s'agit justement de faire la part entre ce qui l'est et ce qui ne l'est pas. Si j'ai certaines sympathies (p. ex. Dasen, 1995) pour le relativisme et le coconstructivisme (Valsiner & Lawrence, 1997), ou ce que certains appellent maintenant *psychologie culturelle* (Krewer & Dasen, 1993), le relativisme absolu et son refus de la comparaison me semblent aberrants. L'unité psychique de l'humanité, au moins au niveau des processus de base et des structures sous-jacentes, me semble maintenant bien démontrée; pourquoi donc n'y aurait-il rien de commun à l'ensemble de l'espèce humaine? Mais de l'autre côté je rejette encore plus vivement l'absolutisme. Peut-être avons-nous passagèrement besoin d'une bonne dose de relativisme pour contrer l'absolutisme dominant en psychologie (Saraswathi & Dasen, 1997). Mais le conflit me semble temporaire, et la convergence plus que probable (Poortinga, 1997).

Certains auteurs qui représentent le courant de la psychologie culturelle (p. ex. Krewer, 1993; Shweder, 1990) ont tendance à classer la psychologie interculturelle comparative, telle que je l'ai présentée ici, comme relevant du positivisme, c'est-à-dire en fait de l'absolutisme. Il me semble qu'ils tronquent la réalité. Il est vrai que le cadre théorique écoculturel, puisqu'il cherche à représenter l'influence des variables au niveau du groupe (contextes et adaptation culturelle) sur les variables au niveau individuel (effets psychologiques), peut sembler refléter un modèle causal linéaire; d'ailleurs, une seule flèche symbolise les rétroactions, alors que celles-ci interviennent bien entendu à l'intérieur du schéma. Une lecture plus interactive est cependant parfaitement possible; dans ce sens, l'analyse systémique de la niche développementale complète le cadre théorique écoculturel, et le rend plus explicitement dynamique. Il est aussi vrai qu'en psychologie interculturelle les méthodes quantitatives prédominent et que les méthodes qualitatives ont encore de la peine à se faire respecter; là encore, une triangulation et une convergence me semblent souhaitables (Miles & Huberman, 1994; Pourtois & Desmet, 1988).

En conclusion, contrairement au relativisme complet qui rejette toute possibilité de comparaison et veut considérer chaque société en elle-même, sans chercher ce qui est commun à plusieurs ou à toutes, et contrairement à l'absolutisme qui considère que tout est universel et que les différences ne sont que quantitatives, je pense qu'il s'agit toujours de faire la part de ce qui est universel et de ce qui est relatif. Il ne s'agit pas d'une conclusion très originale: cela fait longtemps que je professe cette rengaine (p. ex. Dasen, 1983a, 1993b)! Le programme de recherche que j'ai pu exposer ici me semble en être une bonne illustration.

RÉFÉRENCES

Acredolo, L. (1988). Infant mobility and spatial development. In J. Stiles-Davis, M. Kritchevsky, & U. Bellugi (Eds.), *Spatial cognition: Brain bases and development* (pp. 157–166). Hillsdale, NJ: Erlbaum.

Akkari, A. (1993). *La modernisation des petits paysans: une mission impossible?* Tunis, Tunisie: Editions Education et Cultures.

Berry, J. W. (1966). Temne and Eskimo perceptual skills. *International Journal of Psychology, 1,* 207–229.

Berry, J. W. (1971). Ecological and cultural factors in spatial perceptual development. *Canadian Journal of Behavioral Science, 3,* 324–336.

Berry, J. W. (1976). *Human ecology and cognitive style.* New York: Sage/Halsted/Wiley.

Berry, J. W. (1987). The comparative study of cognitive abilities. In S. H. Irvine & S. E. Newstead (Eds.), *Intelligence and cognition* (pp. 393–420). Dordrecht, Netherlands: Martinus Nijhoff.

Berry, J. W. (1995). The descendants of a model. *Culture & Psychology, 1,* 373–380.

Berry, J. W., & Dasen, P. R. (Eds.). (1974). *Culture and cognition: Readings in cross-cultural psychology.* London: Methuen.

Berry, J. W., Poortinga, Y. H., Segall, M. H., & Dasen, P. R. (1992). *Cross-cultural psychology: Research and applications.* Cambridge: Cambridge University Press.

Bril, B., Dasen, P. R., Krewer, B., & Sabatier, C. (Eds.). (sous presse). *Ethnothéories parentales et représentations de l'enfant et de l'adolescent: Une perspective culturelle comparative.* Paris: L'Harmattan.

Bril, B., & Lehalle, H. (1988). *Le développement psychologique est-il universel? Approches interculturelles.* Paris: Presses Universitaires de France.

Bronfenbrenner, U. (1979). *The ecology of human development.* Cambridge, MA: Harvard University Press.

Bronfenbrenner, U. (1989). Ecological systems theory. *Annals of Child Development, 6,* 185–246.

Brown, P., & Levinson, S. C. (1993a). *Linguistic and nonlinguistic coding of spatial arrays: Explorations in Mayan cognition* (Working paper No. 24). Nijmegen, Netherlands: Cognitive Anthropology Research Group, Max Planck Institute for Psycholinguistics.

Brown, P., & Levinson, S. C. (1993b). "Uphill" and "downhill" in Tzeltal. *Journal of Linguistic Anthropology, 3,* 46–74.

Camilleri, C. (1989). Réflexion d'ensemble. In C. Clanet (Ed.), *Socialisations et cultures* (pp. 435–445). Toulouse: Presses Universitaires du Mirail.

Camilleri, C., & Malewska-Peyre, H. (1997). Socialization and identity strategies. In J. W. Berry, P. R. Dasen, & T. S. Saraswathi (Eds.), *Handbook of cross-cultural psychology: Vol. 2. Basic processes and human development* (2nd ed., pp. 41–67). Boston: Allyn & Bacon.

Cole, M., Gay, J., Glick, J. A., & Sharp, D. W. (1971). *The cultural context of learning and thinking: An exploration in experimental anthropology.* New York: Basic Books.

Cole, M., & Scribner, S. (1974). *Culture and thought: A psychological introduction.* New York: Wiley.

Danziger, E. (Ed.). (1993). *Cognition and space kit, version 1.0.* Nijmegen, Netherlands: Cognitive Anthropology Research Group, Max Planck Institute for Psycholinguistics.

Dasen, P. R. (1975a). Concrete operational development in three cultures. *Journal of Cross-Cultural Psychology, 6,* 156–172.

Dasen, P. R. (1975b). Le développement des opérations concrètes chez les Esquimaux canadiens. *Journal international de psychologie, 10,* 165–180.

Dasen, P. R. (1983a). Apports de la psychologie à la compréhension interethnique. In G. Baer & P. Centlivres (Eds.), *L'ethnologie dans le dialogue interdisciplinaire* (pp. 47–66). Fribourg, Suisse: Editions Universitaires.

Dasen, P. R. (1983b). Jeux et jouets chez les enfants africains. *L'éducateur: Revue suisse de pédagogie et d'éducation, 9,* 10–12.

Dasen, P. R. (1984a). The cross-cultural study of intelligence: Piaget and the Baoule. *International Journal of Psychology, 19,* 407–434.

Dasen, P. R. (1984b, January/February). The value of play / Jouer est amusant, mais pas seulement / La importancia del juego / Brincar é importante. *World Health / Santé du Monde / Salud Mundial / A Saude Do Mundo,* pp. 11–13.

Dasen, P. R. (1985). Gestes et activités quotidiennes chez l'enfant africain. In Groupe consultatif du Comité français pour l'UNICEF (Eds.), *Maîtrise du geste et pouvoirs de la main chez l'enfant* (pp. 151–155). Paris: Flammarion Médecine-Sciences.

Dasen, P. R. (1988a). Cultures et développement cognitif: La recherche et ses applications. In R. Bureau & D. de Saivre (Eds.), *Apprentissages et cultures: Les manières d'apprendre (Colloque de Cerisy)* (pp. 123–141). Paris: Karthala.

Dasen, P. R. (1988b). Développement psychologique et activités quotidiennes chez des enfants africains. *Enfance, 41,* 3–24.

Dasen, P. R. (1993a, November 29). How ethnocentric is developmental psychology? *Current Contents, 48,* 8.

Dasen, P. R. (1993b). L'ethnocentrisme de la psychologie. In M. Rey (Ed.), *Psychologie clinique et interrogations culturelles* (pp. 155–174). Paris: L'Harmattan.

Dasen, P. R. (1993c). Schlusswort. Les sciences cognitives: Do they shake hands in the middle? In J. Wassmann & P. R. Dasen (Eds.), *Savoirs quotidiens: Les sciences cognitives dans le dialogue interdisciplinaire* (pp. 331–349). Fribourg, Suisse: Presses de l'Université de Fribourg.

Dasen, P. R. (1994). Culture and cognitive development from a Piagetian perspective. In W. J. Lonner & R. S. Malpass (Eds.), *Psychology and culture* (pp. 145–149). Boston: Allyn & Bacon.

Dasen, P. R. (1995). Préface à l'édition française. In E. E. Boesch, *L'action symbolique: Fondements de psychologie culturelle* (pp. 13–16). Paris: L'Harmattan.

Dasen, P. R., & Bossel-Lagos, M. (1989). L'étude interculturelle des savoirs quotidiens: Revue de la littérature. In J. Retschitzki, M. Bossel-Lagos, & P. R. Dasen (Eds.), *La recherche interculturelle* (Vol. 2, pp. 98–114). Paris: L'Harmattan.

Dasen, P. R., Dembélé, B., Ettien, K., Kabran, K., Kamagate, D., Koffi, D. A., & N'Guessan, A. (1985). N'glouèlê, l'intelligence chez les Baoulé. *Archives de psychologie, 53,* 293–324.

Dasen, P. R., & de Ribaupierre, A. (1987). Neo-Piagetian theories: Cross-cultural and differential perspectives. *International Journal of Psychology, 22,* 793–832.

Dasen, P. R., & Heron, A. (1981). Cross-cultural tests of Piaget's theory. In H. C. Triandis & A. Heron (Eds.), *Handbook of cross-cultural psychology: Vol. 4. Developmental psychology* (pp. 295–342). Boston: Allyn & Bacon.

Dasen, P. R., Lavallée, M., & Retschitzki, J. (1979). Training conservation of quantity (liquids) in West African (Baoulé) children. *International Journal of Psychology, 14,* 57–68.

Dasen, P. R., Ngini, L., & Lavallée, M. (1979). Cross-cultural training studies of concrete operations. In L. Eckensberger, Y. Poortinga, & W. Lonner (Eds.), *Cross-cultural contributions to psychology* (pp. 94–104). Amsterdam: Swets & Zeitlinger.

Fournier, M., Schurmans, M.-N., & Dasen, P. R. (1994). Utilisation de langues différentes dans l'étude des représentations sociales. *Papers on Social Representations: Textes sur les représentations sociales, 3,* 152–165.

Greenfield, P. M. (1997). Culture as process: Empirical methods for cultural psychology. In J. W. Berry, Y. H. Poortinga, & J. Pandey (Eds.), *Handbook of cross-cultural psychology: Vol. 1. Theory and method* (2nd ed., pp. 301–346). Boston: Allyn & Bacon.

Guba, E. G. (1990). The alternative paradigm dialog. In E. G. Guba (Ed.), *The paradigm dialog* (pp. 17–30). Thousand Oaks, CA: Sage.

Harkness, S., & Super, C. M. (Eds.). (1995). *Parents' cultural belief systems: Their origins, expressions, and consequences.* New York: Guilford Press.

Inhelder, B., Sinclair, H., & Bovet, M. (1974). *Apprentissage et structures de la connaissance.* Paris: Presses Universitaires de France.

Jahoda, G. (1995). The ancestry of a model. *Culture & Psychology, 1*, 11–24.

Kağıtçıbaşı, C. (1997). Individualism and collectivism. In J. W. Berry, M. H. Segall, & C. Kağıtçıbaşı (Eds.), *Handbook of cross-cultural psychology: Vol. 3. Social behavior and applications* (2nd ed., pp. 1–49) Boston: Allyn & Bacon.

Kağıtçıbaşı, C. (this volume). Human development: Cross-cultural perspectives. In J. G. Adair, D. Bélanger, & K. L. Dion (Eds.), *Advances in psychological science: Vol. 2. Developmental, personal, and social aspects.* Hove, UK: Psychology Press.

Krewer, B. (1993). Psychologie transculturelle ou psychologie culturelle: L'homme entre une nature universelle et des cultures spécifiques. In F. Tanon & G. Vermès (Eds.), *L'individu et ses cultures* (pp. 79–90). Paris: L'Harmattan.

Krewer, B., & Dasen, P. R. (1993). La relation psychisme–culture: un problème d'équivalence des termes dans la discussion internationale. In F. Tanon & G. Vermes (Eds.), *L'individu et ses cultures* (pp. 53–61). Paris: L'Harmattan.

Lavallée, M., & Dasen, P. R. (1980). L'apprentissage de la notion d'inclusion de classes chez de jeunes enfants Baoulés (Côte d'Ivoire). *Journal international de psychologie, 15*, 27–41.

Lefebvre, M., & Pinard, A. (1972). Apprentissage de la conservation des quantités par une méthode de conflit cognitif. *Revue canadienne des sciences du comportement, 4*, 1–12.

Levinson, S. C. (1992a). *Language and cognition: The cognitive consequences of spatial description in Guggu Yimithirr* (Working paper No. 13). Nijmegen, Netherlands: Cognitive Anthropology Research Group, Max Planck Institute for Psycholinguistics.

Levinson, S. C. (1992b). Primer for the field investigation of spatial description and conception. *Pragmatics, 2*, 5–47.

Levinson, S. C. (1996). Frames of reference and Molyneux's question: Cross-linguistic evidence. In P. Bloom, M. Peterson, L. Nadel, & M. Garrett (Eds.), *Language and space* (pp. 109–169). Cambridge, MA: MIT Press.

Lincoln, Y. S. (1990). The making of a constructivist: A remembrance of transformations past. In E. G. Guba (Ed.), *The paradigm dialog* (pp. 67–87). Thousand Oaks, CA: Sage.

Lonner, W. J., & Adamopoulos, J. (1997). Culture as antecedent to behavior. In J. W. Berry, Y. H. Poortinga, & J. Pandey (Eds.), *Handbook of cross-cultural psychology: Vol. 1. Theory and method* (2nd ed., pp. 43–84). Boston: Allyn & Bacon.

Miles, M. B., & Huberman, M. (1994). *Qualitative data analysis: A sourcebook of new methods* (2nd ed.). London: Sage.

Miller, J. G. (1997). Theoretical issues in cultural psychology. In J. W. Berry, Y. H. Poortinga, & J. Pandey (Eds.), *Handbook of cross-cultural psychology: Vol. 1, Theory and method* (2nd ed., pp. 85–128). Boston: Allyn & Bacon.

Mishra, R. (1997). Cognition and cognitive development. In J. W. Berry, P. R. Dasen, & T. S. Saraswathi (Eds.), *Handbook of cross-cultural psychology: Vol. 2. Basic processes and human development* (2nd ed., pp. 143–175). Boston: Allyn & Bacon.

Mundy-Castle, A. C. (1975). Social and technological intelligence in Western and non-Western cultures. In S. Pilowsky (Ed.), *Cultures in collision* (pp. 46–52). Adelaide, Australia: Australian National Association for Mental Health.

Munroe, R. H., & Munroe, R. L. (1971). Effects of environmental experience on spatial ability in an East African society. *Journal of Social Psychology, 83*, 3–13.

Munroe, R. H., & Munroe, R. L. (1980). Household structure and socialization practices. *Journal of Social Psychology, 3*, 293–4.

Munroe, R. H., Munroe, R. L., & Michelson, C. (1983). Time allocation in four societies. *Ethnology*, *22*, 355–370.

Munroe, R. L., & Munroe, R. H. (1997). A comparative anthropological perspective. In J. W. Berry, Y. H. Poortinga, & J. Pandey (Eds.), *Handbook of cross-cultural psychology: Vol. 1: Theory and method* (2nd ed., pp. 171–214). Boston: Allyn & Bacon.

Pick, H. L. (1993). Organization of spatial knowledge in children. In N. Eilan, R. McCarthy, & B. Brewer (Eds.), *Spatial representation: Problems in philosophy and psychology* (pp. 31–42). Oxford: Blackwell.

Poortinga, Y. H. (1997). Towards convergence? In J. W. Berry, Y. H. Poortinga, & J. Pandey (Eds.), *Handbook of cross-cultural psychology: Vol.1. Theory and method* (2nd ed., pp. 347–387). Boston: Allyn & Bacon.

Pourtois, J.-P., & Desmet, H. (1988). *Epistémologie et instrumentation en sciences humaines*. Liège, Belgique: Mardaga.

Rogoff, B., & Lave, J. (Eds.). (1984). *Everyday cognition: Its development in social context*. Cambridge, MA: Harvard University Press.

Sabatier, C., & Bril, B. (1996, August). *Psychologie du développement: ethnothéories parentales*. Paper presented at the meeting of the International Union of Psychological Science, Montréal.

Saraswathi, T. S., & Dasen, P. R. (1997). Introduction. In J. W. Berry, P. R. Dasen, & T. S. Saraswathi (Eds.), *Handbook of cross-cultural psychology: Vol. 2. Basic processes and human development* (2nd ed., pp. i–xxxvii). Boston: Allyn & Bacon.

Saxe, G. B. (1981). Body parts as numerals: A developmental analysis of numeration among remote Oksapmin village populations in Papua New Guinea. *Child Development*, *52*, 306–316.

Saxe, G. B. (1983). Culture, counting and number conservation. *International Journal of Psychology*, *18*, 313–318.

Schliemann, A., Carraher, D., & Ceci, S. (1997). Everyday cognition. In J. W. Berry, P. R. Dasen, & T. S. Saraswathi (Eds.), *Handbook of cross-cultural psychology: Vol. 2: Basic processes and human development* (2nd ed., pp. 177–216). Boston: Allyn & Bacon.

Schurmans, M.-N., & Dasen, P. R. (1992). Social representations of intelligence: Côte d'Ivoire and Switzerland. In M. von Cranach, W. Doise, & G. Mugny (Eds.), *Social representations and the social bases of knowledge* (pp. 144–152). Bern, Switzerland: Hogrefe & Huber.

Schurmans, M.-N., Dasen, P. R., & Vouilloz, M.-F. (1990/91). Composantes des représentations sociales de l'intelligence: Kpouebo (Côte d'Ivoire) et Evolène (Suisse). In N. Bleichrodt & P. Drenth (Eds.), *Contemporary issues in cross-cultural psychology* (pp. 347–358). Amsterdam: Swets & Zeitlinger.

Segall, M. H., Dasen, P. R., Berry, J. W., & Poortinga, Y. H. (1990). *Human behavior in global perspective: An introduction to cross-cultural psychology*. Boston: Allyn & Bacon.

Serpell, R. (1989). Dimensions endogènes de l'intelligence chez les A-chewa et autres peuples africains. In J. Retschitzki, M. Bossel-Lagos, & P. Dasen (Eds.), *La recherche interculturelle* (Vol. 2, pp. 164–179). Paris: L'Harmattan.

Serpell, R. (1993). *The significance of schooling: Life-journeys in an African society*. Cambridge: Cambridge University Press.

Shweder, R. A. (1990). Cultural psychology: What is it? In J. W. Stigler, R. A. Shweder, & G. Herdt (Eds.), *Cultural psychology: Essays on comparative human development* (pp. 1–42). Cambridge: Cambridge University Press.

Super, C. M. (1983). Cultural variations in the meaning and uses of children's "intelligence". In J. B. Deregowski, S. Dziurawiec, & R. C. Annis (Eds.), *Expiscations in cross-cultural psychology* (pp. 199–212). Lisse, Netherlands: Swets & Zeitlinger.

Super, C. M., & Harkness, S. (1986). The developmental niche: A conceptualization at the interface of child and culture. *International Journal of Behavioral Development*, *9*, 545–570.

Super, C. M., & Harkness, S. (1997). The cultural structuring of child development. In J. W. Berry, P. R. Dasen, & T. S. Saraswathi (Eds.), *Handbook of cross-cultural psychology: Vol. 2. Basic processes and human development* (2nd ed., pp. 1–40). Boston: Allyn & Bacon.

Tapé, G. (1994). *L'intelligence en Afrique: Une étude du raisonnement expérimental.* Paris: L'Harmattan.

Troadec, B. (1996). *Emboîtements, collections et inclusion: Etude interculturelle du développement de la catégorisation. L'apport du contexte tahitien à une théorie générale.* Thèse de doctorat non publiée, Université de Paris V.

Tshingeji, M. (1989). Savoirs quotidiens relatifs à l'agriculture chez les Bashi des hautes terres du Kivu (Zaïre). In J. Retschitzki, M. Bossel-Lagos, & P. R. Dasen (Eds.), *La recherche interculturelle* (Vol. 2, pp. 151–163). Paris: L'Harmattan.

Tshingeji, M. (1993). *Savoirs quotidiens des paysans bashi du Kivu (Zaïre): Fondements d'un enseignement agricole approprié.* Thèse de doctorat non publiée, Université de Genève.

Valsiner, J., & Lawrence, J. (1997). Human development in culture across the life span. In J. W. Berry, P. R. Dasen, & T. S. Saraswathi (Eds.), *Handbook of cross-cultural psychology: Vol. 2. Basic processes and human development* (2nd ed., pp. 69–106). Boston: Allyn & Bacon.

van de Vijver, F. J. R., & Leung, K. (1997). Methods and data analysis of comparative research. In J. W. Berry, Y. H. Poortinga, & J. Pandey (Eds.), *Handbook of cross-cultural psychology: Vol. 1. Theory and method* (2nd ed., pp. 257–300). Boston: Allyn & Bacon.

Verhelst, T., & Sizoo, E. (Eds.). (1994). *Cultures entre elles: Dynamique ou dynamite? Vivre en paix dans un monde de diversité* (Vols. 1–2). Paris: Fondation pour le progrès de l'homme.

Wassmann, J. (1988). Methodische Probleme kulturvergleichender Untersuchungen im Rahmen von Piagets Theorie der kognitiven Entwicklung—aus der Sicht eines Ethnologen. *Zeitschrift für Ethnologie, 113*, 21–66.

Wassmann, J. (1993). Der kognitive Aufbruch in der Ethnologie. In J. Wassmann & P. R. Dasen (Eds.), *Alltagswissen / Les savoirs quotidiens / Everyday cognition* (pp. 95–133). Fribourg, Suisse: Editions universitaires.

Wassmann, J., & Dasen, P. R. (1994a). "Hot" and "cold": Classification and sorting among the Yupno of Papua New Guinea. *International Journal of Psychology, 29*, 19–38.

Wassmann, J., & Dasen, P. R. (1994b). Yupno number system and counting. *Journal of Cross-Cultural Psychology, 25*, 78–94.

Wassmann, J., & Dasen, P. R. (1996). Comment ne pas perdre le Nord à Bali. Processus cognitifs: Une combinaison de méthodes ethnographiques et psychologiques. *Bulletin de l'Académie suisse des sciences humaines et sociales, 1*, 17–26; *2*, 13–16.

Whiting, B. B., & Whiting, J. W. M. (1975). *Children of six cultures: A psycho-cultural analysis.* Cambridge, MA: Harvard University Press.

CHAPTER ELEVEN

Cultural diversity and psychological invariance: Methodological and theoretical dilemmas of (cross-)cultural psychology

Ype H. Poortinga
Tilburg University, Netherlands and University of Leuven, Belgium

Many cross-cultural studies can be criticized for naive empiricism: instruments are believed to yield equivalent, unbiased results in different cultural populations, and differences in scores are attributed *post hoc* to some seemingly plausible, cultural factor. Three strategies are discussed that are meant to lead to better interpretation: (1) improving the design and data analysis of quantitative studies; (2) contextualization of methods and the use of qualitative approaches; and (3) searching for cross-culturally invariant patterns of scores to determine the limits of influence of cultural factors. It is argued that the different conceptions of the relationship between behavior and culture that lie at the basis of the various methodological approaches should be seen as complementary rather than incompatible.

On peut reprocher à plusieurs études interculturelles leur empiricisme naïf: on considère que les instruments donnent des résultats équivalents et impartiaux lorsqu'appliqués à des populations de cultures différentes et on attribue, après le fait, les différences de score à quelque facteur culturel, apparemment plausible. On traite ici de trois stratégies qui se veulent inductrices de meilleures interprétations soit: (1) améliorer le plan et l'analyse de données des études quantitatives; (2) situer les méthodes dans le contexte et utiliser des approches qualitatives; (3) rechercher des patterns de scores interculturellement invariants afin de définir les limites de l'influence des facteurs culturels. On soutient que les différentes conceptions de la relation entre comportement et culture qui se trouvent à la base des diverses approches méthodologiques devraient être considérées comme complémentaires plutôt qu'incompatibles.

NAIVE EMPIRICISM

Many cross-cultural studies take the following form. There is some psychological variable on which a difference in score distributions is found between samples of subjects that have been drawn from at least two cultural populations. This difference is interpreted in terms of some cultural variable. Often such research is characterised by *ad hoc* selection of cultural populations. An opportunity that arises is used to administer an existing instrument outside one's own country, usually to students supplied by a colleague. Needless to say, the interpretation of a difference in the score distributions obtained by local and foreign subjects is also *ad hoc*. Cultures differ from each other in many ways, and it is often unclear how other interpretations than the one preferred by a researcher can be ruled out (Campbell, 1961). It can be said that culture serves in such studies as a "deus ex machina." In classical Greek and Latin dramas human beings would mess up their affairs and in the last act a god would be lowered on to the stage "ex machina" (from the crane) and settle things. This is what cross-cultural researchers often tend to do: they invoke some cultural factor as a mythical solution to explain cross-cultural differences in data.

The interpretation of results in cross-cultural research is affected by another problem: namely, that measurement procedures are likely to lead to scores that are biased or inequivalent across cultures. Inequivalence means that a given score does not have the same meaning for a subject from one cultural population as it has for a subject from another population.

Given the range of possible cultural factors that can lead to a score difference and the likelihood of measurement bias, the a priori probability of finding a statistically significant cross-cultural difference between two randomly chosen cultural populations with some randomly selected instrument or observation procedure is far higher than the 5% or 1% level of confidence at which null hypotheses are formally tested in psychology (Finifter, 1977). In fact, this probability can be much higher than finding no difference (Malpass & Poortinga, 1986). This risk of misinterpretation is especially serious as the cumulative effect over a large number of studies will be a systematic overestimation of the impact of cultural variation on psychological variables.

In this chapter three strategies will be examined that seek to avoid the pitfalls of this naive empiricism in cross-cultural psychology. Although the emphasis is on methodology, it has to be recognized that method and theory are strongly interrelated in each instance. The first strategy is to follow the traditional culture-comparative framework that is based on the experimental paradigm of mainstream psychology, but to incorporate extensive methodological controls. The second strategy is a more far-reaching alternative, known as cultural psychology. This approach emphasizes that behavior is fully contextualized: i.e. behavior is cultural in essence and as a consequence, methods have to be culture-specific. The third strategy makes explicit that cross-cultural psychology has to deal with similarities in human behavior and understanding around the world, as well as with differences between cultural populations. It amounts to an explicit search for psychological invariance as a complementary strategy to the other traditions in which differences occupy most of the researcher's interests. In the concluding comments, it is suggested that approaches are needed that can transcend controversies between the strategies.

THE CULTURE-COMPARATIVE FRAMEWORK

One illustration of the use of this framework is the landmark study by Segall, Campbell, and Herskovits (1966) into the influence of ecological factors on the perception of visual illusions, like the Müller-Lyer, the Sander parallelogram and the horizontal–vertical illusion. There were contrasting opinions as to whether exposure to different ecological environments (i.e. environments with or without rectangular buildings and street plans, presence or absence of wide vistas) leads to differences in susceptibility to such illusions. Specific hypotheses were formulated and tested with an extensive set of samples, mainly from Africa and the USA. The findings, by and large, supported the hypotheses, pointing clearly to the role of ecological factors. The study is also of interest because a few years later an alternative explanation was suggested, to the effect that differences in illusion susceptibility could also be due to differences in retinal pigmentation between the predominantly black and white samples. Subsequent research in which skin color and environment were both varied systematically showed that ecology rather than pigmentation was the crucial antecedent (see Deregowski, 1989 for a summary).

Characteristics

Cross-cultural studies like that of Segall et al. (1966) are modeled on the experiment (Strodtbeck, 1964). The dependent or consequent variable is the aspect of the behavior repertoire that is being assessed, usually by means of a psychometric method (i.e. a questionnaire, an observation schedule, a standardized test, etc.). The independent variable or antecedent is an aspect of the culture of the populations concerned. Differences in score distributions are due to differences in the treatment that various ecological or social circumstances provide. In order to make observed differences interpretable, there is a strong tendency towards the use of formally identical instruments and procedures (in the study of Segall et al., there was a standard test booklet for all samples).

The experimental paradigm, including quasi-experimental as well as experimental research, presumes control by the experimenter of the various treatment conditions and the random assigment of subjects to these conditions. However, in cross-cultural studies there are essential difficulties with both forms of control. Subjects are inherently linked to the cultural population to which they belong and thus to one of the "treatments." (Note that in the case of Segall et al., the nonrandom allocation of subjects to environments implied the presence of systematic differences between samples in skin color as well as ecological factors.) As far as control over the treatment is concerned, more often than not the cross-cultural researcher is interested in long-term effects of antecedent experiences that cannot be manipulated in a laboratory. An example is the (retrospective) explanation of behavior patterns of adults in terms of earlier socialization practices. The various cultural "treatments" are not observed directly; they can only be inferred *post hoc* from current practices and memories of subjects.

Quality controls

It has long been recognized that the aforementioned difficulties impose limitations on meaningful cross-cultural comparison of psychological data, and a fairly elaborate technology has been developed to rule out or control alternative explanations. In general terms, one can distinguish two aspects: namely, improving the design of studies and improving the equivalence of the data. Both forms of controls have been reviewed by Malpass and Poortinga (1986; Poortinga & Malpass, 1986) and, more recently and extensively, by Van de Vijver and Leung (1997a; 1997b).

As far as design is concerned, the first and most important form of control lies in the selection of cultural populations. A well designed study will be based on populations which differ systematically on the cultural factor that is believed to be the antecedent to some expected difference in psychological data. It is essential to ascertain that postulated antecedent differences are indeed present. In the study by Segall et al., this was done by asking the collaborators in the various countries to complete a questionnaire on features of the natural environment for each sample of subjects.

A second form of control is the formulation of research questions in such a way that interpretation does not depend on a single score variable, but on patterns of scores or on structural relationships between variables. Patterns and structures are less sensitive than separate variables to many forms of bias. A third form of control is to rule out competing explanations by including in the design of an investigation measurements of presumably relevant context variables (i.e. other than antecedent variables related to a dependent variable). If differences are found on these context variables, multivariate statistical analysis can help to estimate their effects on the dependent variable.

As far as controls on the equivalence of data are concerned, in a well designed study it is recognized that methods are likely to result in cultural bias. In a set of standards for adaptation of tests that are presently being developed (Hambleton, 1995), it is recommended to involve in the construction of instruments members of the various populations taking part in a project, rather than to use existing instruments originally developed for one country. If an existing instrument is preferred for some reason, judgements can be made of the appropriateness of items for a new population. In addition, translation equivalence of the items can be investigated. Various techniques are available of which the translation from source to target language followed by an independent back translation from target to source language is the most widely used (Brislin, 1980).

Finally, there is an elaborate set of procedures to investigate cultural bias in data *after* they have been collected (Van de Vijver & Leung, 1997b). For each of these various techniques, a certain state of affairs is postulated that should be met by unbiased or equivalent data, but is unlikely to be met by data that are biased or inequivalent. For example, it can be postulated that the relative difficulty of items should be approximately equal in the cultural samples for which data are compared, or that correlations between item parameters should be equal. Such conditions can be formally tested. Nowadays, sophisticated statistical analyses are possible, based on Item Response Theory and analysis of covariance structures.

Problems

It is a frequent complaint that only token tribute is paid by cross-cultural researchers to cultural context (e.g. Boski, 1996; Georgas & Berry, 1995; Jahoda, 1992). There are extensive theories, for example, on cognitive processes or emotions, but efforts to develop models of culture are scarce in the comparative tradition. In this respect the research by Segall et al. on visual illusions is not representative of the field. Another complaint is that limited use is made of the available methodological tools to improve the quality of culture-comparative research. The proportion of studies is small in which additional variables are introduced to rule out alternative explanations and in which proper checks are made on the equivalence of the data for the interpretations that were derived. The quality of culture-comparative research would improve considerably if both shortcomings would be dealt with optimally.

However, there are limits to these refinements. The number of context variables that can be added to a design to control for alternative interpretations is limited and they come with their own problems of measurement and interpretation, especially if there are interrelationships between these variables. According to Jahoda (1984), the comparative framework is suitable only for the study of psychologically simple phenomena such as visual illusions.

Also, procedures for the identification of bias are not without difficulties. When evidence of bias is found, one solution is to develop culturally appropriate instruments and procedures that differ in item content. But this diminishes dramatically the scope for comparison. Obviously, if items are not the same, it becomes difficult to establish a common scale in terms of which an accurate comparison can be made. Moreover, a distinction should be made between item bias, method bias, and construct bias. The possibility of item bias is well recognized, especially for cognitive tests, but effects of bias can reach much further.

When all (or most) items of an instrument lack equivalence, there is method bias. This bias can be due to a host of factors, including response tendencies such as social desirability or acquiescence, speed versus accuracy trade-off, and familiarity with response procedures. Construct bias occurs when the definition of a concept or its operationalization is inappropriate for some culture. Bias at this level cannot be established directly; it can only be inferred from persistent failure to avoid item and/or method bias.

Quite a few of these difficulties can be resolved when cultural bias is not seen as a fixed property of an instrument or method vis à vis certain cultural populations, but as a function of the interpretations or inferences derived from a data set. For example, low scores of children in some cultural group on a cognitive test could be interpreted in terms of: (1) the quality of school education they received; (2) the probability of future success in higher education; or (3) their intellectual capacities. Obviously, a test which adequately reflects performance as a function of prior school quality does not necessarily provide an unbiased estimate of future school success, let alone the intellectual capacities of the children.

The distinction between levels of bias has led to the recognition that there are limitations to bias analysis. There are statistical limitations. An analysis showing little evidence of bias at the item level does not rule out the possibility of a method bias effect that influences all items to a similar extent. There are also conceptual limitations. Any comparison presumes concept or construct equivalence; it is meaningful only if concepts are identical across cultural populations. After all, it makes logically as little sense to make cross-cultural comparisons in terms of inequivalent psychological concepts as to compare the height of subjects with the weight of other subjects.

The question has to be asked whether bias can be so pervasive that attempts at comparison have to be given up. One can merely note that few comparative researchers seem inclined to abandon interpretation of differences for reasons of bias, and there are no procedural rules for this. As a result, the basic premise of the culture-comparative framework of universal psychological functions usually escapes rigorous testing in concrete instances. For example, one of the issues in emotion research concerns the noncorrespondence of emotion words in different languages. What are the implications if a certain language does not have a word for a certain (shade of) emotion? Is there a set of basic and universal emotions, or are untranslatable words indicative of differences in the meaning and structure of emotions (Russell, 1991)?

CONTEXTUALIZATION OF BEHAVIOR

One study that rejects the notion that emotions are invariant across cultures is an ethnographic analysis by Lutz (1988) of emotional life among the Ifaluk in Micronesia. She argues (p. 5) that "emotional meaning is fundamentally structured by particular cultural systems and particular social and material environments". Indigenous models about self and social interaction should be used to understand emotion terms. Lutz concentrates her analysis on two emotions that are not found in the USA: namely, "fago" (an amalgam of what in English is expressed as compassion, love and sadness) and "song." She translates song as "justifiable anger." It is described (p. 156) as "an unpleasant emotion that is experienced in a situation of perceived injury to the self or to another". But unlike anger, the emotion of *song* is not so much about what is personally disliked as about what is socially condemned. The Ifaluk have other words for anger, but they are distinguished from (p. 157) "the anger which is a righteous indignation, or justifiable anger (*song*), and it is only this anger which is morally approved".

Characteristics

Like Lutz, many researchers in the school of cultural psychology reject, or at least de-emphasize, the axiom of comparativists that psychological functions are universal. Whereas the latter take the "psychic unity of mankind" for granted, cultural psychologists emphasize context as a constitutive aspect of psychological functioning. Culture and behavior tend to be seen as so inextricably linked that they are inseparable. Behavior has to be analyzed in terms of the meaning that it has for the actors and their understanding. Thus, the meaning of behavior can be understood only within the cultural context in which it occurs (Miller, 1997). Shweder (1991) talks about the co-construction of culture and behavior; there is an essential interaction in which person and culture mutually form each other. In such conceptualizations there is scope for intentionality and historicity of behavior. For example, Eckensberger (1979) describes the person as a self-reflective and active agent with goals and intentions. In the Marxist tradition of Vygotsky (1978) and Luria (1971), new mental functions are the outcome of historical processes. These functions develop first at the societal level before they can become properties of individuals. In Gergen's (1982) social constructionist theory, historicity becomes the central feature of social behavior, leaving no room for psychological constancies. Another characteristic of cultural psychology is the position in scientific analysis of the unique event, or unique constellation of events; the single event is treated as a source of valid knowledge rather than of preliminary knowledge that needs further validation.

Methodologically, cultural psychology tends to adhere to a phenomenological mode of interpretation rather than to the experiment, although there are clear exceptions, like the work of Cole (e.g. Scribner & Cole, 1981). Cultural psychologists tend to object to the rigid harness of the standardized test and experimental procedures, and even to the epistemological principles of objectivity in measurement. Some even question the adequacy of scientific knowledge as a representation of external reality (see Miller, 1997).

The main orientation of cultural psychologists is towards qualitative research. The term "qualitative" has somewhat different meanings, partly dependent on the field of science (e.g. Denzin & Lincoln, 1994). In psychology, the term is used in two ways. At a mundane level of data analysis, it refers to measurement on nonparametric scales. Examples can be found in a book edited by Asendorpf and Valsiner (1992), in which there is emphasis on nominal scales. One of the uses of such scales is to map processes of ontogenetic development across stages that defy definition in terms of the same parameters and quantitative measurement. Although psychologists tend to accept too easily that their data meet the requirements for interval scale measurement, there is no major disagreement in principle. Virtually all researchers using quantitative scales will admit that the level of measurement has to be considered carefully.

More crucial is the second way in which the term "qualitative" is used, namely as referring to a contextual description and interpretation of behavior as it presents itself to the researcher (often identified as "understanding"). Qualitative research in this sense implies the absence of preconceived scales or standards in terms of which an event is assessed. In cross-cultural research, this means the absence of a common standard in terms of which similarities and differences in behavior between cultural populations can be assessed. In short, the emphasis on contextual interpretation is associated with more reliance on the insights of the researcher and less on the formalized aspects of the research process (namely, standardized instruments and quasi-experimental manipulation) that are characteristic of the culture-comparative framework.

Quality controls

There are various concepts that refer to quality control in qualitative research. Examples are "transparency" and "credibility" (Lincoln & Guba, 1985). It should be clear how the account of an event has been arrived at. Transparency has a similar meaning to "plausibility." Van de Vijver and Poortinga (1990) point out that in many areas of life we assume high plausibility of the interpretation of a single event, as in the case of a judicial trial where the sentence is based on the reconstruction of a criminal act.

In a review of qualitative research methods for cross-cultural psychology, Greenfield (1997) has emphasized that these methods allow for monitoring events in context and for observation of change and development. She stresses the importance of analysis of culture as an ongoing process, drawing heavily on information provided by members of the community studied. Many of the methods Greenfield describes fall in the general category of participant observation. One outstanding method is the use of video recording; it provides fairly direct access to ongoing behavior. At the same time, the video tape is a permanent record available for later inspection by other researchers, and thus for independent evaluation.

Problems

The contrast between quantitative and qualitative research is an expression of a basic preoccupation in much of the history of psychology that is also indicated with the terms *nomothetic* and *idiographic*, or "naturwissenschaftlich" and "geisteswissenschaftlich." The difficulties with qualitative research in cross-cultural psychology can be summarized in two points. The first concerns the question as to how there can be understanding of persons from another cultural background unless there is some form of invariance in psychological functioning. The second point is the strength of quality controls, as mentioned.

From the elaborate description by Lutz I have the impression that I can understand the Ifaluk emotion of *song*. How is such an understanding possible if their psychological processes in attributing meaning differ in essential ways from mine? Moreover, the description reminds me of the indignation that is displayed, for example, by a trade union leader who strongly condemns in public an unacceptable salary offer made by management. Does my perception of this similarity mean that I essentially misunderstand the description by Lutz? Whatever the case, it can be argued that the very attempt to describe Ifaluk emotions for a Western readership seems to imply a form of comparison: namely, how there exist cross-cultural differences and what these entail.

The second problematic aspect of qualitative research is the issue of validity. As mentioned previously, in extreme forms of social constructionism or post-modernism, scientific statements do not refer to knowable reality, in which case the question of validity becomes trivial. However, many cultural psychologists continue to accept that scientific statements should reflect more than time-and-location bound accounts. Evidently, for them the requirement of validity is as crucial as it is in the traditional culture-comparative framework. Unfortunately, qualitative methodology tends to dodge the question of validity. Most quality controls mentioned earlier in this section hardly provide for procedures to decide between valid and invalid interpretations. Forms of validity distinguished in the qualitative research literature, like "interpretive" validity or "ecological" validity (Greenfield, 1997), are defined in such a way that interpretations are beyond empirical scrutiny. Interpretative validity is concerned with, and limited to, subjective meaning for research participants. A method has ecological validity if it elicits data that are representative of behavior beyond the research context. Greenfield (1997, p. 316) is of the following opinion: "In studying naturally occurring rather than laboratory behavior, ecological validity is insured." However, this belief seems to ignore the fact that there can be varied and even contrasting interpretations of behavior observed in real-life settings, not only between cultural insiders and outsiders, but also among the insiders themselves.

Perhaps the contrast between quantitative and qualitative analysis is given too much emphasis. In the area of evaluation research, Reichardt and Rallis (1994) have pointed to similar concerns in both forms of enquiry. In psychometrics,

Messick (1995) has argued for an integrated approach to validity in which values are seen as an intrinsic part of testing. Also, in the present chapter the potential of qualitative analysis is not questioned. When a distinction is made between discovery and justification in the scientific process (paraphrasing Reichenbach, 1938), exploration has qualitative features. Approaches in which context is emphasized are rich in potential for exploration. However, researchers who advocate qualitative analysis also tend to incorporate the phase of justification. Dispensing with limitations of methods that are meant to safeguard independence of data from the researcher, they overextend the reach of exploratory analysis. Findings that cannot be validated with independent methods are frowned upon in culture-comparative research, but they tend to be given credibility in cultural psychology.

SEARCHING FOR INVARIANCE

Van de Vijver (1991) investigated inductive thinking in samples of primary and secondary school children in Zambia, Turkey, and The Netherlands. In the latter country separate samples of Turkish migrant children and Dutch autochthonous children were taken. In order to assess various phases of the inductive reasoning process, Van de Vijver constructed eight tasks. The items in each task were designed to follow a facet design, with systematic variations in expected difficulty. Additional information was collected on context variables at the individual level (e.g. education of parents), and at the level of schools (e.g. teaching style and equipment). Apart from differences between age levels, substantial differences in mean scores were found between the cultural groups, part of which could be explained in terms of the context variables. However, the observed relative difficulty of the items in any of the eight inductive reasoning tasks was very much the same across all samples. Thus, the amount of variance attributable to culturally specific ways of cognitive reasoning was negligible. Table 11.1 shows that the difference between *within* and *between* coefficients of item difficulty in the four cultural populations is very small, both for item difficulty indices based on proportions of correct responses and for difficulty estimates based on a model derived from Item Response Theory. Apparently, inductive reasoning is a highly similar process, at least in the populations studied. Van de Vijver's study was explicitly designed to allow for finding invariance as well as variations in the inductive reasoning process. The design also offered a possibility to explain observed cross-cultural differences in score levels in terms of context variables that were likely to affect test performance and that were taken from the immediate home and institutional environment.

Characteristics

One of the surprising aspects of cross-cultural research following the culture-comparative framework is the emphasis on cultural differences. It is acknowledged that differences can be explained only against the background of similarities

TABLE 11.1
Median correlations of difficulty indices
(observed, and estimated in an IRT model)
for eight inductive reasoning tests.

tests	Proportion correct responses		Estimated basic parameters	
	within	*between*	*within*	*between*
Inductive Thinking Figures	.91	.86	.92	.87
Rule Classification Figures	.85	.78	.89	.83
Rule Generating Figures	.96	.95	.98	.97
Rule Testing Figures	.92	.86	.84	.78
Inductive Thinking Letters	.96	.92	.99	.97
Rule Classification Letters	.88	.79	.92	.90
Rule Generating Letters	.95	.91	.98	.96
Rule Testing Letters	.95	.92	.95	.91
Median	.93	.89	.95	.91

NOTE:
    Correlations were computed within and between samples of Zambian, Turkish, Turkish-Dutch and Dutch children (Copied with permission from Van de Vijver, 1991, p. 170).

(e.g. Berry, Poortinga, Segall, & Dasen, 1992), but almost without exception, hypotheses are formulated to test for differences, with rejection of the null hypothesis as the desired outcome. An explicit search for cross-cultural similarities or invariance in psychological functioning entails an empirical challenge, both to the emphasis on cross-cultural differences and to the primacy of co-construction of culture.

A major characteristic of such a search is a skeptical attitude towards broad generalizations. Often data are interpreted in terms of broad and comprehensive psychological dispositions. Coherence of divergent aspects of context is assumed in notions such as cultural syndromes (Triandis, 1996) and culture-as-a-system. In the area of cognition, essential differences in modes of thinking have been postulated between literates and illiterates (e.g. Luria, 1976; Tulviste, 1991). In the area of social behavior, a host of differences, including mate selection (Buss, 1989) and the incidence of cardiovascular diseases (Triandis, 1989) has been related to the dimension of individualism–collectivism. However, differences in abstract thinking can also be explained as a function of specific algorithms taught in Western-type schools (Scribner, 1979; Scribner & Cole, 1981), and Western (individualistic) subjects show mutual commitment and pursue common goals (Jansz, 1991). Segall (1984) has pointed out that high-level variables (in particular the notion of "culture" itself) used to explain virtually everything, in fact explain nothing.

In searches for invariance, it is recognized that there are obvious cross-cultural differences in manifest behavior, but the possibility is left open that underlying psychological processes are the same universally. Consequently, there is a tendency to interpret differences as reactions to specific situations, or even as measurement artifacts, and to restrict interpretation to low-level generalizations. It may be noted that the present strategy is in direct contrast with research on intelligence (e.g. Jensen, 1985) and personality dimensions (e.g. Eysenck & Eysenck, 1983) in which universality of concepts is taken for granted, and sweeping generalizations are made from differences in score levels to inborn characteristics of subject populations, without regard for less comprehensive explanations or measurement bias.

In short, as an alternative to system-oriented and high-level conceptualizations, culture is considered as a (large) collection of domain-specific differences in knowledge, customs and beliefs that have the character of conventions: i.e. historically grown, agreed upon ways as to what is appropriate in social interactions or in a field of activity.

The methodological basis of an explicit search for similarities is the a priori low probability of finding *no differences* in results between subjects from cultural populations that are as far apart as Japan and the USA or India and Nigeria. Whatever way data are collected (experiments, tests, questionnaires, observation), it is much safer to bet that some cross-cultural difference will be found in a study with not too small samples than to bet that there will be no difference. Thus, a search for invariance amounts to predicting a low probability outcome. If found to be correct, such an outcome has high information value.

Invariance can be predicted for a specific set of cultural populations: for example, the countries of Western Europe. When stipulated for all cultural populations, this amounts to a claim of universality. It is in principle irrelevant whether invariance is predicted for scores as they are obtained, or for scores that have been corrected for the effects of some context variable. Researchers should make explicit which populations are included in a claim of invariance. They should also indicate for which variables invariance is expected and the effects of which context variables should be eliminated before a cross-cultural comparison is made. Moreover, the "level of invariance" has to be specified. Various levels can be distinguished, such as: (1) conceptual invariance, when the same label is used, but no empirical referents are specified; (2) structural invariance, when correlations between variables are the same across cultural populations; (3) metric invariance, when patterns of scores are the same cross-culturally; and (4) strict invariance when the score distributions on a single score variable are the same cross-culturally (Van de Vijver & Poortinga, 1982).

In the 1980s various projects were initiated at Tilburg University in which metric or strict invariance was recognized as a possible outcome, and sometimes even predicted explicitly. The aforementioned study by Van de Vijver on inductive reasoning was one of these. Support for similarity was also shown in other projects. For example, in a series of studies in India and The Netherlands on reactions to intergroup norm violations, it was found that situational factors like the perceived power of a social group were important determinants, but not internal factors like own-group identity (DeRidder & Tripathi, 1992). Contrary to suggestions about the sweeping effects of tonality in language (Van Lancker & Fromkin, 1973; Wober, 1975), Joe (1992) found that differences between tonal and non-tonal speaking subjects from the Antilles were limited to the mere recognition of tonality in words. There were no indications of a more general sensitivity for tonal information in either verbal or non-verbal stimuli. Between six so-called individualistic and collectivistic countries Fijneman et al. (1996) found no difference in the ratio of readiness to provide support for others over expectations to receive support from others—a result that goes against the belief that collectivists should be more inclined to provide for others, notably for members of their ingroup. In short, the data of these studies were interpretable without any reference to cross-cultural differences in (broad) internalized dispositions.

Quality controls

The interpretation of results that point to invariance is rather straightforward: namely, that there is no differential effect of cultural factors. Since it is unlikely that a finding of "no difference" is due to effects of a cultural antecedent or to cultural bias, there is usually no need to rule out alternative explanations.

Problems

A potential methodological threat to studies searching for invariance is the failure to find cross-cultural differences because of poor design or lack of precision in the instruments that were used. It is not without reason that in traditional methodology, rejection of the null hypothesis is more easily interpretable than a failure to find significant differences. Through careful design this difficulty can be resolved. For example, the size of an expected difference can be stipulated in advance (Cohen, 1988), and if scores are shown to be reliable, the absence of a mean difference cannot be attributed to inaccurate methods.

The strategy of searching for invariance is primarily a reaction against the presumed overinterpretation of cross-cultural differences in data, but so far there appears to be no consistent psychological theory to demarcate in which respects human behavior is psychologically the same and in which respects it is different. The studies mentioned in this section pay little attention to this problem. In the end, a search for invariance that is not guided by theory is exposed to the danger of overlooking higher order coherence in cross-cultural differences of various conventions.

CONCLUDING COMMENTS

Methodology and theory are interrelated. The differences in research strategies discussed in this chapter are rooted in beliefs about the relationship between behavior and culture. It should be realized that theorizing about this relationship is not merely an academic pursuit. Presumed knowledge determines how we talk about cross-cultural differences and what recommendations we make about interventions—for example, in the sphere of education and health care for disadvantaged groups, intercultural communication, or assessment for placement and selection in multicultural societies (Berry et al., 1992).

Most cross-cultural research follows the experimental paradigm of mainstream psychology. By postulating culture as a set of antecedent factors and differences in behavior as their consequences, a framework is created for empirical research. A strong point of this research strategy is the availability of elaborate controls to protect the researcher's preferred interpretation against alternative interpretations. Unfortunately, such controls are underutilized. On the other hand, methodological difficulties in this approach arise from the fact that methods are embedded in culture in multiple ways and that score differences which are the focus of measurement are confounded with unwanted differences (i.e. cultural bias).

In cultural psychology, behavior and culture are defined as being inseparable. The presence of bias is seen as a reflection of the futility of constructing methods that can be applied across (a wide range of) cultural populations. Cultural psychology is non-comparative; each culture has to be understood in its own terms. The methodology tends to be interpretive and linked to the person of the researcher; qualitative approaches are prominent. The major problem with cultural psychology is that interpretations tend to be *ad hoc*, and controls on validity weak, if not entirely absent.

The search for invariance is an amendment on the culture-comparative framework. It starts from the assumption that there should be evidence of the invariance expressed in the notion of the psychic unity of mankind, not only at the level of hypothetical psychological concepts but also at the level of data. Various levels of invariance can be distinguished, and the effects of context variables on scores can be eliminated to find cross-cultural similarities rather than differences. Findings of invariance are not very sensitive to method artifacts; it is unlikely that effects of bias will obscure existing differences and lead to similarities in outcome. However, psychological theories demarcating cross-cultural variations from similarities in behavior are still lacking.

Much of the current debate in cross-cultural psychology concerns the question as to whether a nomothetic or an idiographic perspective is the *via regia*, the royal road to knowledge and understanding. In methodology this debate is focused on the controversy between qualitative and quantitative approaches, or between comparative and non-comparative research. The debate is challenging, but perhaps the time has come to conclude that it has outlived its usefulness, and that theoretical orientations have to be developed in which these approaches can be seen as complementary rather than mutually exclusive. In a concrete sense this can be done by every researcher in any study: namely, by looking at one's own approach in the light of the criticisms from other perspectives.

At a more general level, there are various ways to make distinctions in the field of cross-cultural research that allow for integration. One major dimension suggesting itself is a dimension which ranges from distal variables defined in phylogenetic terms to proximal variables that refer to immediate context. Inasmuch as behavior is considered in terms of distal variables, lawful psychological relationships can be anticipated that should be the same in all human populations (Tooby & Cosmides, 1992). On the other hand, when behavior is studied in real-life settings, the complexity of behavior tends to be so great that prediction easily becomes meaningless and descriptive methods are indicated. Another distinction is between the traditional domains of psychology. These domains can be ordered according to the extent that they are subject to biological and cultural constraints on behavioral manifestations. Biological constraints limit cross-cultural variation. Cultural constraints that are the outcome of socialization processes limit individual variation within cultures (Child, 1954). Therefore, the ratio of anticipated *between* culture differences over *within* culture (i.e. between individual) differences should increase from the domain of psychophysiology and psychophysics, via perception, cognition, and personality, to social psychology (Poortinga, 1992). Still another distinction is between universal features of the environment and culture as historically specific features of the environment (Cole, 1992). This distinction suggests a demarcation between a domain of psychological laws lending itself to (quasi-)experimental methods, and a domain where cultural rules prevail, lending itself more to interpretive methods. In summary, the most important condition for methodological advancement in cross-cultural psychology is perhaps modesty among researchers in recognizing that their preferred methodological approach may have a limited reach.

REFERENCES

Asendorpf, J. B., & Valsiner, J. (Eds.). (1992). *Stability and change in development: A study of methodological reasoning.* Thousand Oaks, CA: Sage.

Berry, J. W., Poortinga, Y. H., Segall, M. H., & Dasen, P. R. (1992). *Cross-cultural psychology: Research and applications.* Cambridge: Cambridge University Press.

Boski, P. (1996). Cross-cultural psychology at the crossroads. In H. Grad, A. Blanco, & J. Georgas (Eds.), *Key issues in cross-cultural psychology* (pp. 25–41). Amsterdam: Swets & Zeitlinger.

Brislin, R. W. (1980). Translation and content analysis of oral and written material. In H. C. Triandis & J. W. Berry (Eds.), *Handbook of cross-cultural psychology* (Vol. 2, pp. 389–444). Boston: Allyn & Bacon.

Buss, D. M. (1989). Sex differences in human mate preferences: Evolutionary hypotheses tested in 37 cultures. *Behavioral and Brain Sciences, 12,* 1–49.

Campbell, D. T. (1961). The mutual methodological relevance of anthropology and psychology. In F. L. K. Hsu (Ed.), *Psychological anthropology* (pp. 333–352). Homewood, IL: Dorsey.

Child, I. L. (1954). Socialization. In G. Lindzey (Ed.), *Handbook of social psychology* (Vol. 2, pp. 655–692). Cambridge, MA: Addison-Wesley.

Cohen, J. (1988). *Statistical power analysis for the behavioral sciences* (2nd ed.). Hillsdale, NJ: Erlbaum.

Cole, M. (1992). Context, modularity, and the cultural constitution of development. In L. T. Winegar & J. Valsiner (Eds.), *Children's development within social context* (Vol. 2, pp. 5–31). Hillsdale, NJ: Erlbaum.

Denzin, N. K., & Lincoln, Y. S. (Eds.). (1994). *Handbook of qualitative research.* Thousand Oaks, CA: Sage.

Deregowski, J. B. (1989). Real space and represented space: Cross-cultural perspectives. *Behavioral and Brain Sciences, 12*, 51–119.

DeRidder, R., & Tripathi, R. C. (Eds.). (1992). *Norm violations and intergroup relations.* Oxford: Clarendon Press.

Eckensberger, L. H. (1979). A metamethodological evaluation of psychological theories from a cross-cultural perspective. In L. Eckensberger, W. Lonner, & Y. H. Poortinga (Eds.), *Cross-cultural contributions to psychology* (pp. 255–275). Amsterdam: Swets & Zeitlinger.

Eysenck, H. J., & Eysenck, S. B. G. (1983). Recent advances in the cross-cultural study of personality. In J. N. Butcher & C. D. Spielberger (Eds.), *Advances in the study of personality assessment* (Vol. 2, pp. 41–69). Hillsdale, NJ: Erlbaum.

Fijneman, Y. A., Willemsen, M. E., Poortinga, Y. H., in cooperation with Erelcin, F. G., Georgas, J., Hui, H. C., Leung, K., & Malpass, R. S. (1996). Individualism-collectivism: An empirical study of a conceptual issue. *Journal of Cross-Cultural Psychology, 27*, 381–402.

Finifter, B. M. (1977). The robustness of cross-cultural findings. *Annals of the New York Academy of Sciences, 285*, 151–184.

Georgas, J., & Berry, J. W. (1995). An ecocultural taxonomy for cross-cultural psychology. *Cross-Cultural Research, 29*, 121–157.

Gergen, K. (1982). *Towards transformation in social knowledge.* New York: Springer.

Greenfield, P. M. (1997). Culture as process: Empirical methods for cultural psychology. In J. W. Berry, Y. H. Poortinga, & J. Pandey (Eds.), *Handbook of cross-cultural psychology* (2nd ed., Vol. 1, pp. 301–346). Boston: Allyn & Bacon.

Hambleton, R. K. (1995). Guidelines for adapting educational and psychological tests: A progress report. *European Journal of Psychological Assessment (Bulletin of the International Test Commission) 10*, 229–244.

Jahoda, G. (1984). Do we need a concept of culture? *Journal of Cross-Cultural Psychology, 15*, 139–151.

Jahoda, G. (1992). *Crossroads between culture and mind.* New York: Harvester Wheatsheaf.

Jensen, A. R. (1985). The nature of black–white differences on various psychometric tests: Spearman's hypothesis. *Behavioral and Brain Sciences, 8*, 193–263.

Joe, R. C. (1992). Cognitive consequences of tonality in language: A cross-cultural investigation. *Cross-Cultural Psychology Monographs, 2* (whole issue).

Jansz, J. (1991). *Personal self and moral demands: Individualism contested by collectivism.* Leiden, The Netherlands: DSWO Press.

Lincoln, Y. S., & Guba, E. G. (1985). *Naturalistic Inquiry.* Thousand Oaks, CA: Sage.

Luria, A. R. (1971). Towards the problem of the historical nature of psychological processes. *International Journal of Psychology, 6*, 259–272.

Luria, A. R. (1976). *Cognitive development: Its cultural and social foundations.* Cambridge, MA: Harvard University Press.

Lutz, C. (1988). *Unnatural emotions.* Chicago: University of Chicago Press.

Malpass, R. S., & Poortinga, Y. H. (1986). Strategies for design and analysis. In W. J. Lonner & J. W. Berry (Eds.), *Field methods in cross-cultural research* (pp. 47–84). Thousand Oaks, CA: Sage.

Messick, S. (1995). Validity of psychological assessment. *American Psychologist, 50*, 741–749.

Miller, J. G. (1997). Theoretical issues in cultural psychology. In J. W. Berry, Y. H. Poortinga, & J. Pandey (Eds.), *Handbook of cross-cultural psychology* (2nd ed., Vol. 1, pp. 85–128). Boston: Allyn & Bacon.

Poortinga, Y. H. (1992). Towards a conceptualization of culture for psychology. In S. Iwawaki, Y. Kashima, & K. Leung (Eds.), *Innovations in cross-cultural psychology* (pp. 3–17). Amsterdam: Swets & Zeitlinger.

Poortinga, Y. H., & Malpass, R. S. (1986). Making inferences from cross-cultural data. In W. J. Lonner & J. W. Berry (Eds.), *Field methods in cross-cultural research* (pp. 17–46). Thousand Oaks, CA: Sage.

Reichardt, C. S., & Rallis, S. F. (1994). Qualitative and quantitative inquiries are not incompatible: A call for a new partnership. In C. S. Reichardt & S. F. Rallis (Eds.), *The qualitative–quantitative debate: New perspectives* (pp. 85–91). San Francisco: Jossey-Bass.

Reichenbach, H., (1938). *Experience and prediction*. Chicago: University of Chicago Press.

Russell, J. A., (1991). Culture and the categorization of emotions. *Psychological Bulletin, 110,* 426–450.

Scribner, S. (1979). Modes of thinking and ways of speaking: Culture and logic reconsidered. In R. O. Freedle (Ed.), *New directions in discourse processing* (pp. 223–243). Norwood, NJ: Ablex.

Scribner, S., & Cole, M. (1981). *The psychology of literacy*. Cambridge: MA: Harvard University Press.

Segall, M. H. (1984). More than we need to know about culture, but are afraid not to ask. *Journal of Cross-Cultural Psychology, 15,* 153–162.

Segall, M. H., Campbell, D. T., & Herskovits, M. J. (1966). *The influence of culture on visual perception*. Indianapolis, IN: Bobbs-Merrill.

Shweder, R. A. (1991). *Thinking through cultures: Expeditions in cultural psychology*. Cambridge, MA: Harvard University Press.

Strodtbeck, F. L. (1964). Considerations of metamethod in cross-cultural studies. *American Anthropologist, 66 (3, P. 2),* 223–229.

Tooby, J., & Cosmides, L. (1992). The psychological foundations of culture. In J. Barkow, L. Cosmides, & J. Tooby (Eds.), *The adapted mind: Evolutionary psychology and the generation of culture* (pp. 19–136). New York: Oxford University Press.

Triandis, H. C. (1989). The self and social behavior in differing cultural contexts. *Psychological Review, 96,* 506–520.

Triandis, H. C. (1996). The psychological measurement of cultural syndromes. *American Psychologist, 51,* 407–415.

Tulviste, P. (1991). *The cultural-historical development of verbal thinking*. New York: Nova Science Publishers.

Van de Vijver, F. J. R. (1991). *Inductive thinking across cultures*. Helmond, The Netherlands: Wibro.

Van de Vijver, F. J. R., & Leung, K. (1997a). Methods and data analysis of comparative research. In J. W. Berry, Y. H. Poortinga, & J. Pandey (Eds.), *Handbook of cross-cultural psychology,* (2nd ed., Vol. 1, pp. 257–300). Boston: Allyn and Bacon.

Van de Vijver, F. J. R., & Leung, K. (1997b). *Methods and data analysis for cross-cultural research*. Thousand Oaks, CA: Sage.

Van de Vijver, F. J. R., & Poortinga, Y. H. (1982). Cross-cultural generalization and universality. *Journal of Cross-Cultural Psychology, 13,* 387–408.

Van de Vijver, F. J. R., & Poortinga, Y. H. (1990). A taxonomy of cultural differences. In F. J. R. Van de Vijver & G. J. M. Hutschemaekers (Eds.), *The investigaton of culture: Current issues in cultural psychology* (pp. 91–114). Tilburg, The Netherlands: Tilburg University Press.

Van Lancker, D., & Fromkin, V. A. (1973). Hemispheric specialization for pitch perception: Evidence from Thai. *Journal of Phonetics, 1,* 19–23.

Vygotsky, L. S. (1978). *Mind in society: The development of higher social processes*. Cambridge, MA: Harvard University Press.

Wober, M. (1975). *Psychology in Africa*. London: International Africa Institute.

CHAPTER TWELVE

Permanence and modification in national identities

José Miguel Salazar
Universidad Central de Venezuela, Caracas, Venezuela

Miguel A. Salazar
Harvard University, Cambridge, Massachusetts, USA

In reviewing studies published in the last 10 years regarding national identity, three different but interrelated meanings of the term were distinguished: identity as objective chacteristics, as subjective representations, or as inter-subjective identification. Studies are considered illustrating these different perspectives. Account is also taken of the fact that, both at the individual and social level, observable changes are taking place; so consideration is given to studies related to acculturation, assimilation, and societal changes regarding national identities. Finally consideration is also given to studies related to the processes of emerging supranationalisms. The conclusion of this review is that the questions of national identity are still very much on the agenda, and that contrary to some prophets of globalization, its demise is still very far off.

En passant en revue les études publiées au cours des 10 dernières années sur l'identité nationale, on constate que ce terme a trois sens différents mais intimement reliés: l'identité en tant que caractéristiques objectives, en tant que représentations subjectives, ou encore comme identification inter-subjective. On considère ici des études illustrant ces différentes perspectives. On fait état du fait que, tant au niveau individuel qu'au niveau social, des changements visibles prennent place. De ce fait, une considération spéciale est accordée aux études portant sur l'acculturation, l'assimilation et les changements sociétaux se rattachant à l'identité nationale. En dernier lieu, considération est aussi accordée aux études reliées aux processus de supranationalismes émergents. La conclusion de cette revue est que les questions d'identité nationale sont encore très présentes à l'agenda et que, contrairement à certains prophètes de la globalisation, leur mort est encore très loin à l'horizon.

THE VARIED SOCIAL SCIENCE DISCOURSES ON NATIONAL IDENTITY

Within the Social Sciences the opinions regarding national identity and nationalism can be seen as forming a continuum. On the one hand, we find those who think national identity is a necessary and essential phenomenon, connected to the very nature of humanity. Indeed, the political scientist Connor (1994, p. 203) even suggests that it is not explainable in rational terms: "The dichotomy between the realm of national identity and that of reason has proven vexing to students of nationalism ... They are inclined to seek rational explanations for the nation in economic and other 'real' forces. But national consciousness resists explication in such terms". Some authors avoid such tendencies to consider nationalism an insoluble mystery, while retaining a sense of the essential nature of national identity. For example, the Italian psychologist Guerra (1992, pp. 122 & 126) states that "In the case of nations, we suggest that belonging is, on the one hand, a fundamental and historical human need, while on the other it is conditioned by historical circumstances", and that "the functional value of belonging is as central to the development of the subject as it is to the cohesion of the society".

At the other extreme, we find what we could call the "instrumental contingency" idea of national identity. Probably the best example of this approach comes from the historian Hobsbawm (1990). Starting with a minimalist definition of nation and nationalism as the political project of providing one state to every "nation" (a definition originally developed by the British sociologist and anthropologist, Ernest Gellner), and an elaborate idea of nation as a fully constructed ideological concern, Hobsbawm criticizes all considerations of "nation" based on pre-existing "essential characteristics" that define a Nation and give identity to its members (e.g. common language). More specifically, he states (p. 57) that "the mystical identification of nationality with a sort of platonic idea of language, existing behind and above all its variants and imperfect versions, is much more characteristic of the ideological construction of nationalistic intellectuals of whom Heider is the prophet, than the actual grass-roots users of the idiom".

Whether intrinsically human or historically constructed, the fact is that nationalism and national identity constitute very important actual phenomena. Hobsbawm (1990) argues that there has been a "decoupling" of nationality and political citizenship, that will ultimately lead to the progressive marginalization of nationalism as a political force. Without necessarily disagreeing with this analysis, it is imposible to deny that nationalism still commands today a significant amount of power to mobilize. We consider that Hobsbawn undestimates the attachment generated by the image of the nation. At the same time, we cannot accept the extreme form of essentialism which suggests that nations are the natural expression of innate, atemporal human nature. To a large degree, the difference between these two positions is found in the definitions used for the two basic concepts that we need to explore the phenomenon: *National* and *Identity*.

There has been a long catalogue of definitions for "a nation" in the history of the social sciences, and those that emphasize the political aspects of real or potential power for a social group or conglomerate are found most frequently. Other definitions restrict themselves to underscoring the element of common birth or ancestry (real, acquired, or based on myths). The most common usage of "nation" is as a political concept, and most studies of national identity investigate "nations" in political terms. Considering nations as political ideological constructs is bound to create a very incomplete view, since it obviates a complete set of social and psychological factors that help to establish the boundary for what counts as "nation" and "national." Authors like the historian and linguist Fishman (1972) try to emphasize these other dimensions by differentiating between "nationism," which refers to the acquisition, maintenance, and development of political independent territory, and "nationalism" which refers to ethnocultural solidarity.

This second type of national solidarity, proto-political in nature, must be be kept well in mind, given its socio-psychological significance. These "nations" without nationalism are the raw material of ideological political nationalism. For example, from very vague conceptions of being "North Italian", a concept all but meaningless without the existence of an Italian nationalism, clever political operators like Umberto Bossi of the separatist Lega Nord can succeed in creating an image of a "Padanian" nation. Indeed, there is a large continuum of "nation-related identities" extending from both sides of the prototypical case of the nation state. From ethnic groups and regional grouping to supranational conglomerations, these "nation-like" identities are as abundant as they are theoretically problematic. Limiting our exploration of national identity exclusively to the case of the imagined nation state as center of political loyalty, would limit the socio-psychological interest of the phenomenon. Therefore, we will cover other "nation-related" identities, like ethnicity and supernationalism as well as the specific case of "nation-state" nationalism.

The term "identity" is also problematic. In its pure philosophical usage, it implies "uniqueness," the concept of being equal to oneself, and nothing else. From this basic concept, implying "sameness and difference," identity has come to refer to individuals, groups or conglomerates; it can also be used to refer to something externally or consensually defined, or to something subjective or individually experienced (Mach, 1993; Salazar, 1994).

Some authors consider the "group" to be a real (not nominal) category. From this perspective, identity can be "identified" externally by the individual possession of relevant traits. Personal characteristics, behavioral patterns, etc., provide the necessary and sufficient rules to define membership to a unique group. The validity of these definitions may be ascertained through objective, consensually accepted ways. This was the view of the Culture and Personality school of mid-century, with their emphasis on national character as the nucleus of the identity of a particular group. Even though the terminology may have changed, there are authors who still think of identity in terms of national characteristics.

Alternatively, national identity may refer to the subjective feelings people have about a national group. This is the degree to which they identify themselves with a particular nominal category, using "cultural markers" and "family resemblance" rules, rather than substantive content to create the boundaries of the category (Barth, 1969). This is more along the lines of Social Identity theorizing (Tajfel, 1981).

There is a third approach to national identity theorizing, which centers on the way groups are perceived by others and particularly by themselves. This approach has produced a copious literature on stereotype research and helps to link the two previous conceptions. The way a group is perceived is not the same as the way a group is (unless one takes an extreme constructionist position), yet continually, research gives support to formulations that suggest that, contrary to being totally disjointed, unreal constructions, stereotypes contain a "grain of truth" (Lee, Jussim, & McCauley, 1995). Thus, we can see stereotypes as grounded in objective characteristics of the members of the group, and the nominal and real categories do overlap. Unfortunately, it is common to loosely consider stereotypes as describing the "real" characteristics of a national entity.

Likewise, when identity is conceived as the acceptance of ascription to a social category, this ascribed category is perceived to entail certain characteristics. The category is construed on the basis of a label, but goes well beyond that; it incorporates images, stereotypes, and representations. Again, differentiations must be established between stereotypes (in this case, group self-stereotypes) and social identity because the perception of characteristics attributed to one's group does not imply wholehearted acceptance of such characteristics as one's own.

The three conceptions of national identity found in the literature are linked, and, hence, should be considered to be a trinity of valid perspectives. Identity as "objective" group characteristics; identity as "subjective" group self-images or stereotypes; and identity as "intersubjective" identification with a social category are all valid and useful conceptions. In terms of behavioral consequences, probably the last one is the most useful, but since we did not want to restrict ourselves when giving an overview of research on the area, we opted to include studies that define national identity in any of these three ways.

National identities can also be considered along the temporal dimension of permanence and modification or change. There can hardly be any doubt that the issue of differentiating the "new" from the "old" in a national identity has powerfully exercised theorists since Ernest Renan, the 19th-century French historian who is one of the fathers of the study of nationalism. We need to explore this continuum of opinion, which stretches from conceptions of nations as an eternal, essential unit with a continuous history extending centuries or millennia, to conceptions of nations as one of the freshly minted "invented traditions" produced, quite recently, as part of the ideological baggage of modernity.

On the question of persistence and continuity, let us consider the study of Ocampo, Bernal, and Wright (1993). This study follows Piagetian theory, and describes the processes of acquisition of identities. According to this model, the sequential stages in the acquisition of social identities in children are: awareness, self-identification, and constancy. Children become aware of the existence of certain categories in a first stage; subsequently they acquire identification with the category; and finally, they come to realize that there is consistency in such identity, and that it doesn't change from one moment to the other. Ocampo et al. (1993) found that American children acquire constancy in their gender identities by age 4, and in their race and ethnic identities after age 8.

Just as the child acquires the idea that his or her sexual, racial, ethnic, or national identity persists over time, social groups similarly acquire the idea that the group identity has persisted and will persist through generations. This idea of continuity is better expressed in the form of myths of ethnic descent and the ethnic nationalism described by the sociologist Anthony Smith (1991). The community of nationals are united by a common descent, and by inference, a common destiny. However, while this phenomenon gives national identities extension in time, it does not preclude that, just as nations persist, they can appear and disappear (Fishman, 1972). National identities are subject to change and modification as they "move" along the line of time.

We have organized this chapter based on the following dimensions: first by giving an overview of recent work (after 1985) regarding persisting national identities defined in any of the three aforementioned ways (as objective common characteristics, as subjective self images or as the intersubjective identifications); then, we look at changes of identities occurring at the individual and societal levels; and finally, we discuss the question of supranational identities. The limits imposed on this chapter made it impossible to be exhaustive, so our approach will tend to be illustrative. Attempts will be made to include examples from different regions of the world, although most material will come from Latin American studies. This bias comes, naturally, from the authors' familiarity with the region, but also from a desire to exemplify the phenomenon with data from a region relatively unknown to the rest of the world.

STUDIES DEVELOPED AROUND THE THREE MEANINGS OF NATIONAL IDENTITY

National identity as substantive, differentiating characteristics

As mentioned earlier, this approach is implicit in the workings of authors of the Culture and Personality school which flourished during the middle of the century. These kinds of study try to identify the basic personality structures that create a distinct national character. Often, what is actually researched are differentiating values and traits. Good examples of these are some of the differentiating dimensions identified by Hofstede (1980), Schwartz (1992), or Triandis (1988). Yet their work is not presented as centering on national identity, which is the case for that of Díaz-Guerrero (1991; 1995). He began his work focusing on what he calls "socio-cultural premises," in an attempt to describe and operationalize the measurement of Mexican national identity. He started with socio-cultural premises related to the family, which are statements (some of the prescriptive type like, "A man should wear the pants in the family") for which there is a high agreement among the members of a culture. These premises are interrelated and could be conceived of as integrated. In the Mexican case, these seem to reflect the dominance of the father and the abnegation of the mother within the family structure. In his early work, carried out in the 1950s, Díaz-Guerrero identifies 123 premises of this type which, when submitted to a factor analysis, yielded several factors, three of which are machismo, affiliative obedience, and virginity. Other socio-cultural premises related to the relationship with the environment, and yielded a measure of active vs. passive confrontation. Traditional Mexican culture, according to Díaz-Guerrero, is characterized by "affiliative obedience" and also by a "passive style of confrontation."

In this approach, national identity is ascertained by the degree to which the individuals internalize the traditional Mexican socio-cultural premises. There is evidence that the degree of acceptance is related to several personality measures, like field-dependence and low autonomy. There is also evidence that affiliative obedience tends to decrease with age, educational level, and socio-economic status. At the same time, a dialectic interplay seems to exist between what Díaz-Guerrero calls "culture-counter culture." This is the idea that not everybody accepts the sociocultural premises to an equal degree. More recently, followers of Díaz-Guerrero's school have carried out work on the trait of abnegation (self-denial) (Avendaño & Díaz-Guerrero, 1992), connected to affiliative obedience. Experimental and field evidence of the frequency of this trait among diverse Mexican groups studied has led Díaz-Guerrero (1993) to consider it a cardinal factor in Mexican personality, and hence, a defining characteristic of Mexican national identity.

National identity as self-stereotype

Studies centered on self-stereotypes or self-images have been numerous, although not as widespread as those on stereotypes held by external observers. Some authors believe that these self-stereotypes provide the basis for national identity. Marques and Oliveira (1988, p. 31) state that "the construct of Social Identity refers to the sum of self-stereotypes held by social actors, and National Identity can be conceived as of a subset of this construct (i.e. the national self stereotype)". Similarly, Montero (1984, p. 76) defines national identity as "meanings and representations . . . that permit the members of a social group . . . to recognize themselves as biographically related".

Larsen et al. (1992) provide a recent example of self-stereotype research. They asked students from the three countries to give their national self-descriptions by listing the three words that best describe being an American, a Hungarian, and a Bulgarian with. The results indicated a very positive self-image for the Americans, but the Hungarian self-image tended to be self-derogatory, indicated by the fact that negative character traits accounted for almost half (49%) of the responses. What was interesting was that the Hungarians defined "being a Hungarian" in personality trait terms, while "being an American" was defined in more socio-political terms (freedom, national development). Bulgarians were somewhat more positive, but again concentrated on personality traits. In Portugal, Marques and Oliveira (1988) reported a positive self-image of the Portuguese, which contrasted with a more negative social image of the Spaniards.

In Latin America, a great amount of information has been collected working with self-stereotypes. Salazar's (1988) surveys conducted in 1979, 1982, and 1986 in Venezuela, consistently yielded negative self-perceptions of the people and of the country. Representative samples drawn from the population residing in Caracas considered Venezuelans to be, on the one hand, lazy and irresponsible, and on the other, hospitable, helpful, and "simpaticos" (roughly translated as "possessing likeable niceness"), the trait that yielded the highest loadings in the evaluative dimension in semantic differential studies carried out in the country (Santoro, 1975). The country was considered by the majority in the study as backward and anarchical, with poor public services, the only positive trait being freedom of speech. At the same time, an overwhelming majority indicated that they like Venezuela despite these negative characteristics. It is interesting to note that the relative persistence of the negative self-image has been evidenced by Montero (1984) through her content analysis of sociological writings over a period of time, starting in the later part of the nineteenth century.

Quintero (1993) traced the acquisition of this negative self-image through an analysis of history texts used in primary schools in Venezuela. The results of this study showed evidence of high Eurocentrism in these textbooks, and a corresponding "colonizing education" in Venezuelan primary schools, which both help to create and reinforce the negative self-image.

The negative self-image of the Latin American ethnonational self is almost universal. D'Adamo and Garcia (1995) even found evidence of negative self-evaluations in the case of the Argentineans (regarded by other Latin Americans as arrogant and self-confident, in itself an interesting phenomenon of stereotyping). In this multinational study, these researchers found that the Argentineans' self-perception emphasized negative attributes: they saw themselves as underdeveloped, corrupt, dependent, and unstable. Yet their particular self-perception seems to be associated with the history of European immigration at the beginning of the century, which gave Argentina a whiter and more European population

than the rest of Latin America. D'Adamo and Garcia argue that with this identification with European forefathers comes an inferiority complex, but at the
same time, this "Europeanness" allows Argentineans to feel superior in comparison to other Latin American countries.

There are certain limitations that must be identified with respect to self-
images, since there seems to be a difference between the individual and the
social image. Rivera (1982), working with Puerto Rican children from rural and
urban contexts, found that self-description associated with the prompt "I am"
included the use of positive adjectives. When parents were asked to describe
their children, similar positive adjectives were used. Yet when teachers and
parents were asked to consider the Puerto Rican child in general, the description
emphasized negative traits. This is a replication of what this researcher found
to be occurring in adults (Rivera, 1991), with negative collective self-images
occurring hand-in-hand with positive individual self-images. She interpreted
the situation as evidence of breaking with the "image of the colonized," which
is also found in other Third World countries.

Studies carried out in El Salvador regarding the negative own-group images
in Latin America are also of interest. Azucena et al. (1989) and Martin-Baró
(1990) found that in the self-descriptions of the Salvadorean, the adjectives most
used were hard-working, simpatico, and benevolent. The meaning of this result,
atypical in the area, was further analyzed by Martin-Baró (1990), who used
group discussions to obtain the meaning of "hard-working" among his subjects.
This term was defined by his subjects as "exploited" or "hard-worker in order
to survive" under the very adverse conditions of their country. So, the seemingly
positive image turned again into a negative one.

Some discrepant results were obtained by Sorin (1991) in a study carried out
in Cuba. She found that in all groups studied, there was a high valuation of the
Cuban, with the following qualities as more frequent in self-descriptions: hospitable, internationalist, loved, helpful, brave, etc. This was in sharp contrast with
results obtained previously in Cuba (Bustamante, 1959) which yielded the negative self-image observed frequently in Latin American countries. Sorin interpreted
these results as reflecting the changed socio-political situation in that country.

Banchs (1992) evaluated the social representation of Venezuelans about
Indians, Blacks, and Spaniards—who are the main elements of the Latin American
mixed heritage. Looking at the content of the characteristics enumerated, it was
concluded that these characteristics correspond with historical stereotypes of the
country: the naive Indians; the strong hard-working Black slaves; the arrogant
Spanish conquistador. These archetypes or images of the ancestry of the nation
play a significant role in explaining the origins of the national characteristics
of most Latin American countries. The critical idea for making the transition
between these archetypical ancestors and the modern traits is the idea of mixture.

Dominguez' (1993) study illustrates this concept. After obtaining a list of
traits attributed to Venezuelans, she asked her subjects to identify whether the

TABLE 12.1
The ten traits most frequently assigned to
Venezuelans and their origin

Traits attributed to Venezuelans	Origin of traits		
	Spanish	Indian	Black
Merry	41%	23%	57%
Spendthrift	72%	10%	24%
Disorganized	38%	24%	43%
Not law-abiding	70%	12%	26%
"Simpático"	42%	29%	46%
Loving	30%	52%	43%
Violent	54%	18%	40%
Intelligent	60%	48%	24%
Generous	17%	67%	24%
Lazy	37%	45%	22%

NOTES:

Traits could be assigned to more than one origin; hence rows do not add to 100%.

From *Diversidad Cultural y Construcción de Identidades* (pp. 107–108), by Dominguez (1993) Caracas: Tropykos. Copyright 1993 by Fondo Editorial Tropykos. Adapted with permission.

origin of those traits can be attributed to the Indian, the Black, or the Spanish ancestry. The results are presented in Table 12.1.

The research question may sound odd in some cultural contexts, but it was quite understandable to the subjects, because it fits in with the dominant ideology regarding race in the country. The dominant ideology encourages racial mixture to the extent that, since 1892, the 12th of October has been known as the "Day of the Race," celebrating the creation of a new (mixed) race, which started with the arrival of Columbus.

This romanticized idea of the "cosmic race" (Vasconcelos, 1958), which is an historical conception of "nationhood" as an evolved mixture of disparate elements that jell together to form a new national "essence," seems to be one of the main theories behind the Latin American conception of nationhood and ethnicity. It goes much further than the "melting pot" idea of the USA, and the "mongrel nation" idea entertained by the British. Of course, this mixed race ideology makes sense only in the context of the concept of race used in Europe and the USA, the reference groups of choice for most of Latin America. Since the concept of race in these countries has, at its core, the idea that "white is good," it follows that the proper mix of races is seen to be one with a heavy white component: coffee with milk, but "to dilute the *café* as much as possible with more *leche*" (Wright, 1990, p. 2; in Spanish in the original).

Self-stereotype or image research, apart from providing the occasional eye-catching headline, is only part of the story. The subjective images of nationhood and ethnicity are "grounded" in social reality. In which way are those "images" of nation connected to actual social behavior and communication? Other approaches must be used to extend our view of the phenomenon.

Social identity approaches

Although an orthodox social identity approach takes as its starting point the acceptance of a national category, a similar way of tackling the problem is by studying the acceptance or identification with national symbols and institutions. With this broad conceptualization in mind, it has been possible to identify at least five different lines of research, which we shall briefly describe.

Experimental minimal group situations.   An experimentally centered approach to ascertain national identity, using an extension of Tajfel's (1978) minimal group paradigm, has been used by Gallagher (1989) in Northern Ireland. He created experimental situations requiring the assignment of points to the ingroup and the outgroup, defined in religious (Catholic vs. Protestant), national (Irish vs. British), and political (Unionist vs. Nationalist) terms. This procedure made it possible to evaluate ingroup favoritism and discrimination against the outgroup. In this study, which was complemented by in-depth interviews, it was concluded (p. 933) that "for minority group members, the identities provided by religion (Catholic) and political (Nationalist) aspirations appeared to have a similar impact over time. It was argued that these identities may have an essential unity, perhaps within some notion of what constitutes the Irish nation".

Self-labeling.   A more direct and less sophisticated approach consists of obtaining the self-labeling of subjects, and attempting to relate this identification to other variables. In a study carried out in Australia, Feather (1993) included an evaluation of national identity by asking subjects to indicate to which national group they consider themselves to belong. The choices were: Australian, British, Vietnamese, Polish, Italian, Greek, Yugoslavian, Chinese, or Other. Their answers enabled subsequent classification into Australian versus non-Australian national identity. Besides this, a measure of identification with Australia was obtained, based on two questions: "In general, how much would you say being an Australian means to you? How much do you care about being an Australian?" and "How proud are *you* to be a member of the Australian nation?" He found that those subjects who identified with Australia, both by labeling themselves as Australians and by being proud of being Australian, tended to value their country and its achievements. It was also found that there was no relationship between identity and general self-esteem or personal standing. In another analysis, Feather (1994) looked for evidence of the moderating effect of values in the relationship between in-group bias and identification, postulated by classical social identity theory. Using Schwartz' value survey, he ascertained that some collectivist values (conformity, security) increased the positive relationship between in-group bias and identification.

Salazar (1989), in studying Latin American identity among Venezuelan, Colombian, and Chilean students, had his subjects indicate on a rating scale the extent to which they agreed with the statement: "I feel that I am, first of all, Latin American." Also, distance scores in Semantic Differential scales in rating the concepts "the Latin Americans" and "I" were analyzed. From these measures, the subjects were classified as "identified with Latin America" or "unidentified". It was possible to ascertain differences in their cognitive structures regarding their world views as a function of the degree of identification: subjects who identified with Latin America perceived relationships in political terms more often, and had a more positive image of the Latin American.

Jenson (1993, p. 337) makes an interesting theoretical analysis in considering the importance of the creation and utilization of self-naming in social movements. According to to her, self-naming involves four elements: "It generates strategic resources; it defines some claims as meaningful and others as less relevant; it locates the community in relation to allies and opponents; and it has consequences for routing claims through state institutions". Her examples refer to the Canadian situation and the effect that the Québecois designation, and more recently the Aboriginal one, has on social processes in the country. In this regard, Oboler (1992), empirically studied the problem of labeling in relation to the Latino cultural identity with middle- and working-class Latinos living in New York City. In this qualitative study, it became evident that even though the term Hispanic is increasingly used by Hispanics and non-Hispanics alike to establish the idea of a homogeneous Hispanic ethnic group, the term was generally rejected and considered to be a term of abuse or of discrimination. On the other hand, Calderón (1992), working in California, found that using the term "Latino" to label Hispanics actually tended to build panethnic unity around issues that threatened the interest of the entire Hispanic community.

Consciousness of national affiliation. In Germany, Gallenmüller and Wakenhut (1992) developed an instrument, inspired by the theorizing of Piaget and Kohlberg, to evaluate "consciousness of national affiliation." Using this instrument, respondents were presented a list of national symbols and asked to state whether these represented national symbols for them personally or not, and then to judge them favorably or unfavorably. Three possible interpretations or functions are attributed to the symbols that reflect three qualitatively social perspectives with regard to the concept of nation. The first is personal interests and needs (associated with strength, power, superiority, and advantage); the second is the member-of-society perspective ("cultural nationalism"); and the third is the prior-to-society perspective (refers to a "universalizable national affiliation"). An example of the use of the instrument comes from Forsthofer and Martini's (1992) report on comparisons carried out in Germany and Italy. It was found that in the Italian students, national pride, satisfaction with life in their own country, and the emotional relationship to their country (the member-of-society perspective) was more pronounced than among the German students. In Germany, national pride was related to right-wing orientations, while in Italy, national pride was less related to political orientation. They also found that consciousness of national affiliation was not related to moral development. This study concluded that national pride can hardly be considered a one-dimensional construct, but rather, must be divided into different, clearly defined qualities of national consciousness.

Relationship with social, cultural, and political elements and institutions. Bejar and Capello (1986) define national identity by making reference to the institutions of the society, and the people's "sense of participation" and "sense of belonging" towards them. Further, they classified institutions as either "expressive" (regional dances, music, etc.) or "directive" (political parties, industry, etc.). Among inhabitants of the northern frontier of Mexico, they found a greater sense of "belonging" than of "participation" in the institutions, and that when this participation occurs, it is more likely to be in relation to the expressive institutions. According to Bejar and Cappello, this indicated a very low level of national identity. In a replication study (Cappello, 1995), the situation was similar, or worse, as a result of the economic changes that had taken place in the country.

Cadenas (1992) took a similar approach. He made a list of cultural objects and symbols, and asked his subjects (young Venezuelan students) to indicate whether they considered the objects alien or of their own, and the degree of affect felt towards each. The objects were connected to Indian, Black, or Spanish cultures. Subjects tended to consider the Indian objects to be elements of their own culture, and to like them. To a lesser degree, elements of the Black culture were considered part of their own culture and were liked. Finally, there was a tendency to consider alien and to dislike those elements associated with Spanish culture, the only exception being the Catholic religion. However, there was a large consensus in considering Latin America as their own, and to like it.

Language and identity. Studies that approach national identity on the basis of language identity or usage are particularly relevant because language is perhaps the most important cultural element differentiating or bringing groups together. Ros, Cano and Huici (1987) studied the case of the languages in Spain, where at least five languages are recognized. In their study, languages were classified according to their "linguistic vitality," from Castilian (high) to Galician (med.-low). They found that there is a tendency among speakers of languages with lower vitality to upgrade outgroups on status dimensions, and ingroups in solidarity dimensions. Ingroup members compensate for their inferior position by enhancing interpersonal attraction this way. Thus it is not uncommon to find individuals who, despite their clear identification with the ingroup (subjects identified more with their communities than with Spain), acknowledge its inferiority (at least in some dimensions). They also found that degree of identification was related to attitude towards language use, but not to actual usage. In other words, they found that language was being used as a symbol of nationalism.

In a similar vein, Keefe and Padilla (1987) found that, in the USA, "ethnic identity" was not related to "cultural knowledge" among members of the Latino community they studied, and that the self-identification as Latin could in many cases exist without knowledge or usage of the language.

The role of language in identity is often mixed with other elements, as evidenced by a case study reported by Mach (1993) about a Lutheran Polish community in Taschen, southern Poland. In this community, identity has been defined in different historical moments either in terms of language (Polish speaking vs. others), or religion (Lutheran vs. Catholic). Mach (1993, p. 231) concluded that, "The identity of the Protestant-Teschenian is therefore simultaneously local and abstract: they are Teschenians, Lutherans, and Poles, and in their isolated enclave they cultivate all those components in a unique combination".

The various studies enumerated in this section point to the sustained interest in approaches related to social identity, and the creativity of the researchers working in such varied socio-cultural contexts. It is this ability to account for variation of form and strategy in self-identification, that substantiates the viability of the social identity approach. Moreover, from a social action perspective, perceptions, characteristic ways of behaving, values, and even generalized traits, are closely associated with a category, and the act of accepting the category has clear behavioral consequences. Taking a social identity perspective, broadly speaking, gives us the opportunity to integrate the three disparate approaches identified.

THE MANIFESTATIONS OF CHANGE

Acculturation and assimilation

National identity is a phenomenon which is continually changing. One of the ways in which this change comes about is when individuals move around the world and change their social, national, or cultural context. Berry (1993) defines four acculturation strategies: assimilation, integration, separation, and marginalization. In the cases of integration and separation, maintaining cultural identity and characteristics is considered to be of value, the difference being that the separation strategy leads to the formation of enclaves, while integration tends towards bi-culturalism. Taylor (1991) contends that the multiculturalist ideology, with all its implications (e.g. affirmative action), runs counter to the meritocracy (liberal) ideology of North America, which centers on the individual, rather than on groups or categories. Yet, this ideology has been implemented in North America as a means of redressing injustices. Taylor believes that the important factors used to analyze the level of multicultural ideology in a country are the motives for heritage culture maintenance. The psychological needs that are met through symbolic ethnicity may be fundamental. That is, since the individual needs a cultural context to develop and strengthen its identity (something the host society does not always provide), a heritage culture emerges within the context of a new society. It is not necessary that the emerging heritage culture be true to the original, since what is important is that the individual be socialized through a culture that provides a framework from which to define and evaluate the self.

In the literature, many examples can be found of instruments and methodologies designed to evaluate the degree of adaptation to a new culture. Wong-Rieger and Quintana (1987) consider a consistency model of adaptation that includes behavioral, cognitive, and identification variables, and develop a multicultural acculturation scale. In a study carried out in Oklahoma with South East Asian (mostly Vietnamese) and Hispanic immigrants, they found that the Hispanic immigrants scored higher in overall integration (tended towards bi-culturalism), while the South East Asian immigrants tended towards a separatist orientation. Cultural similarity and permanent status increased assimilation, whereas extended kin group network fostered ethnic maintenance. Marín et al. (1986) and Sabogal et al. (1987) working with different groups of Hispanics developed a measure of cultural values (using factor analysis), which related cultural values to behavioral acculturation (e.g. preferences in use of language). Three factors were identified: familial obligations, support from the family, and family as referent. When they compared subjects who were highly acculturated on the behavioral scale with those who showed low acculturation, significant differences were found in family as referents and in familiar obligations. Sabogal et al. concluded (1987, p. 409) that "Hispanic families do not resemble white non-Hispanic families, even though acculturation has taken place. There seems to be an interaction between original and new cultural patterns rather than a unidirectional process of total assimilation".

Cuéllar, Arnold, and Gonzalez (1995) also sought to establish relationships between behavioral acculturation to cognitive changes, and not only familism, but also other aspects of social construction. In their study, they used five generation groups, from those born in Mexico to those whose parents and all their grandparents had been born in the USA. A scale was used to measure acculturation (behavioral), and five types of cultural constructs: familism, fatalism, folk beliefs, machismo, and personalism. These constructs map the changes that occurred. In all the scales, there were differences corresponding to the transitions of the generations: changes in personalism and fatalism occured between generations 1 and 2; familism and machismo changed between generations 3 and 4; and folk beliefs changed only between generations 4 and 5. The data point out the complexity of the acculturation process. Marín (1993) considered the preferred ethnic label to be a function of acculturation, and found evidence of important shifts in preferred ethnic labels between generations. The first generation preferred Mexican (89%), while the second generation preferred Mexican American (81%), with the degree of acculturation increasing through the following labels: Mexican, Mexican American, Chicano, Spanish American, and Anglo American.

A recent paper by Georgas et al. (1996) also considered the question of family values in the context of acculturation. Using a 65-item questionnaire, with items very similar to some of Díaz-Guerrero's (1972) socio-cultural premises about the Mexican family, these researchers evaluated changes in Greek immigrants living in Europe and Canada, to evaluate the importance of the policies or ideological definitions of the host societies. There was evidence that, in Canada, policy is defined in terms of integration and not assimilation, and that the changes of values regarding the family were less pronounced than in Germany or the Netherlands. The relevance of the characteristics of the policies and philosophy of the recipient countries is underlined in the work of Soysal (1994), who considered the situation of immigrants in European countries, and created a comprehensive four-fold typology of the host countries: Corporatist (Sweden, Netherlands); Liberal (Switzerland, Britain); Statist (France); and Fragmental (Gulf oil countries). The work by Ward and Kennedy (1993) considered two cases: Malaysian and Singaporean students in New Zealand. In both groups the relationship to the host country rather than the relationship to the original culture (termed cultural identity) appeared to be the significant predictor of sociocultural adaptation. Similarly, the relationship to the host country is underlined in the work of Tsai (1995) who considered the question of the adaptation of foreigners to Japan. Attitude scales submitted to factor analysis yielded four factors: attitudes towards Japan; nativism (my country is better); Japan as a model; and alienation to Japan. Subjects were divided in terms of time of stay, and there was no evidence of the U-curve of adjustment (that is, a very positive early "honeymoon" stage, followed by a negative stage, and then a moderately positive one again) The relationship was found to be lineal and consistent for all time periods: the longer you are in Japan, the less you like it, although the decrease tends to taper off after three years. When subjects classified as Asians were investigated, no such change was observed. This was explained by the lack of a honeymoon phase in the case of the Asians.

Liebkind (1996) worked with young Vietnamese refugees (average age of 17) and their adult care-givers in Finland. As the result of interviews and some questionnaires, several indexes were calculated relating to their experience in Vietnam as well as to their acculturation experiences in Finland. The results suggested that acculturation attitudes and degree of acculturation exert different and distinct influences on acculturation stress, depending on gender and generation. It is interesting to note that, even in this probably very traumatized group of subjects, pre-emigration traumatic experiences had less impact than post-migration contingencies. Again, as in some of the previous studies, the present situation, the way they are received, and their experience in host country seem to be the most important variables in the process of adaptation.

Altrocchi and Altrocchi (1995) reported an interesting case which gives emphasis to the other side of the coin: the attitudes towards the original country. This study focused on the acculturation of Cook Islanders in New Zealand. Four groups were contrasted: the first from a small economically backward island; the second from Raratonga (the capital and most developed island); the third, islanders who had migrated to New Zealand; and the fourth made up of Cook Islanders born in New Zealand. The degree of acculturation was measured by acceptance of some traditional customs (e.g. having their children brought up by foster (relatives) parents), and an acculturation index was devised. A direct measure ("To what degree do you consider yourself a Cook Islander?") was also obtained, as well as a measure of time lived in Cook Island. The results of the study indicated (Altrocchi & Altrocchi, 1995, p. 437) that "Cook Islanders who had emigrated to New Zealand and who were heavily involved in Cook Island activities were, on the average, higher in sense of belonging and more willing to give children to feeding parents than were Raratongans".

To conclude this section, a very important study by Keefe & Padilla (1987) combined ethnological-qualitative interviews with quantitative survey research of Chicanos in southern California. Keefe and Padilla posited that acculturation is different from assimilation: You *can* have one without the other. They developed measures of culture awareness (acculturation), ethnic loyalty (ethnic identity), and ethnic social orientation (social assimilation). Using cluster analysis, five types of Chicanos emerged based on different combinations of cultural awareness and ethnic loyalty. These types were related to generation, with social assimilation occurring primarily in the second generation and leveling off thereafter. The strongest relationship that emerged in the analysis of ethnic loyalty was "barrio [Hispanic neighborhood] residence." Familism was evaluated using behavioral reports. It was found that Mexican-Americans exchange aid with two to three times as many secondary kin as Anglos, and that local extended families grow stronger, despite the impact of many processes assumed to promote family breakdown (e.g. acculturation, social and economic assimilation, and urbanization). Loyalty toward Mexican heritage persisted through the fourth generation, although a slight shift occurred between first and second generation respondents. Social assimilation followed a similar course, with Chicano interaction with Anglos increasing somewhat in the second generation, and no significant change occurring afterwards. On the other hand, awareness of Mexican cultural traits declined steadily with each successive generation. Based on these findings, the authors contended that as long as ethnically segregated communities persist, it is easy to understand why Chicanos may be acculturated, but not socially assimilated. They concluded that their results did not support the acculturation–assimilation model, and that the pluralism model is best suited to their findings.

Societal changes

Sometimes the changes occurring are not the result of individuals moving to a different culture, but can be identified as occurring in a society as a whole. The work of Laroche et al. (1996) attempted to provide evidence of ethnic changes that French Canadians in Quebec experience when they come into contact with English Canadian influences. Although they recognized that the process operates in both directions, they concentrated on the French Canadian population of Montreal. On the basis of factor analysis of five ethnic identifiers (language use, social networks, attitude towards outgroups, spouse ethnic identity, and self-identification), they obtained two factors: French Canadian ethnic identification, and an acculturative tendency. Using cluster analysis on the basis of the two factors, a typology of subjects was created. Among the five clusters identified, the one that incorporated the largest number of subjects was the one characterized by a very high degree of French Canadian ethnic identification, and a moderate or low degree of acculturative tendency. The authors concluded that both ethnic identification and acculturation have to be taken into account, and in line with Keefe and Padilla (1987), emphasized the need to sustain a multidimensional perspective in studying ethnic change.

Another example of the process of change occurring within a society comes from a study investigating the socio-cultural changes taking place in Peru (Herencia, 1991). Herencia found that, in Peru, there exists a situation best described as "two systems of life essentially different in confrontation and with unequal power relationships". Based on a qualitative study in a poor community in Lima, this researcher identified two national identities: one present in Quechua speaking, recent immigrants from the Andes, characterized by a clearly organized vision of the world and the cosmos, and a strong identification with very positive traits; the other identity, the "standard" Peruvian identity, characterized by a very negative image of themselves (a phenomenon we have already seen as characterizing other Latin American populations). In between these two poles, she describes three other transitional types which express the gradual breakdown of the Andean (Native American) identity, and the changes towards the Peruvian (Creole) identity.

Related to these considerations of society-level changes, Lara-Tapia, Gómez, and Fuentes (1992), and Lara-Tapia and Gómez (1991) reported changes that have taken place in Mexico in a follow-up study (35 years after the original study) regarding the socio-cultural premises among Mexican secondary school children. In the original study carried out in the mid-1950s, (Diaz-Guerrero, 1955), the widespread acceptance of certain statements were taken as the basic elements defining the Mexican national identity. Standardized instruments were then developed based on these statements (Diaz-Guerrero, 1972). Through factor analysis, one instrument yielded several factors, one of which was designated "affiliative obedience" and most of the items related to obedience were widely accepted. When the instruments were applied to similar populations in the 1980s, there were significant changes in relation to many of the statements. For example, while in the original study 86% agreed that "A daughter should always obey her parents," this percentage fell to only a 49% agreement in the later study. Likewise, the statement "One should never put in doubt our father's word" changed from 77% to 31% agreement. Similar changes were found when machismo and virginity, two other factors which were very important in the original research, were considered. Here again, changes were evident and the support for socio-cultural premises like "The man should wear the pants in the house" and "It is better to marry a woman who is a virgin" was found in the later study to be minimal. Evidently, Mexican national identity, as defined by the acceptance of some socio-cultural premises, has definitely changed in the last 35 years. This does not mean that we cannot speak of Mexican national identity any more, but rather that we should explore other ways of defining identity. Although many changes were identified, there were still some consistencies. For example, the statement "A person should always respect his parents" was still found to be a socio-cultural premise after 35 years.

Of relevance to this discussion of permanence and change is Lew's (1988) report which gave an overview of the important changes that have taken placed in South Korea since 1945 in religion, family, kinship, education, housing, etc. In spite of all these changes, the author says (p. 164) that "Koreans have preserved a strong sense of national identity ... that provides them with some leverage in a world that is sometimes friendly and other times hostile. With this national identity, Koreans hope to realize their own ideals and to contribute to the progress of the world community".

SUPRANATIONALISM

Parellel to the evidence of changes in national identities, there is growing evidence of the development of identities that transcend the existing national states. The "imagined communities" (Anderson, 1991) that elicit allegiance and provide a focus for mobilization are progressively more likely to be situated at a higher level than the traditional nation, a phenomenon we may call supranationalism. Several examples come to mind: Europe and the emergence of a European consciousness, the pan-Arabic movements, and the revival of ideas of Latin American integration.

In a special issue of the *International Journal of Psychology*, devoted to the problem of European identity, Fells and Niznik (1992, p. 206) came to the following conclusions based on each of the presented papers:

> According to the analysis of students' responses from nine countries, there is no doubt that European identity is a fact. There were respondents who considered themselves to be European and who affirmed their membership in a supranational European Community ... Nevertheless, the basis of European identity is much

more difficult to define. We have tried to show how inadequate are such putative bases as the geographical boundaries of Europe or other more subjective boundaries. However, the elements most often mentioned as contributing to European identity are communality of culture and common history.

Quadrio and Magrin (1992) carried out a study with Italian children (10 and 13 years old) to investigate the evolution of the supranational consciousness of Europe. They state (p. 90) that "The geophysical aspects form the first and simplest method of approaching an outside and complex object such as Europe ... as they become older, we see a gradual construction of European image through political traits and an affective motion that is translated in the exaltation of Europe". Considering the whole sample, more than 50% of the adjectives were placed in the Geo-ethnical category (density, extension, beauty), and the socio-political category (united–divided, military, sociopolitical) appeared in second place (15%). They came to the conclusion (p. 94) that "The young Eurocentric feeling does in fact require a proper stimulation which promotes the development of a more solid structure of categories". Personnaz (1993), working with French students found that, when indexes of favoritism (using trait lists) were calculated in relation to the European, the French, the Germans, the English, and the Danish; the European was more highly regarded than the French, and there was no difference when specific countries were considered alone or collectively. This points towards an emerging tendency towards a supranational identity.

Similar results have been obtained in Latin America. Salazar (1992) synthesized the results of several studies, and evidence from students in six Latin American countries showed that the attitude towards the Latin American was more positive than the one expressed towards their own specific country. This suggested a more positive social identity when construed at this level, rather than at the national level, where there is a tendency towards a negative self-image (see Fig. 12.1).

In another study (Salazar, 1993) an analysis was made of research reports investigating national identity in Latin American countries over a period of 15 years, using the value categories of Schwartz (1992). The most frequent underlying values evidenced in the studies were benevolence, autonomy, and achievement, with some evidence that achievement is tending to displace autonomy as an underlying value.

SYNTHESIZING THE DIVERSITY

When putting together this review of recent psychologically relevant work on the topic of national identity, we had to begin by pointing out the different usages of the terms in the current literature. We tried to respect the researchers' own definitions of the topic, and not to exclude them on account of their "not fitting" our definition. We tentatively grouped their work into three broad categories depending on whether "national identity" was for them defined by: (1)

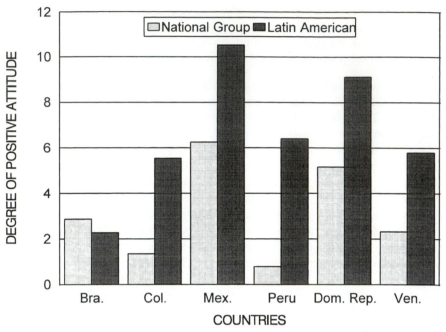

FIG. 12.1   Attitudes toward the Latin American and own National Group by students of six Latin American countries.

objective common characteristics; (2) subjective self images; or (3) intersubjective identification with the national category or some national symbols or institutions. We believe these are complementary ways to approach this complex phenomena.

Nevertheless, the objectivist approach, connected as it is with classical "essentialist" nationalism, is the one we consider most open to criticism. The Personality and Culture perspective simply does not give sufficient emphasis to the differences within complex modern societies, and it is not flexible enough to take into account rapid social change. The "essences" of nationhood change so fast they behave like a peculiar kind of substance indeed; more like predicates than essences.

Being simpler in its implementation, the self-stereotypes approach (which considers self-images or stereotypes) has resulted in a large amount of work, but has the danger of taking images for realities. Although we are aware that from a constructivist perspective this should not worry us too much, the frequent examples of behavioral observations that contradict commonly held stereotypes should make us very cautious regarding their validity. The main result of this line of work that we wanted to communicate is the recurrence of negative national self-images in Latin American research, not accompanied by negative feelings: This "decoupling" contradicts the affective–cognitive balance model of much of mainstream social psychology. This result from Latin America is also not in line with the ethnocentric element incorporated into Social Identity theory. As we have argued elsewhere (Salazar, 1996), social comparisons do not necessarily have to imply perceived superiority of the ingroup.

Finally, we looked at varied contributions that emphasized the identification element, which forms the core of the Social Identity approach. This approach is, to our understanding, the one with the most potential, since it is the most flexible and can more readily take change into account. At the same time, its subjective conceptualization avoids the "reality" questioning; that is, the objectiveness of the social constructs that individuals identify with (in this case, the reality of the nation). Yet it is as powerful as any other conceptualization in terms of possible behavioral predictions. We examined several methodological variants, not all orthodox, but all yielding interesting results. In keeping with the title of this paper, we went on to examine the question of change of national identity, first at the level of individuals moving into foreign cultures, and then at the level of societal changes. In the first case, evidence pointed to the need to consider a complex model that differentiates between acculturation and assimilation. Again, in the background, there is the question of social identity, and the persistence of the original ethnic identity in some societies given the different circumstances encountered in the recipient countries. When considering the changes occurring at the societal level, again the social identity perspective is useful in the face of evident changes in customs, values, etc. The important, consistent factor is the maintenance of the identification with the national category, with all its behavioral implications. Finally, we looked at the question of supranational identities. In terms of what has come to be called the globalization process, these supranationalisms could be seen as intermediate stages to the ultimate goal of a cosmopolitan identity, an identity of being "Citizen of the World". However, there is very little direct evidence that this is indeed what is occurring. Supranational identities, both in Europe and in Latin America, point to a broader definition of nation, not to its eradication. It seems to indicate a redefinition of the national "imagined communities", not to their elimination.

It is fashionable nowadays to predict that the process of globalization will mark the death-knell of nationalism. News of the demise of nationalism has been exaggerated on many previous occasions and none of the evidence presently available to us suggests that it will stop playing anything other than a critical role in framing the political and social development of the modern, or even postmodern world.

REFERENCES

Altrocchi, J., & Altrocchi, L. (1995). Polyfaceted psychological acculturation in Cook Islanders. *Journal of Cross-Cultural Psychology*, 26, 426–440.

Anderson, B. (1991). *Imagined communities*. London: Verso.

Azucena, S. E., Cortez, G., Guevara, M., Pocasangre, C., & Solano, N. (1989). La identidad nacional del salvadoreño. *Revista de Psicología de El Salvador*, 8, 135–146.

Avendaño, R., & Díaz-Guerrero, R. (1992). Estudio experimental de la abnegación. *Revista Mexicana de Psicología*, 9, 15–19.

Banchs, M. A. (1992). Representación social de la identidad venezolana desde la perspectiva de sus vínculos con indios, negros y blancos españoles. *Boletín de la Avepso*, 15, 3–23.

Barth, F. (1969). Introduction. In F. Barth (Ed.), *Ethnic groups and boundaries*. Boston: Little, Brown.

Béjar, R., & Cappello, H. M. (1986). La identidad y carácter nacionales en México: La frontera de Tamaulipas. *Revista de Psicología Social*, 1, 153–166.

Berry, J. (1993). Ethnic identities in plural societies. In M. E. Bernal & G. P. Knight (Eds.), *Ethnic identities*. Albany, NY: State University of New York.

Bustamante, J. A. (1959). *Raices psicológicas del cubano*. La Habana: Editorial Edibesa.

Cadenas, J. M. (1992). Estudio de la identificación con lel significado de palabras de origen indígena, negro y español en jovenes de padres venzolanos y padres españoles. *Boletín de la Avepso*, 15, 24–38.

Calderón, J. (1992). "Hispanic" and "Latino": The viabililty of categories for panethnic unity. *Latin American Perspectives*, 19, 37–44.

Cappello, H. M. (1995). Processes of change in the civic–political identity and character of two cities from the northeast of Mexico: Revisiting the theory. *Sociotam*, 5, 9–55.

Connor, W. (1994). Beyond reason: The nature of the ethnonational bond. In W. Connor, *Ethnonationalism: The quest for understanding*. (pp. 196–209). Princeton, NJ: Princeton University Press.

Cuéllar, I., Arnold, B., & González, G. (1995). Cognitive referents of acculturation: Assessment of cultural constructs in Mexican Americans. *Journal of Community Psychology*, 23, 339–356.

D'Adamo, O., & Garcia-Beaudoux, V. (1995). *El Argentino Feo*. Buenos Aires: Losada.

Díaz-Guerrero, R. (1955). Neurosis and the Mexican family structure. *American Journal of Psychiatry*, 112, 411–417.

Díaz-Guerrero, R. (1972). Una escala factorial de premisas histórico-socioculturales de la familia mexicana. *Revista Interamericana de Psicología*, 6, 235–244.

Díaz-Guerrero, R. (1981). *Psicología del Mexicano*. México: Trillas.

Díaz-Guerrero, R. (1991). El problema de al definición operante de la identidad mexicana. *Revista de Psicología Social y Personalidad*, 7, 23–61.

Díaz-Guerrero, R. (1993). Un factor cardinal en la personalidad de los mexicanos. *Revista de Psicología Social y Personalidad*, 9, 1–19.

Díaz-Guerrero, R. (1995). Una approximación científica a la etnopsicología. *Revista Latinoamericana de Psicología*, 27, 359–389.

Dominguez, D. (1993). Atributos asignados a negros, indios y blancos españoles en relación con la imagen del venezolano. In D. Matos (Ed.), *Diversidad cultural y construccion de identitades* (pp. 99–112). Caracas, Venezuela: Tropykos.

Feather, N. T. (1993). Devaluing achievement within a culture: Measuring the cultural cringe. *Australian Journal of Psychology*, 45, 182–188.

Feather, N. Y. (1994). Values, national identification and favouritism towards the ingroup. *British Journal of Social Psychology*, 33, 467–476.

Fells, J., & Niznik, J. (1992). Conclusion: What is Europe? *International Journal of Sociology*, 22, 201–206.

Fishman, J. (1972). *Language and nationalism*. Rowley, MA: Newbury House.

Forsthofer, R., & Martini, M. (1992). A comparative study of the consciousness of national affiliation in German and Italian students. *Ricerche di Psicología*, 16, 29–47.

Gallagher, A. M. (1989). Social identity and the Northern Ireland conflict. *Human Relations*, 42, 917–935.

Gallenmüller, J. & Wakenhut, R. (1992). The conceptualization and development of questionnaire for analyzing conciousness of national affiliation. *Richerche di Psicologia*, 16, 9–27.

Georgas, J., Berry, J. W., Shaw, A., Christakopoulou, S., & Mylonas, K. (1996). Acculturation in Greek family values. *Journal of Cross-Cultural Psychology*, 27, 329–338.

Guerra, G. (1992). Psychosocial aspects of national belonging. *Ricerche de Psicologia*, *16*, 121–138.

Herencia, H. C. (1991). Identidad social en la dominación cultural y de clases en el Perú: Consecuencias para la Identidad Nacional. In M. Montero (Ed.), *Acción y discurso: Problemas de Psicología Política en América Latina*. Caracas, Venezuela: Eduven.

Hofstede, G. (1980). *Culture's consequences*. Thousand Oaks, CA: Sage.

Hobsbawm, E. (1990). *Nations and nationalism since 1780*. Cambridge: Cambridge University Press.

Jenson, J. (1993). Naming nations: Making nationalist claims in Canadian public discourse. *Canadian Review of Sociology and Anthropology*, *30*, 337–358.

Keefe, S. E., & Padilla, A. M. (1987). *Chicano ethnicity*. Alburquerque, NM: University of New Mexico Press.

Kohr, H. U., & Wakenhut, R. (1992). Social morality and consciousness of national affiliation. *Richerche de Psicologia*, *16*, 49–63.

Lara-Tapia, L., & Gómez, P. (1991). Cambios socioculturales con respecto al machismo y la virginidad. *Revista Mexicana de Psicología*, *8*, 17–32.

Lara-Tapia, L., Gómez, P., & Fuentes, R. (1992). Cambios socioculturales en los conceptos de obediencia y respeto en la familia Mexicana: Un estudio en relación con el cambio social. *Revista Mexicana de Psicología*, *9*, 21–26.

Laroche, M., Kim, C., Hui, M. K., & Joy, A. (1996). An empirical study of multidimensional ethnic change: The case of French Canadians in Quebec. *Journal of Cross-Cultural Psychology*, *27*, 114–131.

Larsen, K. S., Killifer, C., Csepelli, G., Krumov, K., Andrejeva, L., Kashlakeva, N., Russinova, Z., & Pordany, L. (1992). National Identity: A new look at an old issue. *Journal of Social Behavior and Personality*, *7*, 309–322.

Lee, Y. T., Jussim, L. J., & McCauley, C. R. (1995). *Stereotype accuracy: Towards appreciating group differences*. Washington, DC: American Psychological Association.

Lew, S. C. (1988). Life in South Korea today. *The Social Studies*, *79*, 161–164.

Liebkind, K. (1996). Acculturation and stress: Vietnemese refugees in Finland. *Journal of Cross-Cultural Psychology*, *27*, 161–180.

Mach, Z. (1993). *Symbols, conflict and identity*. Albany, NY: State University of New York.

Marín G. (1993). Influence of acculturation on familism and self-identification among Hispanics. In M. Bernal & G. P. Knight (Eds.), *Ethnic Identity*. Albany, NY: State University of New York.

Marín, G., Marín, B. V., Sabogal, F., Otero-Sabogal, R., & Perez-Stable, E. J. (1986). *Intracultural differences in values among Hispanics: The role of acculturation* (Tech. Rep. No. 15). San Francisco, CA: University of San Francisco, Hispanic Smoking Cessation Project.

Marques, L. G., & Oliveira, J. M. P. (1988). National identities and levels of categorization: Self-stereotypes, attitudes and perception of other nationalities. In D. Canter, J. C. Jesuino, L. Soczka, & G. M. Stephenson (Eds.), *Environmental Social Psychology* (pp. 312–319). Dordrecht, Netherlands: Kluwer.

Martin-Baró, I. (1990). ¿Trabajador alegre o trabajador explotado? La identidad nacional del salvadoreño. *Revista Interamericana de Psicología*, *24*, 1–24.

Montero, M. (1984). *Ideología, alienación e identidad nacional*. Caracas, Venezuela: EBUC.

Ocampo, K. A., Bernal, M. E., & Knight, G. P. (1993). Gender, race and ethnicity: The sequencing of social constancies. In M. E. Bernal & G. P. Knight (Eds.), *Ethnic Identity*. Albany, NY: State University of New York.

Oboler, S. (1992). The politics of labeling: Latino cultural identities of self and others. *Latin American Perspectives*, *19*, 18–36.

Personnaz, B. (1993). Relations intergroupes et Europe. *Cahiers de sociologie economique et culturelle*, 177–183.

Quadrio, A., & Magrin, M. E. (1992). Development of a trans-national European consciousness in a sample of Italian children. *Ricerche di Psicologia*, *16*, 83–105.

Quintero, M. P. (1993). *Psicología del colonizado*. Mérida, Venezuela: Universidad de los Andes.

Rivera, A. N. (1982). La autoimagen del puertorriqueño. *Revista Latinoamericana de Psicología*, *14*, 81–92.

Rivera, A. N. (1991). Psicología y colonización. In M. Montero (Ed.), *Acción y discurso: Problemas de psicología política en América Latina*. Caracas, Venezuela: Eduven.

Ros, M., Cano, J. I., & Huici, C. (1987). Language and intergroup perception in Spain. *Journal of Language and Social Psychology*, *6*, 243–259.

Sabogal, F., Marín, G., Otero-Sabogal, R., Marín, B. V., & Perez-Stable, E. J. (1987). Hispanic familialism and acculturation: What changes and what doesn't? *Hispanic Journal of Behavioral Sciences*, *9*, 397–412.

Salazar, J. M. (1988). Cambio y permanencia en creencias y actitudes hacia lo nacional (1982–1986). *Boletín de la Avepso*, *11*, 3–13.

Salazar, J. M. (1989). Niveles de identificación y estructura cognocitiva en relación con el Latinoamericano. *Revista de Psicología Social*, *4*, 13–21.

Salazar, J. M. (1992). Dos acercamientos a la identidad latinoamericana. *Boletín de la Avepso*, *15*, 75–86.

Salazar, J. M. (1993). La especificidad latinoamericana desde una perspectiva psico-social. In H. Acosta (Ed.), *Una mirada humanistica* (pp. 57–80). Caracas, Venezuela: Universidad Central de Venezuela.

Salazar, J. M. (1994). Investigaciones psicológicas acerca de la identidad Latinoamericana. *Tribuna del Investigador*, *1*, 26–35.

Salazar, J. M. (1996). Identidad social e identidad nacional. In J. F. Morales, D. Ptez, J. C. Deschamps, & S. Worchel (Eds.), *Identidad social: Aproximaciones psicosociales a los grupos y a las relaciones entre grupos*. Valencia, Spain: Promolibro.

Santoro, E. (1975). *El diferencial semántico*. Caracas, Venezuela: UCV

Schwartz, S. (1992). Universals in the content and structure of values. *Advances in Experimental Social Psychology*, *25*, 1–65

Smith, A. C. (1991). *National identity*. Harmondsworth, UK: Penguin.

Sorin, M. (1991). Identidad nacional, identidad Latinoamericana y desarrollo moral de la personalidad en el cubano de hoy. In M. Montero (Ed.), *Acción y Discurso: Problemas de Psicología Política en América Latina*. Caracas, Venezuela: Eduven.

Soysal, Y. N. (1994). *Limits of citizenship: Migrants and postnational membership in Europe*. Chicago, ILL: The University of Chicago.

Tajfel, H. (1978). *Differentiation between social groups: Studies in the social psychology of intergroup relations*. London: Academic Press.

Tajfel, H. (1981). *Human groups and social categories*. Cambridge: Cambridge University Press.

Taylor, D. M. (1991). The social psychology of racial and cultural diversity: Issues of assimilation and multiculturalism. In A. G. Reynolds (Ed.), *Bilingualism, multiculturalism, and second language learning: The McGill conference in honour of Wallace E. Lambert* (pp. 1–9). Hillsdale, NJ: Erlbaum.

Triandis, H. (1988). Collectivism and individualism: A reconceptualization of basic concepts in cross-cultural psychology. In G. K. Verma & C. Bagley (Eds.), *Personality, attitudes and cognitions* (pp. 60–95). London: Macmillan.

Tsai, H. Y. (1995). Sojourner adjustment: The case of foreigners in Japan. *Journal of Cross-Cultural Psychology*, *26*, 523–536.

Vasconcelos, J. (1958). La raza cósmica. In *Obras completas*, *Tomo II* (pp. 918–923). México: Libreros Mexicanos Unidos.

Ward, C., & Kennedy, A. (1993). Where is the "culture" in cross-cultural transition? Comparative studies of sojourner adjustment. *Journal of Cross-Cultural Psychology*, *24*, 221–249.

Wong-Rieger, D., & Quintana, D. (1987). Comparative acculturation of Southern Asian and Spanish immigrants and sojourners. *Journal of Cross-Cultural Psychology*, *18*, 345–362.

Wright, W. P. (1990). *Café con leche: Race, class and national image in Venezuela*. Austin: University of Texas Press.

CHAPTER THIRTEEN

China's reform and challenges for psychology

Qicheng Jing
Institute of Psychology, Chinese Academy of Sciences, Beijing, China

Houcan Zhang
Department of Psychology, Beijing Normal University, China

The introduction of China's economic reform and its opening up to the outside world in recent years has resulted in dramatic and rapid economic growth. Through this, conflict between a new global culture and China's traditional culture and values has been created, giving rise to a host of social and psychological problems. The new challenges for psychology in the fields of population, education, mental health, and social stability are reviewed in the context of China's social development. The issues presented in this paper pose far more questions than solutions. The task which lies before social scientists is to study the psychology of a people comprising one fifth of the world's population, and undergoing a process of rapid social change.

L'introduction de la réforme économique de la Chine et son ouverture au monde extérieur durant les dernières années a eu pour conséquence une croissance économique à la fois dramatique et rapide. De ce fait, un conflit a été créé entre la nouvelle culture globale et la culture et les valeurs traditionnelles de la Chine. Ceci a donné lieu à une foule de problèmes sociaux et psychologiques. Les nouveaux défis pour la psychologie dans les domaines de la population, de l'éducation, de la santé mentale et de la stabilité sociale sont examinés dans le contexte du développement social de la Chine. Les points soulevés dans cet article suscitent beaucoup plus de questions qu'ils offrent de solutions. La tâche qui se présente aux spécialistes des sciences sociales est d'étudier la psychologie d'un peuple qui représente un cinquième de la population mondiale et qui subit un processus de changement social rapide.

Over the past two decades, China has adopted a policy of reform, which includes opening further to the outside world, promoting development, and maintaining stability. In recent years, China was rated as one of the countries with the highest rate of economic growth in the world. According to initial statistics, the gross domestic product (GDP) reached $815.66 billion in 1996, an increase of 9.7% over the previous year (Li, 1997). Moreover, China's economic growth had shown an average increase of over 10% since 1992 (State Statistical Bureau, 1996). State foreign exchange reserves exceeded $105 billion by the end of 1996 (Chen, 1997). However, there are pressing problems facing the nation. Prices are increasing at an annual average rate of around 10%, while the natural increase in the population rate is still 10.55 per thousand (State Statistical Bureau, 1996). There is a floating migrant population of 60 million who have no permanent jobs, moving into towns; and the trend is on the increase. In 1995, there were 65 million people still living in poverty-stricken areas, whose living standard was below the poverty line of a per capita income of less than 550 Yuan (US $68) per year ("Poverty Elimination", 1996).

GLOBAL CULTURE AND INDIGENOUS CULTURE

Traditional Chinese culture

China maintains its distinctive cultural heritage as a fairly non-religious and state-oriented society. China has had a predominantly secular culture for 2500 years. Bureaucratic authority developed within the Confucian system long before it reached the West. The cultural system stresses strong familial values and harmony in worldly and personal relations. From 1000 years ago until 200 to 300 years ago, China was one of the most prosperous and culturally advanced countries in the world. China's contributions included the Chinese classics of Confucius, the Yong Le Encyclopedia, the earliest astronomical instruments, and the four great inventions of gun powder, the compass, printing, and paper-making. China was also well-known for its extensive waterworks, the Great Wall, and the Silk Road. When Marco Polo returned to Venice in the 13th century, he described China as a paradise on earth, and in later centuries, travelers and missionaries introduced Chinese culture to the West. In 17th- and 18th-century Europe, elegant Chinese artwork, known as Chinoiserie, was extremely fashionable in elite society.

In the late Qing dynasty (1644–1911), Westerners came again to China, this time armed with gunboats and rifles. They initiated the Opium War, demanded concessions, and obtained extra-territorial rights, causing China to become a half-feudal and half-colonial state. Chinese intellectuals see modernization as the way to a strong China and, thus, believe it is important to learn from the West. At this point, Chinese reformers were confronted with two dilemmas. The first was the realization that to modernize, they must take Western nations as models and learn their science, technology, and modern management skills. Meanwhile, they also recognized that it was these Western teachers who came with rifles, traded opium, demanded concessions, and tried to subdue China's development. The second dilemma involved the contradiction between egalitarianism and inequality. For most of this century, China persistently attempted to build an egalitarian society. For China to modernize in the Western way, it had to develop capitalism; although this promoted social progress, it also brought about exploitation and polarization of the rich and poor. For the past 100 years, these two dilemmas have been haunting Chinese intellectuals. Thus, China's state policy has swayed between the two extremes of "opening doors" and "Westernizing" on the one hand, and "closed doors", "anti-foreign" on the other.

A new turn in modern Chinese history was the founding of the People's Republic of China in 1949. The Marxist ideological basis of this socialist society during the past five decades established a cultural tradition specific to China, greatly accentuating China's traditional emphasis on the state and the implementation of an egalitarian system. The general characteristics of this culture are the respect for authority, even distribution of wealth, and stress on interpersonal relations. To understand China, it is important to know these characteristics.

Modernization

There are two main theoretical schools of modernization: (1) The Marxist school, which claims that economic development determines the political and cultural characteristics of a society; and (2) the Weberian school, which claims that culture shapes economic and political life. Both schools agree on the point that socio-economic change follows coherent and relatively predictable patterns (Inglehart, 1995). As most social theorists have pointed out, modernization involves the familiar phenomena of industrialization, urbanization, bureaucratization, mass mobilization, occupational specialization, increased literacy, and a new configuration of beliefs and values closely linked with high rates of economic growth.

About two decades ago, China opened itself to the outside world and implemented reform. While keeping its cultural heritage of high respect for authority and a strong bureaucratic tradition, China adopted a market economy and experienced dramatic economic development. How is Chinese culture doing in the context of this fledgling market economy? Successful industrialization requires an impersonal, bureaucratic, competitive, achievement-oriented form of social relations that tends to be dehumanizing, to run contrary to traditional interpersonal relations, and to increase the gap between rich and poor. In China, this trade-off is seen as worthwhile. Starvation and scarcity of the past have been alleviated by individual achievement and economic growth, since production has been increasing much faster than the rate of population growth. The modernization process brought substantial gains in reducing the mortality rate and increasing life expectancy, making it possible to reduce the two leading causes of death in preindustrial societies: malnutrition and disease. With the emergence of an advanced industrial society, a small sector of Chinese entrepreneurs formed the "newly rich" group who strives for extravagance and high consumption.

With an increasing share of the public having higher education, and with work being professionalized, the demand for a feeling of subjective well-being and better quality of life emerged.

The past 20 years have also witnessed the rise of what is called a new global culture, marked by Karoake singing, disco dancing, McDonald's, and Coca Cola. This culture, created for the most part by US and Japanese multinationals, is currently gaining popularity at a rapid rate in newly industrialized countries, and tends to homogenize the behavior of young people. Western values, beliefs, and habits are imposed through the media; many young people have now become fascinated with ways of acquiring wealth. All these conflict and compete with traditional value systems.

Western psychology has adopted and propagated the position of methodological individualism, which assumes that all groups or holistic concepts can be understood in terms of individual behavior (Kim, 1995). This increased emphasis on individualism generates negative side effects which can be a real threat to morality. Modern individualized societies lack shared moral principles, because the individual's judgment of what is right and wrong ranks above traditional collective norms (Halman, 1995). Also, corruption is becoming a widespread phenomenon. It is no longer exclusively a national problem intrinsic to the political system, but instead, its international dimension is becoming increasingly apparent (Meny, 1996). In contemporary China, there are widespread complaints of a decline in moral values in the younger generation, and corruption is becoming a major problem, causing dissatisfaction among the population. In a recent survey (Minjian, 1996), people were asked which problems most affected social stability in China. The problem considered most pressing was corruption, and specifically, the abuse of powers by State employees for personal benefits. Rated second was the gap between the rich and the poor. The "newly rich" lives in extravagance, whereas in some remote parts of the country people are still very poor, with 6% of the total population still living below the poverty line. China is now at a crossroads: It can either become an individualistic, morally declined society, or it can re-establish a firm moral order according to traditional values.

In October 1996, the Central Committee of the Communist Party of China passed a resolution regarding "Important questions of promoting socialist ethical and cultural progress" (CPC, 1996). It proclaimed that promoting socialist ethical and cultural progress is a strategically important task. It was noted that most of the serious errors in the previous 10 years had been made in education, and primarily in the weakening of ideological and political education. These errors were manifest mainly in the spheres of moral conduct. The practice of worshipping money, seeking pleasure and individualism had grown, and feudal superstitions and social vices such as pornography, gambling, and drug abuse had resurfaced. The Communist Party made efforts to raise the promotion of ethical and cultural progress to a new level, and prevent decadent ideas and social evils from spreading, while establishing a socialist market economic structure. It was concluded that extensive education in patriotism, collectivism, and socialism should be carried out, as well as education in social moral standards, professional ethics, and family virtues, particularly for the younger generation. Further, advocating a civilized and healthy lifestyle was deemed necessary to form a relationship among people characterized by unity and mutual help, equality and affection, and common progress. China has come to realize that materialism alone does not guarantee a collective high quality of life, but that the Chinese must enrich themselves spiritually before they can succeed in building modernization. Despite the fact that China boasts the world's most dynamic economic growth, it is still a developing country with a huge population, making it among the lowest in the world in terms of overall development.

New trends

Three salient features of China's modernization can be identified. First, China's modernization brings with it most of the usual features characteristic of other modernized societies: industrialization, urbanization, mass mobilization, increased literacy, occupational specialization, increasing crime, and corruption. However, what is particularly striking about China's modernization is the aggressive influence of a new individualistic value system, which results in the moral decline of the general public, and particularly of the younger generation. Secondly, diminishing effectiveness of centralization and authority has characterized China's modernization. Large, state-owned enterprises are facing great difficulties, causing workers to turn towards running small individual businesses, which are far more flexible in responding to a market economy, or to being hired in the labor market. There is a shift in governmental institutions towards a focus on individual concerns. This reflects a systematic decline in mass support for established political effectiveness, and in the acceptance of massive, centralized, bureaucratic authority, indicating a tendency towards democratization. Finally, what has remained unchanged is the traditional Chinese family value system and the ways of interpersonal relationship. With the weakening dependency on the governmental system for livelihood and security, Chinese familial values have remained intact. Family members make up a web of kin relations that holds strong, especially in times of need, and people continue to interact with one another by way of family relationships and personal friendship.

In his speech delivered at the 21st Century Forum in Beijing, Mr Lee Kuan Yew (1996), Senior Minister of Singapore, stated that the 21st century will see Asia recover its place in the world. At present rates of growth extrapolated for 25 years, East Asia's GDP will be 40% of the world's total GDP, as compared to North America's 18% and the European Union's 14%, by the year 2020. It is only a question of time before the Chinese people re-organize, re-educate, and train themselves to take full advantage of modern science and technology. China will quicken the pace of its development by using inputs from industrialized countries to become a fully industrialized nation. This change in economic weight will likely be accompanied by a parallel change in cultural influences. China can acquire "hard power" (economic and military strength) in 30 years, but it will take much longer to acquire "soft power" (cultural influence). Soft power, or the influence of culture, becomes as important as hard power in international affairs.

For 300 years, the Europeans, and later the Americans, dominated the world. They made scientific discoveries, enjoyed the highest standard of living, and their lifestyle, fast foods, and entertainment became dominant throughout the world. The English language that the British spread throughout their empire became the international language. By learning this language, people have access to an enormous range of scientific, technological, and economic information. The Japanese were the first non-white people to catch up with the Americans and Europeans. They dominate world markets in cameras, watches, consumer electronics, and even in Sushi restaurants and Karaoke singing. Soft power is achieved when other nations admire and want to absorb another culture that is seen as superior. Some believe that Eastern culture will become popular in the world. Indeed, in recent years, there has been a trend in the world to learn the Chinese language, either for trade or for interest in its culture. The Confucian ideology, as well as China's socialist market economy, are attracting more attention around the world. China has become popular for tourism, and Chinese cuisine has already won the greatest share of world restaurants. It should be noted that Chinese culture may, by recreating itself and adopting useful elements of other highly developed cultures, be one of the advanced cultures of the world in the 21st century.

POPULATION AND ONLY CHILDREN

The one-child family policy

The population of China stood at 400 million in 1947. Several decades of unrestrained birth increase, and improvements in health care and in agricultural and industrial technology resulted in an explosive population growth. In 30 years, the population doubled, reaching close to one billion in 1980, making it the most populated nation in the world. In response, the Chinese government implemented a policy limiting the number of children per family. In 1971, a State Family Planning Commission was established and China instituted its first national family planning program. Although family planning has been proclaimed a fundamental state policy, controlling population growth was difficult. Hence in 1981, the government intensified the family planning program and launched the single-child family planning program: each couple should give birth to only one child. This program was successfully carried out in the cities. However, in the rural areas where 74% of the Chinese people reside, the implementation of this program has encountered many difficulties. In spite of this, the policy has dramatically decreased the birth rate: now many rural families have two children instead of many more (Jing, 1994). In the past two decades, China's population growth rate plummeted from 26 per thousand in 1970 to 10.5 per thousand in 1994. In 1995, China's population exceeded 1.2 billion and is still increasing by 13 million people a year (State Statistical Bureau, 1996). It has been predicted that the national population will be 1.4 billion by 2010. Although China has been successful in supporting 22% of the world's population with a mere 7% of the arable land on Earth, it is now facing the challenge of achieving a higher standard of living under the immense pressure of a growing population and dwindling natural resources.

The new family policy altered Chinese family structure, as noted by an increased number of only children in China. Chinese feudal society lasted for over 2000 years, and the traditional Chinese patrilineal family structure present in this society emphasized primogeniture, or the rights of inheritance of the eldest son. When a daughter married, she married into her husband's family and was no longer considered a member of her original family. Following tradition, having many children ensured having sons to perpetuate the family. For rural families, a son was particularly important because he became another worker for the land who earned a living and supported the extended family. A family with several sons provided greater security, particularly for its elderly members. Evidently, the new family-planning policy of restraining family size and reproductive behavior resulted in a departure from cultural tradition and was confronted by social and psychological hurdles. Presently, over 95% of preschool children in urban areas are only children. Livi-Bacci (1994) summarizes the reasons for the success of this mandate. First, he says that Chinese social transformation proceeded more quickly and efficiently in the area of public health care which resulted in a rapid decline in mortality. A second factor he describes is the Chinese political system, where government authority extends through all levels of the administrative hierarchy down to the grass roots, allowing for the quick execution of demographic policy directives. Finally, he notes that an efficient distribution and assistance network has been established, employing a variety of birth control methods.

Another societal phenomenon related to population growth and to the weakening of authoritative government control is the increase of surplus laborers in rural districts. There are far more farm hands than necessary for doing farm work in the fields. These laborers have become a "transient population," leaving their rural homes to find work in cities. Notwithstanding reduced population growth, 72 million youth will be seeking to join the labor force by the end of this century. These young people, plus the country's growing transient population— some 80 million peasants—have saturated the job market and exerted pressure on the nation's already overburdened urban infrastructure. In 1995, there was a 9.5% increase in the transient population. It is estimated that by the end of this century, this population will reach 100 million. This transient population has become one of the most difficult groups with which to carry out family planning. In some areas, about two-thirds of the reported unplanned births occur in transient families.

The only child: Cognitive and social aspects

Recent evidence has suggested an advantage for only children in certain cognitive, emotional, and physical domains. A host of evidence pointed out that only children appear to be superior in intellectual matters, and that boys obtained higher scores on some cognitive tasks (Jiao, Ji, & Jing, 1996; Jing, Jiao, & Ji, 1993). Children from high achievement expectancy parents tend to have better developed cognitive skills (Ji, Jiao, & Jing, 1993). The Chinese government advocates the single-child family policy to reduce the quantity of Chinese population and to upgrade the quality of Chinese population. Population quality includes physical, cognitive, and cultural aspects of the people. When the birth-rate is low, meaning that there are fewer people, more can be invested in the promotion of health, education and culture to improve the general quality of life of the people.

Although the population control policy has had many desired effects, there have also been some unexpected consequences. Because the implementation of the policy was successful in the cities, urban Chinese have relatively higher education and a higher standard of living. By contrast it has not been successful in rural areas, thus creating fear among some Chinese demographers of a so-called "counterculling effect" of the population control policy—that the disadvantaged rural parents, who comprise about 74% of the total population, will produce a greater number of offspring who will be relatively more disadvantaged than their more educated urban counterparts (Jing, 1994). In the long run, this would result in the deterioration of the general population quality, and in a population composed of a minority of urban intellectual elite and a majority of intellectually disadvantaged rural people.

The policy of restricting family size has not only great immediate effects on the child, but also on parental childrearing practices, perceptions, and ultimately on the hopes and aspirations they have for their children. In traditional China, social competence is judged by adherence to agreed-upon norms and by how well one gets along with others. Parents exert great control over the child's behavior, and reinforcement is given to obedience, good behavior, and compliance with group authority. Chinese children are expected to serve societal goals, and there is little tolerance for individuality. Now, because of the new family policy, the only child becomes so precious that parental overprotectiveness or overindulgence is more common, and these altered childrearing practices lead to negative behavior, such as selfishness, in the child. For example, Jiao, Ji and Jing (1986) have found, through peer ratings, that certain personality problems, such as egocentrism and willfulness, are common to only children. In other studies (e.g. Fan et al., 1994; Wan et al., 1994), only children were found to be less independent.

Contemporary parents seem not to realize the importance of social development, nor the importance of providing the child with role models of discipline and integrity. Modern Chinese families are comprised of parents who both work, and their preschool children are usually cared for by grandparents who devote even more attention to the children. Thus the single-child government mandate is so central to family life that it alters the nature of the child, the parents, their interaction, and the overall family structure and social relations in the community.

Aged society

The population explosion in the early 1950s and late 1960s, coupled with a decrease in the birth-rate in succeeding years due to the implementation of the single-child family planning program, means that the number of aged people will increase in the coming years. It is predicted that the number of people over 60 will increase from the present 120 million to 280 million by the year 2025 (i.e. from 10% to 19% of the total population), and by 2040 China's elderly population is expected to peak at 380 million, or about 25% of the total population (Niu, Guan & Jia, 1992). Accordingly, there will be a rapid change in the proportions of children to adults and adults to elders in the coming years.

A number of consequences may result from this change in age structure in China. For example, in the middle of the next century, there will be a workforce consisting of fewer than half of the total population supporting the majority population. Because the proportion of the three sectors of people (children/ adults/aged) will change with time, attitudes and values of people in different age groups towards people in other age groups will also change. When there is a great number of elderly people in the Chinese society, they will be less valued and negligence may occur. Even today, signs of this trend already exist. For example, there is an emphasis on young people in the job market, giving them priority for promotion, while elderly people are encouraged into early retirement. In September 1996, however, China passed a law to protect the rights and interests of the aged population. The new law was enacted in order to foster a social environment in which elderly people are respected and treated with consideration and dignity, and to guarantee good living conditions for them. In urban China, most senior residents rely on government pensions, while in rural areas, they depend on their families. The law stipulates that most aged people remain with their families and that their children are responsible for supporting them. This requires a harmonious intergenerational relationship, and also has added to the burden on the workforce.

Stateways vs. folkways

City dwellers support a tough family planning policy, and believe that the drop in fertility is helping to produce a historic economic boom, and a rise in education and health standards. Thus, these people feel that, by restricting couples to one child, the government is leading China out of poverty and into a modern industrialized state. It is apparent that in urban areas, traditional beliefs and enduring patterns of behavior are certainly changing. However, 75% of China's population reside in rural areas. For several of the reasons acknowledged earlier, rural families rely more on their offspring and, thus, often have two and sometimes even three children with little regard for governmental interference.

China has a history of strict hierarchical social system with a strong emphasis on the family as the hierarchical model. As family composition changes, there will be more emphasis on the child, a more interactive parent–child relationship; and, as the number of aged people increases, there will be a decline in authority of aged members in the family. These changes in the social structure of the family may be reflected in a weakening of the traditional hierarchical social system which may lead to changes in the social structure of the society, such as a change from centralized to more democratic forms, and a change in social values from collectivism to more individualism (Rosenberg & Jing, 1996).

EDUCATION

Education and the imperial examination system

China has had a tradition for learning since ancient times. For example, Confucius stressed the importance of learning. Connected with this tradition was the complex governmental hierarchy and highly sophisticated administration system present in imperial China. During these times, the quality of leadership was very important, since administrators were given much greater power than those in the West. In the year 606 AD, the emperor decreed that officials were to be selected by a civil service examination. This new arrangement was much more egalitarian since any man (*sic*) could be promoted to high officialdom (e.g. minister or provincial governor) if he passed the various levels of examinations. Thus, the Chinese civil service examination represented the first merit-based selection of administrators in the hierarchical government system. For the underclass in particular, this represented an opportunity to become part of the ruling class. To take the civil service examination, one had to know the Chinese classics and be able to write essays in a required formal way. To achieve this goal, children began learning the required skills at a very young age. They first underwent instruction for careful, intensive reading, and continued with this until the text could be memorized. Then, at a later date, the focus of instruction was on comprehension, thus increasing the depth of learning.

One can still see traces of the imperial examination system in modern China, particularly in the university system. In each city there are a number of better supported prestigious "key" secondary schools, which have experienced teachers and good facilities, and only a small number of qualified students gain entrance into these schools. Also, China has a certain number of better supported state-controled prestigious "key" universities, and a great number of other universities at the provincial level. All high school graduates in China are required to take the Unified National College Entrance Examination. The key universities choose the students with the best scores, and the other students are admitted to provincial universities. Just as success in the civil service examinations in the past assured the candidate a lifelong high post, so enrolling into a prestigious "key" university today can assure lifelong success. Most students from these universities go on to pursue graduate studies, good government positions, and higher status jobs.

Educational reform

The importance of education in the process of China's modernization has been duly recognized by the Chinese government. In 1993, the government announced the "National Program for Education Reform and Development," which stressed the priority of developing education. In September 1995, the "Education Law of the People's Republic of China" was passed, in which education was considered to be the basis for socialist construction. In recent years, there has been a decrease in the number of primary and secondary schools, owing to the decreased birth-rate caused by China's family planning policy. Currently there is a new emphasis on reforming basic education—i.e. education in primary and middle schools. The central government's goal is to create a nine-year compulsory education program, and eliminate illiteracy among young and middle-aged people by the end of this century. There is also a plan to change the curriculum structure and teaching methods. For example, the number of years currently required to complete the curriculum in primary, junior, and senior middle schools are six, three, and three, respectively. The proposed change is five years in primary school, four in junior school, and three at the middle-school level. This change will cut down the years in primary school, and will have students learn more practical skills at the end of the ninth grade. Further, the change in curriculum structure should reduce the number of basic courses, giving the students the opportunity to take practical courses, such as computer knowledge and healthcare courses.

China's economic development requires large numbers of skilled laborers. This imposes increasingly greater demands on the country's vocational education, which has remained weak in the educational system. In 1996, the "Vocational Education Law" was promulgated. To stress the significance of vocational education, the government is introducing a professional certificate system, which will make a professional certificate as important as a college diploma. At present, most vocational schools are made up of students from senior high schools, and about half of the junior middle-school graduates are diverted to vocational schools. By the year 2000, vocational schools are expected to make up 60 to 70% of the total number of secondary schools in the rural areas, but remain as 50% of the total number of secondary schools in the cities. In 1995, mid-level vocational schools numbered 17,000, with 9.4 million students (Zhang, 1996).

To promote science and technology, there has been a great increase in the number of institutes of higher education, which has resulted in a dramatic increase in the enrollment of graduate students. From 1980 to 1995, the number of institutes of higher learning increased from 675 to 1054, and the number of enrolled students increased from 1,144,000 to 2,906,000. However, there are still very few relative to the population size. The enrollment of graduate students increased from 21,604 in 1980 to 145,443 in 1995, a sevenfold increase (State Statistical Bureau, 1996).

Another striking phenomenon of this reform period is the brain drain of young scientists. Now there are about 280,000 students studying in Western countries (Zhang, 1997), but the number of students returning from study abroad is relatively small. The low wage system, lack of financial support for research, and poor facilities in the home country have little attraction for their return. Recently, the government has been trying to solve this problem by providing more generous support to foreign trained students, including higher salary, creating special research grants and providing housing for students who earned advanced degrees abroad. Unfortunately, this causes inequality between the majority of the locally trained students and their foreign trained counterparts, and could further motivate more Chinese students to go abroad. It remains to be seen if this new system will work smoothly. The brain drain problem demonstrates the intellectual resource advantage which highly developed industrial countries have over developing nations, and the effect the brain drain has on the development of science and technology in China.

With the establishment of a market economy, the problems associated with merely stressing the intellectual aspects of education are becoming evident. In the traditional education system, which made college attendance its ultimate goal, all teaching activities were focused on how to prepare students for the college entrance examination. The negligence of the social aspects of education has resulted in negative trends in the social and moral development of the students. Now, there is a shift from "education for examination" to "education for human quality," giving equal emphasis to intellectual, moral, physical, aesthetic, and labor education. Labor education is considered important in China, because it allows students to experience the hardship of manual labor in farms and factories, to sympathize with the mass labor force, and to cultivate the spirit of mutual cooperation in team work. To endure hardship and to cooperate with others are major aspects of socialist ethics. Thus, the goal of today's education is to develop the holistic personality of children, to train good citizenship, to cultivate the comprehensive development of a new generation, and finally, to promote the overall quality of the people.

Educational psychology

The highly selective examination system has led Chinese schools to stress the significance of intellectual learning, and parents at home to sacrifice much time and effort for the benefit of their children's learning. The emphasis on learning in Chinese society has promoted the rapid development of educational psychology. A statistical study of the contents of five psychology periodicals published in China over the past 10 years showed that about one third of the articles were on child development and educational psychology (Duan et al., 1995). In the past, psychological research has been centered on the cognitive aspects of learning, such as promoting learning efficiency and investigating the developmental stages of children's learning. Some cross-cultural studies have focused on comparisons of the cognitive development in Chinese children and Western children, and it is generally found that Chinese children surpass Western children in mathematics and in reading (Stevenson et al., 1985).

In order to achieve better performance in schools and to increase children's motivation, self-learning is encouraged as a supplement to teaching in the classroom. For example, one influential teaching method was initiated by Lu Zhongheng's experiments in mathematics self-learning (Lu, 1987). Based on some of the principles of programmed instruction and the teaching experience of outstanding teachers, Lu formulated several psychological principles of guided self-learning, of which "appropriate pacing" and "immediate knowledge of results" are examples. In this teaching method, instruction is geared towards the development of pupils' knowledge and aptitude, to ensure that pupils are interested and motivated. Today, more than 5000 classes in 28 provinces and cities throughout the country are using Lu's learning method. Liu Jinghe's experiments in mathematics teaching are another example (Liu et al., 1982). After her investigation into the developmental process of mathematics learning in primary schools, she has proposed revising the way in which mathematical knowledge is currently structured. By using the unit "1" as the basis and relating other numbers to "1", and by making "part–whole" relationship the main thread in mathematical thinking, she has successfully produced teaching materials for nationwide experimental use.

Currently, with the new emphasis on the cultivation of the whole personality in Chinese education, the emphasis in educational psychology has also shifted from merely highlighting knowledge acquisition, to investigating both knowledge acquisition and character cultivation. The fostering of non-intellectual factors, particularly the development of children's moral character and the whole personality, is now emphasized.

Moral education

In ancient China, morality was considered to be at the heart of knowledge, and hence, moral education was emphasized. Morality in China is related to both knowledge and ethical judgment. This model emphasizes the acquisition of knowledge and ethical rules through self-cultivation—that is, through awareness and self-analysis. Some of the most outstanding research in moral psychology concerns the levels of development of moral judgment in children. In keeping with the Chinese social context, Li Boshu (1992) explored the development of some specific moral conceptualizations held by Chinese children, such as their conceptualization of public, private, collectivism, friendship, patriotism, love of labor, etc. In terms of taking responsibility for one's behavior and the development of the concepts of fairness and punishment, Chinese children were generally found to mature one to three years earlier than Piaget had found for Western children. Research on intervention in moral development has confirmed that praise and reasoning are more effective than providing reward in encouraging children to make correct moral judgments. Zhang Zhiguang (1993) studied the ways in which external conditions exert influence on the internal psychological structures used in forming and transforming moral character. The general findings in moral education indicate that children's moral knowledge is primarily based on their perception, knowledge, and understanding of moral models and norms in society.

In 1984, some primary schools in Shanghai, Beijing and other cities initiated a personality-based teaching method which stresses the emotional side of learning. With this method, called "joy education," emphasis is placed on the emotional side of learning, and on the need for the teacher to create a harmonious, relaxed educational environment so that pupils feel they are able to participate actively and positively in the educational process. Four basic needs are identified for children's physical and psychological development: love, beauty, interest, and creativity. These have become the four key elements of joy education. At present, experiments in joy education have been extended to a number of primary schools throughout the country (Duan et al., 1995).

The current trend in education in China is an emphasis on the harmonious development of the whole personality. This trend is in response to the complaints of the general public regarding the moral decline of young Chinese people since the opening up of the country to the outside world. To cultivate the whole personality, Chinese educational psychologists must acknowledge the need to consider the child as a human being in a social environment. It is important to provide an ideal educational environment for the development of a child's whole personality; that is, to acquire all aspects of knowledge and at the same time to cultivate good social behavior to enable them to become responsible citizens.

MENTAL HEALTH

Psychological testing and counseling

Psychological testing and counseling were forbidden areas since the People's Republic of China was founded in 1949. Only in the late 1970s, after the Cultural Revolution, were these two practices rehabilitated. Mental counseling clinics were first established in 1985, the same year that the Chinese Mental Health Association was founded. The first clinic was the Psychometrics and Counseling

Service Center, which was established at Beijing Normal University. Today, most hospitals, universities, and high schools in big cities have mental health clinics. Also, offering mental health courses to students at universities and high schools is currently under consideration as a part of China's educational reform program.

In psychological clinics where psychologists and medical doctors work towards the prevention and cure of behavioral disorders, psychological tests are widely applied in diagnosis. Some Chinese clinical psychologists who specialize in testing have introduced and revised some Western tests, and have also provided training courses to enable medical workers to use these tests. The psychological tests most frequently used in China are WISC-CR, EPQ, WAIS-RC, MMPI and WPPSI. All these tests have been revised so that they adhere to Chinese norms. Hospitals use these tests most frequently, followed by universities and colleges. Child care institutions make use of tests for children, such as the RAVEN and DDST tests (Gong & Li, 1996).

According to a survey (Dai et al., 1993) of 183 medical test-using institutions, psychological tests are used in the medical field mainly for the following three purposes: clinical diagnosis; counseling and psychotherapy; and psychological research. In 1990, over 80 types of test were used, the most common being intelligence tests and non-projective tests. Some rating scales for personality assessment were also commonly used, but the use of projective tests was rare, and psychoanalysis in general was not a very popular technique in China.

Counseling for college and high school students is becoming common in China. Some of the most common complaints of students are compulsive behavior, interpersonal relationship problems, reactance, anxiety, inferiority, and pessimism. The main causes of mental health problems in young Chinese people come from the pressure for learning in schools, tensions in student–teacher relationships, and child abuse in the family. Some believe that many psychological problems of young people have their roots in overprotection and indulgence of the only child by parents and grandparents at home. The increase in scenes of sex, terror, violence, and crime on TV and other media also have affected children's behavior, and at present, there is no rule imposing restrictions on TV programs for children.

Over the last decade, adolescent crime-rate has increased, and mental and personality ailments have been the causes of adolescent crimes. Thus, psychological clinics offering counseling for the prevention and cure of behavioral disorders are becoming important. Counseling by correspondence and through telephone hotlines is also becoming popular in China. The *Chinese Journal of Mental Health* correspondence hotline is well known. Other mental health institutions and women's federations have established hotlines such as the "Hope Hotline," "Juvenile Hotline," and "Woman Hotline." There is even a TV counseling program available. Many psychologists participate in these counseling programs. Research in mental health is increasing in universities and in mental health institutions, and some special treatments (e.g. group therapy and music therapy) are being tried out. However, more work needs to be put into building up the theoretical framework of Chinese mental health. At present, there is a trend to overemphasize the medical aspect in mental health treatment and to neglect psychological treatment. This can be solved only by improving psychological theory and skill in China.

Psychotherapy and Chinese Qigong

Western psychotherapy methods are used in China. The types of psychotherapy most frequently used are behavioral therapy, cognitive therapy, and supportive therapy. Occasionally psychoanalysis and Morita therapy are also used. Some therapies are especially effective for certain disorders, such as behavioral therapy for treating compulsion, cognitive therapy for treating depression, and hypnosis for treating hysteria. Other techniques such as progressive desensitization, music therapy, movement therapy (e.g. gymnastics and dancing), and family therapy are also being experimented with, and Chinese psychiatrists have integrated some of these techniques into Chinese conventional methods (Gong & Li, 1996).

Chinese traditional medicine also has its own principles as a special branch of medical science, different from Western medicine. *Qigong* is a Chinese relaxation technique often used as a method of psychotherapy in China. Relaxation techniques appeared as behavioral therapeutic methods in both the East and the West several thousand years ago, and have been used to cure diseases and to promote health ever since. Relaxation techniques in the East are represented by Chinese Qigong, Taijiquan, and Indian Yoga. Qigong (pronounced Chee Gong) is a Chinese term applied to all forms of exercise which develop an individual's Qi. According to Oriental medicine, *Qi* is everything from the air we breathe to the vital energy which animates our bodies. *Gong* means to work with or to do training exercises. Even though Qigong essentially means "breath training," it covers a very broad scope of exercises and practices from ancient Taoist mysticism to painkilling practices by unconventional methods in the operating rooms of modern hospitals. Qigong has proved effective in the treatment of chronic diseases, such as neurosis, hypertension, ulcers, gastroptosis, and constipation (Chen & Chen, 1995). In recent years, Chinese cancer patients performed Qigong exercises under the guidance of Qigong experts. This training produced higher immunological resistance in these patients, and noticeably improved their physical condition. Thus, Qigong plays an active role in protecting and strengthening health.

Chinese traditional relaxation techniques rely mainly on the regulation of posture, respiration, and mental functions. Through monitoring cognitive functions, such as imagination, suggestion, and mediation, an individual regulates his or her internal perceptions and feelings in order to reach a state of total relaxation. For example, to cure hypertension, Chinese relaxation techniques utilize a stable state of psychophysiological activity, which requires the patient to concentrate continuously on his or her internal mental and bodily states until blood pressure is lowered. Chinese traditional physicians are sensitive to the emotional aspects of diseases, and special attention is given to the development of a trusting doctor–patient relationship. Western biofeedback techniques similarly require the regulation of posture, respiration, and mental state, to tranquilize oneself and reach a base level for training. However, such regulations are based mainly on visible or audible external signals, rather than on internal regulation. For example, in biofeedback, the physician reinforces the patient by encouraging him or her to do his or her best to establish a lower blood pressure, continuing until the lowered blood pressure is achieved. In summary, Chinese relaxation techniques emphasize the holistic integration of mind and body, Western biofeedback emphasizes psycho–physiologic activities. This discrepancy reflects the different ideologies of the East and West, Orientals analyze events in their entirety, holistic and ambiguous, whereas Westerners prefer to grasp an event partly, precisely and exactly.

SOCIAL STABILITY

Criminal offense

The trends of criminal offenses in China since 1949 can be divided into three periods: The early years (1949–1965), the Cultural Revolution period (1966–1976), and the years of reform (1978-present). In the early years of the People's Republic since 1949, criminal cases were very rare. For example, in 1956, the total number of criminal cases was only 180,000, amounting to 0.29 per thousand of the population. The government at this time took strong measures to eradicate crimes and other social maladies, such as gambling, prostitution, and drug addiction. The society was peaceful and people felt secure. However, this was achieved at the cost of strong social control and severe punishment for wrongdoing. Thanks to the residence registration rule which stipulates that household members and visitors have to be registered in local police stations, criminal conduct can be easily discovered. For the Cultural Revolution period, it was very hard to define what were considered criminal offenses, because the Red Guards themselves robbed people's homes, arrested people at will, and inflicted physical and mental tortures on anyone regarded as political deviants, especially intellectuals. Therefore, the number of crimes may have been underestimated during the Cultural Revolution period. During the reform period, there has been a powerful rebound in crime-rate. This recent increase can be linked to the new market economy system, which brought about the loosening of central control, an inept legal system, opening of stock exchange and real estate markets, influence from overseas, and a striving for wealth. In 1991, criminal offenses reached a peak number of 2.4 million cases which amounts to 2.1 per thousand of the population (Shao, 1996).

A market economy leads to a greater mobility of members of society, particularly of young people. The trend in crimes is toward an increase in crimes committed by this "floating population." It was claimed that 80% of crimes committed in the cities are by these people. In 1994, about 649,000 temporary residents violated laws, an increase of 14% over the previous year (Chen, 1996). In Beijing, 70% of crimes committed are by young people from other parts of the country. In Shanghai, the floating population contributes to about 39% of the crime rate; in Guangzhou, they contribute to about 65% (Kang, 1996). These criminals move to other parts of the country after committing a crime, and return to the city again at a later date to commit more crimes. Another characteristic of criminal offenses is that crimes are taking on more and more of an intellectual nature. Crimes are now committed by people using modern technology, like the electronic pager, cellular phones, and other modern communication facilities. Computer crimes are becoming more common. Also, fake credit cards and fake bank notes are commonly used. Young people form groups in carrying out misconduct, causing an increase in organized crimes. Gangs from outside of mainland China are beginning to infiltrate into the mainland, some of whose crimes are of an international nature. Drug trafficking and antique smuggling usually involve accomplices in Hong Kong or in other parts of the world.

Crime as a social psychological phenomenon

The Chinese Cultural Revolution, which occurred from 1966 to 1976, was one of the most astonishing social political movements in history. It resulted in a reversal of moral values and the disruption of normal social life. Aside from political reasons, such as the personality cult of Mao Zedong who initiated the revolution, it remains a mystery as to how such a large-scale movement could have occurred. So far, no plausible social psychological theory exists to explain the motives behind the movement, but the social and psychological consequences of the revolution are clear. Juvenile crime provides a good example of these consequences.

In China, people aged 14 to 25 are in the adolescent and youth (Qing Shao Nian) period. The number of offenses committed by this age group has shown a steady increase since the 1970s. For example, the juvenile crime rate from 1979 to 1993 increased threefold, with juvenile crime comprising about 75% of the total number of criminal cases during this period (Shao, 1996). The increase in juvenile delinquency can be attributed to the social and psychological effects that the Cultural Revolution had on this age group. Most of these young offenders were born during or immediately after the Cultural Revolution and deprived of a proper education during their primary and secondary school years. During the revolution, schools were suspended, teachers were persecuted, and children were separated from their parents and sent to the remote countryside to do farm labor. This led to a lack of education and professional skills training for young people, resulting in difficulties obtaining stable employment and a corresponding feeling of desperation. Together with the great number of young rural migrant workers who moved into cities competing for jobs, these adolescents and youth formed a group which is prone to commit crimes in times of frustration. Thus, it seems that the opening up of the country after the Cultural Revolution had a dual effect: it exposed young people to the opportunities that accompany wealth and luxurious lifestyles; but made it more difficult for them to obtain such prosperity without taking risks and committing crimes.

CONCLUSION

China's reform and modernization have brought about great changes in China's economy and society. The conflict between China's ancient heritage and values on the one hand, and modern global culture on the other hand, has given rise to a host of social and psychological problems awaiting study by social scientists. The issues presented in this paper are examples of some of these problems, and pose far more questions than solutions. What are the challenges for psychology? The task which lies before us is to study the psychology of a people comprising one-fifth of the world's population, and undergoing a process of rapid social change. A consideration of the issues discussed in this chapter may provide, at least in part, some solutions to China's social problems, and contribute to the development of international psychology as a whole.

ACKNOWLEDGEMENTS

The authors wish to thank Professor John G. Adair for his constructive comments in the revision of the manuscript; his polishing of the English language was especially helpful in upgrading this paper.

REFERENCES

Chen, J. H. (1997, March). *Report on the implementation of the 1996 plan for national economic and social development and the 1997 plan for national economic and social development*. Paper presented at the 5th Session of the 8th National People's Congress, Beijing, China.

Chen, S. J., & Chen Z. K. (1995). Comparison of relaxation techniques in the East and in the West: Chinese traditional relaxation techniques and biofeedback. In T. Kikuchi, H. Saduma, I. Saito, & K. Tsubar (Eds.), *Biobehavioral self-regulation: Eastern and Western perspectives* (pp. 79–82). New York: Springer Verlag.

Chen, Y. (1996, April 3). Transient population gets extra attention. *China Daily*, p. 2.

Communist Party of China (1996, October). *Resolutions of the CPC Central Committee on certain important questions on promoting socialist ethical and cultural progress*. The 6th Plenum of the 14th Central Committee of Communist Party of China, Beijing, China.

Dai, X. Y., Deng, L. X., Ryan, J. J., & Paolo, A. M. (1993). A survey of psychological tests used in clinical psychological practice of China and its comparison with the data of United States. *Chinese Journal of Clinical Psychology, 1*, 47–50.

Duan, H. F., Zhang, S. Y., Wu, Z. Q., Shen, Z. F., & Xu, M. D. (1995). Educational psychology and teaching methods in China: Developments and trends. In *Educational Studies and Documents 61: Recent trends and developments in educational psychology: Chinese and American perspectives*. Paris: UNESCO Publishing.

Fan, C. R., Wan, C. W., Lin, G. B., & Jing, Q. C. (1994). A comparative study of personality characteristics between only and non-only children of primary schools in Xian. *Psychological Science, 17*, 70–74.

Gong, Y. X., & Li, Q. Z. (1996). Survey and perspective of current condition of China's clinical psychology. *Chinese Clinical Psychology Journal, 4*, 1–9.

Halman, L. (1995). Is there a moral decline? A cross-national inquiry into morality in contemporary society. *International Social Science Journal, 145*, 419–439.

Inglehart, R. (1995). Changing values, economic development and political change. *International Social Science Journal, 145*, 379–404.

Ji, G. P., Jiao, S. L., & Jing, Q. C. (1993). Expectancy of Chinese parents and children's cognitive abilities. *International Journal of Psychology, 28*, 821–830.

Jiao, S. L., Ji, G. P., & Jing, Q. C. (1986). Comparative study of behavioral qualities of only children and sibling children. *Child Development, 57*, 357–361.

Jiao, S. L., Ji, G. P., & Jing, Q. C. (1996). Cognitive development of Chinese urban only children and children with siblings. *Child Development, 67*, 387–395.

Jing, Q. C. (1994). The Chinese single-child family programme and population psychology. *Psychology and Developing Societies, 6*, 29–53.

Jing, Q. C., Jiao, S. L., & Ji, G. P. (1993). Relationship between children's birth category and cognitive development. *Child Development in China, 8*, 24–26.

Kang, S. H. (1996). Characteristics of contemporary China's juvenile delinquency. *Changan Journal, 33*, 28–29.

Kim, U. (1995). Psychology, science, and culture: Cross-cultural analysis of national psychologies. *International Journal of Psychology, 30*, 663–679.

Lee, K. Y. (1966). Asia and the world in the 21st century. In *Collection of presentations of the 21st century forum* (pp. 22–34). Beijing: China Culture and History Publishers.

Li, B. S. (1992). *Moral psychology*. Shanghai, China: East-China Chemical Engineering College Press.

Li, P. (1997, March). *Report on the work of the government*. Paper presented at the 5th Session of the 8th National People's Congress, Beijing, China.

Liu, J. H., Wang, X. D., Zhang, M. L., He, J. Q., & Lin, J. S. (1982). The development of children's cognition of the part–whole relationship concerning number and arithmetic. *Acta Psychologica Sinica, 3*, 263–271.

Livi-Bacci, M. (1994). Population policies: A comparative perspective. *International Social Science Journal, 141*, 317–330.

Lu, Z. H. (1987). *Psychology of guided self-teaching*. Beijing: Geological Publishing House.

Meny, Y. (1996). "Fin de siecle" corruption: Change, crisis and shifting values. *International Social Science Journal, 149*, 309–335.

Minjian, Z. Y. (1996). Survey on problems in current reform and construction. *Economic Affairs, 3*, 66–69.

Niu, D., Guan, S., & Jia, L. (1992). *Studies of international experience on modern social development*. Beijing: Hai Yang Publishers.

Poverty elimination still hard. (1996, July 24). *China Daily*, p. 4.

Rosenberg, B. G., & Jing, Q. C. (1996). A revolution in family life: The political and social structural impact of China's one child policy. *Journal of Social Issues, 52*, 51–69.

Shao, D. S. (1996). *Perplexities of Chinese society*. Beijing: Social Science Literature Publishers.

State Statistical Bureau (1996). *China Statistical Yearbook 1996*. Beijing: China Statistical Publishing House.

Stevenson, H. W., Stigler, J. W., Lee, S. Y., Lucker, G. W., Kitamura, S., & Hsu, C. (1985). Cognitive performance and academic achievement of Japanese, Chinese, and American children. *Child Development, 56,* 718–734.

Wan, C. W., Fan, C. R., Lin, G. B., & Jing, Q. C. (1994). Comparison of personality traits of only and sibling school children in Beijing. *Journal of Genetic Psychology, 155,* 377–388.

Zhang, X. (1996, July 22). Trade schools to be upgraded. *China Daily,* p. 4.

Zhang, Y. (1997, May 11). Returning students eligible for higher salaries, incentives. *China Daily,* p. 6.

Zhang, Z. G. (1993). On the psychological structure of moral traits. In Z. G. Zhang (Ed.), *The formation of students' character* (pp. 445–462). Beijing: Beijing Normal University Press.

PART THREE

Work and Organizational Psychology

Psychology of work and organizations: Scientific inquiry and professional care

P. J. D. Drenth
Vrije Universiteit, Amsterdam, The Netherlands

In this paper the relationship between the two goals of psychology of work and organizations is discussed: the contribution to the scientific body of knowledge and the assistance in solving practical problems. Five types of scientific and professional activities—pure research, strategic research, applied research, diagnosis, and professional use of research—are distinguished and ranked with an increasing emphasis on utility as a criterion, and at the same time a decreasing emphasis on veracity as a criterion. It is further defended that, for an optimal contribution to the solution of numerous problems in organizations and society at large, psychology should retain an independent identity. Its added value stems from the interest in both intra- and interindividual phenomena, as well as the expertise in both structural analyses and processes of development and change.

Cet article traite des rapports entre les deux objectifs de la psychologie du travail et des organisations soit: la contribution au fonds des connaissances scientifiques et la participation à la solution de problèmes pratiques. On y identifie cinq types d'activités scientifiques et professionnelles: la recherche pure, la recherche stratégique, la recherche appliquée, le diagnostic et l'utilisation professionnelle de la recherche; ils sont ainsi présentés dans un ordre de classification basé sur un critère d'utilité croissante en même temps que sur un critère de véracité décroissante. On soutient de plus que, pour apporter une contribution optimale à la solution de nombreux problèmes dans les organisations et la société dans son ensemble, la psychologie devrait maintenir une identité indépendante. La valeur ajoutée de sa contribution découle de son intérêt pour les phénomènes tant intra-individuels qu'interindividuels, de même que de son expertise dans l'analyse structurale comme dans les processus de développement et de changement.

At the end of the 19th century, psychology was full of optimism about its contribution to the proper functioning of societies and the well-being of humankind.

Scientific psychological knowledge was expected to provide individuals with the insights they needed to be aware of in regard to their qualities as well as the limitations of these qualities. In the process of building a life and career, an individual would both rely on these qualities and make allowances for these limitations, as Gerard Heymans (1909), the pioneer of Dutch psychology, predicted in his 1909 inaugural address as professor at the University of Groningen. A few years earlier, G. Stanley Hall had been equally optimistic about psychology as "the long hoped for, long delayed science of man to which all other sciences are bringing their ripest and best thoughts" (Fowler, 1990, p. 1).

Now, some 100 years later, psychology is sadder and wiser. The world is still full of personal and group conflicts, and our societies still show an appalling lack of tolerance and acceptance. Exploitation and misuse of power is the order of the day, both at the interpersonal and the national or international levels. Human beings are still capable of atrocious acts, as wars and ethnic or racial outbursts have repeatedly demonstrated throughout this century.

In his valedictory address as Professor of Psychology at the University of Amsterdam, Nico Frijda (1992) asked himself whether psychology was any use at all, if we looked only at what it had brought about. Initially he did not seem to go beyond an attempt to ascribe this value *ex nihilo*: the world may not become a better place thanks to psychology, but it does become inferior without it—more stupid, more vulgar and more vulnerable to tyranny. At the end of his address, however, he was a little more hopeful: psychology can contribute to the advancement of truth, human dignity, and compassion. Let us hope that his optimism is not unjustified.

The discussion of the supposed contribution of psychology to society is naturally relevant to organizational psychology, which from the outset has seen itself as one of the practical and useful, applied disciplines within psychology, and claims to further both the effectiveness of organizations and the well-being of their members. The interesting question then arises, from *whom* should we expect this supposed beneficial effect: from the contributions of scientists in the field of work and organizational psychology, or from practitioners employing scientific insights but who attach more emphasis to professional care aspects than to scientific knowledge?

VERACITY AND UTILITY

The title of this presentation refers to the two aspects of the psychology of work and organizations: its contribution to the scientific body of knowledge and its assistance in solving practical problems. Let us have a closer look at the relationship between these two goals and make some distinctions for further clarification.

First, let us rank five types of scientific and professional activities of psychologists, with an increasing emphasis on utility as a criterion and a decreasing emphasis on veracity as the (sole) criterion: *Pure Research*, *Strategic Research*,

TABLE 14.1
Five types of psychologists' activities, ranked by veracity and utility

	Veracity as criterion	Utility as criterion	Generalizable knowledge?	Science driven	Problem driven
Pure research	+	−	+	+	−
Strategic research	+	(+)	+	+	(+)
Applied research	+	+	+	−	+
Diagnosis	+	+	−	−	+
Professional use of research	−	+	−	−	+

NOTES:
+ = applicable
(+) = somewhat applicable
− = not applicable

Applied Research, *Diagnosis*, and *Professional Use of Research*. Table 14.1 lists these five types, together with an indication of the applicability of the two criteria, *veracity* and *utility*. To provide some further insight into the nature and definition of these five activities, three further indicators are given in Table 14.1.

First is the extent to which these activities generate generalizable knowledge and insights: in other words, whether an activity contributes to scientific knowledge. Second and third, there is the motive for the activity: is it curiosity, the stimulus of an intellectual riddle, the scientific challenge of an unsolved problem, the need to solve a practical question, difficulty or dilemma? For the second indicator the term *science driven* is selected (other terms used in the literature are "curiosity driven", "conclusion oriented", "precompetitive", "untargeted" or "unfettered"). The third indicator is named *problem driven* (alternative terms in use are "field induced", "decision oriented", "competitive" or "targeted", "market driven").

Using the information from Table 14.1, the following descriptions of the five distinguished activities can be given:

1. *Pure research.*   The issue as stated by the researcher is prompted purely or primarily by scientific curiosity or by questions raised in previous research because of insufficient evidence or incomplete theoretical explanation. Pure scientific research is carried out for the sake of acquiring insights and generating generalizable laws or relationships, not to find out whether these have any practical usefulness or whether they yield applicable results.

Although the majority of the research work carried out in work and organizational psychology is of an applied character, the literature in this field provides numerous examples of pure research. Research work on personality (Maslow, 1954), achievement motivation (McClelland, 1961), evaluation and appraisal processes (Frank & Hackman, 1975; Schmitt, 1976), decision making (Heller, Drenth, Koopman, & Rus, 1988), group processes (Janis, 1982) or cross-cultural comparisons of organizational behavior (Hofstede, 1983) are just a few illustrative cases in point.

The fact that pure research does not aim at applicable results does not imply it does not or cannot have social or organizational relevance. Both the process and results of pure research do have an important and useful social function. First, they satisfy human curiosity, a very basic human need. Second, they educate the next generation of psychological scientists. Wherever good research is carried out in an inspiring scientific climate, we also find young researchers being trained for scientific careers. Given the social impact of preparing a future generation of high-level scientific psychologists, this educational function of basic and pure research certainly deserves attention. Third, pure research is needed to further our scientific insights, expand the frontiers of our knowledge, and find new technological and instrumental applications of our scientific insights. Let us not forget what Pasteur once said: if we over-emphasize the importance and priority of applied research, the time will come when there is nothing left to apply. In a recent report on the competitiveness of European research and technology, the European Commission emphasized the importance of the creation of new knowledge industries (European Commission, 1995). For new knowledge industries, we need new knowledge, not merely the application of existing knowledge. Here again the importance of basic, pure research is accentuated. This point also applies to psychology in industry.

2. *Strategic research.*   This type of research, described in the OECD Frascati manual as "fundamental strategic research," refers to research at the meeting point of supply (universities, research institutes) and demand (society, industry). In certain cases fundamental, pure research can nevertheless be directed toward problem areas which have been selected as being of general interest. In the case of organizational psychology, these areas would include the multicultural workforce, the meaning of work and non-work (including problems of unemployment), gerontological problems with respect to work, equal opportunities in selection, and the like. Strategic research is oriented towards application, but has such a fundamental character that it furthers pure science at the same time. It is research that takes place within a long-term program, even if it deals with urgent societal problems. A good deal of the more fundamental research in work and organizational psychology belongs to this category.

Veracity is the main criterion for strategic research, with societal utility as a secondary consideration: in other words, societal utility is only indirectly important because of the priority given to the general theme or problem area. Research projects are primarily science-driven, and to a lesser degree initiated or justified by the saliency of a particular organizational problem. It is certainly an objective of this type of research that it leads to generalizable knowledge.

3. *Applied research.* As has already been indicated, the origin of this type of psychological research is a question, problem or difficulty in the functioning of individuals in a societal or organizational context. Applied research in organizational psychology is concerned with objectives external to scientific research itself: organizational policies, economic, marketing or personnel decisions, technological development and the like.

Various types of research can be further distinguished within this category, such as the generation of specific applied programmes, the development of new products, of instruments, and new processes or interventions, operations research (i.e. analyzing, in an objective and quantitative way, the decision-making problems that used to be tackled by experience or intuition), as Rothschild (1972) indicated.

Obviously, the majority of research in work and organizational psychology will be of this applied type. Most of the research in the well-known areas of testing and selection, training, performance appraisal, ergonomics, worker motivation, leadership, intergroup relations, safety and accidents, organizational processes, decision making, consumer behavior and the like is either initiated by practical problems or requests, or leads to practical decisions, procedural advice or applicable instruments, or both.

Two further observations should be made in this respect. First, while the origin and objective of a piece of research may stem from the need for its practical utilization, the research process itself is subject only to the norm of veracity. Identical scientific rules and norms are applied in both pure scientific and applied research. In applied research, just as in "pure science" research, questions are posed and the design is planned in an unbiased way. Empirical data are used to sustain or disconfirm hypotheses Standardization and objectivity are the aims in data collection. The analysis and interpretation of the data are executed in a "value-free" way (that is to say, no ideology, values, interests, power, or external pressure may play a role in the explanation and interpretation of the research findings), and important criteria in the formulation and testing of the hypotheses or expectations are explicitness, testability, and replicability.

Second, applied research also leads to generalizable laws and relationships. This is why, ideally, applied research is not secondary to pure research in terms of its contribution to the body of psychological knowledge. In fact, a great deal of what is now known about the nature of intelligence, the structure of personality and individual differences, the behavior of individuals in groups or organized systems, man–machine interfaces, and collective behavior is the product of applied research in work and organizational psychology. There is nothing inferior about applied research in psychology. It may even make a genuinely fundamental contribution to the discipline, as the afore-mentioned examples show. The only difference is that its origin and intention is to offer a "helping hand" in the solution of a practical problem.

4. *Diagnosis.* With this type of activity the psychologist leaves the field of research in the strictest sense and enters the area of care for and interest in the individual case, person, or system. This activity is a prevalent orientation in professional psychology. Testing a job applicant, analyzing the culture of an organization, unravelling a conflict situation, evaluating the style of a particular leader—all these activities are concerned with individual cases, persons or social systems.

In this area we no longer speak of scientific research, defined as leading to and aiming at generalizable laws and insights into human behavior. Occasionally, studies of individual cases may be directed at seeking general principles (as, for instance, in exemplary case studies, in-depth analyses of individuals aiming at the generation of hypotheses, or the validation of specific interpretations). However, this is not usually the case; the intention is usually to gain insight into a single individual (in order to advise, help or cure that individual) or a single system (in order to change or improve that system), making conscientious and critical use of existing scientific knowledge. This type of activity is no longer scientific research, but rather its application to particular, individual cases.

It is important to realize that, as Table 14.1 shows, veracity remains a valid criterion for this category. One still adheres to the norms and rules of the "scientific game" such as accuracy, the need for precision of observation, the avoidance of gratuitous statements, and the requirement to verify the surmised. One is still seeking for correct understanding and truthful knowledge, but the objective is no longer a generalizable insight into human behavior. Sometimes, however, the dividing-line between diagnosis and the applied research becomes indistinct. The experience of a proficient organizational advisor, the "stored information" of an experienced selection psychologist, or the "tacit knowledge" of a competent therapist may approach general laws of understanding generated by scientific research. If these experienced practitioners take the trouble to write up their accumulated insights, it often enriches the existing scientific literature, as is demonstrated by well-known organizational scientists like Drucker, Morgan, Kets de Vries, and others.

There is one other aspect of this type of understanding an individual case which should be mentioned, which may carry it beyond the status of application of science. Most individual cases do not fit exactly into the categories developed in scientific research to which validated laws and relationships apply. The problems with which they are faced are often difficult to define, and fixed solutions do not usually apply. Many organizational situations are uncertain, complex, unstable, and have to be contextualized in order to be understood. In a sense they are frequently distinctive and unique. A skilled professional does more than merely apply in each individual situation that which is known to hold for a category of cases or organization to which the case in question belongs. In trying to understand fully the individual phenomenon or person, he or she uses general scientific insights, but also personal wisdom and experience; he or she tries to place the case in the context of the specific environment and time, and he or she may even develop (and test!) new theories for that individual case. In other words, professional activity goes beyond what Schön (1987) calls (and rejects as) "technical rationality", and develops into an intellectual process which Peterson (1995) describes as "reflection-in-action".

In my view, there are no grounds for demeaning this practice from an arrogant scientific perspective, but we must guard against the temptation to drift off into an "intuitive never-never-land" (Peterson, 1995). Accepting veracity as an important criterion means adhering to the scientific rules described earlier. Wherever possible, independent validating indicators and supporting information should be sought and hypotheses and assumptions should be subjected to systematic scientific scrutiny.

We must ask the serious question as to whether today's university training in organizational psychology sufficiently acknowledges this need for individualized, contextualized knowledge and whether we prepare our graduates adequately for this professional responsibility. Too many organizational psychology programs exude the spirit of traditionalism rather than tradition. In McCall's (1996, p. 380) humorous description of these two concepts ("Traditions are the living ideas of the dead, traditionalism consists of the dead ideas of the living"), we can hear an implicit denunciation of the former. Whether it is possible to teach this professional skill or whether it can be developed only through practical experience is the subject of continuing debate.

5. *Professional use of research.* This last category is principally different from the others. It concerns the use of scientific information: that is, the utilization of knowledge in decisions, actions, and interventions. The criterion is no longer scientific veracity, but a value-based outcome, such as greater economic growth, a more effective change process, a higher degree of well-being in the workforce, an improved corporate image, and the like. In this vein it can be said that organizational developers, personnel selection psychologists, management developers and trainers (like psychotherapists and pedagogues) are, in this capacity, not scientists but social practitioners. Personal, social, or economic norms and values ultimately determine the decisions arrived at and the actions taken. The critical question is no longer *Is it true?* but *Does it work?*

The epithet "professional", however, implies a number of further qualifications and restrictions. After all, not everything that works is admissible. The professional psychologist's responsibilities pertain to at least the following restrictive consequences:

• Adherence to the principles of scientific reasoning and evaluation in the selection and use of theories, approaches and methods. This responsibility also implies refraining from the use of unscientific methods, even if they are popular, such as graphology, astrology, homoeopathy, healing by praying, neurolinguistic programming, and the like.

- Adherence to the principles of proper ethical behavior, as prescribed by most professional psychological associations. The national associations of many countries have an "ethical code" for psychologists. Sometimes, as in the Code of the Netherlands Institute of Psychologists (NIP), there are additional specifications for work and organizational psychologists.
- Meeting the requirements of a proper education and training in psychology and the relevant specialization within psychology. These requirements may vary in different countries, but the basics are generally accepted. (For instance, the Dutch NIP has recently formulated the following requirements for the training of psychologists: (1) thorough knowledge in five basic subjects: experimental, developmental, personality, social, and abnormal psychology; (2) sufficient knowledge in supporting subjects: methods and statistics, history of psychology, biology, sociology, cultural anthropology, and philosophy; (3) familiarity with the three main fields of application: education, work and organizations, and health care; (4) thorough training in the principles of empirical science; and (5) some training in professional skills: e.g. interviewing, testing.)

Further specific requirements have been formulated for independent practice in one of the psychological specializations.

This last issue brings us to the next point in our discussion. Should psychology retain an independent identity, both in its professional organization and its education of psychologists, or should we gradually dissolve the sharp demarcation lines between psychology and its related disciplines?

AN INDEPENDENT IDENTITY?

Let us first now turn to the question with which the previous section concluded, the question of whether psychology should retain an independent identity. This issue has become rather controversial of late. We see a growing interest in psychology (especially organizational psychology) in areas "outside" mainstream psychology and psychology training. Work and organizational psychologists are identifying themselves less and less as *psychologists*. They see themselves as organizational specialists, organizational consultants, organizational analysts, but not psychologists. They tend to go to management conferences rather than psychology conferences. Social and organizational psychology is now taught in engineering and business schools, in management science and MBA programs, in university economics and technical science departments, in polytechnics and other higher vocational institutes for technical and commercial posts, and so on. These days, work and organizational psychology is probably being taught more often outside conventional disciplinary training programs in psychology than within them.

These developments have been welcomed by some of our colleagues. Psychology training has been accused in the past of one-sidedness, stricture, and insufficient problem-orientation. Real problems, the argument goes, seldom bother about the disciplinary borderlines that traditional sciences happen to have drawn. In a recently organized series of workshops on the changing nature of the profession of work and organizational psychology, de Wolff and Hurley (1994) conclude that a lack of knowledge of organizational practices is seen as the most common weakness of organizational psychology. Work and organizational psychologists are seen as having an overly narrow view of organizational life, caused, amongst other things, by a clear gap between the content of university courses and actual practice in organizations.

Such attitudes and opinions have created centrifugal forces which have driven organizational psychology beyond its original domain, both in training and education and in its professional orientation and organization. "Interdisciplinarity" has become a fashionable motto. Qualifications such as "relevant", "problem-oriented", "meaningful", "concerned with real-life issues" and the like are often associated with interdisciplinary training and research.

Let me not be misunderstood. Naturally, the idea that organizational psychologists should broaden their orientation to include societal and industrial viewpoints should be acclaimed and encouraged. The spreading of the organizational psychology "gospel" in other faculties and schools should also be welcomed. It is not difficult to demonstrate insights into, and consequent improvements in, the decisions taken in adjacent scientific fields. In economics, for instance, notions such as saving, product choice, brand loyalty, stock market crashes and the like, while central to the dynamics of economic processes, are actually psychological and social phenomena. Nowadays, in the technology of task and machine design, it is acknowledged that the incorporation of the "human factor", preferably at an early stage, always bears fruit. Decision-making processes, whether in management, the judiciary, or medical practice, are clearly improved when use is made of psychological insights. Environmental science and research into global change have correctly acknowledged the importance of the human dimension in the control and prevention of further environmental impairment.

None of this need obscure the borders between disciplines, or lead to problem-oriented, cafeteria-type educational programmes, and the negation of the unique contribution of psychology. It need not lead, in short, to an abandonment of a monodisciplinary, psychological identity. Admittedly, the practical organizational psychologist should certainly develop a more problem-oriented attitude and should expand his or her knowledge of and feeling for the type of scientific reasoning in other disciplines, particularly colleagues with whom he or she has to collaborate in multidisciplinary teams, such as marketing, finance, engineering, and strategic management. He or she should also develop more of the political skills needed to operate in a business environment, more sensitivity in the identification of specific problems, a greater capacity to translate problems into analyzable questions, and more of the skills required to implement the findings in everyday practice. This recommendation will naturally require changes, some of them radical ones, in many existing curricula. I would nevertheless reiterate that the contribution of the organizational psychologist can best be guaranteed if his or her training is based on a solid, disciplinary education in psychology.

My first argument for this view is a general one. Both researchers and professional workers need a number of generic aptitudes, such as conceptual thought, the ability to abstract, to distinguish between matters of primary and secondary importance, to integrate, and so on. These aptitudes are developed primarily in disciplinary training and research. Too early a participation in interdisciplinary training and discussion leads to superficiality and shallow chatter.

My second argument is that the contribution made by organizational psychologists ideally has an added value derived from a special combination of knowledge and skills. We may identify three dimensions to this combination, each having a dichotomous character. The first dimension is the attention given to both the intra- and interindividual aspects of human behavior. We know that organizational processes are influenced by personal motives, needs, fears and expectancies as well as interpersonal conflicts, rivalries and other group or social processes. Knowledge of both the structure and dynamics of personality and socio-psychological mechanisms is needed for a fuller understanding of organizational behavior. The second dimension is the emphasis given to descriptive, structural aspects as opposed to processes of development and change. The latter can be brought about by natural growth or by deliberate (e.g. experimental) interventions. The third dimension refers to the typical training given to psychologists, and consequently to their experience. This dimensions concerns, on the one hand, knowledge of and insight into the background and determinants of human functioning, resulting from a long tradition of scientific experimentation and scholarly reflection in psychology. On the other hand, it includes a strong methodological and empirical approach, emphasizing instrument development, research design, data analysis and interpretation. This qualification is fostered by a combination of statistics, experimental design and psychometrics (tests and measurement), all of which are part of regular psychology training in most countries.

These three dimensions can be illustrated as a cube encompassing the basic psychological scientific competencies, as illustrated in Fig. 14.1.

Figure 14.1 also shows another vertical dimension, indicated by dotted lines. This dimension contains the professional skills needed for the analysis of individual cases (individual and organizational diagnosis) or for change processes in individuals (therapy, training, counselling) or in groups and organizations (team building, organizational development). As I have said, neither the analysis of individual cases as such, nor the utilization of insight and experience in therapy and change, necessarily lead to generalizable psychological knowledge. Needless to say, however, these practical diagnostic or remedial competencies make up a significant part of the special value of the contribution made by the psychological profession to organizations and society.

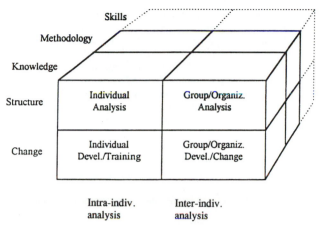

FIG. 14.1   Cube illustrating psychological scientific and professional competencies.

Clearly, the organizational psychologist who is armed with these scientific and professional competencies and who puts them to practical use can continue to make a significant contribution to the solution of numerous theoretical and practical problems in organizations and society at large. The added value provided by the profession results, then, from its unique combination of competencies represented by different boxes within this cube. It is important that psychological training acknowledges this insight and continues to pay attention to a proper balance among all these competencies represented in the cube. In this way psychology, including organizational psychology, will be able to retain its own identity. In this way it will also continue to contribute to the discovery of the truth and to the growth of human dignity and compassion to the end of this century and beyond into the next millennium.

REFERENCES

Drenth, P. J. D. (1995). Psychology as a science: Truthful or useful? *European Psychologist, 1*, 3–13.

European Commission (1995). *Green paper on innovation*. Brussels: E.C. DG XII.

Fowler, B. D. (1990). Psychology: The core discipline. *American Psychologist, 45*, 1–6.

Frank, L. L., & Hackman, J. R. (1975). Effects of interviewer–interviewee similarity on interviewer objectivity in college admission interviews. *Journal of Applied Psychology, 60*, 366–368.

Frijda, N. H. (1992). *Heeft de psychologie wel zin?* [Does psychology make sense?] Afscheidsrede, Universiteit van Amsterdam (valedictory address to the Psychology Department at the University of Amsterdam).

Heller, F. A., Drenth, P. J. D., Koopman, P. L., & Rus, V. (1988). *Decisions in organizations*. London: Sage.

Heymans, G. (1909). *De toekomstige eeuw der psychologie* [The next centennium of psychology]. Rectorale rede, Universiteit van Groningen (inaugural address as Rector Magnificus at the University of Groningen).

Hofstede, G. A. (1983). *Culture's consequences*. London: Sage.

Janis, I. L. (1982). *Victims of groupthink.* Boston: Houghton Mifflin.

Maslow, A. H. (1954). *Motivation and personality.* New York: Harper.

McCall, R. (1996). The concept and practice of education, research, and public service in university psychology departments. *American Psychologist, 51*, 379–388.

McClelland, D. C. (1961). *The achieving society.* Princeton, NJ: Van Nostrand.

Nederlands Instituut van Psychologen. (1995). *De kwaliteit van de psychologie beoefening.* (The quality of practicing psychology). Amsterdam: Netherlands Institute of Psychologists.

Peterson, D. R. (1995). The reflective educator. *American Psychologist, 50*, 975–983.

Rothschild, Lord (1972). Forty-five varieties of research (and development). *Nature, 2399*, 373–378.

Schmitt, N. (1976). Social and situational determinants of interview decisions: Implications for the employment interview. *Personnel Psychology, 29*, 79–101.

Schön, D. A. (1987). *Educating the reflective practitioner: How professionals think in action.* San Francisco: Jossey-Bass.

Wolff, Ch. J. de, & Hurley, J. (1994). The changing nature of the profession of work and organizational psychology. Overview of a panel discussion study in six European countries. *European Work and Organizational Psychologist, 4*, 343–353.

CHAPTER FIFTEEN

Basic issues in occupational stress research

Anna B. Leonova
Department of Work and Engineering Psychology,
Moscow State Lomonosov-University, Russia

The chapter is devoted to the recent developments in the field of occupational stress. An overview of main findings and directions of research is done in the framework of three research paradigms that dominate in the contemporary literature: (1) person–environment-fit; (2) transactional; and (3) state regulation approaches. Benefits and limitations of these approaches are exemplified by results of field studies in different occupational groups such as blue-collar workers, operators of highly automated systems, and fire-fighters. The explication of relationships between these approaches shows that they are complementary by representing successive stages in investigation of stress mechanisms in real-world setting.

Ce chapitre passe en revue les développements récents dans le domaine du stress associé au métier. On y présente une vue d'ensemble des données et des directions principales de la recherche dans ce domaine, utilisant les trois paradigmes de recherche qui dominent la littérature contemporaine: (1) l'ajustement personne-environnement; (2) l'approche transactionnelle; et (3) l'approche régulation de l'état. Les avantages et les limitations de ces approches sont illustrés par l'entremise de résultats d'études sur le terrain auprès de différents groupes de métiers tels les cols bleus, les opérateurs de systèmes automatisés, et les pompiers. Les relations entre ces approches indiquent qu'elles se complètent entre elles puisqu'elles représentent toutes des stages successifs dans l'étude des mécanismes du stress.

In recent years, occupational stress has become one of the most popular topics for applied research in psychology, and in the broader areas of social and medical sciences (Cooper & Payne, 1988; Jenkins, 1991; Karasek & Theorell, 1990; Levi, 1981; Salvendy, Sauter, & Hurrel, 1987). The concept of stress, introduced by Hans Selye (see e.g. Selye, 1976), has had many connotations, and occupational stress research can be seen as a natural extension of this classical concept to a specific form of human activity, namely work (Appley & Trumbull, 1986).

Problems implied by the stress concept are highly relevant to problems arising in individuals' professional lives. For instance, the types and stages of an individual's adaptation to a demanding environment or the deterioration in health are seen as "the price" for the extraordinary mobilization of psychophysiological resources. On the other hand, the great variety and complexity of real work situations has restricted any direct transfer of the original stress concept to occupational stress, and stimulated an intensive, independent development of occupational stress research.

This chapter is devoted to an overview of the main approaches to the modern investigation of occupational stress. In discussing these approaches, I shall use the notion of occupational stress as a generic term subsuming many relevant concepts which co-exist in the literature, such as work stress, job stress, professional stress, operator's stress, and managerial stress (Cooper & Payne, 1988; House, 1981; Levi, 1981; Spielberger & Reheiser, 1994a). The obvious reason for this generalization is that in all these cases, relationships between a person and his/her professional activity are emphasized.

EMPIRICALLY RICH AND CONCEPTUALLY POOR?

When studies on occupational stress began 25 to 30 years ago, they made up only one among several domains of stress-related research. At the same time, however, they demonstrated extensive development which by and large outstripped the amount of stress investigations in more traditional biological areas. According to the PsycLIT data for 1993–1995, the term "occupational stress" was mentioned 1860 times in different publications (together with references to "work stress" and "job stress," this number was 2489). In comparison, the term "family stress" appeared only 280 times. This tendency was clearly represented in Spielberger and Reheiser's (1994a) analysis of publication rates in different domains of stress research, which we have revised for the last 25 years (see Fig. 15.1).

Of course, it is not an accident that occupational stress became the dominant topic in applied stress research starting in the 1980s. During this time, the wave of automation in most areas of professional activity resulted in several unanticipated consequences that actually increased and changed personnel work load (see Kantowitz & Campbell, 1996; Leonova, 1996). The exploding number of publications on occupational stress was accompanied by a considerable increase in subject topics covered by these studies. Today, one can observe a wide spectrum of investigations, from large-scale, demographic, and so-called "epidemiological" studies on whole populations and occupational groups (Karasek & Theorell, 1990; Kasl, 1978; Levi, Frankenhaeuser, & Gardell, 1982; Sauter, 1992), to case studies (Leonova, 1996; Schmidt & Daune, 1993; Spielberger & Reheiser, 1994b) and in-depth laboratory simulations (Broadbent, 1985; Hockey

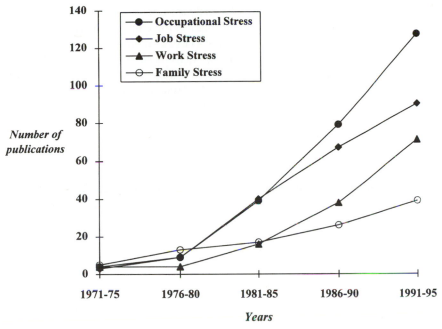

FIG. 15.1 Dynamics in publication rates in different stress-related topics during last 25 years.

& Hamilton, 1983). The majority of the publications have an overtly empirical character, and make up a rich collection of loosely connected facts, concrete methods, and research procedures that are in need of theoretical integration.

Although the findings are applicable to professional life, a generally accepted theory of occupational stress has not been developed. There is need for a clear conceptual definition, including how occupational stress relates to cognate concepts like work stress, job stress, workloads, environmental stressors, and occupational health. Several previous overviews on relevant topics began with the assumption that the basic propositions are obscure and varied, making a discussion of analyzed problems difficult. For instance, Spielberger and Reheiser (1994b, p. 20) note that "a major limitation of research on sources of stress in the workplace stems from ambiguity in the conceptual definition of occupational stress, which often differs from study to study". Working on the conceptual framework for studies of work and mental health, Warr (1994, p. 84) similarly stated: "There are many different views about the components and processes of mental health. The concept is heavy value-laden, so that a single agreed definition is unlikely to be attained".

The list of such examples can be continued. However, many authors not only noted the lack of an appropriate conceptualization of the field but also concentrated their efforts on a search for methodological solutions to this problem. These efforts have resulted in the development of different groups of explanatory models and analytical schemes for data analysis. Looking at the literature (both Western and Eastern), one can easily distinguish three main research approaches widely used in occupational stress studies: (1) Person-environment-fit approach (Caplan et al., 1975; Cox & Ferguson, 1994; Karasek & Theorell, 1990; Kasl, 1978; Levi, 1981; Warr, 1994; Zinchenko & Munipov, 1978); (2) transactional approach (Cox, 1987; Cox & Mackay 1981; Coyne & Downey, 1991; Franken-haeuser, 1986; Lazarus, 1991; Leonova, 1984; Schoenpflug, 1986; Zarakovsky & Pavlov, 1987); and (3) state-regulation approach (Appley & Trumbull, 1986; Broadbent, 1971; Gaillard & Wientjes, 1994; Gopher & Kimchi, 1989; Hockey, 1993; Leonova, 1994; Spielberger, 1972). In the subsequent sections, I attempt to analyze the types of reasoning and main findings within each of these approaches. I also try, where possible, to delineate links between them in order to identify the main perspectives on the development of a more comprehensive methodology for occupational stress research.

PERSON–ENVIRONMENT-FIT APPROACH

The development of the person–environment-fit approach began in the late 1960s to the early 1970s, when the first systematic investigations of relations between demanding work conditions and risk factors for occupational health took place (Caplan et al., 1975; Jenkins, 1991; Kasl, 1978). As Appley and Trumbull (1986, p. 9) have noted, stress research has changed since that time, shifting ". . . from laboratory studies and interpretation of catastrophic events to the full life spectrum . . . [which] brought new meaning to concepts like intensity, duration, and *normal*". Different aspects of the ordinary work situation started to be treated as stressful. The negative consequences for job performance and worker's health were considered to be a result of imbalanced interactions between a person and the specificity of work environment. A variety of socio-demographic and epidemiological studies, based on a comparison of different occupational groups, stimulated the development of an appropriate research methodology (Caplan et al., 1975; Cox & Ferguson, 1994; French, Caplan, & Van Harrison, 1982; Jenkins, 1991; Kasl, 1978; Levi, 1981).

Within this framework, occupational stress is defined in terms of job/environmental characteristics that can threaten the behavior, health, and well-being of a working person (French et al., 1982). According to this supposition, negative stress outcomes arise when individual capacities are incompatible with job/environmental demands or, in other words, when there is no longer a person-environment-fit (Cox & Ferguson, 1994; Levi et al., 1982; Warr, 1987). A schematic model of this approach is presented in Fig. 15.2.

A macro-level analysis predominates in person-environment-fit models, where "input" and "output" characteristics of stress reactions are the focus of attention for investigators. This type of analysis helps to clarify links between demanding job conditions and a multitude of negative stress outcomes caused by

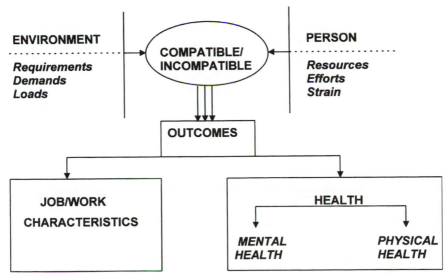

FIG. 15.2   A schematic model of person–environment-fit approach.

occupational activities (Kasl, 1978; Karasek & Theorell, 1990; Marsella, 1994; Sauter et al., 1992). The negative stress outcomes most frequently considered in empirical research can be grouped according to the following three topics: work outputs, mental health, and physical health (see Table 15.1). The data for such an approach is provided by interdisciplinary studies, which combine demographic and medical data in an attempt to provide a psychological interpretation of the observed phenomena. One can find these procedures in different surveys and reports under keywords such as "occupational health," "quality of working life," "healthy work," and so on (for representative overviews, see Caplan et al., 1975; Kasl, 1978; Karasek & Theorell, 1990).

It is not a purpose of our paper to concentrate attention on analyses of these data. Since the time of the classic work of Caplan et al. (1975), publications on

TABLE 15.1
Three groups of stress outcome indicators

Work/ job outputs	Mental health	Physical health
Productivity	Well-being	Morbidity/mortality rates
Human reliability	Job/life satisfaction	Vital signs profiles
Work behavior	Motivation	Injuries and traumas
Accident rate	Social integration	Organic diseases
Turnover	Health risk behavior	Psychosomatic disorders
Absenteeism	Negative chronic states	
Organizational climate		

related topics have appeared systematically in Western literature. Prominent contemporary reviews are presented in Karasek and Theorell (1990), Northwestern National Life review (1991), and Sauter et al. (1992). Less known but equally interesting results of occupational studies for East European countries (see, e.g. Sudakov, 1994) also cannot be discussed, but for an additional reason. At present, it is virtually impossible to differentiate the effects of occupational stress from the dramatic consequences of social and economic transformation in these countries. For the purpose of our analysis, it is important to emphasize that a common finding of most of these publications is that an employee's "burn out" under demanding job conditions has a multidimensional nature and includes parameters of work performance as well as those of mental and physical health.

The conceptualization of basic definitions in person–environment-fit models took place at the same time that empirical knowledge was being accumulated. First of all, the concept of person-environment-fit requires that principal notions such as "optimal" and "non-optimal" work be differentiated (Marsella, 1994; Warr, 1994; Zarakovsky & Pavlov, 1987). Although specialists pay more attention to analyzing the sources of negative stress outcomes, it is necessary also to understand the "optimal" or "normative" conditions in which job demands and individual capacties to cope with them are harmonized. In this sense, a set of positive outcomes could be defined in reference to indicators of high job efficiency, improved job/life satisfaction, heightened scores of well-being, and an absence of illness or health deterioration (Hacker, Fritsche, Richter, & Iwanowa, 1995; Leonova, 1994; Marsella, 1994; Warr, 1987). Marsella (1994) has summarized the findings concerning optimal and non-optimal work conditions by working out the idea of "work salutogenesis." Looking on a disposition, characterized as "salutogenic-stressful work places," he outlined a hierarchy of indicators for optimal and non-optimal work. His model includes a representation of workers' reactions on different levels, including behavioral, emotional, cognitive, interpersonal relations, mental health/well-being, and biological functioning. It is a good example of a descriptive scheme for data analysis which can be highly sufficient for the solution of many practical problems, like demarcating zones of normal versus potentially dangerous and pathogenic job environments. The criteria for adequate work redesign and stress management are particularly valued in the person–environment-fit approach (Cooper & Payne, 1988; Gopher & Kimchi, 1989; Zinchenko & Munipov, 1978).

The more implicit concepts of mental health and workers' well-being have also been substantially elaborated within the person-environment-fit approach. One of the most interesting attempts in this direction was Warr's (1987; 1994) "vitamin model." This author has shown that the term "mental health" has a complex structure, which includes five main components: affective well-being, competence, aspiration, autonomy, and integrated functioning. Each of these components can be represented by numerous psychological parameters. In view of the mostly non-linear relationships between these parameters and objective work conditions, it is useful, for predictive and preventive purposes, to determine the type of dependence between the principal features of job environment and the different components of mental health (Warr, 1994).

The "vitamin model" distinguishes nine factors as constituents of any job environment. These factors are then subdivided into two groups according to their influence on mental health, and these effects are analogous to the effects that vitamins have on physical health. The two groups are: (1) those factors which lead to a decrement in mental health, if their intensity is too low or too high (e.g. opportunity for control, opportunity for skill use, externally generated goals, variety, environmental clarity, and opportunity for interpersonal contact); and (2) those factors which have a constant negative effect on mental health when their intensity exceeds some critical level (e.g. physical security, availability of money, and valued social position). This categorization shows that specific "curvilinear" relationships exist between features of the job environment and indicators of mental health. Also, in a more general context, "this categorization appears to be useful in three main ways. It conveniently groups the principal variables; it emphasizes that we should always think of the full set, rather than concentrating only on one or two features in isolation; and it provides a framework within which we can locate sub-categories of variables" (Warr, 1994, p. 88).

The implementation of the job analysis methodology has promoted the development of the person–environment-fit approach by helping to make clear the content of "input" characteristics of the job environment (e.g. job demands, work loads, requirements to personnel). Two different paradigms are used for this purpose. The first one is oriented towards a precise analysis of each concrete job situation. Appropriate methods were created for such a purpose in different traditions, and are widely used in applied studies. For example, the Activity Evaluation System is used by German authors (Hacker et al., 1995), and similar "professiographic" procedures are used in Russian research (Zinchenko & Munipov, 1978; Zarakovsky & Pavlov, 1987). In the second paradigm, the intention is to give a more general description of the job situation (Algera, 1988). Such methods are based on revealing the major dimensions of a variety of job/ task characteristics including their subjective meaning for workers (Karasek, 1978; Karasek & Theorell, 1990). The Job Characteristics Model by Hackman and Oldham (1980) is one of the best known examples of these methods. This model distinguishes five main dimensions of job/task characteristics: (1) skill variety; (2) task variety; (3) task significance; (4) autonomy; and (5) feedback. The clarity and empirical validity of this model makes it especially attractive to applied stress research (Duncham, 1976; Marsella, 1994; Schmidt & Daune, 1993).

Unfortunately, even the advanced version of the person–environment-fit approach cannot provide answers to many questions arising in the applied setting. The main weakness in this approach is the gap in the methodological description of links between the stress precursors, defined by environmental demands and individual capacities, and the postponed effects, outwardly presented in performance and health indicators. In fact, the interaction between a person and his/her environment is postulated but not specially analyzed using this approach. Particularly, the "compatibility/incompatibility" component involved in assessing actualized human resources has never been operationally defined (see Fig. 15.2). This problem cannot be solved by lengthening the list of "input" characteristics (i.e. by including some additional information about individuals, such as sex, age, education, and personality traits). Instead, the role of these characteristics in developing stress reactions has to be further clarified.

This position can be exemplified by various data from recent empirical studies. For instance, Schmidt and Daune (1993) applied the Job Characteristics Model for predicting negative stress outcomes, such as turnover. The study was carried out with a group of blue-collar workers (n = 120) in a medium-sized car supply factory. An index of turnover was correlated with indicators of the main job characteristics from the model, and, in addition, with several demographic parameters (age, job tenure, martial status) and one personality variable (growth need strength, GNS). In general, the data showed that direct links between turnover and job characteristics were rather weak; a significant correlation was found only for the index of job autonomy ($\alpha = -0.25$, $p < 0.01$). On the other hand, significant correlations ($p < 0.01$) were found between turnover and demographic characteristics, and turnover and GNS. Differences were also found in correlational links among the subjects with high and low GNS. In the group of workers with the high level of GNS, several correlations between turnover and job characteristics were significant, while in the opposite group, no significant correlations were found. Thus, the study clearly demonstrated the mediating effects of individual characteristics on turnover, especially on the personality and motivational variables.

Recently, researchers have started to treat personal characteristics and motivational attitudes as moderator variables that define the type of stress response (Cox & Ferguson, 1994; Parkes, 1994). The influence of these variables cannot be considered in a simplified manner, as some additional source of increasing efforts, mental strain, or exhaustion of internal resources. In a flow of activity regulation, the processes such as goal orientation, subjective appraisal of the situation, life/work preferences, and expectations, individual characteristics change relationships between "input" and "output" components of stress reactions (Frese, 1986; Johanssen & Gardell, 1988; Lazarus, 1991; Parkes, 1994). A more precise analysis of these interactive processes at the level of an acting person is beyond the scope of the person–environment-fit approach. The "transactional" or "cognitive" models of stress have been developed to suit this specific purpose.

TRANSACTIONAL APPROACH

At this time, the transactional approach may well be the most developed conceptual framework in applied stress research. In the famous work by Lazarus (1966), a new perspective on the nature of psychological stress was proposed.

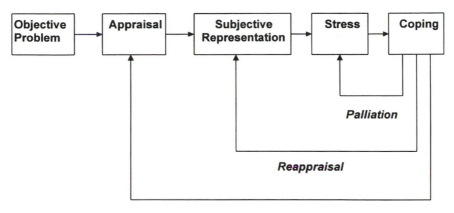

Problem Solving

FIG. 15.3 Synopsis of cognitive stress theories. From "Behavior Economics as an Approach to Stress Theory," by W. Schoenpflug, 1986, in *Dynamics of Stress* (pp. 81–97), M. H. Appley & R. Trumbull (Eds.), New York: Plenum Press. Copyright 1986 by *name of copyright holder*. Reprinted with permission.

The focus of interest was shifted to individual susceptibility and different modes of coping with stress. This orientation differs substantially from the classical descriptions of stress in terms of homeostatic mechanisms and the incongruity of environmental requirements and internal resources (cf., for example, Selye, 1976). By considering the stress reaction to be a result of "what the individual demands of himself" (Lazarus, 1966, p. 296), researchers began to concentrate on pathways that link the situation and observed stress reactions to subjective needs and values, mental representation of the problem, and an individual's "ability to cope effectively with the perceived threat" (Appley & Trumbull, 1986, p. 11).

The processes of subjective representation and cognitive appraisal of a situation played a central role in Lazarus' (1966, 1991) model of psychological stress. This model stimulated the development of cognitive theories of stress as part of the transactional approach (Lehman, 1972). One of the best examples of this development is the behavior economics approach proposed by Schoenpflug (1986). This researcher extended and operationalized some of the basic propositions of the earlier cognitive models (see Fig. 15.3).

In cognitive models, stress is considered to be a process of interactions between the person and the situation in which he/she acts. As a result of a "subjective interpretation" of the situation, an individual repertoire of coping strategies is generated. Depending on the adequacy of actualized coping mechanisms, one can observe positive ("getting over" stress) or negative (prolonging and intensifying the stress) solutions to the subject's problem. Insufficient coping leads to further iterations or changes in the stress-processing operations (e.g. reappraisal, new mental representation of the problem, detection of additional threats, etc.) through feedback loops. An accumulation of negative stress outcomes often takes place in the course of such iterative processing, demonstrating deterioration in mental health and aggravation of behavioral disorders (Coyne & Downey, 1991; Frankenhaeuser, 1986; Siegrist & Peter, 1994).

One type of transactional model has been proposed by Cox and co-workers (Cox, 1987; Cox & Mackay, 1981). This model is suitable for practical applications, and incorporates elements of the person-environment-fit approach. The input characteristics (job/situational demands and support, actual internal resources and individual values/motives) are considered to be initial interactive variables that can be evaluated from the point of view of their "balance" or "imbalance." The addition of the subjective appraisal component provides an opportunity to analyze observed stress reactions in psychological terms; for instance, by describing the nature of conflicts in actualized motivation and emotional attitudes.

The use of this model is productive for different purposes. First of all, it provides an impetus for creating new diagnostic methods (Cox & Ferguson, 1994; Parkes, 1994). Secondly, this model can be used as an analytic scheme for the interpretation of empirical data, including information obtained in field studies. We attempted to use this model to interpret findings of several investigations of fire-fighting jobs, especially with specialists who had participated in the liquidation of large-scale conflagration and fire accidents (Leonova, Maryin, & Lovchan, 1996).

Fire-fighting jobs are extremely demanding. Typical stress factors in this profession are the high-risk environment, excessive physical overloads, time limits, strong social expectations and control over quality of work, task complexity, unpredictability of the situation, high level of responsibility, and personal involvement (Maryin & Sobolev, 1990; Leonova et al., 1996). Based on each of these factors, we were not surprised to find fire-fighters' occupational health to be at a problematic level. It has been shown, for example, that their sick rate increases gradually over time. Specifically, fire-fighters who serve for more than 7 to 10 years fall ill 2.5 to 3 times more frequently than those who serve under 3 years. The rate of cardiovascular disease among fire-fighters is approximately 1.7 times higher than in the same age group in the general population (Maryin, Lovchan, & Ephanova, 1992; Leonova et al., 1996).

Although these trends seem dramatic, they are comparable to the statistics for other high-demand occupational groups (e.g. medical doctors and police officers; see Sudakov, 1994). More dangerous and unexpected is the impact that this job has on mental health and social/behavioral adaptation. For instance, the suicide rate in fire-fighters corresponds to the number of servicemen who have died as a result of fire accidents, and this rate has the potential for further growth. Also, approximately 50% of the personnel were found to have family problems, 37% had problems with alcohol consumption, and 43% had little contact with friends or manifested social disintegration in other ways (Alexandrovsky, Lobastov,

TABLE 15.2
Rates of mental health deterioration depending
on the type of fire-fighting jobs

Type of job	Rates of mental deterioration (in %)			
	Border states, behavioral accentuation	Neurosis and psychosomatic disorders	Clinical forms of mental diseases	Total
Large-scale accidents (n = 53)	28.3	52.8	13.2	94.3
"Ordinary" fires (n = 40)	22.5	15.1	2.5	40.1

Spivak, & Schukin, 1991; Maryin et al., 1992). Behavioral and mental disorders observed in fire-fighters range from short-term behavioral deviations (impulsive actions, affective reactions, etc.) and border states (asthenic syndrome, neurotic reactions), to clinical forms of mental diseases (mainly depression and reactive psychosis; see Alexandrovsky et al., 1991).

To some extent, the manifestation of mental and behavioral disorders depends on the type of fire-fighting job. In a recent study (Maryin et al., 1992), two groups of fire-fighters were examined using medico-psychological screening. These two groups were: (1) fire-fighters who systematically participated in large-scale fire accidents (so called "liquidators"; n = 53); and (2) fire-fighters who participated in relatively "ordinary" fires ("firemen"; n = 40). Though a number of symptoms were found in both groups, the group of liquidators had more difficulties. About 90% of them had mental health problems, 66% of which could be qualified as illnesses (see Table 15.2). The difference between the groups shows that increasing the complexity of the job leads to a breakdown in mechanisms used for psychological adaptation. This is interesting, considering the fact that liquidators have a higher level of professional expertise and better protective equipment.

To identify reasons for such pronounced negative effects on mental health, we used a modified version of Cox's transactional model to analyze the psychological risk factors for liquidators who had worked in the Chernobyl Zone in 1992–1994 (i.e. more than 5 years after the disaster; Leonova et al., 1996). This analysis revealed conflict between subjective appraisals, represented by the incongruity of job-oriented motivation and basic safety needs. A personal commitment to work and persistent feelings of individual defenselessness with respect to "evil radiation" came into conflict and led to serious psychological problems. Since there were no resources available to cope with this problem during the work and even after it, stress reactions became a regular occurrence, and caused a variety of problems with respect to reliable job performance and mental health.

TABLE 15.3
Manifestations of acute stress symptoms in the fire-fighting
shift depending on anticipation of environmental dangers

	Percent of acute stress symptoms		
Fire accident	Physiological	Mental	Behavioral
Nuclear power plant	36	48	16
Electrical power plant	16	21	8

The validity of this explanation can be further illustrated by the data on stress reactions in situations with different levels of risk predictability. The frequency of acute stress symptoms experienced by liquidators was measured during fire-fighting shifts in two accidents: (1) after a further accident at the Chernobyl Nuclear Power Plant; and (2) in a large conflagration at the Smolensky Electrical Power Plant (Leonova et al., 1996). The three different groups of acute stress symptoms evaluated were physiological, mental, and behavioral (see Table 15.3).

A comparison of the data obtained at the two accidents indicated that the personnel in the Chernobyl liquidator troop experienced an average of twice the acute stress symptoms than the fire-fighters who worked at the Smolensky Electrical Power Plant. This difference was not related to the gravity of the accidents: the Chernobyl accident was a rather minor one, and the troop arrived at the accident site 4 days after it began; on the other hand, the Smolensky conflagration was a large disaster where the liquidators worked in the open fire. It seems that the presence of invisible radiation danger, and the uncertainty about the developing situation in the Chernobyl Zone were more stressful for the professionals than the heavier work in more predictable conditions. Thus, "the person's subjective model of work environment" (Cox & Ferguson, 1994, p. 100) was found to have an overwhelming influence on the stress reaction.

Although transactional models are better suited to an analysis of everyday work stressors than are classical theories, their simplified versions are not comprehensive enough to provide an understanding of the complex interplay of sociopsychological and physiological events (Coyne & Downey, 1991; French et al., 1982). New paradigms have to be developed for these purposes. For instance, in longitudinal studies a methodology of "widespread netting" (Leonova, 1996) can be implemented. This methodology includes several aspects of occupational stress research:

1. *Detailed job analysis* which provides a description of the work demands that may evoke stress reactions (Algera, 1988; Salvendy et al., 1987; Warr, 1994).
2. *Multidimensional assessment* which is needed to evaluate various manifestations of stress and their effects on performance and health (Cox, 1985; 1987; Frankenhaeuser, 1986; Leonova, 1994).

3. *Integrative description* of data in order to reveal relationships between heterogeneous facts and events (Cox & Ferguson, 1994; Hockey & Hamilton, 1983; Leonova, 1993; Parkes, 1994).
4. *Dynamic patterns of change* over time that help to differentiate situational reactions from stable tendencies in adaptation and coping (Johanssen & Gardell, 1988; Leonova, 1996; Siegrist & Peter, 1994).

This methodology was used in one of our longitudinal studies with operator managers who worked in a complex telecommunication network (Leonova, 1993; 1996). A group of thirty-one well-educated and highly experienced specialists was followed for more than 6 years in their real work conditions. The automated control system was modernized during the course of this study, and this produced substantial changes in the operator's job. Before modernization, the operators worked in a semi-automated regime where the routine functions of monitoring and control were dominant. The implementation of new computerized technology placed the operator in a supervisory position, whereby functions of decision making and strategy planning became dominant.

The effects of job modernization were evaluated by the multidimensional assessment of performance, psychological manifestations, and health outcomes. For this purpose five main groups of indicators were used: parameters of job performance; indexes of job satisfaction; manifestations of current psychological state; indicators of chronic negative states; and symptoms of psychosomatic disorders. Three sets of data were collected during the following 3 critical periods: (1) 9 to 12 months before modernization; (2) 6 to 8 months after the installation of the new equipment (i.e. during adaptation to the new job conditions); and (3) 18 to 20 months after completion of modernization. The dynamics of the measured indicators during these 3 stages are presented in Table 15.4.

A kind of dissociation of the indicators can easily be discovered in the data. All parameters of job performance and work satisfaction significantly improved after the implementation of new technology. However, this improvement was paradoxically associated with increased emotional strain, an accumulation of chronic negative states, and health deterioration (particularly in the cardiovascular domain). These dynamic changes were provoked by major modification in groups of job-related stress factors at the different stages of job modernization.

In the initial stage of the study, the stressful work environment contributed mainly to a fatigue–boredom syndrome, which is typical for jobs in semi-automated systems (Kantowitz & Campbell, 1996; Salvendy et al., 1987). This syndrome is characterized by feelings of monotony, fatigue, and a lowered state of well-being. After modernization, the enriched job content and more efficient tools reduced the monotonous and exhaustive workloads, but the more demanding cognitive tasks and personal responsibility for critical decisions became important sources of job stress. The inherent conflict between the enrichment of job content and the increased cognitive complexity produced the emotional

TABLE 15.4
Changes in indicators of work performance, job satisfaction,
psychological states and health in a group of operator-
managers during different stages of job modernization

Measures/indicators	Trends in dynamics	Significance
Work outputs		
Productivity	positive	$p < 0.001$
Speed	positive	$p < 0.001$
Errors	positive	$p < 0.001$
Job satisfaction	positive	$p < 0.05$
(General index)		
Current psychological states		
Well-being	none	—
Emotional tension	negative	$p < 0.01$
Acute fatigue	none	—
Monotony	positive	$p < 0.05$
Negative chronic states		
Prolonged stress reactions	negative	$p < 0.05$
Chronic fatigue	none	—
Trait anxiety	negative	$p < 0.05$
Psychosomatic symptoms		
Cardiovascular	negative	$p < 0.05$
Gastric	none	—
Neurotic	none	—
Hormonal	none	—

NOTES:
    Trends in dynamics for each indicator were evaluated by one-way
ANOVA design; $n = 31$, $df = 2/30$ (for more details, see Leonova, 1996).

hypermobilization which forces adaptation to greater psychological requirements. However, when the non-stop emotional hypermobilization is coupled with an inadequate release, the result is a chronic imbalance in basic regulatory mechanisms, both emotional and somatic (Frankenhaeuser, 1986; Siegrist & Peter, 1994).

These examples of field studies were presented and analyzed in the framework of a transactional approach. The results demonstrate that negative stress outcomes originate from the conflicting nature of human responses in the job situation. The data also indicate that there are a variety of qualitatively different stress forms. If we want to know more about the microstructure of coping strategies and their dynamics, it is important to look more precisely at the flow of activity regulation underlying overt stress manifestations (Gaillard & Wientjes, 1994; House, 1981; Hockey, 1993). Activity regulation has to be considered from the perspective of its multilevel organization, in a tight interplay of behavior with motivation, cognition, and available operational resources (Leont'ev, 1981).

This type of research is the main concern of the third major approach to the study of occupational stress.

STATE-REGULATION APPROACH

The state-regulation approach is perhaps the oldest method used in applied psychological studies (Appley & Trumbull, 1986; Cox & Mackay, 1981; Zinchenko & Munipov, 1978). It originated in the tradition of work and engineering psychology, where attempts are made to analyze different types of worker's states—fatigue, monotony, vigilance, physical and mental overloads, etc. (Gopher & Kimchi, 1989; Zarakovsky & Pavlov, 1987). The early "organism versus environment" debate led to a simplified understanding of the notion of "state" as a combination of physiological reactions and subjective feelings. This understanding was justifiably criticized in the literature (see, for instance, Cox & Mackay, 1981) because to some extent, it restricted the use of the "state" concept in contemporary models of occupational stress. Since then, several new approaches to the analysis of human states have been developed (for review, see Hockey et al., 1986; Gopher & Kimchi, 1989; Leonova, 1994; Sanders, 1983). All of these approaches are based on deeper insights into regulatory mechanisms of actual human activity.

In the state-regulation approach, particular attention is given to the process of actualization of individual resources in the concrete situation that defines the choice of coping mechanism. Work efficiency and current socio-motivational feedback also have greater value in this case. Comparing a transactional model ("job-strain model" by Karasek, 1978) and a state-regulation model ("effort–reward imbalance model"), Siegrist and Peter (1994, p. 132) note that the difference between them "concerns the role of personal coping characteristics . . . The amount of an individual's efforts spent at work is not simply a function of the intensity and quality of external demands, but demand appraisal and energy mobilization are modulated by motivational states of the individual . . . Thus, we assume that the combined effect of extrinsic workload and of intrinsic effort due to the coping pattern "high need for control" is the critical in triggering distress and autonomic arousal under conditions of low reward".

Cognitive and energetic aspects of the ways in which people attempt to manage their work are analyzed in a multilevel state-regulation framework, inspired by Donald Broadbent (1971; 1985). In Hockey's (1993) control model of demand-management, the idea of having two levels of control mechanisms was operationally defined. It was shown that the functional structure of task execution changes under the influence of alterations in internal loads and individual task goals. These changes are described by a shift from low-level control operations to a higher control level that includes so-called "supervisory controler" and "effort monitor" mechanisms when the situation becomes more complex. Based on a higher control level, performance strategies become more

TABLE 15.5

Changes in memory search strategies in several stress inducing situations

Stress Inducing Situation (SIS)	Linear equations of reaction time in Sternberg-type of memory search task		Dynamics in memory search strategies
	Beginning of SIS	End of SIS	
Fatigue in prolonged working shift (desk-top operators)	$RT(+) = 417 + 93n$ $RT(-) = 484 + 101n$	$RT(+) = 498 + 48n$ $RT(-) = 527 + 99n$	Exhaustive successive search $\rightarrow$ Self-terminating successive search
Emotional distortion by examination stress (university students)	$RT(+) = 463 + 38n$ $RT(-) = 509 + 59n$	$RT(+) = 427 + 37n$ $RT(-) = 501 + 78n$	Mixed search strategy $\rightarrow$ Self-terminating successive search
Positive mobilization by examination stress (university students)	$RT(+) = 451 + 38n$ $RT(-) = 523 + 41n$	$RT(+) = 483 + 11n$ $RT(-) = 561 + 40n$	Exhaustive successive search $\rightarrow$ Trend toward parallel processing mode

NOTES:

According to the Sternberg model, coefficients of linear equations of reaction time ($RT = a + bn$, where 'n' is the size of memory set) were used as predictors of the type of actualized memory search strategy. The strategies are differentiated by the relative size of 'a' and 'b' coefficients in probes with positive (RT+) and negative (RT−) responses (for more details, see Sternberg, 1975).

The trend toward parallel processing mode was identified according to Zinchenko, Velichkovsky, & Vuchetich (1980).

"costly" from the point of view of applied attentional resources (Broadbent 1985; Kahneman, 1973). This model can be used to explain patterns of performance deterioration and consequent impacts on mental health observed in real life situations (Hockey, 1993; Hockey & Hamilton, 1983; Schoenpflug, 1986).

The most important issue for the state-regulation approach is the development of sensitive methods for assessing human states. The analysis of changes in microstructure of cognitive processes has been successfully used for this purpose (Broadbent, 1985; Leonova, 1993; Sternberg, 1981, Wierwille, Rahimi, & Casali, 1985). It has been shown that specific stressors can selectively affect different stages of human information processing (Broadbent, 1985; Eysenck, 1982; Leonova, 1994). For instance, the effects of fatigue on symbolic information processing in short-term memory (according to the multistore memory model, Atkinson & Shiffrin, 1971) seem to be mainly related to distortions in control operations such as rehearsal, simple serialization, and processing in working memory (Zinchenko, Leonova & Strelkov, 1985). Other types of stressors have distinct effects on the same processing system. For example, monotony affects the operations of recovery and masking of information in sensory memory, phonologic encoding, and preparation of a motor response. Also, negative emotional strains destroy the retrieval operations and organization of motor responses. All these facts were obtained from both laboratory experiments and field studies of operator and clerical jobs (Leonova, 1984; 1993).

A further illustration of the microstructural changes, in terms of shifts in control operations and required mental efforts, is connected with applications of the Sternberg memory search task (e.g. Sternberg, 1975). It is well established that the task is usually solved by using a sequential exhaustive search which is stable, fast, and the most "economic" among the other successive search strategies (Sternberg, 1975; Zinchenko, Velichkovsky, & Vuchetich, 1980). Nevertheless, empirical data suggest that different stressors can influence the priority of this strategy, as summarized in Table 15.5. For example, the state of fatigue after depleted working shifts can be associated with a different dominant strategy, such as the exhaustive self-terminating search (Leonova, 1994). This is a more costly strategy because it requires the utilization of additional conscious resources. Negative emotional strains (for example, stress caused by a difficult examination) produced a deterioration in search strategies, and influenced the process of decision making. On the other hand, positive emotional mobilization in the same situation strengthened the optimal search strategy and even gave impetus to a more efficient, parallel processing mode (Gordon, 1988).

It is obvious that diagnostic properties of cognitive methods have to be validated. In the literature, one can find several structural cognitive tests that are sensitive to particular effects of workloads and are implemented in practice (Derrick, 1988; Leonova, 1993; Schlegel, Gilliland, & Schlegel, 1987; Wierwille et al., 1985). More comprehensive than traditional performance tests, these methods enrich the psychological interpretation of stress types and of evoked coping mechanisms. The same tendency is observed in the development of more satisfactory subjective tests, such as structural checklists, subjective scales, and questionnaires (for review, see Cox & Ferguson, 1994; Leonova, 1993; Marsella, 1994; Spielberger & Reheiser, 1994a). The following factors are presented in all contemporary subjective tests: (1) Symptoms of subjective well-being and physiological discomfort; (2) emotional reactions and dominant affective tone; (3) main motivational orientation; and (4) personality and attitudes towards the situation.

In theory, almost all authors consider "human state" to be an integrative concept. A necessity to analyze worker's states in a multidimensional way (i.e. in terms of specific syndromes) was declared in practical work long ago (Simonson & Weiser, 1976; Zinchenko & Munipov, 1978). In contemporary research, this orientation is realized in attempts to coordinate various symptoms and state manifestations with different levels of activity regulation (Cox & Ferguson, 1994; Gopher & Kimchi, 1989; Hockey & Hamilton, 1983; Leonova, 1994; Marsella, 1994). Accordingly, the inclusion of a number of tests in diagnostic procedures will produce information about a measured state on several levels, including: (1) energetic support of activity (physiological and psychophysiological measures); (2) mental/cognitive functioning (cognitive tests); (3) subjective/reflexive evaluation (subjective tests); and (4) task performance and job outputs.

Despite the development of more sophisticated diagnostic procedures, the problem of integrative evaluation of states is not yet solved. After decades of debate, it has been shown only that an integrative diagnostic solution cannot be found by means of any single method or some universal "formula" (Hockey & Hamilton, 1983; Zinchenko, Leonova, & Strelkov, 1985). It seems that a more constructive method lies in classifying the types of diagnostic tasks, supported by a selection of formal procedures suitable for integrating the initial sets of indicators. Three typical classes of applied diagnostic tasks can be set apart (see, for example, Gopher & Kimchi, 1989; Leonova, 1993; Zarakovsky & Pavlov, 1987) and stated in the following questions:

1. Are the worker's states similar or different (e.g. in comparison with a "normal" or "normative" state)?
2. Are the worker's states changing over time (e.g. are there dynamics in work ability or acute stress reactions)?
3. What is the worker's state (e.g. what we can say about the concrete form of fatigue, emotional mobilization, distress, or monotony)?

The differences between these tasks becomes obvious if one looks specifically at their content. In the first case, it is necessary only to compare two states without any deep qualitative characteristic; in the second case, to define the main tendency in changes over time; and in the third case, to give an indepth description of the state's syndrome by explaining the relationships between different symptoms. The type of solutions for each of these tasks can be called "strategies of data integration" (Leonova, 1993).

The first strategy is needed only to detect either the similarity or the difference between states (usually an "optimal" prototype and the state), developed in critical work conditions. Differentiation of the states is usually carried out using rough empirical scales such as "positive–negative," or "allowed–prohibited." Such estimations are useful when general indexes of job complexity, health and well-being status, or quality of work conditions have to be evaluated. Justification of need and general directions of job optimization can be worked out using this method (Hacker et al., 1995; Zarakovsky & Pavlov, 1987; Zinchenko & Munipov, 1978).

The second strategy is used most frequently. It is related to estimations of state dynamics at different times: in the course of an actual stress episode, over shifts, during a working day, or more prolonged stress effects observed in longitudinal studies (Gaillard & Wientjes, 1994; Leonova, 1996; Levi et al., 1982). The goal is to reveal the main trends and to fix gradual stages in change beyond variability in isolated stress indicators. A summary of dynamic parameters is usually determined using trend analysis and regression statistics (Derrick, 1988; Wierwille et al., 1985). This method of integration is helpful for the reorganization of temporal and intensive structure of workloads. This is done, for example, by improving "work–rest" schedules or by preparing timetable programs for preventive and psychotherapeutic interventions (Leonova & Kouznetcova, 1993; Schreus, Winnubst, & Cooper, 1996).

Finally, the third strategy concerns an indepth characterization of states. A qualitative specification of the state syndrome includes structural patterning of symptoms and its psychological interpretation. This problem does not involve simple labeling or categorization of states in general terms such as "fatigue," "emotional stress," or "optimal state." Coordination of changes in or between different state indicators uses a whole picture of actualized regulatory processes for reconstruction. This helps to explain an individual's method of adaptation to a current situation. Depiction of main factors (or vectors) in the multidimensional representation of a state syndrome provides the basis for an integrative solution (Derrick, 1988; Hockey, 1993; Leonova, 1996). This diagnostic orientation is closer to the needs of the state-regulation approach to occupational stress.

"Sketch maps" (Hockey & Hamilton, 1983) give an opportunity to realize this strategy with qualitative characteristics. The formal methods of data structuralization (factor analysis, cluster analysis, multidimensional scaling) make the qualitative diagnosis much more substantiated. For instance, these methods can be successfully applied in our longitudinal study with operator managers of a telecommunication network that has been discussed above in connection with the transactional approach (Leonova, 1996). The data obtained on the effects of job modernization on the different states were first standardized and then

A. Before modernization
(2-D solution, Kruskal's stress formula 1, p < 0.019)

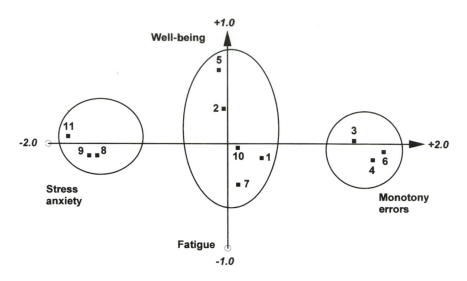

B. After modernization
(1-D solution, Kruskal's stress formula 1, p < 0.026)

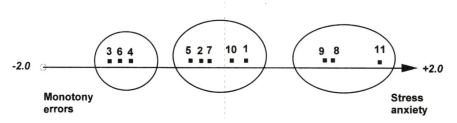

FIG. 15.4 Structural representation of indicators of operator manager's states at the different stages of job modernization by the means of multidimensional scaling (Euclidean model). 1 = productivity; 2 = speed; 3 = errors; 4 = job satisfaction; 5 = actual well-being; 6 = monotony; 7 = acute fatigue; 8 = state anxiety; 9 = trait anxiety; 10 = chronic fatigue; 11 = prolonged stress reactions.

processed using multidimensional scaling. Some of the results of this analysis are presented in Fig. 15.4.

One can easily see that these "space-state" representations allow us to confirm the hypothesis that there is a transformation of stress syndromes at different stages of the described technological innovation. At the beginning of the study (i.e. "before modernization"), the measured indicators of functional states were located in a two-dimensional space. The distribution of parameters between two vectors, "monotony versus anxiety" and "well-being versus fatigue," corresponds to the prevalence of the fatigue-boredom syndrome. In the condition "after modernization," the structural representation of the "space-state" changed. All indicators changed to a unidimensional scale, and the manifestations of prolonged overstrain and anxiety took over the dominant position.

The recent achievements of the state-regulation approach are grounded in better psychological methods of stress management and stress prevention. In addition to earlier tasks using ergonomic and organizational redesign of the work environment, contemporary occupational research pays more attention to individualized procedures used to cope with stress (Alexandrovsky et al., 1991; Jenkins, 1991; Karasek & Theorell, 1990; Lazarus, 1991). Specialized techniques of stress management can be used not only in individual psychological consulting, but also as a part of larger training and health assistance programs (Hamberger & Lohr, 1984; Leonova & Kouznetcova, 1993; Schreus et al., 1996). The applicability of these efforts depends on the quality of basic psychological concepts and their professional implementation in practical settings.

CONCLUSIONS

In this chapter, I have presented an overview of the major approaches to occupational stress that co-exist in contemporary literature. Rather than consider them to be contradictory and competing, I should like to emphasize the fact that each approach represents a different stage of research and is directed towards different aspects of stress mechanisms:

1. The person–environment-fit models provide a macro-outlook of occupational stress and give a global description of risk factors, by linking together sources and negative consequences of the stress experience.
2. The transactional models show the intermediate methods used to analyze an individual vulnerability to stress and to enhance psychological management of stress initiation and coping strategies.
3. The state-regulation approach presents a microanalysis of individual modes of adaptation and helps to develop powerful diagnostic tools for integrative stress assessment.

The big picture will not change much in the future, although new emphases and directions are possible. Longitudinal studies will certainly play a more important role because they provide the best opportunity to assimilate requests and facilities of different approaches. Phenomena such as the dissociative influence of human functional states on some but not other mechanisms of activity regulation will receive increasing attention (Leonova, 1996; Proffitt et al., 1995). Improvment in methodology will make possible questions about interactions with non-occupational stress sources (as rooted in ecology, social life, and family events), and will lead to an increasing number of around-the-clock stress studies (Richter & Rohlandt, 1996). It should also become possible to implement the state-trait paradigm for analyzing changes in temperament and even changes in personality, a negative stress consequence that has seldom been examined empirically (see Spielberger, 1972; Rodina & Leonova, 1987). Besides an enrichment of knowledge necessary for practical work, this research will stimulate solutions to basic psychological problems (e.g. concepts of adaptation, motivation and personality, and cognitive architecture) more applicable to real-life human experience.

ACKNOWLEDGEMENTS

Thanks are due to John Adair, Fergus Craik, and Charles Spielberger for valuable editorial comments as well as to our co-workers for their contribution to the described investigations. Our studies in occupational stress and health have been supported by the Commission of European Community (INTAS 93–3493, Brussels), Dutch Foundation for Advancement of Scientific Research (NWO, den Hague), and the Russian State Institute for Medico-Biological Problems (IMBP, Moscow).

REFERENCES

Algera, J. A. (1988). Task analysis and new technologies. In V. de Keyser, T. Qvale, B. Wilpert, & S. A. R. Quintanilla (Eds.), *The meaning of work and technological options* (pp. 131–145). Chichester, UK: Wiley.

Alexandrovsky, Yu. A., Lobastov, O. S., Spivak, L. I., & Schukin, B. P. (1991). *Psichogenicheskie rasstroistva v extremal'nych usloviyach* [Psychogenic disorders in extreme conditions]. Moscow: Medicina.

Appley, M. H., & Trumbull, R. (1986). Development of the stress concept. In M. H. Appley & R. Trumbull (Eds.), *Dynamics of stress* (pp. 3–18). New York: Plenum Press.

Atkinson, R. C., & Shiffrin, R. M. (1971). The control of short-term memory. *Scientific American*, *225*, 82–90.

Broadbent, D. E. (1971). *Decision and stress*. New York: Academic Press.

Broadbent, D. E. (1985). The clinical impact of job design. *British Journal of Clinical Psychology*, *24*, 33–44.

Caplan, R. D., Cobb, S., French, J. R. P., Van Harrison, R., & Pinneau, S. R. (1975). *Job demands and worker health*. Washington, DC: US Government Printing Office.

Cooper, C. L., & Payne, R. (Eds.). (1988). *Causes, coping, and consequences of stress*. Chichester, UK: Wiley.

Cox, T. (1985). The nature and measurement of stress. *Ergonomics*, *28*, 1155–1163.

Cox, T. (1987). Stress, coping, and problem solving. *Work and Stress*, *1*, 5–14.

Cox, T., & Ferguson, E. (1994). Measurement of the subjective work environment. *Work and Stress*, *8*, 98–109.

Cox, T., & Mackay, C. (1981). A transactional approach to occupational stress. In E. N. Corlett & J. Richardson (Eds.), *Stress, work design, and productivity* (pp. 91–113). Chichester, UK: Wiley.

Coyne, J., & Downey, G. (1991). Social factors and psychopathology: Stress support and coping processes. *Annual Review of Psychology*, *41*, 401–425.

Derrick, W. L. (1988). Dimensions of operator workload. *Human Factors*, *30*, 95–110.

Duncham, R. B. (1976). The measurement and dimensionality of job characteristics. *Journal of Applied Psychology*, *61*, 404–409.

Eysenck, M. W. (1982). *Attention and arousal: Cognition and performance*. Heidelberg: Springer.

Frankenhaeuser, M. (1986). A psychobiological framework for research on human stress and coping. In M. H. Appley & R. Trumbull (Eds.), *Dynamics of stress* (pp. 101–116). New York: Plenum Press.

French, J. R. P., Caplan, R. D., & Van Harrison, R. (1982). *The mechanisms of job stress and strain*. Chichester, UK: Wiley.

Frese, M. (1986). Coping as a moderator and mediator between stress at work and psychosomatic complaints. In M. H. Appley & R. Trumbull (Eds.), *Dynamics of stress* (pp. 183–206). New York: Plenum Press.

Gaillard, A. W. K., & Wientjes, C. J. E. (1994). Mental load and work stress as two types of energy mobilization. *Work and Stress*, *8*, 141–152.

Gopher, D., & Kimchi, R. (1989). Engineering psychology. *Annual Review of Psychology*, *40*, 431–455.

Gordon, I. V. (1988). Vliaynie kachestvenno raznorodnych nagruzok na processy opoznaniya v kratkovremennoi pamayti [Influence of heterogeneous loads on recognition in short-term memory]. *Ergonomics: Proceedings of All-Russian Institute of Technical Design*, *27*, 90–103.

Hacker, W., Fritsche, B., Richter, P., & Iwanowa, A. (1995). *Taetigkeits-Bewertungssystem (TBS): Verfahren zur Analyse, Bewertung und Gestaltung von Arbeitstaetigkeiten* [Activity evaluation system (TBS): Procedures of analysis, evaluation and design of work activities]. Stuttgart: Teubner.

Hackman, J. R., & Oldham, G. R. (1980). *Work redesign*. Reading, MA: Addison-Wesley.

Hamberger, L. K., & Lohr, J. M. (1984). *Stress and stress management*. New York: Springer.

Hockey, G. R. J. (1993). Cognitive-energetical control mechanisms in the management of work demands and psychological health. In A. Baddeley & L. Weisnkrantz (Eds.), *Attention, selection, awareness, and control: A tribute to Donald Broadbent* (pp. 328–345). Oxford: Clarendon Press.

Hockey, G. R. J., Gaillard, A. W. K., & Coles, M. G. H. (Eds.). (1986). *Energetics and human information processing*. Dordrecht: Nijhoff.

Hockey, G. R. J., & Hamilton, P. (1983). The cognitive patterning of stress states. In G. R. L. Hockey (Ed.), *Stress and fatigue in human performance* (pp. 331–362). New York: Academic Press.

House, J. S. (1981). *Work stress and social support*. Reading, MA: Addison-Wesley.

Jenkins, R. (1991). Demographic aspects of stress. In C. L. Cooper & R. Payne (Eds.), *Personality and stress: Individual differences in the stress process* (pp. 107–132). Chichester, UK: Wiley.

Johanssen, G., & Gardell, B. (1988). Work–health relations as mediated through stress reactions and job socialization. In S. Maers (Ed.), *Topics in health psychology* (pp. 271–285). Chichester, UK: Wiley.

Kahneman, D. (1973). *Attention and effort*. Englewood Cliffs, NJ: Prentice Hall.

Kantowitz, B., & Campbell, J. L. (1996). Pilot workload and flightdeck automation. In R. Parasuranam & M. Mouloua (Eds.), *Automation and human performance* (pp. 117–136). Hillsdale, NJ: Lawrence Erlbaum Associates.

Karasek, R. A. (1978). Job demands, job decision latitude and mental strain: Implications for job redesign. *Administrative science quarterly*, *24*, 285–308.

Karasek, R., & Theorell, T. (1990). *Healthy work, stress, productivity, and the reconstruction of working life*. New York: Basic Books.

Kasl, S. V. (1978). Epidemiological contributions to the study of work stress. In C. L. Cooper & R. Payne (Eds.), *Stress at work* (pp. 3–48). Chichester, UK: Wiley.

Lazarus, R. S. (1966). *Psychological stress and the coping process.* New York: McGraw-Hill.

Lazarus, R. S. (1991). *Emotion and adaptation.* New York: Oxford University Press.

Lehman, E. C. (1972). An empirical note on the transactional model of psychological stress. *The Sociological Quarterly, 13,* 484–495.

Leonova, A. B. (1984). *Psichodiagnostika funkcional'nych sostoyanii cheloveka* [Psychodiagnostics of human functional states]. Moscow: Moscow University Press.

Leonova, A. B. (1993). Psychological means for the control and prevention of industrial stress in computerized working places. *European Work and Organizational Psychologist, 3,* 11–27.

Leonova, A. B. (1994). Industrial and organizational psychology in Russia: The concept of human functional states and applied stress research. In C. L. Cooper & I. T. Robertson (Eds.), *International review of industrial and organizational psychology: 1994* (Vol. 9, pp. 183–212). Chichester, UK: Wiley.

Leonova, A. B. (1996). Occupational stress, personnel adaptation, and health. In C. D. Spielberger & I. G. Sarason (Eds.), *Stress and emotion: Anxiety, anger, and curiosity* (Vol. 16, pp. 109–125). Washington, DC: Taylor & Francis.

Leonova, A. B., & Kouznetcova, A. S. (1993). *Psichoprophilaktika stressov* [Psychoprophylactics of stress]. Moscow: Moscow University Press.

Leonova, A. B., Maryin, M. I., & Lovchan, S. I. (1996). *Risk factors and human reliability in fire-fighting job* (Research Rep. No. 4/96, INTAS 93–3493). HCM-CEC, Program of the Commission of European Community.

Leont'ev, A. N. (1981). *Activity, consciousness, personality.* Englewood Cliffs, NJ: Prentice Hall.

Levi, L. (1981). *Society, stress and disease: Vol. 4. Working.* London: Oxford University Press.

Levi, L., Frankenhaeuser, M., & Gardell, B. (1982). Work-stress related to social structures and processes. In G. Elliot & C. Eisdorfer (Eds.), *Research on stress and human health* (pp. 173–189). New York: Springer.

Marsella, A. J. (1994). The measurement of emotional reactions to work: Conceptual, methodological and research issues. *Work and Stress, 8,* 153–176.

Maryin, M. I., Lovchan, S. I., & Ephanova, N. I. (1992). Funkcional'nye sostoyaniya personala protivopojarnoi slujby v processe likvidacii posledstvii avarii na Chernobyl'skoi atomnoi stancii [Functional states of personnel of the fire-fighting service at the Chernobyl Nuclear Plant during the liquidation of the consequences of the accident]. In M. I. Bobneva (Ed.), *Chernobyl'skii sled: Medicinskie i psichologicheskie posledstviya avarii* [The Chernobyl's trace: Medical and psychological consequences of the accident] (pp. 108–187). Moscow: Nauka.

Maryin, M. I., & Sobolev, E. S. (1990). A study of the influence of work conditions on the functional state of fire-fighters. *Soviet Journal of Psychology, 11,* 62–70.

Northwestern National Life (1991). *Employee burnout: America's newest epidemic.* Minneapolis, MN: Northwestern National Life Insurance Company.

Parkes, K. R. (1994). Personality and coping as moderators of work stress process: Models, methods and measures. *Work and Stress, 8,* 110–129.

Proffitt, D. R., Bhalla, M., Gossweiler, R., & Midgett, J. (1995). Perceiving geographical slant. *Psychonomic Bulletin and Review, 2,* 419–428.

Richter, P., & Rohlandt, A. (1996). Assessment of task design and mental load. In P. Ullsperger, M. Ertel, & G. Freude (Eds.), *Occupational health and safety aspects of stress at modern workplaces* (pp. 28–38). Bremenhafen: Bundesanstalt fuer Arbeitsmedizin.

Rodina, O. N., & Leonova, A. B. (1987). Vliyanie trudovoi deyatel'nosti na dinamiku lichnostnych characteristik v processe professional'noi adaptacii [Influence of work activity on personality traits during professional adaptation]. In V. S. Aseev (Ed.), *Adaptaciya molodeji k trudovoi i uchebnoi deyatel'nosti* [Youth's adaptation to work and learning activities] (pp. 19–32). Irkutsk: Nauka.

Salvendy, G., Sauter, S. L., & Hurrel, J. J. (Eds.). (1987). *Social, ergonomic and stress aspects of work with computers.* Amsterdam: Elsevier.

Sanders, A. F. (1983). Towards a model of stress and human performance. *Acta Psychologica, 53*, 61–97.

Sauter, S. L., Murphy, L. R., & Hurrel, J. J. (1992). Prevention of work-related psychological disorders: A national strategy proposed by the National Institute for Occupational Safety and Health (NIOSH). In G. P. Keita & S. L. Sauter (Eds.), *Work and well-being: An agenda for the 1990s* (pp. 17–40). Washington, DC: American Psychological Association.

Schlegel, R. E., Gilliland, K., & Schlegel, B. (1987). Factor structure of the criteria task set. *Proceedings of the 31st Annual Meeting of Human Factors Society* (pp. 389–393). Santa Monica, CA: Human Factors Society Press.

Schoenpflug, W. (1986). Behavior economics as an approach to stress theory. In M. H. Appley & R. Trumbull (Eds.), *Dynamics of stress* (pp. 81–97). New York: Plenum Press.

Schreus, P. G., Winnubst, J. A. M., & Cooper, C. L. (1996). Workplace health programmes. In M. J. Schabracq, J. A. M. Winnubst, & C. L. Cooper (Eds.), *Handbook of work and health psychology* (pp. 462–485). Chichester, UK: Wiley.

Schmidt, K. H., & Daune, B. (1993). Job characteristics and voluntary employee turnover: Direct and moderated relationships. *The European Work and Organizational Psychologist, 3*, 29–44.

Selye, H. (1976). *Stress in health and disease*. London: Butterworth.

Siegrist, J., & Peter, R. (1994). Job stressors and coping characteristics in work-related disease: Issues of validity. *Work and Stress, 8*, 130–140.

Simonson, E., & Weiser, P. C. (1976). *Psychological aspects and physiological correlates of work and fatigue*. Springfield: Thomas.

Spielberger, C. D. (1972). Anxiety as an emotional state. In C. D. Spielberger (Ed.), *Aniety: Current trends in theory and research* (Vol. 1, pp. 23–49). New York: Academic Press.

Spielberger, C. D., & Reheiser, E. C. (1994a). The job survey: Measuring gender differences in occupational stress. *Journal of Social Behavior and Personality, 9*, 199–218.

Spielberger, C. D., & Reheiser, E. C. (1994b). Job stress in universities, corporate, and military personnel. *International Journal of Stress Management, 1*, 19–31.

Sternberg, R. (1981). Testing and cognitive psychology. *American Psychologist, 83*, 171–192.

Sternberg, S. (1975). Memory scanning: New findings and current controversies. *Quarterly Journal of Experimental Psychology, 27*, 1–32.

Sudakov, K. V. (Ed.). (1994). *Social'naya phisiologiya: Ocenka sostoyaniya cheloveka. Trudy nauchnogo komiteta po eksperimental'noi i prikladnoi phisiologii* [Social physiology: Assessment of human state. Proceedings of the Scientific Committee of Experimental and Applied Physiology] (Vol. 4, pp. 6–150). Moscow: Academy of Medical Sciences.

Warr, P. (1987). *Work, unemployment, and mental health*. Oxford: Oxford University Press.

Warr, P. (1994). A conceptual framework for the study of work and mental health. *Work and Stress, 8*, 84–97.

Wierwille, W. W., Rahimi, M., & Casali, J. G. (1985). Evaluation of 16 measures of mental workload using a simulated flight task emphasizing mediational activity. *Human Factors, 27*, 489–502.

Zarakovsky, G. M., & Pavlov, V. V. (1987). *Zakonomernosti funkcionirovaniya ergaticheskich system* [Principles in functioning of ergatic systems]. Moscow: Nauka.

Zinchenko, V. P., Leonova, A. B., & Strelkov, Yu. K. (1985). *Psychometrics of fatigue*. London: Taylor & Francis.

Zinchenko, V. P., & Munipov, V. M. (1978). *Osnovy ergonomiki* [Foundations of ergonomics]. Moscow: Moscow University Press.

Zinchenko, V. P., Velichkovsky, B. M., & Vuchetich, G. G. (1980). *Funkcional'naya struktura zritel'noi pamyati* [Functional structure of visual memory]. Moscow: Moscow University Press.

CHAPTER SIXTEEN

Work culture in a developing country: The case of India

Jai B. P. Sinha
ASSERT Institute of Management Studies, Patna, India

An overview of work culture in Indian organizations by the end of the 1980s identified the presence of a non-work culture, fostered by socio-cultural factors such as familism, paternalism, patronage, and centralization of power. Further examination differentiated the non-work, or "soft" work culture, as it is called, from the synergetic work culture which reflects a philosophy of self-reliance, strong work norms, and humane practices, leading to greater viability and satisfaction. The synergetic work culture enabled many large organizations to take advantage of the liberalization of the economy in the 1990s. This focus has often resulted in the neglect of smaller organizations, many of which are still maintaining an exploitative work culture where profit is made by extracting maximum work from workers without paying any attention to either work and service conditions or human resources. This chapter argues for vertical networking of large and small organizations, as well as horizontal alliances among smaller ones, in order to share resources for development in coming years.

Une vue d'ensemble de la culture du travail dans les entreprises Indiennes jusqu'à la fin des années 1980 dénote la présence d'une culture autre que celle du travail, favorisée par des facteurs socio-culturels tels le familialisme, le paternalisme, le patronage, et la centralisation du pouvoir. Un examen plus approfondi permet de distinguer cette culture, ou culture "molle" du travail, telle qu'on l'appelle, de la culture du travail coopératif qui reflète une philosophie d'indépendance, de normes rigoureuses de travail, d'usages humains, menant à une plus grande viabilité et satisfaction. La culture du travail coopératif a permis à plusieurs grandes entreprises de tirer avantage de la libéralisation de l'économie dans les années 1990. Cette concentration a souvent abouti au délaissement des petites entreprises, plusieurs d'entre lesquelles maintiennent encore une culture exploitatrice du travail et une perspective à court terme de la rentabilité. Ce chapitre prône la gestion verticale de réseaux de grandes et petites entreprises, ainsi que des alliances horizontales au sein des plus petites d'entre elles, afin de mettre en commun les ressources nécessaires au développement dans les années à venir.

It is hazardous to talk about work culture in India which is so huge, hetero-geneous, and rapidly developing. In the beginning of the 1990s, the country was rated 13th in industrial production, but remained 10th poorest in the world with 34 million unemployed. There were about 260 million people in the work force, but only one tenth of them belonged to the organized sector. The remaining ones in the unorganized sector were either self-employed or worked casually for petty contractors. Organized labor was reported to earn over three times more than unorganized labor. Further, India was the third largest in the world in skilled labor, but the skilled laborer earned only about US$ 100 per month, while the salaries of high level executives were about US$ 25,000 per year. This amount may look very small by Western standards, but shows a disparity of about 21 times between an average skilled worker and the highly paid executives (Billmoria, 1994). The public sector accounted for over two-thirds of industrial activity and employment, but only 55% (131 out of 237) of the public sector was making a profit by 1992–1993. As a whole, the ratio of their net profit to capital was only 1:2.43. By the end of March 1992, over 221 thousand small enterprises, and 2200 medium and large units were running into losses (Ministry of Finance, 1994).

This large and varied industrial structure was subjected to structural adjust-ments through the New Economic Policy (Ministry of Finance, 1991) which opened the economy to global market forces by lowering various barriers and constraints imposed by the government. After a long protective and restrictive period, the economy began to show signs of rapid growth. By 1994–1995, the GNP growth rate had increased by about 6%, the rate of export (in dollars) by about 20%, and industrial production by 8%. Foreign private investment, which was less than a billion in 1991–1992, climbed to five billion dollars. Compared to the period before 1990, the capital raised through public issues of stocks and bonds was 13 times higher (Khandwalla, 1996). As a result, a new wave of opportunities and challenges has appeared on the industrial landscape.

We have yet to systematically examine the impact of these changes on the work culture. The best I can do at this point is to: (1) provide an overview of the work culture as it has been evolving within the industrial growth we have experienced over the 49 years since our Independence; and (2) report the emerg-ing trends which are likely to gain momentum in the coming years. I intend to start with a sample of generalized observations made in the early years of our industrial activity. This will be followed by a report of our studies from the 1980s which identified two dominant cultural profiles in large industrial organ-izations. It was the presence of one of the cultural profiles which is now recog-nized as the ground for building the new edifice. We have also taken a look beyond the large industrial organizations in order to understand the prevailing work culture in relatively smaller organizations, which are expected to function at the cutting edge, but are often forgotten in deliberations on work culture in India. At the end, I shall attempt to outline the task of building a work-conducive culture in Indian organizations.

GENERALIZED EARLY OBSERVATIONS

Industrial growth in India was planned through a large-scale import of Western technology and managerial practices for building a dominant public sector, which was then expected to feed other sectors. Apart from generating wealth for nation building, the industries in all sectors were envisaged to transform the traditional values, work habits, and life styles of Indians. It was further hoped that the changes would cascade over the various rungs of Indian society. Inkeles and Smith (1974), for example, strongly advocated the salience of industrial experience as the most potent instrument for inculcating modernity in people. The outcome, however, did not meet the expectations.

Instead of transforming people and the surrounding culture, industrial organizations were themselves encroached upon by socio-cultural forces. Several decades back, for example, Weber (1958) doubted whether Hindu religion was conducive to economic activities. Myers (1960), Lambert (1963), and Myrdal (1968) similarly reported that the habits and social systems which employees brought to their organizations were contrary to the requirements of industrial organizations. McClelland (1975) contended that Indians performed work as a favor to others: work was believed to exhaust a person by draining his energy and was, therefore, to be expended only for someone who could return the favour.

Some Indian scholars supported the Western view. Sinha (1985) observed that, despite what Shri Bhagawadgita prescribed in the ancient past, work was intrinsically not valued in India because of the culture of *aram* (i.e. preference for rest and relaxation not preceded by hard work). It is common to find a large number of people in all parts of India sitting here and there doing nothing. Even those who have a job often come late to work and leave early, unless they have special reasons to remain punctual. At the work place, they receive friends and relatives who feel free to call on them at any time without any prior appointment or purpose. While people relish chatting and talking over a cup of tea or coffee, their work suffers. No one objects if employees leave work to visit and attend ailing friends and relatives, go out of their way to help them in their personal matters, or perform personal errands. Naturally, it is not uncommon to find a large number of chairs empty in offices. Even when the occupants are present, they are found to work in slow and clumsy ways, look indifferent to what they are doing, seem more concerned about procedures and rules rather than outcomes, and lack consideration for others. The number of holidays and festivals, and the fact that the occasions of both joy and sorrow lead to stopping work, indicate the low priority that work assumes in comparison to socio-personal obligations. Consequently, it is natural to find that Indian organizations have assumed *social* rather than *work* identities (Parikh, 1979), and that work behavior is determined socially rather than technologically. Kanungo (1990, p. 803) explained this phenomenon in terms of people's generalized helplessness and family ethic. He observed that:

Indian workers ... manifest a family-centred ethic ... There is an emphasis on idle leisure pursuits that satisfy security and affiliative needs, rather than creative leisure pursuits that achieve work objectives; on maintaining status positions rather than task goal accomplishment; on performing socially approved duties in inter-personal contexts rather than in the job contexts.

Ganesh (1982, p. 5) went even further: he contended that it is not only the family ethic, but the whole gamut of caste, religion, language, and politics which erode work culture in Indian organizations:

... organizations in this country have "fuzzy" boundaries. Essentially, organiza-tions have come to represent settings in which societal forces interact. Thus, our organizations have provided settings for interaction of familial forces, interest groups, caste conflicts, regional and linguistic groups, class conflicts, and political and religious forces among others ... Therefore, organizations do not concern themselves with work ... but seem to concern themselves more with those activ-ities which maintain "equilibrium" of the social forces.

The fact that these scholars were located in different places and were writing independently of each other suggests a convergence of views regarding the work culture in Indian organizations. However, there were some disagreements too. Some scholars (Singh, 1979; Soares, Valecha, & Venkataraman, 1981) showed that Indian managers had values similar to their Western counterparts, and they cultivated a strong work ethic (Sinha & Sinha, 1990; Tripathi, 1990). Virmani and Guptan (1991) studied 44 organizations drawn from public and large private sectors, family owned, and multinationals. They found that all organizations had adopted Western systems of management, but in each case ". . . the structure has to be bypassed to keep the system going and to get work done" (p. 136). There were also reports of sectorial differences in organizational practices (Khandawalla, 1988). The multinationals and their subsidiaries were found to maintain their corporate culture and Western type of managerial practices to a great extent. The public sector, on the other hand, being vulnerable to surrounding socio-political forces, was often more bureaucratic than entrepreneurial. The large private sector organizations were also bureaucratic, but many of them maintained their profit orientation and remained viable. The family-owned enterprises were found to be personalized, flexible, and susceptible to local imperatives. Virmani and Guptan contended that, despite these variations, all organizations took cultural detours by subscribing to familism, patronage, personalized relationships, obedi-ence to authority, and so on.

In conclusion, it seemed to us that Indian organizations by and large adopted Western formal systems, but used the Indian cultural ethos to make them work effectively in some situations, and ineffectively in other situations. Therefore, my colleagues and I wanted to explore how those situations were different, and how they evolved to create different work cultures.

SOFT AND SYNERGETIC WORK CULTURES

We studied two steel plants (one in the public sector and one in the private sector), two fertilizer companies (one in the public and one in the cooperative sector) and two nationalized banks (one having rural thrust and the other having more commercial interests; Sinha, 1990). Altogether six studies were conducted between 1983 and 1987. Five of them were conducted to supplement a major survey which was designed to map work culture and relate it to the contextual factors.

Work culture was conceptualized as the meaning and importance attached to work in terms of: (1) centrality of work rather than of the family, in the life space of managers; (2) extent to which managers worked hard; (3) hours they spent at work; (4) clarity of their roles; (5) job affect (i.e. feeling about their job); and (6) satisfaction with their job outcomes. These variables were related to six organizational factors including: (1) physical condition of work; (2) superior–subordinate relationships; (3) work pressure; (4) work norms; (5) upkeep and age of technology; and (6) performance-based rewards. In addition, items were developed to ascertain the extent to which the managers: (1) glossed over their job requirements in order to meet their socio-personal obligations to their friends and family members; and (2) yielded to such influences on their work-behavior as caste, religion, language groups, region, and political affiliations. Five-hundred and twenty middle-level managers were interviewed in five organizations. As soon as the project was started, we realized that supplementary studies were required to: (1) include a public sector steel plant to match with its private counterpart with respect to important variables; and (2) collect information about history, philosophy, norms and managerial practices, major critical events, financial health, and relationship with the financing institutions in the same six organizations in order to be able to develop their cultural profiles. Supplementary studies were designed to fill these gaps.

As we waded through the accumulating mass of data, we felt that the most appropriate way to identify the work culture of an organization would be to allow the pieces of evidence to fall into a pattern unique to the organization. As the profiles were mapped, they displayed, despite their uniqueness, some meaningful overlaps. The profiles are reported in Table 16.1.

The *public steel* and the *public fertilizer* organizations differed in their history, technology, and product mix. Yet, there were a number of common features. Both were commissioned to meet the national need for expanding industrial activities and for functioning as model employers by giving generous welfare to employees. Profit was not the primary motive. The losses, if any, were to be borne by the Government of India either directly or through financing institutions. The organizations began to incur heavy losses, and yet the employees kept mounting pressure for all kinds of benefits. The pressure, instead of resulting from their work performance, emanated from the clout they had in the organization.

TABLE 16.1
A comparative picture of organizations

Organization	Technology	Loss-bearing capacity	Main concerns	Management styles
Cooperative Fertilizer	Modern	Low	Productivity & welfare	Assertive & humane
Private Steel	Quite old	Low	Productivity & welfare	Assertive & humane
Bank-B	Old	High	National development & then profit	Assertive but getting pliant
Public Fertilizer	Getting old	High	Welfare & peaceful industrial relations	Pliant
Public Steel	Modern	High	Welfare & then productivity	Pliant
Bank-A	Old	High	National development & then profit	Pliant

NOTES:

Number of managers interviewed: Cooperative Fertilizer = 107; Private Steel = 150; Bank-B = 57; Public Fertilizer = 150; Public Steel = 100; Bank-A = 56.

This caused indiscipline, militancy, rowdyism, and irresponsible trade unionism among workers. The top leadership was rendered pliant by the workers. It adopted an appeasing attitude, disregarding organizational goals and objectives, and even undermining the authority of lower level managers. As a result, the lower-level managers felt alienated from the management and powerless in the face of their workers. Consequently, they too were forced to form their own power bases by either patronizing their loyal subordinates or colluding with some of the trade union leaders.

In contrast, the *cooperative fertilizer* and the *private steel* organizations maintained a different approach. They too differed in size, technology, and product mix, but they both established strong norms of high productivity. In the case of the cooperative fertilizer, the norm was cultivated and handed down by its apex body which was already running two productive units elsewhere in the country. The founder of the private steel company, on the other hand, had envisioned a management philosophy in which the interests of the shareholders were integrated with the welfare of the employees; and thus, both profit and welfare were contingent on productivity. This caused a sense of interdependence between the workers, the managers, and the top management for generating profit, which then led to a wide range of welfare measures, some of which were introduced even before the government framed rules about them. The management established an effective joint consultative system by inviting workers and managers for a "partnership in growth." In both organizations, the management remained assertive by maintaining systems of close supervision, adequate incentives, generous bonuses, and a number of fringe benefits.

The *two banks* started as private enterprises with commercial interests. They were nationalized in 1969 to serve less profitable priority sectors in the rural areas. Bank-A succumbed to social pressure, thus following the course of the public steel and public fertilizer organizations. The top management became increasingly pliant and yielded to the demands of fragmented and militant trade unions. Bank-B was also under pressure, and the management had to yield on several counts because of the changing nature of banking organizations. However, Bank-B was fortunate to have a few stabilized trade unions and strong leadership at the top, helping it retain parts of its commercial interests. As a result, Bank-B maintained an edge over Bank-A, although the work climate, and its profitability were eroded over the years.

The six organizations presented two extremes of a continuum of the way work was viewed and valued, and the extent to which organizational and socio-cultural factors were related to this viewing and valuing process. The first (the two banks, public steel, and public fertilizer) reflected a *soft work culture* while the second (cooperative fertilizer and private steel) manifested a *synergetic work culture*.

In the organizations with a *soft work culture*, work received a lower priority than social–personal obligations. Non-work interests and activities displaced work from its central place in the life space of managers. They neither worked hard, nor felt positive affect for their jobs, nor derived any satisfaction from their work. They worked in a leisurely way, and many of them just put in their time. They were not clear about their roles. They often came late to work, left early, and took time off to do their personal work or to visit friends and relatives. This same scenario was observed in earlier investigations conducted by Indian (Ganesh, 1982; Kanungo, 1990; Parikh, 1979) and Western scholars (Lambert, 1963; McClelland, 1975; Myers, 1960; Myrdal, 1968; Weber, 1958).

Characteristically in the organizations with a soft work culture, superiors did not normally ask subordinates to do what they were hired to do, and those who did ask were ignored. Work norms were weak and work pressure was low. The subordinates believed that politics and personal connections mattered more than merit or hard work. Those who could pressurize their superiors or cultivate personal connections with them received more benefits than those who maintained a low profile. Some of the common comments were quite revealing: "It is a place where action, not inaction, has to be defended"; "It is a place where some work sincerely while others are praised and promoted." Relationships were plagued with suspicions and misgivings. Factories and machines were poorly maintained, and the climate was not perceived to be conducive to work.

The managers in the *synergetic work culture*, by contrast, perceived that their organization rewarded hard work, recognized merit, established clear norms of performance, and gave the employees adequate work load. The superiors demanded hard work from their subordinates, provided them with close supervision and direction, and differentially rewarded those who worked harder. In the cooperative fertilizer, where technology was up-to-date and work facilities were adequate, managers perceived the climate highly conducive to work. But even when the technology was old and the physical condition of work was less than satisfactory (as in the case of private steel), managers reported making up deficiencies by maintaining good interpersonal relationships, conforming to strong work norms, and responding to work pressure. In sum, the organizational climate was such that work seemed to be a natural behavior.

The two types of organizational climate, it may be recalled, evolved out of the history, philosophy, and practices of the top management. It is worth noting that both soft and synergetic cultures were contextualized in the same socio-cultural milieu, comprising a high rate of unemployment, political pressures, restrictive government rules, short span of familiarity with Western technology, and personal and social obligations. All of the organizations had to employ or retain more people on the workforce than was necessary; and the socio-cultural values of personalized relationships, patronage, hierarchy, and ingroup orientation had permeated all of the organizations. However, the organizations having either soft or synergetic work cultures differed in the way they used these values. The synergetic work culture enabled the managers to use socio-cultural values to mobilize human resources to get the best out of their employees. The soft work culture, in contrast, rendered the managers so vulnerable that they did not feel comfortable in discharging their legitimate role, and workers got away with not meeting their obligations. The critical factor in both cases was the top leadership. It functioned, in the first case, not only as a custodian of organizational interests and as a role model, but also created systems and norms to make their organization highly purposive, task-oriented, and humane. In the soft work culture, top leadership lost its grip, and tended to drift with the flow of pressures and counter pressures.

Lest we generalize from our findings that public sector organizations have a soft work culture and the private and cooperative sectors have a synergetic work culture, I must point out that the sectorial differences were more accidental than veridical. As stated in the beginning, 55% of public sector organizations were making profits and a large number of private enterprises were reported to be running into losses. This is enough to suggest that the specific configurations of the forces of history, critical events, and strategic policy decisions played a more crucial role in creating one or the other kind of culture than did the nature of ownership. We have no way of knowing the percentage of Indian organizations having synergetic and soft work cultures. However, given the large industrial base, we may safely assume that there are many examples of both in the country.

TRENDS IN LARGE, LEADING ORGANIZATIONS

It is the presence of this synergetic work culture in many organizations which has enabled them to take advantage of the effects of economic liberalization since 1991. The emerging trends are not yet stabilized, but they do appear quite promising. There is evidence of recovery not only in the economy, but also in the performance of both public and private sectors. Khandwalla (1996) examined a number of sources and found that that sales and profit of the private sector had doubled from the period between 1991–1992 and 1995–1996. The public sector also increased its profitability. A number of corporations made vigorous efforts to upgrade productivity, operating efficiency, process and product quality, etc. Many introduced quality circles, computerization, and obtained ISO 9000 certification.[1] There were about a dozen ISO 9000 certificate holders in 1990. The number by 1995 was 800, and is likely to triple by the end of 1996. There was virtually no private company in 1991 that could claim to be the largest in the world in a specific product line. By 1995, however, there were fifteen. Khandwalla (1996, p. 22) referred to a number of large private enterprises to conclude the following:

> The preference seems increasingly for organizational differentiation through decentralization and organizational integration through setting up self-contained, autonomous units with bottom line responsibility, supplemented by an overall coordinative system-building, and vision and core values institutionalizing role played by the corporate or business house headquarters.

In a study of 20 organizations, Khandwalla (1995) identified four managerial styles, namely participative, altruistic, professional, and organic. These styles, singly or in combination, contributed to "outstanding strengths" in the effectiveness of organizations. The criteria for assessing effectiveness were an organization's: (1) learning ability; (2) smooth and stress-free functioning; (3) capacity to yield excellent performance; and (4) capacity to "gel" and have synergy with the ingrained mode of management.

The participative style, as we know, involves sharing of information, power, and responsibilities as well as team-building, collaboration, and so on. This does not, however, suggest an over-reliance on committees. Altruism, on the other hand, implies that management is a trustee for various groups of people who have stakes in the organization. It maintains honesty, dedication, welfare to employees, and business ethics. Professionalism lies in systematic search and management of information, growth opportunities, costs and benefits, and long term planning. The organic management style emphasizes flexibility, openness, innovation, improvisation, and the like. It seemed that the styles made significant improvements in the organizational culture, which is reflected in the rhetoric such as "Change is the only constant", "Only quality ensures survival", "Information is everything", and "People, not products, are paramount." Khandwalla

---

[1] The ISO 9000 was set up by the International Organization For Standardization in Geneva in 1987 to set out guidelines for evaluating all parts of the manufacturing process from start to finish including creation, design, calibration of equipment, training, suppliers' performance, production, and shipping.

(1995, p. 18) did find a gap between rhetoric and reality, but indicated that the gap is narrowing and that "... the change in corporate culture seems distinctly to be compatible with a free, more competitive market environment".

A NEGLECTED BACKYARD: THE SMALLER ENTERPRISES

All deliberations have so far pertained to large and leading organizations which are more visible than smaller ones—the latter often lie unseen and ignored in the backyard of the former ones. Liberalization of the economy has brought this neglected sector into sharper focus. They are now increasingly recognized as the cutting edge due to the changing perspective on development, which can be realized through people's participation. Small enterprises are deeply embedded in their community. Their boundaries are permeable, structures are loose and improvised, relationships are personalized, and managers are likely to be more flexible. They have the potential to respond quickly to the business environment, play the ancillary role to the larger businesses, and provide quality products and services to people. Because they are rooted in a local environment, smaller organizations can initiate locally relevant economic activities, generate employment, and meet the needs of their surroundings. However, their capital base is generally weak, making them unable to acquire high technology and take a great deal of risk. Furthermore, societal forces are likely to encroach upon their boundaries freely by diluting their work identity and viability.

We wanted to know the nature of the existing work culture in smaller organizations, and to estimate the prospect of their cultivating a culture more conducive to realizing their potential. To investigate these, we (Sinha, 1997) have studied 28 organizations in the state of Bihar, which is located in the eastern part of India. Bihar has three geographical zones. The northern part is plains and mostly agricultural; the south is a plateau and endowed with natural resources; and the central part, between the river Ganges and the plateau, is also plains. Twelve organizations were selected from the north, 10 from the south, and six from the central zones. Each had capital ranging from US$ 250,000 to 1.56 million. They were all medium-sized enterprises according to the specification of The Reserve Bank of India.

The organizations represented a wide spectrum of manufacturing activities: sugar, beverage, dairy, distillery, flour, forging, tool-making, auto parts, cement, electrical, tiles, chemical, pharmaceutical, and motor vehicle body-building. While the food-processing industries were more concentrated in the north, iron- and steel-related activities were more visible in the south. The central zone had a mixture of the two. Their diverse nature was accompanied by wide variations in their wage and benefit structure, recruitment policy, growth rate, work climate, and so on. For example, the monthly salary of managers ranged from US$ 60 to 350, with an average of US$ 200. Supervisors reported receiving US$ 60 to

225, with an average of US$ 100; and workers were paid anywhere between US$ 30 and 75, with an average of US$ 50 per month (although one central government factory paid up to US$ 140). It may be noted that the workers got half of the national average wage received by skilled workers and the managers received one-tenth of what the top managers in the country were getting.

We started the investigation with an implicit assumption that the smaller organizations would manifest shades of soft and synergetic work culture. However, we soon realized that most of them deviated significantly from either of the two. Because the majority were headed by the owners, who were primarily interested in maximizing their profit, the work culture turned out to be exploitative. In the exploitative work culture, the management tended to extract maximum work from workers without caring to provide adequate facilities, safety measures, appropriate physical conditions of work, or sufficient training to the employees. Pay and perks were disproportionately asymmetrical: where owners made a profit, managers and supervisors tried to earn more money and favour from the owners by maintaining close supervision, strict discipline, and strong task orientation; and because of their smaller number, workers were not unionized, and therefore, felt dependent on the management for their wages, benefits, and favours.

The exploitative culture was similar to the synergetic in terms of maintaining strong work norms and discipline, consistently making profit, and manifesting a high growth rate. However, unlike the synergetic work culture, human resources were grossly neglected. Employees in an exploitative work culture were dissatisfied just as they were in the soft work culture. There were, of course, variations. The work culture in public enterprises, for example, indeed ranged from somewhat soft to somewhat synergetic. Of the 28 small organizations sampled, six were in the public sector, two controlled by the central and four by the state government. Four of these public enterprises were accumulating losses while the remaining two were making profits. They were managed by bureaucrats on deputation from the government, or by professionals appointed through advertisement. The latter were generally appointed on merit and were much less bureaucratic in their managerial styles than those placed on deputation from the government. Lower level functionaries were appointed through advertisement and the Employment Exchanges, although unfair means were alleged to be frequently used in recruiting them.[2] Most of these public enterprises had spacious premises with a well-maintained garden. One of them had houses for managers and small quarters for workers, each having space for a garden. Some of the workers from the neighbouring villages did not need any quarters, and rented their quarters to those who were working elsewhere. Privileges were steeply

---

[2] Employment Exchange is an office of the government where unemployed persons register themselves for jobs. The employers approach the Exchange for a list of suitable candidates, out of which they select the most appropriate people.

asymmetrical with managers claiming many more benefits than workers, who got pay, perks, and other benefits according to the government rules.

The most critical factor in determining profitability in these public enterprises was the style of the top executive.[3] If he took initiative, personal interest, and asserted his role, he mobilized his work force and made them work hard. The executives in two profit-making enterprises seemed to have the nurturant task style (Sinha, 1980) and were able to motivate their workforce to render the organizations profitable while gaining respect and obedience from their workers. They often bent rules and procedures to meet small needs of the workers, removed their minor irritants, provided personal help, support, and counseling, and were thereby able to get work done. The work culture was somewhat synergetic.

By contrast, the four chief executives in the remaining public enterprises were typical bureaucrats who did not pay adequate attention to managing their organizations. They collected their pay and benefits, adopted laissez-faire style, and enjoyed a peaceful and comfortable life. Their organizations drifted into losses. Invariably, the machines and equipment in these four loss-incurring public enterprises were old. The top executive in these organizations did not make any effort to upgrade them. Three of the four organizations were frequently closed. In two of them, workers' salaries were frequently not paid on time, while the managers and the chief executives were alleged to have claimed their full benefits. Workers were hired only when the factory was in a position to run. They came from the neighbouring rural areas and returned to their villages whenever there was no work for them. Naturally, the main concerns of the workers were having a regular and secure job, pay and perks, housing, medical care, and other benefits. The workers' benefits in two large central enterprises were relatively greater, because they had trade unions which were on good terms with the management. However, in this situation, whatever grievances the workers had were pinned on the government for its faulty policies and interference in the working of the organizations. The workers in the four smaller state enterprises did not have a trade union, and hence, the workers approached their superiors directly for redressal or favour. The work culture was somewhat soft, except that the workers were not in a position to bully the management as they did in the larger organizations.

Now let us turn to the private enterprises which were by and large characterized by varying degrees of exploitative culture. There were twenty-two private enterprises in our sample. Of these, three were incurring losses year after year; two at times made profit and at times losses; and the remaining 17 were consistently making a profit.[4] The private enterprises as a whole shared many

---

[3] The top person and senior managers in all 28 organizations were male. Henceforth "he" will be used without implying any gender bias.

[4] Loss-incurring enterprises were generally closed, and hence, were not always available for the study.

common features, although there were some variations in the patterns of management practices. One of the loss-incurring organizations, for example, was being run in a feudal fashion. The owner had a flourishing transport service in northern Bihar. He started this enterprise as a support company to build the bodies of his buses and trucks. Only surplus time was commercially utilized. He appointed one of his relatives with an engineering degree to manage the company. This chief manager bossed others, made all decisions, and enjoyed the confidence of the owner who behaved like a feudal lord. The salary and wages of all employees (including the chief manager) were low. The chief manager was very strict in the matters of work and time-keeping, although he was not himself known for either punctuality or work commitment. He tended to take on as much work as he could, except that his planning was so poor that the workers were often idle because the raw materials were not available on time. The whole place looked quite shabby. The workers were still grateful to the company for the livelihood and the patronage that the owner had provided to them. Since there was no trade union, workers approached the owner through the chief managers to redress their grievances, or to ask for an occasional loan or favour.

There were four private enterprises which were being run by the companies having factories elsewhere in the country. Two of them had appointed professionals as the managing directors, through advertisement. The remaining two, just like other private companies, had recruited family members as the directors and one of the directors as the managing director. The common pattern in the rest of the 19 private enterprises was to have either a single owner or a dominant partner, who drew a few other partners, mostly from family members or close friends, but ran the enterprise like a single owner. In most of the private enterprises, the owner or the dominant partner was the second generation technocrat or a son of the first generation business man. He pooled his (and/or his partners') resources, procured a loan from a bank, and started the enterprise. He centralized all power. He often chose his family members or junior partners for key positions. If they were indifferent or incapable, he recruited a competent technical person as a senior manager through personal contacts, and after thorough investigation of the latter's background.

Together they manifested a clear pattern of dual leadership. The senior manager was given the responsibility for internal management, including monitoring of work flow, accounts, administration, industrial relations, personnel, supervision, reward, and punishment. The top man kept himself free for managing external affairs such as procurement of capital goods, purchase of important raw materials, marketing, cash flow, bank loans, recruitment of managers, contacts with government officers, etc. He visited the factory when he had time, but did not get involved unless there were major events such as misbehavior of a worker, a serious accident, or visits by important government officers or political leaders. However, he invariably had the means to know what was happening on the shop floor. In sum, the power was totally centralized, and whatever power the next person had was, in fact, more manifest than real. Together, they recruited other managers, supervisors, and workers. Managers and supervisors were expected to get maximum work out of the workers. Thus, they maintained heavy work pressure, close supervision, tight work schedule, strict discipline, and rarely allowed workers to go out of the factory premises on personal errands or to loiter around.

The workers, indeed, were entitled to and were given wages, bonuses, medical insurance, leave, and similar benefits according to government rules. The factories, which were being run by the companies also having factories elsewhere, provided a few more benefits which still were generally inadequate. Workers in most of the organizations wanted to have job security, better pay and perks, housing, and medical care. About 75% of all 22 private enterprises did not have a trade union. A few allowed workers to form a grievance-handling committee, which discussed individual and common problems with the management. Workers were reported to be docile and hard working. They did not defy authority, nor did they avoid work. By and large, they considered their employer to be the "provider" who was expected to take care of them.

Physical conditions at work were bad in 68% of 22 private enterprises. Exceptions were those dealing with beverages, dairy, distillery, and electrical goods, where physical condition was not a problem. In 18 out of 22 enterprises, where safety was an important concern, over 75% did not adopt adequate safety measures. Even at the places where helmets, shoes, and goggles were available, neither the workers were keen nor the managers were insistent on using them. Workers' indifference to safety measures was often an excuse not to supply them in adequate number or on time. Flying ashes, smell of paints, glare and sparks from welding, deafening noise, and inadequate illumination were typical features, particularly in those factories which manufactured cement, tools, nuts and bolts, auto parts, and chemicals. In cement and flour mills, workers were found covering their mouth and nose with a towel. The owner and managers, on the other hand, generally had well-furnished offices with air conditioning, fans, and good furniture. A number of owners had acquired their engineering degree in the West. Some professed to be concerned about their workers' safety, health and well-being, but they hardly did anything to follow up their intentions.

Many of these private enterprises did acquire new machines. Roughly 35% of the machines were new, and about 60% of them were properly maintained. About 65% of the machines were old but well maintained. All of them had one or more power generators to cope with the chronic energy problem in Bihar. All private enterprises had added managers, supervisors, and workers over the years. Most of them also reported varying rates of growth in terms of activities, sales, and profit. However, they did not consider it necessary to maintain a healthy and dedicated workforce. They hired managers and supervisors who were already trained in engineering institutes and polytechnics or were working somewhere else in the same line. Workers were trained on the job itself and their training was limited to the routine operation of the machines. It seemed that the owners' main concern was to make money by being exploitative. Obviously, the private enterprises in this exploitative culture were profit-driven.

It may be noted that none of the six state and central enterprises in the sample was exploitative in taking work, although four of them had non-conducive work environments, and all six had unequal power and privileges between managers and workers. Two of them, as stated earlier, created a better work place by utilizing nurturant task leadership in order to render the enterprises profitable.

In sum, of 28 medium-sized organizations, all 22 private enterprises had an exploitative work culture, 4 public sector organizations had a culture which was rather soft, and only 2 public enterprises had a culture which was somewhat synergetic. Probably, size and ownership are the critical factors which lead to one or the other kind of work culture. Public sector organizations often have diffused leadership. Even large private sector organizations have diffused ownership because of the large number of shareholders. A major part of equity often comes from financing institutions which are directly or indirectly controlled by the government. They also have access to information about the time-tested systems of management. They become soft or synergetic primarily because of the policy decisions, history, philosophy, and top leadership. The smaller organizations are, on the contrary, individually owned. Hence, profit motive dominates other considerations. Because their technology is relatively simple, they do not require complex skills. As unskilled or semi-skilled labor is cheap and plenty, there is no pressure to build up and retain a healthy and dedicated labor force. All these factors seem to lead to an exploitative culture.

THE INTERDEPENDENCY OF SMALL AND LARGE ORGANIZATIONS

It is not altogether unexpected to find a profit-making exploitative work culture in smaller organizations coexisting with soft and synergetic work cultures in large organizations. Indian culture itself has a long tradition of people living with conspicuous inequality and large power distance. Hierarchy reflects this cultural ethos (Sinha, 1995). Disparities between top executives, lower level managers, and their workers are invariably enormous. Organized labor earns disproportionately more than its unorganized counterpart. Similarly, large organizations have many more resources, as well as more access to information regarding modern management practices than do the smaller ones, which have limited capabilities and narrow vision. They are unaware of the importance of human resources in sustaining a high level of productivity over a long period of time.

We could have lived with these two different worlds, except that the synergetic edifice that is being erected is likely to crumble unless supported by viable, smaller organizations, which are less visible but indispensable. Smaller organizations have to play an ancillary role to large ones, taking the pressure of over-staffing off the organizations, using their end products for rapidly expanding domestic and foreign markets, and creating a symbiotic relationship with the large organizations. Large organizations, in turn, will have to reach out to help the smaller ones to renovate their technology, manage and develop their human resources, and above all, create a synergetic work culture. What is needed is the backward and forward networking between large and small enterprises for interdependence and mutual support. Smaller organizations too will have to forge alliances among themselves to pool their meagre resources for mutual support and growth. The role of social scientists as well as government agencies is to facilitate the development of this vertical and horizontal networking.

ACKNOWLEDGEMENTS

The author wishes to thank Rabindra N. Kanungo and Zeynep Aycan for their comments and suggestions on an earlier draft of this chapter.

REFERENCES

Billmoria, S. B. (1994). *Doing Business in India*. New York: Ernst & Young International.
Ganesh, S. R. (1982). *Quality of life in Indian organizations: An irrelevant view* Working Paper No. 407. Ahmedabad, India: Indian Institute of Management.
Inkeles, A. & Smith, D. H. (1974). *Becoming modern*. London: Heinemann.
Kanungo, R. N. (1990). Culture and work alienation: Western models and eastern realities. *International Journal of Psychology*, *25*, 795–814.
Khandwalla, P. N. (1988). Organizational effectiveness. In J. Pandey (Ed.), *Psychology in India: The state-of-the-art* (Volume 3, pp. 97–216). New Delhi: Sage.
Khandwalla, P. N. (1995). *Management styles*. Delhi: Tata-McGraw-Hill.
Khandwalla, P. N. (1996). Effective corporate response to liberalization: The Indian case. *The Social Engineer*, *5*, 5–33.
Lambert, D. (1963). *Workers, factories, and social change in India*. Princeton, NJ: Princeton University Press.
McClelland, D. C. (1975). *Power: The inner experience*. New York: Free Press.
Ministry of Finance. (1991). *The New Economic Policy*. New Delhi: Publication Division, Government of India.
Ministry of Finance. (1994). *Economic Survey, 1993–1994*. New Delhi: Publication Division, Government of India.
Myers, C. A. (1960). *Industrial relations in India*. Bombay: Asia Publishing House.
Myrdal, G. (1968). *Asian Drama*. New York: Twentieth Century.
Parikh, I. J. (1979). *Role orientation and role performance of Indian managers* Working Paper No. 300. Ahmedabad, India: Indian Institute of Management.
Singh, P. (1979). *Occupational values and styles of Indian managers*. New Delhi: Wiley Eastern.
Sinha, D. & Sinha, M. (1990). Dissonance in work culture in India. In A. D. Moddie (Ed.), *The concept of work in Indian society*. Shimala: Indian Institute of Advance Study.
Sinha, J. B. P. (1980). *The nurturant task leader*. New Delhi: Concept.
Sinha, J. B. P. (1985). Psychic relevance of work in Indian culture. *Dynamic Psychiatry*, *18*, 134–141.
Sinha, J. B. P. (1990). *Work culture in the Indian context*. New Delhi: Sage.
Sinha, J. B. P. (1995). *The cultural context of leadership and power*. New Delhi: Sage.

Sinha, J. B. P. (1997). *Work culture in medium-size organizations*. New Delhi: Indian Council of Social Science Research.

Soares, R., Valecha, G., & Venkataraman, R. (1981). Values of Indian managers: The basis of progress. *Indian Management*, *20*, 32–38.

Tripathi, R. C. (1990). Interplay of values in the functioning of Indian organizations. *International Journal of Psychology*, *25*, 715–734.

Virmani, B. R. & Guptan, S. U. (1991). *Indian management*. New Delhi: Vision.

Weber, M. (1958). *The religion of India: The sociology of Hinduism and Buddhism* (H. H. Gerth & D. Martindale, Trans. & Eds.). Glenocoe, IL: C.T. Press.

PART FOUR

Research Methods/Statistics

Causal modeling: New interfaces and new statistics

Peter M. Bentler
University of California, Los Angeles, USA

Structural equation modeling, as implemented with computer programs such as EQS and LISREL, is becoming the major multivariate analysis methodology for the analysis of nonexperimental data in the social and behavioral sciences. Recent and current developments in the human factors and statistical aspects of this methodology are reviewed. The user interface for these methods permits an improved ability to specify and test theories with easy-to-use graphical tools. These are illustrated using the EQS for Windows environment and with a political example based on hypothesized effects of proposed tax cuts in the United States. The technical statistical accuracy for these methods is good under ideal conditions but has been shown to break down with typical psychological data. Certain existing methods and various new developments that promise greater accuracy in the evaluation of causal hypotheses are reviewed. Among these are the Satorra–Bentler corrected chi-square statistic, robust standard error estimates, the Yuan–Bentler finite sample distribution-free test, and a variety of improved methods that will become available to researchers in the next few years.

La modélisation structurale d'équations, telle qu'appliquée dans les programmes informatiques comme l'EQS et le LISTEL, est en cours de devenir la principale méthodologie d'analyse multivariée pour le traitement des données non-expérimentales en sciences sociales et comportementales. Dans cet article, on examine les développements actuels et récents des aspects de cette méthodologie qui portent sur les facteurs humains et la statistique. L'interface de l'usage de ces méthodes permet d'améliorer la capacité de préciser et de vérifier les théories, au moyen d'outils graphiques faciles à utiliser. L'auteur illustre ce point en se servant de l'EQS pour l'environnement Windows et d'un exemple en politique, basé sur les effets hypothétiques de propositions de réduction d'impôts aux États-Unis. Dans des conditions idéales, l'exactitude statistique et technique de ces méthodes est bonne, mais on a constaté qu'elle se détériorait dans le cas de données psychologiques typiques. On examine certaines méthodes existantes et divers nouveaux procédés susceptibles d'améliorer l'évaluation exacte des hypothèses causales. Parmi celles-ci on retrouve la statistique du chi-carré de Satorra–Bentler, des estimations solides de l'erreur type, le test Yuan–Bentler d'échantillon limité non assujetti à l'influence de la distribution et une gamme de méthodes améliorées qui deviendront accessibles aux chercheurs, au cours des quelques prochaines années.

INTRODUCTION

Structural equation modeling is a dynamic field of ever greater importance to the understanding and analysis of psychological data (e.g. Faulbaum & Bentler, 1994; Tremblay & Gardner, 1996). The field has become so active that a new journal, *Strutural Equation Modeling: A Multidisciplinary Journal*, was recently created. I use the name *causal modeling* in my title because the main thrust of this methodology is to evaluate a series of causal hypotheses, collectively called a model, based on nonexperimental data (Bullock, Harlow, & Mulaik, 1994; Steyer, 1993). Some good introductory overviews that provide a balance of theory and practice in this field are Arminger, Clogg, and Sobel (1995), Byrne (1994), Dunn, Everitt, and Pickles (1993), Hoyle (1995), Loehlin (1992), Marcoulides and Schumacker (1996), Mueller (1996), Schumacker and Lomax (1996), and Ullman (1996). However, because of the rapid pace of developments, even these recent sources need to be supplemented by information about new interfaces and new statistics that have, or shortly will, become available in this field. These developments substantially improve the user-friendliness of the methodology, and certainly will promote greater scientific accuracy in conclusions drawn with it.

Historically, as popularized by the LISREL program (Jöreskog & Sörbom, 1993), the causal modeling process required using matrix algebra and arcane commands to specify a model. The idea of automatic creation of path diagrams to simplify modeling was initiated by Huba and Palisoc (1983), but computer graphics were primitive at that time. McArdle and Boker (1990) extended this work by incorporating drawing features in their procedures, yielding a diagram in which the screen objects appear quite similar to the printed diagram. However, these approaches were output oriented and were not designed to yield a complete graphical modeling system in which model input is a drawing as well. Recently, a revolution in interfaces has been created, and a variety of nonalgebraic options for model specification has become possible. The one that especially appeals to researchers who are not specialists in multivariate analysis is a graphical technology based on easy-to-use Windows and Macintosh interfaces such as can be found in EQS for Windows, EQS for Macintosh (Bentler & Wu, 1995a; 1995b), and AMOS (Arbuckle, 1995). In the first part of this paper, I shall illustrate some aspects of the modeling process using EQS, and I will illustrate the model specification process using a recent example from politics.

On the other hand, a revolution in the use of statistics for structural equation modeling remains to be carried out. The most widely used estimation and testing methodology, which has been used in this field for several decades, is based on the theory of maximum likelihood. This theory is implemented only under the assumption that data are multivariate normally distributed. However, psychological data are rarely normal, and one should wonder what the consequences of violating these assumptions might be. It turns out that the consequences are drastic, in that true models may often be rejected, while coefficients that seem to be highly significant actually may be marginal or statistically unimportant (Bentler & Dudgeon, 1996). In the final part of the paper, I shall describe this problem, as well as some existing and newly proposed solutions. Several of these solutions are already implemented in the EQS programs and hopefully will be added to other programs as well.

A GRAPHICAL ENVIRONMENT

Rather than talk about modeling in the abstract, I shall illustrate how it is approached in today's Windows (and similarly, Macintosh) environment, using EQS as an example. When the program is started and a data file is opened, the screen shown in Fig. 17.1 appears. In this example, *File* was clicked and the file *exercise.ess* was opened in the usual way. This is an EQS system file of 40 participants on 6 variables, containing the variable labels shown along with data. Figure 17.1 shows only the first two participants. Once data are active, a variety of procedures become available as indicated in the written menu choices and the graphical plot procedures. For example, under *Data*, there are a variety of data handling options such as randomly splitting the sample, recoding or transforming variables, and so on. Under *Analysis*, there are options such as exploratory factor analysis, which can be used to help build a model. *Build EQS* is a procedure for building a model using the equations language to be described later.

The plotting options, available by clicking on any of the icons, allow various views of the data. Plots are dynamically recomputed. For example, the scatterplot option (9th in sequence from the left) permits one to mark outlier cases in the plot, remove such cases by a few clicks, thereby instantaneously generating a

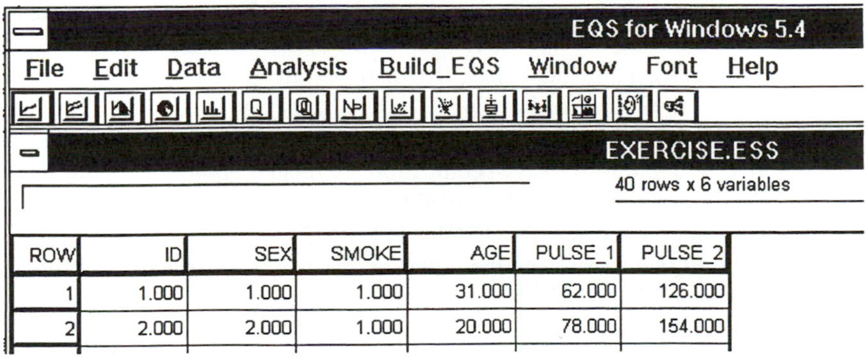

							EQS for Windows 5.4
File	Edit	Data	Analysis	Build_EQS	Window	Font	Help

EXERCISE.ESS

40 rows x 6 variables

ROW	ID	SEX	SMOKE	AGE	PULSE_1	PULSE_2
1	1.000	1.000	1.000	31.000	62.000	126.000
2	2.000	2.000	1.000	20.000	78.000	154.000

FIG. 17.1   An open data file in EQS.

recomputation of the regression and squared correlation. The 3-D plot (10th in sequence) allows dynamic rotation of all three axes in a three-dimensional space. This type of graphical presentation is helpful for finding clusters in data.

EQS models can be set up with *Build EQS* or using *Diagrammer*, EQS' plotting tool. This is activated by clicking on the last plot icon, the factor structure with its 3 indicators. This brings up a drawing screen; see Fig. 17.2.[1]

EQUATIONS AND DIAGRAMS

Equations and diagrams are completely synonymous in causal modeling. To explain this point, let me review some basic ideas from the field. Structural equation models, including covariance structure analysis, path analysis, confirmatory factor analysis, and their many variants that are used to model a hypothesized set of relations among variables, are fundamentally algebraic in nature. All such models are made up of a series of regression-like equations to which most researchers will have been exposed. These equations are of the form:

$$V4 = \beta_1 V1 + \beta_2 V2 + \beta_3 V3 + E4$$

This example indicates that *V4* is to be predicted with optimal weights by *V1*, *V2*, and *V3*. Since the prediction may not be perfect, an error term *E4* is added. When a model requires a series of such equations, historically they have been collected into a set of matrix equations to describe the model structure (e.g. eight matrices in the standard LISREL model by Jöreskog & Sörbom, 1993). This technically demanding approach was simplified by Bentler and Weeks (1980) using a three matrix form and a coherent conceptual approach to describing all such models. In their approach, *the parameters of any model are the unknown coefficients in the equations as well as the variances and covariances of the independent variables.* Thus, in the regression example, the coefficients β_1, β_2, β_3, and the variances of *V1*, *V2*, and *V3* and their covariances are the parameters. The Bentler–Weeks approach also requires recognition that residual variables such as *E4* are almost always also independent variables. This is not surprising since the variance of *E4* (relative to the variance of *V4*) carries information about the R^2, which is not known before the analysis. Although a matrix form for the Bentler–Weeks model exists, the matrices are hidden from the user in all versions of EQS. The mainframe, UNIX, and personal computer versions of EQS (Bentler, 1995) accomplish this by using an equation language similar to the above example for model specification. A related approach was recently developed for LISREL using the SIMPLIS language (Jöreskog & Sörbom, 1993). A distinction between the AMOS and SIMPLIS approaches, on the one hand, and the EQS approach, on the other, is that the basic principles of model

---

[1] The reader who wants to more actively follow the description can download a free copy of EQS from http://www.mvsoft.com.

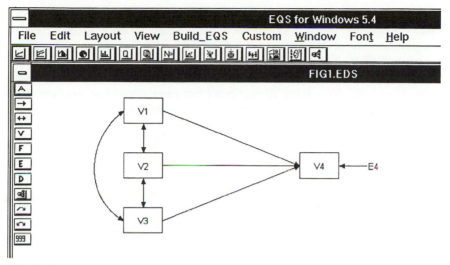

FIG. 17.2 EQS' path diagram for regression equation.

construction are always visible to the researcher in the former but not in the latter. Further, in the graphical EQS approach, a wide variety of additional plotting and analysis tools are an integral part of the modeling environment. For example, there is a procedure for automatically creating a confirmatory model from an exploratory factor analysis solution.

Although an algebraic representation of a model is informative, it is not the only approach. In fact, Wright (1921), a major inventor of this methodology, preferred his path diagram representation to an equations representation for showing the causal flow among variables. The path diagram in Fig. 17.2 is the counterpart to the regression equation above. It clearly shows the causal flow from *V1*, *V2*, and *V3* to *V4*, and shows how the independent variables *V1*, *V2*, and *V3* are correlated. However, since there is no two-way arrow relating {*V1*, *V2*, *V3*} to *E4*, it is apparent that the predictors and the residual error are not correlated. This is the typical assumption of regression, required to yield an identified model. Actually, the regression model is *just identified*, meaning that it has the same number of parameters as data points, and hence it is theoretically uninteresting since any set of data always can be transformed into a regression model.

As usual, two-way arrows are covariances, and one-way arrows are the regression coefficients. Each independent variable also has a variance; this is typically not shown, though McArdle and Boker (1990) use a two-way arrow from a variable to itself to show a variance.

Figure 17.2 shows not only the regression model, but also the EQS for Windows drawing environment (which is almost identical in the EQS for Macintosh environment) called *Diagrammer*. The top of the screen shows various menu options that are available within *Diagrammer*. These options permit editing a diagram, selection of objects in the diagram, rotating selected parts of a figure, and so on. They also permit beautifying the diagram for publication, by controlling the spacing, alignment and size of objects, and choosing what aspects are to be displayed (e.g. the variables *V1*, *V2* . . . or variable labels, latent or measured variables, types of parameter estimates, etc.). The drawing tools that are used to build a diagram are shown in the left-hand side of the screen. The drawing area is initially blank, and clicking on *V* and then clicking in the screen area brings up the first variable, *V1*. A complete latent factor with its indicators can be drawn at once using the factor structure option that shows the tiny circle and the three tiny squares. Arrows are drawn by clicking on the chosen type, and then clicking on the variables to be connected. Variables can be renamed and renumbered, as desired. After the diagram is finished, the model can be estimated by clicking on *Build EQS* and choosing the estimation option. The results (estimates, test statistics) then come back directly to the diagram as well as to an output text file that gives a vast amount of information about the quality of the model. However, as noted before, a regression model is usually uninteresting. To illustrate a more interesting, potentially testable model, I shall use a political example.

THE TAX RATES ISSUE IN US POLITICS

The talk on which this paper is based was given just before the 1996 US presidential election, and hence it may be appropriate to use a political example to illustrate how to conceptualize competing models and express them in a simple way with *Diagrammer*. I should like to show how one would use causal modeling to understand the claim made by candidate Dole, and the Republican party, that cutting tax rates will *increase* the amount of money the government receives in revenues. Their claim is associated with an idea that was popular a few years ago (but never officially adopted by the US government), about "dynamic scoring" of budget consequences.

The position that President Clinton and the Democratic party espoused is shown in Fig. 17.3.

Figure 17.3 is just a bivariate regression, a special case of Fig. 17.2. The direction of the arrow implies a causal impact of Tax Cut on Revenue, rather than the other way around, and implies that the anticipated path or impact is negative: greater tax cut, less revenue. The directional arrow represents a quantitative

FIG. 17.3 Democratic theory for effect of Tax Cut.

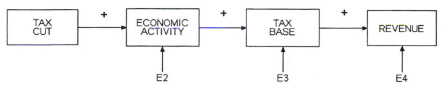

FIG. 17.4   Republican theory for effect of Tax Cut.

regression coefficient, which is an impact multiplier whose magnitude reflects the strength of effect. Evidently, the Democrats would argue that the relation is strongly negative: that is, cutting taxes will strongly and negatively impact government revenues.

By itself, this model is also not very interesting, since it too is just identified, but it does have two conceptually valuable features. At least, it predicts that there is an effect of Tax Cut. If none were predicted, there would be no one-way arrow. Further, the effect is predicted to be of a particular sign. An observed zero or positive coefficient would lead to rejection of this model.

On the other hand, former Senator Dole and the Republicans had quite a different model in mind. They proposed that cutting taxes would lead the government to receive more, rather than less, revenue. However, I believe they never convinced the American public that this proposal made logical sense. I suspect if the Republicans had used a path diagram, the public might have believed this claim more. In particular, the Republicans proposed a dynamic series of conseuences of a tax cut that I interpret with the model shown in Fig. 17.4.[2]

That is, they proposed that two additional variables must be considered: Economic Activity and Tax Base. The first would be an aggregate measure of sales volume, number of new firms, new products, and so on. The second would be a measure of the number of citizens paying taxes, or perhaps also the average income of workers. Then this theory claims that Tax Cut stimulates Economic Activity positively. In turn, increased Economic Activity means increases in the Tax Base of the economy. In turn, as the Tax Base increases, the government takes in more Revenue. Thus, the Republican proposal is a causal chain of effects among four variables, each coefficient in the chain being positive.

Evidently, this model is a mediation model, since the new variables, Economic Activity and Tax Base, mediate the effect of Tax Cut on Revenue. Unlike the multiple and bivariate regressions earlier, it is a multiple equation model. In this model, there are three dependent variables. Hence, to set up and run this model in EQS or any other program, one must use three equations. (In EQS, *Diagrammer* will create them automatically.) By itself, the model in Fig. 17.4 is a testable model because it predicts that there is no direct effect of Tax Cut on Revenue—rather, it is mediated by the two intervening variables. Path

---

[2] Richard Scheines also has suggested this interpretation.

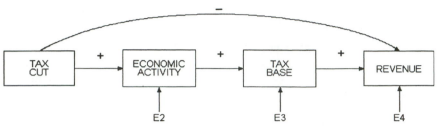

FIG. 17.5 Combined model for effect of Tax Cut.

analysis, as invented by Sewell Wright (1921), is a way of doing algebra with such diagrams. He showed that, if each of the three paths in the chain is positive, then the impact of Tax Cut (as mediated by Economic Activity and Tax Base) on Revenue also would be positive. In fact, if each of the paths has a quantitative regression coefficient, the overall mediated effect, called the *indirect effect*, of Tax Cut on Revenue is the product of the three coefficients.

Of course, it is unlikely that the Republicans would totally disregard the *direct effect* model of Fig. 17.3. Since both Democratic and Republican arguments may each have merit, a combined model must also be considered. This model, which is in principle testable, can be diagrammed as in Fig. 17.5.

The combined model reflects the possibility that both theories may have some truth: that is, Tax Cut is expected to have a negative direct effect on Revenue, while the indirect effect is positive. Sewell Wright's algebra, then, gives the *total effect* as the sum of the direct effect plus the indirect effect. Thus, under the complete model, the actual effect of the Tax Cut would depend on the relative size of the positive and negative effects. If the direct negative effect were large, and the indirect positive effect small, the overall total effect would be a loss of Revenue. On the other hand, if the direct effect were small, and the indirect effect large, there would be a gain in Revenue. Or, both effects could cancel each other.

Thus, we can see the Democratic argument is that the direct effect of a tax cut would be large and the indirect effect would be zero or very small. In contrast, the Republican argument is that the indirect positive effect would be much larger than the direct negative effect. I think that this analysis, conceptualized in terms of path analysis, makes clear some of the murky claims about tax cuts that are only vaguely understood by the American public. In fact, in November 1996 the American public elected a Democratic president and a largely Republican Congress. If this were the only issue on which they voted, it would seem that the American public is ambivalent about what to expect from tax cuts.

As a scientist, I would say that the path diagram makes explicit two alternative theories on the effect of tax cuts, but that arguments about which theory is correct cannot be based on political beliefs or the strength of arguments, as was done in the American elections. Policy decisions should be based, if possible, on data rather than speculation. Ideally, theories should be tested with experiments, but it is difficult or impossible to do experiments with economies. So methods are needed to test theories with nonexperimental data such as those obtained from economies as they evolve naturally across time. These tax cut theories presumably apply to any market economy. In order to test these contrasting theories, one would want to obtain a data base taken from, say, 100 market economies, each of which implemented a tax cut under relatively similar general conditions. In each economy, one would have to quantify the size of a tax cut and also quantify subsequent changes in amount of economic activity, tax base, and revenues. Then the unknown paths in these models can be quantified, and these contrasting models could be tested.

Although I have no such data, the model of Fig. 17.5 can be used to create the command language to create the setup for a model run, by clicking on the *Build EQS* option shown in Fig. 17.1. After giving a title and accepting the program defaults, the following model file is created:

```
/TITLE
Effects of a Tax Cut
/SPECIFICATIONS
 DATA='';
 METHODS=ML;
 MATRIX=RAW;
/EQUATIONS
V2 = + *V1 + E2;
V3 = + *V2 + E3;
V4 = + *V1 + *V3 + E4;
/VARIANCES
V1 = *;
E2 = *;
E3 = *;
E4 = *;
/COVARIANCES
```

It is apparent in line 4 of this file that the data file was not specified. An actual modeling run testing this hypothetical model on real data, of course, would need to have this file specified. As was noted earlier, the model has three dependent variables, and hence three equations. It has four independent variables, each of which has a variance to be estimated. There are no two-way arrows or covariances. The remaining point to note is that an asterisk ("*") represents a parameter to be estimated: that is, an unknown. Thus there are four regression coefficients (one-way arrows) as well as four variances to be estimated, for a total of eight unknown parameters. Since with four variables there are ten data variances and covariances altogether, a model that tests Fig. 17.5 would have two degrees of freedom. These two degrees of freedom would test a missing connection between Tax Cut and Tax Base and also between Economic Activity and Revenue. If empirical data were not consistent with the model, leading to model rejection, additional paths between these variables might have to be considered. Finally, in mainframe and UNIX versions of EQS, where *Diagrammer* is not available, a model is specified by simply typing the input file as shown earlier (Bentler, 1995).

TOWARD A REVOLUTION IN STATISTICAL PRACTICE

Normal theory maximum-likelihood methods form the practical statistical basis of causal modeling practice. All the critical statistics derived from this method, such as the χ^2 goodness-of-fit test to evaluate the entire model and the z-statistics that test hypotheses on particular parameters in models, are based on the assumption of independent observations drawn from a population in which variables are multivariate normally distributed. In most areas of psychology, it is easy to assure that participants' data are independent, but it is quite a bit harder to assure that data are multivariate normal. To illustrate, Micceri (1989) reported that all 440 tests and measures he reviewed were significantly nonnormally distributed. In my drug abuse research (e.g. Newcomb & Bentler, 1988), I hardly ever find multivariate normal distributions.

As reviewed by Bentler and Dudgeon (1996), the typical consequence of ignoring the normality assumption is that true models will be falsely rejected, and effects will appear more important than they really are. Stated differently, scientific conclusions will be compromised. In fact, the literature must be strewn with questionable results, since most researchers do not bother to evaluate this very strong assumption and simply accept normal theory statistics (Breckler, 1990; Gierl & Mulvenon, 1995). It would seem that a revolution in practice is needed to assure statistical soundness in the use of causal modeling for understanding relationships among nonexperimental data. However, such a revolution can occur only if structural modeling programs provide researchers with appropriate alternative methods. Some good alternatives have been around for a long time, new methods were recently developed, and many promising alternatives will be published in the next few years. I shall say a bit about these methods in the next sections.

Current practice

If F is the function to be minimized in maximum likelihood (ML), taking on the value F_{min}, the ML assumptions are met, the model is correct, and the sample size n is large enough, at the minimum $T_{ML} = nF_{min}$ is distributed as a goodness-of-fit χ^2 variate with $(p^* - q)$ degrees of freedom, where $p^* = p(p + 1)/2$ is the number of variances and covariances to be fit and q is the number of free parameters estimated. Thus T_{ML} is the test statistic used to evaluate the null hypothesis, which is rejected if T_{ML} exceeds a critical value in the χ^2 distribution at an α-level of significance, and accepted otherwise. Unfortunately, as already noted, T_{ML} is not necessarily a chi-square variate with nonnormal data (although under very special circumstances it can be), and hence scientific conclusions based on it must be suspect. Various studies have shown how misleading T_{ML} can be (e.g. Curran, West, & Finch, 1996; Hu, Bentler, & Kano, 1992). Unfortunately, T_{ML} is routinely computed by computer programs, implying that it has some meaning even when it does not.

Once a model is accepted, the relative size and significance levels of particular parameter estimates θ_i are evaluated to see if they differ significantly from zero. Typically, this involves evaluating a null hypothesis on the population value $\theta_{iPOP} = 0$ using the statistic $z = (\theta_i - \theta_{iPOP})/SE(\theta_i)$, where $SE(\theta_i)$ is the standard error estimate. Again, computer programs calculate this standard error estimate by a default ML "information matrix" -based procedure which does not correctly estimate the true $SE(\theta_i)$. Typically, the estimate of $SE(\theta_i)$ is too small, and hence the z statistic is inflated, making parameters seem more important than they are. Hence, tests of parameters will be incorrect in the typical case where a normal theory method is used, but the data are not normal.

Today's correct statistics

Developed about a decade ago, and incorporated into the EQS program in 1989 (with full technical documentation), the Satorra–Bentler (1994) scaled test statistic T_{SB} has been found to correct the bad behavior of T_{ML} under distributional violations. In principle, T_{SB} is simple to compute, via $T_{SB} = T_{ML}/c$, where c is a scaling constant that corrects T_{ML} so that the mean of the sampling distribution of T_{SB} will be closer to the expected mean under the model. Chou and Bentler (1995), Chou, Bentler, and Satorra (1991), and Curran, West, and Finch (1996) showed with simulation studies that T_{SB} performed very well under a wide variety of nonnormal conditions, as well as with normal data. It remains the best test statistic for ML estimation in practice at this writing.

It is difficult to provide an explanation for the problems with the standard error estimates obtained from ML without resorting to matrices. If A is the large sample information matrix, the usual variance–covariance matrix of the ML estimator is obtained from the inverse of this matrix as $\text{acov}(\theta_i) = A^{-1}/n$. Standard errors, of course, are square roots of the variances which are on the diagonal of this matrix. This is what is computed with most programs, but this matrix has no special meaning if the data are not multivariate normal. It does not give standard errors. The correct large sample covariance matrix is given by $\text{acov}(\theta_i) = A^{-1}BA^{-1}/n$, where B is a matrix that takes the nonnormality into account. When data are normal, $A = B$ and the usual formula is correct. The correct covariance matrix has been known for more than a decade; see Bentler and Dudgeon (1996) for the precise formula and many early references to it (e.g. Bentler & Dijkstra,

1985; Browne, 1984). The correctness of these standard errors has been verified in simulations (e.g. Chou & Bentler, 1995). In EQS, the correct standard errors, known as the "robust" standard errors, have been available since 1989.

Surprisingly, however, T_{SB} and robust standard errors are not available in any other structural equation program, though LINCS (Schoenberg & Arminger, 1988) evidently does give the robust standard errors. This is in spite of the fact that these statistics have been known for many years, the issues and solutions were discussed in the 1989 EQS manual, and a thorough review about correct inference with nonnormal data was made by Bentler and Dudgeon (1996). It is hard to understand why various computer programs have not yet corrected their statistics for this typical scenario in which data are nonnormal but ML is used. I have concluded that program developers will continue to ignore technical accuracy until journal editors and reviewers insist on the use of correct statistics. If editors and reviewers were to insist on the use of more reliable statistics in journal articles, users certainly would put pressure on program publishers to provide such statistics.

An alternative way to deal with nonnormal data is to use Browne's (1984) asymptotically distribution-free (ADF) approach. In the ADF approach, no assumption is made about the distribution of the variables, and hence it should be the ideal method to use with nonnormal data. Unfortunately, ADF is useless in practice (e.g. Curran, West, & Finch, 1996; Hu, Bentler, & Kano, 1992). That is, its test statistic T_{ADF} yields completely distorted conclusions about the adequacy of a model in all but impractically large sample sizes. For example, in the simulation study of Hu et al. (1992), at the smallest sample sizes the ADF test statistic virtually always rejected the true model, and sometimes 5000 cases were needed to yield nominal rejection rates. Yung and Bentler (1994) proposed some computationally intensive modifications to the ADF test statistic, which improved its performance, but these are not fully adequate either.

A new radically improved version of the ADF statistic was developed by Yuan and Bentler (1997a). Their approach is a simple correction to the ADF test statistic $T_{YB} = T_{ADF}/(1 + T_{ADF}/n)$. As sample size gets large, T_{YB} becomes equal to the standard ADF test, but at smaller sample sizes it corrects the typical inflation of the ADF test. At present, this is the best ADF test available, performing very much better than the classical ADF test in simulations under a variety of conditions. The Yuan–Bentler test has been available in EQS since 1995. As with the corrected normal theory statistics, so far T_{YB} has not made its way into other modeling programs.

It seems hard to believe that there should be so few trustworthy methods. In fact, there are many new developments on the horizon that will, in the future, provide still better statistical tools for structural modeling. Such tools have to be able to handle the most difficult, realistic data analysis conditions found in practice, such as nonnormal data or data with outliers. I turn to these methods in the concluding section.

RESEARCH FRONTIERS IN MODELING STATISTICS

The work that I shall summarize here is based on collaboration with Ke-Hai Yuan, one of the bright new stars in this field. As above, I shall concentrate first on corrections to normal theory statistics such as ML, and then discuss more general alternative approaches.

Frontiers with normal theory statistics

Evidence indicates that the normal theory ML estimator is well behaved not only under classical situations, but also when assumptions are violated. That is, the parameter estimates are really very good, no matter what. The problem lies with the test statistics and standard errors. Is the Satorra–Bentler corrected ML test, T_{SB}, really the only one to work well under violation of assumptions? Actually, T_{SB} should be only approximately chi-square distributed in large samples, so in principle it should be possible to develop a better test. Such a better test was, theoretically, developed by Browne (1984). He had developed a general residual-based test statistic, T_B, that should be exactly chi-square distributed in large samples, and hence it should work for any type of data. Surprisingly, this statistic has hardly been studied. Arguing that Browne's residual test shares some key similarities with his ADF test, Yuan and Bentler (1996a) agreed that it would be excellent in extremely large samples but suspected it would also break down in all but the largest sized samples. In a series of simulation studies, they found that Browne's residual-based T_B statistic behaved badly at almost all practical sample sizes. In order to correct this problem, they developed two new versions of this statistic as well as a new F-test. For example, one of their statistics is of the form T_{YB} described earlier: that is, it corrects Browne's residual test as $T_{ResYB} = T_B /(1 + T_B /n)$. This new test, and the others, were found to be very promising indeed.

It is not a minor matter to discover conditions under which a test may be robust to violation of distributional assumptions. Yuan and Bentler (1997b) proposed two new ways to generate nonnormal data while maintaining a specified structural model. An important feature of these nonnormal distributions is that their fourth-order moment matrices can be precisely stated. As a result, the performance of test statistics that depend on these fourth-order moments can be predicted, and simulation methods can evaluate the correctness of these predictions. Yuan and Bentler (1996b) then studied several test statistics derived from the normal theory likelihood ratio with these new classes of nonnormal distributions and obtained conditions for the validity of the statistics under these distributions. Using some common models, they showed that these statistics are valid under much wider classes of distributions than previously assumed. Interestingly, this new theory also provided an explanation for previously reported Monte Carlo results on some statistics.

Turning next to the other critical issue, the correctness of the standard error estimates, Yuan and Bentler (1996c) evaluated some correction formulas that have been proposed for the ML estimator covariance matrix to handle nonnormal data. The classical correction is one that was developed for elliptically symmetric distributions (e.g. Browne, 1984). Yuan and Bentler found that the asymptotic distribution of the ML estimator, when computed for a sample from an elliptical distribution, is valid in a larger class of pseudo-elliptical distributions, which can have arbitrary marginal skewnesses. In addition, the covariance matrix of the estimator under these skewed distributions was found to have as simple a form as when the sample is from an elliptical distribution. Finally, they found that, while the covariance submatrix for a subset of the parameter estimator can be obtained by rescaling the corresponding normal-based matrix, Browne's proposed scaling factor based on Mardia's multivariate kurtosis parameter cannot be used, while the Satorra–Bentler scaling factor remains valid.

Frontiers with distribution-free statistics

Although the distribution-free test T_{YB} performs very well, it is not the only one. As part of this research program, other alternatives to Browne's ADF statistic were developed. By comparing mean and covariance structure analysis with its analogue in the multivariate linear model, Yuan and Bentler (in press a) modified the ADF test statistic to yield an F-test. The natural approach of using an F-distribution to approximate the distribution of this test turned out to be excellent. In simulation work, they found that the distributions of the new F-tests are much more closely approximated by F-distributions than the original ADF statistics are approximated by chi-square distributions. This paper also provided a detailed analysis as to why the ADF statistic fails on large models and why F-tests and corrections should give better results.

A related problem is that the standard errors computed from the ADF method are not very good, which in turn means that parameter tests based on z-statistics will also not be very good. For example, Curran (1994, p. 198) found that ADF standard errors were significantly negatively biased in normal samples with Ns of 100 and 200, but also "cannot be trusted even under conditions of multivariate non-normality at samples of $N = 1000$ or less." Yuan and Bentler (in press c) also found that these estimates are much more biased than has been suspected. Because they tend to underestimate actual sampling variability, parameters in models that should truly be considered as nonexistent or zero are taken as statistically significant instead. As a result, models in practice will contain many superfluous parameters that not only make the models much more complex than necessary, but also most likely have the effect that the models will not replicate when evaluated on new samples. Using a simple correction to the ADF inverse weight matrix, motivated by admissible estimators of inverse covariance matrices, a new ADF standard error was proposed that was found to be a substantial improvement over current practice.

Frontiers with messy data distributions

It is necessary to acknowledge that, in spite of their differences in assumptions about distributional shape, ML and ADF methods both assume that data are fairly well behaved. Neither theory makes any real allowance for bizarre or strange observations. Since data sets with small proportions of outliers usually exist in practice, Yuan and Bentler (1996d) evaluated the effect of outliers on estimators and tests in covariance structure analysis. Their simulation results show that, even if a proposed structure is correct for a sample without data contamination, a small percentage of outliers will lead the estimators to be biased and the test statistics to reject a true model. This suggests that new methods based on robust procedures are required. Yuan and Bentler (in press b) developed such methods.

There are many ways to think about lack of robustness of estimators and tests for outlying cases. In a regular case, it will be appropriate to base an analysis on the usual ML sample covariance matrix, which is the typical input matrix to both ML and ADF estimation. This matrix is computed based on the standard formula in which every observation is treated with equal weight. However, when the data generating mechanism is not well behaved, the sample covariance matrix may not be an adequate unstructured estimator of the population covariance matrix, and hence any procedure based on it is liable to be inadequate. Using influence functions, the authors show that the standard procedures can totally fail because of their quadratic influence functions. While robust methods have been used in principal components and canonical variates, the technical development of robust methods in covariance structure analysis is new. Yuan and Bentler (in press b) studied M-estimators and S-estimators and developed the relevant theory to permit model goodness-of-fit tests and to yield correct standard error estimates. Simulation results permit optimistic conclusions about improvements in correct inference that are possible with this approach in situations where data quality may not be very good.

CONCLUSIONS

In this report, I have discussed the simple as well as the complex aspects of causal modeling. Almost anyone can be an expert on the human interface involved in structural modeling—that is, they can judge whether or not a computer implementation is easy and fun to use. As was shown in the first part of this paper, substantial strides have been made in user-friendliness of causal modeling programs.

On the other hand, the correct handling of psychological data to yield statistically reliable conclusions is a much more complex and technical area. It is also an area where the field is still critically underdeveloped. As reviewed in this chapter, technical improvements with great practical importance have been made, but much more remains to be done. For example, new results have not yet made it into the practitioner's hands. However, I am hoping that many of the successful methods mentioned here will make it into the next release of EQS. That release will also contain other new technical developments which space limitations precluded me from discussing. For example, coherent approaches to dealing with missing data that are normally distributed (Jamshidian & Bentler, in press; Tang & Bentler, in press) and nonnormally distributed (Yuan & Bentler, 1996e) are also on the horizon for EQS. Of course, I shall continue to strive to make EQS even more user-friendly than it already is. No doubt, competitive program developers will also do their best to make their approaches to causal models more friendly, useful, and accurate. Such friendly competition among developers brings ever better methods into the hands of researchers.

ACKNOWLEDGEMENTS

The research reported here was supported in part by grants DA01070 and DA00017 from the National Institute on Drug Abuse.

REFERENCES

Arbuckle, J. (1995). *AMOS 3.5*. Chicago: Smallwaters.

Arminger, G., Clogg, C. C., & Sobel, M. E. (Eds.). (1995). *Handbook of statistical modeling for the social and behavioral sciences*. New York: Plenum.

Bentler, P. M. (1995). *EQS structural equations program manual*. Encino, CA: Multivariate Software.

Bentler, P. M., & Dijkstra, T. (1985). Efficient estimation via linearization in structural models. In P. R. Krishnaiah (Ed.), *Multivariate analysis VI* (pp. 9–42). Amsterdam: North-Holland.

Bentler, P. M., & Dudgeon, P. (1996). Covariance structure analysis: Statistical practice, theory, and directions. *Annual Review of Psychology, 47*, 563–592.

Bentler, P. M., & Weeks, D. G. (1980). Linear structural equations with latent variables. *Psychometrika, 45*, 289–308.

Bentler, P. M., & Wu, E. J. C. (1995a). *EQS for Windows user's guide*. Encino, CA: Multivariate Software.

Bentler, P. M., & Wu, E. J. C. (1995b). *EQS for Macintosh user's guide*. Encino, CA: Multivariate Software.

Breckler, J. (1990). Applications of covariance structure: modeling in statistics: Cause for concern? *Psychological Bulletin, 107*, 260–273.

Browne, M. W. (1984). Asymptotically distribution-free methods for the analysis of covariance structures. *British Journal of Mathematical and Statistical Psychology, 37*, 62–83.

Bullock, H. E., Harlow, L. L., & Mulaik, S. A. (1994). Causation issues in structural equation modeling research. *Structural Equation Modeling, 1*, 253–267.

Byrne, B. (1994). *Structural equation modeling with EQS and EQS/Windows: Basic concepts, applications, and programming*. Thousand Oaks, CA: Sage.

Chou, C.-P., & Bentler, P. M. (1995). Estimates and tests in structural equation modeling. In R. Hoyle (Ed.), *Structural equation modeling: Concepts, issues, and applications* (pp. 37–75). Thousand Oaks, CA: Sage.

Chou, C.-P., Bentler, P. M., & Satorra, A. (1991). Scaled test statistics and robust standard errors for nonnormal data in covariance structure analysis: A Monte Carlo study. *British Journal of Mathematical and Statistical Psychology, 44*, 347–357.

Curran, P. J. (1994). *The robustness of confirmatory factor analysis to model misspecification and violations of normality*. Unpublished doctoral dissertation, Arizona State University, Tempe.

Curran, P. J., West, S. G., & Finch, J. F. (1996). The robustness of test statistics to nonnormality and specification error in confirmatory factor analysis. *Psychological Methods, 1*, 16–29.

Dunn, G., Everitt, B., & Pickles, A. (1993). *Modelling covariances and latent variables using EQS*. London: Chapman & Hall.

Faulbaum, F., & Bentler, P. M. (1994). Causal modeling: Some trends and perspectives. In I. Borg & P. Mohler (Eds.), *Trends and perspectives in empirical social research* (pp. 224–249). Berlin, Germany: Walter de Gruyter.

Gierl, M. J., & Mulvenon, S. (1995, April). Evaluating the application of fit indices to structural equation models in educational research: A review of the literature from 1990 through 1994. Paper presented at the annual meeting of the American Educational Research Association, San Francisco, CA.

Hoyle, R. H. (Ed.). (1995). *Structural equation modeling: Concepts, issues, and applications*. Thousand Oaks, CA: Sage.

Hu, L., Bentler, P. M., & Kano, Y. (1992). Can test statistics in covariance structure analysis be trusted? *Psychological Bulletin, 112*, 351–362.

Huba, G. J., & Palisoc, A. L. (1983). Computerized path diagrams on a line printer. *Computational Statistics & Data Analysis, 1*, 137–140.

Jamshidian, M., & Bentler, P. M. (in press). ML estimation of mean and covariance structures with missing data using complete data routines. *Journal of Educational and Behavioural Statistics*.

Jöreskog, K. G., & Sörbom, D. (1993). *LISREL 8 structural equation modeling with the SIMPLIS command language*. Hillsdale, NJ: Erlbaum.

Loehlin, J. C. (1992). *Latent variable models: An introduction to factor, path, and structural analysis*. Hillsdale, NJ: Erlbaum.

Marcoulides, G. A., & Schumacker, R. E. (Eds.). (1996). *Advanced structural equation modeling techniques*. Hillsdale, NJ: Erlbaum.

McArdle, J. J., & Boker, S. M. (1990). *RAMpath: Path diagram software*. Denver, CO: Data Transforms.

Micceri, T. (1989). The unicorn, the normal curve, and other improbable creatures. *Psychological Bulletin, 105*, 156–166.

Mueller, R. O. (1996). *Basic principles of structural equation modeling*. New York: Springer-Verlag.

Newcomb, M. D., & Bentler, P. M. (1988). *Consequences of adolescent drug use: Impact on the lives of young adults*. Thousand Oaks, CA: Sage.

Satorra, A., & Bentler, P. M. (1994). Corrections to test statistics and standard errors in covariance structure analysis. In A. von Eye & C. C. Clogg (Eds.), *Latent variables analysis: Applications for developmental research* (pp. 399–419). Thousand Oaks, CA: Sage.

Schoenberg, R., & Arminger, G. (1988). LINCS: Linear Covariance Structure Analysis. *Multivariate Behavioral Research, 23*, 271–273.

Schumacker, R. E., & Lomax, R. G. (1996). *A beginner's guide to structural equation modeling*. Hillsdale, NJ: Erlbaum.

Steyer, R. (1993). Principles of causal modeling: A summary of its mathematical foundations and practical steps. In F. Faulbaum (Ed.), *SoftStat '93: Advances in Statistical Software* (pp. 107–114). Stuttgart, Germany: Fischer.

Tang, M.-L., & Bentler, P. M. (in press). Theory and method for constrained estimation in structural equation models with incomplete data. *Computational Statistics & Data Analysis*.

Tremblay, P. F., & Gardner, R. C. (1996). On the growth of structural equation modeling in psychological journals. *Structural Equation Modeling, 3*, 93–104.

Ullman, J. (1996). Structural equation modeling. In B. G. Tabachnick & L. S. Fidell, (Eds.), *Using multivariate statistics* (3rd Ed., pp. 709–811). New York: HarperCollins.

Wright, S. (1921). Correlation and causation. *Journal of Agricultural Research, 20,* 557–585.

Yuan, K.-H., & Bentler, P. M. (1996a). *Normal theory based test statistics for nonnormal data* (Tech. Rep.). Los Angeles, CA: University of California, Psychology Department.

Yuan, K.-H., & Bentler, P. M. (1996b). *On normal theory and associated test statistics in covariance structure analysis under two classes of nonnormal distributions* (Tech. Rep.). Los Angeles, CA: University of California, Psychology Department.

Yuan, K.-H., & Bentler, P. M. (1996c). *On asymptotic distributions of normal theory mle in covariance structure analysis under some nonnormal distributions* (Tech. Rep.). Los Angeles, CA: University of California, Psychology Department.

Yuan, K.-H., & Bentler, P. M. (1996d). *Effect of outliers on estimators and tests in covariance structure analysis* (Tech. Rep.). Los Angeles, CA: University of California, Psychology Department.

Yuan, K.-H., & Bentler, P. M. (1996e). Mean and covariance structure analysis with missing data. In A. Gupta & V. Girko (Eds.), *Multidimensional statistical analysis and theory of random matrices* (pp. 307–326). Amsterdam: VSP.

Yuan, K.-H., & Bentler, P. M. (1997a). Mean and covariance structure analysis: Theoretical and practical improvements. *Journal of the American Statistical Association, 92,* 767–774.

Yuan, K.-H., & Bentler, P. M. (1997b). Generating multivariate distributions with specified marginal skewness and kurtosis. In W. Bandilla & F. Faulbaum (Eds.), *SoftStat '97: Advances in statistical software 6* (pp. 385–391). Stuttgart: Lucius & Lucius.

Yuan. K.-H., & Bentler, P. M. (in press a). *F* tests for mean and covariance structure analysis. *Journal of Educational and Behavioral Statistics.*

Yuan. K.-H., & Bentler, P. M. (in press b). Robust mean and covariance structure analysis. *British Journal of Mathematical and Statistical Psychology.*

Yuan, K.-H., & Bentler, P. M. (in press c). Improving parameter tests in covariance structure analysis. *Computational Statistics & Data Analysis.*

Yung, Y. F., & Bentler, P. M. (1994). Bootstrap-corrected ADF test statistics in covariance structure analysis. *British Journal of Mathematical and Statistical Psychology, 47,* 63–84.

CHAPTER EIGHTEEN

Meta-analysis: Concepts, corollaries and controversies

Robert Rosenthal

Harvard University, Cambridge, Massachusetts, USA

In this paper, the history and current status of the meta-analytic enterprise is reviewed. Newer views of the concept of replication are considered and their relationship to the development of meta-analytic procedures is examined. Common criticisms and benefits of meta-analysis are considered, as are some less obvious consequences flowing from the development of a meta-analytic perspective. Meta-analytic procedures are seen to be tools useful to all researchers, even when the goal is not to do a full-scale review of the literature. Finally, the special value of meta-analytic procedures for investigators working with very small sample sizes is described.

Dans cet article, l'histoire et l'état actuel de l'entreprise méta-analytique sont réexaminés. Des opinions récentes sur le concept de la reproduction sont considérées et leur lien au développement de procédures méta-analytiques est examiné. Les critiques courantes et les avantages de la méta-analyse sont pris en considération, ainsi que certaines conséquences moins évidentes qui découlent du développement d'une perspective méta-analytique. Les procédures méta-analytiques sont perçues comme des outils utiles à tout chercheur, et ce même lorsque le but n'est pas de faire une revue complète de la documentation. En dernier lieu, on traite de la valeur spécifique de procédures méta-analytiques pour les chercheurs qui doivent utiliser de très petits échantillons.

CUMULATING SCIENTIFIC EVIDENCE

The fundamental problem addressed by meta-analytic procedures is the cumulation of evidence. There has long been a pessimistic feeling in the softer social, behavioral, and biological sciences that our progress has been exceedingly slow, at least when compared to the progress of harder sciences, such as physics and chemistry. In particular, it has seemed that the softer (and newer) sciences do not show the orderly progress and development of the harder (and older) sciences.

In other words, the more recent work of the harder sciences seems to build directly on the older work of those sciences, whereas the more recent work of the softer sciences seems often to be starting from scratch.

Those who have looked closely at the issue of cumulation in the physical sciences have pointed out that these disciplines have ample problems of their own (Collins, 1985; Hedges, 1987; Mann, 1990; Pool, 1988). Nonetheless, in the matter of cumulating evidence the softer sciences have much to be modest about.

Poor cumulation does not seem to be due primarily to lack of replication, or to the failure to recognize the need for replication. There are many areas of the softer sciences for which we have the results of many studies, all addressing essentially the same question. Our summaries of the results of these sets of studies, however, have not been nearly as informative as they might have been, either with respect to summarized significance levels or with respect to summarized effect magnitudes. Even the best reviews of research by the most sophisticated workers have rarely told us much more about each study in a set of studies than the direction of the relationship between the variables investigated, and whether or not a given significance level was attained. This state of affairs is beginning to change. More and more reviews of the literature are moving from the traditional literary approach to quantitative approaches to research synthesis described in an increasing number of textbooks of meta-analysis (Cooper, 1989; Cooper & Hedges, 1994; Glass, McGaw, & Smith, 1981; Hedges & Olkin, 1985; Hunter & Schmidt, 1990; Light & Pillemer, 1984; Rosenthal, 1991a). The goals of these quantitative approaches of meta-analysis are to help us discover what we have learned from the results of the studies conducted, and to help us discover what we have not yet learned.

Defining research results

Before we can consider various issues and procedures in the cumulation of research results, we must become quite explicit about the meaning of the concept "results of a study." It is easiest to begin with what we do not mean. We do not mean the prose *conclusion* drawn by the investigator and reported in the abstract, the results, or the discussion section of the research report. We also do not mean the results of an omnibus F test with $df > 1$ in the numerator or an omnibus χ^2 test with $df > 1$.

What we do mean is the answer to the question, *What is the relationship between any variable X and any variable Y?* The variables X and Y are chosen with only the constraint that their relationship be of interest to us. The answer to this question should normally come in two parts: (1) the estimate of the magnitude of the relationship (the effect size); and (2) an indication of the accuracy or reliability of the estimated effect size (as in a confidence interval placed around the effect size estimate). An alternative to the second part of the answer is one not intrinsically more useful, but one more consistent with the existing practices of researchers; that is, the examination of the significance level of the difference between the obtained effect size and the effect size expected under the null hypothesis (usually an effect size of zero).

Because a complete reporting of the results of a study requires the report of both the effect size and level of statistical significance, it is useful to make explicit the relationship between these quantities. The general relationship is given by:

Test of Significance = Size of Effect × Size of Study

In other words, the larger the study in terms of the number of sampling units, the more significant the results will be. This is true unless the size of the effect is truly zero, in which case a larger study will not produce a result that is any more significant than a smaller study. However, effect magnitudes of zero are not encountered very often.

Meta-analysis: A brief historical note

We are inclined to think of meta-analysis as a recent development, but it is older than the t test, which dates back to 1908 (Gosset, 1908)! Let me simultaneously describe the early history of meta-analysis, while providing a classic illustration of the meta-analytic enterprise. In 1904, Karl Pearson (1904) collected correlation coefficients; there were six of them with values of .58, .58, .60, .63, .66, and .77. The weighted mean of these six correlation coefficients was .64, the unweighted mean was .63, and the median was .61.

Karl Pearson was collecting correlation coefficients because he wanted to know the degree to which inoculation against smallpox saved lives. His own rough and ready summary of his meta-analysis of six studies was that there was a .6 correlation between inoculation and survival—a truly huge effect.

When Karl Pearson quantitatively summarized six studies of the effects of smallpox inoculation, a meta-analysis was an unusual thing to do. It is unusual no longer. Indeed, there is an explosion of meta-analytic research syntheses such that a rapidly increasing proportion of all reviews of the literature are in the form of quantitative reviews. In other words, they are meta-analyses. Despite its increasing frequency in the literature, meta-analysis is not without controversy and criticism, and we shall be examining some of this criticism.

Before we do that, however, it will be useful to examine a little more closely the concept of replication. Meta-analysis, after all, involves the summarizing or synthesizing of studies that are thought of broadly as replications. However, studies included in a meta-analysis are not replications in a narrow sense. Rather, they are replications in the sense that they examine the same underlying relationships even if the independent and dependent variables of the replications are operationally defined in different ways.

HOW SHALL WE THINK OF SUCCESSFUL REPLICATION?

There is a long tradition in psychology of our urging one another to replicate each other's research. Although we have been very good at calling for replications, we have not been very good at deciding when a replication has been successful. The issue we now address is, *When shall a study be deemed successfully replicated?*

Successful replication is ordinarily taken to mean that a null hypothesis that has been rejected at time (1) is rejected again, and with the same direction of outcome, on the basis of a new study at time (2). We have a failure to replicate when one study was significant and the other was not. Let us examine more closely a specific example of such a "failure to replicate".

Pseudo-failures to replicate

The saga of Smith and Jones.   Smith has published the results of an experiment in which a certain treatment procedure was predicted to improve performance. She reported results significant at $p < .05$ in the predicted direction. Jones published a rebuttal to Smith, claiming a failure to replicate (i.e. "I couldn't get it"; "It's not there"). In this type of situation, it is often the case that, although the p value associated with Smith's results is smaller than Jones's, the studies were in quite good agreement as to their estimated sizes of effect as defined either by Cohen's d [$(Mean_1 - Mean_2)/\sigma$] or by r, the point biserial correlation between group membership (coded 0 or 1) and performance score (a more continuous score; Cohen, 1988; Rosenthal, 1991a). Thus, studies labeled as "failure to replicate" often turn out to provide strong evidence for the replicability of the claimed effect.

On the odds against replicating significant results.   A related error often found in the behavioral and social sciences is the implicit assumption that if an effect is "real," we should expect it to be found significant again on replication. Nothing could be further from the truth.

Suppose there is, in nature, a real effect with a true magnitude of $d = .50$ (i.e. [$Mean_1 - Mean_2$]$/\sigma = .50$ σ units), or, equivalently, $r = .24$, a difference in success rate of 62% versus 38% as shown in the Binomial Effect Size Display in which r is the difference between the success rates of the two conditions. The success rates are given as $.50 + r/2$ and $.50 - r/2$; hence for this example, .62 $- .38 = .24$, the value of r. For further details, see Rosenthal and Rubin (1982). Further, suppose an investigator studies this effect with an N of 64 subjects or so, giving the researcher a level of statistical power of .50, a very common level of power for behavioral researchers of the last 35 years (Cohen, 1962; Sedlmeier & Gigerenzer, 1989). Even though a d of .50 or an r of .24 can reflect a very important effect, there is only one chance in four ($p = .25$) that both the original investigator and a replicator will get results significant at the .05 level; i.e. the probability (power) for the first study ($p = .50$) is multiplied by the probability for the second study ($p = .50$) to yield $.50 \times .50 = .25$. If there were two replications of the original study, there would be only one chance in eight ($p = .125$) that all three studies would be significant (i.e. $p = .5 \times .5 \times .5 = .125$), even though we know the effect in nature is very real and very important.

Contrasting views of replication

The traditional, less useful, view of replication has two primary characteristics: (1) it focuses on significance level as the relevant summary statistic of a study; and (2) it makes its evaluation of whether replication has been successful in a dichotomous fashion. For example, replications are successful if both or neither $p < .05$, and they are unsuccessful if one $p < .05$ and the other $p > .05$. Psychologists' reliance on a dichotomous decision procedure accompanied by an untenable discontinuity of credibility in results varying in p levels has been well documented (Nelson, Rosenthal, & Rosnow, 1986; Rosenthal & Gaito, 1963; 1964).

The newer, more useful views of replication success have two primary characteristics: (1) a focus on effect size as the more important summary statistic of a study, with a relatively more minor interest in the statistical significance level; and (2) an evaluation of whether replication has been successful made in a continuous fashion. For example, two studies are not said to be successful or unsuccessful replicates of each other, but rather the degree of failure to replicate is specified.

What should be reported?

Effect size and significance tests.   If we are to take seriously our newer view of the meaning of the success of replications, *what should be reported by authors of papers that are replications of earlier studies?* Clearly, reporting the results of tests of significance will not be sufficient. The effect size of the replication and of the original study must be reported. It is not crucial which particular effect size is employed, but the same effect size should be reported for the replication and the original study. Complete discussions of various effect sizes and when they are useful are available from Cohen (1977; 1988) and elsewhere (e.g. Rosenthal, 1991a; 1994). If the original study and its replication are reported in different effect size units, these can usually be translated into one or the other (Cohen, 1977; 1988; Rosenthal, 1991a; Rosenthal & Rosnow, 1991; Rosenthal & Rubin, 1989).

Power.   The statistical power at which the test of significance was made (assuming, for example, a population effect size equivalent to the effect size actually obtained) should be reported, especially if the results of either the original study or its replication were not significant (Cohen, 1988). In addition to reporting the statistical power for each study separately, it would be valuable to report the overall probability that both studies would have yielded significant results, given, for example, the effect size estimated from the results of the original and the replication study combined.

The counternull value of an effect size. Recently, Don Rubin and I introduced a new statistic, the counternull value of an obtained effect size. This is the non-null magnitude of effect size that is supported by exactly the same amount of evidence as supports the null value of the effect size (Rosenthal & Rubin, 1994). In other words, if the counternull value were taken as the null hypothesis, the resulting p value would be the same as the obtained p value for the actual null hypothesis. Reporting the counternull, in addition to the p value, virtually eliminates the common error of equating failure to reject the null with the estimation of the effect size as equal to zero. In many common situations, with a one degree of freedom effect size, the value of the counternull is simply twice the magnitude of the obtained effect size. For example, suppose a replicator, Jones, did not reject the null but obtained an effect size of $d = .50$. If Jones had been required to report that his d of .50 was just as close to a d of 1.00 as it was to a d of zero, Jones would have been less likely to draw his wrong conclusion that he had failed to replicate Smith's work, which had a very similar effect size.

CRITICISMS OF META-ANALYSIS

Does the enormous increase in the number of meta-analytic reviews of the literature represent a giant stride forward in the development of clinical psychology, and of the behavioral and social sciences generally, or does it signal a lemming-like flight to disaster? Judging from reactions to past meta-analytic enterprises, there are at least some who take the more pessimistic view. Some three dozen scholars were invited to respond to a meta-analysis of studies of interpersonal expectancy effects (Rosenthal & Rubin, 1978a). Although much of the commentary dealt with the substantive topic of interpersonal expectancy effects, a good deal of it dealt with methodological aspects of meta-analytic procedures and products. Some of the criticisms offered were accurately anticipated by Glass (1978) who had earlier received commentary on his meta-analytic work (Glass, 1976) and that of his colleagues (Glass et al., 1981; Smith & Glass, 1977). Because these criticisms have been addressed elsewhere in detail (Rosenthal, 1991a, Rosenthal & Rubin, 1978b) they will be summarized here briefly, organized into half-a-dozen conceptual categories.

Sampling bias and the file drawer problem

This criticism holds that there is a retrievability bias such that studies retrieved do not reflect the population of studies conducted. One version of this criticism is that the probability of publication is increased by the statistical significance of the results, so that published studies may not be representative of the studies conducted. This is a well-taken criticism, though it applies equally to more traditional narrative reviews of the literature. Procedures that can be employed to address this problem have been described elsewhere (Rosenthal, 1979; 1991a; Rosenthal & Rubin, 1988).

Loss of information

One criticism has been that summarizing a research domain by a single value, such as a mean effect size, loses valuable information. However, comparing studies, which means trying to understand differences between their results, is as much a part of meta-analytic procedures as is summarizing the overall results of the set of studies. We should also note that even *within* a single study we have historically found it quite helpful to compute the mean of the experimental and control groups, despite the fact that computing a mean always involves a "loss of information."

Heterogeneity of method and quality

Meta-analysts summarize studies with different operationalizations of independent and dependent variables, and different types of sampling units. Well-done meta-analyses take these differences into account by treating them as moderator variables. Meta-analyses are also criticized for throwing together good and bad studies. Aside from some difficulties in defining bad studies (e.g. the studies of my "enemies" as Glass et al. (1981) have put it), we can deal with this problem quite simply by weighting studies by their quality. Such weighting includes a weight of zero for the truly terrible study (Rosenthal, 1991a; 1991b).

Problems of independence

Sometimes the same subjects generate multiple effect sizes within the same study, often creating a problem for significance testing in particular. Technical procedures are available for adjusting for nonindependence (Rosenthal, 1991a; Rosenthal & Rubin, 1986). More subtle problems of possible nonindependence arise because different studies conducted in one laboratory may yield results that are more correlated with each other than with different studies conducted in another laboratory. In other words, there may be "laboratory effects" (Jung, 1978; Rosenthal, 1966; 1969; 1976). These can be handled by treating laboratory effects as moderator variables, and by analyzing research domains by laboratory as well as by study (Rosenthal, 1969; 1991a).

Exaggeration of significance levels

Perhaps the only criticism of meta-analysis that is based entirely on a misunderstanding of the fundamental equation of data analysis (i.e. *Test of Significance = Size of Effect × Size of Study*) is the criticism that, as more and more studies are added to a meta-analysis, the results are more and more significant. That is certainly true, but difficult to perceive as a negative feature!

Small effects

The final criticism is that the results of socially important meta-analyses show only "small effects" because the r^2's obtained are small. This criticism has been addressed in detail elsewhere, where it has been shown that r^2s of nearly zero can save 34 lives per 1000 (Rosenthal, 1995; Rosenthal & Rubin, 1979; 1982).

BENEFITS OF META-ANALYSIS

There are several fairly obvious benefits of meta-analysis. Our summaries of research domains are likely to be more complete, more explicit, more quantitative, more powerful (in the sense of decreasing type II errors), and, for all these reasons, helpful to the process of cumulation. Moderator variables are more easily spotted and evaluated in a context of a quantitative research summary, thereby aiding theory development and increasing empirical richness. There are also some less obvious benefits.

Decreased overemphasis on single studies

One less obvious benefit that will accrue to psychological science is the gradual decrease in the overemphasis on the results of a single study. There are good sociological grounds for our preoccupation with the results of a single study. Those grounds have to do with the reward system of science where recognition, promotion, reputation, and the like depend on the results of the single study, the smallest unit of academic currency. The study is "good," "valuable," and above all, "publishable" when $p \le .05$. Our discipline would be further ahead if we adopted a more cumulative view of psychology. With such a view, the impact of a study would be evaluated less on the basis of p levels, and more on the basis of its own effect size. In addition, such a view would lead us to evaluate the revised effect size and combined probability that resulted from the addition of the new study to any earlier studies investigating the same or a similar intervention or other relationship.

Decreased "differentiation drive"

Related to the problem of overemphasis on single studies is the problem of "differentiation drive," a motivational state (and trait) frequently found among scientists in all fields. This is the drive to be more different, more ahead, more right, and more unique than others. Priority strife is one reflection of the differentiation drive. Another reflection is the occurrence of "renomination," the mechanism by which a well-known process is given a new name in hopes of effecting "concept capture." Concept capture is the mechanism by which ownership of a concept is claimed by virtue of the renaming of the concept. Differentiation drive keeps us from viewing the world meta-analytically, or in a more Bayesian way, by keeping us from seeing the similarity of our work to the work of others. B. F. Skinner (1983, p. 39) has spoken eloquently, if indirectly, on this matter:

> In my own thinking, I try to avoid the kind of fraudulent significance which comes with grandiose terms or profound "principles." But some psychologists seem to need to feel that every experiment they do demands a sweeping reorganization of psychology as a whole. It's not worth publishing unless it has some such significance. But research has its own values, and you don't need to cook up spurious reasons why it's important.

"The new intimacy"

This new intimacy is between the reviewer and the data. We cannot do a meta-analysis by reading abstracts and discussion sections. We are forced to look at the numbers and, very often, compute the correct ones ourselves. Meta-analysis requires us to cumulate *data*, not *conclusions*. "Reading" a paper is quite a different matter when we need to compute an effect size and a fairly precise significance level—often from a results section that does not include effect sizes, or precise significance levels (and was not prepared following the APA publication manual)!

The demise of the dichotomous significance testing decision

Far more than is good for us, social and behavioral scientists operate under a dichotomous null hypothesis decision procedure in which the evidence is interpreted as anti-null if $p \leq .05$ and pronull if $p > .05$. If our dissertation p is $< .05$ it means joy, a PhD, and a tenure-track position at a major university. If our $p > .05$ it means ruin, despair, and our advisor suddenly thinking of a new control condition that should be run. That attitude is not helpful. God loves the .06 nearly as much as the .05. Indeed, there is good information that God views the strength of evidence for or against the null as a fairly continuous function of the magnitude of p. As a matter of fact, two .06 results are much stronger evidence against the null than one .05 result, and 10 p's of .10 are stronger evidence against the null than 5 p's of .05.

The overthrow of the omnibus test

It is common to find specific questions addressed by F tests with $df > 1$ in the numerator or by χ^2 tests with $df > 1$. For example, suppose the specific question is whether increased frequency of meeting improves the effectiveness of therapy groups. We employ four levels of frequency so that our omnibus F test would have 3 *df* in the numerator, or our omnibus χ^2 would be on at least 3 *df*. Common as these tests are, they reflect poorly on our teaching of data analytic procedures. The diffuse hypothesis tested by these omnibus tests usually tells us nothing of importance about our research question. The rule of thumb is unambiguous: whenever we have tested a fixed effect with *df* > 1 for χ^2 or for the numerator of *F*, we have tested a question in which we are almost surely not really interested.

The situation is even worse when there are several dependent variables as well as multiple *df* for the independent variable. The paradigm case here is canonical correlation, and special cases are MANOVA, MANCOVA, multiple discriminant function, multiple path analysis, and complex multiple partial correlation. While all of these procedures have useful exploratory data analytic applications, they are commonly used to test null hypotheses which are, scientifically, almost always of doubtful value. The effect size estimates they yield (e.g. the canonical correlation) are also almost always of doubtful value.

The increased recognition of contrast analysis

Meta-analytic questions are basically contrast questions. *F* tests with *df* > 1 in the numerator or χ^2's with *df* > 1 are useless in meta-analytic work. That leads to the following additional scientific benefit: meta-analytic questions require precise formulation of questions, and contrasts are procedures for obtaining answers to such questions, often in an analysis of variance or table analysis context. Although most statistics textbooks describe the logic and the machinery of contrast analyses, one still sees contrasts employed all too rarely. That is a real pity given the precision of thought and theory they encourage, and (especially relevant to these times of publication pressure) given the boost in power conferred with the resulting increase in .05 asterisks (Rosenthal & Rosnow, 1985; 1991; Rosenthal, Rosnow, & Rubin, 1997).

Meta-analytic procedures are applicable beyond meta-analyses

Many of the techniques of contrast analyses among effect sizes, for example, can be used within a single study (Rosenthal & Rosnow, 1985). Computing a single effect size from correlated dependent variables, or comparing treatment effects on two or more dependent variables serve as illustrations (Rosenthal & Rubin, 1986).

The decrease in the splendid detachment of the full professor

Meta-analytic work requires careful reading of research and moderate data analytic skills. We cannot send an undergraduate research assistant to the computer or the library with a stack of 5 × 8 cards to bring us back "the results." With narrative reviews that seems often to have been done. With meta-analysis, the reviewer must get involved with the actual data, and that is all to the good of science.

EVERY RESEARCHER A META-ANALYST

Any researcher considering a review of a literature, or a specifiable subset of literature, might as well do this review quantitatively instead of nonquantitatively. All the virtues of narrative reviews can be preserved in a meta-analysis, which merely adds the quantitative features as a bonus. The level of quantitative skill and training required to employ meta-analytic procedures is so modest that any researcher capable of analyzing the results of their own research will be capable of learning the small number of calculations required to answer standard meta-analytic questions (e.g. what is the mean and standard deviation of this list of correlation coefficients or other effect size estimates?).

Indeed, keeping the meta-analytic procedures descriptive, simple, and clear, is a positive virtue. We never see a meta-anlysis that is too simple, but we often see a meta-analysis that is very "fancy" and very wrong.

The most important part of a meta-analysis is the descriptive part, in which the effect sizes (e.g. correlation coefficients) are displayed and their distribution and central tendency are summarized. Good meta-analytic practice, like good data-analytic practice in general, adopts an exploratory orientation toward these displays and summaries (Tukey, 1977); and for this valuable enterprise, little "high-tech statistication" is required. Indeed, the basic computations required for most meta-analytic work are so trivial that there is little need for specialized software that "does meta-analysis."

The one drawback to the development of sophisticated software for the computation of meta-analytic (or any other data-analytic) computations is that researchers who feel less expert than they might like, believe the software will "do the analysis." Alas, that is not the case. The software will do some computations and it will do them fast, but for any given application, the computations may be wise or they may be foolish. Staying simple, staying close to the data, and emphasizing description avoids most serious errors.

Any behavioral researcher might as well do a meta-analysis as a narrative review of the literature. But there is a special incentive for *clinical* researchers to employ meta-analytic procedures.

Pooling pilots

It is often the case in clinical research that the number of patients available may be very small; so small that all we seem able to do is conduct pilot studies. Once we adopt a meta-analytic world view in which our science really does cumulate, this situation appears far more benign. A little pilot here, a little pilot there, and we can cumulate some knowledge despite the virtual certainty that not one of our pilots will ever reach $p \leq .05$.

An illustration of pooled pilots

In a recent issue of *Science*, Jon Cohen (1993) described two pilot studies in which experimental monkeys were vaccinated using SIV (akin to HIV), while control monkeys were not. In the first pilot, 6 animals were available: 3 vaccinated and 3 controls. With a dichotomous outcome variable of better versus worse health, it would take an effect size *r* of 1.00 to yield a significant result. The actual result showed 2 of 3 experimentals and 0 of 3 controls in better health ($p = .20$, one-tailed). In the second pilot 11 animals were available. Of the experimentals, 2 of 5, and of the controls, 0 of 6, wound up in better health ($p = .18$, one-tailed). Results of these tiny pilot studies treated meta-analytically, showed dramatic benefits of vaccination.

CONCLUSION

We have come full circle. Having begun with Pearson's 1904 meta-analysis of vaccination benefits, we conclude with the meta-analytic benefits available in the fight against an affliction more recent than smallpox. Whether samples are huge or tiny in size, whether there are hundreds of studies or only two, meta-analytic procedures are available, when used wisely, to assist in the development of science, medicine, and human welfare.

ACKNOWLEDGEMENT

Preparation of this paper was supported in part by a sabbatical award from the James McKeen Cattell Fund. Some of the ideas presented here were presented earlier in Rosenthal 1989a; 1989b; 1990; 1991a; 1993; 1994; 1995. I thank Frederick Mosteller for having enlarged my horizons about meta-analytic and other procedures over a quarter of a century ago; Jacob Cohen, a fine colleague I have only recently met but whose writings about power and effect size estimation have influenced me profoundly over the years; and Donald B. Rubin, a frequent collaborator and my long-standing tutor on matters meta-analytic and otherwise data-analytic. Our collaboration proceeds as follows: I ask him questions, he answers them and he then insists we publish alphabetically. What a country!

REFERENCES

Cohen, J. (1962). The statistical power of abnormal-social psychological research: A review. *Journal of Abnormal and Social Psychology*, 65, 145–153.

Cohen, J. (1977). *Statistical power analysis for the behavioral sciences* (Rev. ed.). New York: Academic Press.

Cohen, J. (1988). *Statistical power analysis for the behavioral sciences* (2nd ed.). Hillsdale, NJ: Erlbaum.

Cohen, Jon (1993). A new goal: Preventing disease, not infection. *Science*, 262, 1820–1821.

Collins, H. M. (1985). *Changing order: Replication and induction in scientific practice*. Thousand Oaks, CA: Sage.

Cooper, H. M. (1989). *Integrating research: A guide to literature reviews* (2nd ed.). Thousand Oaks, CA: Sage.

Cooper, H., & Hedges, L. V. (Eds.). (1994). *Handbook of research synthesis*. New York: Russell Sage.

Glass, G. V. (1976). Primary, secondary, and meta-analysis of research. *Educational Researcher, 5*, 3–8.

Glass, G. V. (1978). In defense of generalization. *The Behavioral and Brain Sciences, 3*, 394–395.

Glass, G. V., McGaw, B., & Smith, M. L. (1981). *Meta-analysis in social research*. Thousand Oaks, CA: Sage.

Gosset, W. S. (Student) (1908). The probable error of a mean. *Biometrika, 6*, 1–25.

Hedges, L. V. (1987). How hard is hard science, how soft is soft science? *American Psychologist, 42*, 443–455.

Hedges, L. V., & Olkin, I. (1985). *Statistical methods for meta-analysis*. New York: Academic Press.

Hunter, J. E., & Schmidt, F. L. (1990). *Methods of meta-analysis: Correcting error and bias in research findings*. Thousand Oaks, CA: Sage.

Jung, J. (1978). Self-negating functions of self-fulfilling prophecies. *The Behavioral and Brain Sciences, 3*, 397–398.

Light, R. J., & Pillemer, D. B. (1984). *Summing up: The science of reviewing research*. Cambridge, MA: Harvard University Press.

Mann, C. (1990). Meta-analysis in the breech. *Science, 249*, 476–480.

Nelson, N., Rosenthal, R., & Rosnow, R. L. (1986). Interpretation of significance levels and effect sizes by psychological researchers. *American Psychologist, 41*, 1299–1301.

Pearson, K. (1904, November). Report on certain enteric fever inoculation statistics. *British Medical Journal*, 1243–1246.

Pool, R. (1988). Similar experiments, dissimilar results. *Science, 242*, 192–193.

Rosenthal, R. (1966). *Experimenter effects in behavioral research*. New York: Appleton-Century-Crofts.

Rosenthal, R. (1969). *Interpersonal expectations*. In R. Rosenthal & R. L. Rosnow (Eds.), *Artifact in behavioral research* (pp. 181–277). New York: Academic Press.

Rosenthal, R. (1976). *Experimenter effects in behavioral research* (Rev. ed.). New York: Halsted Press.

Rosenthal, R. (1979). The "file drawer problem" and tolerance for null results. *Psychological Bulletin, 86*, 638–641.

Rosenthal, R. (1989a, April). *Research: How are we doing?* Distinguished Lecture presented at the meeting of the Eastern Psychological Association, Boston, MA.

Rosenthal, R. (1989b, August). *Experimenter expectancy, covert communication, and meta-analytic methods*. Paper presented as the Donald T. Campbell Address at the Annual Meeting of the American Psychological Association, New Orleans.

Rosenthal, R. (1990). Replication in behavioral research. *Journal of Social Behavior and Personality, 5*, 1–30.

Rosenthal, R. (1991a). *Meta-analytic procedures for social research* (Rev. ed.). Thousand Oaks, CA: Sage.

Rosenthal, R. (1991b). Quality-weighting of studies in meta-analytic research. *Psychotherapy Research, 1*, 25–28.

Rosenthal, R. (1993). Cumulating evidence. In G. Keren & C. Lewis (Eds.), *A handbook for data analysis in the behavioral sciences: Methodological issues* (pp. 519–559). Hillsdale, NJ: Erlbaum.

Rosenthal, R. (1994). Parametric measures of effect size. In H. Cooper & L. V. Hedges (Eds.), *Handbook of research synthesis* (pp. 231–244). New York: Russell Sage.

Rosenthal, R. (1995). Progress in clinical psychology: Is there any? *Clinical Psychology: Science and Practice, 2*, 133–150.

Rosenthal, R. & Gaito, J. (1963). The interpretation of levels of significance by psychological researchers. *Journal of Psychology, 55,* 33–38.

Rosenthal, R., & Gaito, J. (1964). Further evidence for the cliff effect in the interpretation of levels of significance. *Psychological Reports, 15,* 570.

Rosenthal, R., & Rosnow, R. L. (1985). *Contrast analysis: Focused comparisons in the analysis of variance.* Cambridge: Cambridge University Press.

Rosenthal, R., & Rosnow, R. L. (1991). *Essentials of behavioral research: Methods and data analysis* (2nd ed.). New York: McGraw-Hill.

Rosenthal, R., Rosnow, R. L., & Rubin, D. B. (1997). *Contrasts and effect sizes in behavioral research: A correlational approach.* Manuscript in preparation.

Rosenthal, R., & Rubin, D. B. (1978a). Interpersonal expectancy effects: The first 345 studies. *The Behavioral and Brain Sciences, 3,* 377–386.

Rosenthal, R., & Rubin, D. B. (1978b). Issues in summarizing the first 345 studies of interpersonal expectancy effects. *The Behavioral and Brain Sciences, 3,* 410–415.

Rosenthal, R., & Rubin, D. B. (1979). A note on percent variance explained as a measure of the importance of effects. *Journal of Applied Social Psychology, 9,* 395–396.

Rosenthal, R., & Rubin, D. B. (1982). A simple, general purpose display of magnitude of experimental effect. *Journal of Educational Psychology, 74,* 166–169.

Rosenthal, R., & Rubin, D. B. (1986). Meta-analytic procedures for combining studies with multiple effect sizes. *Psychological Bulletin, 99,* 400–406.

Rosenthal, R., & Rubin, D. B. (1988). Comment: Assumptions and procedures in the file drawer problem. *Statistical Science, 3,* 120–125.

Rosenthal, R., & Rubin, D. B. (1989). Effect size estimation for one-sample multiple-choice-type data: Design, analysis, and meta-analysis. *Psychological Bulletin, 106,* 332–337.

Rosenthal, R., & Rubin, D. B. (1994). The counternull value of an effect size: A new statistic. *Psychological Science, 5,* 329–334.

Sedlmeier, P., & Gigerenzer, G. (1989). Do studies of statistical power have an effect on the power of studies? *Psychological Bulletin, 105,* 309–316.

Skinner, B. F. (1983, August). On the value of research. *APA Monitor,* p. 39.

Smith, M. L., & Glass, G. V. (1977). Meta-analysis of psychotherapy outcome studies. *American Psychologist, 32,* 752–760.

Tukey, J. W. (1977). *Exploratory data analysis.* Reading, MA: Addison-Wesley.

Health Psychology

CHAPTER NINETEEN

Quality of life: Concept and assessment

Rocío Fernández-Ballesteros
Universidad Autónoma de Madrid, Spain

Quality of Life (QoL) could be considered one of the new concepts in psychology (as well as in other sciences) on which research has increased dramatically in the last decades. In the attempt to define the state of the art regarding QoL, its historical background is provided and, in order to arrive at a conceptual definition, a revision of the main dimensions defined as QoL domains is introduced. Secondly, controversies such as whether QoL is mainly subjective or objective, or diographic or nomothetic are examined. In the assessment section, a list with selected QoL instruments is provided and methodological aspects such as psychometric guarantees, methods and sources of data, and data quality are discussed. Finally, suggestions concerning new directions on the research and assessment of QoL are presented.

On peut regarder la qualité de vie (QV) comme l'un des nouveaux concepts en psychologie (de même que dans d'autres domaines scientifiques) à propos desquels il y a eu une augmentation dramatique de la recherche au cours des dernières décennies. Cette tentative de description de l'état actuel de nos connaissances sur la QV la situe d'abord dans son contexte et, afin d'en arriver à une définition conceptuelle, présente une révision des principales dimensions considérées comme sphères de la QV. En second lieu, on considère les controverses comme la question de savoir si la QV est plutôt subjective ou objective, ou encore idéographique ou nomothétique. La section sur l'évaluation offre une liste choisie d'instruments de mesure de la QV et traite d'aspects méthodologiques tels que garanties psychométriques, méthodes et sources de données et qualité des données. En conclusion, on présente des suggestions pour de nouvelles orientations de la recherche et l'évaluation de la QV.

INTRODUCTION

Quality of Life (QoL) is an extremely complex, abstract and scattered concept with a high impact on research and practice. However, it is a key concept in environmental, social, medical and psychological sciences, as well as in public policy and in the minds of the population at large.

TABLE 19.1
Growth of citations in Quality of Life in five databases:
Urban, Biosis, Medline, PsycLIT, & Sociofile

	Urban	Biosis	Medline	PsycLIT	Sociofile
1969	1	1	1	3	2
1995	112	1,379	2,242	187	127
1967–1974	—	20	61	62	109
1975–1979	14	160	1,051	162	346
1980–1984	33	394	1,695	404	507
1985–1989	200	1,575	3,685	877	640
1990–1995	593	5,821	10,641	1,583	881

Urban = Urbater, Urbamet, Urbaline, Genie Urbain, Docet, Bibliodata, Docet & Acompline.

The importance, multicontextuality and growth of QoL may be assessed by looking at the number of citations in urban, biological, medical, psychological and social database literature. Table 19.1 shows the progression of citations in these five databases. For example, in 1969 there is 0 citation in Urban, 1 in Biosis, 1 in Medline, 3 in PsycLIT and 2 in Sociofile; in 1995 we can find, respectively, 112, 1379, 2242, 187 and 137 citations. From these cumulative frequencies, we can conclude that there has been a constant increase of interest in QoL in different scientific fields, but while in the urban, psychological and social fields we obseve an arithmetical progression, growth in the biological and medical literature has been exponential.

From a semantic point of view, the term "quality" refers to certain attributes or characteristics of a given object (in this case, life), and "life" is a wide category which includes all living beings. The problem is that life can be analyzed from different perspectives, and QoL is therefore a multicontextual concept. Ecologists are concerned about the quality of the environment that harbors life; from this point of view thousands of national and international laws have been developed in order to protect the quality of life around the world (CEOTMA & CIFCA, 1982). Measurements such as air and water pollution, energy consumption, deforestation, etc., are taken as indicators of the quality of life in a given territory. From a social point of view, economists, sociologists, political scientists and public agencies are concerned with the welfare and the well-being of a given society. Statistics of crime, suicide, public violence, family disintegration, as well as *per capita* income or GDP (Gross Domestic Product), are used as measures of the *welfare* and *well-being* of a given society. Finally, from a medical point of view, health quality has been assessed through epidemiological indices such as mortality, morbidity and/or life expectancy rates.

In recent decades, QoL has emerged as a key concept representing an ideological change of socio-political (and human) goals: the improvement of economic welfare, in developed countries, does not, automatically, lead to the well-being of the population.[1]

Medical developments have had an extreme influence in standard indicators of health quality but, for example, a decline in mortality rates (as an aggregate measure) is not correlated with improvement of the patients' well-being but rather with the progression of chronic disease. Surgical, pharmacological, and other aggresive interventions can have side effects. Moreover, these interventions are extremely expensive.[2] As Kaplan (1995, p. 3) emphasized "We know remarkably little about the relationships between expenditures on health care and health outcomes". Therefore, since the World Health Organization defines health as a physical, psychological and social condition, in addition to the traditional measurements, we must take psychological and social indices into account.

Scientists, professionals and policy makers are interested not only in providing economic goods, health and human services, but in the impact of these goods and services on human subjects and in how they *perceive* their lives. Aggregated data such as environmental quality, *per capita* income, or mortality rate may be indices of physical, economic or medical conditions, but do not reflect, exactly, the subjects' well-being.[3] As Tolman (1941) emphasized decades ago, the concept of an "economic man" has been substituted by the relevance of a "psychological man" (see also Campbell, 1981): control perception, self-efficacy, social support, are important ingredients, as are other "psychological qualities", of subjects' well-being.

These new ideas, these considerations about the importance of subjective aspects of life—beyond any political rhetoric—perhaps express a new phylogenetic step via a new paradigm in which QoL is the expression of human development, as well as the prototype of new human goals.[4]

In summary, in spite of the fact that QoL involves mainly psychological components, it is a multicontextual concept that arises from several disciplines: biology, medicine, psychology and sociology. Nevertheless, there is no balance

---

[1] As Campbell (1981) has shown, as economic welfare increased during the postwar period in the USA, psychological well-being declined.

[2] Kaplan (1995, p. 3) gives the following estimate of resource allocations: "The United States spent an estimated $838 billion for health care in 1992, and these expenditures are expected to be well over $1 trillion by 1995 and may be $2 trillion by the turn of the century".

[3] Of course, this conceptual evolution occurs mainly in developed countries. International authorities must achieve the generalization of human development throughout the world. In the Third and Fourth Worlds thousands of people die due to extremely poor physical and economic conditions; in such situations we cannot avoid looking for socio-economic and traditional health indicators. Unfortunately, QoL seems to be a concept which is applied only in developed societies.

[4] As quoted by Campbell (1981 p. 37), US President Johnson's *Great Society* expresses this idea: "... the Great Society is concerned not with how good, not with the quantity of goods, but the quality of our lives". This idea is also present in the formal objectives of political programs (see EU, Maastricht Treaty, 1978 Spanish Constitution, etc.).

between these fields, and the exponential growth of interest in the medical context is reinforcing a reductionistic conception of QoL. This is the main reason why psychology must become more involved in the formulation and assessment of this new concept.

LOOKING FOR A DEFINITION

QoL is considered by different authors as an "abstract", "soft", "amorphous" concept (Birren and Dieckmann, 1991, pp. 344–345); as one that "has no fixed boundaries" (Hughes, 1990, p. 47); that "has been exceedingly difficult to define (it) precisely" (Andersen, Davidson, & Ganz, 1994, p. 367); that is "difficult to operationalize" (Lawton, 1991); and, even, as one whose "meaning is dependent of the user of the term" (Fowlie & Berkeley, 1987, p. 226). QoL has been defined as equivalent to well-being in the social domain (Campbell, 1981), to the health status in the bio-medical field (also called health-related QoL; for example, Naughton & Wiklund, 1993), and to life satisfaction in the psychology field (Palys & Little, 1983).

However, in spite of such reductionism and the fact that the difficulties in finding a general definition are commonly accepted, we can—in accordance with Birren and Dieckmann (1991)— establish what *is not* quality of life: QoL is not equivalent of quality of the environment, is not equal to the quantity of material goods, is not equivalent to the physical health status, or to the quality of health care, just as it is distinct from subjective constructs such as life satisfaction, morale or happiness (Campbell, 1981; George & Bearon, 1980; Naughton & Wiklund, 1993). As Browne et al. (1994, p. 235) stated: "Quality of Life (QoL) is (the product) of the dynamic interaction between external conditions of an individual's life and the internal perceptions of those conditions". Thus, we cannot reduce this concept to life's external conditions or to personal characteristics (even the perception of external conditions), just as QoL cannot be reduced to only one condition.

Working from these distinctions, we arrive at a general, commonly accepted, characteristic of QoL: its multidimensionality. That is, like life, QoL is multidimensional by nature. Even if we are applying this concept in a specific context, QoL must be operationalized by means of a set of dimensions. What are these dimensions; in other words, what are the "ingredients" of QoL?.

The ingredients of QoL

Two strategies have been used in the definition of the constituent elements, domains, aspects, components, factors, or content areas of QoL: theoretical and empirical.

From a theoretical perspective, several authors have formulated models of QoL; for example, Lawton (1991, p. 8) proposed a four-sector model in which psychological well-being, perceived quality of life, behavioral competence, and objective environment are hypothesized as the four general evaluative sectors: "Each of the four sectors may in turn be differentiated into as many dimensions as the details of one's attention demand".

On similar lines, the World Health Organization (1993) has conceptualized QoL in terms of five broad domains: physical health, psychological health, level of independence, social relationship, and environment.

Finally, other authors have tried to develop categories of QoL dimensions. For example, Hughes (1990) defined seven categories:

1. Individual characteristics (functional activities, physical and mental health, dependency, etc.).
2. Physical environmental factors (facilities and amenities, comfort, security, etc.).
3. Social environmental factors (levels of social and recreational activity, family and social network, etc.).
4. Socio-economic factors (income, socio-economic status, etc.).
5. Personal autonomy factors (ability to make choices, exercise control, etc.).
6. Subjective satisfaction.
7. Personality factors (psychological well-being, morale, life satisfaction, happiness, etc.).

A second strategy used for defining QoL components is empirical. That is, since QoL refers to individuals' lives, individuals must be asked to state the implicit domains of their QoL concept. For example, Flanagan (1978) assessed QoL components through a US survey of three age group samples. Fifteen critical components were grouped into five main categories:

1. Physical and material well-being (material well-being and financial security).
2. Relations with other people (relations with spouse and having and raising children, relations with parents, siblings, or other relatives, relations with friends).
3. Social, community and civic activities (activities related to helping or encouraging other people, activities related to local and national governments).
4. Personal development and fulfillment (intellectual development, personal understanding and planning, occupational role, creativity and personal expression).
5. Recreation (socializing, passive and observational activities, active and participatory recreational activities).

Also, from an empirical perspective, Fernández-Ballesteros (1993; Fernández-Ballesteros & Macia, 1993; Fernández-Ballesteros, Zamarrón, & Maciá, 1997) has tried to identify the "popular" concept of QoL in the elderly, by asking a representative sample of the Spanish population what are its fundamental ingredients (or domains):

Health status, functional abilities, financial resources, family and social relationships, daily-living and recreational activities, social and health services, life

FIG. 19.1   Quality of Life multidimensionality: Personal and socio-environmental factors (Fernández-Ballesteros, 1992)

satisfaction, cultural resources, and environmental quality seem to be, in that order, components of QoL.

In this "pop" conceptualization among Spaniards, no differences were found across gender, age, and socio-economic status. Moreover, when all these components were assessed in several samples of the Spanish elderly population and factorial analysis was carried out, a factorial structure close to these QoL components emerged in several samples.

As we can see, with both strategies (theoretical and empirical) there is a moderate consensus regarding both the multidimensionality and the main dimensions of QoL. For the majority of the authors, these components include both external variables (socio-economic or environmental factors) and intraindividual or personal factors (life satisfaction, perceived health, motor behaviors).[5] As an example, Fig. 19.1 presents a graphical representation of the QoL multidimensionality, as well as of the presence of personal and socio-environmental factors

---

[5] Nevertheless, Stewart and King (1994) consider that only the "personal" factors belong to the domains of QoL and that the "external" factors are determinants of the QoL.

of the QoL. Personal factors (e.g. health, functional abilities, social relationships, recreational activities, life satisfaction) interact with socio-environmental conditions (e.g. health and social services, financial conditions, cultural factors, social support, environmental quality. Both types of factor are constituents of QoL and we can state that QoL cannot be reduced to any one of its components (from Fernández-Ballesteros, 1993).

Nevertheless, authors do not agree either about the nature of these dimensions nor about the way they should be selected. In other words, they do not agree as to whether those dimensions are subjective and/or objective, and as to whether they should be selected nomothetically or idiographically.[6] In this respect, there are in this field two main debates: subjective vs. objective QoL, and nomothetic vs. idiographic QoL.

DEBATES IN QoL RESEARCH

Subjective or objective nature of the QoL ingredients

Although in QoL conceptualization authors introduce external dimensions (e.g. financial resources), we can state that this inclusion does not necessarily imply that they are to be considered objectively. For example, since the World Health Organization (1993, p. 153) has defined QoL as "an individual's perception of his/her position in life", when the environment is included as a QoL component it refers only to the subject's evaluation.

Unfortunately, there is confusion between type (external vs internal) and nature (objective vs subjective) of dimension. External variables (such as environmental quality) can be operationalized by means of external criteria or by means of a subject's perception or appraisal. Likewise, we have to be aware that in the latter case we would be assessing a personal/subjective condition. Also, health can be considered both objectively and subjectively; measures drawn from physical examinations or/and from clinical analysis can be taken into consideration, as well as those drawn from self-perception of one's state of health. Figure 19.2, presents examples of subjective elements superimposed on objective factors that define QoL (perceived/objective health, health and social services evaluation/social and health services availability, etc.)

Although several authors recognize only the subjective nature of all dimensions of QoL (even external ones), others, such as Lawton (1991, p. 7), maintain that "objectively measurable or consensual evaluations of facets of life must also

---

[6] Among other authors, Lawton (1991) confuses the *subjective* nature of intrapersonal QoL dimensions with their *idiosyncratic* character. In other words, intrapersonal dimensions can be selected either in a standard (the same intrapsychic components for all subjects) or in a specific (idiosyncratic intrapsychic component) way. For example, we can decide to introduce for all subjects their perception about their health, just as we can ask the subject what makes his/her life pleasant.

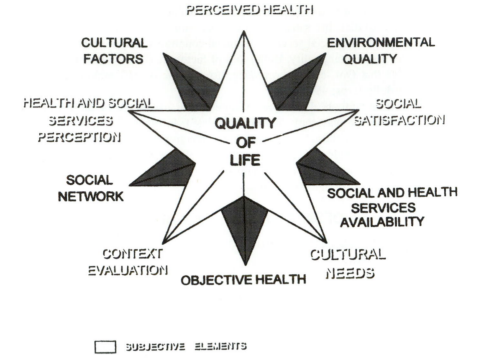

FIG. 19.2   Objective and subjective factors defining Quality of Life (Fernández-Ballesteros, 1992)

be considered in assessing quality of life" (see also, Birren & Dieckmann, 1991; Hughes, 1990).

In our opinion, in spite of the fact that the concept of QoL emphasizes the "psychological" aspects of life (that is, personal and subjective conditions), external/objective conditions of life cannot be ignored. As has been pointed out by Neisser (1976), Gibson (1966) and Sampson (1981), although it is extremely important, in order to avoid reductionism, to take into account the subjectivity of the individual's perception of the world, some consideration must also be given to his or her objective world. The real world also needs to be transformed in order to improve human welfare, well-being and quality of life. Scientists and policy-makers must be aware of this necessity.

We must note that this definition of the QoL is the product of theoretical conceptualization and empirical research, as well as of lay opinion originating, mainly, in developed countries; this raises the question as to whether these dimensions should be given the same weight and importance as they apply to individuals all over the world. Are they universal? Can we use the same dimensions to assess individuals across age groups, health status, or cultures?

Nomothetic vs idiographic concept of QoL

Up to this point we have established a social-normative (Lawton, 1991) or nomothetic approach to QoL. However, several authors have pointed out that the subject is the only one capable of defining his or her QoL. From this perspective, Browne and colleagues (1994, p. 235) pointed out that "although some domains tend to be nominated more than others, no taxonomy suits all individuals", and the World Health Organization (1993, p. 153) defined the QoL of a given individual "in the context of the culture and value systems in which they live, and in relation to their goals, expectations, standards and concerns". In other words, for these and other authors the QoL is idiographic in nature. The old controversy from Windelband (1904) between nomothetic and idiographic sciences is also present in the QoL literature.

The idiographic approach to QoL maintains that: "Given that the list of domains relevant to the QoL of all individual remains indefinable, it is not surprising that a universally applicable means of weighting the relative importance of such domains does not exist" (Browne et al., 1994, p. 236). From a rational point of view, it seems to be true that, depending on the base line of the individual's conditions and functioning (age, health, economic status, personal characteristics, etc.), a given subject can consider some QoL domains more important than others for his/her QoL. However, human needs and human life are not so diverse as to make QoL totally idiographic.

The main problem concerns not domains, but the *weight* that a given domain has at a specific time for a specific subject. In our opinion, a (relatively) nomothetic concept of QoL (based on a variety of dimensions or conditions) can be adjusted idiographically. From this perspective, several instruments have been developed (McGee et al., 1991; NERI, 1992), and other standard devices also take into consideration the importance for the subject of the listed domains (World Health Organization, 1993). In this respect, Fernández-Ballesteros, Zamarrón & Macia (1997) have pointed out that a standard QoL instrument can be used both from a nomothetic and an idiographic point of view. Moreover, in a representative sample of Spanish subjects older that 65, the comparison between the two types of score was not significant.

Nevertheless, in order to arrive at a universal concept of QoL, cross-cultural research is needed and the World Health Organization (1993) is making progress in this respect.

Summarizing, we can make four general statements about QoL:

1. Like life, QoL is by nature a multidimensional construct: it cannot be reduced to any one of its components (health, psychological well-being, etc.).
2. QoL contains personal as well as socio-environmental dimensions.
3. Emphasis on the subjective appraisal of external life conditions must not eliminate consideration of objective life circumstances.

4. A nomothetic or standard QoL concept is compatible with an individually weighted one.

THE MEASUREMENT OF QUALITY OF LIFE

In spite of the fact that there is no commonly accepted definition of QoL, there are dozens of QoL instruments, and most of them come from the medical domain.[7] In Table 19.2, a list of the selected QoL measures is presented on the basis of target population, administration procedure and their psychometric properties. In Table 19.3, the same instruments are analyzed through the domains they include.

For reasons of space and time, it is impossible to review each selected measure but, in order to help in the selection of a given instrument we will deal with the following topics: *reasons for measuring QoL*; *target population*; *method of administration and source of data*; *psychometric guarantees*; and *data quality*.

Reasons for measuring QoL

As previously pointed out, QoL has had an exponential growth. This growth is related to several scientific and social needs. Thus, as Arnold (1991) pointed out, in order to select a QoL instrument, assessment purposes or objectives have to be considered. QoL measurement is conducted for five purposes:

1. Understanding the causes and consequences of differences in QoL between individuals or groups of individuals.
2. Assessing the impact of social and environmental conditions on QoL.
3. Estimating the needs of a given population.
4. Evaluating the efficiency or effectiveness of health interventions and/or the quality of the health care system.
5. Improving clinical decisions.

On the basis of these five objectives, different instruments can be selected depending on their characteristics. For example, if we are going to evaluate a given health intervention, we must select a health-related quality of life instrument; therefore, sensitivity will be one of the required psychometric properties.

Target population

Beyond the basic (standard) QoL domains, a first question is whether QoL can be assessed with the same instrument across populations. Although several efforts have been made to assess QoL in the general population (for example,

---

[7] Naughton and Wiklund (1993) review six dimension-specific health-related QoL instruments, cross-culturally assessed. These instruments assess pain (McGill Pain Questionnaire (MPQ)) or psychopathology (the General Health Questionnaire (GHQ); the Beck Depression Inventory (BDI); the Center for Epidemiologic Studies-Depression (CES-D); and the Zung Self-Rating Depression Scale (SDS).

TABLE 19.2
Selected Quality of Life measures

Measure	Population	Administration	Reliability	Validity
* A Generic health-related Quality of Life Instrument (CCV; Ruiz & Baca, 1993)	General population	Interviewer	Extensive data available	Extensive data available
* Elderly community reactions to the nursing home (Biedwenharn & Baslin, 1991)	Institutionalized residents	Interviewer and self-administered	Limited	Limited
* Evaluating the efficacy of physical activity for influencing quality of life outcomes in older adults (Stewart & King, 1991)	Elderly	Interviewer	Limited	Limited
* Initial psychometric evaluation of a qualitative well-being measure: The Integration Inventory (Ruffining-Rahal, 1991)	Elderly	Interviewer	Limited	Limited
* Multitrait-multimethod analysis of health-related quality of life measures (HRQOL; Hadorn & Ron, 1991)	General population and elderly	Interviewer	Limited	Limited
* Older Americans resources and services instrument (OARS; Duke University, 1978)	Elderly	Most experience obtained from interviewer-administered version	Extensive data available	Extensive data available
* Perceived Quality of Life scale (PQoL; Patrick et al., 1988)	Former intensive care patients	Interviewer-administered	Limited	Limited
* Nothingan Health Profile (PSN) (NHP; Hunt et al., 1981)	Health related	Interviewer and Self-administered	Extensive data available	Extensive data available
* Quality of life in elderly, chronically ill outpatients (Pearlman & Uhliman, 1991)	Elderly and chronically ill	Interviewer	Extensive data available	Extensive data available
* Rand health status measures (Ware et al., 1981)	Community-dwelling population, including elderly and those with chronic disease	Self-administered	Extensive data available	Extensive data available
* Sickness Impact Profile (SIP; Bergner et al., 1981)	Extensive use in many populations, including chronically ill	Interviewer and self-administered versions	Extensive data available	Extensive data available

(continued)

TABLE 19.2
(continued)

Measure	Population	Administration	Reliability	Validity
* Subjective well-being instrument for the chronically ill (Gill, 1984)	Chronically ill	Interviewer	Limited	Limited
* Swedish health-related Quality of Life Survey (Swed-Qual; Brorsson et al., 1993)	General population	Self-administered	Extensive data available	Extensive data available
* Quality of Well-Being Scale QWE (Kaplan and Bush, 1982)	Numerous populations, including chronically ill and frail elderly	Interviewer and self-administered versions	Extensive data available	Extensive data available
* Reintegration to normal living index (Wood-Dauphinee et al., 1988)	Rehab patients	Interviewer administered	Limited	Limited
* City of Hope medical center Quality of Life survey (Ferrell et al., 1989)	Cancer patients	Interviewer	Limited	Limited
* WHOQoL-100 (WHO, 1993)	General population	Interviewer and self-administered	Limited	Limited
* Multidimensional QoL questionnaire (NERI, 1992)	HIV patients	Interviewer and self-administered	None	None
* Schedule for evaluation of individual QoL (SEIQoL; McGee et al., 1991)	Elderly	Interviewer	Limited	Limited
* Sixteen-dimensional health-related measure (16 D) (Apajasalo et al., 1996)	Adolescent	Self-Administered	Limited	Limited
* Euro QoL (1990)	Health related	Self-Administered	Limited	Limited
* Spitzer Quality of Life (QL) index (Spitzer et al., 1981)	Chronically ill	Self-Administered	Limited	Limited
* Dartmouth COOP function CHARTS (Nelson et al., 1987)	Health related	Interviewer	Extensive data available	Extensive data available
* Elderly Cruz Roja Quality of Life (Guillén et al., 1990)	Elderly	Interviewer	None	None
* CUBRECAVI (Fdez-Ballesteros et al., 1997)	Elderly	Interviewer	Limited	Limited

TABLE 19.3
Domains in selected Quality of Life measures

Measure	Physical Functioning	Emotional Functioning	Cognitive Functioning	Social Functioning	Life Satisfaction	Health Perception	Functional Skills	Economic Status	Cultural Status	Recreation	Sexual Functioning	Energy and Vitality	Physical environment	Self-Esteem	Risk factors	Services
* A Generic Health related Quality of Life Instrument (CCV)	x	x		x	x	x	x				x	x				
* Elderly community reactions to the nursing home	x	x				x	x					x				
* Evaluating the efficacy of physical activity for influencing quality of life outcomes in older adults	x	x	x			x				x		x		x		
* Initial psychometric evaluation of a qualitative well-being measure: The integration inventory		x		x	x	x	x					x		x		
* Multitrait-Multimethod analysis of Health-related quality of life measures (HRQOL)	x			x	x	x	x					x				
* Older Americans Resources and Services Instrument (OARS)	x	x	x	x		x	x	x		x						
* Perceived Quality of Life Scale	x	x	x	x	x	x	x	x		x						
* Nothingan Health Profile (PSN)	x	x		x		x	x			x	x	x				
* Quality of life in elderly, chronically ill outpatients	x	x	x	x	x	x	x	x		x	x	x				x
* Rand Health Status Measures	x	x	x	x	x	x	x	x		x	x	x				
* Sickness Impact Profile	x	x		x		x	x	x		x		x				
* Subjective well-being instrument for the chronically ill	x	x	x	x			x				x					
* Swedish Health-Related Quality of Life Survey (Swed-Qual)	x	x		x		x	x				x	x				
* Quality of Well-Being Scale	x															
* Reintegration to Normal Living Index	x							x		x						
* City of Hope Medical Center Quality of life Survey	x	x		x												
* WHO Qol-100	x	x		x		x	x					x		x		
* Multidimensional Qol. NERI	x	x		x		x	x			x	x	x			x	
* Schedule for evaluation of Individual QoL	x	x	x	x	x	x	x	x	x	x		x			x	x
* Sixteen-Dimensional Health	x	x		x		x	x		x	x	x	x		x	x	
* Euro QoL		x		x		x	x			x	x					
* Spitzer Quality of Life (QL)				x		x	x	x	x		x					
* Dartmouth COOP function CHARTS	x	x		x			x	x								
* Elderly Quality of Life. Cruz Roja	x					x	x				x					
* CUBRECAVI	x	x	x	x	x	x	x	x		x	x	x	x	x	x	x

399

Campbell, 1981), a review of QoL instruments indicates that age and health conditions are two important differential components.

With regard to age, a relevant group of QoL instruments has been developed for the elderly. By contrast, very few instruments have been developed for children, adolescents, or middle-aged people (an exception is the 16D by Apajasalo et al., 1996).

As mentioned previously, the QoL concept has had its most important impact in the medical domain. Thus, the majority of QoL instruments are *"health-related measures"*. These measurement devices have been developed in order to assess the impact of illness and medical treatment on a given patient. Within this field, *generic* and *specific* health-related QoL measures have been developed in order to assess clinical populations or particular diseases (cancer, AIDS, chronic diseases, etc.).

In summary, we have to take into consideration our target population when we select a QoL measure.

Method of administration and source of data

As was emphasized by Campbell (1981), if QoL is reduced to subjective components of the individual, self-report is the most "direct" way to assess this condition. In other words, a single procedure and a single source of data is the common rule in QoL measurement.

Nevertheless, since external/objective variables are also components of life, in order to have a more complete picture, other sources of data and other methods have to be considered. For example, in assessing environmental conditions, Fernández-Ballesteros, Zamarrón, and Maciá (1997) used both observational procedures and self-report evaluation of environment quality.

Also, other methods (such as expert rating scales) have been proposed. For example, Birren and Dieckmann (1991) emphasized that, for assessing health status, physicians' ratings are a better measure than self-rating.[8]

As Stewart and King (1994 p. 29) have pointed out, "special problems of some subgroups of older populations, such as cognitive difficulties or sensory limitations, may affect the choices regarding the optimal method". From this point of view, several methods are available: performance-based testing, medical exams, clinical analysis, etc. For example, since data from proxy and from subjects were found to be equivalent (Fernández-Ballesteros & Maciá, 1996), in a subsequent study on older persons with cognitive impairment (assessed by a performance test), Fernández-Ballesteros (1996) asked family members to answer objective questions (number of pills taken, number of visits to physician, etc.) of the elder's life.

---

[8] The fact that we are defending the utilization of subjective as well as objective measures (in health as well as in other domains), in the QoL assessment, does not mean that both can have different predictive values. For example, the Bonn Longitudinal Study (BOLSA; Lehr, 1993) found that subjective health was a better predictor of longevity than objective health.

Although several problems arise with the use of several methods/several sources of data, the complexity of the QoL construct requires a multimethod/ multidatasource approach, at least for the basic investigation when an instrument is being developed.

Psychometric guarantees

As in the measurement of other constructs, QoL instruments must present certain psychometric properties. *Reliability* (internal consistency and test–retest correlations), *validity* (criterion-related and construct validity), and *sensitivity to change* are the most important psychometric properties reported in QoL measurement (Cronbach et al., 1972; Messik, 1995).

Internal consistency (that is, item generalizability assessed through the association across items in a given instrument) has been reported in the majority of QoL instruments. Since QoL is a multidimensional construct, internal consistency is not applicable to the whole QoL instrument but to its subscales. For example, in the case of the Rand Health Status Measure-36 (MOS-36; Ware, 1989) internal consistency reliability coefficients range from moderate to high (from .67 to .90) in its different subscales. Internal consistency varies with the extent of the domain assessed and, therefore, a longer subscale has better reliability coefficients.

Test–retest (or time generalizability) is assessed through the administration of a given instrument (or subscale) at two points in time. For example, test–retest reliability for the six Nothingan Health Profile (NHP; Hunt et al., 1981) domains ranged from .77 (energy subscale) to .85 (physical mobility and sleep subscales). Test–retest reliability depends on the stability of a given domain; for example, cultural or financial resources are usually very stable ingredients of QoL, while pain is strongly related to health and illness. Also, life satisfaction is a very stable personality characteristic. For example, the reported life satisfaction of several representative sample of the Spanish population from 18 to more than 85 years does not yield age differences (CIRES, 1995). In other words, the nature of a given domain—as a trait or as a state—must be taken into consideration when test–retest reliability correlations are considered and interpreted (Fernández-Ballesteros, 1992).

Criterion-related validity has been tested with well-known groups (age groups, different levels of pathology groups, etc.). For example, in rheumatoid arthritis and hip replacement, the Sickness Impact Profile (SIP; Bergner et al., 1981) total score correlates above .80 with specific measures of patients' functioning (Anderson, Aaronson, & Wilkin, 1993). But, these high correlations depend on the nature of the construct assessed for a given domain. When SIP emotional domains are correlated with another instrument assessing the same variables (e.g. anxiety or depression) correlations are only moderate.

Since QoL is a construct with different domains, construct validity is one of the most important ways of testing it. Factorial analysis, convergent and discriminant analysis, multimethod-multitrait matrices are very good avenues for assessing QoL instruments. For example, as mentioned earlier, in our QoL Questionnaire validation studies, for different samples and different sources of data, we obtained a very close factorial structure (Fernández-Ballesteros & Maciá, 1996; Fernández-Ballesteros, Zamarrón, & Maciá, 1997).

Finally, several authors emphasize the importance of QoL measures for program evaluation (e.g. Kaplan & Bush, 1982), since QoL measures are used to monitor change over time, sensitivity to treatment/program is one of the most important characteristics. For example, Ruiz and Baca (1993) assessed the Quality of Life Questionnaire's ("Cuestionario de Calidad de Vida", CCV) sensitivity to change by comparing treated and non-treated insomnia subjects. Significant differences ($p < .001$) between pre- and post-treatment scores, in the predicted direction, were found both in CCV total score and in all domain scores (social support, general satisfaction, physical/psychological well-being, and absence of work overload/free time).

Data quality

Data quality depends on several conditions, including who is assessed, who assesses, the assessment situation, and, of course, the instrument used (see Arnold, 1991). Since we are dealing with the measurement of QoL, we are going to consider only two sources of error: influence of response biases and the widespread use of a given instrument.

Responses to questionaires or interviews unrelated to any non-test conditions of interest constitute, by definition, data error variance. As was emphasized by Lanyon and Goodstein (1971, p. 141), "strong effort must be exerted to eliminate or to substantially reduce them". Since QoL instruments are mainly based on self-report and interviews, sets of responses such as social desirability, lying, faking, self-deception, acquiescence are sources of error in QoL data. In spite of the importance of these sources of distortion, very little research has been conducted in this area.

For example, Fernández-Ballesteros, Zamarrón, and Maciá (1997) found that, a representative sample of 65-year-old subjects with high scores on a Lying Scale reported significantly better health (perceived health, chronic diseases, number of drugs taken, pain, and mental health), and higher life satisfaction than those scoring low on Lying. Since we are not sure about the real meaning of Lying Scales in gerontology research, it is difficult to conclude either that liars distort their responses or that liars are really healthier and happier. In any case, however, more research must be conducted in order to clarify and control this and other similar sources of error.

Linked to the universal character of the QoL concept, the international literature, defined mainly on health-related QoL research, is vast and rapidly expanding. Instruments developed in a specific language/culture have been translated and/or adapted to other languages/contexts. As Anderson et al. (1993, p. 390) point out: "It is difficult, if not impossible to make definitive statements about cross-cultural equivalence of measures". A review of the cross-cultural QoL literature points to the existence of two main problems: inappropriate translation/ adaptation methods and the lack of investigation on psychometric properties in the new culture. The conclusion from the analysis of the most widely used QoL instruments was that "none of the instruments reviewed were judged to have data available for all aspects of measurement equivalence considered ... too often, health-related QoL measures have simply been translated into another language, linguistically, and immediately used in research with the assumption that the essential properties of the original instrument have been preserved" (Anderson et al., 1993, p. 390). As is well known, psychometric properties in the "original" (domain) version are not guaranteed in the new target version. Since international guidelines have been developed for test translation/adaptation, much more attention must be paid to this process in cross-cultural research on QoL (Hambleton, 1994). In sum, much more concern must be given to the psychometric properties of QoL instruments.

CONCLUSIONS

Quality of Life is becoming an increasingly important multicontextual and multidimensional concept. In spite of the fact that QoL is defined mainly through psychological components, Psychology seems to be less involved than other scientific disciplines. Although multidimensionality is commonly accepted, the majority of instruments are so-called health-related quality of life measures, and have been developed exclusively in the medical field.

Although there is no commonly accepted QoL definition, there is some consensus regarding the dimensions involved in QoL, but several problems exist with regard to its conceptualization. Despite the fact that there is agreement that QoL includes both personal and external components, as well as subjective and objective indices, self-reports about subjective conditions are the basic method for collecting QoL data, but observational methods must be used in assessing environmental QoL factors. In this respect, a more ecological approach, the recourse to triangulation and to the use of a diversified methodology or multi-methodism are required.

Several authors emphasize the idiographism of QoL and our conclusion is that a normative perspective does not prevent the idiographic use of standard domains.

The field of QoL measurement is changing rapidly and several dozens of instruments have been developed in recent decades. However, although some of them inform about psychometric properties, others are in a very immature state as scientific measurement devices. In spite of the fact that the majority of instruments are self-report measures, very few results about potential response distortions have been provided. On the basis of beliefs about the universality of this construct, several instruments have been translated into different languages/ cultures without having been submitted to a rigorous process of test adaptation and psychometric evaluation. We have no proof as yet of the universal character of QoL; there are critical problems of instrument translation/adaptation and lack of psychometric guarantees. The generalization of QoL research is extremely limited.

For all these reasons, psychology and psychologists should be much more involved in QoL conceptualization and assessment.

REFERENCES

Abeles, R. P., Gift, H. C., & Ory, H. G. (Eds.). (1994). *Aging and quality of life*. New York: Springer.

Andersen, R. M., Davidson, P. L., & Ganz, P. A. (1994). Symbiotic relationships of quality of life, health services research and other health research. *Quality of Life Research, 3*, 365–371.

Anderson, R. T., Aaronson, N. K., & Wilkin, D. (1993). Critical review of the international assessments of health-related quality of life. *Quality of Life Research, 2*, 369–395.

Apajasalo, M., Sintonen, H., Holmberg, C., Sinkkonen, J., Aalberg, V., Pihko, H., Siimes, M. A., Kaitila, I., MäKelvi, A., Rantakari, K., Antila, R., & Rautonen, J. (1996). Quality of life in early adolescence: A sixteen-dimensional health-related measure (16D). *Quality of Life Research, 5*, 205–211.

Arnold, S. B. (1991). Measurement of quality of life in frail elderly. In J. E. Birren, (Eds.), *The concept and measurement of quality of life in the frail elderly* pp. 28–73. San Diego, CA: Academic Press.

Bergner, M., Bobbit, R., Carter, W., & Gilson, B. (1981). Sickness impact profile: Development and final version of a health status measure. *Medical Care, 19*, 787–805.

Biedwenharn, J., & Baslin, B., (1991). Elderly community residents' reactions to the nursing home: An analysis of nursing home-related beliefs. *The Gerontologist, 31*, 1, 107–115.

Birren, J. E., & Dieckmann, L. (1991). Concepts and content of quality of life in later years: An overview. In J. E. Birren (Ed.), *The concept and measurement of quality of life in the frail elderly* (pp. 344–360). San Diego, CA: Academic Press.

Brorsson, B., Ifver, J., & Hays, R. D. (1993). The Swedish health-related quality of life survey (SWED-QUAL). *Quality of Life Research, 2*, 33–45.

Browne, J. P., O'Boyle, C. A., McGee, H. M., Joyce, C. R. B., McDonald, N. J., O'Malley, K., & Hiltbrunner, B. (1994). Individual quality of life in the healthy elderly. *Quality of Life Research, 3*, 235–244.

Campbell, A. (1981). *The sense of well-being in America*. New York: McGraw-Hill.

CEOTMA, & CIFCA. (1982). *Calidad de vida, medio ambiente y ordenación del territorio: Textos internationales* [Quality of life, environment and territory: International documents]. Madrid: MOPU.

Cronbach, L. J., Gleser, G. C., Nando, H., & Rajaratman, N. (1972). *The dependability of behaviour measurements theory of generalizability for series and profiles*. New York: Wiley.

CIRES. (1995). *Estudio sobre la realidad social española 1993–94* Madrid: Centro de Investigación de la realidad social española.

Dimsdale, J. E., & Baum, A. (Eds.). (1995). *Quality of Life in Behavioral Medicine*. Hillsdale, NJ: Erlbaum.

Duke University. (1978). *Multidimensional functional assessment: The OARS methodology*. Durham, NC: Center for the Study of Aging and Human Development.

EuroQoL group. (1990). EuroQoL: A new facility for the measurement of health-related quality of life. *Health Policy*, *2*, 153–159.

Fernández-Ballesteros, R. (1992). *Mitos y realidades sobre la la vejez y la salud* [Myth and reality about aging and health]. Barcelona: SG Ed.

Fernández-Ballesteros, R. (1993). The construct of quality of life among the elderly. In E. Beregi, I. A. Gergely, & K. Rajzi (Eds.), *Recent Advances in Aging and Science* (pp. 1627–1630). Milano: Monduzzi.

Fernández-Ballesteros, R. (1996). Las demandas de servicios sociales por la población mayor. In J. Díez Nicolás (dir.), *Los mayores [The elders]*. Madrid: Fundación Caja Madrid.

Fernández-Ballesteros, R., & Maciá, A. (1993). Calidad de vida en la vejez [Quality of life in the elderly]. *Revista de Intervención Psicosocial*, *5*, 77–94.

Fernández-Ballesteros, R., & Maciá, A. (1996). Informes de allegados sobre los mayores y de estos sobre sí mismos [Proxys' reports about the elderly and elders' self-reports]. *Revista de Gerontología*, *6*, 20–29.

Fernández-Ballesteros, R., Zamarrón, M. D., & Maciá, A. (1997). *Calidad de vida en la vejez en distintos contextos* [Quality of life among the elderly in different contexts]. Madrid: INSERSO.

Ferrell, B. R., Wisdom, C., & Wenzl, C. (1989). Quality of life as an outcome variable in the management of cancer pain. *Cancer*, *63*, 2321–2327.

Flanagan, J. C. (1978). A research approach to improving our quality of life. *American Psychologist*, *33*, 138–147.

Fowlie, M., & Berkeley, J. (1987). Quality of life: A review of the literature. *Family Practice*, *4*, 226–234.

George, J. K., & Bearon, L. B. (1980). *Quality of life in older persons: Meaning and measurement*. New York: Human Science Press.

Gibson, J. J. (1966). *The senses considered as perceptual systems*. Boston: Houghton Mifflin.

Guillen, F., Caballero, J. C., Guijarro, J. L., Reus, J. M., Sempere, R., Sagués, F., Tobares, N., Viguera, S., & Rodríguez, L. (1990). Escalas de valoración en geriatría. *Revista Española de Geriatría y Gerontología*, *25*, 1, 683–691.

Gill, W. M. (1984). Subjective well-being: properties of an instrument for measuring this (in the chronically ill). *Social Science Medicare*, *18*, 683–691.

Hadorn, D. C., & Hays, R. D. (1991). Multitrait-multimethod analysis of health-related quality of life measures. *Medical Care*, *29*, 9, 829–840.

Hambleton, R. K. (1994). Guidelines for adapting educational and psychological tests: A progress report. *European Journal of Psychological Assessment*, *19*, 229–244.

Hughes, B. (1990). Quality of life. In S. M. Sheila & M. Peace (Eds.), *Researching social gerontology: Concepts, methods and issues* (pp. 46–58). Thousand Oaks, CA: Sage.

Hunt, S. M., McKenna, S. P., McEwen, J., Backett, E. M., Williams, J., & Papp, E. (1981). A quantitative approach to perceived health status: A validation study. *Journal of Epidemiology and Community Health*, *34*, 281–286.

Kaplan, R. M. (1995). Quality of life, resource allocation, and the US health-care crisis. In J. E. Dimsdale & A. Baum (Eds.), *Quality of Life in Behavioral Medicine Research*. Hillsdale, NJ: Erlbaum.

Kaplan, R. M., & Bush, J. (1982). Health-related quality of life measurement for evaluation research and policy analysis. *Health Psychology*, *1*, 61–80.

Lanyon, R. L., & Goodstein, L. D. (1971). *Personality assessment*. New York: Wiley.

Lawton, M. P. (1991). A multidimensional view of quality of life in frail elders. In J. E. Birren (Eds.). *The Concept and Measurement of Quality of Life in the Frail Elderly* (pp. 3–27). San Diego: Academic Press.

Lehr, U. (1993). A model of well-being in old age and its consequences for further longitudinal studies. In J. J. F. Schoroots (Ed.). *Aging, health and competence* (pp. 293–302). Amsterdam: Elsevier.

Messick, S. (1995). Validity of psychological assessment. *American Psychologist, 50,* 741–749.

McGee, H. M., O'Boyle, C. A., Hickey, A., O'Malley, K., & Joyce, C. R. B. (1991). Assessing the quality of the individual: The SEIQoL with healthy and gastroenterology unit population. *Psychological Medicine, 21,* 749–759.

Naughton, M. J., & Wiklund, I. (1993). A critical view of dimension-specific measures of health-related quality of life in cross-cultural research. *Quality of Life Research, 2,* 397–432.

Neisser, U. (1976). *Cognition and reality.* San Francisco, CA: Freeman.

Nelson, E., Wasson, J., & Kirk J. (1987). Assessment of function in routine clinical practice: Description of the COOP chart method and preliminary findings. *Journal of Chronic Disease, 40,* 55S–63S.

NERI. (1992, Winter). Neri HQL. *New England Research Institute Newsletter,* 1–3.

Palys, T. S., & Little, B. R. (1983). Perceived life satisfaction and the organization of personal project system. *Journal of Personality and Social Psychology, 44,* 1221–1230.

Patrick, D. L., Danis, M., Southerland, I., & Hong, G. (1988). Quality of life following intensive care. *Journal of General Internal Medicine, 3,* 218–223.

Pearlman, R. A., & Uhlmann, R. E. (1991). Quality of life in elderly chronically ill outpatients. *Journal of Gerontology: Medical Sciences, 46,* 2, M31–M38.

Rufining-Rahal, M. A. (1991). Initial psychometric evaluation of a qualitative well-being. *Health Values, 15,* 2, 10–20.

Ruiz, M. A., & Baca, E. (1993). Design and validation of the "Quality of Life Questionnaire": A generic health-related perceived quality of life instrument. *European Journal of Psychological Assessment, 9,* 19–32.

Sampson, E. E. (1981). Cognitive psychology as ideology. *American Psychologist, 36,* 730–743.

Spitzer, W. O., Dobson, A. J., Hall, J., Chesterman, E., Levi, J., Shepherd, R., Battista, R. N., & Catchlove, B. R. (1981). Measuring the quality of life of cancer patients. *Journal of Chronic Disease, 34,* 585–597.

Stewart, A. L., & King, A. C. (1991). Evaluating the efficacy of physical activity. *Annals of Behavioral Medicine, 13,* 3, 108–116.

Stewart, A. L., & King, A. C. (1994). Conceptualizing and measuring quality of life in older populations. In R. P. Abeles, H. C. Gift, & H. G. Ory (Eds.), *Aging and Quality of Life* (pp. 27–54). New York: Springer.

Tolman, E. C. (1941). Psychological man. *Journal of Social Psychology, 13,* 205–218.

Ware, J. E., Brook, R. H., Davies, A. R., & Loht, K. N. (1981). Choosing measures of health status for individuals in general populations. *American Journal of Public Health, 71,* 620–625.

Ware, J. (1989). *A short form general health survey* (P-7444). Santa Monica, CA: The RAND Corporation.

Windelband, W. (1904). *Geschichte und Naturwissenschaft.* Estrasburg: Heitz.

Wood-Dauphinee, S. L., Optzoomer, M. A., Williams, J. J., Marchand, B., & Spitzer, W. O. (1988). Assessment of global function: The reintegration to normal living index. *Archives of Medicine and Rehabilitation, 69,* 583–590.

World Health Organization. (1993). Study protocol for the World Health Organization project to develop a quality of life assessment instrument (WHOQOL). *Quality of Life Research, 2,* 153–159.

CHAPTER TWENTY

Alcohol and intentions to engage in risky health-related behaviors: Experimental evidence for a causal relationship

Tara K. MacDonald
University of Lethbridge, Alberta, Canada

Mark P. Zanna
University of Waterloo, Ontario, Canada

Geoffrey T. Fong
University of Waterloo, Ontario, Canada

There is a common assumption that alcohol is a general disinhibitor, sometimes causing people to be more relaxed and outgoing, and sometimes causing antisocial behavior. Prior research has shown that alcohol is associated with numerous harmful behaviors that are costly to individuals and to society. Most of this research, however, has been correlational; thus, the nature of the relationship between alcohol and risky behaviors is not clear. In this chapter, we review experimental evidence demonstrating that alcohol intoxication can cause greater intentions to engage in risky health-related behaviors, such as drinking and driving, or having unprotected sexual intercourse. We hypothesize that the mechanism underlying the relationship between alcohol and intentions to engage in risky behavior is alcohol myopia (Steele & Josephs, 1990). Alcohol intoxication restricts cognitive capacity, so that people attend to the most salient cues in a situation. Implications of this theoretical perspective for designing effective change programs are discussed.

On suppose généralement que l'alcool est un disinhibiteur général qui rend parfois les gens plus relaxes et plus extravertis, provoquant parfois un comportement anti-social. Les recherches antérieures ont démontré que l'alcool est associé à plusieurs comportements nuisibles qui sont coûteux pour l'individu et pour la société.

Cependant, la plupart de ces recherches sont de type corrélationnel. Par conséquent, la nature du lien entre l'alcool et les comportements hasardeux n'est pas claire. Dans ce chapitre, nous passons en revue les données expérimentales démontrant que l'intoxication alcoolique peut susciter des désirs plus intenses de s'adonner à des comportements dangereux pour la santé, tels que conduire en état d'ébriété, ou encore avoir des relations sexuelles sans protection. Nous formulons l'hypothèse que le mécanisme sur lequel repose la relation entre l'alcool et l'intention de s'engager dans des comportements hasardeux est la "myopie alcoolique" (Steele & Josephs, 1990). L'intoxication alcoolique réduit la capacité cognitive, de telle sorte que les individus concentrent leur attention sur les indices les plus saillants dans une situation. Les implications de cette perspective théorique dans la conception de programmes efficaces de changements sont discutées.

Ellen is a healthy, attractive, and intelligent 19-year-old university freshman. In her high school health class, she learned about the sexual transmission of HIV and other sexually transmitted diseases (STDs). In her orientation week at University, senior students presented a seminar about the dangers of having unprotected sex, and provided the freshmen in her residence with free condoms and safe sex literature. It is safe to say that Ellen knows the facts about unprotected sex, and is cognizant of the dangers associated with this behavior. Indeed, she holds negative attitudes toward having unprotected sex, does not intend to have unprotected sex, and has always practiced safe sex behavior: She and her former boyfriend were always careful to use latex condoms when having intercourse. At a homecoming party in her residence, Ellen had a great time, drinking and dancing with her friends, and meeting new people. She was particularly taken with Brad, a sophomore at her college, and the two of them decided to go back to her room to order a pizza. One thing led to another, and Ellen and Brad ended up having sex without using a condom. The next morning, Ellen woke up, dismayed and surprised at her behavior, and very concerned that she might be pregnant, or may have contracted a STD. Even worse, she was terrified that she might have contracted AIDS.

What happened? Why would Ellen engage in unprotected casual sex, despite her knowledge of the risks associated with this behavior? This type of scenario is frustrating to health educators, who attempt to inform people about the dangers of unsafe sex. People generally hold negative attitudes about engaging in sexual intercourse without a condom. Unfortunately, people's negative attitudes toward unsafe sex do not always translate into safe-sex behavior. The incidence of AIDS continues to grow at an alarming rate, particularly among adolescents and young adults. Recent estimates report that the majority of newly infected HIV cases occur in the 15–24 age group (World Health Organization, 1996).

In this chapter, we shall discuss one possible explanation for the finding that people sometimes engage in risky health-related activities, despite their negative attitudes toward these behaviors. We hypothesize that alcohol intoxication affects the decision-making process, increasing the likelihood that people will engage in these potentially destructive behaviors. Indeed, alcohol is associated with many dangerous and harmful behaviors that are costly to individuals and to society, including unprotected sexual intercourse, drinking and driving, date rape, child or spousal abuse, and other forms of aggression.

Past research that has examined the effects of alcohol on the decisions to engage in risky behaviors has been largely correlational in nature (see Abbey, 1991; Leigh & Stall, 1993, for reviews of the effects of alcohol on date rape and condom use). The results of many correlational studies do support the notion that alcohol is associated with risky behaviors. For example, in a review of over 90 published studies assessing the relationship between alcohol or drug use and risky sex, Leigh and Stall (1993) concluded that in general, there is a positive relationship between substance use and risky sexual behavior.

As Leigh and Stall note in their review, however, there are numerous limitations inherent in any type of correlational design. These authors categorized prior research assessing the relationship between alcohol and risky sexual behavior into the three following design categories. *Global association studies*, in which general measures of substance use and general measures of sexual behavior are correlated, are limited in that they cannot demonstrate that substance use and risky behavior occur concurrently. Moreover, these designs are subject to third-variable explanations (e.g. it could be that people who consume alcohol take more risks in general than people who do not consume alcohol, and having a "risky" personality might also be associated with a propensity to engage in unsafe sex). *Situational association studies*, in which general measures of risky sexual activity within a specific time frame and the number of times in which sex and alcohol have been combined are correlated, are similarly limited in that it is not possible to determine whether the occasions when one had unsafe sex were the same ones when alcohol was used. Finally, *event analyses*, in which respondents are asked to think of a specific sexual event and report whether they had engaged in risky behavior and whether they had consumed alcohol, are somewhat better than the other techniques because they can demonstrate that alcohol and risky sexual behavior coincided, but are limited because they are subject to third-variable explanations and reporting biases. Thus, it is impossible to draw causal inferences from past research examining alcohol and risky sexual behavior.

In our research, we have used randomized experiments to establish a causal relationship between alcohol intoxication and intentions to drink and drive (MacDonald, Zanna, & Fong, 1995), or have casual sexual intercourse without a condom (MacDonald, Zanna, & Fong, 1996). Moreover, we hypothesize that alcohol myopia (Steele & Josephs, 1990) may be the cognitive mechanism that underlies the relationship between alcohol and the decision to engage in risky behaviors.

ALCOHOL MYOPIA

Alcohol myopia (Steele & Josephs, 1990) can account for the seemingly contradictory findings that alcohol can cause people to behave more aggressively (Zeichner & Pihl, 1979), or more prosocially (Steele, Critchlow, & Liu, 1985).

Thus, alcohol myopia can explain why alcohol might cause a person to don a lampshade and become the life of the party in some social situations, whereas alcohol might cause that same person to get involved in a bar brawl in other situations. The theory of alcohol myopia simply states that alcohol causes social behaviors to become more extreme, and the direction of the behavior will be determined by whatever cues are most salient in the environment.

Why does alcohol myopia cause social behavior to become more extreme? Steele and others (e.g. Steele et al., 1985; Steele & Southwick, 1985; Steele & Josephs, 1990) have demonstrated that alcohol intoxication impairs decision-making processes because it limits cognitive capacity. An intoxicated individual is simply not able to attend to all of the information in the environment. Instead, that person is likely to attend to, and act on, the cues that are most salient in the environment. Furthermore, the alcohol myopia perspective makes a specific prediction about *when* alcohol will cause a person's behavior to become more extreme. A central tenet of the alcohol myopia account is that the effect of alcohol on social behavior varies as a function of inhibitory response conflict, or the extent to which there are competing types of cues in the environment, ones that would facilitate a social behavior, and ones that would inhibit it. Alcohol myopia predicts that *when response conflict is low* (e.g. when there are no competing cues in the environment), intoxicated people should behave no differently than sober people. In contrast, *when response conflict is high* (e.g. when there are competing cues in the environment), intoxicated people will engage in more extreme behavior, because an intoxicated person cannot attend to both types of cue, and thus will be strongly influenced by whatever cues are most salient.

To test their hypothesis that the effects of alcohol on social behaviors are more pronounced when inhibitory response conflict is high, Steele and Southwick (1985) conducted a meta-analysis including 34 studies that assessed the effects of alcohol on social behaviors. In sum, there were 121 comparisons between sober and intoxicated participants. They categorized these comparisons according to whether response conflict was high or low (as rated by independent judges), and assessed differences between sober and intoxicated participants using standard deviation scores. When response conflict was low, there was little difference between sober and intoxicated participants (*M* standard deviation = 0.14). In contrast, when response conflict was high, there was a striking difference between sober and intoxicated participants (*M* standard deviation = 1.06). Thus, looking across a variety of social behaviors such as aggression, gambling, and sexual interest, intoxicated people responded one full standard deviation more extremely than their sober counterparts to experimental situations only when response conflict was high.

Inhibitory response conflict can also be used to explain other social effects of alcohol intoxication. For example, Steele and Josephs (1990) maintain that alcohol will alleviate or exacerbate anxiety, depending on whether the intoxicated person engages in a distracting activity (e.g. watching television). Because of the cognitive limitation associated with alcohol myopia, an intoxicated person who is engaged in a highly engrossing activity no longer has the cognitive capacity necessary to focus on anxiety-provoking worries, enabling that person to "drown his or her sorrows." In contrast, alcohol can increase anxiety when no other distraction is present, because this lack of response conflict might cause one to focus on anxiety-provoking worries at the expense of any other stimuli, causing what Steele and Josephs (1990, p. 929) call the "crying-in-one's-beer effect."

The notion of inhibitory response conflict can be readily applied to the behavior of drinking and driving. When a person is deciding whether to drive home, there are both impelling cues and inhibiting cues present. Impelling cues are those that would lead a person to drive (e.g. getting home quickly, not having to spend money on a taxi or bus, not having to worry about the hassle of picking up the car later). Inhibiting cues are those that would prevent a person from driving when intoxicated (e.g. the possibility of being fined by the police, being in a car accident, injuring or killing oneself or others). A sober person possesses the requisite cognitive capacity to weigh the impelling and the inhibiting cues. Because the potential costs of drinking and driving tend to outweigh the benefits, a sober person would tend to hold negative attitudes toward this behavior, and would be very unlikely to report intentions to drink and drive. An intoxicated person, however, may not possess the cognitive capacity necessary to weigh the impelling and the inhibiting cues of drinking and driving. Instead, that person may be more likely to attend to impelling cues, because the benefits of drinking and driving are more immediate than the costs (e.g. an intoxicated person may focus on the fact that he or she is tired, and simply wants to get home as quickly and conveniently as possible). Thus, an intoxicated person might decide to get into a car and drive home, without questioning his or her decision. This is consistent with the notion of myopia in that people are not able to see the potential long-term costs of their decisions, attending instead to the short-term benefits.

In this chapter, we review experimental evidence for a causal relationship between alcohol and intentions to engage in two risky behaviors: drinking and driving, and having unprotected sex. In both programs of research, we have based our hypotheses in terms of alcohol myopia. We shall discuss implications that the alcohol myopia perspective holds for designing effective change programs, and explore potential avenues for future research.

DRINKING AND DRIVING

Despite public safety campaigns designed to reduce the incidence of drinking and driving, this behavior remains a serious societal problem. Most people have negative attitudes toward drinking and driving, and are unlikely to report intentions to engage in this behavior. Unfortunately, however, statistics tell another story. It is estimated that between 40 and 70% of all traffic fatalities in Canada and the United States are related to driving under the influence of alcohol (Ministry of Transportation, 1990; Steele & Josephs, 1990). We were interested in examining why alcohol might cause people to drink and drive, when their normal, or "sober" attitudes toward drinking and driving are negative.

Recall that the alcohol myopia theory posits that alcohol should cause people to behave more extremely than sober people only when response conflicts are high. Thus, we speculated that alcohol should cause people to hold more positive attitudes and intentions toward drinking and driving only in the presence of cues that would dispose them to drive while intoxicated, such as an excuse, or justification for doing so (i.e. a contingency). When such a contingency is not present, alcohol may have no effect on attitudes and intentions, because both sober and intoxicated people should be able to access the relevant inhibiting cues that would prevent them from drinking and driving.

To test the alcohol myopia hypothesis, we assessed participants' attitudes and intentions using two types of questions. In the *non-contingent* items, we simply asked participants to respond to items asking whether they would drink and drive. An example of a non-contingent intention item is, "I will drink and drive the next time that I am out at a party or bar with friends." Similarly, an example of a non-contingent attitude item is, "If I drink and drive the next time that I am out at a party or bar, I would find it acceptable." For these non-contingent items, where no justification to drink and drive is made salient, we predicted that both sober and intoxicated participants would be able to access the relevant inhibiting cues, such as the possible negative outcomes of drinking and driving, and would therefore be quite negative about doing so.

We also asked participants *contingent* questions assessing their attitudes and intentions toward drinking and driving, where we embedded an excuse, or justification in the items. An example of a contingent intention item is, "If I only had a short distance to drive home, I would drive while intoxicated the next time that I am out at a party or bar," and an example of a contingent attitude item is, "Supposing I drive some friends the next time that I go out to a party or bar, and I tell my friends that I will drive them home. I consume alcohol that evening, but feel obligated to drive my friends from the party or bar. If I were to drink and drive in this situation, my behavior is foolish." For these contingent items, we predicted that intoxicated participants would be highly influenced by the salient impelling cues to drink and drive (e.g. having only a short distance to drive) instead of the less apparent inhibiting cues (e.g. being in a car accident). Therefore, we expected that in response to these items, intoxicated participants would be less negative about drinking and driving than sober participants, who can attend to both types of cue.

It is important to note that the alcohol myopia perspective differs from the commonly held hypothesis that alcohol acts as a general disinhibitor. Indeed, people tend to think about the effects of alcohol in terms of disinhibition as Critchlow (1986, p. 753) noted: "The belief that alcohol, by way of its pharmacological

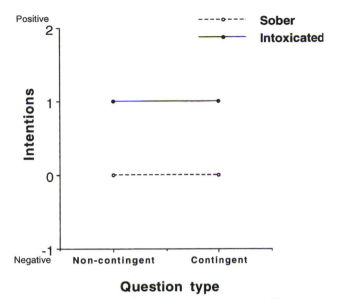

FIG. 20.1   Main effect of intoxication level, as predicted by the disinhibition account.

effects of the brain, causes the drinker to lose inhibitions and engage in behaviors that would never be done when sober has become the conventional wisdom of our society." A disinhibition account would predict that alcohol simply makes people more risky and impulsive; intoxicated people should become more likely than sober people to get up and dance on a table, or to choose to drink and drive. Thus, disinhibition would predict a main effect of intoxication level such that intoxicated people would be more likely to express favorable attitudes and intentions toward drinking and driving, regardless of question type (see Fig. 20.1).

In contrast, the alcohol myopia account makes a more specific hypothesis, in the form of an *interaction*. In accordance with the alcohol myopia perspective, we predicted an interaction between intoxication level (sober or intoxicated) and question type (contingent or non-contingent). We expected that for the non-contingent items, there would be no difference between sober and intoxicated participants, whereas for the contingent items, intoxicated people would express more favorable (or, at least, less unfavorable) attitudes and intentions toward drinking and driving (see Fig. 20.2).

We conducted two laboratory studies and two field studies assessing attitudes and intentions toward drinking and driving. In each study, we compared sober and intoxicated participants' attitudes and intentions toward drinking and driving, using both contingent and non-contingent questions. We shall describe the methodologies of the four studies, and present the aggregated results (for a complete description of the procedures and the results obtained in the individual studies, see MacDonald et al., 1995).

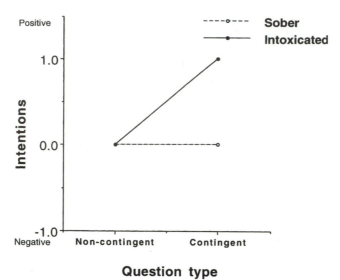

FIG. 20.2   Interaction between intoxication level and question type, as predicted by alcohol myopia.

Drinking and driving: Laboratory studies

Study 1: Laboratory experiment

In all laboratory studies, we selected only males for participation (because of the potential health consequences of administering alcohol to female particip-ants who may be pregnant, we chose not to administer alcohol to females). The participants were at least 19 years old (the legal drinking age in Ontario), owned a car, and reported spending at least $20.00 on alcohol each month.

Participants were assessed in groups of two or three. Each group was ran-domly assigned to the sober ($n = 29$) or the intoxicated ($n = 28$) condition. Participants in the sober condition simply completed the dependent measures. Those in the intoxicated condition were weighed at the beginning of the experi-mental session, and were given enough alcohol so that, based on their weight, their blood alcohol level (BAL) would reach .08% (the legal intoxication limit in Ontario). Three alcoholic beverages (alcool, which is 40% alc/vol., was diluted with Wink brand soda with a ratio of 1 part alcohol to 2 parts soda) were admin-istered in 20 minute intervals over a one-hour period. Fifteen minutes after their third drink, participants completed the dependent measures. After doing so, their BAL was assessed using a breathalyzer ($M = .074\%$, SD = .010).

Study 2: Placebo experiment

In this experiment, we replaced the sober condition with a placebo condition, in which participants were led to believe that they were consuming three alco-holic beverages when, in fact, they were consuming only a minute amount of alcohol. The purpose of a placebo control condition is to rule out expectancy effects as a plausible alternative explanation for the findings of an alcohol experiment. That is, any differences between sober and intoxicated participants may reflect participants' *beliefs* about the effects of alcohol, rather than the effects of the alcohol itself. Comparison of the differences between a placebo condition and an intoxicated condition allows a test of the extent to which alcohol affected attitudes and intentions toward drinking and driving (i.e. because both groups believe that they had consumed alcohol, expectancies were present in both the placebo and the intoxicated conditions, thus any differences between the two groups can be attributed to alcohol intoxication).

Participants were selected using the same criteria as that described in Study 1, and were randomly assigned to the intoxicated ($n = 27$) or the placebo ($n = 23$) condition. Participants in the intoxicated condition were administered three alcoholic beverages using the protocol described earlier. Those in the placebo condition were led to believe that they were consuming three alcoholic beverages through smell, sight, and taste cues. While subjects were completing a measure in another room, we sprayed the room where they would be consuming their drinks with a mixture of water and alcohol in order to provide smell cues. In addition, we put alcohol around the rim of the glass that each participant would drink from, so that when the participant raised the glass to drink from it, the smell of alcohol would be on the top rim, near his nose. We also mixed the drinks in front of the participants. In the placebo condition, we put flattened tonic water into an alcohol bottle, so that participants could see us pouring a clear liquid from an alcohol bottle into their drinks. Finally, we put a very small amount of alcohol (1 teaspoon) disguised as lime juice on top of the drinks. Because the alcohol is less dense than the soda, it floats on top of the drink, so that the first sip is mostly alcohol. Indeed, this was a very compelling cue to our participants. The fact that the first sip of their drinks was unmistakably alcohol persuaded them to believe that their entire drink contained alcohol.

Our manipulation did indeed convince placebo subjects that they had consumed alcohol: Despite the fact that their actual breathalyzer readings were .000% or .001% in all cases, the average BAL estimate for the placebo group was .072%, which was comparable to the actual BAL of participants in the intoxicated condition. None of our placebo subjects expressed any suspicion during the debriefing—a number of them reacted with surprise and disbelief that they were not actually intoxicated. One participant actually refused to believe that he was not intoxicated. After the experimenter showed him the breathalyzer, indicating that he was perfectly sober, he argued that the equipment must be "rigged," and insisted on remaining in the laboratory until he felt sober enough to leave.

Drinking and driving: Field studies

Studies 3 and 4 were field studies, where we assessed participants' attitudes and intentions toward drinking and driving in a real-world context, where intoxicated participants would actually be in a situation where they would have to decide whether to drink and drive. Additionally, it was possible to use female participants in the field studies because the ethical considerations of administering alcohol to females did not apply, as we were in no way encouraging participants to consume alcohol. In Study 3, we used a diary methodology (Reis & Wheeler, 1991; Wheeler & Reis, 1991). Study 4 was an experiment conducted at a campus pub.

Study 3: Diary study

For this correlational study, we wanted participants to complete the measures while they were at a party or a bar. At an introductory meeting, participants were given a package containing a questionnaire, and a quarter. The instructions on the package specified that the participants should bring the package with them the next time that they drove their car to a party or bar where alcohol was to be consumed. At the party or bar, participants were asked to open the package, use the quarter to call a telephone answering machine that we had hooked up at the university, and to read and answer the questionnaire onto the telephone answering machine.

After the participants had completed the questionnaire, they were asked to report their weight, the number and type of alcoholic beverages they had consumed, and the number of hours that it had taken to consume the drinks. This self-reported information was used to estimate the BAL for each participant. On the basis of their estimated BAL, participants were assigned to the sober ($n = 37$, mean estimated BAL $= .01$) or the intoxicated condition ($n = 13$, mean estimated BAL $= .11$).

The diary methodology proved to be a viable way to assess attitudes and intentions outside the laboratory. Participants did not seem to mind calling in and answering questions onto a telephone answering machine while engaging in a social activity. They reported that this procedure was convenient and relatively non-intrusive.

Study 4: Campus pub experiment

The next field study employed an experimental methodology. An experimenter waited in the lobby of a campus bar, and approached patrons as they entered, asking if they had driven to the bar that evening, and, if so, whether they would participate in an attitude survey. Participants who agreed were randomly assigned to the early or the late condition. Participants in the early condition completed the dependent measures as soon as they entered the bar, before they had an opportunity to consume any alcohol. Participants in the late condition completed the dependent measures after 11:30 p.m. The experimenter assessed each participants' BAL with a breathalyzer at the end of the evening. Only participants whose BAL was at least .05% at the end of the evening were included in the analyses. In this way we were able to ensure that the early (sober) and the late (intoxicated) condition were comparable. Early participants ($n = 14$) were sober when they completed the questionnaires, but intoxicated at the end of the evening. Late participants ($n = 12$) were intoxicated when they completed the questionnaire. At the end of the evening, the BAL of the early group ($M = .086$) did not differ significantly from that of the late group ($M = .095$).

Of course, there is an intentional confound built into this methodology. The sober participants were all assessed early in the evening, and the intoxicated participants were all assessed late in the evening. To be certain that alcohol intoxication, and not time of assessment accounted for our findings we compared those who were assessed early and were sober at the end of the night with those who were assessed late and were sober at the end of the night. If we found that sober participants assessed at the end of the evening reported less negative attitudes and intentions toward drinking and driving than sober participants assessed early in the evening, then time of assessment would be a plausible alternative explanation for our findings. We found no interactions between time of assessment (early, late) and question type (contingent, non-contingent). Moreover, there was a main effect of time of assessment for the intention items. This could not account for our findings, however, because sober participants tested early in the evening were *less* negative toward drinking and driving than sober participants tested late in the evening, thus ruling out time of assessment as a viable alternative explanation.

Results

To make the data from each of the studies comparable, we created standardized scores for all participants, using the mean and standard deviation of the sober group; that is, for each participants' score we subtracted the mean of the sober condition, and divided that by the standard deviation of the sober condition (Glass, McGaw, & Smith, 1981; Steele & Southwick, 1985). In this way, the overall mean and standard deviation of the sober condition became 0 and 1, respectively, and the scores for each sober participant reflected the difference in standard scores from the group mean. Similarly, the scores for the intoxicated participants reflected the magnitude and direction (in standard units) of the differences from the mean of the sober group. Therefore, we expected that for the non-contingent items, scores for the intoxicated group would be very close to zero (reflecting little difference between the groups), whereas for the contingent items, we expected that scores for the intoxicated group would be positive and significantly greater than zero (reflecting more positive attitudes and intentions toward drinking and driving, see Fig. 20.2).

Across the four studies, the hypothesis that intoxicated participants would hold less negative attitudes and intentions toward the behavior of drinking and driving than sober/placebo participants only when a contingency (i.e. an impelling cue to drink and drive) was made salient was generally supported (see

MacDonald et al., 1995). We conducted meta-analyses using the terms from the expected interaction between condition (sober, intoxicated) and intention type (contingent, non-contingent). For the attitude subscale, we conducted the meta-analysis on the four aforementioned studies. For the intention subscale, we conducted the meta-analysis on five studies: the four studies just presented in addition to a pilot study that was similar in design to Study 1 (MacDonald, Zanna, & Fong, 1993).

Using the method of weighted zs for the predicted interaction (Mosteller & Bush, 1954, as described in Rosenthal, 1984), we found that the expected interaction was reliable for the attitude subscale ($z = 2.97$, $p = .003$) and the intention subscale ($z = 2.93$, $p = .003$). Direct comparisons between the sober and the intoxicated groups on the contingent and non-contingent scales were analyzed using the method of adding ts (Winer, 1971, as described in Rosenthal, 1978; 1984). In this method, the sum of t values from independent studies are divided by the square root of the sum of their corresponding degrees of freedom (df), after dividing the df by (df − 2), to produce a z value. Controlling for past drinking and driving behavior, we found that for the attitude subscale, there was a significant difference between the sober and intoxicated groups for the contingent items ($z = 3.29$, $p < .001$) such that intoxicated people reported less negative attitudes toward drinking and driving, but that there was no difference for the non-contingent items ($z < 1$, ns.). Similarly, for the intentions subscale, there was a significant difference between groups for the contingent items ($z = 4.21$, $p < .0001$) in the predicted direction, but not for the non-contingent items ($z = 1.42$, ns.). The sober/placebo groups differed for the contingent items, but not for the non-contingent items, thus supporting the alcohol myopia hypothesis.

In summary, across four studies comparing sober and intoxicated participants, the pattern of results was consistent with alcohol myopia. We found that when asked general, non-contingent questions, there were no differences in participants' attitudes and intentions to drink and drive. Presumably, in the absence of competing cues, all participants were able to access, and attend to, cues that would prohibit driving while intoxicated. When asked questions that contained a relevant contingency, however, intoxicated participants reported less negative attitudes and intentions toward drinking and driving than did their sober counterparts. We believe that the presence of impelling cues created a high-conflict situation, and thus prevented intoxicated participants from attending to cues that would prohibit drinking and driving.

CONDOM USE

Condom use is another domain where, like drinking and driving, there is often a discrepancy between people's attitudes and their behavior. It is accepted that outside of abstinence, latex condoms are the most effective way to prevent STDs including HIV, the virus that causes AIDS. Great efforts are taken to educate people about the value of condom use and the dangers associated with unprotected sexual intercourse, and people do typically report positive attitudes and intentions toward condom use. When they are in a situation where they have to decide whether to have unprotected sex, however, many people decide to do so. Numerous studies have found that in North American high school and university samples, only 15 to 38% of sexually active young people use a condom every time they have sexual intercourse (Baldwin & Baldwin, 1988; Butcher, Manning, & O'Neal, 1991; Campbell, Peplau, & DeBro, 1992; Fong, Parent, & Poppe, 1994; Levin, 1993; Poppen & Reisen, 1994).

We applied the alcohol myopia perspective to the domain of condom use. We hypothesized that alcohol may cause people to hold more favorable attitudes and intentions toward having sexual intercourse without a condom because the immediate physical cues (e.g. being sexually aroused, being with an attractive person) may be more salient than the potential outcomes of having unprotected sex (e.g. causing an unwanted pregnancy, contracting an STD or HIV). Thus, intoxicated people may attend to, and act on the impelling cues in the situation, without recognizing the relevant inhibiting cues.

One important strength of this research is that we used experimental methodologies to establish a causal relationship between alcohol intoxication and intentions to have sexual intercourse without a condom (see also Gordon & Carey, 1996). Of course, one may wonder how we were able to study condom use in the laboratory. Even the most ambitious researcher would have to concede that it is virtually impossible (and if not impossible, highly unethical) to observe the effects of alcohol on actual condom use behavior. Instead, we chose to compare sober and intoxicated participants' intentions to engage in unprotected sex by setting up a realistic, engaging scenario, which we presented in a video. The video depicts two attractive University of Waterloo undergraduates, Mike and Rebecca, and is presented in three scenes. In Scene 1, Mike and Rebecca meet after a class, and he invites her to join him and some friends at a campus bar. In Scene 2, Mike and Rebecca are shown at the bar, where they are dancing, engaging in small talk, and drinking alcohol. At the end of this scene, Mike asks if he can walk Rebecca home. The critical part of the video, Scene 3, occurs in Rebecca's apartment. After talking briefly, they begin to kiss passionately on the couch. Rebecca then suggests that they move to her bedroom, where they will be more comfortable. After some embarrassed pauses, Mike tells Rebecca that he does not have any condoms with him. Rebecca admits that she does not have any either. However awkwardly, the two characters discuss how to resolve this dilemma. The video ends with a freeze frame, and participants immediately complete the dependent measures while the freeze frame is still in view.

We attempted to create the video so that it was very engaging, and so that the situation presented was very enticing to participants. As stated earlier, the actors portraying Mike and Rebecca are very attractive. Additionally, Rebecca discloses to Mike that she is taking birth control pills, which effectively rules out pregnancy as an inhibiting cue. Finally, it is clear in the video that both Mike and Rebecca are very interested in having sex, precluding a potential date rape situation. Thus, we created a high-conflict situation, where the impelling cues presented in the video would compete with the relevant inhibiting cues. Colleagues who have viewed the video are impressed with its high quality, and participants generally report finding the video entertaining and realistic.

Here, we present a brief description of each of three experiments, and report the aggregated results (for a complete description of the procedures and the results obtained in the individual studies, see MacDonald et al., 1996).

Primary dependent measures

Intentions. The first question, presented immediately after the freeze frame, assessed participants' intentions to have sexual intercourse with Rebecca, the female character in the video. Participants were asked to respond to the item, "If I were in this situation, I would have sexual intercourse with Rebecca" on a 9-point rating scale with endpoints labeled 1 (strongly disagree) and 9 (strongly agree). We hypothesized that intoxicated participants would be more likely to endorse this item than sober participants. We believed that the intoxicated participants would focus on the many impelling cues presented in the video, and would thus be unable to attend to the relevant inhibiting cues.

Justifications. Each of the next five items contained an impelling cue to engage in sexual intercourse, taken from the information presented in the video (e.g. "Because Rebecca's on the pill and won't get pregnant, there's little for me to worry about if we have intercourse," and "A situation like this occurs only once in a while, so it would be worth the risk involved for me to have intercourse"). These five items were aggregated to form an index of justifications (Cronbach's $\alpha = .86$). We hypothesized that intoxicated participants would indicate more agreement with these justifications than sober participants.

Study 1: Laboratory experiment

For Studies 1 and 2, we chose participants based on their responses to a mass testing questionnaire administered at the beginning of term. We chose males who were at least 19 years old, were social drinkers, were sexually active, and were not in an exclusive romantic relationship of more than two years. Importantly, we chose only those males who reported that they *usually use condoms* when having sexual intercourse. Thus, all of the males in our laboratory studies were "true believers" in the benefits of condom use, and reported that they regularly practiced safe sex.

Participants were randomly assigned to the sober ($n = 24$) or the intoxicated ($n = 30$) condition. Those in the sober condition viewed the video and completed the dependent measures. Those in the intoxicated condition were first given three alcoholic beverages, using the protocol as described earlier in the drinking and driving laboratory experiment.

Study 2: Placebo experiment

Participants were randomly assigned to the sober ($n = 20$), placebo ($n = 16$), or intoxicated ($n = 19$) conditions. The procedures were identical to those described in the placebo study for drinking and driving.

Study 3: Field experiment

Patrons were approached as they entered the bar and asked if they would complete a brief questionnaire for the Psychology Department. Among other questions, the questionnaire asked whether the patron was sexually active and consumed alcohol. The experimenter quickly scanned the surveys, and patrons who were at least 19 years old, consumed alcohol, were sexually active, and not in an exclusive dating relationship were asked if they would like to participate in the study. Those who agreed were randomly assigned to be assessed early in the evening (sober condition) or late in the evening (intoxicated condition). The BAL of each participant was assessed at the outset of the study and at the end of the evening. Only participants who were sober at the beginning of the evening (BAL = 0.03% or below) and intoxicated at the end of the evening (BAL = 0.06% or above) were included in the analyses, thus ensuring that the two groups were comparable in terms of drinking behavior.[1] As in the laboratory studies, we were interested in assessing only people who usually use condoms. To reduce demands for consistency, however, we chose not to inquire about condom use on the evening of participation. Instead, we contacted participants two months after they took part in the study, and asked them to report how frequently they used condoms, on a scale ranging from 0% ("I never use condoms when having sex") to 100% ("I always use condoms when having sex"). Only those participants who reported using condoms at least 70% of the time were included in the analyses.

Results

We conducted a meta-analysis, comparing the mean differences between the sober/placebo conditions and the intoxicated condition. For the intention item, we included the three condom use studies described earlier. For the justification items, we also included a preliminary laboratory study (Koch, 1994), for a total

---

1. As in Study 4 of the drinking and driving research, to rule out the confound of time assessment as a plausible alternative explanation we compared people who participated early in the evening, but were sober at the end of the night with those who participated late in the evening, but were sober at the end of the night. There were no differences between these groups on the dependent measures, thus eliminating time of assessment as a threat to the validity of our findings.

of four studies. Using the method of adding ts, we found a highly significant difference between the sober/placebo and intoxicated condition for the intention item ($z = 5.43$, $p < .0001$) and for the justification items ($z = 4.89$, $p < .0001$), such that intoxicated participants reported more positive intentions, and were more likely to endorse justifications to have sexual intercourse than were their sober counterparts. Recall that in these experiments, we had selected only participants who report that they usually use condoms. Our findings are therefore quite provocative: Alcohol intoxication caused a decrease in intentions to use condoms, even among those participants who claimed to practice safe sex on a regular basis.

Moreover, we conducted mediational analyses to determine whether our data were consistent with the notion that agreement with impelling cues mediates the relationship between level of intoxication (sober/placebo vs. intoxicated) and intentions to have unprotected sex. When our measure of justifications was partialed out of the correlation between level of intoxication and intentions, the intoxication–intention relation became nonsignificant (placebo and field experiments) or less significant (laboratory experiment), suggesting that agreement with impelling cues may mediate, in part, the effect of alcohol on intentions to have unprotected sexual intercourse.

DISCUSSION

Alcohol myopia

In two separate programs of research, using a variety of methodologies (experimental and correlational, laboratory and field studies), our findings have converged to show a pattern consistent with alcohol myopia. Sober participants tended to report extremely negative intentions to drink and drive or to engage in unprotected sex, presumably because they could attend to the negative consequences that could result from these actions, and decide that the potential costs would outweigh any benefits. The intoxicated participants, however, were significantly less negative about both of these behaviors. We believe that the intoxicated participants did not possess the requisite cognitive capacity to attend to both the costs and the benefits of drinking and driving, and having unprotected sex. Alcohol myopia may have caused intoxicated participants to focus on salient impelling cues, at the expense of the relevant inhibiting cues.

To date, we have presented participants in our studies with *impelling cues* (i.e. cues that emphasize the benefits of risky behaviors), and have found that, as hypothesized, intoxicated participants report more favorable intentions to engage in these risky health-related behaviors than do sober participants. Importantly, however, the alcohol myopia perspective makes another intriguing prediction: because alcohol intoxication causes people to attend to, and act on the most salient cues in their environment, it should be possible to demonstrate that if we present participants in our studies with *inhibiting cues* (i.e. cues that emphasize the costs of risky behaviors), intoxicated participants should be even *less* likely than sober participants to report intentions to engage in risky health-related behaviors.

In the data that we have collected so far, we have found limited support for the notion that in the presence of inhibiting cues, intoxicated participants will report less positive intentions to engage in risky behaviors. In the drinking and driving studies, we had included some items to test subjective norms, or the extent to which participants believed that significant referents would approve of drinking and driving (cf. Ajzen & Fishbein, 1980). For these items (e.g. "If I were to drink and drive the next time that I am out at a party or bar, my parents would find it acceptable"), intoxicated participants tended to report *less* positive intentions than sober participants, though not significantly so. We believe that the subjective norm items acted as inhibiting cues (i.e. the recognition that one's parents would disapprove of drinking and driving may decrease the likelihood that one would decide to do so), and that making this type of inhibiting cue salient caused the intoxicated participants to focus on relevant subjective norms, thus decreasing their capacity to attend to impelling cues. Similarly, in an initial pilot study for the condom use research (Koch, 1994), the intention item was worded in such a way to emphasize the fact that sex with Rebecca would be unprotected ("If I were in this situation, I would engage in sexual intercourse with Rebecca *without* a condom"). In response to this question, intoxicated males tended to be more negative toward having unprotected sex than were sober males, although the effect was only marginal. Again, we believe that by making inhibiting cues salient, alcohol myopia may prevent intoxicated participants from attending to the impelling cues in the situation.

We are currently conducting laboratory experiments designed explicitly to test the hypothesis that alcohol intoxication can cause an increase or a decrease in reports of intentions to engage in risky behaviors, depending on the types of cues that are made salient. In these studies, we manipulate whether participants are exposed to impelling or inhibiting cues. We hypothesize that if impelling cues are made salient, then intoxicated people should be *more* likely than sober people to express positive intentions to engage in risky behaviors. Following the logic of alcohol myopia, we also hypothesize that if inhibiting cues are made salient, then intoxicated people should be *less* likely than sober people to express positive intentions to engage in risky behaviors. For example, in the condom use domain, we are presently conducting an experiment where impelling cues or inhibiting cues are presented to participants by a confederate. In this study, participants are randomly assigned to the sober, placebo, or intoxicated condition. In each experimental session, two participants view the video with one male undergraduate confederate. Each session is randomly assigned to an impelling or inhibiting cue condition. In the impelling cue condition, the confederate makes three statements that emphasize the positive aspects of the situation (e.g. the attractiveness of the female character, "Man, she's good-looking," or how enticing the situation is, "I know what I'd do . . . I'd go for it"). In the inhibiting condition, the confederate makes three statements that emphasize the negative aspects of the situation (e.g. "Too bad she smokes," or "I wouldn't do it . . . too risky"). We expect an interaction consistent with alcohol myopia. That is, we expect that intoxicated males in the impelling condition will be more likely than those in the sober/placebo condition to hold positive intentions to have unprotected sex. Importantly, we expect that intoxicated males in the inhibiting condition will be less likely than those in the sober/placebo condition to hold positive intentions to have unprotected sex, because alcohol myopia will cause them to focus on the inhibiting cues that are made salient, and may counteract the impelling cues in the video.

It is very important and worthwhile to demonstrate that alcohol intoxication can actually be associated with a *decrease* in risky behavior if inhibiting cues are made salient. Such findings would lead to an increased understanding of risk behavior, and would hold immediate implications for designing effective programs for condom use and other dangerous and costly behaviors associated with alcohol intoxication. If the data support our hypotheses, then it may be possible to decrease the likelihood that intoxicated people will engage in dangerous and untoward behaviors by ensuring that the appropriate cues are present in the environment in places and situations where alcohol and risky behaviors are likely to coincide (e.g. college residences, campus or singles' bars, fraternity houses).

Expectancy effects

For both the drinking and driving, and condom use domains, we tested for expectancy effects using a placebo control group. In both programs of research, we found no evidence for alcohol expectancies. The placebo groups did not differ from the sober groups, and taken together, the sober and placebo groups were less likely to report intentions to engage in risky behaviors than were the intoxicated groups.

In fact, within the placebo condition, our findings are exactly opposite to the hypothesis that people view alcohol intoxication as a license to act irresponsibly. Those participants who believed that they were the most intoxicated tended to be the least likely to report intentions to engage in risky behaviors. Among placebo participants, there was a *negative* correlation between estimated BAL and intentions to drink and drive, $r(21) = -.42$, $p = .045$ (non-contingent), or have unprotected sexual intercourse, $r(17) = -.54$, $p = .017$. Interestingly, then, participants who believe that they are intoxicated, but still possess the requisite cognitive capacity to weigh the costs and benefits of engaging in risky behaviors, tend almost to bend over backwards to report intentions to avoid these activities. We are intrigued by these findings, and hypothesize that the negative correlation between perceived BAL and intentions to engage in risky behaviors may be related to participants' beliefs that alcohol will impair their judgment. If a participant believes that alcohol will greatly affect his intentions, and believes that he is intoxicated (but is in fact sober), he may overadjust his intentions to be consistent with his "sober" intentions (cf. Wegener & Petty, 1995). Intoxicated participants, however, may not overcompensate in this way, because alcohol myopia precludes the extra cognitive resources necessary to engage in this process. In future studies, we shall test this hypothesis by assessing participants' beliefs about how alcohol will affect their attitudes and intentions.

Gender differences

As already mentioned, in the field studies we were able to assess both males and females, because the ethical considerations of administering alcohol to a female who may be pregnant did not apply. Gender did not interact with intoxication level on any of the primary dependent measures for the drinking and driving field studies (telephone diary and campus pub study) or the condom use field study (campus pub study). Thus, the findings presented in this research were not moderated by gender.

Social desirability

We considered the possibility that social desirability could mediate the observed relationship between alcohol intoxication and intentions to engage in risky behaviors. It is conceivable that intoxicated participants would be less concerned about engaging in a socially desirable manner than sober participants. In a number of the studies reported here, participants completed the Marlowe–Crowne Social Desirability Scale (Crowne & Marlowe, 1964) as one of the dependent measures. There were no differences between sober/placebo and intoxicated participants on this measure. Moreover, scores on this scale were not correlated with the other dependent measures for either group. Therefore, social desirability may be ruled out as an alternative explanation for our findings.

Implications

Our studies have implications for designing effective change programs. We do not think that people are simply unaware of the costs associated with risky behaviors, or that they usually condone behaviors such as drinking and driving and having unprotected sexual intercourse. Indeed, sober and intoxicated people are equally and highly aware of the potential consequences of drinking and driving (see MacDonald et al., 1993), and people tend to report believing that having sex without a condom is foolish and irresponsible (see MacDonald et al., 1996). Instead, we believe that when intoxicated, alcohol myopia causes people to attend to cues that would lead them to engage in these behaviors, rather than to those cues that would inhibit such actions.

The fact that people hold different attitudes and intentions toward these risky behaviors when they are drunk suggests that interventions designed to reduce the incidence of these behaviors may be most effective if implemented in places and situations where people will be making the decision whether to drink and drive, or have unprotected sex. It may be possible to increase the likelihood that one will attend to the potential costs of these behaviors, to counteract any impelling cues that may be present. For example, inhibiting cues, such as signs warning people about the potential costs of drinking and driving posted at the exits of bars, may be helpful in reducing the probability that an intoxicated person will decide to drive away.

By educating people about the effects of alcohol, it may be possible to teach them to anticipate the effects that alcohol will have on their decision-making abilities, and they might in turn plan ahead, and make the decision while they are sober *not* to engage in these risky behaviors. For example, in the domain of drinking and driving, people could *commit* to their decision not to drink and drive before they begin to consume alcohol: they could appoint a designated driver, or take a taxi to their destination.

It could be that people fail to commit to their decision to avoid drinking and driving, not because they have intentions to drive while intoxicated, but because they do not have definite plans to become intoxicated in the first place. A common scenario is that people may go out, planning to "see how they feel" at the end of the night, and then make the decision whether to drive home. This plan may sound reasonable, but at the end of the night, after drinking, alcohol myopia may set in, causing a person to make a different decision than they may expect to while sober. For example, while sober, a person might usually think that after 6 beers, she would be far too intoxicated even to contemplate driving home. After actually consuming 6 beers, however, alcohol myopia may cause that person to pay attention to impelling cues that would lead her to drink and drive, and she might decide that she is in fine shape to drive home. People should know they need to have a plan set for the night, before they consume any alcohol. Similarly, in the condom use domain, people could plan ahead and have a condom available, to decrease the likelihood that they will encounter a situation where unsafe sex is an issue. In any event, people should know that their attitudes and intentions toward high-risk health behaviors may change when they are intoxicated.

SUMMARY

Through experimental laboratory and field studies, we have demonstrated that alcohol *causes* people to be more likely to hold positive (or, at least, less negative) attitudes and intentions toward risky health-related behaviors. We have suggested that alcohol myopia is the process mediating the relationship between alcohol intoxication and the decision to engage in risky behaviors. What makes the alcohol myopia perspective so intriguing, and potentially important, is that this perspective predicts that alcohol intoxication will make a person more or less likely to engage in risky behaviors, depending on the types of cues that are salient in the environment. Accordingly, we have speculated that if *inhibiting* cues are made salient, then alcohol intoxication may actually be associated with more *negative* intentions to engage in drinking and driving, unprotected sexual intercourse, and other types of risky behavior that are associated with alcohol. If this hypothesis is supported, it would hold both theoretical and practical implications for the study of alcohol, and for interventions designed to reduce the incidence of alcohol-related, detrimental behaviors.

ACKNOWLEDGEMENTS

Preparation of this article was supported in part by a Social Sciences and Humanities Research Council of Canada (SSHRC) Doctoral Fellowship to Tara K. MacDonald and SSHRC research grants to Mark P. Zanna and Geoffrey T. Fong.

REFERENCES

Abbey, A. (1991). Acquaintance rape and alcohol consumption on college campuses: How are they linked? *Journal of American College Health, 11*, 173–194.

Ajzen, I., & Fishbein, M. (1980). *Understanding attitudes and predicting social behavior*. Englewood Cliffs, NJ: Prentice Hall.

Baldwin, J. D., & Baldwin, J. I. (1988). Factors affecting AIDS-related sexual risk-taking behavior among college students. *Journal of Sex Research, 25*, 181–196.

Butcher, A. H., Manning, D. T., & O'Neal, E. C. (1991). HIV-related sexual behaviors of college students. *Journal of American College Health, 40*, 115–118.

Campbell, S. M., Peplau, L. A., & DeBro, S. C. (1992). Women, men, and condoms: Attitudes and experiences of heterosexual college students. *Psychology of Women Quarterly, 6*, 273–288.

Critchlow, B. (1986). The powers of John Barleycorn: Beliefs about the effects of alcohol on social behavior. *American Psychologist, 41*, 751–764.

Crowne, D., & Marlowe, D. (1964). *The approval motive*. New York: John Wiley.

Fong, G. T., Parent, M., & Poppe, C. (1994, April). *Predicting and understanding condom intentions and condom use among university students: A test of the theory of planned behavior*. Paper presented at the Annual Meeting of the Society of Behavioral Medicine, Boston, MA.

Glass, G. V., McGaw, B., & Smith, M. L. (1981). *Meta-analysis in social research*. Thousand Oaks, CA: Sage.

Gordon, C. M., & Carey, M. P. (1996). Alcohol's effects on requisites for sexual risk-reduction in men: An initial experimental investigation. *Health Psychology, 15*, 56–60.

Koch, A. (1994). *The effects of alcohol intoxication on attitudes and intentions towards condom use among male university students*. Unpublished undergraduate dissertation, University of Waterloo, Canada.

Leigh, B. C., & Stall, R. (1993). Substance use and risky sexual behavior for exposure to HIV. *American Psychologist, 48*, 1035–1045.

Levin, B. (1993, February). The world of teens. *Macleans*, p. 27.

MacDonald, T. K., Zanna, M. P., & Fong, G. T. (1993, August). *The effects of alcohol on intentions to drink and drive*. Paper presented at the meeting of the American Psychological Association, Toronto, Ontario.

MacDonald, T. K., Zanna, M. P., & Fong, G. T. (1995). Decision making in altered states: The effects of alcohol on attitudes toward drinking and driving. *Journal of Personality and Social Psychology*, *68*, 973–985.

MacDonald, T. K., Zanna, M. P., & Fong, G. T. (1996). Why common sense goes out the window: Effects of alcohol on intentions to use condoms. *Personality and Social Psychology Bulletin*, *22*, 763–775.

Ministry of Transportation. (1990, March). *Smashed: The magazine on drinking and driving*. Ottawa, Ontario. Author.

Poppen, P. J., & Reisen, C. A. (1994). Heterosexual behaviors and risk of exposure to HIV: Current status and prospects for change. *Applied and Preventive Psychology*, *3*, 75–90.

Reis, H. T., & Wheeler, L. (1991). Studying social interaction with the Rochester Interaction Record. In M. P. Zanna (Ed.), *Advances in experimental social psychology* (Vol. 24, pp. 269–318). San Diego, CA: Academic Press.

Rosenthal, R. (1978). Combining results of independent studies. *Psychological Bulletin*, *85*, 185–193.

Rosenthal, R. (1984). *Meta-analytic procedures for social research*. Thousand Oaks, CA: Sage.

Steele, C. M., Critchlow, B., & Liu, T. J. (1985). Alcohol and social behavior: II. The helpful drunkard. *Journal of Personality and Social Psychology*, *48*, 35–46.

Steele, C. M., & Josephs, R. A. (1990). Alcohol myopia: Its prized and dangerous effects. *American Psychologist*, *45*, 921–933.

Steele, C. M., & Southwick, L. (1985) Alcohol and social behavior: I. The psychology of drunken excess. *Journal of Personality and Social Psychology*, *48*, 18–34.

Wegener, D. T., & Petty, R. E. (1995). Flexible correction theories in social judgment: The role of naive theories in corrections for perceived bias. *Journal of Personality and Social Psychology*, *68*, 36–51.

Wheeler, L., & Reis, H. T. (1991). Self-recording of everyday life events: Origins, types, and uses. *Journal of Personality*, *59*, 339–354.

World Health Organization. (1996, July). *The HIV/AIDS Situation in Mid-1996*.

Zeichner, A., & Pihl, R. O. (1979). Effects of alcohol and behavior contingencies on human aggression. *Journal of Abnormal Psychology*, *88*, 153–160.

CHAPTER TWENTY-ONE

Experimental approaches to the anxiety and mood disorders

Susan Mineka
Northwestern University, Evanston, Illinois, USA

Richard Zinbarg
University of Oregon, USA

Conditioning models of anxiety disorders have increased their explanatory power in the past decade because of recognition that the effects of stressors can be predicted only if one examines the dynamic context in which they occur in a person's life. Studies of observational conditioning, immunization, and preparedness have also expanded the scope of these models to account for individual differences in the development of specific and social phobias. Moreover, such models have now been expanded to explain important features of PTSD through inclusion of the extensive animal research implicating uncontrollable and unpredictable stress in this disorder. In addition, extensive work on cognitive biases associated with anxiety and depression has important implications for understanding the maintenance of these disorders. Mood-congruent biases of attention, memory, and interpretation are discussed.

La puissance explicative des modèles de troubles d'anxiété s'est accrue au cours de la dernière décennie, alors qu'on en est venu à reconnaître que l'on ne saurait prévoir les effets des agents de stress qu'à l'examen du contexte dynamique dans lequel ils se présentent dans la vie de l'individu. Les études sur l'observation du conditionnement, de son immunisation et de sa préparation ont également accru la capacité qu'ont ces modèles de rendre compte des différences individuelles dans la formation de phobies spécifiques et sociales. En outre, ces types de modèles ont été maintenent amenés à expliquer d'importantes caractéristiques des troubles post-traumatiques associés au stress, grâce à l'inclusion de nombreuses recherches sur les animaux mettant en cause le rôle du stress imprévisible et incontrôlable dans ce genre de troubles. S'ajoute à ceci le fait que le nombre considérable de travaux portant sur les préjugés d'ordre cognitif associés à l'anxiété et à la dépression a des implications importantes pour notre compréhension de la persistance de ces troubles. On traite également des préjugés d'attention, de mémoire et d'interprétation liés à l'humeur.

Some of our most prominent early-learning theorists such as Pavlov (1927) and Watson (Watson & Rayner, 1920), and later Mowrer (1947) and Solomon (e.g. Solomon, Kamin, & Wynne, 1953), to name a few, were confident that the study of fear conditioning and avoidance learning was highly relevant to understanding what was then called neurotic behavior. In addition, numerous other investigators including Pavlov, Gantt, Liddell, Masserman, Wolpe also argued for the relevance of a wide range of paradigms that produced in animals symptoms of so-called "experimental neurosis" in understanding the genesis of neurotic behavior in humans (see Mineka & Kihlstrom, 1978, for a review). The term neurosis was used to refer to a wide range of not very clearly defined anxiety and depressive symptoms.

Initially there was a good deal of enthusiasm for the relevance of this work to understanding the origins and maintenance of neurotic behavior on the part of psychopathologists. However, by the 1970s and 1980s enthusiasm began to wane and criticisms of the limitations of these models became widespread in clinical psychology textbooks. During the same time period, a great deal of work in descriptive psychopathology was beginning to appear that led in 1980 with the publication of the third edition of the American Psychiatric Association's *Diagnostic and Statistical Manual* (*DSM-III*; 1980) to virtually abolishing the term neurosis in favor of more discrete and reliably diagnosed categories of different anxiety and mood disorders. Thus, "experimental neurosis" was no longer a viable topic of study. Separate models were now needed for phobias, post-traumatic stress disorder, obsessive-compulsive disorder, major depression, to name a few of these disorders.

In the meantime, two other quite separate forces were developing within experimental psychology that were both ultimately going to have a major impact on understanding the psychopathology of anxiety and depression. First, a virtual revolution in the study of learning was going on spearheaded by leading learning theorists such as Rescorla, Wagner, Dickinson, Mackintosh, Garcia, LoLordo, Seligman, Maier, and Overmier, to name a few. One important theme of this revolution was that the nature of the conditioning process is actually quite cognitive (usually not blind S-R associations based on contiguity alone as was thought previously; e.g. Delamater & LoLordo, 1991; Mackintosh, 1983). That is, conditioning involves the development of expectancies about the nature of the unconditioned stimulus (UCs); the emergence of a conditioned response (CR) is a sign that the conditioned stimulus (CS) has associatively primed the representation of the UCS (Wagner 1979; 1981). Moreover, according to helplessness theorists animals can also learn rather abstract expectancies about the effects that their responses have on outcomes (e.g. Maier, Seligman, & Solomon, 1969). A second important theme was that evolutionary principles of belongingness or selective associations dramatically affect which associations are learned easily and which are learned only with great difficulty (e.g. Rozin & Kalat, 1971; Seligman, 1970). However, few *clinical* theorists were very aware of the major new theories and findings in learning, and so they continued their criticisms based on earlier principles of learning from the 1940s and 1950s. At the same time, fewer and fewer *learning* theorists had maintained the interests of their founding fathers in the clinical relevance of work on fear conditioning or avoidance learning, and few of them were very attuned to the work on the descriptive psychopathology of the different anxiety disorders that began to emerge in the 1970s and 1980s. The first goal of this paper is to try to begin to redress these imbalances by showing how contemporary theory and research on conditioning and learning has relevance for understanding many of the causal factors for the different anxiety disorders.

However, before turning to that topic, it should be noted that there was also a second discipline emerging in the 1980s which has had a major impact on understanding other aspects of both the anxiety and the mood disorders. This is research on the emotion–cognition interaction. This work was initially inspired by Beck's seminal work on cognitive theories of depression and anxiety (e.g. Beck, 1967; 1976; Beck & Emery, 1985). Beck clearly spelled out the impact that one's thoughts or interpretations of a situation can have on one's feelings or emotions about the situation. In particular, he articulated how anxiety and depression may fundamentally derive from cognitive biases or distortions that lead people to interpret their environment in threatening or catastrophic ways in the case of anxiety, and in negative or pessimistic ways in the case of depression. By the early 1980s, beginning with Bower's seminal studies (e.g. 1981), this area of research on the emotion–cognition interaction became informed by sophisticated theories and paradigms from cognitive psychology and began to document that the anxiety and depressive disorders are all associated with cognitive biases for emotion-relevant material. Moreover, as documented by Teasdale, Mathews, MacLeod, Williams, and Watts, there is reason to believe that the functions served by these cognitive biases are to reinforce, confirm and even enhance these emotional states and so they may play a very important role in the maintenance of these disorders, and perhaps play an etiological role as well (e.g. MacLeod & Mathews, 1991; Mineka, 1992; Williams, Watts, MacLeod, & Mathews, 1988). Thus, the second part of this paper will describe the highlights of some of this experimental work on the cognitive biases associated with anxiety and depression. As will become apparent, these disorders appear to be associated with somewhat different types of cognitive bias—results that underscore some of the evolutionary/functional differences in these two emotional states and disorders (e.g. Mathews, 1993; Mineka, 1992).

CONDITIONING MODELS OF THE ANXIETY DISORDERS

Returning to the first theme of the paper, we consider what the problems were with the early conditioning approaches to the anxiety disorders, and how they can be redressed within the framework of contemporary research on conditioning and learning. We have argued that the central shortcoming of traditional conditioning models for anxiety disorders was their failure to consider the dynamic context in which stressors occur in an individual's life (Mineka & Zinbarg, 1996). Dynamic contextual factors can have powerful effects on the impact of those stressors, and by ignoring these factors, conditioning models appeared to be much more simplistic than necessary. As a result, they did not come close to realizing their full explanatory potential. We referred to the traditional models as "Stress-in-Total-Isolation Anxiety models" (SITIA models). By contrast, we argued that stress must always be considered in a dynamic context in order to predict or understand what the outcome of exposure to stress will be. This was referred to as the "Stress-in Dynamic-Context Anxiety model" (SIDCA model) (Mineka & Zinbarg, 1996). Some of the relevant dynamic contextual factors that were considered included: constitutional factors such as temperament, past experiential history, current contextual factors at the time of a stressor, and future modification of the impact of the stressor through modification of the representation of the stressor in memory. Although the effects of each of such contextual factors may have been studied only singly, we assume that in real life any one such contextual factor would act in conjunction or interaction with other factors in determining the outcome of exposure to the stressor; for example, whether no disorder develops, whether a mild disorder develops, or whether a severe disorder develops. Assuming that such interactions occur is a core feature of SIDCA models, even though at present little may be known about precisely what kinds of interactions of causal factors may be involved in the etiology of these disorders (Mineka & Zinbarg, 1996). Nevertheless, enough is known to present hypotheses for future research.

In discussing these models, highlights of research and theory are presented from the contemporary conditioning and learning literatures—both animal and human—that are relevant to understanding three of the six currently identified anxiety disorders: *specific phobias*, *social phobia*, and *post-traumatic stress disorder*. Their relevance to understanding the other three anxiety disorders is also described by Mineka and Zinbarg (1996).

Specific phobias

Individuals with specific phobias exhibit intense or irrational fears of various circumscribed objects or situations, and they typically avoid encounters with these objects or situations. Watson and Rayner (1920) first clearly articulated the view that phobias are simply intense classically conditioned fears that develop when a neutral object is paired with a traumatic event, and for years this view was enormously influential (although it was later modified by Eysenck and Rachman, 1965, and others into an avoidance learning model). However, for the past 20 to 25 years, conditioning and avoidance models of specific phobias have been severely criticized for a number of different reasons (see Mineka, 1985; Mineka & Zinbarg, 1991, for criticisms of avoidance models). Yet, as will be elaborated later, each of the major problems with the traditional behavioral approaches occurred because they were developed in the tradition of SITIA models. It is understandable that SITIA models emerged, given that Pavlovian methodoloy demanded that naive animals be studied in soundproof rooms where they were isolated from all stimuli that were extraneous to the conditioning process (including the experimenter). Yet humans who are exposed to Pavlovian conditioning events in the course of their everyday lives are neither naive nor isolated from extraneous stimuli. Therefore today, SIDCA models of fears and phobias must build on advances in knowledge about the theoretical and empirical foundations of conditioning that address the greater complexities of the conditioning process as it occurs in everyday life (Mineka, 1985; Mineka & Zinbarg, 1991, 1996).

Mineka and Zinbarg (1996) addressed four major kinds of criticisms of conditioning models from the SITIA tradition, only three of which will be mentioned here. The *first* problem comes from research suggesting that in many cases people with these disorders may not have any known traumatic conditioning history, leaving the question of how to account for the origins of their specific phobias from the standpoint of traditional conditioning models. There has long been speculation that observational or vicarious conditioning experiences might play an important role in the origins of some phobias. Indeed, based on retrospective self-report measures Öst and Hugdahl (1981) estimated that 17% of all specific phobics, and 40% of small animal phobics recalled a vicarious conditioning incident as having been involved in the origins of their specific phobia. In addition, there is now ample experimental evidence that strong and persistent phobic-like fears can indeed be learned through observation alone. This evidence comes from a series of experiments in which Mineka and Cook showed that laboratory-reared observer rhesus monkeys who were not initially afraid of snakes showed rapid acquisition of an intense and persistent fear of snakes simply as a result of watching a wild-reared model monkey behaving with intense fear in the presence of real and toy snakes. In fact, after a total of only 24 minutes of observing the models behave fearfully in the presence of the snake object, the observers were showing a level of fear that was nearly as strong as that of the wild-reared models (e.g. Cook, Mineka, Wolkenstein, & Laitsch, 1985). Another experiment demonstrated that the lab-reared monkeys also acquired the fear simply through watching a videotape of a model monkey behaving fearfully in the presence of snakes (Cook & Mineka, 1990). This latter finding suggests that humans are also likely to be susceptible to acquiring fears vicariously through television and movies. Such results make it evident that conditioning models from the SITIA tradition erred by not attending to the important role that observational or vicarious conditioning often plays in the origins of fears and phobias.

A *second* problem with SITIA conditioning models is their inability to clearly explain why some individuals having traumatic experiences in the presence of specific objects or situations do *not* acquire fears or phobias. For example, a number of researchers have noted that many nonphobics have had traumatic experiences in the presence of some potentially phobic object and yet not acquired a fear or phobia (e.g. Di Nardo, Guzy, & Bak, 1988; Ollendick & King, 1991). Such findings are perplexing from the perspective of SITIA conditioning models and are often cited as highly problematic for any conditioning account of phobias (e.g. Rachman, 1990). Interestingly, however, such findings are actually predicted by SIDCA models (cf. Mineka & Zinbarg, 1996).

For example, SIDCA models acknowledge that personality and temperamental variables affect the dynamics of conditioning, and the origins of fear (e.g. Pavlov, 1927); thus, individuals with different temperaments will react differently to ostensibly identical traumatic experiences. In addition, however, SIDCA models acknowledge that people come to traumatic conditioning experiences with widely differing experiential histories, which constitute an important part of the dynamic context in which conditioning is occuring. The experiential variables of interest can occur before, during, or following a traumatic event, or an observational fear-conditioning experience; they can act alone or in concert to affect the amount of fear that is experienced, acquired, or maintained into the future (Mineka, 1985). In other words, if we want to understand why only some people undergoing similar traumatic experiences develop fears or phobias, we must first understand a wide range of experiential variables on which individuals undergoing the same stress or trauma may differ. The earlier conditioning theories on which SITIA models were based generally did not overtly acknowledge this fact. However, one might surmise that there was suspicion that this might be the case because traditional Pavlovian methodologies dictated that *naive* animals be studied in *isolated* conditioning chambers. This methodology certainly allowed the study of the fundamentals of conditioning without extraneous potentially confounding variables such as prior experiences on which animals might differ. However, it was very risky to extrapolate directly from the results of such studies to how conditioning experiences might affect humans who are neither "naive" nor isolated from the world during conditioning. Such complexities are fully appreciated by SIDCA models (Mineka & Zinbarg, 1996).

One important *pre-experiential* variable that affects how much conditioning accrues to a CS is the amount and kind of prior experience the organism has had with the to-be-CS. For example, if an individual has been previously exposed to a CS (before the CS and UCS are ever paired together), there will subsequently be less conditioning to the CS (cf. the well-known phenomenon of latent inhibition; e.g. Lubow, 1973; Mackintosh, 1983). Mineka and Cook (1986) showed that even stronger attenuation of vicarious fear conditioning can occur if the prior exposure to a CS had occurred in the context of the observer watching a nonfearful model monkey behaving nonfearfully with snakes (as opposed to the latent inhibition procedure of simply exposing the observer monkey to the snake without a nonfearful model). Such prior exposure to a nonfearful monkey behaving nonfearfully with snakes resulted in complete immunization against the acquisition of fear when observers were subsequently exposed to a fearful model. This suggests that having extensive preexposure to others behaving non-fearfully with some potentially phobic object or situation can prevent the effects of later seeing a fearful or phobic individual behaving fearfully with that object.

Experiential variables that occur *during* a conditioning experience are also an important part of the dynamic context that affect levels of fear conditioning. Classical conditioning of fear was traditionally studied only in paradigms where the organism has no control over the presentation of either the CS or the UCS. Yet it is evident that many of the everyday events during which Pavlovian conditioning occurs involve situations in which organisms do have some control over the US, such as being able to escape it. For many years it has been known that much lower levels of fear are conditioned to neutral stimuli paired with escapable or controllable as opposed to inescapable or uncontrollable shock (e.g. Mineka, Cook, & Miller, 1984; Mowrer & Viek, 1948). In other words, the dynamics of fear conditioning are powerfully affected by the controllability of the UCS.

One example of a variable suggesting the importance of what happens *following* conditioning on the level of fear that is maintained over time is what kind of post-conditioning experiences with the UCS the organism has. For example, Rescorla's inflation effect (1974) showed that mild fears can become strong fears if, following conditioning of the mild fear, the rats were later exposed simply to a more intense traumatic US than was involved in the original conditioning—even though the CS was never paired with the more intense shock. To the extent that parallel effects occur in humans, a person who had a conditioning experience and acquired a fear of non-phobic intensity might be expected to show an increase in that fear, perhaps to phobic intensity, if a noncontingent highly traumatic experience occurred at a later point in time (see Mineka, 1985; Mineka & Zinbarg, 1996).

This small sample of experiential variables occurring prior to, during, and following a stressful experience should suffice to illustrate how much they can affect the level of fear that is conditioned, or that is maintained over time (see Mineka, 1985; Mineka & Zinbarg, 1996, for further examples). One certainly must acknowledge that the factors involved in the origins and maintenance of fears and phobias are considerably more complex than was generally assumed by earlier learning theorists. Nevertheless, all of the complexities discussed above are predicted from the perspective of contemporary research on conditioning and learning.

The *third* problem with traditional conditioning models was that they could not account for observations that fears and phobias are not randomly distributed across any arbitrary group of objects or situations associated with trauma (Seligman, 1971). Seligman (1971) and Öhman (1986; 1996) have hypothesized that primates and humans have a biologically based preparedness to rapidly associate certain kinds of objects that may frequently have been dangerous or posed a threat to our early ancestors—such as snakes, spiders, water, enclosed spaces—with aversive events. The idea is that this evolutionarily based preparedness evolved because there may have been a selective advantage in the course of evolution for primates and humans who rapidly acquired fears of such objects.

Öhman and his colleagues in Sweden have conducted a fascinating series of experiments over the past 20 years generally supportive of this hypothesis. Numerous experiments have found superior conditioning—as evidenced by enhanced resistance to extinction—using slides of snakes and spiders as conditioned stimuli, and mild shock as an unconditioned stimulus, compared to what is found more fear-irrelevant CSs such as slides of flowers and mushrooms (see Öhman, 1996, for a recent review). In addition, several experiments have also shown that such superior conditioning does not generally occur when more ontogenetically fear-relevant stimuli such as guns or damaged electric outlets are used as CSs (e.g. Hugdahl & Kärker, 1981).

Cook and Mineka (1989; 1990; 1991) provided a conceptual replication and extension of these findings using a variant on their observational fear-conditioning paradigm in monkeys. Naive observer monkeys who were not afraid of snakes watched one of two kinds of videotapes: one in which model monkeys appeared to be reacting fearfully to toy snakes, and one in which model monkeys appeared to be reacting fearfully to artificial brightly colored flowers. To do this experiment correctly, it was necessary to *equate the model's* fear performance in the presence of flowers with his fear performance in the presence of snakes through the use of edited videotapes. Thus both groups saw the exact same fear performance; they differed only in whether the fear appeared to be elicited by a toy snake or by flowers. Monkeys who saw models reacting fearfully to toy snakes did indeed acquire a significant fear of toy snakes, but monkeys in the second group who watched models reacting fearfully to flowers did not acquire a fear of flowers. In a closely related study, observer monkeys acquired a significant fear of a toy crocodile but did not acquire a fear of a toy rabbit. Thus, both monkeys and humans seem to selectively associate certain fear-relevant stimuli with aversive outcomes. Such findings are not surprising to contemporary learning researchers who know that for a given species certain CS-US combinations are more easily learned about than are other CS-US combinations (e.g. LoLordo, 1979; LoLordo & Droungas, 1989).

To summarize what is known about the origins and maintenance of specific phobias, it is clear that the factors involved are considerably more complex than has often been assumed by traditional conditioning models from the SITIA tradition. However, conditioning models in the SIDCA tradition actually predict these complexities because they emphasize that a large variety of dynamic contextual variables, and their interactions, have important effects on the outcome of conditioning experiences (see Mineka & Zinbarg, 1996).

Social phobia

Social phobia is diagnosed in people who fear one or more social situations where they are afraid they may be evaluated negatively or where they believe they might do or say something to embarrass or humiliate themselves; these fears must be markedly distressing and/or interfere with functioning. Öhman, Dimberg, and Öst (1985) extended the preparedness theory of specific phobias, and argued that social phobia should be studied in an adaptive/functional frame-work. They further hypothesized that social fears evolved as a by-product of dominance hierarchies. They noted that ritualized displays of threat on the part of a dominant animal, and of fear and submissiveness on the part of a defeated animal, are a common component of competitive encounters within members of a social group when dominance hierarchies are being established and main-tained. Given this evolutionary framework, Öhman and Dimberg (1978) rea-soned that prepared stimuli for social anxiety should involve social stimuli signaling dominance or intraspecific aggression such as facial expressions of anger or threat. Thus, they predicted, and found (using their electrodermal con-ditioning paradigm), that superior conditioning would occur when slides of angry faces were used as CSs, relative to what would be seen with slides of happy or neutral faces. Thus the work of Öhman and colleagues on preparedness and social phobias suggests that humans have an evolutionarily based predisposi-tion to acquire readily fears of angry, critical, or rejecting faces (see Mineka & Zinbarg, 1995, for further discussion). Nevertheless, these fascinating laboratory experiments cannot tell us specifically whether such conditioning does indeed play a role in the origins of full-blown social phobia. However, results of at least two studies consistent with this idea found that 56–58% of their samples of people with social phobia recalled direct traumatic conditioning experiences as having played a role in the origins of their social phobia (Öst & Hugdahl, 1981; Townsley et al., 1995).

But how do we explain the origins of social phobia for individuals who do not recall direct traumatic experiences prior to the onset of their social phobia? Although there are no studies on vicarious conditioning of social fears parallel-ing those on the observational conditioning of snake fear described earlier, there is some direct and some indirect evidence suggesting that such learning could indeed occur. For example, Öst and Hugdahl's (1981) found 13% of their sub-jects with social phobia recalled vicarious learning experiences as having played a role in the origin of their social phobia. In addition, in discussing how domin-ance hierarchies are passed down from one generation to the next in at least some species, de Waal (1989) argued that "The status tradition is primarily a *social* institution" rather than being based on some inborn predisposition. He also observed that in all three instances in which rhesus infants were adopted, their rank was not based on that of their own biological parents, but rather on that of their adoptive parents. Such evidence is at least consistent with the hypothesis that observational learning of social behaviors relating to dominance and submissiveness can indeed occur (see Mineka & Zinbarg, 1995; 1996, for further discussion).

Regarding experiential variables occurring prior to and following a conditioning event that can affect the amount of fear that gets acquired or maintained into the future, the research described earlier for specific phobias is highly relevant and more detailed discussion can be obtained in Mineka and Zinbarg (1995). Briefly, one would expect immunization, inflation, controllability, etc., to operate in basically the same way in moderating levels of fear conditioning for social fears and phobias as they operate for specific fears and phobias.

There are also undoubtedly temperamental contributions to the origins of social fears and phobias, as for specific phobias. There has been increasing consensus in recent years that behavioral inhibition is the temperamental construct that is most relevant for the study of anxiety in animals and humans (e.g. Gray, 1982; Kagan, 1994). Of particular relevance for models of social phobia is the fact that many of these animal studies explicitly demonstrated that behavioral inhibition is related to reactivity to conspecific stressors as well as to nonsocial stressors. For example, Hall and Klein (1942) reported that rats bred for timidity and fearfulness in nonsocial situations were also significantly more *socially* submissive than rats bred for fearlessness in nonsocial situations. Related findings have also been reported for rhesus monkeys (e.g. Chamove, Eysenck, & Harlow, 1972).

Individual differences in timidity in nonsocial situations are also negatively correlated with copulation frequency (Hall, 1941), suggesting that the timid animals are not as bold with the opposite sex as their less inhibited counterparts. Social anxiety in humans has also been found to be negatively correlated with sexual experience (e.g. Leary & Dobbins, 1983). Moreover, at least for men, sexual dysfunction has been thought of by theorists such as Barlow and Heimberg as a form of social phobia given the prominent role that evaluation anxiety appears to play in many cases of male sexual dysfunctions (e.g. Barlow, Chorpita, & Turkovsky, 1996; Heimberg & Barlow, 1988). Thus, the social behavior of animals high on behavioral inhibition seems to parallel some of the more common features of people with social phobia who are often fearful of asserting themselves, submissive, and fearful of dating and talking with the opposite sex.

Perceived uncontrollability also appears to play an important role in the etiology and maintenance of social phobia. First, numerous animal studies have demonstrated that inescapable shock, but not escapable shock, increases submissiveness, using several rather different measures (e.g. Maier, Anderson, & Lieberman, 1972; Rapaport & Maier, 1978). There is also a more ecologically valid line of animal research bearing on the role of uncontrollability in the onset of social phobias involving studies of the effects of social defeat. Repeated social defeat, but not repeated victory, leads to an increase in submissive behavior and lowering of position in a dominance hierarchy, as well as many of the traditional learned helplessness effects (e.g. Ginsburg & Allee, 1942; Scott & Marston, 1953; Uhrich, 1938; Williams & Lierle, 1988). Particularly noteworthy is that the defeated animals do not just become submissive to the specific animals by which they had formerly been defeated, but rather become more generally submissive toward any dominant conspecific (Ginsburg & Allee, 1942; Uhrich, 1938). This suggests another parallel between the behavior of defeated, submissive animals and people with social phobias because it is rare that socially anxious people are frightened only of a specific individual. Rather, people with social phobias are typically apprehensive regarding interactions with certain classes of people, such as people in authority or strangers (see Mineka & Zinbarg, 1995, for further discussion).

In summary, SIDCA learning models of social phobia are capable of accounting for the complexities and individual differences involved in the etiology of social phobia. This is because they acknowledge the important role of both temperamental and experiential variables occurring prior to, during, and following both direct and vicarious conditioning experiences in determining the outcome of those learning experiences. Moreover, these models also acknowledge that there may be a biologically based preparedness of certain cues for social anxiety. Finally, these models also incorporate the role that perceptions of uncontrollability over important life events have in the origins and/or maintenance of social phobia.

Post-traumatic stress disorder

Post-traumatic stress disorder (PTSD) occurs in a subset of individuals who have been exposed to a highly traumatic situation in which they have experienced or witnessed one or more events that involved actual or threatened death or serious injury, and when they responded with intense fear or horror to those events. The symptoms of PTSD are arranged into three categories. First, arousal and anxiety symptoms include sleeping difficulties, concentration difficulties, exaggerated startle, and hypervigilance. Second, re-experiencing symptoms include intrusive recollections of the trauma, nightmares, flashbacks, and intense distress during exposure to reminders of the trauma. The third, avoidance category includes both avoidance of trauma-related situations and/or thoughts, and numbing of emotional responsiveness.

A number of theorists have proposed that the animal literature on unpredictable, uncontrollable aversive events can shed light on some of the most important mechanisms involved in the development of PTSD symptoms (e.g. Başoğlu & Mineka, 1992; Foa, Zinbarg, & Olasov-Rothbaum, 1992; Mineka & Zinbarg, 1996). Başoğlu and Mineka noted that one obvious parallel is that the intense physical stressors used in the animal literature (e.g. electric shocks and defeats in physical fighting) very closely resemble those in at least one form of human traumatization that often leads to PTSD—torture. Moreover, intense physical harm is also often present, or at least threatened, in several other form of human traumatization commonly associated with the onset of PTSD, including child and spouse abuse, and various kinds of assault.

In addition, there are compelling similarities between the symptoms of PTSD and the behavioral and physiological disturbances observed in animals exposed to unpredictable and/or uncontrollable aversive stimulation. The most obvious similarity is the heightened generalized anxiety and arousal characteristic of both PTSD and animals exposed to unpredictable and/or uncontrollable aversive stimulation, but strong functional similarities for each of the other symptoms categories have also been detailed in several reviews (e.g. Başoğlu & Mineka, 1992; Foa et al., 1992; Mineka & Zinbarg, 1996).

Given the strong similarities between the symptoms of PTSD and the effects created by unpredictable and uncontrollable stress, what are the implications and specific predictions of this model for understanding other aspects of human PTSD? For this purpose it is useful to divide the experience of trauma survivors into three broad phases: (1) the pre-trauma phase; (2) the traumatization phase; and (3) the post-trauma phase (Başoğlu & Mineka, 1992; Mineka & Zinbarg, 1996). Similarly the literature on the effects of uncontrollable aversive events can be divided into three corresponding phases. The experimental analogue of the pre-trauma phase involves studies of the pre-treatment variables that either immunize or sensitize the organism to the negative effects of subsequent exposure to uncontrollable aversive events. The traumatization phase itself has as its experimental analogue questions concerning the acute reactions to uncontrollable and/or unpredictable aversive events, as well as what variables affect these reactions. Finally, the post-trauma phase has as its experimental analogue the long-term consequences of uncontrollable stress, as well as which variables that occur, following the experience of uncontrollable stress, influence the intensity and duration of future emotional and behavioral disturbances (Başoğlu & Mineka, 1992; Mineka & Zinbarg, 1996).

Regarding the traumatization phase itself, this model would suggest that the degree to which traumas are perceived to be uncontrollable and/or unpredictable should have a significant impact on the likelihood that a survivor will develop PTSD symptoms. Although prospective studies on this topic are unfortunately not yet available, there is some suggestive cross-sectional evidence by Foa and Zinbarg that the severity of PTSD symptoms is associated with diminished perceptions of controllability, as would be expected from this model (e.g. Boldstad & Zinbarg, in press; Kushner, Riggs, Foa, & Miller, 1993).

One important study illustrates an example of a variable during the traumatization phase that can reduce the negative effects of uncontrollable trauma. This study by Weiss and colleagues on stress-induced ulceration in rats showed that the expression of aggression can reduce the stress associated with uncontrollable shock (Weiss, Glazer, & Pohorecky, 1976). Rats exposed to uncontrollable shock that were given the opportunity to aggress against a conspecific showed less stress-induced ulceration relative to rats not given the opportunity to display aggressiveness. These and other findings suggest the hypothesis that the trauma survivor's attitude of resistance versus defeat may be an important determinant of the intensity of post-traumatic stress reactions (see Başoğlu & Mineka, 1992). Extrapolating from this finding to human torture, Başoğlu and Mineka (1992, p. 193) hypothesized that the amount of trauma inflicted during torture *per se* "may be less predictive than is the victim's psychological state of resistance and fighting back versus giving up and conceding defeat". This was consistent with reports of a good number of torture survivors who said that expression of anger and hostility toward their torturers helped to alleviate the distress during torture.

As already noted, examination of the experimental literature also reveals pre-trauma variables that should impact the development and/or maintenance of PTSD. Animal studies by Maier and colleagues show that prior experiences with uncontrollable stressors can sensitize the organism toward the negative consequences of a subsequent experience with uncontrollable trauma (e.g. Drugan, Moye & Maier, 1982; Moye, Hyson, Grau, & Maier, 1983). Such findings led Foa et al. (1992) to hypothesize that repeated abuse during childhood—an uncontrollable stressor—should make it more likely that the victims would develop PTSD later on following an uncontrollable trauma. As predicted by this hypothesis, childhood abuse has been found in two separate studies to be associated with greater PTSD severity in response to sexual and nonsexual assault in adulthood (Boldstad & Zinbarg, in press; Dancu, Shyer, Riggs, & Foa, 1991, cited in Foa et al., 1992).

By contrast, there are also findings illustrating that the effects of uncontrollable stress can sometimes be prevented. Many experimental studies have shown that a prior history of control can immunize against the negative effects of subsequent uncontrollable stress (e.g. Hannum, Rosellini, & Seligman, 1976; Mineka, Gunnar, & Champoux, 1986; Seligman & Maier, 1967; Williams & Maier, 1977). Such immunization procedures not only prevent behavioral but also physiological indices of learned helplessness. In addition, studies by Seligman (1968), Weiss (1968), and Overmier (1985) have shown that uncontrollable stressors which are predictable have significantly less aversive impact than do uncontrollable stressors which are also unpredictable.

Such findings lead to the hypothesis that prior psychological preparedness for trauma should relate to less perceived distress during torture (Başoğlu & Mineka, 1995; Başoğlu et al., in press). This hypothesis was tested using a sample of 55 carefully studied torture survivors who had been political activists in Turkey before being imprisoned and tortured. Başoğlu and colleagues had previously reported that only 33% of this sample had ever qualified for a diagnosis for PTSD (based on a lifetime structured interview), and at the time of the interview—which was an average of 5 years following their last experience with torture—only 18% qualified for a diagnosis of PTSD (Başoğlu et al., 1994a; 1994b). This low rate of PTSD seemed very surprising given the extreme amounts of torture that these torture survivors had experienced: an average of 23 different forms of torture and a mean total number of exposures to various kinds of torture of 291. However, this was an unusual sample given that they all had been political activists. Başoğlu and Mineka (Başoğlu & Mineka, 1995; Başoğlu et al., in press) hypothesized that their political activism was likely to have led them to have had a greater sense of predictability regarding their torture experience, as well as greater perceived control over their environment than a random person who had been imprisoned and tortured would have had. So they developed a psychological preparedness scale that assessed preparedness for arrest and torture, based on an evaluation of their degree of predictability of being imprisoned and tortured, their political views, degree of commitment to a cause, awareness of possible consequences of this commitment, and any training in physical or mental stoicism the survivor might have had as part of political group activity. Results showed that psychologically more prepared participants had experienced a greater variety of forms of torture and had more exposures to torture events than less prepared participants. Interestingly, however, there was a marginal trend for the more prepared subjects to have given *lower* global overall distress ratings for their entire torture experience (Başoğlu & Mineka, 1995).

Unfortunately, the power of this study was limited by the fact that there was a fairly restricted range on the preparedness scale, given that all participants had been political activists and were relatively high on the scale. Thus, it is important to compare these results with those from a sample of prisoners who are not political activists at all but who have also experienced torture. Başoğlu has very recently collected results from such a sample, also in Turkey. As predicted, even though these citizens who were arrested and tortured for alleged crimes (none were convicted) received much less torture, over a much shorter period of time than had the sample of political activists, they showed higher rates of PTSD and depression and general psychopathology than were seen in the political activist sample (Başoğlu et al., in press). Başoğlu and Mineka hypothesized that this is because the nonactivist sample had a diminished sense of psychological predictability or immunization, the torture experience coming "out of the blue", so to speak, without any prior training in stoicism or commitment to a cause. Indeed, when the results from the two studies were collapsed, ratings on this psychological preparedness scale were the only significant predictor of levels of psychopathology. Specifically, when nine independent variables, reflecting various aspects of the torture experience and demographic variables (e.g. education, ethnic status, income, duration of imprisonment, number of torture events), were entered first in hierarchical regression analyses predicting both general psychopathology and PTSD symptoms, these did not have significant predictive value. However, when psychological preparedness for trauma was entered next in the regression analyses, it accounted for 4% of the variance in general psychopathology (marginally significant) and 9% of the variance in PTSD symptoms ($p < .01$; Başoğlu et al., in press).

What about the post-trauma phase and implications of the animal literature for predicting the course of PTSD symptoms? One example is recent evidence from animals suggesting that the reexperiencing symptoms of PTSD might be involved in mediating the often persistent course of this disorder. In particular, Maier (personal communication, May 1995) found that the usual time course of some of the classic learned helplessness effects in rats can be greatly prolonged if the rats are simply exposed at regular intervals to the context in which they had previously experienced uncontrollable stress. In other words, exposure to the context in which the original trauma occurred seems to serve as a reminder of the trauma and is sufficient to prolong the time period during which learned helplessness deficits can be observed. By extension, such findings suggest that humans who exhibit a large number of reexperiencing symptoms (e.g. flashbacks, nightmares, or simple reexposure to cues for trauma) might be expected to show a more persistent time course for the disorder relative to those with fewer reexperiencing symptoms (see Mineka & Zinbarg, 1996).

In summary, the behavioral disturbances produced by uncontrollable and unpredictable shock in animals bear some compelling similarities to the chronic symptoms of PTSD in humans. This supports the hypothesis that perceptions of uncontrollability and unpredictability may play an important role in the development and maintenance of PTSD symptoms. The animal literature on pretreatment variables that sensitize the organism to the negative consequences of subsequent exposure to uncontrollable and unpredictable aversive events also helps to illuminate why histories of child abuse appear to predispose survivors to the development of PTSD following later victimization. Finally, the literature on predictability and immunization may help explain why torture survivors who were political activists showed such low rates of PTSD.

Summary

This section of the paper has reviewed some highlights of conditioning and ethological research from animals and humans that seem highly relevant to understanding important features of each of the different anxiety disorders, although only three have been addressed here (see Mineka & Zinbarg, 1996, for further discussion). Most criticisms of conditioning models have been based on long-outmoded contiguity views of conditioning that considered only the effects of stress in isolation in producing anxiety and anxiety disorders (Stress-in-Total-Isolation Anxiety models). By contrast, contemporary conditioning theory recognizes the many dynamic contextual variables influencing the outcome of exposure to stressful life events (Stress-in-Dynamic-Context Anxiety models). Clinical theorists interested in anxiety and the anxiety disorders should abandon their critiques of outmoded SITIA models and explore the many promising hypotheses for further understanding of the anxiety disorders that stem from the SIDCA models we have presented here and elsewhere.

COGNITIVE BIASES IN ANXIETY AND DEPRESSION

As noted earlier Beck (1967; 1976; Beck & Emery, 1985) is the seminal theorist who first clearly articulated the idea that emotional disorders (anxiety and depression) may fundamentally derive from cognitive biases or distortions that lead people to interpret their environment in threatening or catastrophic ways (in the case of anxiety) or negative and pessimistic ways (in the case of depression). However, Beck did not make his case based on sophisticated experiments using paradigms and theories from cognitive psychology. That approach began in the 1980s and soon a major theme of experimental research on the emotion–cognition interaction emerged, showing that anxiety and depression do indeed have prominent effects on cognitive processing. Moreover, it seems likely that these effects appear to serve the function of confirming, reinforcing or enhancing the emotional state (MacLeod & Mathews, 1991; Mathews & MacLeod, 1994; Mineka & Tomarken, 1989; Mineka, 1992; Mineka & Sutton, 1992; Williams et al., 1988). This work involves what many have called cognitive biases, which we define as any selective or non-veridical processing of emotion-relevant information (Mineka & Tomarken, 1989). The three main types of cognitive bias that have been identified are *attentional bias*, *memory bias*, and *judgmental or interpretive bias*.

Attentional bias.   A substantial amount of work has now documented that anxiety appears to have a pre-conscious, automatic influence on attention, resulting in attention being directed toward potentially threatening stimuli in the environment. Clinically, anxious patients seem to have a tendency toward heightened perception of, and vigilance for threat and danger cues. Mathews and MacLeod and their colleagues have provided elegant experimental confirmation of such a bias in their work with patients with generalized anxiety disorder (e.g. MacLeod & Mathews, 1991; Mathews & Macleod, 1994; Mathews, 1993). Numerous experiments using a number of different kinds of experimental tasks have demonstrated that anxious patients show evidence of their attention being drawn toward threatening cues when there is a mixture of threatening and non-threatening cues in the environment. This attentional bias appears to occur preconsciously; that is, without awareness. Non-anxious individuals, if anything, direct attention away from threatening stimuli. One possible explanation of these results is that anxious patients have danger schemata which lead to preattentive shifts of information-processing resources toward threat cues. It is easy to see how anxiety is likely to be maintained or exacerbated as one tends to see in generalized anxiety disorder if, when one is anxious, one's attention is focused more and more on threat and danger cues. Whether such a vicious cycle does indeed occur is not yet known but it certainly seems quite likely.

Moreover, there is now evidence gathered by MacLeod suggesting that the tendency to exhibit this preconscious attentional bias toward threat cues predicts subsequent reactions to a stressful life event (MacLeod & Hagan, 1992). Women in this study were given a test for this preconscious attentional bias at the time they underwent a test for cervical cancer. The greater their tendency to show this attentional bias for threat, the more severe their subsequent emotional distress if they received a diagnosis of cervical pathology.

By contrast to this strong evidence for an attentional bias in anxiety, MacLeod and Mathews have noted that there is little convincing evidence for a similar attentional bias for negative information in depression (e.g. MacLeod & Mathews, 1991; Mathews & MacLeod, 1994). Even in the few studies that have found a relative bias, it is the nondepressed individuals who have their attention drawn to positive words relative to neutral or negative words (e.g. Gotlib, McLachlan & Katz, 1988). Depressed individuals tend to show even-handed attention. However, if we now look at memory biases the pattern of results is in one sense the opposite.

Memory bias. Specifically, there are many experiments showing that depression is associated with a bias to recall mood-congruent information; by contrast, there is little consistent evidence that anxiety is associated with a similar memory bias (e.g. MacLeod & Mathews, 1991; Mathews & MacLeod, 1994; Mineka & Nugent, 1995). Studies of mood-congruent memory in depression usually compare individuals who experience high levels of depression with matched nondepressed controls. The memory tasks usually involve lists of words which vary in affective content and the encoding task usually needs to be a self-referential one. Subjects with clinical depression show a significant bias to recall negative, especially self-referential information (see Matt, Vazquez, & Campbell, 1992). The negative material can either be experimentally presented or it can be autobiographical. By contrast, nondepressed individuals generally exhibit a bias favoring positive material (see MacLeod & Mathews, 1991; Mineka & Nugent, 1995). Teasdale (1988) hypothesized that this memory bias for negative self-referential material can be seen as creating a vicious cycle of depression. When one is already depressed and one's memory is strongly biased so that primarily the bad things that have happened to one are remembered, this is only going to help perpetuate the depression. Consistent with this idea, Dent and Teasdale (1988) found that the degree of memory bias shown by depressed individuals at Time 1 predicted how depressed the subjects were 5 months later, even when subjects were matched on Time 1 depression level. In addition, Brittlebank, Scott, Williams, and Perrier (1993) found the presence of an autobiographical memory bias to be the *best* predictor of a failure to recover from depression in 22 depressed patients at 3- and 7-month follow-up. Indeed, their measure of memory bias at Time 1 accounted for 33% of the variance in depression levels at follow-up. Finally, Bellew and Hill (1991) showed that the presence of a memory bias predicts onset of depression as well as course of the disorder.

By contrast, the majority of studies examining whether anxiety is also associated with a memory bias for threatening information have not found such an effect (see Macleod & Mathews, 1991; Mathews & MacLeod, 1994; Mineka & Nugent, 1995). Although there have been a few studies reporting such a bias in anxious individuals, the majority have not found such an effect. And when significant findings have been obtained, they have often failed to replicate. For example, Mathews, Mogg, May, and Eysenck (1989) reported that anxious patients may show an *implicit* but not an explicit memory bias for threatening information. However, Mathews, Mogg, Kentish, and Eysenck (1995) later reported a failure to replicate that effect, and Nugent and Mineka (1994, and unpublished data) failed to find evidence for an implicit memory bias in high trait anxious subjects in at least 5 different studies, using both data-driven and conceptual memory tasks, of both an implicit and an explicit nature (Mineka & Nugent, 1995; Roediger & McDermott, 1992).

Thus anxiety and depression appear to have somewhat different effects on cognitive processing. There is strong evidence that anxiety is associated with a preconscious attentional bias for danger or threat cues, and that depression is associated with a memory bias for negative self-referential information. Theories of the effects of emotion on cognition need to be able to account for this apparent dissociation between the most prominent biases for these two different emotional disorders (Williams et al., 1988). The two original theories that were used to account for the relationship between affect and cognition—one being a semantic associative network model like Bower's (1981) and one being a schema model like Beck's (1967; 1976)—predict that evidence for both memory *and* attentional biases should be evident in both anxiety *and* depression. This is because in both of these models different emotions are all thought to have the effect of giving priority to mood-congruent information at each stage of the information-processing continuum—from early perceptual detection to subsequent recall and judgment. Only in the past decade have models been developed that may eventually help us to understand these differential effects of anxiety and depression on attention versus memory (e.g. Williams et al., 1988). Although their framework does a better job of accounting for these differences, it still does have some difficulties in accounting for certain aspects of the results in this complex array of findings (Mineka & Nugent, 1995, and see later).

The Williams et al. (1988) model draws on the distinction made by Graf and Mandler (1984) between the *activation* or *integration* of mental representations, which is a relatively automatic process, and the *elaboration* of mental representations, which is a more strategic process. Graf and Mandler proposed that integration results when exposure to a stimulus automatically activates an associated schema, leading to a strengthening of the internal organization of the schema. Integration makes the activated schema and its components more readily accessible, facilitating perception of schema-congruent information, and implicit memory performance. Because explicit memory requires more elaborative processing, integration does not, however, necessarily facilitate explicit memory (e.g. recall or recognition). Elaboration involves developing and strengthening connections between the schema and other contextual cues at encoding, and with other associated representations in memory; the effects of elaboration are reflected by explicit memory test performance.

Williams et al. (1988) also integrated the activation/elaboration distinction of Graf and Mandler (1984) with Oatley and Johnson-Laird's proposal (1987) that there may be unique modes of cognitive operation associated with the different primary emotions. They proposed that anxiety selectively activates mood-congruent (e.g. threatening) representations, but reduces the tendency to elaborate mood-congruent representations. This would account for the consistent pattern of preconscious (i.e. automatic) attentional biases for threatening material seen in anxious subjects, and the relative paucity of findings for explicit memory biases for threatening material seen in anxious subjects. It would also predict the findings of implicit mood-congruent biases in anxiety (e.g. Mathews et al., 1989). However, this account has difficulty in explaining the inconsistency of such results unless this inconsistency stems from the failure to use conceptual implicit memory tests in any studies published to date (see Mineka & Nugent, 1995; Roediger & McDermott, 1992, for discussion).

In contrast to anxiety, Williams et al. (1988) proposed that depression is characterized by a tendency to elaborate mood-congruent material to a disproportionate degree. This over-elaboration of depression-relevant material would account for the consistent evidence seen in the depression literature for mood-congruent explicit memory biases (Matt et al., 1992). However, this elaboration does not stem from any special early activation of mood-congruent material. This would explain failures to find mood-congruent implicit memory biases (cf. Denny & Hunt, 1992; Watkins et al., 1992), and the relatively sparse and inconsistent evidence for attentional biases for negative information. However, it may not as easily account for why an implicit memory bias seems to emerge when a conceptual implicit memory task is used (Watkins et al., 1996).

The idea that anxiety is characterized by an early, selective attentional bias for threat and avoidance of more elaborate processing of this threat, and that depression is associated with greater elaboration of and memory for depression-relevant information can be understood from the vantage point of psycho-evolutionary theories of cognition and emotion (Mineka, 1992; Mineka & Gilboa, in press; Plutchik, 1984). According to these theories, cognition has developed as a means of shaping and regulating the adaptive function of emotions. Given that there were probably quite different pressures which shaped the evolution and development of depression and anxiety, it is not surprising that distinct modes of information processing would facilitate the function of different emotions (e.g. Mathews, 1993; Oatley & Johnson-Laird, 1987). For example, anxiety, like fear, would seem to require a cognitive system which could quickly scan for and perceive cues for danger, allowing for continuous monitoring of the environment for signals of potential threat. Depression, by contrast, involves reflective consideration of events that have led to failure and loss, and would

seem to require a cognitive system adept at remembering vital information concerning loss and failure in order to facilitate reflection on those factors which
resulted in failure and/or loss. Thus, anxiety as a forward-looking emotion may
have evolved to be associated with attentional biases because such biases facilitate the rapid detection of threat and its subsequent avoidance (Mathews, 1993).
By contrast, depression as a more backward-looking emotion may be associated
with memory biases, perhaps because as Mathews (1993) has argued, reflecting on past events is more relevant to the function of sadness than would be
vigilance for future threat.

Judgmental or interpretative bias.   Several forms of judgmental or interpretive bias are also associated with both depression and anxiety and phobias.
For example, both anxiety and depression are associated with biased judgments
of the likelihood that negative events will happen to the individual (e.g. Butler
& Mathews, 1983; MacLeod & Mathews, 1991). Anxiety is also associated with
an increased tendency to interpret ambiguous information in a threatening manner. For example, Eysenck, Mogg, May, Richards and Mathews (1991) showed
that when clinically anxious subjects read a series of ambiguous sentences such
as, "The men watched as the chest was open," or "The Doctor examined Little
Emma's growth" or "They discussed the priest's convictions," they are more
likely to remember the threatening meaning of the sentence than are normals.
Having a bias to interpret ambiguous information in a threatening manner and
overestimating the likelihood of negative events can once again be seen as
serving to reinforce or enhance the anxiety or depression that drives the bias in
the first place.

From these highlights of research on the emotion–cognition interaction conducted in individuals with emotional disorders, it appears that anxiety is associated with an attentional bias for threatening material, and depression with a
memory bias for negative self-referential information. Both anxiety and depression
appear to be associated with various interpretive or judgmental biases. Although
much work remains to be done to establish the real consequences of these
cognitive biases, it seems likely that all of these biases for emotion-relevant
material can be expected to have the effect of reinforcing or even enhancing the
current emotional state. Thus they may play important roles in the maintenance
of these disorders, and perhaps in their etiology as well.

CONCLUSIONS

In conclusion, this chapter has provided highlights of two different experimental
approaches to understanding anxiety disorders, as well as how one of these
approaches has been applied to understanding depression. Both of these experimental approaches began to emerge along with concurrent developments in the
descriptive psychopathology of these disorders—wherein the old generic term

neurosis was virtually abolished in the *DSM-III* in 1980 and replaced with more specific and concretely defined categories of anxiety and depressive disorders. Although research in these two different traditions has generally proceeded along independent and quite unrelated paths, some attempts to integrate them have been made and are likely to be fruitful paths for future research (e.g. Chan & Lovibond, 1996; Tomarken, Mineka, & Cook, 1989; Zinbarg & Mohlman, in press).

The first part of the chapter demonstrated that the causal role of stress and traumatic events for the anxiety disorders can be understood only if one considers the many dynamic contextual variables that affect the outcome of exposure to stressful life events. These included temperamental variables, the controllability of the UCS, prior experiences with the CS, etc., as well as evolutionary principles of belongingness or selective associablity. In addition, the vast animal literature on the effects of exposure to uncontrollable and unpredictable aversive events has a great deal of relevance for understanding many of the anxiety disorders—perhaps PTSD most strongly. In the second part of the chapter, we demonstrated the importance of research on the emotion-cognition interaction as studied with paradigms from cognitive psychology for understanding important features of both anxiety and depression. As first suggested by the pioneering cognitive theorist of the emotional disorders—Aaron Beck—there is now ample experimental evidence that anxiety and depression are both characterized by cognitive biases for emotion-relevant material. These include biases of attention, memory and judgement. Moreover, there is good reason to believe that these biases serve the function of confirming or maintaining these emotional states, and some preliminary evidence that they may also play an important role in etiology.

REFERENCES

American Psychiatric Association (1980). *Diagnostic and statistical manual of mental disorders* (3th ed.). Washington, DC: American Psychiatric Association.

Barlow, D. H., Chorpita, B., & Turovsky, J. (1996). Fear, panic, anxiety, and disorders of emotion. In D. Hope (Ed.), *Perspectives on Anxiety, Panic, and Fear: 43rd Annual Nebraska Symposium on Motivation* (pp. 251–328). Lincoln, NE: University of Nebraska Press.

Başoğlu, M., & Mineka, S. (1992). The role of uncontrollability and unpredictability of stress in the development of post-torture stress symptoms. In M. Başoğlu (Ed.), *Torture and its consequences: Current treatment approaches*. Cambridge: Cambridge University Press.

Başoğlu, M., & Mineka, S. (1995). Perceived distress during torture and its relationship to post-traumatic stress responses. Unpublished manuscript.

Başoğlu, M., Mineka, S., Paker, M., Aker, T., Gok, S., & Livanou, M. (in press). Psychological preparedness for trauma as a protective factor in survivors of torture. *Psychological Medicine*.

Başoğlu, M., Paker, M., Paker, O., Ozmen, E., Marks, I., Incesu, C., Sahin, D., & Sarimurat, N. (1994a). Psychological effects of torture: A comparison of tortured with nontortured political activists in Turkey. *American Journal of Psychiatry, 151*, 76–81.

Başoğlu, M., Paker, M., Tasdemir, O., Ozmen, E., & Sahin, D. (1994b). Factors related to long-term traumatic stress responses in survivors of torture in Turkey. *Journal of the American Medical Association, 272*, 357–363.

Beck, A. T. (1967). *Depression: Clinical, experimental, and theoretical aspects*. New York: Harper & Row.

Beck, A. T. (1976). *Cognitive therapy and the emotional disorders*. New York: International Universities Press.

Beck, A. T., & Emery, G. (1985). *Anxiety disorders and phobias: A cognitive perspective*. New York: Basic Books.

Bellew, M., & Hill, B. (1991). Schematic processing and the prediction of depression following childbirth. *Personality and Individual Differences, 12*, 943–949.

Bolstad, B., & Zinbarg, R. (in press). Sexual victimization, generalized perception of control and post-traumatic stress disorder symptom severity. *Journal of Anxiety Disorders*.

Bower, G. H. (1981). Mood and memory. *American Psychologist, 36*, 129–148.

Brittlebank, A. D., Scott, J., Williams, J. M., & Perrier, I. N. (1993). Autobiographical memory in depression: State or trait marker? *British Journal of Psychiatry, 162*, 118–121.

Butler, G., & Mathews, A. (1983). Cognitive processes in anxiety. *Advances in Behaviour Research and Therapy, 5*, 51–62.

Chamove, A. S., Eysenck, H. J. & Harlow, H. F. (1972). Personality in monkeys: Factor analyses of rhesus social behavior. *Quarterly Journal of Experimental Psychology, 24*, 496–504.

Chan, C., & Lovibond, P. (1996). Expectancy bias in trait anxiety. *Journal of Abnormal Psychology, 105*, 637–647.

Cook, M., & Mineka, S. (1989). Observational conditioning of fear to fear-relevant versus fear-irrelevant stimuli in rhesus monkeys. *Journal of Abnormal Psychology, 98*, 448–459.

Cook, M., & Mineka, S. (1990). Selective associations in the observational conditioning of fear in monkeys. *Journal of Experimental Psychology: Animal Behavior Processes, 16*, 372–389.

Cook, M., & Mineka, S. (1991). Selective associations in the origins of phobic fears and their implications for behavior therapy. In P. Martin (Ed.), *Handbook of behavior therapy and psychological science: An integrative approach* (pp. 413–434). New York: Pergamon.

Cook, M., Mineka, S., Wolkenstein, B., & Laitsch, K. (1985). Observational conditioning of snake fear in unrelated rhesus monkeys. *Journal of Abnormal Psychology, 94*, 591–610.

Dancu, C. V., Shoyer, B., Riggs, D. S., & Foa, E. B. (1991). [*Childhood sexual abuse and crime-related PTSD*]. Unpublished raw data.

Delamater, A., & LoLordo, V. (1991). Event revaluation procedures and associative structures in Pavlovian conditioning. In L. Dachowski, & C. Flaherty (Eds), *Current topics in animal learning: Brain, emotion, and cognition* (pp. 55–94). Hillsdale, NJ: Erlbaum.

Denny, E., & Hunt, R. (1992). Affective valence and memory in depression: Dissociation of recall and fragment completion. *Journal Abnormal Psychology, 101*, 575–582.

Dent. J., & Teasdale, J. (1988). Negative cognition and the persistence of depression. *Journal of Abnormal Psychology, 97*, 29–34.

de Waal, F. (1989). *Peacemaking among primates*. Cambridge, MA: Harvard University Press.

Di Nardo, P. A., Guzy, L. T., & Bak, R. M. (1988). Anxiety response patterns and etiological factors in dog-fearful and non-fearful subjects. *Behaviour Research and Therapy, 26*, 245–252.

Drugan, R. C., Moye, T. B., & Maier, S. F. (1982). Opioid and nonopioid forms of stress induced analgesia: Some environmental determinants and characteristics. *Behavioral and Neural Biology, 35*, 251–264.

Eysenck, H., & Rachman, S. J. (1965). *Causes and cures of neurosis*. London: Routledge & Kegan Paul.

Eysenck, M., Mogg, K., May, J., Richards, A., & Mathews, A. (1991). Bias in interpretation of ambiguous sentences related to threat in anxiety. *Journal of Abnormal Psychology, 100*, 144–150.

Foa, E., Zinbarg, R., & Olasov-Rothbaum, B. (1992). Uncontrollability and unpredictability in post-traumatic stress disorder: An animal model. *Psychological Bulletin, 112*, 218–238.

Ginsburg, B., & Allee, W. C. (1942). Some effects of conditioning on social dominance and subordination in inbred strains of mice. *Physiological Zoology, 15*, 485–506.

Gotlib, I., MacLachlan, A., & Katz, A. (1988). Biases in visual attention in depressed and non-depressed individuals. *Cognition and Emotion*, *2*, 185–200.

Graf, P., & Mandler, G. (1984). Activation makes words more accessible, but not necessarily more retrievable. *Journal Verbal Learning and Verbal Behavior*, *23*, 553–568.

Gray, J. A. (1982). *The neuropsychology of anxiety: An enquiry into the functioning of the septo-hippocampal system*. Oxford: Oxford University Press.

Hall, C. S. (1941). Temperament: A survey of animal studies. *Psychological Bulletin*, *38*, 909–943.

Hall, C. S., & Klein, S. J. (1942). Individual differences in aggressiveness in rats. *Journal of Comparative Psychology*, *33*, 371–383.

Hannum, R., Rosellini, R., & Seligman, M. (1976). Retenion of learned helplessness and immunization in the rat from weaning to adulthood. *Developmental Psychology*, *12*, 449–454.

Heimberg, R. G., & Barlow, D. H. (1988). Psychosocial treatments for social phobia. *Psychosomatics*, *29*, 27–37.

Hugdahl, K., & Kärker, A.-C. (1981). Biological vs. experiential factors in phobic conditioning. *Behaviour Research and Therapy*, *19*, 109–115.

Kagan, J. (1994). *Galen's prophecy*. New York: Basic Books.

Kushner, M. G., Riggs, D. S., Foa, E. B., & Miller, S. M. (1993). Perceived controllability and the development of posttraumatic stress disorder (PTSD) in crime victims. *Behaviour Research & Therapy*, *31*, 105–110.

Leary, M. R., & Dobbins, S. E. (1983). Social anxiety, sexual behavior and contraceptive use. *Journal of Personality and Social Psychology*, *45*, 1347–1354.

LoLordo, V. (1979). Selective associations. In A. Dickinson & R. Boakes (Eds.), *Mechanisms of learning and motivation: A memorial to Jerzy Konorski* (pp. 367–398). Hillsdale, NJ: Erlbaum.

LoLordo, V., & Droungas, A. (1989). Selective associations and adaptive specializations: Food aversion and phobias. In S. Klein & R. Mowrer (Eds.), *Contemporary learning theories: Instrumental conditioning theory and the impact of biological constraints on learning* (pp. 145–179). Hillsdale, NJ: Erlbaum.

Lubow, R. E. (1973). Latent inhibition. *Psychological Bulletin*, *79*, 398–407.

Mackintosh, N. (1983). *Conditioning and associative learning*. New York: Oxford University Press.

MacLeod, C., & Hagan, R. (1992). Individual differences in the selective processing of threatening information, and emotional responses to a stressful life event. *Behaviour Research and Therapy*, *30*, 151–161.

MacLeod, C., & Mathews, A. M. (1991). Cognitive-experimental approaches to the emotional disorders. In P. Martin (Ed.), *Handbook of behavior therapy and psychological science* (pp. 116–150). New York: Pergamon Press.

Maier, S. F., Anderson, C., & Lieberman, D. (1972). Influence of control of shock on subsequent shock-elicited aggression. *Journal of Comparative and Physiological Psychology*, *81*, 94–100.

Maier, S. F., Seligman, M. E. P., & Solomon, R. L. (1969). Pavlovian fear conditioning and learned helplessness: Effects on escape and avoidance behavior of a) the CS-US contingency and b) the independence of the US and voluntary responding (pp. 299–342). In B. A. Campbell & R. M. Church (Eds.), *Punishment*. New York: Appleton-Century-Crofts.

Mathews, A. (1993). Anxiety and the processing of emotional information. In L. Chapman, J. Chapman, & D. Fowles (Eds.), *Models and methods of psychopathology: Progress in experimental personality and psychopathology research*. New York: Springer.

Mathews, A., & MacLeod, C. (1994). Cognitive approaches to emotion and emotional disorders. *Annual Review of Psychology*, *45*, 25–50.

Mathews, A., Mogg, K., Kentish, J., & Eysenck, M. (1995). Effect of psychological treatment on cognitive bias in generalized anxiety disorder. *Behaviour Research and Therapy*, *33*, 293–303.

Mathews, A., Mogg, K., May, J., & Eysenck, M. (1989). Implicit and explicit memory bias in anxiety. *Journal of Abnormal Psychology*, *98*, 236–240.

Matt, G., Vazquez, C., & Campbell, W. K. (1992). Mood-congruent recall of affectively toned stimuli: A meta-analytical review. *Clinical Psychology Review*, *12*, 227–255.

Mineka, S. (1985). Animal models of anxiety-based disorders: Their usefulness and limitations. In J. Maser & A. Tuma (Eds.), *Anxiety and the anxiety disorders* (pp. 199–244). Hillsdale, NJ: Erlbaum.

Mineka, S. (1992). Evolutionary memories, emotional processing and the emotional disorders. In D. Medin (Ed.), *The psychology of learning and motivation* (Vol. 28, pp. 161–206). New York: Academic Press.

Mineka, S., & Cook, M. (1986). Immunization against the observational conditioning of snake fear in rhesus monkeys. *Journal of Abnormal Psychology, 95,* 307–318.

Mineka, S., & Gilboa, E. (in press). Cognitive biases in anxiety and depression. In W. F. Flack & J. L. Laird (Eds.), *Emotions and psychopathology.* Oxford: Oxford University Press.

Mineka, S., & Kihlstrom, J. (1978). Unpredictable and uncontrollable aversive events. *Journal of Abnormal Psychology, 87,* 256–271.

Mineka, S., & Nugent, K. (1995). Mood-congruent memory biases in anxiety and depression. In D. Schacter (Ed.), *Memory distortion: How minds, brains, and societies reconstruct the past* (pp. 173–193). Cambridge, MA: Harvard University Press.

Mineka, S., & Sutton, S. (1992). Cognitive biases and the emotional disorders. *Psychological Science, 3,* 65–69.

Mineka, S., & Tomarken, A. J. (1989). The role of cognitive biases in the origins and maintenance of fear and anxiety disorders. In T. Archer & L.-G. Nilsson (Eds.), *Aversion, avoidance, and anxiety: Perspectives on aversively motivated behavior* (pp. 195–221). Hillsdale, NJ: Erlbaum.

Mineka, S., & Zinbarg, R. (1991). Animal models of experimental psychopathology. In C. E. Walker (Ed.), *Clinical psychology: Historical and research foundations* (pp. 51–86). New York: Plenum.

Mineka, S., & Zinbarg, R. (1995). Animal-ethological models of social phobia. In R. Heimberg, M. Liebowitz, D. Hope, & F. Schneier (Eds.), *Social phobia: Diagnosis, assessment and treatment* (pp. 134–162). Guilford Press.

Mineka, S., & Zinbarg, R. (1996). Conditioning and ethological models of anxiety disorders: Stress-in-Dynamic-Context Anxiety models. In D. Hope (Ed.), *Perspectives on anxiety, panic, and fear: 43rd Annual Nebraska Symposium on Motivation* (pp. 135–211). Lincoln, NE: University of Nebraska Press.

Mineka, S., Cook, M., & Miller, S. (1984). Fear conditioned with escapable and inescapable shock: The effects of a feedback stimulus. *Journal of Experimental Psychology: Animal Behavior Processes, 10,* 307–323.

Mineka, S., Gunnar, M., & Champoux, M. (1986). Control and early socioemotional development: Infant rhesus monkeys reared in controllable versus uncontrollable environments. *Child Development, 57,* 1241–1256.

Mowrer, O. H. (1947). On the dual nature of learning: A reintepretation of "conditioning" and "problem solving". *Harvard Educational Review, 17,* 102–148.

Mowrer, H., & Viek., P. (1948). An experimental analogue of fear from a sense of helplessness. *Journal of Abnormal and Social Psychology, 43,* 193–200.

Moye, T., Hyson, R., Grau, J., & Maier. S. (1983). Immunization of opioid analgesia: Effects of prior escapable shock on subsequent shock-induced and morphine-induced antinociception. *Learning and Motivation, 4,* 238–251.

Nugent, K., & Mineka, S. (1994). The effects of high and low trait anxiety on implicit and explicit memory tasks. *Cognition and Emotion, 8,* 147–163.

Oatley, K., & Johnson-Laird, P. (1987). Towards a cognitive theory of emotions. *Cognition and Emotion, 1,* 29–50.

Öhman, A. (1986). Face the beast and fear the face: Animal and social fears as prototypes for evolutionary analyzes of emotion. *Psychophysiology, 23,* 123–145.

Öhman, A. (1996). Preferential preattentive processing of threat in anxiety: Preparedness and attentional biases. In R. Rapee (Ed.), *Current controversies in the anxiety disorders* (pp. 253–290). New York: Guilford Press.

Öhman, A., & Dimberg, U. (1978). Facial expressions as conditioned stimuli for electrodermal responses: A case of "preparedness"? *Journal of Personality and Social Psychology, 36,* 1251–1258.

Öhman, A., Dimberg, U., & Öst, L.-G. (1985). Animal and social phobias: Biological constraints on the learned fear response. In S. Reiss, & R. Bootzin (Eds.), *Theoretical issues in behavior therapy* (pp. 123–175). New York: Academic Press.

Ollendick, T. H., & King, N. J. (1991). Origins of childhood fears: An evaluation of Rachman's theory of fear acquisition. *Behaviour Research and Therapy, 29,* 117–123.

Öst, L.-G., & Hugdahl, K. (1981). Acquisition of phobias and anxiety response patterns in clinical patients. *Behaviour Research and Therapy, 16,* 439–447.

Overmier, J. B. (1985). Toward a reanalysis of the causal structure of the learned helplessness syndrome. In F. R. Brush & J. B. Overmier (Eds.), *Affect, conditioning and cognition: Essays on the determinants of behavior* (pp. 211–228). Hillsdale, NJ: Erlbaum.

Pavlov, I. (1927). *Conditioned reflexes.* London: Oxford University Press.

Plutchik, R. (1984). Emotions: A general psychoevolutionary theory. In K. Scherer. & P. Ekman (Eds.), *Approaches to emotion.* Hillsdale, NJ: Erlbaum.

Rachman, S. J. (1990). *Fear and courage.* New York: Freeman.

Rapaport, P., & Maier, S. (1978). Inescapable shock and food-competition dominance in rats. *Animal Learning and Behavior, 6,* 160–165.

Rescorla, R. (1974). Effect of inflation of the unconditioned stimulus value following conditioning. *Journal of Comparative and Physiological Psychology, 86,* 101–106.

Roediger, H. & McDermott, K. (1992). Depression and implicit memory: A commentary. *Journal of Abnormal Psychology, 101,* 587–591.

Rozin, P., & Kalat, J. W. (1971). Specific hungers and poison avoidance as adaptive specializations of learning. *Psychological Review, 78,* 459–487.

Scott, J. P., & Marston, M. (1953). Nonadaptive behavior resulting from a series of defeats in fighting mice. *Journal of Abnormal and Social Psychology, 48,* 417–428.

Seligman, M. E. P. (1968). Chronic fear produced by unpredictable shock. *Journal of Comparative and Physiological Psychology, 66,* 402–411.

Seligman, M. E. P. (1970). On the generality of the laws of learning. *Psychological Review, 77,* 408–418.

Seligman, M. (1971). Phobias and preparedness. *Behavior Therapy, 2,* 307–320.

Seligman, M. E. P., & Maier, S. F. (1967). Failure to escape traumatic shock. *Journal of Experimental Psychology, 74,* 1–9.

Solomon, R. L., Kamin, L. J., & Wynne, L. C. (1953). Traumatic avoidance learning: The outcomes of several extinction procedures with dogs. *Journal of Abnormal and Social Psychology, 48,* 291–302.

Teasdale, J. D. (1988). Cognitive vulnerability to persistent depression. *Cognition and Emotion, 2,* 247–274.

Tomarken, A. J., Mineka, S., & Cook, M. (1989). Fear-relevant selective associations and covariation bias. *Journal of Abnormal Psychology, 98,* 381–394.

Townsley, R., Turner, S., Beidel, D., & Calhoun, K. (1995). Social phobia: An analysis of possible developmental factors. *Journal of Abnormal Psychology, 104,* 526–531.

Uhrich, J. (1938). The social hierarchy in albino mice. *Journal of Comparative Psychology, 25,* 373–413.

Wagner, A. R. (1979). Habituation and memory. In A. Dickinson & R. A. Boakes (Eds.), *Mechanisms of learning and motivation* (pp. 53–82). Hillsdale, NJ: Erlbaum.

Wagner, A. R. (1981). SOP: A model of automatic memory processing in animal behavior. In N. Spear & R. Miller (Eds.), *Information processing in animals: Memory mechanisms* (pp. 5–47). Hillsdale, NJ: Erlbaum.

Watkins, P., Mathews, A., Williamson, D. A., & Fuller, R. D. (1992). Mood-congruent memory in depression: Emotional priming or elaboration? *Journal of Abnormal Psychology, 101,* 581–586.

Watkins, P., Vache, K., Verney, S., Muller, S., & Mathews, A. (1996). Unconscious mood-congruent memory bias in depression. *Journal of Abnormal Psychology, 105,* 34–41.

Watson, J. B., & Rayner, R. (1920). Conditioned emotional reactions. *Journal of Experimental Psychology, 3,* 1–14.

Weiss, J. (1968). Effects of coping response on stress. *Journal of Comparative and Physiological Psychology, 65,* 251–260.

Weiss, J. M., Glazer, H. I., & Pohorecky, L. A. (1976). Coping behavior and neurochemical changes: An alternative explanation for the original "learned helplessness" experiments. In A. Serban & A. Kling (Eds.), *Animal models in human psychobiology* (pp. 141–173). New York: Plenum Press.

Williams, J. L., & Lierle, D. M. (1988). Effects of repeated defeat by a dominant conspecific on subsequent pain sensitivity, open-field activity, and escape learning. *Animal Learning and Behavior, 16,* 477–485.

Williams, J., & Maier, S. (1977). Transsituational immunization and therapy of learned helplessness in the rat. *Journal of Experimental Psychology: Animal Behavior Processes, 3,* 240–252.

Williams, M., Watts, F., MacLeod, C., & Mathews, A. (1988). *Cognitive psychology and the emotional disorders.* Chichester, UK: Wiley.

Zinbarg, R., & Mohlman, J. (1997). *Individual differences in the acquisition of affectively valenced associations.* Manuscript Submitted for Publication.

CHAPTER TWENTY-TWO

Sexual and reproductive health education in Latin America: What next?

Susan Pick
Universidad Nacional Autónoma de México and Instituto Mexicano de Investigación de Familia y Población, Mexico City, Mexico

The main problems affecting reproductive and sexual health in Latin America and their implications for research design in the areas of sexuality education and reproductive health are presented, beginning with an overview of sexual and reproductive health in Mexico and Latin America. The sexuality education programs designed in Latin America are described, outlining problems with design and application. The third section describes a methodological research–action model used to design a sexuality and family life education program for adolescents called "Planeando tu Vida" (Planning your Life), which has been tested in Mexico and other Latin American countries, and the United States. The paper also presents results from recent studies in Mexico and Latin America on sexuality, sexually transmitted diseases (STDs), Acquired Immune Deficiency Syndrome (AIDS), and contraceptive use. Last, the problems and needs faced by current research and design of programs in the areas of sexuality and reproductive health education in Latin America are considered.

A partir d'une vue globale de l'état de la santé dans le domaine de la sexualité et de la reproduction au Mexique et en Amérique latine, l'auteur décrit les principaux problèmes qui ont une incidence sur la santé sexuelle et le processus de reproduction et leur effet sur la planification de la recherche en éducation sexuelle et en hygiène de l'activité de reproduction. Elle présente les programmes d'éducation sexuelle conçus en Amérique latine et dresse un bref bilan des problèmes de planification et d'application. La troisième partie présente un modèle méthodologique de recherche–action utilisé dans la conception d'un programme d'éducation de la sexualité et de la vie de famille à l'intention des adolescents, programme nommé "Planeando tu Vida" (En planifiant ta vie), qui a été mis à l'épreuve au Mexique, en Amérique latine et aux Etats-Unis. Cet article donne aussi les résultats d'études récentes, faites au Mexique et en Amérique latine, sur la sexualité, les maladies à transmission sexuelle, le Syndrome d'immunodéficience acquise (SIDA) et l'utilisation de contraceptifs. Il traite, en dernier lieu, des problèmes et des besoins qui confrontent la recherche actuelle et la création de programmes dans les domaines de l'éducation de la sexualité et de l'hygiène de l'activité de reproduction en Amérique latine.

OVERVIEW OF SEXUAL AND REPRODUCTIVE HEALTH IN LATIN AMERICA

Historically, public policy in Latin America has been based on a reproductive health model that emphasizes the promotion of contraceptive use and mother–infant health care, especially during pregnancy, birth, and post-partum. As a consequence, during the 1970s, contraceptive use increased significantly and birthrates dropped, as did the average number of children per family through-out the population of reproductive age (Langer & Romero, 1995). However, the concept of reproductive health has broadened in recent years, allowing the integration of new strategies, such as educational programs aimed at different social groups and the incorporation of new personnel as health promoters. The new model defines reproductive health as the ability and right to have safe sexual relations, to experience pregnancy free of medical complications, and to raise children in favorable conditions (Madaleno et al., 1995).

This new approach suggests that in order to achieve reproductive health, women should be able to regulate their fertility without risk, to make an edu-cated choice about the method of contraception they wish to use, and to enjoy a sexual life safe from sexually transmitted diseases (STDs) and the Human Immune Deficiency Virus (HIV). Thus, attention to reproductive health implies considering not only the biological and physical aspects of reproduction, but also the distinct cultural contexts, societies, families, and actions that play a role in safe and risky sexual behaviors engaged in by the individual. The starting point, therefore, is the assumption that human sexuality and reproduction are social and cultural constructs, which are regulated by social norms and conven-tions in a specific historical period.

Despite significant advances in reproductive health care and promotion, cer-tain problems still continue to affect the reproductive health of men, women, and adolescents in Latin America. It was estimated that in 1994, between 20% and 35% of women aged from 15 to 44 years in Mexico, Brazil, Chile, Peru, and the Dominican Republic faced the risk of an unwanted pregnancy because they did not use contraception or used rhythm or withdrawal methods, providing less protection against pregnancy than other methods (Alan Guttmacher Institute, 1994).

Reports also show that between 40% and 60% of all registered pregnancies in the region are unwanted, which leads women either to have an unwanted child or to choose abortion (Bidegain Greising, 1992). In Latin America, with the exception of Cuba, abortions continue to be illegal, and therefore must be per-formed clandestinely, which increases the health risk to the mother. Such abor-tions are often performed by unqualified personnel with unsafe procedures, or by the women themselves with traditional methods such as abortive herbs and medicines easily available without prescription. The large number of such abortions, represents a substantial health risk to these women. In 1991, an estimated four million abortions were carried out in the region (Alan Guttmacher Institute, 1994).

In Mexico, there are more than 22 million women of reproductive age (Conferencia sobre Maternidad sin Riesgos en México, 1995). According to a survey completed in 1995 (CONAPO, 1995), it was estimated that in 1994 nearly 6.7 million women in Mexico aged from 15 to 44 needed family planning services or to replace their traditional contraception with more effective methods. Of all registered pregnancies in 1990, 23% were unwanted and another 17% ended in abortion (CONAPO, 1995). An estimated 850,000 abortions are performed annually (López-García, 1993), which makes abortion the fourth largest cause of death among women of all economic levels, ages, and civil status. It also means that for every 100 births, there are 21 abortions. Medical complications of abortion are the second largest cause of hospitalization in the gynecological and obstetric areas (regular births being the leading cause).

Unplanned pregnancies among adolescents represent a major public health problem throughout Latin America. Of the total number of births reported in the region in 1990, 15% were to women under the age of 20, representing 450,000 births (Welti, 1992). According to the World Bank (1992), in 1990 there were approximately 137 million individuals between the ages of 10 and 24—equivalent to 31% of the total population of Latin America and the Caribbean. It is expected that by the year 2000, that number will have risen to 172 million. Although the birthrate in this age group diminished in the majority of countries in the region, there was an increase in the absolute number of children born to adolescents and in their proportion of children born to women of all ages (Munist, Giurgiovich, Solís, & Mora, 1995). This increase is partially due to between 14% and 36% of adolescents having their first sexual experience before the age of 16 (Atkin, Ehrenfeld, & Pick, 1996).

In Mexico's case, men and women under the age of 25 represent 59.8% of the total population; and out of those, one in every four is between the ages of 10 and 19 (INEGI, 1990). In Mexico, adolescents between the ages of 15 and 19 have the lowest levels of contraceptive use; and only 34% of women who live with their partners use any method of family planning (Atkin et al., 1996). Throughout the world, STDs and HIV are most prevalent among sexually active adolescents aged between 15 and 24. It is estimated that half of all cases of HIV will occur in persons under the age of 25 (Conasida-Epidemiología, 1996); and up to 65% of women who get infected with the virus do so before their 20th birthday.

Mexico has the third highest number of cases of HIV infection in the Americas after the United States and Brazil. According to information released by Conasida-Epidemiología (1996) in the second quarter of 1996, there were 27,950 cases of HIV, although it is estimated that there are really 39,939 cases. In just one decade, the number of women in Mexico infected with HIV has doubled. The sex ratio for those infected has changed from fourteen men to one woman in 1985 to six men to one woman in 1995. Among men between the ages of 25 to 34, AIDS is the third leading cause of death (Conasida-Epidemiología, 1996).

During the first half of 1996, there were 435 reported cases of AIDS among adolescents between the ages of 14 and 19, which represents only 1.6% of the total number of cases. It is very likely that a large percentage of the adolescents who now have AIDS contracted the virus even earlier (Conasida-Epidemiología, 1996). More than half the men contracted the virus through homosexual and bisexual relations; while more than half of the women did so through heterosexual relations. Sexual relations are the most common means of contracting the virus; and the risks of contracting HIV differ by gender.

Even with the impact of AIDS on sexual practices among the population in general, there is still only limited use of condoms among adolescents (12.3%), because they are principally used as a means of contraception (García & Figueroa, 1994). Safe sexual practices and use of a condom are the most effective means of preventing the spread of HIV. Therefore, it is necessary for men and women of all ages and marital statuses to learn to discuss safe sexual practices with their partners, in order for them to take an active role in making decisions regarding their health and sexuality.

Studies (Pick, Givaudan, & Aldaz, 1996a; 1996b) have uncovered that one of the factors hindering the acceptance of safe sexual practices among couples is the traditional idea that values vaginal penetration as the ultimate pleasure in a heterosexual relationship, bringing with it the perception that any deviation from this practice is incomplete (Holland et al., 1991).

In heterosexual relationships, beliefs surrounding women's passive sexual role can become an impediment to condom use. If a woman requests a man to use a condom, it is taken as a threat to the man's power over decisions about sexuality in the relationship. Although women understand the importance of using a condom with men they have had little contact with or at the beginning of a relationship, most are not able to negotiate the use of condoms with their steady or long-term partners (Pick et al., 1996a; 1996b). They feel embarrassed and fear that such a request would question their trust of their partner or arouse suspicions of infidelity for both parties (Fernández, 1992).

Although men and women in Latin America may understand the methods of transmission and prevention of HIV, their prejudices regarding sexual identity and immoral sexual relations lead them to the misconception that they are not at risk for contracting the virus because their sexual practices fall within the norm. As Sontag (1988) proposed, having AIDS implies belonging to a high-risk group, and one who seeks information and protects oneself from HIV can be seen as a person who cannot be trusted.

SEXUAL AND REPRODUCTIVE HEALTH
EDUCATION PROGRAMS IN LATIN AMERICA

National and international organizations have advocated the development and implementation of family life and sexuality education programs as one of the most important tools in promoting responsible, protected sexual conduct among diverse groups. Interventions in this field can be framed in the context of the "Life and Health Education" model which seeks to diminish risk factors by generating positive attitudes toward health and self-protection (Rodríguez, Corona, & Pick, 1996).

Sexuality education consists of an ongoing process of developing and changing values, knowledge and behaviors, which influence relations between men and women within a given social and cultural context (Rodríguez et al., 1996). These types of program aim to deliver information and tools to teach people to improve their sexual and reproductive health. In order to create favorable conditions for the acceptance of sexuality education programs, it is important to convey messages that sensitize the population to the importance of being informed about sexuality. Furthermore, it is important to recognize the population's actual beliefs and behaviors about sexuality.

Most research that exists on sexuality education programs has been conducted in developed countries where sex education has been institutionalized as a part of the educational system. In the United States and Europe, sex education was introduced into the school system earlier than in Latin America. In Latin America, population and family planning programs of sex education were created in order to modify the fertility patterns in large segments of the population. They have focused mainly on reproductive issues, leaving aside sexual health (including the social, cultural, psychological, and physical factors that make up sexuality), thus separating sex from reproduction (Corona, 1995). Using the argument that sexuality education programs encourage the initiation of sexual relations, conservative and religious groups from countries throughout the region have hindered the inclusion of sexuality education programs into official curricula. Until a few years ago, sexuality education programs in the school system were very rare and, when provided, were given primarily to students in the form of study plans and books in the final years of primary and secondary school. The educational model focused on physical aspects of reproduction, changes during puberty, venereal diseases, and contraception (Rodríguez et al., 1996).

Non-Governmental Organizations (hereafter, NGOs) have played a central part in implementing sexuality education programs into the school systems of many Latin American countries (IPPF, 1995). They have used diverse negotiation strategies with the authorities in charge of designing public policy in order to promote educational programs with a broader conception of sexuality, by introducing subjects such as gender relations, sex roles, self-esteem, and decision making. In spite of the advances and achievements obtained in implementing sexuality education programs in Latin America, there are few; and the ones that exist face problems including a lack of theoretical bases and program evaluation.

Some of the most common problems with sex education programs in Latin America include: (1) an emphasis on descriptive instead of explanatory research; (2) assumption of a medical-biological conception of sexuality; (3) failure to include life and health education; (4) lack of a solid theoretical base due to assigning more importance to technical matters; (5) paucity of systematic program evaluations; (6) methodological problems with the evaluations that are done, such as inconsistency in course content, absence of baseline studies and control groups; and (7) evaluations focused on an increase in knowledge but not behavior change.

PLANEANDO TU VIDA: A MODEL SEXUALITY AND FAMILY LIFE EDUCATION PROGRAM FOR ADOLESCENTS

In this section, I shall illustrate the methodological process leading to the elaboration, implementation, evaluation, and dissemination of sex education programs. I shall refer to the research–action model to develop and apply a sexuality and family life program for adolescents that has been implemented and evaluated in Mexico, nine other Latin American countries, and the United States.

In 1986, the Instituto Mexicano de Investigacion de Familia y Poblacion (IMIFAP) began developing Planeando tu Vida, a sexuality and family life education program for adolescents in Mexico, which has served as the basis for courses targeting other populations: children, parents, teachers, pharmacy workers, and dotors (Pick de Weiss et al., 1988). The development of the Planeando tu Vida program initiated a process of research and action, consisting of the following stages: (1) diagnostic research into the behavior of Mexican adolescents; (2) development and evaluation of the first program; (3) implementation and evaluation within various settings and samples; (4) national opinion surveys; (5) massive implementation through "waterfall" multiplication (explained later); and (6) development of educational programs for other populations.

Diagnostic research. Few sex education programs have been based on the results of diagnostic studies about factors associated with sexual and reproductive behavior among adolescents. The first step in developing the Planeando tu Vida program was to carry out two diagnostic studies in Mexico City with male and female adolescents. The first study surveyed 1420 female adolescents between 12 and 19 years of age from low and lower middle socioeconomic levels (Pick de Weiss, Atkin, Gribble, & Andrade Palos, 1991; Pick de Weiss, Díaz Loving, Andrade Palos, & Atkin, 1988). The sample was made up of three groups of adolescents: (1) those who had not begun to have sexual relations; (2) those who had begun to have sexual relations but had not become pregnant; and

(3) those who were in the last trimester of an unwanted pregnancy. These three groups were matched for age, education, and socioeconomic level in order to make them comparable for the study.

Logistic regression analyses indicated that six variables were related with the young women not having begun sexual relations: (1) high submission to family and sociocultural norms and rules; (2) high scholastic aspirations; (3) perception of conservative attitudes among girlfriends; (4) high level of communication about sexuality with the mother; (5) not discussing sex with girlfriends; and (6) using instrumental measures vs. emotional blackmail to achieve objectives. Variables related to the young women having sexual relations but using contraceptives and not becoming pregnant were: (1) low submission to family and sociocultural norms; (2) high level of communication with girlfriends about sexuality; (3) knowledge of contraceptive methods and their use; (4) high orientation towards the future; and (5) using instrumental measures vs. emotional blackmail to achieve objectives. Other variables related to contraceptive use were the perception of liberal attitudes regarding sexuality among girlfriends and the rejection of erroneous beliefs about sexuality, contraception and pregnancy.

A second study with 338 male adolescents compared the psychosocial differences between a group of young men who had impregnated an adolescent female (some of whom lived with their partner) to those who had not (some of whom had not yet begun to have sexual relations; Pick de Weiss, Andrade Palos, Alvarez Izazaga, & Gribble, 1990; Pick de Weiss et. al., 1991). As in the study of young women, the two groups of male adolescents were categorized by age, educational level and socioeconomic level in order to make them comparable. Logistic regression was again used to predict the following behaviors for an adolescent male: (1) had not had sexual relations; (2) had not impregnated an adolescent female; and (3) lived with his partner.

Six variables were useful for predicting that the male had not begun to have sexual relations: (1) little or no work experience; (2) being older than the median age of the sample; (3) high scholastic aspirations; (4) high orientation towards the future; (5) rejection of risk taking; (6) and not wanting to take responsibility for an unplanned pregnancy. The prediction of not impregnating an adolescent female was related to the following variables: (1) having experience in the use of contraceptives to prevent pregnancy; (2) not wanting to take responsibility in the event of a pregnancy; and (3) the belief that birth control pills do not provoke illness. Lastly, the prediction of living with a partner related to the variables of being older than the median age of the sample, low scholastic aspirations, and having parents with a low educational level.

Design and evaluation of the first version of Planeando tu Vida.   Results of studies with Mexican adolescents indicate that factors associated with sexual risk behaviors can be prevented and/or modified by sexuality and family life education programs that include biological, personal, family, and social factors related to sexuality. Based on these results, the first version of Planeando tu Vida (Pick de Weiss et al., 1988) was designed to address the following areas:

— Communication, assertiveness and expression of affect.
— Self-esteem.
— Self-control and decision making.
— Activity planning and future goals.
— Anatomy and physiology of the reproductive system.
— Alternatives for the exercise of free and safe sexuality.
— Information regarding contraceptive methods.
— Information regarding pregnancy and the prevention of STDs.

Evaluations of the program measured the effect of Planeando tu Vida on knowledge, attitudes, and behavior of the participants, and also provided information about their needs and doubts. The program evaluations followed a pretest–posttest design with an equivalent control group and participants assigned randomly to the different conditions. The control group received a traditional sexuality education course; and the experimental group received Planeando tu Vida. Both programs included traditional aspects of sexuality education, but Planeando tu Vida also emphasized personal development skills and had a participatory aspect.

Follow-up was carried out over a period of four to eight months in order to measure the impact of information on participants' attitudes towards topics covered in the course. One finding of the first stage of evaluations was that adolescents responded better to participatory exercises than to traditional ones that do not actively encourage active participation. Based on these results, modifications were made to the methodology and content of the course, including adding a greater number of participatory activities like games and role playing, as well as content to provide more detail and depth to the topics of human reproduction, communication, decision making, values and self-esteem, as well as STDs.

The second stage of evaluation was carried out with a pretest–posttest design with two equivalent control groups, with participants assigned randomly to the three different conditions. One control group received a traditional sexuality education course, and the other, no course whatever. Questionnaires were administered eight months after the course's conclusion. At this latter stage, the program's impact on instructors and school principals was also evaluated. Results showed that sexually active adolescents who received Planeando tu Vida increased use of contraceptives, had fewer erroneous beliefs about sex than the control groups, and had increased knowledge regarding the correct use of birth control pills and the perceived accessibility of contraceptive methods. They also reported increased communication with their partners about contraception and with their mothers about sexuality. After the evaluations were concluded, the program was revised and the first manual for instructors, *Planeando tu Vida*, was published (Pick de Weiss et al., 1988).

Implementation and evaluation of the program with diverse samples and in different settings. After the conclusion of the pilot and initial evaluation, two formal evaluations of Planeando tu Vida were carried out, one in Mexico City high schools (Pick de Weiss, Andrade Palos, & Townsend, 1990) and the other in secondary schools throughout the country (Pick, Reyes, Ramírez, & Vernon, 1994). In both cases, the program was evaluated with representative samples of adolescents registered in secondary and high schools at the national level. Results of the evaluations with high school students showed changes in participants' knowledge of sexuality and contraception, their perception of the accessibility of contraceptives, and the probability that they would use them. The evaluations also showed that adolescents who took the program before initiation of sexual activity were more likely to use contraceptives when they did begin sexual relations. There were no observed differences in the age of first sexual experience between experimental and control groups. These findings confirm the importance of sexuality and family life education beginning before the adolescents become sexually active.

The program evaluations also included questions about the use of alcohol, tobacco and drugs. Alcohol and tobacco use were positively correlated with sexual-risk behaviors. In addition, alcohol use was the fourth best predictor of sexual relations, after masturbation, physical contact with a member of the opposite sex, and perceived access to contraceptive methods. Based on these results, basic concepts and information regarding psychoactive substances were added to the program, as well as information regarding risk behaviors associated with their use.

The next step in updating the program was implementing and evaluating it on a national scale in 72 secondary schools in Mexico. In 1991, the Secretary of Public Education (SEP) included Planeando tu Vida in its development of a national family life and health curriculum entitled *Adolescencia y Desarrollo* [Adolescence and development]. The curriculum, which targets 9th graders, has a strong component of sexuality and reproductive health information. During this stage, teachers were trained to spread the program with their students. The same methodological model was used as in previous evaluations, with the addition of: (1) questionnaires for teachers; (2) two supervisory visits during the school year by personnel specializing in courses for adolescents; (3) informal interviews with teachers and principals; (4) a register of problems encountered in each session; (5) focus groups with students; and (6) opinion surveys for students, parents, and teachers.

After the training workshop in Planeando tu Vida, teachers' knowledge of puberty, adolescence, sexuality, pregnancy, self-esteem and assertiveness, as well as the process of making life decisions, was significantly higher. The results of questionnaires administered to a representative sample of students showed increased knowledge of contraception in general, sexuality, and human reproduction, as well at the elements necessary for making decisions, planning their lives, and improving their self-esteem.

Based on focus groups with the students, opinion surveys were developed and administered to teachers, students, and parents in 32 of the 72 schools. It was found that 85.5% of the teachers thought the program should form part of the required curriculum. Among parents, 86.5% favored giving the *Adolescencia y Desarrollo* program in the schools, 86.3% believed it promoted responsibility, and 80.7% believed it promoted communication between adolescents and parents.

As a result of this series of evaluations, the current version of Planeando tu Vida (Pick et al., 1995) now covers the following topics:

— Biological aspects of human reproduction.
— Alternatives for practicing sexuality.
— STDs and AIDS prevention.
— Pregnancy and its consequences.
— Basic concepts regarding psychoactive substances.
— Risk factors and psychoactive substances.
— Gender roles.
— Expressing affection and nonverbal communication.
— Assertiveness and verbal communication.
— Values.
— Self-esteem.
— Controlling your life and making decisions.
— Future expectations.

National opinion surveys.   Based on the results of the opinion surveys carried out with parents, teachers, and secondary school students, national surveys were carried out during four consecutive years with nationally representative samples, by the Gallup organization in Mexico (IMIFAP-Gallup, 1991; 1992; 1993; 1994).

The intensive dissemination of the results of these surveys represents a tremendous tool for sensitizing and educating the public about the importance of implementing sexuality education programs, as well as providing a strong base for negotiating with educational and health authorities to institutionalize sexuality and family life education programs. In general, the 1994 survey revealed that 81.5% of those interviewed considered it necessary to teach children aspects of human reproduction within the formal education system; and 93.7% said adolescents should be taught how to prevent unwanted pregnancy. In the same survey, more than 90% of the sample agreed that teachers should have more knowledge and information about AIDS (98%); sexuality (97.1%); the prevention of sexual abuse (96.4%); how babies are born (95.7%); contraceptive methods (94.9%); menstruation (94.5%); how to eliminate inequality between the sexes (98.8%); and how to use a condom (92.1%). Parents showed particular interest in incorporating into the school programs not only sexuality education but also topics such as personal development, self-knowledge, and skills to help students in their lives, their work, and in family integration and communication. According to some of those surveyed, including these topics in educational programs would result in improved family communication (23.4%) and a fuller development of each individual (22.8%).

Massive implementation through the "waterfall" model.   To achieve large-scale implementation of Planeando tu Vida, a strategy was sought that would reach the greatest number of people, thus optimizing the available resources. The strategies to accomplish this goal are the "waterfall" and "peer educator" models. The waterfall model is a strategy of continuous training, whereby teachers, health workers, community leaders and promoters, NGO members, and other personnel who work directly with young people become trained and go on to multiply and spread their training among their peers and colleagues in schools, communities, youth centers, and diverse state institutions. During the process, aspects that favor or inhibit program multiplication by the instructors are monitored in order to insure program quality. Systematic supervision is carried out by personnel specializing in the application of sexuality and family life programs for youth, who provide "multipliers" with feedback and updated information about course topics and methodology.

This waterfall was initially implemented in the Mexico City area and different states within the country and later extended to other countries in the Americas. Planeando tu Vida has now been implemented in more than 300 health, education, and nongovernmental institutions in countries such as Bolivia, Chile, Colombia, the Dominican Republic, Guatemala, El Salvador, Honduras, Mexico, Peru, the United States, and Uruguay. Ten years after the initial development of the program, there are approximately 20,000 Planeando tu Vida instructors throughout the Americas, who have given the course to three million participants throughout the region.

Development of educational programs for diverse sectors of the population. Using the investigation–action model with which Planeando tu Vida was developed, additional sexuality and family life education programs have been developed, implemented, and evaluated with preschool, primary, and secondary students, with an accompanying series of workbooks containing course topics presented in a manner appropriate to each grade level. Two programs for parents were also developed, one for parents of children aged 12 and under, and one for parents of adolescents. The courses and manuals include diverse topics related to education, parents' relationship with their children, sexuality, discipline, limits, and planning. An AIDS education and prevention program for pharmacy workers was also created, with the aim of promoting condom use. The course is supported by a training manual for pharmacy workers, and a video. Finally, a new program for doctors, nurses, social workers, and other health promoters aims to lead participants to reflect on their role in health care and promotion, as well as provide information regarding the health and sickness process and ethical–legal aspects related to medical practice. The course also provides information about sexuality, AIDS, and family planning.

RESULTS OF SEXUALITY RESEARCH

Major sociodemographic changes in the past several years highlight the need for research on sexual and reproductive conduct based on an integrated conceptualization that seeks to overcome the limitations of a reproductive health focus centered on family planning (Salles & Tuirán, 1995). In this section, I review the results of research carried out in the last several years in various Latin American countries, which illustrate the social, cultural, and individual factors involved in reproduction, sexuality, and health in different sectors of the population.

In the area of adolescent reproductive health, recent studies with male and female adolescents in Mexico (Pick et al., 1996a; 1996b) showed that young people possess several beliefs and values that make it difficult for them to talk about sexuality with partners, teachers, or parents, due to the myths, taboos, and silence surrounding the topic. This situation means that many adolescents confront their first sexual relations without information about how to prevent pregnancy or HIV transmission. In this context, different socialization patterns and norms regarding sexuality and reproduction based on gender have been documented. For young men, norms and values emphasize the exercise of heterosexual sexuality as a fundamental component of masculinity. For young women, on the other hand, maternity is the most important aspect of being a woman. In the exercise of their sexuality, young women are more worried about avoiding unwanted pregnancy than transmission of an STD or HIV.

The growing use of qualitative research in the area of reproductive health has identified a system of beliefs and values that regulates sexual and health practices in specific sociocultural contexts. Studies have shown that preventive practices in the area of reproductive health, including the prevention of STDs and AIDS, are strongly permeated by traditional beliefs regarding the body and health. One community study with women of reproductive age in Mexico reveals a series of beliefs to the effect that having a woman's body, by definition, means being in a permanent state of illness. Thus, many women do not seek to prevent tumors, cancer, or cysts because they perceive them as illnesses that occur naturally due to their being women and are thus out of their personal control (Collado & Pick, 1997).

Traditional beliefs regarding sexuality and the couple also act as barriers to preventing STDs and AIDS in stable or long-term relationships. Studies in Mexico (Rodríguez, Amuchástegui, Rivas, & Bronfman, 1995) and Argentina (Fernández, 1992) indicated that even when women are conscious of their vulnerability to HIV transmission, a significant proportion of them lack the interpersonal power to negotiate sexual practices with their partner, which reflects an unequal system of gender relations in which men have greater social, economic, and sexual power than women. In this regard, it is worth mentioning that women report a low self-perception of HIV transmission risk, and believe men are at higher risk because they are "promiscuous" or "unfaithful," and "need" to have a more active sexual life. Therefore, many women think their partner should protect them and assume a passive and dependent role. The social construction regarding contraceptives, however, dictates that women are the responsible parties, since they are the ones who experience pregnancy and birth.

In Latin America, machismo—male pride regarding men's sexual ability and superiority over women—has impeded the promotion of male-oriented contraceptive methods, especially vasectomy, despite its efficacy as a family-planning method (Alvarado, 1995). Studies have shown that men who agree to a vasectomy are more experienced in the use of male-oriented contraceptive methods and communicate more with their partner about contraception and sexuality, when compared to men who have not had a vasectomy. Men who undergo the procedure believe it does not affect their virility and sexual pleasure and perceive it as socially acceptable (Aldaz, Givaudan, & Pick, 1996).

FUTURE DIRECTIONS

The experience of designing and evaluating educational programs and conducting research in the area of reproductive health has shown the importance of developing educational programs promoting practices to improve reproductive health for specific populations. As the emerging reproductive health model indicates, efforts to promote attitudes and practices to take care of one's self requires the participation of diverse personnel, including NGOs, health promoters, education specialists, and policy makers.

Sexual health should be promoted in the spheres of family, education, mass media, social work, and community. It is important that programs accurately reflect the needs of target groups, which can be achieved through educational models that actively integrate and involve participants in the promotion of reproductive health. The experience derived from Planeando tu Vida underlines the importance of basing programs on diagnostic and explanatory research of factors associated with the sexual and reproductive behaviors that promoters seek to impact. The research–action model represents a useful methodological tool for the future design, application, and evaluation of sex education and reproductive health programs.

One of the greatest challenges facing educational programs in the areas of sexuality and reproductive health is achieving their acceptance and application within the formal educational system, as well as the implementation of training programs for educators in sexuality-related topics and the dissemination with youth of accurate, appropriate educational materials. To reach this goal, it is important that NGOs and other personnel work together to promote public policy favoring sexual and reproductive health care. Another important challenge is the systematic provision of these programs to youth in low-income or rural areas, as well as those who are not in the formal education system. Towards this objective, diagnostic studies on sexual and reproductive practices should be carried out within these contexts. The results would serve as a base for the development of culturally appropriate sexuality-education programs and materials for these populations.

Simple implementation of educational programs does not guarantee an impact on the promotion of healthy sexual and reproductive practices. It is necessary that the programs be systematically evaluated through scientifically rigorous design, sampling, and instrument development, so their effects can be measured and reproduced in other social contexts. Future studies should strive to learn more about participants' expectations, motivations, and interests from their own perspective. During the past several years, this methodological approach has had a strong emphasis in the social sciences, showing itself to be a research strategy useful for learning about processes, mechanisms, and the different connotations of sexual and reproductive behaviors in the sociocultural or historical context of each specific population.

In the future, it will also be necessary to incorporate a gender focus in the sexuality education programs in order to promote more equal relations between men and women. Messages designed in educational programs and campaigns should promote the idea that sexual relations are a natural expression for women, who should therefore take an active role in the prevention of STDs and AIDS. Educational programs should also deal with the values and risk practices stemming from the double standard that leads individuals to use protection with occasional partners but refuse to use a condom with their regular partner.

In order to promote prevention and education activities in the area of sexual and reproductive health more effectively, it is crucial that educational and health institutions, NGOs, human rights groups, and other personnel in the field of sexual and reproductive health participate and cooperate with one another to have an impact on public policy. It is also important to seek negotiation strategies with groups who oppose sexuality education, in order to disseminate sexuality education programs on a national level. A mechanism should also be sought to coordinate the work of public officials responsible for promoting education and health policy at the state and national levels. To maximize impact, a strategy should be sought for diffusing informative materials about topics like sexuality, contraception, and AIDS prevention so that they are easily accessible and informative. These materials should be adapted for the specific needs of each population targeted and distributed in the workplace, schools, and recreation centers.

One recent area of research in Latin America is the study of masculinity from a gender perspective and its relationship to male reproductive behavior. It is important to conduct research on factors that favor the participation of men in contraception and the prevention of STDs/AIDS. It is also necessary to explore the influence of the sociocultural context in the development of early unprotected sexual behavior among adolescent males, as well as the meaning of fatherhood for young men.

Also, further studies are needed to learn more about HIV risk factors related to men's and women's expectations about gender roles, in order to develop strategies to improve the ability of both sexes to negotiate condom use with their partner(s). Within the emerging reproductive health model, it is important and, above all increasingly possible, to carry out studies that examine health and behavior not only during the reproductive age, but in the years before and after this period. Conducting research that does not narrowly focus on the reproductive years will produce new knowledge regarding crucial processes and behaviors for different stages throughout the life cycle.

REFERENCES

Alan Guttmacher Institute. (1994). *Aborto clandestino: Una realidad latinoamericana* [Clandestine abortion: A Latin American reality]. New York: Author.

Aldaz, E., Givaudan, M., & Pick, S. (1996). *Creencias, conocimientos, actitudes, motivaciones e intenciones conductuales hacia la vasectomía en hombres mexicanos* [Beliefs, knowledge, attitudes, motivations and intentions toward vasectomy among Mexican men]. Report presented to World Health Organization, Geneva, Switzerland.

Alvarado, C. (1995). Estudio de aceptantes de vasectomía del Programa AQV del INPPARES [Study of vasectomy acceptance of INPPARES's AQV program]. Lima, Peru: Instituto Peruano de Paternidad Responsable.

Atkin, L., Ehrenfeld, N., & Pick, S. (1996). Sexualidad y fecundidad adolescente [Adolescent sexuality and fecundity]. In K. Tolbert & A. Langer (Eds.), *Mujer: Sexualidad y salud reproductiva en México*. Mexico City: The Population Council/EDAMEX.

Bidegain Greising, G. (1992). Cambios en la reproducción y en al estructura de la familia en América Latina [Changes in reproduction and in the structure of the family in Latin America]. In G. Lopez, J. Yunes, J. A. Solis, A. Omran, (Eds.), *Salud reproductiva en las Americas* [Healthy Reproduction in the Americas]. Washington, DC: Pan-American Health Organization.

Collado, M. E., & Pick, S. (1997). *Factores que afectan el abastecimiento seguro del DIU en contextos de escasos recursos económicos: Un estudio de comunidad en México.* [Factors that affect the secure provision of IUDs in contexts of scarce economic resources: A community study in Mexico.] Report Presented to the International Center for Research on Women, Washington, DC.

CONAPO (Consejo Nacional de Poblacion). (1995). *Encuesta nacional de planificacion familiar* [National survey on family planning]. México, DF: Author.

CEPAL (Comisión Económica para América Latina & el Caribe, División de Desarrollo Social). (1992). *Tendencias actuales y perspectivas de los jóvenes en América Latina & el Caribe* [Current tendencies and perspectives of young people in Latin America and the Caribbean]. Santiago, Chile: Author.

Conasida-Epidemiología. (1996, April–June). Separata de la revista SIDA/ETS [Insert for the magazine AIDS/STDs]. *2*, (2), Mexico City.

Corona, E. (1995). Salud sexual y reproductiva [Sexual and reproductive health]. Report written for UNIFEM in preparation for Beijing 1995, Mexico City.

Conferencia sobre Maternidad sin Riesgos en México [Conference on maternity without risks in Mexico]. (1995). *Mexican Declaration for a Risk-Free Motherhood*. Morelos, Mexico: Author.

Fernández, A. (1992). Mujeres, heterosexualidad y SIDA [Women, heterosexuality and AIDS]. In A. Fernández, *Las mujeres en la imaginación colectiva: Una historia de discriminación & resistencias*. Buenos Aires, Argentina: Paidós.

García, B., & Figueroa, J. (1994). Práctica anticonceptiva en adolescentes y jovenes del área metropolitana de la ciudad de México [Contraceptive practices of adolescents and young people from the metropolitan area of Mexico City]. In Secretaria de Salud, *El Entorno de la regulación de la fecundidad en México*. Mexico City, Mexico: Author.

Holland, J., Ramazonoglu, C., Scott, S., Sharpe, S., & Thomson, R. (1991). *Pressure, resistance, empowerment: Young women and the negotiation of safer sex*. Wrap Paper 6, Women's Risk Aids Project, London: Tufnell Press.

IMIFAP-Gallup. (1991). *Encuesta nacional sobre educación sexual* [National survey on sex education]. Unpublished manuscript.

IMIFAP-Gallup. (1992). *Encuesta nacional sobre educación sexual* [National survey on sex education]. Unpublished manuscript.

IMIFAP-Gallup. (1993). *Encuesta nacional sobre educación sexual* [National survey on sex education]. Unpublished manuscript.

IMIFAP-Gallup. (1994). *Encuesta nacional sobre educación sexual* [National survey on sex education]. Unpublished manuscript.

INEGI. (1990). *Censo general de población* [General population census]. Mexico City: Instituto Nacional de Estadistica y Geografia.

IPPF (International Planned Parenthood Federation). (1995). *Challenges: Women's Rights*. London: Author.

Langer, A., & Romero, M. (1995). Diagnóstico de la salud reproductiva en México [Diagnostic manual of reproductive health in Mexico]. In Colegio de México (Eds.), *Programa Salud y Sociedad Reproductiva: Reflexiones, Sexualidad, Salud y Reproduccion 3*. Mexico City: Author.

López-García, R. (1993). *El aborto como problema de salud pública* [Abortion as a public health problem]. Paper presented at the Safe Motherhood Conference, Cocoyoc, Morelos, Mexico.

Madaleno, M., Munist, M. M., Serrano, C. V., Silber, T. J., Suárez Ojeda, E. N., & Yunes, J. (Eds.). (1995). *La salud del adolescente y del joven* [The health of adolescents and young people]. Washington, DC: Pan-American Health Organization.

Munist, M., Giurgiovich, A., Solís, J., & Mora, G. (1995). Factores relacionados con la fecundidad en la adolescencia [Factors related to adolescent fertility]. In M. Madaleno, M. M. Munist, C. V. Serrano, T. J. Silber, E. N. Suárez Ojeda, & J. Yunes (Eds.), *La salud del adolescente y del joven*. Washington, DC: Pan-American Health Organization.

Ortner, S., & Whitehead, H. (1996). Indagaciones acerca de los significados sexuales [Investigations into sexual meaning]. In M. Lamas (Ed.), *El género: La construcción cultural de la diferencia sexual*. Mexico City: PUEG.

Pick de Weiss, S., Aguilar Gil, J. A., Rodríguez, G., Vargas Trujillo, E., & Reyes Pardo, J. (1988). *Planeando tu vida* [Planning your life]. Mexico City: Editorial Pax.

Pick, S., Aguilar, J. A., Rodríguez, G., Reyes, J., Collado, M. E., Pier, D., Acevedo, M. P., & Vargas, E. (1995). *Planeando tu vida* [Planning your life]. Mexico City: Planeta.

Pick de Weiss, S., Andrade Palos, P., Alvarez Izazaga, M., & Gribble, J. (1990). *Estudio psicosocial comparativo de varones que han y que no han embarazado a una adolescente* [Comparative psychosocial study of men who have and have not impregnated an adolescent]. Report presented to the Pan-American Health Organization, Washington, DC.

Pick de Weiss, S., Andrade Palos, P., & Townsend, J. (1990). *Planeando tu vida: Desarrollo y evaluación de un programa de educación sexual y para la salud para adultos jóvenes* [Planning your life: Development and evaluation of a sexuality and health education program for young adults]. Report presented to the Population Council, New York City.

Pick de Weiss, S., Atkin, L. C., Gribble, J., & Andrade Palos, P. (1991). Sex, contraception and pregnancy among adolescents in Mexico City. *Studies in Family Planning*, *22*, 74–82.

Pick de Weiss, S., Díaz Loving, R., Andrade Palos, P. & Atkin, L. (1988). *Adolescentes en la Ciudad de México: Estudio psicosocial de las prácticas anticonceptivas y embarazos no deseados* [Adolescents in Mexico City: Psychosocial study of contraceptive practices and unwanted pregnancy]. Report presented to the PanAmerican Health Organization, Washington, DC.

Pick, S., Givaudan, M., & Aldaz. E. (1996a). *Adolescent sexuality: A qualitative study in Mexico City*. Report presented to The Rockefeller Foundation, New York City.

Pick, S., Givaudan, M., & Aldaz, E. (1996b). *Sexual conduct and AIDS prevention with men and women in Mexico City*. Report presented to the US Agency for International Development. Washington, DC.

Pick, S., Reyes, J., Ramírez, H., & Vernon, R. (1994). El personal docente como agente de educación sexual: Programa de capacitación a nivel national [Educational personnel as agents of sexual education: National training program]. In *La Psicología Social en México* (Vol.V) Mexico City: AMEPIO

Rodríguez, G., Amuchástegui, A., Rivas, M., & Bronfman, M. (1995). Mitos y dilemas de los jóvenes en tiempos del SIDA [Myths and dilemmas of young people in the time of AIDS]. In Bronfman, M. (Ed.), *SIDA en México: Migración, adolescencia y género*. Mexico City: CONASIDA.

Rodríguez, G., Corona, E., & Pick, S. (1996). Educación para la sexualidad y salud reproductiva [Sexuality and reproductive health education]. In K. Tolbert. & A. Langer (Eds.), *Mujer: Sexualidad y salud reproductiva en México*. Mexico City: The Population Council/EDAMEX.

Salles, V., & Turián, R. (1995). Dentro del laberinto: Primeros pasos en la elaboración de una propuesta teórico-analítica para el programa de salud reproductiva y sociedad de El Colegio de México [Inside the labyrinth: First steps in the elaboration of a theoretical-analytical proposal for the Colegio de Mexico's reproductive health and society program]. In Colegio de México (Eds.), *Programa Salud y Sociedad Reproductiva: Reflexiones , Sexualidad, Salud y Reproduccion 6*. Mexico City: Author.

Sontag, S. (1988). *El SIDA y sus metáforas* [AIDS and its metaphors]. Madrid, España: Muchnik Editores.

Welti, C. (1992). La fecundidad de los adolescentes mexicanos [Fertility among Mexican adolescents]. In H. Muñoz (Ed.), *Población y sociedad en México*. Mexico City, Mexico: Miguel Angel Porrúa.

World Bank. (1992). *Report on world development*. Washington, DC: Author.

World Health Organization. (1989). *La salud de la juventud* [The health of young people]. Geneva: Author.

PART SIX

Social Development

CHAPTER TWENTY-THREE

Human development: Cross-cultural perspectives

Çiğdem Kağıtçıbaşı
Koc University, Istanbul, Turkey

Human development is typically studied from an individualistic perspective ignoring the sociocultural context. Yet fundamental variations are engendered in this process by contextual factors, ranging from the familial to the social structural. Development of competence and development of the self, two areas of extensive research and conceptualization, can benefit greatly from contextual analysis. Though greatly needed, a contextual perspective has its share of challenges and problems. Foremost among these is the relativism implied which, when taken to extremes, precludes all comparison and rejects universal standards. An integrative/functional approach, combining the contextual and the comparative, promises to resolve the controversy. It can shed some light on the complex interactional processes underlying both the commonality and the diversity observed across cultures.

On étudie généralement le développement humain dans une perspective individualiste qui ignore le contexte socioculturel. Cependant plusieurs variations fondamentales sont engendrées dans ce processus par des facteurs contextuels, qui s'étendent du familial au social structural. Le développement des compétences et celui du moi, deux vastes domaines de recherche et de conceptualisation, peuvent tirer grand avantage de l'analyze contextuelle. Quoique grandement nécessaire, une perspective contextuelle comporte sa part de défis et de problèmes. Parmi ceux-ci se trouve en tout premier lieu le relativisme implicite qui, lorsque poussé à l'extrème, exclut toute comparaison et rejette les standards universels. Une approche intégrée et fonctionnelle, qui combine le contextuel et le comparatif, est susceptible de résoudre la controverse. Elle pourrait éclairer les processus complexes interactionnels sous-jacents à la fois la similarité et la diversité observées d'une culture à l'autre.

In her overview, "A Century of Psychological Science," Anne Anastasi (1992, p. 842) described the emergence in mid-century of two new fields of psychology —*life-span developmental psychology* and *cross-cultural psychology*—as a most "significant integrative movement . . . to build bridges between scattered islands of research". This chapter is in line with her observations, as it will attempt to touch on some of the common ground between these two fields of inquiry. They represent an expansion of perspective and data sources, temporally and spatially, to encompass "human development in context," and it is this contextual focus which constitutes the main theme of this chapter. A contextual approach constitutes the backbone of a cross-cultural perspective on human development. I shall, therefore, focus on this approach and shall examine its implications for theory, research, and applications in cross-cultural developmental psychology.

THE INCREASING RELEVANCE OF CONTEXT

A main trend in the study of human development has been the increasing recognition of the importance of context, ranging from the proximal environment of the family all the way to the most encompassing culture. This trend reflects an important change in the main orientations in the study of human development. For a long time, psychological study of human development entailed examining *child development* from an *organismic* and *mechanistic* perspective. The former, as epitomized by Piagetian thinking, was a model of maturational unfolding, assigning a secondary role to context, and the latter, in true behavioristic tradition, reduced context to the proximal environment of *the stimulus* (see Kağıtçıbaşı, 1990 for a discussion of these models).

Because reaching universal laws of development and behavior was the goal, uniformities and generalities were inferred from observations and experiments. Contextual, as well as individual, variation was treated as a source of error. However, discontent was rising with this developmental psychology which, in Bronfenbrenner's (1979, p. 19) words was ". . . the science of the strange behavior of children in strange situations with strange adults for the briefest possible periods of time".

A particularly troublesome outcome of the noncontextual nature of mainstream developmental psychology has been the neglect of culture. Firstly, this has deprived the study of human development of a rich source of information and knowledge, and secondly, it has led to the assumption that findings acquired in one context (typically in the middle-class, white population in the US) apply everywhere. Thus, it has been claimed (Schwartz, 1981, p. 4) that "developmental psychology has largely missed the opportunity to consider the child in the cultural milieu, which is the *sine qua non* of the developmental completion of a human nature". Along the same lines, it is noted (Jahoda & Dasen, 1986, p. 413) that "theories and findings in developmental psychology originating in the First World tend to be disseminated to the Third World as gospel truth".

Notwithstanding the dominance of organismic and mechanistic paradigms within mainstream developmental psychology, contextual or environmental orientations to human development have a long history. Indeed, the organismic (biological) and the environmental approaches have constituted the two main competing perspectives in developmental psychology. The roots of the contextual emphasis can be traced back to the enlightenment period, with the theoretical precursors emerging mid-century in different topic areas of psychology, ranging from social psychology to perception.

AN OVERVIEW OF THE CONTEXTUAL PERSPECTIVES

It may be informative to review briefly the main historical influences, recent developments, and current directions which figure in the increasing relevance of context in developmental psychology. Different lines of theory/research emerge as important. The researchers and references to be cited comprise only a few examples, not at all a representative sample, of the work involved. There is also overlap, and a particular researcher may be seen to belong to another topic area or to more than one area. The number and diversity of the theoretical perspectives and research programs focusing on context is impressive. They each arise from different traditions, but share a common recognition of the significance of context; indeed, an *increasing* relevance of context is apparent with so many current perspectives involved.

Historical antecedents

The historical antecedents of the contextual perspective are to be found in philosophy. Though an environmental emphasis could be traced to Aristotle, Locke and the British Empiricists of the 18th and 19th centuries are more commonly associated with it. Dewey followed suit in the late 19th and the first half of the 20th century, influencing in particular modern education. The philosophical emphasis on learning and experience was reflected in early developmental and comparative psychology (Baldwin, 1895; 1909; Novikoff, 1945; von Bertalanffy, 1933).

Theoretical precursors

Several theoretical perspectives share a contextual approach. They helped to establish the relevance of context in different areas of psychology, as well as in sociology and anthropology. Among these are Lewin's (1951) topological psychology and field theory; Brunswik's (1955) "environment-organism-environment arc"; Barker's (1968) ecological psychology; Berger and Luckmann's (1967) social constructionism; and the Whitings' (Whiting & Child, 1953; Whiting, B. B., 1963) cross-cultural anthropology. The two decades starting mid-century, the 1950s and the 1960s, thus mark the emergence of contextual theories which influenced later thinking in the field.

More recent impetus and current directions

Starting in the 1970s, a number of theories and schools of thought in psychology, as well as in anthropology, were informed by contextual thinking. Among
these the following are notable:

Ecological perspectives.   Ecological theory in child/family studies (Bronfenbrenner, 1979) and ecocultural perspective in cross-cultural psychology (Berry
1976; 1980) fit into this area. Closely parallel are systemic models of person-
environment interaction (von Bertalanffy, 1968). These holistic conceptualizations
focus on context.

Sociohistorical theory.   Vygotsky's work (1962; 1978), translated into English, informs the culture and cognition school (later). Vygotsky added historical
and societal components to the understanding of context.

Life-span developmental theory and developmental contextualism.   These are
basically European theoretical perspectives, reflected mainly in life-span development theory and contextualism (Baltes, 1987; Baltes & Brim, 1979; Baltes,
Reese, & Lipsitt, 1980; Lerner & Busch-Rossnagel, 1981, Lerner, Hultsch, &
Dixon, 1983; Valsiner, 1994).

Interpretive anthropology.   This body of research and theory stresses the
significance of symbols and meanings as constituting culture (context). Subjectivity of experience is seen as inherent in the understanding of reality and in
culture–self interplay (e.g. Marsella & White, 1984; Marsella, DeVos, & Hsu,
1985; Shweder & Bourne, 1984; Shweder & LeVine 1984).

Culture and cognition.   Also known as everyday cognition, this line of
thinking and research is characteristic of the Laboratory of Comparative Human
Cognition (LCHC) group (Cole, Sharp, & Lave, 1976; Cole, 1992; Scribner,
1990) and the more encompassing Cultural Psychologists (e.g. Greenfield &
Lave, 1982; Nunes, 1993; Rogoff, 1981, 1990; Serpell, 1976). This orientation
is informed by Vygotskian sociohistorical theory and interpretive anthropology,
and it stresses an *emic*, rather than an *etic* methodology. *Emic* refers to studying
culture from within and claims the specificity and noncomparability of culturally
relevant learning patterns, while an *etic* approach assumes universality and therefore comparability of psychological processes.

Culture and human development.   This is the more general study of human
development within culture and shares some of the characteristics of the aforementioned perspectives. The work of anthropologist–psychologist teams and
psychologists with different outlooks show a common recognition of the importance of cultural context (e.g. Dasen, 1984; Goodnow, Miller, & Kessel, 1995;

Harkness & Super, 1992; Kağıtçıbaşı, 1996; Munroe, Munroe, & Whiting, 1981; Sigel, McGillicudy-Delisi, & Goodnow, 1992).

Problem- and policy-oriented research.   Emerging from a different tradition than the above cultural and cross-cultural approaches, this body of research has an applied emphasis. Three related research areas can be distinguished within this general rubric.

1. *Family and disadvantage research* is typically conducted in social work, education, and family and child studies, and is informed by Bronfenbrenner's ecological theory (e.g. Bronfenbrenner & Weiss, 1983; Dym, 1988; Huston, 1991; Laosa & Sigel, 1982; Patterson & Dishion, 1988; Sameroff & Fiese, 1992).
2. *Ethnic minority research* in the USA is closely related to 1. it has an applied emphasis and studies ethnic group children and families (e.g. Coll, 1990; Harrison et al., 1990; Laosa, 1980; 1984; McLoyd, 1990; Szapocznik & Kurtines, 1993).
3. *Intervention research*, focuses more than 1. and 2. on intervention in ameliorating the negative effects of poverty and disadvantage. This is an extensive body of applied research and evaluation, spanning health, nutrition, and education interventions. Examples from early educational intervention are found in several reviews (Kağıtçıbaşı, 1995; 1996; Meisels & Shonkoff, 1990; Slaughter, 1988; Zigler & Weiss, 1985).

All these theoretical and research endeavors have brought focus to the context of development, and with it inevitably culture. This increased focus has prompted R. A. LeVine (1989, p. 90) to ask whether there will "be a 'cross-cultural revolution' in thinking about child development". Indeed, recognizing the importance of context is seen as "a clear and discernible trend" (Gupta, 1992, p. 8). This trend is reflected in a number of recent publications, all situating human development within its sociohistorical and cross-cultural context (e.g. Damon, 1989; Greenfield & Cocking, 1994; Kağıtçıbaşı, 1996; LeVine, 1988; Nsamenang, 1992; Valsiner, 1989; Woodhead, Light, & Carr, 1991).

Various features of context are examined. These include societal values and the place of the child in family and society; parental goals, beliefs, and childrearing orientations; and ethnic and social class status. Several attempts have been made to build models relating human development to context. The models typically try to delineate mediating factors between the macro-level variables and the developing person. They attempt to contribute to a better understanding of development in context by bridging the gap between the individual and the culture (e.g. McLoyd, 1990; Patterson & Dishion, 1988; Sameroff & Fiese, 1992). Parenting assumes a special importance here as the key proximal variable (intervening between the child and the larger environment) in both conceptualization and applied work.

TABLE 23.1
Summary of substantive and topical areas within contemporary
developmental psychology that reflect contextual influence

Substantive research areas	Examplar research topics
General development	Socio-emotional, personality, attitudinal Cross-cultural comparisons Life span (adolescence, adulthood, old age)
Cognitive development/Development of competence	School achievement Cognitive development (Piaget) Child language Literacy/numeracy Social competence (social intelligence)
Moral development	Prosocial behavior Personal-moral-conventional spheres Justice norms
Attachment	Parent–infant interaction, infancy Early childhood
Parenting	Parental beliefs and values Parental control/affection Parenting style (authoritative, authoritarian, permissive)
Family and social network	Context (neighborhood, kin, extended family) African American family/other ethnic family Poverty research (social class)
Intervention	Educational (early enrichment, parent education) Parent/family support (empowerment)

Given this trend toward a greater recognition of context, it may be informative to take a cursory glance at some of the current research areas in developmental psychology which have a contextual perspective (see Table 23.1). These research areas reflect some of the main orientations stated above. Thus, the recently emerging contextual perspectives and current directions inform the substantive research areas and the corresponding exemplar research topics given in Table 23.1. The table is based on a general reading of some of the leading child development journals in the last few years; it reflects the diversity of topics in which a great deal of research is currently being carried out. It presents a sample of the most important topics of current research interest and is not meant to be an exhaustive representation of the field of human development in cultural context.

A few observations are in order. First of all, there is a focus on both the developing child/person and the parent/family context, in some areas reaching out to social networks. Secondly, the more comprehensive approaches (e.g. family and social network, and intervention) are seen more readily in the applied research areas of social work, early childhood education, and sociological poverty research, than in psychology. Parenting is studied by both psychologists and others, both from a theoretical and applied perspective, as seen in intervention research involving parent education and support. Finally, in most of the research screened, there is a recognition of the importance of context, if not of culture.

Nevertheless, this recognition is not seen in all developmental research, particularly with the current emphasis on biological factors. For example, in the study of temperament, context may again be relegated to a secondary role. Even though there are some attempts at the integration of the organismic and the contextual approaches (Bronfenbrenner & Ceci, 1993), the age-old controversy of nature vs. nurture continues. However, increased sophistication is seen in theory and methodology in both perspectives, handling complex interrelations among multilayered variables. Biological research, especially in infancy and old age, opens up new vistas, but contextual analysis sheds new light on human development in real-life situations. One significant example is the focus on the interplay between human development and culture.

IMPLICATIONS OF A CONTEXTUAL SHIFT

It may be claimed that the increasing relevance of context in psychological thinking may be akin to a paradigm shift. It is basically a shift from a universalistic/organismic (*etic*) to a contextual/interactional (*emic*) approach in the study of human development. In other words, it involves a shift from an orientation where cultural context is ignored to one where it is stressed. There are some significant implications of such a shift.

A shift from a universal, organismic orientation to a contextual/interactional approach entails the emergence of different challenges in scientific inquiry. The main challenge/problem of a universalistic perspective is the inference of false uniformities across cultures from unicultural studies. In other words, when a research finding obtained in one sociocultural context is assumed to have universal validity, this is an assumption of false uniformities. It is based on the physical science model of universal laws to which psychology has long aspired. Cross-cultural psychology has emerged in reaction to this model, calling the assumption of uniformity an "imposed etic" (Berry, 1989).

A contextual perspective has its own share of challenges and problems. Foremost among these is the assumption of false uniqueness/specificity. This is the opposite of assuming uniformities where there are none; it claims that there are no uniformities where there may, in fact, be some. Taken to its logical extremes, this view considers all findings culturally relative and rejects all comparisons, since every act is assumed to have unique meaning derived from its specific context.

This perspective in psychology reflects an anthropological bias. Cultural and cross-cultural psychologists have typically accepted the assumption of the uniqueness of each culture, an assumption which leads to the expectation that cross-cultural comparisons should reveal differences. Thus, cross-cultural research reports are replete with statements such as "the Indian self", "the Japanese mother", or "the Greek philatimo", "the Latin American simpatia", "the Japanese amae". Yet studies find similar characteristics among behavior patterns in other countries. Thus, Triandis (1989) noted sentiments in other collectivistic groups similar to the "Greek philatimo"; and Aycicegi (1993) found the so-called "Mexican historic-sociocultural premises" (Diaz-Guerrero, 1991) regarding gender to be typical in Turkey!

The assumption of the uniqueness of each cultural context is particularly stressed by interpretive and cognitive anthropology, and is prevalent in the "everyday cognition" orientation in cultural psychology (see, for example, Shweder, 1991; Shweder & Sullivan, 1993). This orientation studies cultural phenomena "from within" (with an *emic* emphasis) and stresses the specific meaning each cultural context imparts on psychological processes. In its extreme form, it considers "culture and psyche to make each other up" and rejects even the use of the term *and* between them which implies their separateness (see Shweder, 1990, pp. 22; 24).

Thus, a shift from universal to contextual may bring with it a shift from an assumption of false uniformities to an assumption of false uniqueness/specificity. Both of these assumptions are unwarranted, and the degree of uniformity or specificity is an empirical issue. The universal approach is more representative of the *etic* orientation in cross-cultural psychology, and the cultural specificity approach of the *emic* orientation in cultural psychology. Nevertheless, the *etic* and the *emic* are not necessarily mutually exclusive.

The issues emerging in this debate are complex and have to do basically with comparability of psychological processes (psychic unity) and relativism. The controversy is seen as a polarity, contrasting cultural psychology and cross-cultural psychology. Cross-cultural psychology is charged by its critics with continuing the outmoded positivist tradition, assuming psychic unity, and employing an *etic* stance in cross-cultural comparison, which inevitably becomes "imposed etic" as it is based mainly on Western experience. Cultural psychology, in turn, while committed to an *emic* approach in studying psychological processes in each culture's own terms, is at times vulnerable to nihilistic relativism (for a review see Kağıtçıbaşı, 1996).

What is the solution to this controversy? I do not see the cultural and cross-cultural approaches as competing, but rather as complementary (Kağıtçıbaşı, 1992; 1996). A comparative approach does not preclude a contextualistic orientation, and contexts are not necessarily unique; they can be compared. All human psychology should indeed be cultural psychology, as human phenomena always occur within culture. Thus, any psychological inquiry that takes cognizance of culture is cultural psychology. If, in such inquiry, more than one culture is implied, then it is cross-cultural psychology.

An integrative approach is needed to resolve the controversy and to avoid the problems of false uniformity and false uniqueness in the study of human development. An integrative approach, combining the contextual and the comparative, would stress the *functional* interrelations among multilayered factors. The goal should be to discover the underlying *reasons* for behavior that may be shared in different contexts. This would provide greater understanding of *why* certain human phenomena are seen in certain contexts. Such an analysis would involve an examination of social structural variables as well as psychological variables, and would provide insights into possible links between them.

Cross-cultural psychology has long been involved in describing differences without going into the questions of why there are these differences or of underlying causes. Labeling rather than explanation is common, for example in terms of individualism–collectivism. There is a need to step out of the psychological mode of inquiry into a more social-structural and economic mode in order to situate psychological processes into context and to form causal links. A functional integrative approach could also deal with *changes* in psychological processes in response to changes in social structural variables constituting the context. To show how an integrative functional approach can be both contextual and comparative, I shall examine the development of competence.

THE DEVELOPMENT OF COMPETENCE

From a contextual perspective, competence is the attainment of what is socially valued (Kağıtçıbaşı, 1996). Socialization of competence in children is goal-oriented, even though this goal is often implicit and not consciously formulated. A great deal of research conducted in non-Western, traditional, socio-cultural contexts has pointed to some characteristic aspects of childrearing and socialization which are different from those seen in Western (American) middle-class contexts. I shall focus on two of these main characteristics: one is obedience-orientation in cultivating social intelligence in children; the other is a teaching style based on demonstration, modeling, and imitation. These qualities are inter-related from a functional point of view, even though the former pertains to social development and socialization while the latter defines cognitive development.

Social intelligence

Obedience expectations of children show systematic cross-cultural variation. In more traditional family contexts, particularly in rural agrarian and low socio-economic conditions, high value is placed on obedience in childrearing. This value is reflected in a cultural conceptualization of cognitive competence, which includes a strong social component. The goal of childrearing in closely knit collectivistic societies is the socialization of a socially responsible and kind person, who is sensitive to the needs of others, and who will uphold harmonious relations with them. Individual independence assumes much lower priority, if any. For example, in a study among families with low levels of income and education in Istanbul, good social relational behavior (including being obedient, showing affection, and getting along well with others) accounted for more than 80% of the desired behaviors in children spontaneously mentioned by mothers (Kağıtçıbaşı, 1991).

Obedience-orientation in childrearing is functional in socio-economic contexts where children have "old-age security value" for their parents (Kağıtçıbaşı, 1982; 1984). This is because obedient children are more likely to develop into loyal adults who take care of their elderly parents, whereas an independent child may leave home and attend to his/her own needs rather than to those of his/her family of origin.

In the nine-country Value of Children Study (Kağıtçıbaşı, 1982; 1984), the majority of adult respondents from Indonesia, the Philippines, Thailand, and Turkey stated "obeying their parents" as the most desired characteristic of children. This contrasted with responses from the USA and Germany, which stressed independence and self-reliance as characteristics desired in children. Other functions of conformity orientations have also been studied. For example, LeVine (1974; 1988) noted the survival value of obedience for young children in hazardous environments, and Kohn (1969) stressed the "anticipatory socialization" for work roles. He reasoned that obedience is functional in working-class (routine) jobs, and is therefore reinforced by working-class parents. This is contrasted with middle-class socialization in autonomy, which is functional for later decision-making skills, required in middle-class jobs.

Obedience is also seen as useful for developing social sensitivity. In socio-cultural contexts where socialization for social sensitivity is stressed, there is also a social definition of intelligence. It is found in a great deal of research from Africa (see review by Berry, 1984) and is best demonstrated by Serpell (1977). He showed that village adults' rating of intelligence in 10-year-old children, in terms of which ones they would choose to carry out an important task, did not correlate with children's scores on intelligence tests. This has been called "African social intelligence" (Mundy-Castle, 1974), but in fact, extends to all collectivistic societies (e.g. Berry & Bennett, 1992; Kim & Choi, 1994).

Childrearing is functional in that it is adaptive to environmental demands, and what is valued is taught to children. In this way, children's cognitive competence in culturally-valued domains is promoted, but cognitive competence in other domains may lag behind. For example, in Harkness & Super's (1992) study with the Kokwet of Kenya, Kokwet children were found to have highly developed skills in carrying out household chores, child care, etc., in comparison to children from the United States. On the other hand, Kokwet children were found to do poorly on simple cognitive tasks (such as retelling a story) on which American children had no difficulty.

A main issue that arises here has to do with changes in environmental demands, which render what was adaptive in one set of circumstances dysfunctional in another. This is particularly the case in the process of culture change through migration or urbanization. Many millions of people in the world have moved from rural areas or small towns into large cities or even to other countries, in search of jobs and better living conditions—and this process is continuing. Urban lifestyles make different demands on people, and some of the traditional values and habits may stop being functional. For example, with socio-economic development and the provision of other sources of old-age support, an obedience orientation in childrearing, serving toward loyalty to the elderly, loses its function. Instead, autonomy of the growing child becomes functional in more specialized urban jobs requiring decision making (Kohn, 1969; Kağıtçıbaşı, 1996).

Such rural to urban mobility, together with the increasing introduction of public schooling into the rural areas and small towns, has meant an unprecedented expansion in schooling for children in the world. There may be a disparity between the requirements of schools and urban lifestyles, and some of the traditional childrearing values, such as complete obedience orientation and an exclusively social definition of intelligence. Research with ethnic minorities in the US provides some evidence. For example, Nunes (1993) noted that immigrant Mexican parents believe, erroneously, that if their children are quiet, obedient, and listen to the teacher, then they will be successful in school. Similarly, Okagaki, and Sternberg (1993) found that for immigrant parents from Cambodia, Mexico, the Philippines, and Vietnam, non-cognitive characteristics such as motivation, social skills, and practical school skills, were as important as, or more important than, cognitive skills such as verbal ability, creative ability, and problem solving. This was not the case for Anglo-American parents. They also showed that American-born parents favored autonomy over conformity, and that beliefs about the importance of conformity correlated *negatively* with children's school performance.

Teaching / learning through modeling

Anthropological research shows that a great deal of learning in non-school contexs involves teaching through demonstration and modeling, and typically without verbal instruction or positive reinforcement. This is particularly the case in families where parents do not have much schooling themselves, and has been observed in studies conducted in Turkey (Helling, 1966), several societies in Africa (Gay & Cole, 1967, LeVine, 1989), and among the Australian Aborigines (Teasdale & Teasdale, 1992). It is also noted among ethnic minorities in the US (Laosa, 1980) and in Europe (Leseman, 1993).

Learning through observation and imitation obviously occurs everywhere. However, there are limitations to observational learning, such as inadequate transfer to new situations. When almost all learning is of this type, there may be serious developmental implications, as adult verbalization with the child is important. In particular, adult communication involving reasoning and decontextualized language is shown to contribute to children's early cognitive development (Snow, 1991; 1993). Similarly, a growing body of literacy research is pointing to the key role of early experience with oral language skills and to the "culture of literacy" (involving familiarity with the printed media, vocabulary, etc.) in the home, in predicting advanced literacy achievement (for reviews see Eldering & Leseman, 1997; Kağıtçıbaşı, 1996).

Research conducted with children from low-income urban groups in Turkey (Ataman & Epir, 1972; Savasir, Sezgin, & Erol, 1992), with Mexican-American mothers and children in the US (Laosa, 1980; 1984), with ethnic migrants in the Netherlands (Leseman, 1993), and with Blacks in the US (Slaughter, 1988) provide evidence for the importance of early verbal stimulation for cognitive development and school achievement. However, anthropologists and cultural psychologists in the "everyday cognition" school, who are informed by the Vygotskian sociohistorical approach, stress the value of everyday learning in an "apprenticeship model" (Rogoff, 1990), which is basically learning through modeling and imitation (e.g. Carraher, Schliemann, & Carraher, 1988; Childs & Greenfield, 1980; Dasen, 1984; Lave, 1977; LCHC, 1983; Nunes, Schliemann & Carraher, 1993; Rogoff, Mistry, Goncu, & Mosier 1991; Scribner & Cole, 1981;).

Recent research has provided some evidence for transfer to new situations in the so-called "street mathematics of the street traders" (Carraher et al., 1988; Nunes et al., 1993). However, this involves transfer of formal reasoning, which includes conceptualization. Apparently, procedural skills (*how* to do something) do not transfer adequately, but if conceptualization is involved, then transfer occurs (Hatano, 1982). At this point, something more than mere imitation probably enters the picture, such as guidance and explanation. On the other hand, Oloko (1994, p. 220) found that non-working students in Nigeria do better than street traders in mathematics, even more than in other subjects, and identified street trading, which interferes with school performance or keeps children out of school, as "maladaptation to a modernizing economic, social and political environment".

IMPLICATIONS FOR AN INTEGRATIVE APPROACH

In examining the development of competence, I have used a contextual approach. I have also looked into the functional reasons underlying the childrearing patterns involved, particularly in the study of the development of social intelligence. The basic guideline emerging is that whatever is valued in a culture is reflected in childrearing, and childrearing, in turn, effectively socializes the human infant to be a competent member of society. There is a caveat here in that, when society changes, the established patterns of a culture (e.g. childrearing values) may not follow suit. A related caveat is that there may be conflicts between social institutions (such as the family and the school) and the demands they put on individuals.

A contextual approach places a phenomenon into a specific context and studies it with a holistic perspective. However, it cannot and should not assume either the uniqueness or the permanence of contexts. As I have mentioned before, there are commonalities among contexts, as well as differences, and all societies change. From this perspective, the issue is no longer that of a contextual versus a non-contextual approach, because the latter lacks basic validity. Rather, it is how a contextual approach can be compatible with generalization and comparison; in other words, how to achieve contextualism without complete relativism.

Recently, Rogoff & Chavajay (1995) reviewed research on culture and cognitive development from a sociohistorical perspective. They pointed to the trend of moving away from cross–cultural comparisons towards a notion that ". . . cognitive development is intrinsically a cultural–historical process" (p. 869), reasserting the importance of everyday cognition/learning, as studied by cultural psychologists. Clearly, cultural psychologists continue to stress specific everyday learning (at home, in the community, in apprenticeship, etc.), relegating schooling to simply another context for learning with its own, specific cognitive outcomes. Though this is an understandable reaction to the overemphasis on school-like tasks in early cross-cultural thinking, which typically assigned "primitive" peoples low capacity, it goes too far in rejecting all bases of comparison.

In fact, pervasive and consistent positive effects of formal schooling are found on diverse cognitive and memory tasks going far beyond specific learning, with generalization and transfer to new learning situations (LCHC, 1983; Oloko, 1994; Scribner & Cole, 1981; Segall et al., 1990; Serpell, 1993). It is also the main vehicle of social mobility, both for societies and for individuals. To claim that in the less-developed contexts, non-cognitive traditional skills are more adaptive and therefore just as good as school-like tasks, is a relativism which assumes that those societies are static, which is not true. It also implies double standards: in the industrial society (comparative, universal) cognitive standards of achievement apply, but in pre- industrial societies, they do not.

In Vygotskian terms, schooling is a most important sociohistorical phenomenon, both in terms of its cognitive psychological connotations and also in terms of its social/economic impact. It is based on comparative standards, which are shared to a large extent and are not context specific. It is part of a shared culture of "development." For example, skills inculcated in schools are functional in urban society, with specialized job patterns increasingly requiring high levels of literacy and numeracy. School failure, a serious problem in the world, is to some extent the result of the mismatch between the (traditional) home culture and the school culture in the context of social change.

As I mentioned before, a complete obedience orientation and an exclusively social definition of intelligence may be some elements of this mismatch.

Another one may be the tradition of non-verbal teaching/learning in the home. Though these patterns/values of childrearing are functional in the cultural contexts in which they originate, with changed circumstances, and particularly in school contexts, they are no longer functional. In fact, they may be detrimental to children's achievement. Adjustment of these patterns to fit new contextual requirements is called for.

What appears to be needed is not a decreased emphasis on social goals in child socialization, but an increased emphasis on cognitive goals (e.g. an *expanded* parental vision in childrearing). Social skills are important also in the school context, as they facilitate school adjustment (Okagaki & Sternberg, 1993). However, the development of cognitive and language skills should *also* be a goal of parents in preparing children for school. Related to this, parents should come to recognize that other forms of teaching and learning in the home, in addition to modeling, contribute to children's cognitive development, school readiness, and eventual school achievement.

Is this "imposing middle-class values" on non-middle-class families, or being unduly demanding of working-class parents with low levels of schooling? I think not. First of all, quite a bit of research shows the positive effects of this type of parenting (e.g. Miller, 1988), which Goodnow (1988) has called "parental modernity", and Applegate, Burleson, and Delia (1992) have termed "refection-enhancing parenting." It is more typical of middle-class homes, but if it is beneficial for children's cognitive development and school performance, it should not be a monopoly of the middle classes. Secondly, a high level of education is not necessary for parents to talk with their children. If they don't normally talk at length with their children, this is because it is not customary, and may appear silly. Thus, it is not because of a lack of responsiveness on the part of the parent, as responsiveness can take different forms (Rabain-Jamin, 1994). But if the importance of early language development and the value of adult–child communication are recognized by parents, this would be reflected in their behavior.

The previous statement assumes an "involved" stance with regard to childrearing contexts. It reflects an outlook of applied research which sees the role of the social scientist as one who helps promote human well-being in addition to understanding human phenomena. This is a role carrying heavy responsibility, and calls for a partnership with the people involved. In my recently published book (Kağitçibaşı, 1996), I have examined one instance of theory and research that can inform applications across cultures. Such applications can take the form of "sensitization" efforts through parent education, media programs, community development programs, etc. to promote children's well-being and adjustment to changing social conditions. An example of this is the Turkish Early Enrichment Project (Kağitçibaşı, Sunar, & Bekman, 1988; Kağitçibaşı, 1995; 1996), which has grown from an experimental intervention research with low-income urban shanty town dwellers into a nationwide informal mother–child education program.

A contextual approach, focusing on the proximal environment of the child, is used; and at the same time, comparative standards of cognitive development and school performance are used, since these have validity in the changing environment of the families and the children involved.

CONCLUSION

In conclusion, I have noted a main trend—a paradigm shift—toward contextualism in the study of human development. This is a healthy trend in the field, but it should not turn into complete relativism. To ensure this, we need to go beyond mere description of context-specific behaviors and reach out into the underlying functional reasons which help us to understand *why* certain behaviors are reinforced in particular contexts. When those contexts change, new types of behaviors will become functional. In particular, when commonly shared standards of competence become relevant in societies undergoing socio-economic development, then comparative (common) behavior patterns may be called for. This appears to be the current situation in the world. Thus, cross-cultural perspectives on human development would benefit from an integration of both a contextual and a comparative orientation.

REFERENCES

Anastasi, A. (1992). A century of psychological science. *American Psychologist, 47*, 842–843.

Applegate, J. L., Burleson, B. R., & Delia, J. G. (1992). Reflection enhancing parenting as an antecedent to children's social-cognitive and communicative development. In I. E. Sigel, A. V. McGillicuddy-DeLisi, & J. J. Goodnow (Eds.), *Parental belief systems* (pp. 3–40). Hillsdale, NJ: Erlbaum.

Ataman, J., & Epir, S. (1972). Socio-economic status and classificatory behavior among Turkish children. In L. J. C. Cronbach & P. J. D. Drenth (Eds.), *Mental test and cultural adaptation* (pp. 329–337). The Hague: Mouton.

Aycicegi, A. (1993). *The effects of mother training program*. Unpublished master's thesis. Bogazici University, Istanbul, Turkey.

Baldwin, J. M. (1895). *Mental development in the child and the race*. New York: Macmillan.

Baldwin, J. M. (1909). *Darwin and the humanities*. Baltimore: Review Publishing.

Baltes, P. B. (1987). Theoretical propositions of life-span developmental psychology: On the dynamics between growth and decline. *Developmental Psychology, 23*, 611–626.

Baltes, P. B., & Brim, O. (Eds.). (1979). *Life-span development and behavior* (Vol. 2). New York: Academic Press.

Baltes, P. B., Reese, H. W., & Lipsitt, L. P. (1980). Life-span developmental psychology. *Annual Review of Psychology, 31*, 65–110.

Barker, R. G. (1968). *Ecological psychology*. Stanford, CA: Stanford University Press.

Berger, P. L. & Luckmann, T. (1967). *The social construction of reality*. New York: Doubleday.

Berry, J. W. (1976). *Human ecology and cognitive style: Comparative studies in cultural and psychological adaptation*. New York: Sage/Halsted.

Berry, J. W. (1980). Ecological analyses for cross-cultural psychology. In N. Warren (Ed.), *Studies in cross-cultural psychology*. (Vol. 2, pp. 157–189). New York: Academic Press.

Berry, J. W. (1984). Toward a universal psychology of cognitive competence. *International Journal of Psychology, 19*, 335–361.

Berry, J. W. (1989). Imposed etics-emics-derived etics: The operationalization of a compelling idea. *International Journal of Psychology, 24*, 721–735.

Berry, J. W., & Bennett, J. A. (1992). Cree conceptions of cognitive competence. *International Journal of Psychology, 27*, 73–88.

Bertalanffy, L. von. (1933). *Modern theories of development.* London: Oxford University Press.

Bertalanffy, L. von. (1968). *General systems theory.* New York: Brazilier.

Bronfenbrenner, U. (1979). *The ecology of human development: Experiments by nature and design.* Cambridge, MA: Harvard University Press.

Bronfenbrenner, U., & Ceci, S. J. (1993). Heredity, environment, and the question "how?" A first approximation. In R. Plomin & G. E. McClearn (Eds.), *Nature–nurture* (pp. 313–324). Washington, DC: American Psychological Association.

Bronfenbrenner, U., & Weiss, H. B. (1983). Beyond policies without people: An ecological perspective on child and family policy. In E. F. Zigler, S. L. Kagan, & E. Klugman (Eds.), *Children, families and government: Perspectives on American social policy* (pp. 393–414). New York: Cambridge University Press.

Brunswik, R. (1955). Representative design and probabilistic theory. *Psychological Review, 62*, 236–242.

Carraher, T. N., Schliemann, A. D., & Carraher, D. W. (1988). Mathematical concepts in everyday life. In G. B. Saxe & M. Gearhart (Eds.), *Children's mathematics: New directions in child development* (pp. 71–87). San Francisco: Jossey-Bass.

Childs, C. P., & Greenfield, P. M. (1980). Informal modes of learning and teaching: The case of Zinacantoco weaving. In N. Warren (Ed.), *Studies in cross-cultural psychology* (Vol. 2, pp. 269–316). London: Academic Press.

Cole, M. (1992). Culture and cognitive development: From cross-cultural comparisons to model systems of cultural mediation. In A. F. Healy, S. M. Kosslyn, & R. M. Shiffrin (Eds.), *Essays in honor of William K. Estes* (pp. 279–305). Hillsdale, NJ: Erlbaum.

Cole, M., Sharp, D., & Lave, C. (1976). The cognitive consequences of education: Some empirical evidence and theoretical misgivings. *Urban Review, 9*, 218–233.

Coll, C. T. G. (1990). Developmental outcome of minority infants: A process-oriented look into our beginnings. *Child Development, 61*, 270–289.

Damon, W. (Ed.). (1989). *Child development today and tomorrow.* San Francisco: Jossey-Bass.

Dasen, P. R. (1984). The cross-cultural study of intelligence: Piaget and the Baoule. *International Journal of Psychology, 19*, 407–434.

Diaz-Guerrero, R. (1991). Historic-sociocultural premises (HSCPs) and global change. *International Journal of Psychology, 26(5)*, 665–673.

Dym, B. (1988). Ecological perspectives on change in families. In H. B. Weiss & F. H. Jacobs (Eds.), *Evaluating family programs* (pp. 477–496). New York: Aldine.

Eldering, L. & Leseman, P. (1997). (Eds.), *Early education and culture: Culture-sensitive strategies for empowering parents and children.* New York: Garland.

Gay, J., & Cole, M. (1967). *The new mathematics and an old culture.* New York: Holt, Rinehart & Winston.

Goodnow, J. J. (1988). Parents' ideas, actions, and feeling: Models and methods from developmental and social psychology. *Child development, 59*, 286–320.

Goodnow, J. J., Miller, P., & Kessel, F. (1995). (Eds.), *Cultural practices as contexts for development.* San Francisco: Jossey-Bass.

Greenfield, P. M., & Cocking, R. R. (Eds.). (1994). *Cross-cultural roots of minority child development.* Hillsdale, NJ: Erlbaum.

Greenfield, P. M., & Lave, J. (1982). Cognitive aspects of informal education. In D. Wagner & H. Stevenson (Eds.), *Cultural perspectives on child development* (pp. 181–207). San Francisco: Freeman.

Gupta, G. C. (1992). *Ecology, cognition, metacognition and mind.* New Delhi, India: B. R. Publishing.

Harkness, S., & Super, C. M. (1992). Parental ethnotheories in action. In I. E. Sigel, A. V. McGillicuddy-DeLisi, & J. J. Goodnow (Eds.), *Parental belief systems* (2nd ed., pp. 373–391). Hillsdale, NJ: Erlbaum.

Harrison, A. D., Wilson, M. N., Pine, C. J., Chan, S. R., & Buriel, R. (1990). Family ecologies of ethnic minority children. *Child Development, 61,* 347–362.

Hatano, G. (1982). Cognitive consequences of practice in culture-specific procedural skills. *Quarterly Newsletter of the Laboratory of Comparative Human Cognition 4* (1), 15–18.

Helling, G. A. (1966). *The Turkish village as a social system.* Los Angeles, CA: Occidental College.

Huston, A. C. (1991). Antecedents, consequences, and possible solutions for poverty among children. In A. C. Huston (Ed.), *Children in poverty: Child development and public policy* (pp. 282–315). Cambridge: Cambridge University Press.

Jahoda, G., & Dasen, P. R. (Eds.). (1986). *International Journal of Behavioral Development, 9* (4), 413–416.

Kağıtçıbaşı, C. (1982). *The changing value of children in Turkey.* Honolulu, Hawaii: East-West Center, Publ. No. 60-E.

Kağıtçıbaşı, C. (1984). Socialization in traditional society: A challenge to psychology. *International Journal of Psychology, 19,* 145–157.

Kağıtçıbaşı, C. (1990). Family and socialization in cross-cultural perspective: A model of change. In J. Berman (Ed.), *Cross-cultural perspectives: Nebraska symposium on motivation* (pp. 135–200). Lincoln, NE: Nebraska University Press.

Kağıtçıbaşı, C. (1991). The early enrichment project in Turkey. *UNESCO-UNICEF-WFP Notes, Comments. (No. 193).* Paris: UNESCO.

Kağıtçıbaşı, C. (1992). Linking the indigenous and universalist orientations. In S. Iwawaki, Y. Kashima, & K. Leung (Eds.), *Innovations in cross-cultural psychology* (pp. 29–37). Lisse: Swets & Zeitlinger.

Kağıtçıbaşı, C. (1995). Is psychology relevant to global human development issues? Experience from Turkey. *American Psychologist, 50,* 293–300.

Kağıtçıbaşı, C. (1996). *Family and human development across cultures: A view from the other side.* Hillsdale, NJ: Erlbaum.

Kağıtçıbaşı, C., Sunar, D., & Bekman, S. (1988). *Comprehensive preschool education project: Final report.* Ottawa: International Development Research Centre.

Kim, U., & Choi, S. H. (1994). Individualism, collectivism, and child development: A Korean perspective. In P. M. Greenfield & R. R. Cocking (Eds.), *Cross-cultural roots of minority child development* (pp. 227–257). Hillsdale, NJ: Erlbaum.

Kohn, M. L. (1969). *Class and conformity: A study in values.* New York: Dorsey.

LCHC (Laboratory of Comparative Human Cognition). (1983). Culture and cognitive development. In W. Kessen (Ed.), *Handbook of child psychology* (14th ed., Vol. 1, pp. 295–356). New York: Wiley.

Laosa, L. M. (1980). Maternal teaching strategies in Chicano and Anglo-American families: The influence of culture and education on maternal behavior. *Child Development, 51,* 759–765.

Laosa, L. M. (1984). Ethnic, socioecenomic, and home language influences upon early performance on measures of abilities. *Journal of Educational Psychology, 76,* 1178–1198.

Laosa, L. M. & Sigel I. E. (1982). *Families as learning environments for children.* New York: Plenum Press.

Lave, J. (1977). Tailor-made experiments and evaluating the intellectual consequences of apprenticeship training. *Quarterly Newsletter of the Institute for Comparative Human Development, 1,* 1–3.

Lerner, R. M., & Busch-Rossnagel, N. A. (1981). *Individuals as producers of their development: A life-span perspective.* New York: Academic Press.

Lerner, R. M., Hultsch, D. F., & Dixon, R. A. (1983). Contextualism and the charater of developmental psychology in the 1970s. *Annals of the New York Academy of Sciences, 412,* 101–128.

Leseman, P. (1993). How parents provide young children with access to literacy. In L. Eldering & P. Leseman (Eds.), *Early intervention and culture* (pp. 149–172). The Hague, The Netherlands: UNESCO.

LeVine, R. A. (1974). Parental goals: A cross-cultural view. *Teachers' College Record, 76*, 226–239.

LeVine, R. A. (1988). Human parental care: Universal goals, cultural strategies, individual behavior. *New Directions in Child Development, 40*, 37–50.

LeVine, R. A. (1989). Cultural environments in child development. In N. Damon (Ed.), *Child development today and tomorrow*. San Francisco: Jossey-Bass.

Lewin, K. (1951). *Field theory in social science*. New York: Harper.

Marsella, A. J., DeVos, G., & Hsu, F. L. K. (Eds.). (1985). *Culture and self: Asian and Western perspectives*. New York: Tavistock.

Marsella, A. J., & White, G. M. (Eds.). (1984). *Cultural conceptions of mental health and therapy*. Boston: Reider.

McLoyd, V. C. (1990). The impact of economic hardship on black families and children: Psychological distress, parenting, and socioemotional development. *Child Development, 61*, 311–346.

Meisels, S. J., & Shonkoff, J. P. (Eds.). (1990). *Handbook of early childhood intervention*. Cambridge, UK: Cambridge University Press.

Miller, S. A. (1988). Parents' beliefs about children's cognitive development. *Child Development, 59*, 259–285.

Mundy-Castle, A. (1974). Social and technological intelligence in Western and non-Western cultures. In S. Pilowsky (Ed.), *Cultures in collision*. Adelaide, Australia: Australian National Association of Mental Health.

Munroe, R. L., Munroe, R. H., & Whiting, B. B. (Eds.). (1981). *Handbook of cross-cultural human development*. New York: Garland.

Novikoff, A. B. (1945). The concept of integrative levels of biology. *Science, 62*, 209–215.

Nsamenang, A. B. (1992). *Human development in cultural context: A third world perspective*. Thousand Oaks, CA: Sage.

Nunes, T. (1993). Psychology in Latin America: The case of Brazil. *Psychology and Developing Societies, 5*, 123–134.

Nunes, T., Schliemann, A. D., & Carraher, D. W. (1993). *Street mathematics and school mathematics*. New York: Cambridge University Press.

Okagaki, L., & Sternberg, R. J. (1993). Parental beliefs and children's school performance. *Child Development, 64*, 36–56.

Oloko, A. B. (1994). Children's street work in urban Nigeria: Dilemma of modernizing tradition. In M. P. Greenfield & R. R. Cocking (Eds.), *Cross-cultural roots of minority child development* (pp. 197–224). Hillsdale, NJ: Erlbaum.

Patterson, G. R., & Dishion, T. J. (1988). Multilevel family process models: Traits, interactions, and relationships. In R. A. Hinde & J. Hinde (Eds.), *Relationships within families* (pp. 283–310). Oxford: Clarendon Press.

Rabain-Jamin, J. (1994). Language and socialization of the child in African families living in France. In P. M. Greenfield & R. R. Cocking (Eds.), *Cross-cultural roots of minority child development* (pp. 147–166). Hillsdale, NJ: Erlbaum.

Rogoff, B. (1981). Schooling and the development of cognitive skills. In H. C. Triandis & A. Heron (Eds.), *Handbook of cross-cultural psychology: Vol. 4. Developmental Psychology* (pp. 233–294). Boston: Allyn & Bacon.

Rogoff, B. (1990). *Apprenticeship in thinking*. New York: Oxford University Press.

Rogoff, B., & Chavajay, P. (1995). What's become of research on the cultural basis of cognitive development? *American Psychologist, 50*, 859–877.

Rogoff, B., Mistry, J., Goncu, A., & Mosier, C. (1991). Cultural variation in the role relations of toddlers and their families. In M. H. Bornstein (Ed.), *Cultural approaches to parenting* (pp. 173–183). Hove, UK: Erlbaum.

Sameroff, A. J., & Fiese, B. H. (1992). Family representations of development. In I. E. Sigel, A. V. McGillicuddy-DeLisi, & J. J. Goodnow (Eds.), *Parental Belief Systems* (pp. 347–369). Hillsdale, NJ: Erlbaum.

Savasýr, I., Sezgin, N., & Erol, N. (1992). 0–6 Yas Cocuklari icin gelisim tarama envanteri gelistirilmesi [Devising a developmental screening inventory for 0–6-year-old children]. *Turk Psikiyatri Dergisi, 3*, 33–38.

Schwartz, T. (1981). The acquisition of culture. *Ethos, 9*, 4–17.

Scribner, S. (1990). A sociocultural approach to the study of mind. In G. Greenberg & E. Tobach (Eds.), *Theories of the evolution of knowing: The T. C. Schneirla Conference series* (Vol. 4, pp. 107–120). Hillsdale, NJ: Erlbaum.

Scribner, S., & Cole, M. (1981). *The psychology of literacy*. Cambridge, MA: Harvard University Press.

Segall, M. H., Dasen, P. R., Berry, J. W., & Poortinga, Y. H. (1990). *Human behavior in global perspective*. New York: Pergamon.

Serpell, R. (1976). *Culture's influence on behavior*. London: Methuen.

Serpell, R. (1977). Strategies for investigating intelligence in its cultural context. *Quarterly Newsletter: Institute for Comparative Human Development, 3*, 11–15.

Serpell, R. (1993). *Significance of schooling*. Cambridge, UK: Cambridge University Press.

Shweder, R. A. (1990). Cultural psychology:—What is it? In W. Stigler, R. A. Shweder, & G. Herdt (Eds.), *Cultural psychology: Essays on comparative human development* (pp. 1–43). Cambridge: Cambridge University Press.

Shweder, R. A. (1991). *Thinking through cultures: Expeditions in cultural psychology*. Cambridge, MA: Harvard University Press.

Shweder, R. A., & Bourne, E. J. (1984). Does the concept of the person vary cross-culturally? In R. A. Shweder & R. A. LeVine (Eds.), *Culture theory: Essays on mind, self and emotion* (pp. 158–199). Cambridge: Cambridge University Press.

Shweder, R. A., & LeVine, R. (1984). *Culture theory*. New York: Cambridge University Press.

Shweder, R. A., & Sullivan, M. A. (1993). Cultural psychology: Who needs it? *Annual Review of Psychology, 44*, 497–523.

Sigel, I. E., McGillicuddy-DeLisi, A., & Goodnow, J. (1992). *Parental belief systems*. Hillsdale, NJ: Erlbaum.

Slaughter, D. T. (1988). Black children, schooling, and educational interventions. In D. T. Slaughter (Ed.), *Black children and poverty: A developmental perspective* (pp. 109–116). San Francisco: Jossey-Bass.

Snow, C. E. (1991). The theoretical basis for relationships between language and literacy in development. *Journal of Research in Childhood Education, 6*, 5–10.

Snow, C. E. (1993). Linguistic development as related to literacy. In L. Eldering & P. Leseman (Eds.), *Early intervention and culture* (pp. 133–148). The Hague, The Netherlands: UNESCO.

Szapocznik, J., & Kurtines, W. M. (1993). Family psychology and cultural diversity. *American Psychologist, 48*, 400–407.

Teasdale, G. R., & Teasdale, J. I. (1992). Culture and curriculum: Dilemmas in the schooling of Australian Aboriginal children. In S. Iwawaki, Y. Kashima, & K. Leung (Eds.), *Innovations in cross-cultural psychology* (pp. 442–457). Lisse, The Netherlands: Swets & Zeitlinger.

Triandis, H. C. (1989). The self and social behavior in differing social contexts. *Psychological Review, 96*, 506–520.

Valsiner, J. (1989). *Child development in cultural context*. Toronto: Hogrefe.

Valsiner, J. (1994). *Comparative-cultural and constructivist perspectives*. Norwood, NJ: Ablex.

Vygotsky, L. S. (1962). *Thought and language*. Cambridge, MA: MIT Press.

Vygotsky, L. S. (1978). *Mind in society: The development of higher psychological processes*. Cambridge, MA: Harvard University Press.

Whiting, B. B. (Ed.). (1963). *Six cultures: Studies in child rearing*. New York: Wiley.

Whiting J. W., & Child, I. (1953). *Child training and personality*. New Haven, CT: Yale University Press.

Woodhead, M., Light, R. C., & Carr, R. (Eds.). (1991). *Growing up in a changing society*. London: Routledge & Kegan Paul.

Zigler, E., & Weiss, H. (1985). Family support systems: An ecological approach to child development. In R. Rapaport (Ed.), *Children, youth, and families: The action–research relationship* (pp. 166–205). Cambridge, UK: Cambridge University Press.

CHAPTER TWENTY-FOUR

The person in developmental research

David Magnusson
Stockholm University, Sweden

Using the total individual as the organizing principle for understanding and explaining psychological phenomena has deep roots in scientific psychology. The traditional holistic model has been given new properties and new content from four sources during recent decades: research on cognitive processes; the rapid development of disciplines concerned with biological aspects of individual functioning and development; the formulation of modern models for dynamic, complex processes; and the revival of longitudinal research. These contributions have enriched the old holistic view in a way which makes it a stable platform for further scientific progress in psychology, enabling us to fall into step with other scientifc disciplines in the life sciences. Aspects of an integrated, holistic model for research on psychological phenomena, in a current and developmental perspective, respectively, are presented and illustrated with data from the Stockholm Laboratory for Developmental Science.

L'utilisation de l'individu global comme principe organisateur pour la compréhension et l'explication des phénomènes psychologiques a de profondes racines en psychologie scientifique. Au cours des récentes décennies, le modèle holistique traditionnel a trouvé de nouvelles propriétés et de nouveaux contenus à partir de quatre sources: la recherche cognitive; l'évolution rapide des disciplines s'intéressant aux aspects biologiques du développement et du fonctionnement individuel; la formulation de modèles modernes de processus dynamiques complexes; le rétablissement de la recherche longitudinale. Ces contributions ont enrichi la vieille conception holistique d'une façon qui fait d'elle une plate-forme stable pour des progrès scientifiques additionnels en psychologie, nous permettant de rejoindre d'autres disciplines dans les sciences de la vie. Des aspects d'un modèle holistique intégré pour la recherche sur les phénomènes psychologiques dans une perspective courante et développementale sont présentés et illustrés à partir de données venant du Laboratoire de Science Développementale de Stockholm.

The following quotation from a leading psychologist in the past raise debate on an issue that has drawn much attention:

An increasing number of investigators are engaging in the problem of classifying and measuring the traits of personality with the result that the advance in method is rapid and gratifying. But with analyzing, testing, and correlating most of these investigators become blind to the true nature of the problem before them. They lose sight of the forest in their preoccupation with individual trees. What they want is an adequate representation in psychological terms of the total personality; what they get is a series of separate measurements which pertain only to isolated and arbitrarily defined traits. No doubt a certain gain comes from studying single traits, but the more important task is to evolve and to standardize methods for the study of the undivided personality. (Allport, 1924, p. 132)

The quotation is from Gordon Allport's speech to the British Psychological Association entitled: "The study of the undivided personality." In a later article, Allport (1937, p. 3) concluded: "Of the several sciences devoted to the study of life-processes, none, peculiarly enough, recognizes as its central fact that life processes actually occur only in unified, complex, individual form."

I did not quote Allport as a contribution to the current debate about traits and the Big Five. My aim is to show that the claim for using the total individual as the organizing principle for understanding and explaining psychological phenomena has deep roots in scientific psychology. Gordon Allport has often been noted as the leading figure in the tradition that we now refer to as the holistic approach to individual functioning and development. However, he was not the first, nor the only one, to claim a holistic approach to personality and developmental research. Binet and Henri (1895) discussed the elemental/holistic duality in understanding children's cognitive functioning and problem solving. The holistic view was fundamental to Stern's (1917) person-oriented theory. Brunswik (1929) argued that the general Gestalt principle that the whole is more than the sum of the parts holds for the functioning of the total individual. Lewin's (1926; 1927) discussion of types and a typological approach belongs to the holistic tradition in psychological research.

But theoretical winds change, and for a long time the holistic approach was out of fashion. Over the last several decades, however, an increasing number of voices have been raised in defense of the neglected perspective. In this reawakened movement, an early proponent for a holistic view was Block (1971) in his book, *Lives Through Time*, and others have followed. Cairns (1979, p. 325) expressed the holistic view in the following statement: "Behavior, whether social or nonsocial, is appropriately viewed in terms of an organized system, and its explanation requires a 'holistic analysis'."

In spite of the early proposals, it was not until rather late that the claim for the holistic perspective had an impact on empirical psychological research. In an article titled "Where is the person in personality research?", Carlson (1971) reported a survey of 226 studies published in 1968 in the two leading journals, *Journal of Personality and Social Psychology* and *Journal of Personality*. Carlson (1971, p. 209) summarized the results in the following words: "Not a single published study attempted even minimal inquiry into the organization of personality variables within the individual." However, since then, at a slowly increasing rate, empirical studies have appeared, which have been planned and implemented from the holistic perspective. As a prerequisite for this development the traditional holistic model for psychological phenomena has been given new properties and has been filled with new content during recent decades. Three main sources have contributed to this new situation.

RECENT CONTRIBUTIONS

The *first* main enrichment comes from cognitive research. During the last three decades, research on cognitive processes has been one of the most rapidly developing fields in psychology. Research on information processing, memory, and decision-making has made dramatic progress and contributed essential knowledge for the understanding and explanation of individual development and functioning. Recently, research on the interface of cognitive and brain studies has helped to bridge the gap between psychological and biological understanding of mental processes.

The *second* contribution stems from the rapid development of research in neuropsychology, endocrinology, pharmacology, developmental biology, and other disciplines in the life sciences. Hull (1943) made a distinction between molar behavior and specific properties of living organisms. He argued (1943, p. 275) that "any theory of behavior is at present, and must be for some time to come, a molar theory. This is because neuroanatomy and physiology have not yet developed to a point such that they yield principles which may be employed as postulates in a system of behavior theory." Almost 30 years later, Russell (1970, p. 211), in an address to the American Psychological Association, concluded, referring to Hull's formulation:

> The situation is now different and is changing so rapidly that the psychologist is hard pressed to keep abreast of even those major developments in other biological sciences that are most relevant to his area of primary competences. Thus, the stage is already set for the play in which the actors are properties of living biological systems and in which the plot unfolds within the concept of the "integrated organism."

Since 1970, research in biological and medical sciences has advanced at an increasing pace in two interrelated directions of interest for our discussion here. First, research in these areas has contributed detailed knowledge about the brain, how it develops from conception and onwards in an interaction process between constitutional factors and contextual factors, and how it functions at each stage of development, as an active organ, selecting, interpreting, and integrating information from the environment. Brain research is now in an almost revolutionary stage of development. Second, research has provided new insights into the role of internal biological structures and processes in the total functioning and development of individuals.

Knowledge from the biological sciences is important for bridging the gap between traditional, competing explanations of individual functioning in terms of mental *or* biological *or* environmental factors. Beyond what appears in neuropsychology, biological research has had a direct impact on developmental research. For example, Kagan (1992) ascribed the strong renewed interest in research on temperament to the extraordinary advances in neuroscience.

The *third* important source for the use of the holistic perspective in psychological research lies in the modern models which have been developed in the natural sciences for the study of complex, dynamic processes: chaos theory, general systems theory, and catastrophe theory. These theoretical models, particularly chaos theory, have had an almost revolutionary impact on theory building and on empirical research in scientific disciplines that focus on multidetermined stochastic processes: that is, meteorology, biology, chemistry, ecology, and others.

In psychology, the general systems view has been applied in theoretical analyses more than chaos theory and catastrophe theory. A growing number of developmentalists have discussed developmental issues in the framework of systems theory (e.g. Thelen, 1989). To an increasing extent, research referring to such a framework is being conducted and reported. Fogel and Thelen (1987) and Lockman and Thelen (1993) have offered examples of the fruitfulness of applying this perspective to research on specific topics: expressive and communicative behavior and motor development, respectively.

The *fourth* main source of enrichment for the holistic perspective on individual development lies in the launching, maturation, and interpretation of modern long-term longitudinal investigations. Some of the most comprehensive longitudinal programs have been planned and implemented with reference to a holistic view (see, for example, Cairns & Cairns, 1994; Magnusson, 1988). In the search for causal mechanisms in developmental processes, well planned long-term longitudinal studies underscore the holistic nature of personality and social development in human beings in ways that could only have been speculated about in cross-sectional research. In tracking individuals over time and context, inadequacies of the piecemeal or variable-oriented approach to the study of developmental issues become obvious because operating factors necessarily shift over time. It is only the organism that remains distinct and identifiable. Recognizing the importance of longitudinal research, the first scientific network established by the European Science Foundation in 1985 had the title, Longitudinal Research on Individual Development (see e.g. Magnusson & Casaer, 1992).

To summarize: the contributions from cognitive research, from neurosciences, from modern models for dynamic complex processes, and from longitudinal research have enriched the old holistic view of individual functioning and development in a way that makes it a fruitful theoretical framework for planning, implementing, and interpreting empirical research. The modern holistic view offers a stable platform for further scientific progress in psychology, enabling us to fall in step with recent developments in other scientific disciplines in the life sciences.

Of course, it is not possible to give a full and comprehensive description of a modern holistic view here and discuss all the essential implications for theory, methodology, and research strategy. I shall draw attention to a few aspects I regard as essential. It is an attempt to bring together what has been said by others before, within the coherent framework of the holistic view on individual functioning and development. I shall fulfill my aim with reference to some figures and empirical studies performed in our research program in Stockholm.

Before going into the substantive issues, let me make a clarification concerning perspectives on psychological phenomena. An individual's thoughts, feelings, actions, and reactions can be the object of study from three perspectives: current, developmental, and evolutionary. My discussion here is restricted to a current and a developmental perspective. I should like to stress the complementarity of these two perspectives. We need both.

A CURRENT PERSPECTIVE OF INDIVIDUAL FUNCTIONING

Let us first consider the way an individual functions in a current perspective. Figure 24.1 gives a simplified (but essentially correct) picture of what happens psychologically and biologically in a situation that an individual interprets as threatening or demanding.

The individual's cognitive act of interpreting the situation stimulates, via the hypothalamus, the excretion of adrenaline from the adrenal glands, which in turn triggers other physiological processes. The cognitive–physiological interplay is accompanied by emotional states of fear and/or anxiety and/or generally experienced arousal. In the next stage of the process, these emotions affect the individual's interpretation of sequences of changes in the situational conditions and, thereby, his/her physiological reactions and adaptive behavioral responses.

The figure illustrates that any general model which seeks to understand and explain why an individual thinks, feels, acts, and reacts as he or she does in everyday situations must integrate mental, biological, behavioral, and social factors. These factors function simultaneously and need to be placed in a coherent theoretical framework, in which the total individual forms the organizing principle. That is, any general framework for psychological research must be holistic.

The way the total system of mental, biological, behavioral, and social factors function in a specific situation and the characteristics of the total process at a certain stage of the life course of an individual is the result of a developmental process starting at conception. From the very beginning of life, constitutional factors form the potentialities and set the restrictions for nested developmental processes of maturation and experiences. The characteristic features of that process are determined in a continuous interaction among mental, biological, and behavioral "person-bound" factors and social factors across time.

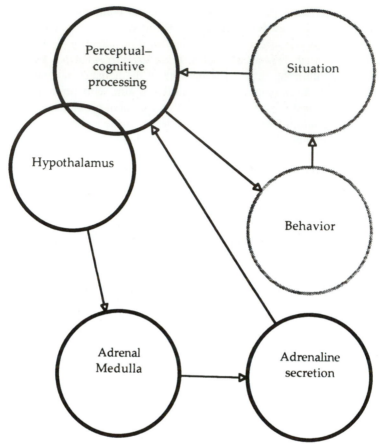

FIG. 24.1   A simplified model of the interplay of environmental, mental, biological, and behavioral factors for an individual in a specific situation.

At the same time, the way a person functions as a total organism at a certain stage of development becomes the platform for his/her further life course. A person's functioning at each stage contains both the potentialities and the restrictions for further development. *Thus, at each stage of the life course of an individual, the present is the child of the past and the parent of the future.* This conclusion leads us to a developmental perspective of individual functioning.

A DEVELOPMENTAL PERSPECTIVE: SOCIALIZATION

Of particular interest in developmental psychology is the process by which socialization takes place: which factors operate and how do they operate together in a holistic process? An empirical study in our longitudinal research program in Stockholm illustrates some aspects of the socialization process. A

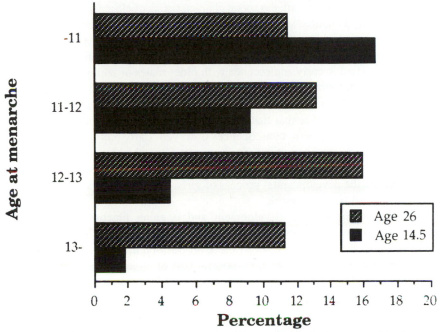

FIG. 24.2   Percentage of girls in four menarcheal groups: (1) with high frequency of drunkenness (10 times) at the age of 26; and (2) with high frequency of drinking (weekly) at the age of 14.5.

cohort of all boys and girls in one community in Sweden were followed from the ages of 10 to 30. At the age of 14.5, a strong correlation was found between the age of menarche and different aspects of norm-breaking behavior among girls, school adjustment, and parent–teacher relations. For example, girls maturing very early reported much greater alcohol comsumption than later maturing girls, as shown in Fig. 24.2.

As seen in the figure, the frequency of alcohol consumption at the age of 14.5 was much higher among girls who had their menarche before the age of 11 than among later maturing girls. The former also reported more strained parent–teacher relations and adjusted less well to school. However, in the follow-up of the same girls at the ages of 26–27, no systematic relation between the age of menarche and frequency of drinking was observed (see Fig. 24.2). Thus, high alcohol consumption at the age of 14 among early maturing girls was not a precursor of alcohol abuse at adult age.

On the other hand, very early biological maturation had long-term consequences in other respects. At adult age, the early maturing girls married earlier, had more children, completed less education, and acquired lower job status relative to average or late maturing girls. *These effects could not be attributed to early maturation per se*; rather they were the result of a net of interrelated factors, linked to biological maturation during adolescence: self-perception, self-evaluation and, above all, the social characteristics of close friends in puberty. The short-term deviances in norm-breaking behavior and the long-term consequences for family life, education, and job status were observed only among early maturing girls who perceived themselves as more mature than their agemates and who affiliated in early adolescence with older males or with peers who were out of school and working.

Two interrelated conclusions can be drawn from this study. First, the biological rate of onset of sexual maturity plays a role but does not alone account for the short- and long-term consequences observed. Early biological maturation provides predisposing conditions for a process in which mental, biological, behavioral, and social factors are involved. In order to understand individual differences in the developmental process of girls, all these factors must be integrated in the holistic framework.

Second, an individual's development and ongoing functioning cannot be understood in isolation from the proximal and distal properties of the environment in which the individual lives. A basic proposition in holistic interactionism is that the individual is an active, purposeful part of an integrated, complex and dynamic person–environment system. Thus, the specific way in which mental, biological, behavioral and social factors operate may differ in cultures with other social norms, rules, and role expectations for teenage girls. The relevance of this proposition has been confirmed in later studies on the same issue in other cultural settings: by the Cairns in the US, by Caspi and Moffit in New Zealand, by Pulkkinen in Finland, and by Silbereisen and Kracke in Germany. The empirical study and the results that I have summarized also have strong implications for research strategy in the study of developmental processes. The first is the need for a longitudinal research design. The second is the importance of cross-cultural research.

METHODOLOGICAL IMPLICATIONS OF A HOLISTIC MODEL

In the introduction I quoted from an address by Gordon Allport in 1924. He ended this quotation by saying: "No doubt a certain gain comes from studying single traits, but the more important task is to evolve and to standardize methods for the study of the undivided personality. To this end we must have a supplementary and very different type of technique" (p. 3). The recommendation by Allport is as relevant and urgent today as it was 1924. The recent contributions to the enrichment of the holistic model have provided conditions which make it possible to meet the need for the development of effective methodological tools.

As mentioned earlier, the formulation of modern models for dynamic complex process has had an almost revolutionary impact on research in the natural sciences and life sciences. As a consequence, it has led to the development of mathematical and methodological tools appropriate for studying such processes. One line is the revival of nonlinear mathematics and methods for the study of patterns of systems. For further scientific progress, it is important for researchers in psychology to take advantage of this development. There is a also a growing interest and application of such models and methods in developmental research. An interesting example is van Geert's (1994) application of a non-linear dynamic model for the redefinition of Vygotsky's "zone of proximal development."

When these methodologies are considered in psychology, we have to avoid the mistake we made when we took over models and methods from the natural sciences, particularly physics, in the beginning of this century in order to strengthen the image of psychology as a scientific discipline. Certain similarities exist between the structures and processes studied in the natural sciences and those investigated in psychological research. However, essential differences also exist, particularly when our focus is on the functioning of the total organism. At that level, a fundamental characteristic and guiding element in individual functioning is *intentionality*, which is linked to *emotions* and *values* and also the fact that the individual *learns from experience*. This fact must be taken into account when methods derived from the study of dynamic, complex processes in the natural sciences, which do not have these elements, are applied in planning and implementing empirical research in psychology.

The variable approach.   A characteristic of much psychological research, including that in developmental psychology, is that it is mainly concerned with the relations among variables studied across individuals by the application of nomothetic statistical methods. The focus of interest is on a single variable or on a combination of variables, their interrelations, and their relationships to a specific criterion. The problems are formulated in terms of variables, and the results are interpreted and generalized in such terms.

Research in this tradition has contributed much to increase our knowledge of psychological phenomena, and the variable approach is indispensable in psychological research, when correctly applied and interpreted. However, for understanding and explaining how individuals think, feel, act, and react as total functioning and developing organisms, we need, as Allport (1924, p. 3) phrased it, "a supplementary and very different technique." This need was observed and discussed by most of the strong proponents of a holistic view in the first part of this century. For example, Lewin (1931) discussed problems connected with a variable approach, with reference to the holistic perspective on individual functioning and development. These problems have become more obvious and strengthened by the formulation of modern models for dynamic complex processes. Thus, an approach which reflects the holistic nature of the functioning of the individual system under consideration and uses the individual as the organizing unit is highly needed (Magnusson & Allen, 1983; see also Bergman, in press, and Magnusson, in press). It has been referred to as a "person approach."

A person approach.   In a person approach, the specific problem under consideration is formulated and the results interpreted in person terms and generalizations of results refer to individuals. Specific problems are studied in terms of patterns of values for variables which are relevant with reference to the character of the problem. In operationalization, individuals are grouped into homogeneous clusters on the basis of similarity in terms of patterns of measures for variables which are relevant for the problem under study.

Studying individuals in terms of characteristic patterns of operating factors has a strong theoretical basis. It would lead us too far astray to describe and discuss it here. Let me give a brief background and two empirical examples of its application. A basic, well-documented principle in the development of biological systems is their ability for self-organization (see e.g. Thelen, 1989). From the beginning of the fetus's development, self-organization is the guiding principle. Within subsystems, the operating components organize themselves in a way that maximizes the functioning of each subsystem with respect to the purpose in the total system. At a higher organizational level, subsystems organize themselves in order to fulfill their role in the functioning of the totality. We find this principle in the development and functioning of biological systems in the brain, the coronary system, and the immune system, respectively. The organization of operating factors within each of these subsystems, as well as the organization of cooperating subsystems can be described in terms of patterns.

In other scientific disciplines concerned with dynamic, complex processes (such as ecology, meteorology, biology, chemistry, and medicine), pattern analysis has become an important research methodology with reference to the holistic character of the processes under investigation. A study of the cardiovascular system by Gramer and Huber (1994) in Graz, Austria, illustrates a pattern analysis of a biological subsystem. In a study of the functioning of the cardiovascular system in a stressful situation, they found that participants could be classified in three groups on the basis of their distinct pattern of values for systolic blood pressure, diastolic blood pressure, and heart rate, as shown in Fig. 24.3.

Among other things, the result presented in Fig. 24.3 demonstrates the problems connected with the application of linear regression methods for the study of relations among variables in a variable approach.

Another demonstration of a pattern analysis can be drawn from a study in our research program concerned with early problem behaviors as precursors of adult adjustment problems (Magnusson & Bergman, 1988). The pattern analysis of data for boys at the age of 13 is presented in Table 24.1. The clusters of boys, presented in Table 24.1, are based on data for six different problem behaviors: *aggressiveness, motor restlessness, concentration difficulties, low school motivation, underachievement,* and *poor peer relations.* Empirical variable-oriented studies indicate that each of them is a possible operating factor in the developmental processes underlying adult maladjustment. Data for each of the variables

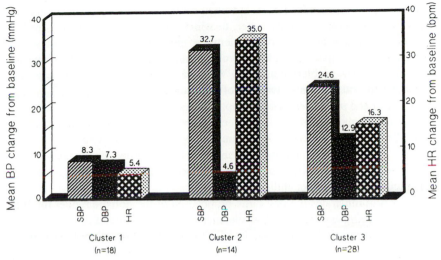

SBP = systolic blood pressure
DBP = diastolic blood pressure
HR = heart rate

FIG. 24.3   Magnitude of SBP, DBP, and HR reactivity in cardiovascular response cluster during "Preparing a Speech" (from Gramer & Huber, 1994).

were transformed to a scale with values 0–3, reflecting levels of seriousness of problem behaviors for boys at the age of 13.

Table 24.1 demonstrates that the boys could be grouped into eight distinctly different clusters with reference to their pattern of values for the variables under

Table 24.1
Clusters of boys at age 13 based on data for problem behaviors

					Cluster means		
Cluster no.	size	Aggressiveness	Motor restlessness	Concentration difficulties	Low school-motivation	Under-achievement	Poor peer relations
1	296	—	—	—	—	—	—
2	23	—	—	—	—	—	2.4
3	40	—	—	—	—	2.6	—
4	61	1.3	1.4	—	—	—	—
5	41	—	1.5	2.3	1.9	—	—
6	12	1.7	1.8	2.3	1.9	2.6	—
7	37	2.3	2.3	1.9	1.3	—	—
8	22	2.2	2.7	2.6	2.4	—	1.9

NOTES:
    — = the cluster mean of a variable is less than 1 in the 4-point scale coded 0, 1, 2, 3.
    From Magnusson and Bergman, (1988)

study. Each cluster of boys has its specific profile of values for the six problem behaviors. The most frequent cluster, to which 296 boys belong, has a profile without indications of behavior problems at the age of 13. The most severe problem cluster, with 22 boys, had a profile which indicates severe problems for five out of the six problem behaviors. With reference to the holistic view, it is of interest to note that only two out of six problem behaviors, namely *under-achievement* and *poor peer relations*, appear as single problem clusters at the age of 13. Each of the the other six problem behaviors occurs only in combination with other problem behaviors in different constellations. For example, *aggressiveness* and *motor restlessness*, which have been studied extensively in the variable-oriented tradition, as separate indicators of maladjustment, appear only in combination with other indicators.

This result illustrates the first basic proposition of the holistic model for individual functioning and individual development: a certain aspect of the total process cannot be meaningfully studied and understood in isolation from its context of other, simultaneously operating factors. A certain factor, say *aggressiveness*, does not have an influence of its own, *per se*, on the functioning and development of the total individual, independent of the context of other factors simultaneously working in the individual. It obtains its psychological significance from its context.

This importance of the context of other simultaneously working factors became even more apparent in the follow-up study to adult age investigating the long-term developmental paths for boys belonging to different clusters of boys at the age of 13. Let me give only one example. With respect to *poor peer relations*, two distinct groups of boys were identified in the pattern analysis: one group with only poor peer relations, and one group with poor peer relations in combination with other serious problem behaviors. In the follow-up, only boys who had poor peer relations in combination with other serious behavior problems at the age of 13 ran an increased risk for later problems in terms of criminality, alcohol abuse, and psychiatric diagnoses. The estimated risk for boys with poor peer relations as the only problem was the same as for those without problem indications. Thus, one and the same indication of poor peer relations at the age of 13 for two boys can have different implications for their further development, depending on the context of other variables in which it appears.

It should be noted that the follow-up of the clustering presented in Table 24.1 says more than the old adage that boys with more problems at an early age runs a stronger risk for adult problems than boys with no or fewor problems at an early age. Beyond information about the range and size of problem behaviors at the age of 14, the profiles for each of the clusters of boys in Table 24.1 contain information about the specific constellation of variables which characterizes the boys belonging to each cluster. It is the specific constellation of variables that is essential in the developmental processes and forms the basis for understanding and explaining them.

To summarize: our concern as psychologists is how individuals function. Thus, in the final analysis, we have to bring together results of analyses of relationships among variables in a person-oriented pattern analysis in order to investigate how these variables simultaneously operate together in individuals.

A GENERAL MODEL OF HUMAN BEINGS AND SOCIETY

In order to answer the questions of why and how individuals think, feel, act, and react, empirical research requires a theoretical framework that takes into account the characteristic features of the functioning and development of "the undivided person," to invoke Allport's (1924) formulation once again. Let us consider that claim with reference to the situation in other empirical sciences. A characteristic feature of scientific progress in empircal sciences is increasing specialization. When specialization in a subfield of the natural sciences has reached a certain level, it becomes apparent that further progress requires integration with what has been achieved in neighboring disciplines. An important step forward in the natural sciences was when such an integration occurred at the interface of physics and chemistry. Later, the important developments have taken place at the interface of biology, chemistry, and physics. The role of the integrative phases of this iterative process of specialization and integration in natural sciences and medicine is explicitly illustrated in the areas for Nobel prizes in these disciplines during the last 40 years.

Thus, we have to answer the following question: why is it that psychological research, including developmental research, is on the whole characterized by specialization with only little integration, when research in the natural sciences is characterized by the iterative process of specialization and integration? The background is certainly complex, but let me try to formulate an answer.

One condition which facilitates the iterative process of specialization and integration in the natural sciences is the existence of a general theoretical framework for theorizing and empirical inquiry, *a general model of nature*. The development of a common, general model of nature has formed the fundamental conditions for continuous progress in the natural sciences in two interrelated respects. First, it has served as the common theoretical framework for planning, implementation, and interpretation of studies on specific problems. Second, it has enabled researchers concerned with very different levels of the physical world (for example, nuclear physicists and astrophysicists) to communicate with and understand each other.

The fact that we, in psychology, lack a corresponding unifying theoretical framework which can offer a common conceptual space for the formulation of problems and interpretation of results from empirical studies is an obstacles for further real progress. Thus, in my opinion, one of the most important tasks in psychological research is the formulation of *a general model of human beings and society*, which can overcome the negative effects of fragmentation. In 1993, Gary Becker received the Nobel prize for his research on economic motives as causal factors in societal processes; for example, in criminal activities. At the same time we had found, in my research group in a comprehensive longitudinal study, that the combination of mental, behavioral, and biological factors in individuals carried a strong explanatory value for understanding the developmental background of adult criminal behavior (Magnusson, 1996a). Both results, Gary Becker's at the societal level, and ours at the individual level, are well founded in solid research, using adequate data and strong methods. A central scientific task then is, to explain and discuss these results in one coherent, integrated theoretical framework. A general model of human beings and society would serve that purpose, if adequately formulated. Such a general model has to build on the holistic nature of psychological processes and integrate mental, biological, and environmental explanatory models into one coherent framework.

To prevent any misunderstanding of the claim for the role and functioning of a general model of human beings and society, let me add two further comments. First, the role and functioning of such a general model is not to offer a hypothesis or an explanation for all specific problems. The Newtonian model did not answer all questions about the structure and functioning of the physical world, but it served the two purposes summarized earlier: it offered a common theoretical framework for planning and implementation of empirical research, and it offered a common conceptual space for communication among researchers. The same would be the case for a common model of human beings and society. Second, the holistic, integrated model for individual functioning and individual development does not imply that the entire system of an individual must be studied in every research endeavor. Acceptance of a common model of nature has never implied that the whole universe should be investigated in every study in the natural sciences.

TOWARDS A DEVELOPMENTAL SCIENCE

A consequence of the holistic view is that for a full understanding and explanation of the developmental processes of individuals, knowledge from what is traditionally incorporated in developmental psychology is not enough. We also need contributions from the interface of a number of other traditional scientific disciplines: developmental biology, physiology, neuropsychology, social psychology, sociology, anthropology, and neighboring disciplines. The total space of phenomena involved in the process of lifelong individual development forms a clearly defined and delimited domain for scientific discovery which has to involve all these and other disciplines for effective investigation. This domain constitutes a scientific discipline of its own, *developmental science* (Cairns, Elder, & Costello, 1996; Magnusson & Cairns, 1996). Indications of the relevance of this proposition are the recent establishment of the Center for Developmental Science at the University of North Carolina in Chapel Hill, and a new scientific journal, *Applied Developmental Science.*

The proposition that research on individual development constitutes a field of research with special demands on theory, methodology, and research strategy does not mean that psychology loses its identity as a scientific discipline. Physics, chemistry, and biology did not lose their special merits as a result of the new developments at the interfaces among them. Rather, by contributing essential knowledge to the field of developmental science, psychology strengthens its position as an active partner in the mainstream of scientific progress in the life sciences. By participating in that collaboration, we can contribute unique knowledge to the understanding and explanation of why individuals think, feel, act, and react as they do; and we can do so more effectively than if we proceed in isolation from the mainstream of research in the life sciences.

THE ZEITGEIST

I began by references to early claims for the holistic view of psychological processes. I have tried to show how, during the last decades, new blood from three main sources has infused the holistic model with substantive content that was lacking in the classical approach and has provided the theoretical and analytical tools for conceptualizing integration. The effect of this development is that the modern holistic model offers new possibilities for effective research on psychological phenomena. The importance of a holistic approach to developmental research has been emphasized by many colleagues during the last few decades. The holistic perspective also formed the theoretical framework for the organization of a Nobel symposium in Stockholm in 1994 convened under the auspices of the Royal Swedish Academy of Sciences, which is responsible for selecting most of the Nobel prize winners. Leading specialists in medical, biological, and psychological fields concerned with different aspects of individual development presented "state of the art" reviews of their specialities and discussed how knowledge from these fields can contribute to the understanding and explanation of developmental processes in a holistic, interactionistic perspective. The papers from the symposium have been published in a volume entitled *The life-span development of individuals: Behavioral, neurobiological and psychosocial perspectives* (Magnusson, 1996b). In the autumn of 1995, research councils and scientific academies in Europe were invited to comment on plans for the Fifth Scientific Framework Programme of the European Union. In a joint response to this invitation, German research councils referred to the Stockholm symposium as an example of recent fruitful developments in the life sciences. This is one among other indications that the holistic view on psychological phenomena not only has deep roots in scientific psychology, but also belongs to the scientific zeitgeist today. As a strong challenge for the future, we must analyze carefully the theoretical, methodological, and research strategy consequences of this conclusion and take these consequences seriously.

ACKNOWLEDGEMENTS

The work presented in this manuscript was supported by grants from the Bank of Sweden Tercentenary Foundation, the Swedish Council for Social Research, and the Swedish Council for Planning and Coordination of Research.

REFERENCES

Allport, G. W. (1924). The study of the undivided personality. *Journal of Abnormal and Social Psychology*, *19*, 131–141.

Allport, G. W. (1937). *Personality: A psychological interpretation*. New York: Holt, Rinehart & Winston.

Binet, A., & Henri, V. (1895). La psychologie individuelle. *L'Année Psychologique*, *2*, 411–465.

Bergman, L. R. (in press). A pattern-oriented approach to studying individual development: Snapshots and processes. In R. B. Cairns, L. R. Bergman, & J. Kagan (Eds.), *The individual as a focus in developmental research*. New York: Sage.

Block, J. (1971). *Lives through time*. Berkeley, CA: Bancroft Books.

Brunswik, E. (1929). Prinzipenfragen der Gestalttheorie [Basic principles in Gestalt theory]. In E. Brunswik, Ch. Bühler, H. Hetzer, L. Kardos, E. Köhler, J. Krug, & A. Willwohl (Eds.), *Beiträge zur Problemgeschichte der Psychologie* [Contributions to the history of problem solving in psychology]. (pp. 78–149). Jena, Germany: Verlag von Gustav Fischer.

Cairns, R. B. (1979). *Social development: The origins and plasticity of interchanges*. San Francisco: Freeman.

Cairns, R. B., & Cairns, B. D. (1994). *Lifelines and risks: Pathways of youth in our time*. Hemel Hempstead: Harvester Wheatsheaf.

Cairns, R. B., Elder, G. H., Jr., & Costello, E. J. (1996). *Developmental science*. Cambridge: Cambridge University Press.

Carlson, R. (1971). Where is the person in personality research? *Psychological Bulletin*, *75*, 203–219.

Fogel, A., & Thelen, E. (1987). Development of early expressive and communicative action: Reinterpreting the evidence from a dynamic systems perspective. *Developmental Psychology*, *23*, 747–761.

Geert van, P. (1994). Vygotskian dynamics of development. *Human Development*, *37*, 346–345.

Gramer, M., & Huber, H. P. (1994). Individual variability in task-specific cardiovascular response patterns during psychological challenge. *German Journal of Psychology*, *18*, 1–17.

Hull, C. L. (1943). The problem of intervening variables in molar behavior theory. *Psychological Review*, *50*, 273–291.

Kagan, J. (1992). Yesterday's premises, tomorrow's promises. *American Psychologist*, *28*, 990–997.

Lewin, K. (1926). Untersuchungen zur Handlungs- und Affekt-Psychologie. I und II. *Psychologische Forschung*, *7*, 294–329, 330–385.

Lewin, K. (1927). *Gesetz und experiment in der psychologie* [Principles and experimentation in psychology]. (Sonderdruck des Symposium, pp. 375–421). Berlin-Schlachtensee: Weltkreis.

Lewin, K. (1931). Environmental forces. In C. Murchison (Ed.), *A handbook of child psychology* (pp. 590–625). Worcester, MA: Clark University Press.

Lockman, J. J., & Thelen, E. (1993). Developmental biodynamics: Brain, body, behavior connections. *Child Development*, *64*, 953–959.

Magnusson, D. (1988). *Individual development from an interactional perspective.* Hillsdale, NJ: Erlbaum.

Magnusson, D. (1995). Individual development: A holistic integrated model. In P. Moen, G. H. Elder, Jr., & K. Luscher (Eds.), *Linking lives and contexts: Perspectives on the ecology of human development* (pp. 19–60). Washington: American Psychological Association.

Magnusson, D. (1996a). The patterning of antisocial behavior and autonomic reactivity. In D. M. Stoff & R. B. Cairns (Eds.), *The neurobiology of clinical aggression* (pp. 291–308). Hillsdale, NJ: Erlbaum.

Magnusson, D. (Ed.) (1996b). *The life-span development of individuals: Behavioral, Neurobiological, and Psychosocial Perspectives. A Synthesis.* Cambridge: Cambridge University Press.

Magnusson, D. (in press). The logic and implications of a person approach. In R. B. Cairns, L. R. Bergman, & J. Kagan (Eds.), *The individual as a focus in developmental research.* New York: Sage.

Magnusson, D., & Allen,V. L. (1983). Implications and applications of an interactional perspective for human development. In D. Magnusson & V. L. Allen (Eds.), *Human development: An interactional perspective* (pp. 369–387). New York: Academic Press.

Magnusson, D., & Bergman, L. R. (1988). Individual and variable-based approaches to longitudinal research on early risk factors. In M. Rutter (Ed.), *Studies of psychosocial risk: The power of longitudinal data* (pp. 45–61). Cambridge: Cambridge University Press.

Magnusson, D., & Cairns, R. B. (1996). Developmental science: Principles and illustrations. In R. B. Cairns, G. H. Elder, Jr., & E. J. Costello (Eds.), *Developmental science* (pp. 7–30). New York: Cambridge University Press.

Magnusson, D., & Casaer, P. (1992). *Longitudinal research on individual development: Present status and future perspectives.* Cambridge: Cambridge University Press.

Magnusson, D., & Stattin, H. (1988). Person–context interaction theories. In W. Damon & R. M. Lerner (Eds.) *Handbook of child psychology: Vol. 1. Theoretical models of human development* (pp. 685–759). New York: Wiley.

Russell, R. W. (1970). "Psychology": Noun or adjective? *American Psychologist, 25,* 211–218.

Stattin, H., & Magnusson, D. (1990). *Pubertal maturation in female development.* Hillsdale, NJ: Erlbaum.

Stern, W. (1917). *Die psychologie under der personalismus* [Psychology from a personality perspective]. Leipzig, Germany: Barth.

Thelen, E. (1989). Self-organization in developmental processes: Can systems approaches work? In M. R. Gunnar & E. Thelen (Eds.), *Systems theory and development* (pp.77–117). Hillsdale, NJ: Erlbaum.

CHAPTER TWENTY-FIVE

Current perspectives on social and emotional development

Carolyn Zahn-Waxler
National Institute of Mental Health, Bethesda, Maryland, USA

Angela McBride
National Institute of Mental Health, Bethesda, Maryland, USA

Research on social–emotional development is increasingly characterized by a multivariate approach, an interdisciplinary focus, and a developmental psychopathology perspective. There is an emphasis on the interaction of biological and environmental factors that produce normative and maladaptive patterns of development. Current conceptual frameworks are reviewed and the range of domains considered within the area of social–emotional development are briefly described. Recent investigations of emotional, prosocial, and antisocial development are examined in greater detail. Exemplars of developmental psychopathology research that are considered focus on outcomes for children and adolescents exposed to marital discord and parental depression. Processes implicated in the development of different types of social, emotional and behavioral styles and problems in males and females are discussed.

La recherche sur le développement socio–émotionnel prend de plus en plus le caractère d'une approche multivariée, à concentration interdisciplinaire, dans une perspective d'évolution psychopathologique. On y insiste sur l'interaction de facteurs biologiques et environnementaux qui débouche sur des patterns de développement normatifs et maladaptés. Ce chapitre fait la critique des cadres conceptuels courants et présente une brève description de l'éventail des domaines pris en considération dans ce champ du développement socio–émotionnel. Les travaux récents sur le développement émotionnel, prosocial et antisocial sont examinés dans le menu détail. Les exemples de recherche en psychopathologie du développement qui sont étudiés mettent l'accent sur les conséquences qu'exercent, sur les enfants et adolescents qui y sont exposés, les désaccords conjugaux et la dépression mentale. On traite des processus en cause dans le développement de divers types de styles et de problèmes sociaux, émotionnels et comportementaux chez les hommes et les femmes.

The field of social–emotional development is in the midst of a new and exciting era (Collins & Gunnar, 1990; Hartup & van Lieshout, 1995; Parke, Ornstein, Reiser, & Zahn-Waxler, 1992). Progress and innovation is evident when current directions are contrasted with work of the previous three decades (see reviews by Hartup & Yonas, 1971; Hetherington & McIntyre, 1975; Hoffman, 1977; Parke & Asher, 1983; Reese, 1993). Interdisciplinary work is now more common, including a developmental interface with such fields as genetics, anthropology, sociology, neurobiology, and ethology. The emergence of a developmental psychopathology perspective reflects increased ties to psychiatry and clinical ·psychology, resulting in a productive integration of research on normative and maladaptive age progressions.

OVERVIEW

Texts and review chapters often link the areas of personality and social development. In the adult literature, enduring personal qualities are characterized, for example, by dimensions such as extraversion, neuroticism, and openness to experience. In infants and young children, dispositions or prototypic responses to the environment are more commonly referred to as temperament than as personality. Temperament includes, for example, irritability, fearfulness, sociability, and activity level. Any review is inevitably selective, and this review will focus more on social than personality development. It will emphasize, in particular, recent research on emotions, as well as prosocial and antisocial development.

Before examining these domains in detail, we shall briefly identify other substantive areas traditionally considered within the broader definition of social–emotional development, describe research methods and paradigms used, and discuss current theoretical approaches and perspectives, using illustrations from recent research. To provide the most current information, many studies reviewed reflect research published in the 1990s to date, but earlier research is also considered where relevant. Because multiple domains of social–emotional development are reviewed, in-depth coverage of particular areas is not possible, nor are themes invariably interwoven tightly.

Because social processes are interpersonal in nature, involving relationships, attachment patterns have been a common topic of inquiry. This latter focus includes the formation of social bonds, the quality and types of attachment relationships formed, what causes infants to become securely or insecurely attached to caregivers, and the implications of early attachment quality for later development within the family and culture. Social development involves, too, the establishment of identity or becoming an individual. Aspects of identity include self-recognition, self-differentiation, self-concept, and self-esteem. The social–emotional domain also incorporates arenas pertaining to achievement, sex differences and sex roles, moral reasoning, and stages of moral development.

Family context is particularly relevant to the process by which the child becomes a social being. Socialization is broadly construed to include not only childrearing practices and discipline but other features of family life such as the affective climate, the marital relationship, and the personalities and interpersonal functioning of caregivers. There has been a burgeoning literature on the effects of discord and divorce, mirroring the high rates of family dissolution in some cultures. Another topic of interest includes the impact of child maltreatment or abuse on children's social and emotional development.

Socialization influences outside the family include the school, television, and peers, especially as children grow older. Peer relations have both adaptive significance in promoting social competence, and potential for promoting deviance (Berndt & Keefe, 1995; Dishion, Andrews, & Crosby, 1995; Hogue & Steinberg, 1995; Mounts & Steinberg, 1995; Rubin, et al., 1994; Tremblay, Masse, Vitaro, & Dobkin, 1995). Children's sociometric status, or standing in the peer group (e.g. Bierman & Wargo, 1995; Black & Logan, 1995; Crick & Ladd, 1993; Hymel, Bowker, & Woody, 1993; Vandell & Hembree, 1994) and their experience with bullying and victimization (Boulton & Smith, 1994; Schwartz, Dodge, & Coie, 1993) are all important elements of children's socialization experiences with age-mates.

There has been a substantial amount of research in the last decade on linkages between parent and peer systems. This includes the different ways parents prepare their children for social relationships with age-mates (Parke & Ladd, 1992). The ways in which parents impart skills, knowledge and abilities, and how processes learned in the family become reflected in peer relations are examined. Both direct and indirect processes are considered (Hart, DeWolf, Wozinak, & Burts, 1992; Pianta & Ball, 1993). We are beginning to see an increased emphasis on parents' emotions as well as behavioral styles that serve to regulate children's emotions, and in turn, their social relationships with peers (Cassidy, Parke, Butkovsky, & Braungart, 1992).

RESEARCH PARADIGMS

A few decades ago laboratory experiments were widely used to simulate and study social processes under rigorously controlled conditions. Criticized for lacking ecological validity, there were paradigm shifts (Grusec & Lytton, 1988). Laboratory research is still common, but now often augmented, and sometimes supplanted, by other approaches, including field experiments and observations of social interactions in natural settings like the home, school, and playground. Standardized self-reports, reports of outside observers, and responses to structured interviews are often part of the armamentarium of approaches used. Multivariate, multimethod studies are now very common. Less effort is expended on isolation of causal processes through experimental manipulations, and more on the use of statistical procedures, like structural equation modeling, to test hypotheses about causal pathways.

Much more than in the past, research on social processes makes use of longitudinal research designs. Earlier, developmental questions focused more on how *groups* change over time: for example, do children in general become more prosocial, or less aggressive, or less inhibited as they grow older? Age cross-sectional research designs can be used to address these kinds of developmental questions. However, an understanding of factors associated with individual variations in continuity and change over time calls for a longitudinal approach.

THEORIES

The era of grand theories and stringent adherence to a particular theory is long past. This reflects a more realistic appraisal of the fact that any given phenomenon is not likely to be well explained with one all-encompassing conceptual framework. Newer formulations emphasize interaction and reciprocity—that is, the dynamic interchange of organism and environment. In the past, psychoanalytic theory with its emphasis on instincts and internal drives was a strong motivating force in research on social development. More current biological perspectives include: (1) evolutionary and ethological viewpoints regarding the development of social motives and behaviors; and (2) the behavior genetics approach, which considers heritability of social and emotional characteristics.

Environmental perspectives now feature: (1) ecological approaches which incorporate broad, complexly textured conceptualizations of the environment in relation to human development, as well as: (2) constructs from social learning theory. Growing interest in relationships and family processes in intergenerational transmission of social behaviors, scripts, and values has expanded social learning approaches beyond the traditional constructs of observational learning, imitation, reinforcement, and punishment (Benoit & Parker, 1994; Putallaz, Costanzo, & Klein, 1993; Putallaz, Klein, Costanzo, & Hedges, 1994). Cognitive developmental theories are also relevant here as organisms respond to or ignore experience, depending on their cognitive stage of development.

No single theoretical position currently dominates the field of social–emotional development (Grusec & Lytton, 1988). A common theme, now, is that nothing can be studied or understood apart from its context. Individuals function in social systems. Systems interact, and adequate knowledge of any one system is not possible unless viewed as part of a larger system. A transactional approach (Sameroff & Chandler, 1975) and ecological, contextual models (Bronfenbrenner, 1979) had their origins in the conceptual work of Bell (1968), who first described the effects of children on parental discipline and socialization practices. The fruits of these conceptual labors, which began over two decades ago, are now clearly being realized in the empirical research and model building of the 1990s.

Contextual, ecological models

In Bronfenbrenner's model, the natural ecology or environment is conceptualized as a set of nested structures that influence each other in the course of
development. The microsystem consists of the child and the immediate environment that is directly experienced (e.g. the family, schools, peers). The mesosystem
reflects the linkages between different microsystems (e.g. a secure attachment
relationship with the parent may pave the way toward cooperative, competent
peer relations). The exosystem may not be experienced directly, yet may still
affect children's development (e.g. the extended family, the parent's work place,
media, and community functions). The macrosystem is the cultural context in
which these other systems are embedded; it provides the overarching ideology
of how children are to be treated.

No individual research project can simultaneously incorporate all of the
dimensions implicated in such an ecological model. However, increasingly multivariate research programs examine potential additive, interactive, and reciprocal
causal influences, often utilizing longitudinal designs. Two recent studies
illustrate the influence of the exosystem on the microsystem. In research on
economic stress, family process, and problems of adolescence (Conger et al.,
1994), economic pressure contributes to parental dysphoria and marital conflict
and predicts parental hostility toward children. Hostile, coercive interchanges
between parents and offspring, in turn, increase the likelihood of adolescent
social and emotional problems. Persistent family economic hardship is linked to
children's difficulties in peer relations, school conduct problems, and low self-
esteem, with the impact of economic hardship being mediated by parental behavior
(Bolger, Patterson, Thompson, & Kupersmidt, 1995).

The contextual approach is a likely intellectual forerunner of an increased
emphasis on diversity (Lerner, 1988). Diversity refers to differences among individuals, including but not restricted to sex/gender, culture, subculture, ethnicity,
socioeconomic status, and accompanying living conditions. Factors influencing
development, organization, and integration of these dimensions may differ in
different contexts and for different groups.

Physical discipline, for example, predicts aggression in children, but not in
a uniform fashion. It is associated with aggression in Euro-American, but not
African-American, children, suggesting that *similar* parenting practices may
have different meanings in different ethnic and cultural contexts (Deater-Deckard,
Dodge, Bates, & Pettit, in press). Antisocial behavior may also be mediated
by *different* caregiver behaviors representative of different cultural values. In
a cross-cultural comparison of Japanese and US preschool children, higher
levels of hostility and aggression in US children could be traced to cross-
cultural differences in the childrearing practices of the mothers (Zahn-Waxler
et al., in press). Different cultural values also may alter relationships found.
Chen, Rubin, and Sun (1992), for example, found shyness to be associated with

lower peer acceptance in North American children, but with higher acceptance in Chinese children. Throughout this chapter, another aspect of diversity is emphasized—namely, sex of child and its role in mediating different developmental outcomes.

Behavior genetics

Specific abilities, traits, and behavior patterns may depend heavily on the particular combination of genes inherited by a given individual. Behavior geneticists advocate the use of research designs for estimating hereditary influence, especially by means of family designs that include monozygotic and dizygotic twins and adoptees, as well as full and half-siblings. Family studies can also help estimate the extent to which the environment influences various social and emotional characteristics (see review by Plomin, 1994). This research orientation is part of a broader interest in neurobiological processes that play a role in the regulation of social organization and social bonds (New York Academy of Sciences Conference, 1996).

Twin and adoption methods provide indirect estimates of genetic variation among individuals and often do not *directly* measure environmental processes. Current research, however, in the area of molecular genetics holds promise for the identification of DNA markers of behavioral traits relevant to social–emotional and personality development. Quantitative trait loci (QTL) analysis involves the search to find multiple (rather than single) genes that affect behavioral traits in a probabilistic rather than a predetermined manner (Plomin, 1994). Behavior genetics designs also are being expanded to include specific measures of environmental processes (Zahn-Waxler et al., 1996), providing increased opportunity to examine transactional questions.

In a recent multivariate genetic analysis of family environment and adolescent depressive symptoms and antisocial behavior, family influence was examined, based on observed family interactions and both parent and child reports (Pike et al., 1996). Parental and sibling negativity were related to adolescent adjustment through nonshared environmental processes, with genetic factors also playing a major role. The interface of nature and nurture can also be considered through examination of parenting practices of adoptive parents and the behavior of their offspring, when biological parents differ in specified ways such as having an antisocial history (e.g. Ge et al., 1996). Harsh parenting by adoptive parents could be predicted from the antisocial histories of biological parents and from the antisocial patterns of their adopted adolescents. However, reciprocal influences between adoptive parent and adolescent behaviors could also be identified, as not all adoptive parents react negatively to aversive child behaviors. Studies such as these begin to move research from simple unidirectional, evocative models to models of mutual and reciprocal influences.

Temperament and environment

This emphasis on organism–environment interaction, is also seen in work on dispositions or temperament styles that may differentially influence (and be influenced by) particular socialization experiences (Kochanska, 1993). Research on shyness, fearfulness, and inhibition serves to illustrate some of these issues. Kochanska (1991; 1995) has studied different pathways to internalization and conscience development. For fearful/anxious children, gentle maternal discipline deemphasizing power predicts internalization. For fearless children, in contrast, internalization is predicted by security of attachment. Parallel themes are found in longitudinal research by Rubin and colleagues on the interaction of child temperament, parent characteristics, and cultural contexts that encourage inhibited and withdrawn versus aggressive behaviors (e.g. Rubin et al., 1995; Rubin, LeMare, & Lollis, 1990).

Research by Kagan, Reznick, and Gibbons (1989) indicates that fearful, inhibited behavior shows stability over time, though socialization experiences may change temperament patterns (Arcus & Kagan, 1995). Rickman and Davidson (1994) report that parents of young, inhibited children show lower extraversion, higher avoidance and shyness, and more anxiety than parents of uninhibited children. Asendorpf (1994) has identified factors in children, including greater social competence and higher IQ, associated with greater malleability in inhibition over time. Inhibition is more stable over time for girls than boys (Kerr, Lambert, Stattin, & Klackenberg-Larsson, 1994), which may reflect culturally shared notions of gender-appropriate behavior, with shyness and dependency more likely to be encouraged in girls. These culturally supported "roles" for females may sometimes have detrimental consequences, as these introverted qualities are associated with anxiety and worry. Already, by middle childhood, worries are more commonly reported for girls than boys (Silverman, LaGreca, & Wasserstein, 1995). By adolescence and adulthood, anxiety disorders are more prevalent in females than males (American Psychiatric Association, *DSM-IV*, 1994). Such studies provide another indication of the relevance of transactional, organism–environment models for elucidating different outcomes in children's social and emotional development.

Group socialization

A group socialization theory of development (Harris, 1995) has attracted recent interest. In this view, parents do not have important long-term effects on their children's personalities and social development except, perhaps, at the extremes. Rather, outside-the-home socialization, which takes place in the peer groups of childhood and adolescence, is emphasized. These intra- and intergroup processes, rather than parent–child relationships, are seen as responsible for transmission of culture and environmental modification of social and personality characteristics. A number of different data sources are used to provide indirect evidence for this proposition. By the time they are adults, adoptive siblings reared in the same home will, on average, bear no resemblance to each other in personality and social characteristics. Biological siblings reared in the same home will be somewhat more alike, but still not very similar. Identical twins reared together will be no more alike than identical twins reared in separate homes. The group socialization theory is based on circumstantial evidence and requires a more substantial database. However, it challenges us both to continue to identify those areas of functioning that are under greater or lesser degrees of genetic influence and to develop better methods to assess the familial and extra-familial environments in which children are reared.

EMOTIONAL DEVELOPMENT

After a long period of neglect, emotions have regained a central role in theories of intrapersonal and interpersonal development (Magai & McFadden, 1995), coinciding with the adoption of a viewpoint that emotions are functional, organized, and generally adaptive action systems. Research now considers the experience, expression, recognition, and control of emotions, as well as their role in social relationships, even in infancy, beginning with the establishment of affectional ties. The newer focus on the importance of emotions in social competence as well as dysfunction is also associated with increased emphasis on the construct of emotion regulation (Cole, Michel, & Teti, 1994; Fox, 1994; Thompson, 1994).

Emotion regulation has been defined (Cole et al., 1994, p. 76) as "the ability to respond to the ongoing demands of experience with the range of emotions in a manner that is socially tolerable and sufficiently flexible to permit spontaneous reactions as well as the ability to delay spontaneous reactions as needed." This full range of emotions includes, but is not restricted to, joy, pride, sadness, anger, guilt, and fear. Emotion dysregulation implies an impairment in the regulatory function. Emotional constriction, such as the inability to express pleasure and joy, is one aspect of dysregulation, while excessive or extreme emotion is another component thought to be maladaptive. In infancy, for example, high emotionality predicts anxiety and depression in early childhood (Rende, 1993). Extreme emotion may be adaptive for some individuals, in some contexts. In a short-term longitudinal study of inner-city teens (Luthar, 1995), high anxiety among ninth grade girls predicted improved performance in school.

Basic and higher-order emotions

The burgeoning of research on affect development first focused mainly on the basic emotions. Sadness, anger, fear, and joy, for example, became more accessible to rigorous study as they became measurable by rules of organization of facial musculature (Ekman & Friesen, 1978). These primary emotions are: (1)

closely linked to underlying physiology; (2) evident in the first year (and some-times, months) of life; and (3) often present in other species as well (Darwin, 1872). Recent research on infants' emotions include demonstrations of: (1) mor-phological stability of facial expressions of joy, sadness, and anger (Izard et al., 1995); (2) differences in specific emotional responses to depressed versus non-depressed mothers (Pickens & Field, 1993); and (3) greater genetic influence on negative than positive emotions (Emde et al., 1992), with genetic influence stronger for some negative emotions (e.g. anger and fear) than others (e.g. sad-ness) (Zahn-Waxler & Robinson, 1995).

A recently emerging theme concerns the appearance of complex new emo-tions, during the transition from infancy to early childhood (Dunn, 1988; 1993). During the second and third years of life, children begin to express emotions not seen earlier, including pride, shame, guilt, empathy, jealousy, and embarrassment, which have been variously termed "secondary," "derived," "higher-order," "moral" or "self-conscious" emotions. They are complex, later to develop, and more likely to occur mainly in humans (Campos, 1995; Kagan & Lamb, 1987; Tangney & Fischer, 1995). The development of higher-order emotions is integral to under-standing other people, the social world, and oneself (Dunn, 1988; 1993).

The expression of higher-order emotions is linked to a new appreciation of standards, development of internalization of rules, expectations of approval and disapproval, increased salience of social relationships, and the development of a sense of self. Because self-development occurs in relation to increased aware-ness of others, vulnerability and suffering in others as well as the self assumes significance. The study of these emotions has revealed previously unidentified social maturity in young children, as seen for example, in their expressions of empathy (Zahn-Waxler, Robinson, & Emde, 1992), or guilt and shame (Cole, Barrett, & Zahn-Waxler, 1992).

Emotion understanding

Emotion understanding includes children's abilities to: (1) recognize and label emotions; (2) identify situational determinants; (3) use information to infer emotional states of others; and (4) recognize outcomes and consequences of emotions. This understanding is evidenced both in children's language and beha-viors. Some preschool children's emotion language is remarkably sophisticated in natural contexts. Almost as soon as children begin to talk, they use emotion words in their everyday conversations with family members. Children as young as 3 can provide relevant causes and consequences of basic emotions, as well as the emotional goals and outcomes of situations. In familiar situations, young children learn: (1) the meanings of emotion words; (2) the contexts that elicit particular emotions; (3) to anticipate the consequences of emotions; and (4) to use emotion language to regulate their own and others' emotions. These capa-cities have direct implications for the quality of children's social relationships.

Socialization of emotion language may differ for young boys and girls. Mothers are more likely to discuss the causes and consequences of emotions with their preschool boys, whereas with girls they focus more on the emotional states and reactions themselves (Fivush, 1989; 1991). In so doing, mothers may be orienting girls more to an interpersonal approach to emotions and also teaching sensitivity to their own and others' emotions. In contrast, mothers may be orienting boys more toward a problem-solving approach to emotions and also teaching about emotional control. With regard to anger, mothers more often accept anger and retaliation as an appropriate response to others' anger in their boys, whereas girls are encouraged to resolve anger by re-establishing the damaged relationship (Fivush, 1989; 1991). Mothers' and fathers' references to emotions are more frequent and varied with daughters than sons, particularly with regard to emotions of sadness and dislike (Adams, Kuebli, Boyle, & Fivush, 1995).

Several aspects of emotion understanding and role-taking have been identified as predictors of social competence. These include children's abilities to identify others' emotions (Cassidy et al., 1992; Dunn & Brown, 1994), to label correctly facial expressions (Cassidy et al., 1992; Denham, McKinley, Couchard, & Holt, 1990), and to use personal information to infer emotions of others (Gnepp, 1989). Emotional role-taking and knowledge of caregiver scripts predict caregiving behaviors toward siblings in preschool children (Garner, Jones, & Palmer, 1994). Development of moral sensibility has been linked to early individual differences in emotion understanding (Dunn, Brown, & Maguire, 1995).

Socialization of emotion

Affective dimensions of the parent–child relationship and family processes also play a role in children's understanding, expression, and regulation of emotion. Through appropriate parental expression of emotion and encouragement of emotional expression in offspring, children may better learn to identify others' emotions, understand the eliciting contexts, and express their own feelings—hence, influencing their social competence. Parents' expressiveness with children (Cassidy et al., 1992), particularly expression of positive emotion (Denham, Renwick, & Holt, 1991), is associated with social competence. In contrast, expressions of negative affect in the family (Dunn & Brown, 1994) and of anger by the mother (Denham, Zollar, & Couchard, 1994), have been linked to children's lowered understanding of emotions and less negotiation in conflict.

Familial emotional expressiveness also has been examined as a predictor of early adolescent social and psychological adjustment (Bronstein et al., 1993). Nonhostile expression of emotion within the family appears to provide a buffer against problems in transition to middle school, indicated in peer popularity, positive self-concept in girls, and positive social behavior in boys. *Mutual* influences of parent and child emotion upon each other are also of interest. There is evidence, for example, that parent and adolescent distress are reciprocally related across time, even after earlier emotional status is controlled (Ge et al., 1995).

PROSOCIAL DEVELOPMENT

Prosocial behavior is voluntary behavior intended to benefit another. It includes sharing, helping, comforting, and cooperation. Prosocial behavior has been of interest in its own right, and as an index of social competence in children. Many studies document the constructive nature of these activities and the positive consequences regarding the child's functioning in the peer group, although prosocial behavior is not invariably linked to good peer relations (e.g. see Wentzel & Asher, 1995). Prosocial development became a major research topic in the late 1960s and 1970s. Initially, primary emphasis was placed on: (1) developmental progressions and (2) socialization experiences associated with individual differences in prosocial activity.

Socialization practices shown to promote concern for the welfare of others have included modeling, reinforcement, discussion of others' feelings, role-playing, appeals to the feelings of others following rule violations, and also a family atmosphere of warmth, affection, and low conflict (see reviews by Eisenberg & Fabes, in press; Grusec & Lytton, 1988; Maccoby & Martin, 1983; Radke-Yarrow, Zahn-Waxler, & Chapman, 1983). Current research in this area emphasizes, in addition, the role of parental emotions, sometimes extreme, as distress stimuli that may alter the nature of empathy in their children. Examination of empathy in children of depressed caregivers, for example, indicates that extremes of parental distress sometimes elicit strong expressions of concern in offspring (Radke-Yarrow et al., 1994; Zahn-Waxler, Cole, & Barrett, 1991). However, this may not continue in the long term and may interfere with peer relations. Children exposed to depressed caregivers (Denham, Zahn-Waxler, Cummings, & Iannotti, 1991) and who witness higher-level maternal sadness or anger (both are emotions associated with parental depression; Denham, Renwick-DeBardi, & Hughes, 1994) are less prosocial with peers and in the classroom.

Many developmental studies of prosocial behavior, including those that have used meta-analytic approaches, document increases with age in children's prosocial behavior (see reviews by Eisenberg & Fabes, in press; Radke-Yarrow et al., 1983). Early conceptualizations focused on young children's egocentrism, impulsivity, and dependency, and hence provided a view of children as incapable of sympathy and compassion. Most developmental studies have made use of age cross-sectional, rather than longitudinal, research designs, and initially young children were mainly excluded from research samples. However, when they were eventually studied, remarkably early origins of concern for others were demonstrated. Our longitudinal studies, guided by Hoffman's (1975) developmental theory integrating the roles of social cognition, emotion, environment, and biology, focused on pivotal transitions in the second year of life

(Zahn-Waxler & Radke-Yarrow, 1982; Zahn-Waxler, Radke-Yarrow, Wagner, & Chapman, 1992; Zahn-Waxler, Robinson et al., 1992).

These studies confirmed the emergence of empathy and prosocial behaviors during the second year of life. There is a transition period during which self-distress wanes, caring behaviors toward victims in distress become more frequent and varied, and sympathetic concern is expressed. These patterns are present when children cause, as well as witness, another's distress. That is, reparative behaviors and remorse for wrongdoing, indicative of early conscience, appear to be on a developmental trajectory parallel to that for compassionate behavior and empathic concern when children are not responsible for others' distress. Follow-up research has identified both genetic influence (Zahn-Waxler, Robinson et al., 1992, 1997) and socialization experiences (Robinson, Zahn-Waxler, & Emde, 1994) that alter the course of prosocial, empathic development. Cumulatively, these studies also confirm the early emergence of sex differences favoring girls in the expression of nurturing behaviors toward others in need.

There has been an increased emphasis on the role of emotion in prosocial development, particularly the emotions of empathy, sympathy and personal distress. The focus in measurement has been both on overt emotion expressions and different patterns of arousal reflected in autonomic nervous system activity thought to be indicative of emotional responses to others' distress (Eisenberg et al., 1988; 1989). In Eisenberg's work, heart-rate deceleration has served as a marker of an other-oriented focus (i.e. attention to the victim's state and needs) in sympathy-inducing contexts (Eisenberg et al., 1991). In these studies, heart-rate deceleration in sympathy-inducing contexts has been associated with empathy and prosocial behavior, whereas heart-rate acceleration more often reflects self-arousal that serves as an index of personal distress.

Personal distress and empathic concern for the victim are viewed as opposites in some conceptualizations of the role of emotion in prosocial development. The contrasting patterns of findings just cited support such a conceptualization. However, others take the position that this contrast need not be so sharply drawn and that the two emotional patterns may not always be in opposition (Zahn-Waxler & Radke-Yarrow, 1990). Under some circumstances, the ability to focus on others, *in conjunction with* anxiety or self-distress, may result in particularly potent forms of empathy (Zahn-Waxler, Cole, Welsh, & Fox, 1995). While 5-year-old girls were found to be more prosocial than boys and to show greater heart-rate deceleration in sympathy-inducing contexts, they also showed overall higher autonomic arousal reflecting anxiety (as indexed by heart rate and skin conductance). This co-occurrence of concern for others and self-distress is also more common in girls than boys in the first years of life (Zahn-Waxler, Robinson et al., 1992) at the point in development when girls also begin to show more prosocial behaviors than boys. In other work, fearfulness (a form of self-distress) predicts empathy at age 7 (Rothbart, Ahadi, & Hershey, 1994). Young children who cry more often are also more prosocial in response to the distress of peers

(Farver & Branstetter, 1994). Cumulatively, these studies of young children indicate that self-distress or personal distress is not invariably an affective state that interferes with empathic concern for others.

Research on the psychophysiology of empathy and prosocial behavior illustrates a growing interest in the biological substrates. Hoffman's (1975) theory implicated the presence of a precursor of empathy at birth, evidenced in the reflexive crying of newborns in response to other infant cries (Sagi & Hoffman, 1976; Simner, 1971). Some sociobiological explanations emphasize the selfish nature of altruism (Dawkins, 1976; Wilson, 1975). Self-sacrificing actions increase an animal's probability that its relatives, who share some of its genes, will survive and reproduce. Hence, even if prosocial acts lead an animal to perish, shared genes are passed on via relatives to future generations. Other sociobiologists have argued that altruism could have evolved through reciprocity, even when giver and receiver are not biologically related (Trivers, 1983): that is, histories of benefit build over time through processes of reciprocal exchange. In MacLean's (1985) view, empathy emerged with the evolution of mammals, developing in the familial context of extended family caregiving, and including patterns of affiliation and responsibility to others. Other approaches have focused on the neurological bases of emotional communication (e.g. Brothers, 1989) and neural circuitry, particularly with regard to the mediating role of the limbic system in the formation of attachments (Panksepp, 1986).

The biology of altruism has been considered in behavior genetics research, as well as in the psychophysiological studies cited. Adolescent and adult monozygotic and dizygotic twins have been compared on their self-reported empathy and altruism (Davis, Luce, & Kraus, 1994; Matthews, Batson, Horn, & Rosenman, 1981; Rushton et al., 1986). A heritable component is identified, suggesting a disposition toward kindness and caring, that characterizes some individuals more than others. The evidence extends downward in age to elementary school children (Segal, 1984) and preschool children (Zahn-Waxler, Robinson et al., 1992), with heritable influence in preschool children now evident in longitudinal as well as cross-sectional genetic analyses (Zahn-Waxler, Robinson, Schmitz, & Emde, 1996).

Evolutionary theories cannot be tested directly, and empirical evidence for biological influence is indirect. Functional unitary brain circuits are unlikely to be discovered for global constructs like altruism, empathy, and prosocial behavior (Panksepp, 1986). These diverse emotional and behavioral patterns may share outward similarities but are likely to arise from several distinguishable neural systems. A realistic research goal, however, is to continue to investigate genetic and environmental sources of influence, including how temperament interacts with socialization to yield individual differences in concern for others (Young, Fox, & Zahn-Waxler, 1996).

Before turning to discussion of antisocial development, other studies indicative of new research trends in the area of prosocial development deserve mention.

Conceptualizations of prosocial attitudes have now been expanded to include protection and concern for the environment (e.g. children's evaluations of polluting a waterway as a violation of a moral obligation; Kahn & Friedman, 1995). The role of intervention, emphasizing the influence of prosocial training on adolescent development, has been examined. Here, the effect of a school-based helper program (engaging in volunteer helping activities) was shown to influence adolescent self-image, attitudes, and behavior (Switzer et al., 1995). Children in the helper program showed positive changes, with effects specific to boys. Identification of personal qualities of highly altruistic adolescents has recently been considered. Care-exemplars were more likely to describe themselves in terms of moral personality traits and goals; view themselves as having closer continuity to past and future; think of themselves as incorporating ideals and parental images; and articulate theories of self (Hart & Fegley, 1995).

ANTISOCIAL DEVELOPMENT

Several schools of thought, including psychoanalytic and ethological approaches, contend that there is an instinct for aggression in humans as well as in animals. Hormones, physical characteristics, neurological factors, and genes, are all thought to play a role in the expression of aggression (see reviews by Coie & Dodge, 1998; Parke & Slaby, 1983). The catharsis hypothesis was developed to describe the proposal that these biologically based aggressive urges are reduced when people witness or commit real or symbolic acts of aggression. This position has not received support: a recent study, for example, indicated that toy gun play strongly predicted real aggression in young boys (Watson & Peng, 1992).

The view that aggression is primarily biologically based was challenged by learning theorists, who proposed that aggression resulted from environmentally imposed frustrations. The frustration–aggression hypothesis was modified when it was shown that frustration could have other outcomes and aggression, other causes. One revision of the hypothesis (Berkowitz, 1974) emphasizes the interaction of an aggressor's internal emotional state and the environment, and their own anger proneness (also see Cole, Zahn-Waxler, & Smith, 1994).

The culture, subculture, and family setting in which children are raised also influence tendencies toward antisocial behavior and violence (see reviews by Coie & Dodge, 1998; Parke & Slaby, 1983). Within the family, physical discipline, lack of warmth, lack of monitoring, escalating coercive exchanges, exposure to marital discord, and antisocial behavior in parents and siblings are all implicated in higher levels of aggression in children. Harsh discipline early in life predicts later aggression in children, controlling for temperament, socioeconomic status, and marital violence (Weiss, Dodge, Bates, & Pettit, 1992). Physical punishment, however, remains a common discipline technique. Spankings are still widely used with young children, with the majority of middle-class, US mothers spanking their children at least a few times a week (Holden, Coleman,

& Schmidt, 1995). This modeling of physical aggression and direct infliction of pain as normative behavior provides a potent stimulus for aggression.

Cognitive contributions to antisocial patterns include, for example, low IQ, learning, and attentional problems. While aggression is inversely related to intellectual functioning, stability of aggression is not attributable to its relation to intelligence (Huesmann, Eron, Lefkowitz, & Walder, 1984). Hostile attributions have also been linked to aggression. "Hostile attribution bias" refers to the fact that aggressive children are likely to perceive hostile intent in others in ambiguous situations. This bias is not unique to antisocial children. It is also present in depressed children (Quiggle, Garber, Panak, & Dodge, 1992). These depressed children differ, however, in that they attribute the negative ambiguous circumstances to something they have done—that is, they assume that they are at fault or to blame in some way. Research on attributions also has now been extended to consider *others'* attributions of aggressive children. Graham and Hoehn (1995), for example, examine when during development and under what circumstances other children begin to see aggressive children as responsible for their actions, as deserving more anger, less sympathy and help, and eliciting less social acceptance.

Development of antisocial patterns. Instrumental aggression emerges at the end of the first year of life, as infants begin to quarrel about possessions with siblings and peers. Temper tantrums and physical aggression diminish over the preschool years. Increasingly with age, children are more likely to resort to verbally aggressive tactics. Although the incidence of physical aggression declines with age, adolescents are not necessarily "better behaved" (Shaffer, 1994). Older children are more likely to engage in covert forms of aggression and antisocial conduct to express their anger or frustrations.

While fewer older children and adolescents engage in overt aggression, children who do continue may be more deviant, and their antisocial behavior more serious. Sociometric studies identify aggressive children, often rejected by peers and who form deviant subgroups, who are particularly at risk. Peer rejection and isolation place children at risk not only for depression, anxiety, and loneliness, but also for early school withdrawal, delinquency, and other externalizing problems (Coie et al., 1995; Hoza, Molina, Bukowski, & Sippola, 1995; Parker & Asher, 1993).

Several longitudinal studies now indicate that externalizing or "acting out" behaviors (i.e. oppositional, antisocial actions) of preschool children do not dissipate with time (Campbell, 1995; Campbell & Ewing, 1990; Caspi, Elder, & Bem, 1987; Cole et al., 1996; Pianta & Caldwell, 1990; Richman, Stevenson, & Graham, 1982; Rose, Rose, & Feldman, 1989; Zahn-Waxler, Iannotti, Cummings, & Denham, 1990). Early onset aggression, in particular, is likely to become entrenched and linked to multiple problems later in development. Precursors can be identified as early as infancy (Shaw, Keenan, & Vondra, 1994). Disruptive behavior in kindergarten predicts aggression between the ages of 10 and 12, as well as early onset of delinquency (Tremblay, Masse, Vitaro, & Dobkin, 1995). Antisocial behavior and impulsivity at ages 8 to 10 predict later delinquency (Farrington, 1995).

Sex differences in antisocial patterns. Although aggression is stable over time in children of both sexes, it may be more stable and predictive of later antisocial patterns in males than females (Huesmann et al., 1984; Olweus, 1981). Males are more physically and verbally aggressive from an early age onward and are likely to become targets of aggression. These sex differences are presumed to reflect complex interactions of biology, family, and culture. It is noteworthy, however, that sex differences in aggression are present well before obvious biological differences (e.g. in testosterone levels, body size, muscle mass).

Males have been studied more than females because of their higher rates of violence, antisocial and delinquent activities. However, antisocial behavior is increasing in females, at least in the United States, including the use of weapons; and some forms of it may be more likely go undetected (Zahn-Waxler, 1993). Women physically abuse children as often as men. Antisocial behavior in some girls may be seen in their harsh treatment of siblings left in their care. Normatively, young adult males report higher levels of physical and verbal aggression, but not more anger than females (Buss & Perry, 1992). The direct translation of hostility from the emotion experienced (i.e. anger) to the behavior overtly expressed (i.e. aggression), thus appears to be less common in females than males. This gender difference raises important developmental questions as to why frustration (commonly reflected in anger, according to the frustration–aggression hypothesis) more often leads to direct expression of aggressive behavior in males than females.

Aggression is most commonly characterized as behavior intended to injure others, with hostile intent implied. Often the focus has been on physical aggression. Crick and Grotpeter (1995) have proposed that when children attempt to inflict harm on peers by aggressing, they do so in ways that damage or thwart goals valued by their peer groups. Boys tend to harm others through physical, and sometimes verbal, aggression. These behaviors are consistent with goals of instrumentality and dominance, shown to be important for boys (see review by Block, 1984). Salient goals for girls pertain to relational issues (e.g. establishing close interpersonal ties). Aggressive behavior of girls would thus be more likely to focus on behaviors intended to damage friendships or create feelings of exclusion by the peer group.

Elementary school girls show more relational aggression than boys (Crick & Grotpeter, 1995). Moreover, relationally aggressive girls are at risk for adjustment problems (i.e. they are more often rejected, lonely, depressed, and isolated). Sex-linked patterns of relational aggression have also been observed during the preschool period (Crick, Casas, & Mosher, in press). Relational aggression is not always more common in females than males, and in some cultures males also may show a lot: for example, Italian boys (Tomada & Schneider, in press).

High arousal, including autonomic arousal (Zahn-Waxler et al., 1995) and the value placed on interpersonal relationships, may divert girls from continued antisocial activity early in development. Anger/aggression is associated with guilt, shame, and reparative actions for girls more than boys, as early as the preschool years (Cummings et al., 1986; Zahn-Waxler et al., 1991; and Zahn-Waxler & Robinson, 1995). Young girls appear to experience more internal distress regarding their "externalizing" emotions. In the early, classic research of Goodenough (1931), girls showed a more marked decrease in anger across the preschool years than did boys. This tendency may reflect a more pronounced presence in girls of feelings of responsibility and anxiety about harming others.

An internalized sense of responsibility can be viewed as one factor that prevents antisocial patterns. While possibly more common in females than males, it is obviously present in many young males as well. Eysenck and colleagues (Eysenck, 1977; Eysenck & Gudjonsson, 1989) note that the development of a strong conscience is critical to socialized behavior. Conditioned anticipatory fear is an incentive for individuals to avoid antisocial stimuli associated with punishment. Increasingly, there is evidence for subtypes of antisocial individuals, including a group that shows high autonomic arousal. Until recently, research on biological substrates of antisocial patterns have emphasized patterns of autonomic *underarousal* (see reviews by Lahey et al., 1993; Quay, 1993). Raine and colleagues (Raine, Venables, & Williams, 1995; 1996) report that antisocial males who are also highly conditionable, and hence more prone to fearfulness, are more likely to desist from antisocial activity in the future. A similar pattern has been found for a subgroup of antisocial boys who show de-escalation of aggression over time. These were boys who had initially shown high levels of guilt (Stouthamer-Loeber et al., 1993). Moffitt (1993) has also described an antisocial subgroup in adolescence who do not go on to manifest criminal behavior in adulthood. This adolescent-limited subgroup may differ psychophysiologically from life-course persistent, antisocial individuals.

These biological differences may provide clues about factors that serve to protect some individuals from continuing maladaptive, antisocial patterns over time. Differences in autonomic activity and expressive styles of subgroups of antisocial children can appear as early as the preschool years, with corresponding implications for differences in later developmental trajectories (Cole et al., 1996). While the emphasis here is on biological substrates, it is important to recognize the relevance also of environmental factors that alter antisocial patterns. Aggressive toddlers of mothers who used proactive childrearing practices (e.g. anticipating the child's point of view; exerting modulated, respectful control; providing structure and organization during peer play) showed reduced aggression and other externalizing problems three years later (Zahn-Waxler et al., 1990).

A DEVELOPMENTAL PSYCHOPATHOLOGY
PERSPECTIVE

Much of the research on aggression and antisocial development illustrates the value of a developmental psychopathology perspective. Developmental clinical and psychiatric research has enriched and informed work on normative social and emotional development, and vice versa, across a variety of domains. This integration of theory and research on adaptive and maladaptive social–emotional development reflects a major, important recent change. Here we consider additional examples of this approach.

Psychiatric disorders are more often studied (as diagnostic categories) within a biomedical framework, while emotional and behavioral problems are more often studied (as dimensions) by psychologists. Often, little or no overlap is assumed, as disorders are characterized as more rare in occurrence. Moreover, studies of psychiatric samples often appear to be based on the assumption that disorders emerging in adulthood appear *de novo* or "out of the blue" with little or no developmental history. A recent epidemiological, longitudinal study (Newman et al., 1996) focused on psychiatric disorder in a birth cohort of young adults (mainly depression, anxiety, substance abuse, and antisocial patterns). Mental health data were collected at ages 11, 13, 15, 18, and 21 using standardized diagnostic instruments. Mental disorders increased over time, reaching a high of around 40% in later adolescence and young adulthood. (This high rate of disorders, in fact, accords with those reported by other epidemiological studies.) Only 10% of the cases were newly diagnosed at age 21. The great majority of cases had a developmental history, and those cases with a developmental history showed greater impairment at age 21. Even though most of the adolescents studied did not have diagnosable problems at any given age, subclinical signs at these time points would likely have been present, as reflected in problematic social and emotional relationships with families, teachers, and peers.

The Newman et al. (1996) study demonstrates the existence of developmental precursors of several adult disorders and suggests chronicity of emotional and behavioral problems that eventually culminate in adult disorders. There likely exists substantial overlap between problems traditionally assessed as dimensions in psychology (i.e. on a quantitative continuum) and psychiatric disorders that are qualitatively assessed in terms of diagnostic categories. This overlap provides an important reminder of the need for a multidisciplinary approach and the integration of quantitative and qualitative approaches in order to understand the adaptive and maladaptive nature of social functioning from a developmental perspective.

We consider next some illustrations of this developmental interface, including research on normative development and the implications for understanding maladaptation as well as adjustment. Two domains are emphasized. One includes sex differences in the development of different types of psychopathology. The other includes the roles of parental depression and marital discord as risk factors in children's social–emotional development. Other risk factors and problems, both constitutional and environmental, could have been chosen as well. Several other areas are not covered here, due to space constraints. Examples include: (1) difficult temperament (Carlson, Jacobvitz, & Sroufe, 1995; Caspi et al., 1995; Caspi & Silva, 1995); and (2) child maltreatment, including the impact of physical, sexual, verbal, and emotional abuse on children's family, peer relations, and friendship patterns (Dodge, Pettit, & Bates, 1994; Parker & Herrera, 1996; Rogosch, Cicchetti, & Aber, 1995).

Sex differences in psychopathology

Sex differences in forms of psychopathology are well documented (Earls, 1987; Eme, 1992). By the time of school entry, rates of externalizing disorders (e.g. oppositional, anti-social, delinquent) are substantially higher in boys than girls, while internalizing disorders (e.g. anxiety, depression) are similar. Boys are overrepresented in disruptive behavior disorders (Robins, 1991). When girls do have externalizing problems, they are more likely to have internalizing problems as well. By adolescence and adulthood, females are two to three times more likely to experience depression and anxiety.

Gender is thus an important organizing construct for investigating the interplay of biology, environment, and cultural processes that shape the different expressions of psychological distress in males and females and may reflect exaggerations of normative patterns (Zahn-Waxler, 1993). Externalizing and internalizing problems often reflect male and female stereotypes. Stereotypes held by both children and adults reflect social constructions that equate sex-role characteristics, present in the extreme, with the different types of problems relatively more likely to characterize males (e.g. aggressive, active, strong, careless, impulsive) and females (e.g. prosocial, submissive, passive, weak, helpless). Even preschool children hold strong gender-based stereotypes, not only about different roles and expectations, but also about emotions, differentially associated with externalizing and internalizing problems (i.e. more anger in males and more sadness in females) (Karbon, Fabes, Carlo, & Martin, 1992). Stereotypes are particularly strong for sadness, including the belief that males are deficient in their capacity to experience sorrow. While these perceptions may be characterized as stereotypes, they may also be rooted in children's realistic appraisals of the emotions they observe in others.

Child characteristics.   The most consistently identified "normative" sex differences pertain to higher levels of aggression, activity, and impulsiveness in boys (see reviews by Block, 1984; Coie & Dodge, 1998; Parke & Slaby, 1983), and higher levels of nurturing patterns and interpersonal sensitivity in girls (e.g. empathy, prosocial behavior, and emotion understanding) (see reviews by Eisenberg & Fabes, in press; Radke-Yarrow et al., 1983). Girls are better able to engage in affective perspective-taking (Denham et al., 1990) and to control feelings of disappointment and display positive emotion instead (Cole, 1986; Cole et al., 1994; Davis, 1995). Girls also show greater discomfort and remorse following transgression (Kochanska, DeVet, Goldman, Murray, & Putnam, 1994), internalization of standards (Zahn-Waxler, Schmitz et al., 1996), empathic concern (Zahn-Waxler, Radke-Yarrow et al., 1992; Zahn-Waxler, Robinson et al., 1992), and emotion regulation (Zahn-Waxler, Schmitz, Fulker, Robinson, & Emde, 1996).

In resolving conflicts with friends, the assertions of girls are more frequently accompanied by rationales than is the case for boys (Hartup et al., Ogawa, 1993). This difference may reflect greater social maturity, or it may indicate greater insecurity and need to justify one's actions. Preschool girls endorse more feelings of sadness and fear in challenging situations, whereas boys are more likely to emphasize anger (Zahn-Waxler, Schmitz et al., 1996). Girls interact in smaller groups than boys, establish more intimate relationships, issue fewer direct commands, and have greater difficulty influencing others (see review by Kavanaugh & Hops, 1994)—patterns that may eventually lead to depressed, unassertive behavioral styles. Early biological advantage in girls may lead them to be more receptive of others' socialization messages and to regulate negative emotion and disruptive behavior. At the same time, it may create greater risk for overregulation of emotion and internalization of distress that is more characteristic of depressed mood and anxiety (Keenan & Shaw, in press).

Socialization.   A diathesis toward different types of emotional and behavioral problems in boys and girls reflects socialization experiences as well as existing predispositions. Several early experiences may function to exaggerate normative sex differences in antisocial versus other-oriented, self-sacrificial behaviors so as to create differential risk. Male children often are more highly valued than female children, which is seen most clearly in families and cultures that practice female infanticide and selective abortion when the (female) sex of the child is known. It is also manifest in subtler forms that might affect the lowered self-esteem more common in females than males and implicated in internalizing problems such as depression (Harter, 1993) and the inflated self-esteem associated with conduct problems (a pattern identified in mainly male samples; Baumeister, Smart, & Boden, 1996).

When young children make causal attributions for their own success and failure on performance tasks, boys show a self-enhancing pattern, whereas girls' attributions are more self-derogating (Burgner & Hewstone, 1993). This sex difference in children may be linked to parental socialization practices regarding achievement issues (Alessandri & Lewis, 1993). Three-year-old girls who achieved as much as boys received more negative evaluations as well as less praise and acknowledgement of their accomplishments from their middle-class parents. By overlooking their success, parents may discourage the incorporation of success into the self-concept in girls and make them less likely to attribute success to their own ability. In a longitudinal study of consistency and change from early adolescence to early adulthood, self-esteem tended to increase over time for males but decrease for females (Block & Robins, 1993).

Shyness and dependency (and the lack of assertiveness implied) are treated more positively in girls than boys (Simpson & Stevenson-Hinde, 1985). Mothers are more likely to support anger expressions in infant and preschool boys than girls (Malatesta & Haviland, 1982; Fivush, 1989; 1991). Assertions of young girls are more likely to be negated by their parents than those of boys (Kerig, Cowan, & Cowan, 1993). Mothers of 2-year-olds are more likely to point out to their daughters than sons the harmful consequences of their aggression (Smetana, 1989). Identical levels of aggression in 3-year-olds are judged to be *less* aggressive and *more* indicative of nurturance when observed in boys (Condrey & Ross, 1985). In other ways as well, including discouragement of exploration of the physical environment in girls and encouragement of sex-stereotyped activities more generally (see review by Siegal, 1987), gender roles may be constructed by caregivers that encourage boys and girls, under certain conditions, to adopt the more extreme behaviors reflected in externalizing and internalizing problems. Images of "appropriate," "acceptable" behaviors in males and females in the media also encourage this diathesis. Subgroups of males and females, who by temperament are already predisposed in a particular direction, may be particularly vulnerable. This process illustrates again the value of a transactional perspective in tracing different developmental outcomes.

Children's perceptions of their socialization experiences may also be implicated in the types of problems they develop. Discrepancies in adolescents' and parents' perceptions, for example, have been examined (Ohannessian, Lerner, Lerner, & von Eye, 1995). While both boys and girls perceived lower levels of family cohesion than did their parents, girls perceived the lowest levels of family adjustment. These discrepant perceptions were related to adolescents' anxiety and depressive symptomatology, particularly for girls. Girls may be more attuned to, and internally distressed by, disturbances in the family environment. Boys also report more "forgetting about" parental negativity than do girls (Herman & McHale, 1993). This may indicate a way in which aversive family conditions are denied or dismissed by males, whereas females more often ruminate (Nolen-Hoeksema, 1987; Nolen-Hoeksema & Girgus, 1994) or dwell on, and hence internalize, negative socialization messages. Early predictors of depressive symptoms in young women are more likely than in young men to reflect autocentric concerns: that is, oversocialization and introspective concern with the self (Gjerde, 1995).

It is noteworthy that much of the research relevant to these arguments about development of different trajectories for different problems in males and females is based on normative samples. Average, "expectable" differences in boys and girls, and the ways they are treated by families and the larger culture are described. In the extreme, and in conjunction with particular conditions of risk, these normative variations in social and emotional development may evolve into different types of problems for males and females.

Family risk conditions: Parental depression and marital discord

A large literature documents the generalization that parental depression has an adverse outcome on offspring (Downey & Coyne, 1990; Gelfand & Teti, 1990; Zahn-Waxler, 1995). Processes of modeling, contagion, direct tuition, maladaptive childrearing practices, as well as genetic factors may be implicated in transmission patterns. While maternal depression has mainly been emphasized in research, Goodman and colleagues (Goodman, Brogan, Lynch, & Fielding, 1993) report that a combination of maternal and paternal psychopathology and marital status best predicts children's behavior outcomes.

Research continues to confirm an early impact of parental depression on offspring that begins early in life. The (dis)organizing role of emotions has received increased emphasis. Infants of depressed mothers show more facial expressions of sadness and anger as well as less interest than infants of nondepressed mothers in face-to-face play (Pickens & Field, 1993). Mothers' simulations of depressed affect with toddlers lead to the latter's withdrawal, negativity, and lack of focus (Seiner & Gelfand, 1995). The aversive, disorganizing nature of this experience for young children implicates processes of contagion as well as modeling in the transmission of negative affect. Some children may be particularly prone to absorb negative parental emotion, indicating an interaction of biological vulnerability and environmental pressures. Infants of depressed mothers show right frontal EEG asymmetry (Field, Fox, Pickens, & Nawrocki, 1995)— a pattern of brain electrical activity similar to that found in inhibited infants and chronically depressed adults. Malatesta and Wilson (1988) discuss the development of biases in the expression of particular discrete emotions. These emotions may become entrenched over time to reflect prevailing personality characteristics or moods that become manifest in specific disorders. The observed distress of some infants of depressed caregivers may indicate early developing sadness and lack of interest in the external environment, which are the principal emotions implicated in depression.

Parental depression does not invariably have a negative impact on offspring; hence, questions regarding protective factors have been of interest. In longitudinal research on 2-year-old children of depressed mothers (Zahn-Waxler et al., 1990), some depressed mothers used childrearing practices identified in other studies as promoting children's social competence. Problems of children of these mothers were more likely to dissipate over time and were less likely to culminate in psychiatric symptoms at the time of school entry. While depressed mothers set a negative tone during interactions with their 5- to 7-year olds

(Nolen-Hoeksema, Wolfson, Mumme, & Guskin, 1995), the strongest effects on child outcomes were found in relation to maternal hostility, negativity, and lack of encouragement of mastery, *regardless* of maternal depression. Negative outcomes included helplessness, lack of competence, and lack of active problem solving—potential precursors of a depressogenic style. Hostile family interaction styles also predict later destructive problem-solving behavior (Rueter & Conger, 1995). Because parental depression and family hostility, especially marital discord, frequently co-occur, their conjoint influences on children's social–emotional development have increasingly been studied.

Harold, Fincham, Osborne, and Conger (in press) report that marital distress plays a significant role in whether parental depression predicts problems for offspring. Maternal depression, shown to predict symptomatology in adolescence, no longer had an influence when marital discord was taken into account. There is substantial documentation of the deleterious effects of parental anger and discord on children of all ages, beginning in infancy (see review by Cummings & Davies, 1994). Parental hostility and discord elicit anger and aggression, fearfulness, emotion dysregulation, and excessive caregiving/peacemaking activities in offspring, and are consistently linked to increased emotional and behavioral problems in children. Mutually hostile marital patterns observed during conflict resolutions predict teachers' ratings of children's internalizing and externalizing problems three years later (Katz & Gottman, 1993). Interparental conflict represents an environmental stress that may even affect biological systems (Belsky, Steinberg, & Draper, 1991): for example, it predicts early menarche (Wierson, Long, & Forehand, 1993).

More intense parental conflicts lead to greater negative affect and perceived threat, as seen in a study of 11- and 12-year-olds (Grych & Fincham, 1993). Children were especially likely to cope by intervening in the conflict and to express shame and fear when the conflict pertained to the child. Explanations that absolved children of blame ameliorated these effects to some degree. In an examination of the organizing role of emotions, mood inductions were performed with 4- to 8-year-olds prior to exposure to interadult anger. The induction of negative emotion increased distress, whereas positive emotions reduced distress reactions and increased children's positive expectations about future adult interactions (Davies & Cummings, 1995).

Maritally distressed dyads show different patterns of interaction with their boys and girls as early as infancy (McHale, 1995). Sex of child becomes an important moderating variable in the literature on martial discord and divorce. Until recently, it has been commonly argued that boys are more adversely affected by hostile family climates, as boys are more directly exposed to the conflicts and girls more shielded. At younger ages, boys are sometimes more likely than girls to act out their distress, overtly displaying disruptive behaviors and other externalizing problems. More recent research, particularly with adolescents, indicates the development of significant problems for females, sometimes more than in males (Davies & Windle, in press). Adolescent girls show greater vulnerability to family discord, with discord mediating the development of delinquency and alcohol problems in these girls. Because young girls are more likely to react in socialized ways (e.g. as caregivers and peacemakers during family discord) (Vuchinich, Emery, & Cassidy, 1988), they may appear more resilient, and their distress may be internalized and less likely to be detected at the time of conflict. In research on the effects of divorce and reconstituted families, as well, young boys initially appear to be more affected, whereas problems in girls become manifest later (Hetherington, Cox, & Cox, 1985; Vuchinich, Hetherington, Vuchinich, & Clingempeel, 1991).

CONCLUSIONS

To reiterate, this is an exciting era in which to be studying social and emotional development in periods of infancy, childhood, and adolescence. The conceptual and paradigmatic changes have advanced our capabilities far beyond what could have been envisioned a few decades ago. There is still a need for further development of additional and alternative conceptual models and research strategies. While most developmental scientists adhere, in principle, to transactional models of developmental processes, optimal translation into research designs is less commonplace. It is very rare for any given study to include the requisite paradigms to measure environment and culture simultaneously, at comparable levels of precision, accuracy, and rigor. Approaches are needed that combine the best features of both genetic and nongenetic research designs if the scientific advantages of multivariate, transactional, interdisciplinary research are to be fully realized.

REFERENCES

Adams, S., Kuebli, J., Boyle, P. A., & Fivush, R. (1995). Gender differences in parent–child conversations about past emotions: A longitudinal investigation. *Sex Roles, 33*, 309–323.

Alessandri, S. M., & Lewis, M. (1993). Parental evaluation and its relation to shame and pride in young children. *Sex Roles, 29*, 335–343.

American Psychiatric Association. (1994). *Diagnostic and statistical manual of mental disorders* (4th ed.). Washington, DC: Author.

Arcus, D., & Kagan, J. (1995, March). *Temperamental contributions to social behavior.* Paper presented at the Biennial Meetings of the Society for Research in Child Development. Indianapolis, IN.

Asendorpf, J. B. (1994). The malleability of behavioral inhibition: A study of individual developmental functions. *Developmental Psychology, 30*, 912–919.

Baumeister, R. F., Smart, L., & Boden, J. M. (1996). Relation of threatened egotism to violence and aggression: The dark side of high self-esteem. *Psychological Review, 103*, 5–33.

Bell, R. Q. (1968). A reinterpretation of the direction of effects in studies of socialization. *Psychological Review, 75*, 81–95.

Belsky, J., Steinberg, L., & Draper, P. (1991). Childhood experience, interpersonal development, and reproductive strategy: An evolutionary theory of socialization. *Child Development, 62*, 647–670.

Benoit, D., & Parker, K.C.H. (1994). Stability and transmission of attachment across three generations. *Child Development, 65*, 1444–1456.

Berkowitz, L. (1974). Some determinants of impulsive aggression: Role of mediated association
with reinforcement for aggression. *Psychological Review, 81*, 165–176.

Berndt, T. J., & Keefe, K. (1995). Friends' influence on adolescents' adjustment to school. *Child
Development, 66*, 1312–1329.

Bierman, K. L., & Wargo, J. B. (1995). Predicting the longitudinal course associated with aggressive-
rejected, aggressive (nonrejected), and rejected (nonaggressive) status. *Development and Psychopathology, 7*, 669–682.

Black, B., & Logan, A. (1995). Links between communication patterns in mother–child, father–
child, and child–peer interactions and children's social status. *Child Development, 66*, 255–271.

Block, J. H. (1984). *Sex role identity and ego development*. San Francisco: Jossey-Bass.

Block, J., & Robins, R. W. (1993). A longitudinal study of consistency and change in self-esteem
from early adolescence to early adulthood. *Child Development, 64*, 901–923.

Bolger, K. E., Patterson, C. J., Thompson, W. W., & Kupersmidt, J. B. (1995). Psychosocial
adjustment among children experiencing persistent and intermittent family economic hardship.
Child Development, 66, 1107–1129.

Boulton, M. J., & Smith, P. K. (1994). Bully/victim problems in middle-school children: Stability,
self-perceived competence, peer perceptions and peer acceptance. *British Journal of Developmental Psychology, 12*, 315–329.

Bronfenbrenner, U. (1979). *The ecology of human development*. Cambridge, MA: Harvard University Press.

Bronstein, P., Fitzgerald, M., Briones, M., Pieniadz, J., & D'Ari, A. (1993). Family emotional
expressiveness as a predictor of early adolescent social and psychological adjustment. *Journal
of Early Adolescence, 13*, 448–471.

Brothers, L. (1989). A biological perspective on empathy. *American Journal of Psychiatry, 146*,
10–19.

Burgner, D., & Hewstone, M. (1993). Young children's causal attributions for success and failure:
"Self-enhancing" boys and "self-derogating" girls. *British Journal of Developmental Psychology, 11*, 125–129.

Buss, A. H., & Perry, M. (1992). The aggression questionnaire. *Journal of Personality and Social
Psychology, 63*, 452–459.

Campbell, S. B. (1995). Behavior problems in preschool children: A review of recent research.
Journal of Child Psychology and Psychiatry and Allied Disciplines, 36(1), 113–149.

Campbell, S. B., & Ewing, L. J. (1990). Follow-up of hard-to-manage preschoolers: Adjustment
at age 9 and predictors of continuing symptoms. *Journal of Child Psychology and Psychiatry,
3*, 871–889.

Campos, J. (1995). Foreword. In J. P. Tangney & K. W. Fischer (Eds.), *Self-conscious emotions:
The psychology of shame, guilt, embarrassment, and pride* (pp. ix-xi). New York: Guilford.

Carlson, E. A., Jacobvitz, D., & Sroufe, L. A. (1995). A developmental investigation of inattentive-
ness and hyperactivity. *Child Development, 66*, 37–54.

Carrey, N. J., Butter, H. J., Persinger, M. A., & Bialik, R. J. (1995). Physiological and cognitive
correlates of child abuse. *Journal of the American Academy of Child and Adolescent Psychiatry,
34*, 1067–1075.

Caspi, A., Elder, G. H., & Bem, D. J. (1987). Moving against the world: Life course patterns of
explosive children. *Developmental Psychology, 23*, 308–313.

Caspi, A., Henry, B., McGee, R. O., Moffitt, T. E., & Silva, P. A. (1995). Temperamental origins
of child and adolescent behavior problems: From age three to fifteen. *Child Development, 66*,
55–68.

Caspi, A., & Silva, P. A. (1995). Temperamental qualities at age three predict personality traits in
young adulthood: Longitudinal evidence from a birth cohort. *Child Development, 66*, 486–498.

Cassidy, J., Parke, R. D., Butkovsky, L., & Braungart, J. M. (1992). Family–peer connections: The roles of emotional expressiveness within the family and children's understanding of emotions. *Child Development, 63*, 603–618.

Chen, X., Rubin, K. H., & Sun, Y. (1992). Social reputation and peer relationships in Chinese and Canadian children: A cross-cultural study. *Child Development, 63*, 1336–1343.

Coie, J., & Dodge, K.A. (1998). Aggression and antisocial behavior. In W. Damon (Series Ed.) & N. Eisenberg (Vol. Ed.), *Handbook of child psychology: Vol. 3. Social, emotional and personality development*, (5th ed.). New York: Wiley.

Coie, J., Terry, R., Lenox, K., Lochman, J., & Hyman, C. (1995). Childhood peer rejection and aggression as predictors of stable patterns of adolescent disorder. *Development and Psychopathology, 7*, 697–713.

Cole, P. M. (1986). Children's spontaneous control of facial expression. *Child Development, 57*, 1309–1321.

Cole, P. M., Barrett, K.D., & Zahn-Waxler, C. (1992). Emotion displays in two-year-olds during mishaps. *Child Development, 63*, 314–324.

Cole, P. M., Michel, M. K., & Teti, L. O. (1994). The development of emotion regulation and dysregulation: A clinical perspective. In N. A. Fox (Ed.), The development of emotion regulation: Biological and behavioral considerations. *Monographs of the Sciety for Research in Child Development, 59*(2–3, Serial No. 240).

Cole, P. M., Zahn-Waxler, C., Fox, N. A., Usher, B. A., & Welsh, J. D. (1996). Individual differences in emotion regulation and behavior problems in preschool children. *Journal of Abnormal Psychology, 105*, 518–529.

Cole, P. M., Zahn-Waxler, C., & Smith, K. D. (1994). Expressive control during a disappointment: Variations related to preschoolers' behavior problems. *Developmental Psychology, 30*, 835–846.

Collins, W. A., & Gunnar, M. R. (1990). Social and personality development. *Annual Review of Psychology, 41*, 387–416.

Condrey, J. C., & Ross, D. F. (1985). Sex and aggression: The influence of gender label on the perception of aggression in children. *Child Development, 51*, 943–967.

Conger, R. D., Ge, X., Elder, G. H., Lorenz, F. O., & Simons, R. L. (1994). Economic stress, coercive family process, and developmental problems of adolescents. *Child Development, 65*, 541–561.

Crick, N. R., Casas, J. F., & Mosher, M. (in press). Relational and over-aggression in preschool. *Developmental Psychology.*

Crick, N. R., & Grotpeter, J. K. (1995). Relational aggression, gender, and social–psychological adjustment. *Child Development, 66*, 710–722.

Crick, N. R., & Ladd, G. W. (1993). Children's perceptions of their peer experiences: Attributions, loneliness, social anxiety, and social avoidance. *Developmental Psychology, 29*, 244–254.

Cummings, E. M., & Davies, P. (1994). *Children and marital conflict: The impact of family dispute and resolution.* New York: Guilford.

Cummings, E. M., Hollenbeck B., Iannotti, R. J., Radke-Yarrow, M., & Zahn-Waxler, C. (1986). Early organization of altruism and aggression: Developmental patterns and individual differences. In C. Zahn-Waxler, E. M. Cummings, & R. J. Iannotti (Eds.), *Altruism and aggression: Biological and social origins* (pp. 165–188). New York: Cambridge University Press.

Darwin, C. (1872). *The expression of the emotions in man and animal.* London: Murray.

Davies, P. T., & Cummings, E. M. (1995). Children's emotions as organizers of their reactions to interadult anger: A functionalist perspective. *Developmental Psychology, 31*, 677–684.

Davies, P. T., & Windle, M. (in press). Gender-specific pathways between maternal depressive symptoms, family discord, and adolescent adjustment. *Developmental Psychology.*

Davis, M. H., Luce, C., & Kraus, S. J. (1994). The heritability of characteristics associated with dispositional empathy. *Journal of Personality, 62*, 369–391.

Davis, T. L. (1995). Gender differences in masking negative emotions: Ability or motivation? *Developmental Psychology, 31*, 660–667.

Dawkins, R. (1976). *The selfish gene.* Oxford: Oxford University Press.

Deater-Deckard, K., Dodge, K. A., Bates, J. E., & Pettit, G. S. (in press). Physical discipline among African-American and European-American mothers: Links to children's externalizing behaviors. *Developmental Psychology.*

Denham, S. A., McKinley, M., Couchard, E. A., & Holt, R. (1990). Emotional and behavioral predictors of preschool peer ratings. *Child Development, 61,* 1145–1152.

Denham, S. A., Renwick, S. M., Holt, R. W. (1991). Working and playing together: Prediction of preschool social–emotional competence from mother–child interaction. *Child Development, 62,* 242–249.

Denham, S. A., Renwick-DeBardi, S., & Hughes, S. (1994). Emotional communication between mothers and preschoolers: Relations with emotional competence. *Merrill-Palmer Quarterly, 40,* 488–508.

Denham, S. A., Zahn-Waxler, C., Cummings, E. M., & Iannotti, R. (1991). Social competence in young children's peer relations: Patterns of development and change. *Child Psychiatry and Human Development, 22,* 29–44.

Denham, S. A., Zoller, D., & Couchard, E. A. (1994). Socialization of preschoolers' emotion understanding. *Developmental Psychology, 30,* 928–936.

Dishion, T. J., Andrews, D. W., & Crosby, L. (1995). Antisocial boys and their friends in early adolescence: Relationship characteristics, quality, and interactional process. *Child Development, 66,* 139–151.

Dodge, K. A., Pettit, G. S., & Bates, J. E. (1994). Socialization mediators of the relation between socioeconomic status and child conduct problems. *Child Development, 65,* 649–665.

Downey, G., & Coyne, J. C. (1990). Children of depressed parents: An integrative review. *Psychological Bulletin, 108,* 50–76.

Dunn, J. (1988). *The beginnings of social understanding.* Oxford: Blackwell.

Dunn, J. (1993). *Young children's close relationships: Beyond attachment.* Thousand Oaks, CA: Sage.

Dunn, J., & Brown, J. (1994). Affect expression in the family, children's understanding of emotions, and their interactions with others. *Merrill-Palmer Quarterly, 40,* 120–137.

Dunn, J., Brown, J. R., & Maguire, M. (1995). The development of children's moral sensibility: Individual differences and emotion understanding. *Developmental Psychology, 31,* 649–659.

Earls, F. (1987). Sex differences in psychiatric disorders: Origins and developmental influences. *Psychiatric Developments, 1,* 1–23.

Eisenberg, N., & Fabes, R. A. (in press). Prosocial development. In W. Damon (Series Ed.) & N. Eisenberg (Vol. Ed.), *Handbook of child psychology: Vol. 3. Social, emotional and personality development,* (5th ed.). New York: Wiley.

Eisenberg, N., Fabes, R. A., Miller, P. A., Fultz, J., Mathy, R. M., Shell, R., & Reno, R. R. (1989). The relations of sympathy and personal distress to prosocial behavior: A multimethod study. *Journal of Personality and Social Psychology, 57,* 55–66.

Eisenberg, N., Fabes, R. A., Nyman, M., Bernzweig, J., & Pinuelas, A. (1994). The relations of emotionality and regulation to children's anger-related reactions. *Child Development, 65,* 109–128.

Eisenberg, N., Fabes, R. A., Schaller, M., Carlo, G., & Miller, P. A. (1991). The relations of parental characteristics and practices to children's vicarious emotional responding. *Child Development, 62,* 1393–1408.

Eisenberg, N., Schaller, M., Fabes, R. A., Bustamante, D., Mathy, R. M., Shell, R., & Rhodes, K. (1988). The differentiation of personal distress and sympathy in children and adults. *Developmental Psychology, 24,* 766–775.

Ekman, P., & Friesen, W. V. (1978). *The facial action coding system (FACS): A technique for the measurement of facial action.* Palo Alto, CA: Consulting Psychologists Press.

Emde, R. N., Plomin, R., Robinson, J., Corley, R., DeFries, J., Fulker, D. W., Reznick, J. S., Campos, J., Kagan, J., & Zahn-Waxler, C. (1992). Temperament, emotion, and cognition at fourteen months: The MacArthur longitudinal twin study. *Child Development, 63,* 1437–1455.

Eme, R. F. (1992). Selective female affliction in the developmental disorders of childhood: A literature review. *Journal of Clinical Child Psychology, 21*, 354–364.

Eysenck, H. J. (1977). *Crime and personality* (3rd ed.). St Albans, UK: Paladin.

Eysenck, H. J., & Gudjonsson, G. H. (1989). *The causes and cures of criminality*. New York: Plenum.

Farrington, D. P. (1995). The development of offending and antisocial behavior from childhood: Key findings from the Cambridge study in delinquent development. *Journal of Child Psychology and Psychiatry, 36*, 929–964.

Farver, J. M., & Branstetter, W. H. (1994). Preschoolers' prosocial responses to their peers' distress. *Developmental Psychology, 30*, 334–341.

Field, T., Fox, N.A., Pickens, J., & Nawrocki, T. (1995). Relative right frontal EEG activation in 3- to 6-month-old infants of depressed mothers. *Developmental Psychology, 31*, 358–363.

Fivush, R. (1989). Exploring sex differences in the emotional content of mother–child conversations about the past. *Sex Roles, 20*, 675–691.

Fivush, R. (1991). Gender and emotion in mother–child conversations about the past. *Journal of Narrative and Life History, 1*, 325–341.

Fox, N. (Ed.). (1994). The development of emotion regulation: Biological and behavioral considerations. *Monographs of the Society for Research in Child Devlopment, 59*(2–3, Serial No. 240).

Garner, P. W., Jones, D. C., & Palmer, D. J. (1994). Social cognitive correlates of preschool children's sibling caregiving behavior. *Developmental Psychology, 30*, 905–911.

Ge, X., Conger, R. D., Cadoret, R. J., Neiderhiser, J. M., Yates, W., Troughton, E., & Stewart, M. A. (1996). The developmental interface between nature and nurture: A mutual influence model of child antisocial behavior and parent behaviors. *Developmental Psychology, 32*, 574–589.

Ge, X., Conger, R. D., Lorenz, F. O., Shanahan, M., & Elder, G. H., Jr. (1995). Mutual influences in parent and adolescent psychological distress. *Developmental Psychology, 31*, 406–419.

Gelfand, D. M., & Teti, D. M. (1990). The effects of maternal depression on children. *Clinical Psychology Review, 10*, 329–353.

Gjerde, P. F. (1995). Alternative pathways to chronic depressive symptoms in young adults: Gender differences in developmental trajectories. *Child Development, 66*, 1277–1300.

Gnepp, J. (1989). Personalized inferences of emotions and appraisals: Component processes and correlates. *Developmental Psychology, 25*, 277–288.

Goodenough, F. (1931). *Anger in young children*. Minneapolis, MN: University of Minnesota Press.

Goodman, S. H, Brogan, D., Lynch, M. E., & Fielding, B. (1993). Social and emotional competence in children of depressed mothers. *Child Development, 64*, 516–531.

Graham, S., & Hoehn, S. (1995). Children's understanding of aggression and withdrawal as social stigmas: An attributional analysis. *Child Development, 66*, 1143–1161.

Grusec, J., & Lytton, H. (1988). *Social development: History, theory, and research*. New York: Springer-Verlag.

Grych, J. H., & Fincham, F. D. (1993). Children's appraisals of marital conflict: Initial investigations of the cognitive–contextual framework. *Child Development, 64*, 215–230.

Harris, J. R. (1995). Where is the child's environment? A group socialization theory of development. *Psychological Review, 102*, 458–489.

Harold, G. T., Fincham, F. D., Osborne, L. N., & Conger, R. D. (in press). Mom and dad are at it again: Adolescent perceptions of marital conflict and adolescent psychological distress. *Developmental Psychology*.

Hart, C. H., DeWolf, D. M., Wozniak, P., & Burts, D. C. (1992). Maternal and paternal disciplinary styles: Relations with preschoolers' playground behavioral orientations and peer status. *Child Development, 63*, 879–892.

Hart, D., & Fegley, S. (1995). Prosocial behavior and caring in adolescence: Relations to self-understanding and social judgement. *Child Development, 66*, 1346–1359.

Harter, S. (1993). Vision of self: Beyond the me in the mirror. In R. Dienstbier (Ed.), *Nebraska Symposium on motivation: Vol. 40. Developmental perspectives on motivation* (pp. 99–144). Lincoln, NE: University of Nebraska Press.

Hartup, W. W., French, D. C., Laursen, B., Johnston, M. K., & Ogawa, J. R. (1993). Conflict and friendship relations in middle childhood: Behavior in a closed-field situation. *Child Development, 64*, 445–454.

Hartup, W. W., & van Lieshout, C. F. M. (1995). Personality development in social context. *Annual Review of Psychology, 46*, 655–687.

Hartup, W. W., & Yonas, A. (1971). Developmental psychology. *Annual Review of Psychology, 22*, 337–392.

Herman, M. A., & McHale, S. M. (1993). Coping with parental negativity: Links with parental warmth and child adjustment. *Journal of Applied Developmental Psychology, 14*, 121–136.

Hetherington, E. M., Cox, M., & Cox, R. (1985). Long-term effects of divorce and remarriage on the adjustment of children. *Journal of the American Academy of Child Psychiatry, 24*, 518–530.

Hetherington, E. M., & McIntyre, C. W. (1975). Developmental psychology. *Annual Review of Psychology, 26*, 97–136.

Hoffman, L. W., & Kloska, D. D. (1995). Parents' gender-based attitudes toward marital roles and child rearing: Development and validation of new measures. *Sex Roles, 32*, 273–295.

Hoffman, M. L. (1975). Developmental synthesis of affect and cognition and its interplay for altruistic motivation. *Developmental Psychology, 31*, 428–431.

Hoffman, M. L. (1977). Personality and social development. *Annual Review of Psychology, 28*, 295–321.

Hogue, A., & Steinberg, L. (1995). Homophily of internalized distress in adolescent peer groups. *Developmental Psychology, 31*, 897–906.

Holden, G. W., Coleman, S. M., & Schmidt, K. L. (1995). Why 3-year-old children get spanked: Parent and child determinants as reported by college-educated mothers. *Merrill-Palmer Quarterly, 41*, 431–452.

Hoza, B., Molina, B. S. G., Bukowski, W. M., & Sippola, L. K. (1995). Peer variables as predictors of later childhood adjustment. *Development and Psychopathology, 7*, 787–802.

Huesmann, R. L., Eron, L. D., Lefkowitz, M. M., & Walder, L. O. (1984). Stability of aggression over time and generations. *Developmental Psychology, 20*, 1120–1134.

Hymel, S., Bowker, A., & Woody, E. (1993). Aggressive versus withdrawn unpopular children: Variations in peer and self-perceptions in multiple domains. *Child Development, 64*, 879–896.

Izard, C. E., Fantauzzo, C. A., Castle, J. M., Haynes, O. M., Rayias, M. F., & Putnam, P. H. (1995). The ontogeny and significance of infants' facial expressions in the first 9 months of life. *Developmental Psychology, 31*, 997–1013.

Kagan, J. (1992). Yesterday's premises, tomorrow's promises. *Developmental Psychology, 28*, 990–997.

Kagan, J., & Lamb, S. (Eds.). (1987). *The emergence of morality in young children.* Chicago: University of Chicago Press.

Kagan, J., Reznick, J. A., & Gibbons, J. (1989). Inhibited and uninhibited types of children. *Child Development, 60*, 838–845.

Kahn, P. H., Jr., & Friedman, B. (1995). Environmental views and values of children in an inner-city Black community. *Child Development, 66*, 1403–1417.

Karbon, M., Fabes, R. A., Carlo, G., & Martin, C. L. (1992). Preschoolers' beliefs about sex and age differences in emotionality. *Sex Roles, 27*, 377–390.

Katz, L. F., & Gottman, J. M. (1993). Patterns of marital conflict predict children's internalizing and externalizing behaviors. *Developmental Psychology, 29*, 940–950.

Kavanaugh, K., & Hops, H. (1994). Good girls? Bad boys? Gender and development as contexts for diagnosis and treatment. In T. H. Ollendick & R. J. Prinz (Eds.), *Advances in clinical child psychology* (Vol. 16, pp. 45–79). New York: Plenum.

Keenan, K., & Shaw, D. (in press). Development and social influences on young girls' early problem behavior. *Psychological Bulletin.*

Kerig, P. K., Cowan, P. A., & Cowan, C. P. (1993). Marital quality and gender differences in parent–child interaction. *Developmental Psychology, 29*, 931–939.

Kerr, M., Lambert, W. W., Stattin, H., & Klackenberg-Larsson, I. (1994). *Child Development, 65*, 138–146.

Kliewer, W., & Sandler, I. N. (1992). Locus of control and self-esteem as moderators of stressor–symptom relations in children and adolescents. *Journal of Abnormal Child Psychology, 20*, 393–413.

Kochanska, G. (1991). Socialization and temperament in the development of guilt and conscience. *Child Development, 62*, 1379–1392.

Kochanska, G. (1993). Toward a synthesis of parental socialization and child temperament in early development of conscience. *Developmental Psychology, 64*, 325–247.

Kochanska, G. (1995). Children's temperament, mothers' discipline, and security of attachment: Multiple pathways to emerging internalization. *Child Development, 66*, 597–615.

Kochanska, G., & Aksan, N. (1995). Mother–child mutually positive affect, the quality of child compliance to requests and prohibitions, and maternal control as correlates of early internalization. *Child Development, 66*, 236–254.

Kochanska, G., DeVet, K., Goldman, M., Murray, K., & Putnam, S. P. (1994). Maternal reports of conscience development and temperament in young children. *Child Development, 65*, 852–868.

Kuczynski, L., & Kochanska, G. (1995). Function and content of maternal demands: Developmental significance of early demands for competent action. *Child Development, 66*, 616–628.

Kupersmidt, J. B., Griesler, P. C., DeRosier, M. E., Patterson, C. J., & Davis, P. W. (1995). Childhood aggression and peer relations in the context of family and neighborhood factors. *Child Development, 66*, 360–375.

Lahey, B. B., Hart, E. L., Pliszka, S., Applegate, B., & McBurnett, K. (1993). Neurophysiological correlates of conduct disorder: A rationale and review of research. *Journal of Clinical Child Psychology, 22*, 141–153.

Lerner, R. M. (1988). Personality development: A life-span perspective. In E. M. Hetherington, T. M. Lerner, & M. Perlmutter (Eds.), *Child development in life-span perspective* (pp. 21–46). Hillsdale, NJ: Erlbaum.

Levine, L. J. (1995). Young children's understanding of the causes of anger and sadness. *Child Development, 66*, 697–709.

Luthar, S. S. (1995). Social competence in the school setting: Prospective cross-domain associations among inner-city teens. *Child Development, 66*, 416–429.

Maccoby, E. E., & Martin, J. A. (1983). Socialization in the context of the family: Parent–child interaction. In P. H. Mussen (Series Ed.) & E. M. Hetherington (Vol. Ed.), *Handbook of child psychology: Vol. 4. Socialization, personality, and social development* (4th ed., pp. 1–101). New York: Wiley.

MacLean, P. D. (1985). Brain evolution relating to family, play and the separation call. *Archives of General Psychiatry, 42*, 405–417.

Magai, C., & McFadden, S. H. (1995). *The role of emotions in social and personality development: History, theory, and research.* New York: Plenum.

Malatesta, C. Z., & Haviland, J. (1982). Learning display rules: The socialization of emotion expression in infancy. *Child Development, 53*, 991–1003.

Malatesta, C. Z., & Wilson, A. (1988). Emotion/cognition interaction in personality development: A discrete emotions, functionalist analysis. *British Journal of Social Psychology, 27*, 91–112.

Matthews, K.A., Batson, C. D., Horn, J., & Rosenman, R. H. (1981). Principles in his nature which interest him in the fortune of others: The heritability of empathic concern for others. *Journal of Personality, 49*, 237–247.

McHale, J. P. (1995). Coparenting and triadic interactions during infancy: The roles of marital distress and child gender. *Developmental Psychology, 31*, 985–996.

Moffitt, T. E. (1993). Adolescence-limited and life-course persistent antisocial behavior: A developmental taxonomy. *Psychological Review, 100*, 674–701.

Mounts, N. S., & Steinberg, L. (1995). An ecological analysis of peer influence on adolescent grade point average and drug use. *Developmental Psychology, 31*, 915–922.

New York Academy of Sciences Conference. (1996, March). *The integrative neurobiology of affili-ation*. Georgetown University, Washington, DC.

Newman, D. L., Moffitt, T. E., Caspi, A., Magdol, L., Silva, P. A., & Stanton, W. R. (1996). Psychiatric disorder in a birth cohort of young adults: Prevalence, comorbidity, clinical signific-ance, and new case incidence from ages 11 to 21. *Journal of Consulting and Clinical Psycho-logy, 64*, 552–562.

Nolen-Hoeksema, S. (1987). Sex differences in unipolar depression: Evidence and theory. *Psycho-logical Bulletin, 101*, 257–282.

Nolen-Hoeksema, S., & Girgus, J. (1994). The emergence of gender differences in depression during adolescence. *Psychological Bulletin, 115*, 424–443.

Nolen-Hoeksema, S., Wolfson, A., Mumme, D., & Guskin, K. (1995). Helplessness in children of depressed and nondepressed mothers. *Developmental Psychology, 31*, 377–387.

Ohannessian, C. M., Lerner, R. M., Lerner, J. V., & von Eye, A. (1995). Discrepancies in adoles-cents' and parents' perceptions of family functioning and adolescent emotional adjustment. *Journal of Early Adolescence, 15*, 490–516.

Olweus, D. (1981). Continuity in aggressive and withdrawn, inhibited behavior patterns. *Psychiatry and Social Sciences, 1*, 141–159.

Panksepp, J. (1986). The psychobiology of prosocial behaviors: Separation distress, play, and altruism. In C. Zahn-Waxler, E. M. Cummings, & R. Iannotti (Eds.), *Altruism and aggressio: Biological and social origins* (pp. 19–57). Cambridge: Cambridge University Press.

Parke, R. D., & Asher, S. R. (1983). Social and personality development. *Annual Review of Psy-chology, 34*, 465–509.

Parke, R. D., & Ladd, G. W. (1992). *Family–peer relationships: Modes of linkage*. Hillsdale, NJ: Erlbaum.

Parke, R. D., Ornstein, P. A., Rieser, J. J., & Zahn-Waxler, C. (Eds.). (1992). *A century of devel-opmental psychology*. Washington, DC: American Psychological Association.

Parke, R. D., & Slaby, R. B. (1983). The development of aggression. In P. H. Mussen (Series Ed.) & E. M. Hetherington (Vol. Ed.), *Handbook of child psychology: Vol. 4. Socialization, person-ality, and social development* (4th ed., pp. 548–641). New York: Wiley.

Parker, J. G., & Asher, S. R. (1993). Friendship and friendship quality in middle childhood: Links with peer group acceptance and feelings of loneliness and social dissatisfaction. *Developmental Psychology, 29*, 611–621.

Parker, J. G., & Herrera, C. (1996). Interpersonal processes in friendship: A comparison of maltreated and nonmaltreated children's experiences. *Developmental Psychology, 32*, 1025–1038.

Perusse, D., Neale, M. C., Heath, A. C., & Eaves, L. J. (1994). Human parental behavior: Evidence for genetic influence and potential implication for gene-culture transmission. *Behavior Genetics, 24*, 327–335.

Pianta, R. C., & Ball, R. M. (1993). Maternal social support as a predictor of child adjustment in kindergarten. *Journal of Applied Developmental Psychology, 14*, 107–120.

Pianta, R. C., & Caldwell, C. B. (1990). Stability of externalizing symptoms from kindergarten to first grade and factors related to instability. *Development and Psychopathology, 2*, 247–258.

Pickens, J., & Field, T. (1993). Facial expression in infants of depressed mothers. *Developmental Psychology, 29*, 986–998.

Pike, A., McGuire, S., Hetherington, E. M., Reiss, D., & Plomin, R. (1996). Family environment and adolescent depressive symptoms and antisocial behavior: A multivariate genetic analysis. *Developmental Psychology, 32*, 590–603.

Plomin, R. (1994). Nature, nurture, and social development. *Social Development, 3*, 37–53.

Putallaz, M., Costanzo, P. R., & Klein, T. P. (1993). Parental childhood social experiences and their effects on children's relationships. In S. Duck (Ed.), *Understanding relationship processes: Vol. 2 Learning about relationships*: (pp. 63–97). Thousand Oaks, CA: Sage.

Putallaz, M., Klein, T. P., Costanzo, P. R., & Hedges, L. A. (1994). Relating mothers' social framing to their children's entry competence with peers [Special Issue: From family to peer group: Relations between relationships systems]. *Social Development, 3,* 222–237.

Quay, H. C. (1993). The psychology of undersocialized aggressive conduct disorder: A theoretical perspective. *Development and Psychopathology, 5,* 165–180.

Quiggle, N. L., Garber, J., Panak, W. F., & Dodge, K. A. (1992). Social information processing in aggressive and depressed children. *Child Development, 63,* 1305–1320.

Radke-Yarrow, M., Zahn-Waxler, C., & Chapman, M. (1983). Children's prosocial dispositions and behavior. In P. H. Mussen (Ed.), *Carmichael's manual of child psychology* (4th ed., Vol. 1, pp. 470–545). New York: Wiley.

Radke-Yarrow, M., Zahn-Waxler, C., Richardson, D. T., Susman, A., & Martinez, P. (1994). Caring behavior in children of clinically depressed and well mothers. *Child Development, 65,* 1405–1414.

Raine, A., Venables, P. H., & Williams, M. (1995). High autonomic arousal and electrodermal orienting at age 15 years as protective factors against criminal behavior at age 29 years. *American Journal of Psychiatry, 152,* 1595–1600.

Raine, A., Venables, P. H., & Williams, M. (1996). Better autonomic conditioning and faster electrodermal half-recovery time at age 15 years as possible protective factors against crime at age 29 years. *Developmental Psychology, 32,* 624–630.

Reese, H. W. (1993). Developments in child psychology from the 1960's to the 1990's. *Developmental Review, 13,* 503–524.

Rende, R. D. (1993). Longitudinal relations between temperament traits and behavioral syndromes in middle childhood. *Journal of the American Academy of Child and Adolescent Psychiatry, 32,* 287–290.

Richman, N., Stevenson, J. E., & Graham, P. J. (1982). *Preschool to school: A behavioral study.* London: Academic Press.

Rickman, M. D., & Davidson, R. J. (1994). Personality and behavior in parents of temperamentally inhibited and uninhibited children. *Developmental Psychology, 30,* 346–354.

Robins, L. N. (1991). Conduct disorder. *Journal of Child Psychology and Psychiatry, 32,* 193–212.

Robins, L. N., & Price, R. K. (1991). Adult disorders predicted by childhood conduct problems: Results from the NIMH epidemiologic catchment area project. *Psychiatry, 54,* 116–132.

Robinson, J. L., Zahn-Waxler, C., & Emde, R. N. (1994). Patterns of development in early empathic behavior: Environmental and child constitutional influences. *Social Development, 3,* 125–145.

Rogosch, F. A., Cicchetti, D., & Aber, J. L. (1995). The role of child maltreatment in early deviations in cognitive and affective processing abilities and later peer relationship problems. *Development and Psychopathology, 7,* 591–609.

Rose, S. L., Rose, S. A., & Feldman, J. R. (1989). Stability of behavior problems in very young children. *Development and Psychopathology, 1,* 5–19.

Rothbart, M. K., Ahadi, S. A., & Hershey, K. L. (1994). Temperament and social behavior in childhood. *Merrill-Palmer Quarterly, 40,* 21–39.

Rubin, K. H., Chen, X., McDougall, P., Bowker, A., & McKinnon, J. (1995). The Waterloo longitudinal project: Predicting internalizing and externalizing problems in adolescence. *Development and Psychopathology, 7,* 751–764.

Rubin, K. H., Coplan, R. J., Fox, N. A., & Calkins, S. D. (1995). Emotionality, emotion regulation, and preschoolers' social adaptation. *Development and Psychopathology, 7,* 49–62.

Rubin, K. H., LeMare, L. J., & Lollis, S. (1990). Social withdrawal in childhood: Developmental pathways to peer rejection. In S. R. Asher & J. D. Coie (Eds.), *Peer rejection in childhood* (pp. 217–252). New York: Cambridge University Press.

Rubin, K. H., Lynch, D., Coplan, R., Rose-Krasnor, L., & Booth, C. L. (1994). "Birds of a feather . . .": Behavioral concordances and preferential personal attraction in children. *Child Development, 65,* 1778–1785.

Rueter, M. A., & Conger, R. D. (1995). Interaction style, problem-solving behavior, and family problem-solving effectiveness. *Child Development, 66,* 98–115.

Rushton, J. P., Fulker, D. W., Neale, M. C., Nias, D.K.B., & Eysenck, H. J. (1986). Altruism and aggression: The heritability of individual differences. *Journal of Personality and Social Psychology, 50,* 1192–1198.

Sagi, A., & Hoffman, M. L. (1976). Empathic distress in the newborn. *Developmental Psychology, 12,* 175–176.

Sameroff, A., & Chandler, M. (1975). Reproductive risk and the continuum of caretaker casualty. In F. Horowitz (Ed.), *Review of child development research* (Vol. 4, pp. 187–244). Chicago: University of Chicago Press.

Schwartz, D., Dodge, K. A., & Coie, J. D. (1993). The emergence of chronic peer victimization in boys' play groups. *Child Development, 64,* 1755–1772.

Segal, N. L. (1984). Cooperation, competition and altruism within twin sets: A reappraisal. *Ethology and Sociobiology, 5,* 163–177.

Seiner, S. H., & Gelfand, D. M. (1995). Effects of mothers' simulated withdrawal and depressed affect on mother–toddler interactions. *Child Development, 66,* 1519–1528.

Shaffer, D. R. (1994). *Social and personality development* (3rd ed.). Pacific Grove, CA: Brooks/Cole.

Shaw, D. S., Keenan, K., & Vondra, J. I. (1994). Developmental precursors of externalizing behavior: Ages 1 to 3. *Developmental Psychology, 30,* 355–364.

Siegal, M. (1987). Are sons and daughters treated more differently by fathers than mothers? *Developmental Review, 7,* 183–209.

Silverman, W. K., La Greca, A. M., & Wasserstein, S. (1995). What do children worry about? Worries and their relation to anxiety. *Child Development, 66,* 671–686.

Simner, M. L. (1971). Newborn's responses to the cry of another infant. *Developmental Psychology, 5,* 136–150.

Simpson, A. E., & Stevenson-Hinde, J. (1985). Temperamental characteristics of three-to-four-year-old boys and girls and child–family interactions. *Journal of Child Psychology and Psychiatry, 26,* 43–53.

Smetana, J. G. (1989). Toddlers' social interactions in the context of moral and conventional transgressions in the home. *Developmental Psychology, 25,* 499–509.

Stouthamer-Loeber, M., Loeber, R., Farrington, D. P., Zhang, Q., van Kammen, W., & Maguin, E. (1993). The double edge of protective and risk factors for delinquency: Interrelations and developmental patterns. *Development and Psychopathology, 5,* 683–701.

Switzer, G. E., Simmons, R. G., Dew, M. A., Regalski, J. M., & Wang, C. (1995). The effect of a school-based helper program on adolescent self-image, attitudes, and behavior. *Journal of Early Adolescence, 15,* 429–455.

Tangney, J. P., & Fischer, K. W. (Eds.). (1995). *Self-conscious emotions: The psychology of shame, guilt, embarrassment, and pride.* New York: Guilford.

Thompson, R. A. (1994). Emotion regulation: A theme in search of definition. In N. A. Fox (Ed.), The development of emotion regulation: Biological and behavioral considerations. *Monographs of the Society for Research in Child Development, 59*(2–3, Serial No. 240).

Tomada, G., & Schneider, B. H. (in press). Relational aggression in gender and peer acceptance: Invariance across culture, stability over time, and concordance among informants. *Developmental Psychology.*

Tremblay, R. E., Masse, L. C., Vitaro, F., & Dobkin, P. L. (1995). The impact of friends' deviant behavior on early onset of delinquency: Longitudinal data from 6 to 13 years of age. *Development and Psychopathology, 7,* 649–667.

Trivers, R. L. (1983). The evolution of cooperation. In D. L. Bridgeman (Ed.), *The nature of prosocial development* (pp. 43–60). Orlando, FL: Academic Press.

Vandell, D. L., & Hembree, S. E. (1994). Peer social status and friendship: Independent contributors to children's social and academic adjustment. *Merrill-Palmer Quarterly, 40,* 461–477.

Vuchinich, S., Emery, R. E., & Cassidy, J. (1988). Family members as third parties in dyadic family conflict: Strategies, alliances and outcomes. *Child Development, 59,* 1293–1302.

Vuchinich, S., Hetherington, E. M., Vuchinich, R. A., & Clingempeel, W. G. (1991). Parent–child interaction and gender differences in early adolescents' adaptation to stepfamilies. *Developmental Psychology, 27,* 618–626.

Watson, M. W., & Peng, Y. (1992). The relation between toy gun play and children's aggressive behavior. *Early Education and Development, 3,* 370–389.

Weiss, B., Dodge, K. A., Bates, J. E., & Pettit, G. S. (1992). Some consequences of early harsh discipline: Child aggression and a maladaptive social information-processing style. *Child Development, 63,* 1321–1335.

Wentzel, K. R., & Asher, S. R. (1995). The academic lives of neglected, rejected, popular and controversial children. *Child Development, 66,* 754–763.

Wierson, M., Long, P. J., & Forehand, R. L. (1993). Toward a new understanding of early menarche: The role of environmental stress in pubertal timing. *Adolescence, 28,* 913–924.

Wilson, E. O. (1975). *Sociobiology: The new synthesis.* Cambridge, MA: Harvard University Press.

Young, S., Fox, N., & Zahn-Waxler, C. (1996). The relations between temperament and empathy in two-year-olds. Unpublished manuscript, University of Maryland, College Park, MD.

Zahn-Waxler, C. (1993). Warriors and worriers: Gender and psychopathology. *Development and Psychopathology, 5,* 79–89.

Zahn-Waxler, C. (1995). Parental depression and distress: Implications for development in infancy, childhood, and adolescence (Introduction to Special Section). *Developmental Psychology, 31,* 347–348.

Zahn-Waxler, C., Cole, P., & Barrett, K. (1991). Guilt and empathy: Sex differences and implications for the development of depression. In K. Dodge & J. Garber (Eds.), *Emotional regulation and dysregulation* (pp. 243–272). New York: Cambridge University Press.

Zahn-Waxler, C., Cole, P. M., Welsh, J. D., & Fox, N. A. (1995). Psychophysiological correlates of empathy and prosocial behaviors in preschool children with behavior problems. *Development and Psychopathology, 7,* 27–48.

Zahn-Waxler, C., Friedman, R. J., Cole, P. M., Mizuta, I., & Hiruma, N. (in press). Japanese and U. S. preschool children's responses to conflict and distress. *Child Development.*

Zahn-Waxler, C., Iannotti, R. J., Cummings, E. M., & Denham, S. A. (1990). Antecedents of problem behaviors in children of depressed mothers. *Development and Psychopathology, 2,* 271–291.

Zahn-Waxler, C., & Radke-Yarrow, M. (1982). The development of altruism: Alternative research strategies. In N. Eisenberg-Berg (Ed.), *The development of prosocial behavior* (pp. 109–137). Orlando, FL: Academic Press.

Zahn-Waxler, C., & Radke-Yarrow, M. (1990). The early origins and development of empathic concern. *Motivation and Emotion, 14,* 107–130.

Zahn-Waxler, C., Radke-Yarrow, M., Wagner, E., & Chapman, M. (1992). Development of concern for others. *Developmental Psychology, 28,* 126–136.

Zahn-Waxler, C., & Robinson, J. (1995). Empathy and guilt: Early origins of feelings of responsibility. In J. P. Tangney & K. W. Fischer (Eds.), *Self-conscious emotions: The psychology of shame, guilt, embarrassment, and pride* (pp. 143–173). New York: Guilford.

Zahn-Waxler, C., Robinson, J., & Emde, R. N. (1992). The development of empathy in twins. *Developmental Psychology, 28,* 1038–1047.

Zahn-Waxler, C., Robinson, J., Schmitz, S., & Emde, R. N. (1997). *Empathy and prosocial patterns in young MZ and DZ twins: Development, genetic and environmental influences.* Unpublished manuscript, National Institute of Mental Health, Bethesda, MD.

Zahn-Waxler, C., Schmitz, S., Fulker, D., Robinson, J., & Emde, R. (1996). Behavior problems in 5-year-old monozygotic and dizygotic twins: Genetic and environmental influences, patterns of regulation and internalization of control. *Development and Psychopathology, 8,* 103–122.

Author Index

Aalberg, V. 398, 400
Aaronson, N. K. 401, 403
Abbey, A. 409
Abel, G. G. 153
Aber, J. L. 531
Abrams, D. 77
Acevedo, M. P. 464
Acker, M. 168, 169, 170, 175, 176
Acredolo, L. 220
Adair, J. 146, 147
Adamopoulos, J. 221
Adams, N. E. 55
Adams, S. 522
Affleck, G. 13
Ageton, S. S. 153
Aguilar Gil, J. A. 462
Aguilar, J. A. 464
Ahadi, S. A. 524
Akande, A. 146, 147
Aker, T. 441, 442
Akkari, A. 216
Akram, A. S. 168
Alan Guttmacher Institute 456, 457
Alcock, J. 154
Aldaz, E. 458, 466, 467
Alden, L. 59
Alessandri, S. M. 532

Alexander, R. D. 159
Alexandrovsky, Yu. A. 316–317, 327
Algera, J. A. 313, 318
Allee, W. C. 439
Allen, V. L. 503
Allen, B. 157
Allen, P. A. 121
Allport, F. H. 73
Allport, G. W. 73, 74, 84, 187, 296,
    502, 503, 507
Altrocchi, J. 262
Altrocchi, L. 262
Alvarado, C. 457
Alvarez Izazaga, M. 461
Amelang, M. 45
American Medical Association 125
American Psychiatric Association 430,
    519
American Psychiatric Association
    Board of Trustees 125
American Psychological Association
    125
Amir, Y. 85
Amuchástegui, A. 466
Anastasi, A. 3, 475
Anastasio, P. A. 85, 86
Andersen, R. M. 390

Anderson, B. 264
Anderson, C. 438
Anderson, J. L. 154
Anderson, K. B. 174
Anderson, R. T. 401, 403
Andrade Palos, P. 460, 461, 463
Andrejeva, L. 253
Andrews, D. W. 515
Aneshansel, J. 190
Angleitner, A. 38, 39, 40, 41, 45
Antila, R. 398, 400
Apajasalo, M. 398, 400
Applegate, B. 529
Applegate, J. L. 488
Appley, M. H. 307, 310, 315, 321
Arbisi, P. 45
Arbuckle, J. 354
Arch, E. C. 60
Arcus, D. 519
Ardelt, M. 63
Arminger, G. 354, 364
Arnold, B. 260
Arnold, S. B. 396, 402
Asai, M. 78
Asberg, M. 45
Asendorpf, J. B. 236, 519
Asher, S. R. 514, 523, 527
Ataman, J. 486
Atkin, L. C. 457, 460, 461
Atkinson, G. 118
Atkinson, R. C. 323
Avendnaño, R. 252
Averill, J. R. 104
Aycicegi, A. 482
Azjen, I. 423
Azucena, S. E. 254

Baca, E. 397, 402
Bachevan, B. A. 85
Bachman, B. 86
Backett, E. M. 397, 401
Bak, R. M. 434
Baldwin, J. D. 419
Baldwin, J. I. 419
Baldwin, J. M. 477
Ball, G. F. 160
Ball, R. M. 515

Ballard-Reisch, D. 164
Ballenger, J. C. 45
Baltes, P. B. 478
Balthazard, C. G. 120
Baltruweit, W. J. 128
Banchs, M. A. 254
Bandura, A. 51, 53, 55, 56, 58, 59, 60, 62, 64
Bantelmann, J. 40
Bányai, É. I. 118, 119, 129
Barbaranelli, C. 64
Barbaree, H. E. 165, 170, 171
Barber, J. 120
Barber, T. X. 127
Bargh, J. 84, 170
Barker, R. G. 477
Barlow, D. H. 153, 438
Barnes 39
Barnes, G. 168, 169, 170, 175, 176
Barnes, R. D. 100
Barongan, C. 166
Barratt 38
Barrett, K. D. 521, 523, 529
Barrett, P. 38, 40
Bart, C. 118, 129
Barth, F. 250
Barton, D. A. 131
Barton, S. 153, 172
Baslin, B. 397
Başoğlu, M. 439, 440, 441, 442
Bates, B. L. 127
Bates, J. E. 37, 517, 526, 531
Batson, C. D. 525
Battista, R. N. 398
Baumeister, R. F. 532
Beahrs, J. O. 124
Bearon, L. B. 390
Beck, A. T. 431, 444, 446
Becker, G. 508
Begley, N. L. 96
Behavioral Science Subpanel of President's Science Advisory Committee 186, 187
Beidel, D. 437
Béjar, R. 258
Bekman, S. 488
Bell, R. Q. 516

Bellew, M. 445
Belmaker, R. K. 10
Belsky, J. 162, 168, 173, 535
Bem, D. J. 527
Bem, S. L. 165, 176
Benjamin, J. 10
Bennett, E. R. 10
Bennett, J. A. 484
Benoit, D. 516
Bentler, P. M. 353, 354, 355, 356, 362, 363, 364, 365, 366, 367, 368
Berger, P. L. 477
Bergman, L. R. 503, 504, 505
Bergner, M. 397, 401
Berkeley, J. 390
Berkowitz, L. 170, 526
Bernal, M. E. 251
Berndt, T. J. 515
Bernier, H. 47
Berry, J. W. 138, 206, 207, 210, 216, 222, 233, 239, 242, 259, 261, 478, 481, 484, 487
Bertalanffy, L. von 477, 478
Bettencourt, B. A. 85
Bhalla, M. 328
Bhawuk, D. S. 141
Bianchi, A. 121, 126
Bidegain Greising, G. 456
Biedwenharn, J. 397
Bierman, K. L. 515
Billig, M. G. 82
Billmoria, S. B. 334
Binet, A. 2, 3, 496
Birch, H. G. 46
Birren, J. E. 390, 394, 400
Black, B. 515
Blaine, D. 10
Blanchard, E. 153
Bless, H. 189
Block, M. L. 131
Block, J. 11, 496, 533
Block, J. H. 528, 531
Bloom, P. B. 125
Bobbit, R. 397, 401
Bobko, P. 56
Bochner, S. 147

Boden, J. M. 532
Bodunov, M. 39, 45
Boker, S. M. 354, 357
Bolger, K. E. 517
Bolstad, B. 440, 441
Bond, M. H. 137, 138, 139, 140, 141, 144, 146, 147
Bonta, B. D. 166
Bontempo, R. 78
Boodoo, G. 9, 10, 11
Booth, C. L. 515
Boski, P. 233
Bossel-Lagos, M. 216
Bothwell, R. K. 189
Bouchard, T. J. 10
Bouchard, T. J. Jr. 9, 10, 11
Bouffard-Bouchard, T. 55
Boulton, M. J. 515
Bourhis, R. Y. 78
Bourne, E. J. 478
Boutin, P. 47
Bovet, M. 209
Bowden, B. 171
Bower, G. H. 60, 431, 446
Bowers, K. S. 118, 123, 126, 128, 130, 131
Bowker, A. 515
Boykin, A. W. 9, 10, 11
Boyle, P. A. 522
Brannon, L. 193–194, 196, 197, 198
Branstetter, W. H. 525
Braungart, J. M. 43, 515, 522
Breckler, J. 362
Brenman, M. 124
Brentar, J. T. 122
Brewer, M. B. 75, 77, 78, 82, 85, 86
Briere, J. 170
Brigham, J. C. 189
Brigham, T. A. 127
Bril, B. 211, 212
Brim, O. 478
Briones, M. 522
Brislin, R. W. 146, 233
Brittlebank, A. D. 445
Broadbent, D. E. 308, 310, 321, 323
Brody, N. 9, 10, 11
Brogan, D. 534

Bromley, S. 82
Bronfenbrenner, U. 211, 476, 478, 479, 481, 516
Bronfman, M. 466
Bronstein, P. 522
Brook, R. H. 397, 401
Brorsson, B. 398
Brothers, L. 525
Broude, G. J. 157
Brown, J. 522
Brown, L. 170
Brown, P. 219, 220
Brown, R. 73, 75, 76, 78, 79, 81, 83, 84, 85, 86
Brown, S. D. 56, 61
Browne, J. P. 390, 395
Browne, M. W. 364, 365, 366
Brownmiller, S. 157
Brunner, J. S. 187
Brunswik, E. 496
Brunswik, R. 477
Bukowski, W. M. 527
Bullock, H. E. 354
Bundy, R. P. 82
Bünning, J. 13
Burgner, D. 532
Buriel, R. 479
Burke, C. H. 153
Burkhart, B. R. 153
Burleson, B. R. 488
Burt, C. 7
Burt, M. R. 153, 170
Burts, D. C. 515
Busch-Rossnagel, N. A. 478
Buse, L. 12, 13, 19
Bush, J. 398, 402, 418
Buss, D. M. 153, 155, 159, 161, 167, 170, 239
Buss, A. H. 35, 36, 38, 40, 43, 528
Bustamante, D. 524
Bustamante, J. A. 254
Butcher, A. H. 419
Butkovsky, L. 515, 522
Butler, G. 448
Byrne, B. 354
Byrne, B. M. 6
Byrne, D. 153, 157

Caballero, J. C. 398
Cacioppo, J. T. 189
Caddick, B. 81
Cadenas, J. M. 258
Cadoret, R. J. 518
Cairns, B. D. 497
Cairns, R. B. 496, 497, 508
Calderón, J. 257
Caldwell, C. B. 527
Calhoun, K. 437
Calkins, S. D. 519
Camilleri, C. 212
Campbell, A. 389, 390, 400
Campbell, D. T. 6, 79, 230, 231
Campbell, J. L. 308, 319
Campbell, S. B. 527
Campbell, S. M. 419
Campbell, W. K. 445, 447
Campos, J. 521
Campos, J. J. 35, 36, 37
Cano, J. I. 258
Caplan, R. D. 310, 311, 318
Capozza, D. 79
Cappello, H. M. 258
Caprara, G.-V. 11, 64
Carey, M. P. 419
Carey, W. B. 46, 47
Carlo, G. 524, 531
Carlson, E. A. 531
Carlson, R. 496
Carment, D. W. 146
Caron, C. 47
Carr, R. 479
Carraher, D. 216
Carraher, D. W. 486
Carraher, T. N. 486
Carroll, J. B. 6, 7, 17
Carter, W. 397, 401
Casaer, P. 498
Casali, J. G. 323, 325
Casas, J. F. 528
Caspi, A. 527, 530, 531
Cassidy, J. 515, 522, 536
Castle, J. M. 521
Catchlove, B. R. 398
Cattell, J. McK. 2
Cattell, R. B. 6, 7, 17, 22

Ceci, S. 216
Ceci, S. J. 9, 10, 11, 481
CEOTMA 388
Cerutti, S. 121, 126
Cervone, D. 55
Chagnon, N. A. 156
Chaiken, S. 186, 187, 189, 191, 194, 198, 199
Chalmers, L. 112
Chalmers, L. J. 158, 167
Chamove, A. S. 438
Champoux, M. 441
Chan, C. 449
Chan, S. R. 479
Chandler, C. 104
Chandler, M. 516
Chaplin, T. C. 165
Chapman, M. 523, 524, 532
Chavajay, P. 487
Chaves, J. F. 118, 119, 127
Check, J. V. P. 153, 170, 171, 172
Chen, J. H. 272
Chen, S. 191
Chen, S. J. 286
Chen, X. 517
Chen, Y. 286
Chen, Z. K. 286
Chess, S. 34, 35, 36, 37, 38, 46, 47
Chesterman, E. 398
Cheung, F. M. C. 144
Cheung, T. S. 147
Chila, A. G. 55
Child, I. L. 243
Child, I. 477
Childs, C. P. 486
Chinese Culture Connection 140, 141
Choi, S. 66
Choi, S. H. 484
Chorney, K. 10
Chorney, M. J. 10
Chorpita, B. 438
Chou, S.-P. 363, 364
Christakopoulou, S. 261
Christopher, F. S. 171, 172
Cicchetti, D. 531
CIFCA 388
Cigada, M. 121, 126

CIRES 401
Clapper 39
Clark, L. A. 140
Clausen, J. A. 11
Cleveland, H. H. 169
Clingempeel, W. G. 536
Clogg, C. C. 354
Cloninger, C. R. 43
Coatsworth, J. D. 171
Cobb, S. 310, 311
Cocking, R. R. 479
Coe, W. C. 120, 121, 125, 127
Cohen, J. 241, 374, 375
Cohen, Jon 382
Coie, J. D. 515, 526, 527, 531
Cole, M. 210, 235, 239, 243, 478, 485, 486, 487
Cole, P. M. 517, 520, 521, 523, 524, 526, 527, 529, 532
Coleman, S. M. 526–527
Coles, M. G. H. 321
Coll, C. T. G. 479
Collado, M. E. 464, 466
Collins, H. M. 372
Collins, P. 45
Collins, W. A. 514
Comer, S. L. 128
Communist Party of China 274
Como, P. G. 45
CONAPO 457
Conasida-Epidemiología 457, 458
Condrey, J. C. 533
Conferencia sobre Maternidad sin Riesgos en México 457
Conger, R. D. 517, 518, 523, 535
Connor, W. 248
Constanzo, P. R. 516
Cook, M. 433, 434, 435, 436, 449
Cook, S. W. 85
Coolen, P. 79
Cooper, C. L. 307, 308, 312, 325, 327
Cooper, H. 174
Cooper, H. M. 191, 372
Coplan, R. 515, 519
Coren 38
Corley, R. 521
Corona, E. 459

Cortez, G. 254
Coser, L. 79
Cosmides, L. 153, 154, 170, 243
Costa, P. T. Jr. 6, 7, 9, 41, 141
Costello, E. J. 508
Coté, R. 47
Couchard, E. A. 522, 532
Council, J. R. 119
Courneya, K. S. 59
Coutts, J. 165
Cowan, C. P. 533
Cowan, P. A. 533
Cox, M. 536
Cox, R. 536
Cox, S. 152
Cox, T. 310, 314, 316, 318, 319, 321, 324
Coyne, J. 310, 316, 318, 534
Crawford, C. B. 154, 159
Crawford, H. J. 120, 126
Crick, N. R. 102, 515, 528
Critchlow, B. 409, 410, 412
Critelli, J. W. 168
Croak, M. R. 85
Cronbach, L. J. 6, 401
Cronin, C. 45
Crosby, F. 82
Crosby, L. 515
Crowne, D. 425
Csepelli, G. 253
Cuéllar, I. 260
Cummings, E. M. 523, 527, 529, 534, 535
Curran, P. J. 363, 364, 366
Cutcomb, S. D. 126
Cutrona, C. E. 61
Cutshall, J. L. 123

D'Adamo, O. 253, 254
Dai, X. Y. 285
Daly, M. 155, 156
Damon, W. 479
Dancu, C. V. 441
Daniels, J. 10
Danis, M. 397
Danziger, E. 219
D'Ari, A. 522

Darley, J. M. 83
Darwin, C. 521
Dasen, P. R. 205, 206, 207, 208, 209, 210, 212, 213, 214, 216, 217, 222, 223, 239, 242, 476, 478, 486, 487
Daune, B. 308, 313, 314
Davidson, B. 80
Davidson, P. L. 390
Davidson, R. J. 519
Davies, A. R. 397, 401
Davies, P. 535
Davies, P. T. 535, 536
Davis, M. H. 525
Davis, T. L. 532
Dawkins, R. 153, 525
de Groh, M. 128
De Monchaux, C. 137
de Ribaupierre, A. 209
de Waal, F. 437
Dean, K. 157, 158, 165, 169, 176, 177
Deater-Deckard, K. 517
Deaux, K. 79
DeBenedittis, G. 121, 126
DeBro, S. C. 419
Debus, R. L. 59
DeFries, J. 43, 521
Delamater, A. 430
Delia, J. G. 488
Dembélé, B. 214
Deng, L. X. 285
Denham, S. A. 522, 523, 527, 529, 532, 534
Denny, E. 447
Dent, J. 445
Denzin, N. K. 236
DePascalis, V. 126
dePaulo, B. M. 102
Depue, R. A. 45
Deregowski, J. B. 231
DeRidder, R. 241
Derrick, W. L. 323, 325
Derryberry, D. 35, 36, 37
Desmet, H. 222
DeVet, K. 532
Devine, P. 83, 84
DeVos, G. 478

Dew, M. A. 525
DeWalt, B. R. 143
DeWolf, D. M. 515
Di Nardo, P. A. 434
Diamond, M. 120
Díaz Loving, R. 460
Diaz-Guerrero, R. 9, 252, 261, 263, 482
Dieckmann, L. 390, 394, 400
Diener, E. 12, 38, 141
Diener, M. 141
Dietze, C. 82
Digman, J. M. 7
Dijkstra, T. 363
Dimberg, U. 437
Dinero, T. 152
Dinges, D. F. 121, 122
Dion, K. K. 141
Dion, K. L. 141
Dishion, T. J. 479, 515
Dixon, R. A. 478
Dobbins, S. E. 438
Dobkin, P. L. 515, 528
Dobson, A. J. 398
Dodge, K. A. 102, 515, 517, 526, 527, 531
Dominguez, D. 254, 255
Dovidio, J. F. 76, 83, 85, 86
Downey, G. 310, 316, 318, 534
Doyle, A. C. 2
Draper, P. 162, 168, 173, 535
Drenth, P. J. D. 295, 298
Drepper, J. 13
Droungas, A. 436
Drugan, R. C. 441
Duan, H. F. 283, 284
Dubin, L. L. 124
DuBreuil, S. C. 128
Dudgeon, P. 355, 362, 363, 364
Dufty, A. M. Jr. 160
Dugan, S. 140, 144, 147
Duijker, H. 137
Duke University 397
Duncan, T. E. 59
Duncham, R. B. 313
Dunn, G. 354
Dunn, J. 521, 522

Dyck, R. J. 101
Dym, B. 479
Dzewaltowski, D. A. 56

Eagly, A. H. 185, 186, 187, 189, 191, 193, 193–194, 194, 196, 197, 198, 199
Earley, P. C. 66
Earls, F. 531
Earls, F. J. 47
Early, J. 168
Eaves, L. J. 10
Ebstein, R. P. 10
Eckensberger, L. H. 235
Edman, G. 45
Edwards, J. A. 46
Edwards, K. 86, 189
Ehrenfeld, N. 457
Eibl-Eibesfeldt, I. 160
Eichhorn, D. H. 11
Eisenberg, N. 104, 523, 524, 532
Eiser, J. R. 189
Ekman, P. 520
Elder, G. H. 63, 517, 527
Elder, G. H. Jr. 508, 523
Eldering, L. 486
Elias, B. 153, 172
Eliasz, A. 47
Ellemers, N. 81
Ellis, B. 157, 170
Ellis, L. 162, 168
Elton, M. 164
Ely, P. G. 78
Emde, R. 518, 532
Emde, R. N. 521, 524, 525
Eme, R. F. 531
Emery, G. 431, 444
Emery, R. E. 536
Endler, N. S. 12
Ephanova, N. I. 316, 317
Epir, S. 486
Epstein, S. 19, 101
Erdelyi, M. H. 119, 121, 122
Erol, N. 486
Eron, L. D. 527, 528
Esses, V. M. 83
Ethier, K. A. 79

Ettien, K. 214
European Commission 298
EuroQol group 398
Everitt, B. 354
Ewing, L. J. 527
Eysenck, H. J. 7, 9, 10, 17, 34, 35, 36, 38, 40, 43, 45, 46, 47, 169, 240, 432, 438, 525, 529
Eysenck, M. W. 9, 323, 446, 447, 448
Eysenck, S. B. G. 17, 38, 40, 240

Fabes, R. A. 523, 524, 531, 532
Fahrenberg, J. 24, 45
Fan, C. R. 278
Fantauzzo, C. A. 521
Farrington, D. P. 528, 529
Farver, J. M. 525
Faulbaum, F. 354
Feather, N. T. 79, 256
Featherman, D. L. 138
Fegley, S. 526
Feldman, J. R. 527
Fellows, B. 118, 127
Fells, J. 264
Ferguson, E. 310, 314, 316, 318, 319, 324
Ferguson, T. 102
Fernández, A. 458, 466
Fernández-Ballesteros, R. 387, 391, 392, 393, 394, 395, 398, 400, 401, 402
Ferrell, B. R. 398
Festinger, L. 186, 187
Field, T. 521, 534
Fielding, B. 534
Fiese, B. H. 479
Figueroa, J. 458
Fijneman, Y. A. 241
Finch, J. F. 363, 364
Fincham, F. D. 103, 535
Finifter, B. M. 230
Fischer, K. W. 521
Fishbein, M. 423
Fishman, J. 249, 251
Fiske, D. W. 6
Fitch, M. 165
Fitzgerald, M. 522

Fivush, R. 522, 533
Flament, C. 82
Flanagan, J. C. 391
Floyd, F. J. 152
Foa, E. 439, 440, 441
Foerster, F. 45
Fogel, A. 497
Foley, M. A. 123
Fong, G. T. 407, 409, 413, 418, 419, 420, 425
Forehand, R. L. 535
Forsthofer, R. 258
Fournier, M. 216
Fowler, B. D. 296
Fowlie, M. 390
Fox, N. 520, 525
Fox, N. A. 519, 524, 527, 529, 534
Fox-Cardamone, L. 78
Frank, L. L. 298
Frankel, F. H. 113, 120
Frankenhaeuser, M. 308, 310, 316, 318, 320, 325
Frederick, E. 56
Freedman, J. L. 187, 188
French, D. C. 532
French, J. R. P. 310, 311, 318
Frese, M. 314
Frey, D. 188
Friedman, B. 525
Friedman, R. J. 517
Friesen, W. V. 520
Frijda, N. 104
Frijda, N. H. 296
Fritsche, B. 312, 313, 325
Fromkin, V. A. 241
Fuentes, R. 263
Fulker, D. 518, 532
Fulker, D. W. 43, 169, 521, 525
Fuller, R. D. 447
Fultz, J. 153, 524
Funder, D. 3, 5

Gabrenya, W. K. Jr. 142, 147
Gaertner, S. 83
Gaertner, S. J. 85, 86
Gaillard, A. W. K. 310, 320, 321, 325

Gaito, J. 375
Galassi, J. P. 56
Galdikas, B. 159
Gale, A. 46
Gallagher, A. M. 256
Gallenmüller, J. 257
Gandour, M. J. 37
Ganesh, S. R. 336, 339
Gangestad, S. W. 161
Ganz, P. A. 390
Garber, J. 527
García, B. 458
Garcia-Beaudoux, V. 253, 254
Gardell, B. 308, 310, 314, 319, 325
Gardner, H. 9
Gardner, R. C. 354
Garner, P. W. 522
Garrison, W. T. 47
Gay, J. 210, 485
Gazzaniga, M. S. 154
Ge, X. 517, 518, 523
Geert, P. van 503
Gelfand, D. M. 534
Gelfand, M. J. 141
Gelles, R. J. 152
Gellner, E. 248
Georgas, J. 233, 261
George, J. K. 390
Gergen, K. 235
Gerong, A. 146, 147
Gibbons, J. 519
Gibbons, R. 60
Gibson, H. R. 125
Gibson, J. J. 144, 394
Gide, André 26
Gidycz, C. A. 152
Gierl, M. J. 362
Gigerenzer, G. 374
Gilboa, E. 447
Gill, M. M. 124
Gill, W. M. 398
Gilliland, K. 323
Gilmore, D. D. 166
Gilson, B. 397, 401
Ginsburg, B. 439
Girgus, J. 533
Gist, M. E. 59

Giurgiovich, A. 457
Givaudan, M. 458, 466, 467
Gjerde, P. F. 533
Glasgow, R. E. 56
Glass, G. V. 372, 376, 377, 417
Glassner-Boyerl, B. 78
Glatt, R. L. 128
Glazer, H. I. 440
Gleser, G. C. 401
Glick, J. A. 210
Glisky, M. L. 121
Gnepp, J. 522
Goffin, R. D. 6
Gok, S. 441, 442
Gold, S. R. 153, 171
Goldberg, L. R. 7
Goldman, M. 532
Goldsmith, H. H. 35, 36, 37, 43
Gómez, P. 263
Goncu, A. 486
Gong, Y. X. 285, 286
González, G. 260
Goodenough, F. 529
Goodman, S. H. 534
Goodnow, J. J. 478, 479, 488
Goodstein, L. D. 402
Gopher, D. 310, 312, 321, 324
Gordon, I. V. 323
Gordon, C. M. 419
Gosi-Gerguss, A. C. 119
Gosset, W. S. 373
Gossweiler, R. 328
Gotlib, I. 445
Gottman, J. M. 535
Graf, P. 446, 447
Graham, P. J. 527
Graham, S. 102, 104, 527
Gramer, M. 504, 505
Grant, P. 79
Grau, J. 441
Gray 35, 36
Gray, J. A. 438
Green, J. P. 122
Greenberg, B. D. 10
Greendlinger, V. 153, 157
Greene, E. 123
Greene, S. J. 157

Greenfield, P. M. 222, 236, 237, 478, 479, 486
Greenland, K. 86
Greenwald, A. G. 187, 190
Gribble, J. 460, 461
Groenewoud, J. T. 86
Gross, P. H. 83
Grossarth-Maticek, R. 47
Grotpeter, J. K. 528
Grove, J. R. 59
Gründemann, U. 13
Grunert, M. 82
Grusec, J. 515, 516, 523
Grych, J. H. 535
Guan, S. 279
Guba, E. G. 221, 236
Gudjonsson, G. 124, 529
Gudykunst, W. B. 141
Guerra, G. 248
Guevara, M. 254
Guijarro, J. L. 398
Guild, D. 153
Guilford, J. P. 7, 9
Guillén, F. 398
Gunn, T. P. 59
Gunnar, M. 441
Gunnar, M. R. 514
Gupta, G. C. 479
Guptan, S. U. 336
Gurtman, M. B. 76, 83
Guskin, K. 535
Guyati, G. H. 112
Guzy, L. T. 434
Gwynn, M. I. 128

Haan, N. 11
Hacker, W. 312, 313, 325
Hackett, G. 61
Hackman, J. R. 298, 313
Haddock, G. 82
Hadorn, D. C. 397
Haeger, G. 82
Hagan, R. 444
Hall, C. S. 438
Hall, G. S. 296
Hall, J. 398
Hall, J. R. 55

Hall, N. G. C. 166, 172
Halman, L. 274
Halpern, D. F. 9, 10, 11
Halverson, C. F. Jr. 37, 41
Hamberger, L. K. 327
Hambleton, R. K. 232, 403
Hamilton, D. L. 80, 83
Hamilton, P. 309, 319, 323, 324, 325
Hamilton, W. D. 159
Hammond, D. C. 123
Hanneke, C. R. 152
Hannum, R. 441
Hanson, R. K. 153
Harkness, S. 206, 211, 212, 479, 484
Harlow, L. L. 354
Harlow, H. F. 438
Harman, H. H. 7, 25
Harmer, D. H. 10
Harold, G. T. 535
Harpending, H. 162, 168
Harris, G. T. 165
Harris, J. R. 519
Harrison, A. D. 479
Hart, C. H. 515
Hart, D. 526
Hart, E. L. 529
Harter, S. 532
Hartmann, G. W. 189, 191, 195
Hartshorne, K. 12
Hartup, W. W. 96, 514, 532
Harvey, O. J. 79
Haslam, S. 80
Haslam, S. A. 80
Hatano, G. 486
Haviland, J. 533
Hayden, B. 102
Haynes, O. M. 521
Hays, R. D. 397, 398
He, J. Q. 283
Heath, A. C. 43
Heavey, C. 161, 168, 169, 170, 175, 176
Hedges, L. V. 372
Hedges, L. A. 516
Hegner, R. E. 160
Heider, F. 97
Heilmann, M. 161

Heimberg, R. G. 438
Heller, F. A. 298
Helling, G. A. 485
Hembree, S. E. 515
Hempel, S. 39, 45
Henri, V. 2, 3, 496
Henry, B. 531
Herencia, H. C. 263
Herman, M. A. 533
Heron, A. 208
Herrera, C. 531
Hershey, K. L. 524
Herskovits, M. J. 231
Hesse, H. 26
Hetherington, E. M. 514, 518, 536
Hettema, J. 12
Hewstone, M. 85, 86, 532
Heymans, G. 296
Hickey, A. 395, 398
Higgins, E. T. 84
Hildebrandt, K. 61
Hilgard, E. R. 118, 119, 121, 123, 124,
    130
Hilgard, J. 127
Hill, B. 445
Hiltbrunner, B. 390, 395
Hinkle, S. 75, 78
Hirsch, L. R. 161, 164, 167
Hiruma, N. 517
Hobsbawm, E. 248
Hockey, G. R. J. 308–309, 310, 319,
    320, 321, 323, 324, 325
Hodkinson, S. 158
Hoehn, S. 527
Hoffman, T. 104
Hoffmann, M. L. 514, 523, 525
Hofstede, G. 139, 140, 141, 144, 146,
    147, 252, 298
Hofstee, W. K. B. 7, 9
Hogg, M. 77, 80
Hogg, M. A. 80
Hogue, A. 515
Holahan, C. J. 61
Holahan, C. K. 61
Holden, G. W. 526–527
Holland, J. 458
Hollenbeck, B. 529

Holm, J. E. 55
Holmberg, C. 398, 400
Holroyd, K. A. 55
Holt, R. 522
Holt, R. W. 522
Holzmuller, A. 165
Hong, G. 397
Honzik, M. 11
Hood, W. R. 79
Hops, H. 532
Horn, J. 525
Horváth, R. 119
Horwitz, M. 82
Hotaling, G. T. 152
House, J. S. 308, 320
Hovland, C. I. 188
Hoyle, R. H. 354
Hoza, B. 527
Hrdy, S. B. 159
Hsu, C. 283
Hsu, F. L. K. 478
Hu, L. 363, 364
Huba, G. J. 354
Huber, H. P. 504, 505
Huberman, M. 222
Hubert, N. C. 37
Hudley, C. 102
Hudson, S. M. 158, 165
Huesmann, R. L. 527, 528
Hugdahl, K. 433, 436, 437
Hughes, B. 390, 391, 394
Hughes, D. E. 126
Hughes, S. 523
Hui, M. K. 263
Huici, C. 258
Hull, C. L. 497
Hultsch, D. F. 478
Hundleby, J. D. 6
Hunt, C. B. 169
Hunt, J. McV. 12
Hunt, R. 447
Hunt, S. M. 397, 401
Hunter, J. E. 372
Hurell, J. J. 307, 308, 311, 312, 318,
    319
Hurley, J. 303
Hursey, K. G. 55

Huston, A. C. 479
Hutson-Comeaux, S. 193–194, 196, 197, 198
Hyman, C. 527
Hymel, S. 515
Hyson, R. 441

Iacono, W. G. 10
Iannotti, R. J. 523, 527, 529, 534
Ickes, W. J. 100
Ifver, J. 398
IMIFAP-Gallup 460, 464
Incesu, C. 441
INEGI 457
Inglehart, R. 273
Inhelder, B. 209
Inkeles, A. 335
IPPF 459
Islam, M. R. 86
Isreal, J. 137
Ivan, C. 165
Iwanowa, A. 312, 313, 325
Izard, C. E. 521

Jacobs, B. 55
Jacobson, K. 169
Jacobvitz, D. 531
Jahoda, G. 206, 233, 476
James, W. 2
Jamieson, G. 122
Jamshidian, M. 368
Janis, I. L. 298
Jansz, J. 239
Jaspars, J. M. 103
Jenkins, R. 307, 310, 327
Jensen, A. R. 240
Jensen, E. 9
Jenson, J. 257
Ji, G. P. 278
Jia, L. 279
Jiao, S. L. 278
Jimerson, D. C. 45
Jing, Q. C. 271, 277, 278, 280
Joe, R. C. 241
Johanssen, G. 314, 319
Johnson, B. T. 191, 193
Johnson, J. R. 168

Johnson, M. K. 123
Johnson-Laird, P. 447
Johnston, M. K. 532
Jones, D. C. 522
Jones, E. E. 190, 192
Jöreskog, K. G. 354, 356
Josephs, R. A. 407, 408, 409, 410, 411, 412
Jourden, F. J. 56
Joy, A. 263
Joyce, C. R. B. 390, 395, 398
Judd, C. M. 83
Jung, J. 377
Junoven, J. 96
Jussim, L. 83
Jussim, L. J. 250

Kabran, K. 214
Kagan, J. 35, 36, 45, 46, 438, 497, 519, 521
Kağitçibaşi, C. 66, 138, 214, 475, 476, 479, 482, 483, 484, 485, 486, 488
Kahn, P. H. Jr. 526
Kahneman, D. 323
Kaitila, I. 398, 400
Kalat, J. W. 430
Kalichman, S. C. 168
Kamagate, D. 214
Kamin, L. J. 430
Kanfer, R. 60
Kang, S. H. 288
Kanin, E. J. 153, 158, 167, 168
Kano, Y. 363, 364
Kant, I. 2
Kantowitz, B. 308, 319
Kanungo, R. N. 335, 339
Kaplan, R. M. 389, 398, 402
Karasek, R. 307, 308, 310, 311, 313, 321, 327
Karbon, M. 531
Karimi, H. 141
Kärker, A.-C. 436
Kasarda, S. 10
Kashlakeva, N. 253
Kasl, S. V. 308, 310, 311
Katz, A. 445
Katz, D. 187

Katz, L. F. 535
Katz, M. Q. 10
Kavanagh, D. J. 60, 61
Kavanagh, K. 532
Keefe, K. 515
Keefe, S. E. 259, 262, 263
Keenan, K. 527, 532
Kelly, J. A. 166
Kennedy, A. 261
Kenrick, D. T. 12, 157
Kent, G. 60
Kentish, J. 446
Kerig, P. K. 533
Kerr, M. 519
Kessel, F. 478
Kessler, S. 82
Khandwalla, P. N. 334, 336, 341
Kidd, R. 100
Kihlstrom, J. 430
Kihlstrom, J. F. 112, 113, 117, 119,
    120, 121, 125, 128, 129
Killifer, C. 253
Kim, C. 263
Kim, K. 169
Kim, S. 171
Kim, U. 66, 274, 484
Kimchi, R. 310, 312, 321, 324
King, A. C. 392, 397, 400
King, G. 84
King, N. J. 434
Kinnunen, T. 131
Kirk, J. 398
Kirmayer, L. J. 118, 120, 121, 128
Kirsch, I. 117, 119, 123, 125, 127, 128
Kitamura, S. 283
Kitano, E. 192
Kitayama, S. 146, 147
Klackenberg-Larsson, I. 519
Klein, S. J. 438
Klein, T. P. 516
Klonowicz, T. 47
Knight, G. P. 251
Knight, R. A. 172
Knox, V. J. 123
Koch, A. 421, 423
Kochanska, G. 519, 532
Koehnken, G. 123

Koffi, D. A. 214
Kohler, R. 192
Kohn, M. L. 484, 485
Kohn, P. M. 39, 45
Kohnstamm, G. A. 41
Konishi, H. 59
Koopman, P. L. 298
Kopp, U. 13
Korn, S. J. 37, 38
Koss, M. P. 152, 158, 161, 168, 169,
    171, 173, 174, 175, 176
Kouznetcova, A. S. 325, 327
Kraft, P. M. 127
Kraus, S. J. 525
Krewer, B. 212, 222
Krishnan, L. 146
Krosnick, J. A. 198
Krumov, K. 253
Kuban, M. 157
Kuebli, J. 522
Kukla, A. 94, 95, 98
Kulesa, P. 193–194, 196, 197, 198
Kumar, V. K. 118, 119, 129
Kunde, W. 13
Kunzendorf, R. G. 123, 126
Kupersmidt, J. B. 517
Kurtines, W. M. 479
Kushner, M. G. 440

La Greca, A. M. 519
Labelle, L. 122
Lacourse, P. 123, 126
Ladd, G. W. 515
Lahey, B. B. 529
Laitsch, K. 433
Lake, C. R. 45
Lalumiere, M. L. 158, 167, 168, 169
Lamb, S. 521
Lambert, D. 335, 339
Lambert, W. W. 519
Langer, A. 456
Lanyon, R. L. 402
Laosa, L. M. 479, 485, 486
Laplante, B. 47
Lara-Tapia, L. 263
Larkin, K. C. 56
Laroche, M. 263

Larsen 38
Larsen, K. S. 253
Latham, G. P. 56, 59
Laurence, J.-R. 118, 122, 127, 130
Laursen, B. 532
Lavallée, M. 209
Lave, C. 478
Lave, J. 216, 478, 486
Lawrence, J. 222
Lawton, M. P. 390, 393, 395
Lazarus, R. S. 310, 314, 315, 327
LCHC 486, 487
Leary, M. R. 438
LeDoux, J. 170
Lee, C. 56
Lee, K. Y. 275
Lee, S. Y. 283
Lee, Y. T. 250
Lefebvre, M. 208
Lefkowitz, M. M. 527, 528
Lehalle, H. 211
Lehman, E. C. 315
Lehr, U. 400
Leigh, B. C. 409
LeMare, L. J. 519
Lenox, K. 527
Lent, R. W. 56, 61
Leon, A. 45
Leonova, A. B. 307, 308, 310, 312,
    316, 318, 319, 320, 321, 323, 324,
    325, 327, 328
Leont'ev, A. N. 320
Lepore, L. 83, 84
Lepper, M. R. 189
Lerner, J. V. 37, 40, 46, 533
Lerner, R. M. 37, 39, 478, 517, 533
Leseman, P. 485, 486
Lettgen, S. 82
Leung, K. 139, 141, 144, 146, 221,
    232, 233
Levey, A. 45
Levi, J. 398
Levi, L. 307, 308, 310, 325
Levin, B. 419
Levine, J. M. 189, 190, 191, 192, 195
Levine, R. 143
LeVine, R. A. 478, 479, 484, 485

Levinson, D. 157
Levinson, S. C. 219, 220
Lew, S. C. 264
Lewin, K. 477, 496, 503
Lewis, M. 532
Li, B. S. 284
Li, L. 10
Li, P. 272
Li, Q. Z. 285, 286
Lichtenstein, P. 10
Lieberman, D. 438
Liebkind, K. 261
Liebrand, W. B. C. 146
Lierle, D. M. 439
Light, R. C. 479
Light, R. J. 372
Lin, G. B. 278
Lin, J. S. 283
Lincoln, Y. S. 221, 236
Linssen, A. C. G. 118, 120
Linton, M. A. 171
Linz, D. 161, 168, 169, 170, 175, 176
Lipsitt, L. P. 478
Lisak, D. 165, 169, 172
Litt, M. D. 55
Little, B. R. 390
Liu, J. H. 283
Liu, T. J. 409, 410
Livanou, M. 441, 442
Livi-Bacci, M. 277
Lobastov, O. S. 316–317, 327
Lochman, J. 527
Locke, E. A. 56, 58, 59
Locke, V. 83
Lockman, J. J. 497
Loeber, R. 529
Loehlin, J. C. 9, 10, 11, 43, 155, 354
Loftus, E. F. 121, 123, 124
Logan, A. 515
Lohr, J. M. 327
Loht, K. N. 397, 401
Lollis, S. 519
LoLordo, V. 430, 436
Lomax, R. G. 354
Long, P. J. 535
Lonner, W. J. 146, 221
López-García, R. 457

Lord, C. G. 189
Lore, R. S. 156
Lorenz, F. O. 517, 523
Lorenz, K. 160
Losoff, M. 171
Lovchan, S. I. 316, 317, 318
Lovibond, P. 449
Lu, Z. H. 283
Lubow, R. E. 434
Lucca, N. 78
Luce, C. 525
Luciana, M. 45
Lucker, G. W. 283
Luckmann, T. 477
Luk, C. L. 140
Luria, A. R. 235, 239
Luthar, S. S. 520
Lutz, C. 234, 237
Lykken, D. T. 10
Lynch, B. 123, 126
Lynch, D. 515
Lynch, M. E. 534
Lynn, S. J. 120, 122, 123, 127
Lytton, H. 515, 516, 523

Maccoby, E. E. 523
MacDonald, T. K. 407, 409, 413, 418,
    420, 425
Mach, Z. 249, 259
Maciá, A. 391, 395, 398, 400, 402
Mackay, C. 310, 316, 321
Mackie, D. M. 80, 83
Mackintosh, N. 430, 434
MacLachlan, A. 445
MacLean, P. D. 525
Macleod, C. 83, 431, 444, 445, 446,
    447, 448
Madaleno, M. 456
Magai, C. 520
Magdol, L. 530
Magnusson, D. 12, 495, 498, 503, 504,
    505, 508, 509
Magnusson, J. 95, 96
Magrin, M. E. 265
Maguin, E. 529
Maguire, M. 522
Maier, S. F. 430, 438, 441, 443

Major, B. 61
MäKelvi, A. 398, 400
Malamuth, N. M. 151, 152, 153, 157,
    158, 161, 165, 168, 169, 170, 171,
    172, 173, 174, 175, 176, 177
Malatesta, C. Z. 533, 534
Malewska-Peyre, H. 212
Maller, J. B. 12
Malpass, R. S. 142, 230, 232
Mandler, G. 446, 447
Manis, M. 83
Mann, C. 372
Mann, J. 86
Manning, D. T. 419
Manzi, J. M. 78
Maras, P. 78, 86
Marchand, B. 398
Marcille, P. J. 55
Marcoulides, G. A. 354
Marín, B. V. 260
Marín, G. 260
Markman, H. J. 152
Marks, I. 441
Markus, H. 146, 147
Marlowe, D. 425
Marques, L. G. 252, 253
Marsella, A. J. 311, 312, 313, 324, 478
Marshall, W. L. 158, 165, 170, 171
Marston, M. 439
Martin, C. L. 531
Martin, J. A. 523
Martin, N. G. 10, 43
Martin, R. P. 37, 41
Martin-Baró, I. 254
Martinez, P. 523
Martini, M. 258
Maryin, M. I. 316, 317, 318
Maslow, A. H. 297
Masse, L. C. 515, 528
Matheson, G. 118, 129
Mathews, A. M. 431, 444, 445, 446,
    447, 448
Mathy, R. M. 524
Matsuda, Y. 59
Matsui, T. 59
Matsumoto, Y. 141
Matt, G. 445, 447

Matthews, K. A. 525
Maucorps, P. H. 137
Mauro, J. A. 37
May, J. 446, 447, 448
May, M. A. 12
Maziade, M. 47
McArdle, J. J. 354, 357
McAuley, E. 59
McBride, A. 513
McBurnett, K. 529
McCall, G. 152
McCall, R. 301
McCann, T. 123
McCaul, K. D. 56
McCauley, C. R. 250
McClearn, G. E. 10
McClelland, D. C. 297, 335, 337
McConkey, K. M. 118, 122, 124, 125, 129
McCormack, J. 165
McCrae, R. R. 7, 41, 141
McDermott, K. 446, 447
McDevitt, S. C. 47
McDonald, N. J. 390, 395
McDougall, W. 73
McElroy, M. 59
McEwen, J. 397, 401
McFadden, S. H. 520
McGarty, C. 80
McGaw, B. 372, 376, 377, 417
McGee, H. M. 390, 395, 398
McGee, R. O. 531
McGillicuddy-DeLisi, A. 479
McGue, M. 10
McGuffin, P. 10
McGuire, S. 518
McGuire, W. J. 187
McHale, J. P. 535
McHale, S. M. 533
McInerney, D. 146, 147
McIntyre, C. W. 514
McKenna, S. P. 397, 401
McKinley, M. 522, 532
McLoyd, V. C. 479
McNeill, P. L. 169
Mehrabian 35, 36, 38, 39
Meisels, S. J. 479

Meny, Y. 274
Merette, C. 47
Messick, D. M. 140
Messick, S. 238, 401
Micceri, T. 362
Michel, M. K. 520, 532
Michelson, C. 211, 213
Midgett, J. 328
Miles, M. B. 222
Miller, J. G. 139, 221, 235
Miller, N. 85, 86
Miller, P. 478
Miller, P. A. 524
Miller, S. 435
Miller, S. A. 488
Miller, S. M. 440
Mineka, S. 429, 430, 431, 432, 433, 434, 435, 436, 437, 438, 439, 440, 441, 442, 443, 444, 445, 446, 447, 449
Ministry of Finance 334
Ministry of Transportation 412
Minjian, Z. Y. 274
Mischel, W. 3, 12, 17, 22
Mishra, R. 209, 210
Mistry, J. 486
Mitchell, T. R. 59
Mizrahi, K. 79
Mizuta, I. 517
Moffitt, T. E. 529, 530, 531
Mogg, K. 446, 447, 448
Moghaddam, F. M. 81, 138
Mohlman, J. 449
Molina, B. S. G. 527
Money, J. 155
Monteith, M. 83
Montero, M. 252, 253
Mora, G. 457
Morrison, D. F. 7
Morrow, J. 37
Mosher, D. L. 171
Mosher, M. 528
Mosier, C. 486
Mosteller 418
Mott, T. Jr. 120
Mounts, N. S. 515
Mowrer, O. H. 430, 435

Moye, T. B. 441
Muehlenhard, C. L. 171
Mueller, P. 61
Mueller, R. O. 354
Mulaik, S. A. 354
Mullen, B. 76, 81
Muller, S. 447
Muller, W. 45
Mulvenon, S. 362
Mumme, D. 535
Mummendey, A. 81, 82
Mundy-Castle, A. C. 214, 484
Munipov, V. M. 310, 312, 313, 321,
    324, 325
Munist, M. M. 456, 457
Munroe, R. H. 211, 213, 479
Munroe, R. L. 211, 213, 479
Murphy, D. L. 10
Murphy, D. 45
Murphy, G. 189, 190, 191, 192, 195
Murphy, L. R. 308, 311, 312
Murray, K. 532
Murrell, A. J. 86
Mussen, P. H. 11
Myers, B. 128
Myers, B. P. 123
Myers, C. A. 335, 339
Mylonas, K. 261
Myrdal, G. 335, 339
Myrtek, M. 24, 45

Nadon, R. 118, 122, 127, 131
Nagler, R. 118, 129
Nando, H. 401
Nasby, W. 102
Nash, M. R. 123
Naughton, M. J. 390, 396
Nawrocki, T. 534
Neale, M. C. 169, 525
Nebylitsyn, V. D. 36, 46
Nederlands Instituut van Psychologen
    302
Neiderhiser, J. M. 518
Neisser, U. 9, 10, 11, 394
Nelson, E. 398
Nelson, N. 375
Nelson, T. E. 83

Nemanov, L. 10
NERI 395, 398
Nesselroade, J. R. 10
Netter, P. 45
New York Academy of Sciences
    Conference 518
Newberry 38
Newcomb, M. D. 362
Newman, D. L. 530
Ngini, L. 209
N'Guessan, A. 214
Nias, D. K. B. 169, 525
Nickel, T. W. 101
Nishida, T. 141
Niu, D. 279
Niznik, J. 264
Noble, J. M. 56
Nolen-Hoeksema, S. 61, 533, 535
Norenzayan, A. 143
Northwestern National Life 312
Novick, O. 10
Novikoff, A. B. 477
Nsamenang, A. B. 479
Nugent, K. 445, 446, 447
Nunes, T. 478, 485, 486
Nuttin, J. 137

Oakes, P. 80
Oakes, P. J. 80
Oatley, K. 447
Oboler, S. 257
O'Boyle, C. A. 390, 395, 398
Ocampo, K. A. 251
Ofshe, R. J. 122, 124
Ogawa, J. R. 532
Ohannessian, C. M. 533
Öhman, A. 435, 436, 437
Ohnishi, R. 59
Okagaki, L. 485, 488
Okamura, L. 174
Olasov-Rothbaum, B. 439, 440, 441
Oldham, G. R. 313
Oliveira, J. M. P. 252, 253
Olkin, I. 372
Ollendick, T. H. 434
Oloko, A. B. 486, 487
Olweus, D. 528

O'Malley, K. 390, 395, 398
O'Neal, E. C. 419
O'Neill, K. 56
Onglatco, M. L. U. 59
Oniszczenko, W. 39, 41, 45
Optzoomer, M. A. 398
Oreland, L. 45
Orne, E. C. 121, 122
Orne, M. T. 121, 122
Ornstein, P. A. 514
Osborne, L. N. 535
Osher, Y. 10
Osland, J. A. 165
Osmer, D. 137
Öst, L.-G. 433, 437
Ostendorf, F. 41
Otero-Sabogal, R. 260
Overmier, J. B. 441
Owen, M. 10
Owens, L. A. 171, 172
Oxman, A. D. 112
Ozer, D. J. 12
Ozer, E. M. 56
Ozmen, E. 441

Padilla, A. M. 259, 262, 263
Paker, M. 441, 442
Paker, O. 441
Paladino, M. P. 79
Palermiti, A. 169
Palisoc, A. L. 354
Palmer, D. J. 522
Palys, T. S. 390
Panak, W. F. 527
Panksepp, J. 525
Paolo, A. M. 285
Papp, E. 397, 401
Parcell, S. R. 167, 168
Parent, M. 419
Parikh, I. J. 335, 339
Park, B. 83
Parke, R. D. 514, 515, 522, 526, 531
Parker, J. G. 527, 531
Parker, K. C. H. 516
Parkes, K. R. 314, 316, 319
Pastorelli, C. 64
Patrick, D. L. 397

Patterson, C. 10
Patterson, C. J. 517
Patterson, G. R. 479
Paul, L. 161, 165, 167
Pavlov, V. V. 310, 312, 313, 321, 324, 325
Pavlov, I. 430, 434
Pawlak, A. E. 128
Pawlik, K. 1, 3, 5, 6, 7, 12, 13, 17, 19, 22, 23, 25
Payne, R. 307, 308, 312
Peake, P. K. 55
Pearlman, R. A. 397
Pearson, K. 373
Pedersen, N. L. 10
Pekala, R. J. 118, 119, 129
Pelto, P. J. 143
Peng, Y. 526
Penzien, D. B. 55
Peplau, L. A. 419
Perdue, C. W. 76, 83
Perez-Stable, E. J. 260
Perline, A. H. 128
Perloff, R. 9, 10, 11
Perrier, I. N. 445
Perry, C. 118, 120, 121, 122, 124, 127
Perry, M. 528
Perry, R. 95, 96
Personnaz, B. 265
Peter, R. 316, 319, 320, 321
Peters-Martin, P. 37
Peterson, D. 156, 157
Peterson, D. R. 301
Peterson, M. F. 140
Pettinati, H. M. 122
Pettit, G. S. 517, 526, 531
Petty, R. E. 189, 198, 425
Pfeffer, J. 37
Pianta, R. C. 515, 527
Pick de Weiss, S. 460, 461, 462, 463
Pick, H. L. 220
Pick, S. 455, 457, 458, 459, 463, 464, 466, 467
Pickens, J. 521, 534
Pickles, A. 354
Pieniadz, J. 522
Pier, D. 464

Pihko, H. 398, 400
Pihl, R. O. 409
Pike, A. 518
Piliavin, I. M. 100
Piliavin, J. A. 100
Pillemer, D. B. 372
Pinard, A. 208
Pine, C. J. 479
Pinneau, S. R. 310, 311
Pliszka, S. 529
Plomin, R. 10, 35, 36, 40, 43, 518, 521
Plutchik, R. 447
Pocasangre, C. 254
Pohorecky, L. A. 440
Ponere, M. 86
Pool, R. 372
Poortinga, Y. H. 206, 207, 210, 216,
    222, 229, 230, 232, 236, 239, 240,
    241, 242, 243, 487
Poppe, C. 419
Poppen, P. J. 419
Pordany, L. 253
Porter, J. F. 168
Post, R. M. 45
Pourtois, J.-P. 222
Poverty Elimination Still Hard 272
Powell, J. W. 121, 122
Pratkanis, A. R. 194
Prentice-Dunn, S. 55
Prentky, R. A. 172
Pribram, K. 126
Priel, B. 10
Prisco, A. G. 153
Proffitt, D. R. 328
Pryor, J. B. 170
Pulkkinen, L. 11
Putallaz, M. 516
Putnam, P. H. 521
Putnam, S. P. 532

Quadrio, A. 265
Quay, H. C. 529
Quiggle, N. L. 527
Quigley, C. A. 128
Quinsey, V. L. 158, 167, 168, 169
Quintana, D. 260
Quintero, M. P. 253

Rabain-Jamin, J. 488
Rabbie, J. M. 82
Rachman, S. J. 432, 434
Radke-Yarrow, M. 166, 523, 524, 529,
    532
Rahimi, M. 323, 325
Raine, A. 529
Rajaratman, N. 401
Rallis, S. F. 237
Ramazonoglu, C. 458
Ramírez, H. 463
Rammsayer, T. 45
Rantakari, K. 398, 400
Rapaport, K. 153
Rapaport, P. 438
Rautonen, J. 398, 400
Ray, W. J. 126
Raye, C. L. 123
Rayias, M. F. 521
Raymond, P. 170
Rayner, R. 430, 432
Reese, H. W. 478, 514
Reese, L. 55
Regalski, J. M. 525
Reheiser, E. C. 308, 309, 324
Reichardt, C. S. 237
Reichenbach, H. 238
Reicher, S. D. 80
Reid, A. 79
Reilley, R. R. 131
Reis, H. 146
Reis, H. T. 416
Reisen, C. A. 419
Reisenzein, R. 104
Reiss, D. 518
Reitz, C. 13
Relich, J. D. 59
Renan, E. 250
Rende, R. D. 520
Reno, R. R. 524
Renwick, S. M. 522
Renwick-DeBardi, S. 523
Rescorla, R. 435
Retschitzki, J. 209
Reus, J. M. 398
Revelle, W. 11, 21
Reyes, J. 463, 464

Reyes Pardo, J. 462
Reznick, J. A. 519
Reznick, J. S. 521
Rhodes, K. 524
Rhue, J. W. 120, 123, 127
Rice, J. M. 59
Rice, M. E. 165
Richards, A. 448
Richardson, D. T. 523
Richman, N. 527
Richter, P. 312, 313, 325, 328
Rickman, M. D. 519
Riemann, R. 39, 45
Rieser, J. J. 514
Rieser-Danner, L. A. 37
Riggs, D. S. 440, 441
Rivas, M. 466
Rivera, A. N. 254
Robbins, M. C. 143
Robbins, A. S. 171
Robert, P. 26
Roberts, J. V. 191
Robertson, P. J. 165
Robins, L. N. 531
Robins, R. W. 533
Robinson, D. N. 2
Robinson, J. 518, 521, 524, 525, 529,
    532
Rodin, J. 100
Rodina, O. N. 328
Rodríguez, G. 459, 462, 464, 466
Rodríguez, L. 398
Roediger, H. 446, 447
Rogers, L. 55
Rogers, R. W. 55
Rogoff, B. 216, 478, 486, 487
Rogosch, F. A. 531
Rohlandt, A. 328
Romero, M. 456
Rommetveit, R. 137
Ron 397
Ros, M. 147, 258
Rose, S. A. 527
Rose, S. L. 527
Rose-Krasnor, L. 515
Rosellini, R. 441
Roseman, I. 104

Rosenberg, B. G. 280
Rosenman, R. H. 525
Rosenthal, R. 371, 372, 374, 375, 376,
    377, 378, 380, 382, 418
Rosnow, R. L. 375, 380
Ross, D. F. 533
Ross, E. A. 73
Ross, G. R. 81
Ross, L. 189
Roth, S. 172
Rothbart, M. K. 35, 36, 37, 524
Rothschild, Lord 299
Rotter, J. B. 97
Rowe, D. C. 10, 169
Royce, J. R. 7
Rozin, P. 430
Rubin, D. B. 374, 375, 376, 377, 378,
    380
Rubin, K. H. 515, 517, 519
Ruch, W. 40
Rueter, M. A. 535
Rufining-Rahal, M. A. 397
Ruiz, M. A. 397, 402
Rule, B. G. 101, 102
Rus, V. 298
Rusalov 35, 36, 39
Rushton, J. P. 169, 525
Russell, D. E. H. 152
Russell, J. A. 234
Russell, R. W. 497
Russinova, Z. 253
Rust, M. C. 85, 86
Ryan, J. J. 285

Sabatier, C. 212
Sabogal, F. 260
Sabourin, M. 126
Sachdev, I. 78
Sackloskie, R. 152, 158, 161, 168, 169,
    171, 173, 174, 175, 176
Sadoff, R. L. 124
Sagi, A. 525
Sagués, F. 398
Sahin, D. 441
Sakumura, J. S. 190
Salazar, J. M. 247, 249, 253, 257, 265,
    267

Salazar, M. A. 247
Salles, V. 466
Salvendy, G. 307, 318, 319
Sameroff, A. J. 479, 516
Sampson, E. E. 394
Sanday, P. R. 153, 157, 165, 166
Sanders, A. F. 321
Santoro, E. 253
Sarason, I. G. 12
Saraswathi, T. S. 222
Sarbin, T. R. 118, 127
Sarimurat, N. 441
Sarwer, D. B. 168
Satorra, A. 363
Sauter, S. L. 307, 308, 311, 312, 318, 319
Savasýr, I. 486
Saxe, G. B. 217
Saxe, L. 82
Schachter, S. 137
Schäfer, R. 13
Schaferhoff, S. 82
Schaller, M. 524
Schalling, D. 45
Scheflin, A. W. 123, 124, 125
Schlegel, B. 323
Schlegel, R. E. 323
Schliemann, A. 216
Schliemann, A. D. 486
Schmidt, F. L. 372
Schmidt, G. 100
Schmidt, K. H. 308, 313, 314
Schmidt, K. L. 526–527
Schmitt, D. P. 161
Schmitt, N. 298
Schmitz, S. 518, 524, 525, 532
Schneider, B. H. 529
Schoenberg, R. 364
Schoenpflug, W. 310, 315, 323
Schön, D. A. 301
Schooler, C. 65
Schreiber, H.-J. 81
Schreus, P. G. 325, 327
Schukin, B. P. 316–317, 327
Schultz, L. 156
Schumacker, R. E. 354
Schunk, D. H. 59

Schurmans, M.-N. 214, 216
Schwartz, D. 515
Schwartz, S. 252, 257, 265
Schwartz, S. H. 75, 79, 140, 141, 147
Schwartz, T. 476
Schwarz, N. 189
Scott, J. 445
Scott, J. P. 439
Scott, S. 458
Scribner, S. 210, 235, 239, 478, 486, 487
Sears, D. O. 187, 188
Sedlmeier, P. 374
Segal, N. L. 525
Segall, M. H. 138, 206, 207, 210, 216, 222, 231, 239, 242, 487
Seibel, C. 152
Seidman, B. T. 165
Seiner, S. H. 534
Seligman, M. E. P. 430, 435, 441
Selye, H. 307, 315
Sempere, R. 398
Serpell, R. 214, 478, 484, 487
Serrano, C. V. 456
Seto, M. C. 157, 158, 165, 167, 168
Sezgin, N. 486
Shaffer, D. R. 527
Shanahan, M. 523
Shao, D. S. 287, 288
Shapiro, P. N. 87
Sharp, D. 478
Sharp, D. W. 210
Sharpe, S. 458
Shaver, K. 103
Shaver, P. R. 169
Shaw, A. 261
Shaw, D. 532
Shaw, D. S. 527
Shaw, J. M. 56
Shaw, J. S. 78
Shaw-Barnes, K. 191, 193–194, 196, 197, 198
Sheehan, P. W. 111, 118, 122, 123, 124, 125, 129
Sheets, V. 157
Shell, R. 524
Shen, Z. F. 283, 284

Shepherd, G. 56
Shepherd, R. 398
Sherif, C. W. 74, 79
Sherif, M. 74, 79, 188
Shields, I. W. 123
Shields, N. 152
Shiffrin, R. M. 323
Shoda, Y. 22
Shonkoff, J. P. 479
Shoyer, B. 441
Shue, K. L. 118, 129
Shweder, R. A. 140, 222, 235, 478, 482
Siegal, M. 533
Siegel, R. G. 56
Siegrist, J. 316, 319, 320, 321
Sigel, I. E. 479
Sigelman, C. K. 96
Signorini, M. G. 121, 126
Siimes, M. A. 398, 400
Silber, T. J. 456
Silva, P. A. 530, 531
Silver, W. S. 59
Silverman, W. K. 519
Simmons, R. G. 525
Simner, M. L. 525
Simon, B. 78, 82
Simons, R. F. 45
Simons, R. L. 517
Simonson, E. 324
Simpson, A. E. 533
Simpson, J. A. 161
Sinclair, H. 209
Singelis, T. M. 141
Singh, P. 336
Sinha, D. 336
Sinha, J. B. P. 333, 335, 337, 342, 344, 347
Sinha, M. 336
Sinkkonen, J. 398, 400
Sintonen, H. 398, 400
Sippola, L. K. 527
Sirkin, M. 171
Sizoo, E. 216
Skinner, B. F. 379
Slabach, E. H. 37
Slaby, R. B. 526, 531

Slaughter, D. T. 479, 486
Smart, L. 532
Smetana, J. G. 533
Smith, D. L. 10
Smith, M. L. 372, 376, 377, 417
Smith, A. C. 251
Smith, C. 76, 81
Smith, D. H. 335
Smith, E. E. 189
Smith, K. D. 526
Smith, M. B. 187
Smith, P. B. 138, 140, 141, 144, 147
Smith, P. K. 169, 515
Smith, R. E. 12
Smuts, B. 157, 159
Snow, C. E. 486
Soares, R. 336
Sobel, M. E. 354
Sobolev, E. S. 316
Soffin, S. 83
Solano, N. 254
Solís, J. 457
Solomon, R. L. 430
Sontag, S. 458
Sörbom, D. 354, 356
Sorin, M. 254
Southerland, I. 397
Southwick, L. 410, 417
Soysal, Y. N. 261
Spaccarelli, S. 171
Spanos, N. P. 118, 119, 127, 128
Spearman, C. 7
Spence, D. P. 123
Spence, J. T. 171
Spiegel, D. 125
Spiegel, H. 120
Spielberger, C. D. 308, 309, 310, 324, 328
Spinath, F. M. 39, 45
Spinhoven, P. 118, 120
Spitzer, W. O. 398
Spivak, L. I. 316–317, 327
Sroufe, L. A. 531
Srull, T. K. 192
Stall, R. 409
Stanley, S. M. 152
Stanton, W. R. 530

State Statistical Bureau 272, 277, 282
Statham, D. 122
Stattin, H. 519
Stecker, H. L. 171, 172
Steele, C. M. 407, 408, 409, 410, 411, 412, 417
Steinberg, L. 162, 168, 173, 515, 535
Steller, M. 123
Stephan, C. W. 83, 86, 87
Stephan, W. G. 83, 86, 87
Stermac, L. E. 158
Stern, E. 13
Stern, W. 2, 4, 6–7, 8, 496
Sternberg, R. 323
Sternberg, R. J. 9, 10, 11, 485, 488
Sternberg, S. 322, 323
Stevenson, H. W. 283
Stevenson, J. E. 527
Stevenson-Hinde, J. 533
Stewart, A. L. 392, 397, 400
Stewart, M. 518
Steyer, R. 354
Stigler, J. W. 283
Stiglmayer, A. 157
Storaasli, R. D. 152
Stouthamer-Loeber, M. 529
Strack, F. 170
Stratenworth, I. 78
Straus, M. A. 152
Strauss, B. 131
Strelau, J. 33, 35, 36, 37, 38, 39, 40, 41, 45, 46, 47
Strelkov, Yu K. 323, 324
Strodtbeck, F. L. 231
Struch, N. 75, 79
Sturgis, L. M. 121, 125
Stürzebecher, G. 13
Suárez, Ojeda 456
Sudakov, K. V. 312, 316
Suengas, A. G. 123
Sugarman, D. B. 152
Sullivan, M. A. 482
Suls, J. 13
Sumner, W. 73, 75
Sun, T. 137, 139, 140, 141, 143, 144, 145, 147, 148
Sun, Y. 517

Sunar, D. 146, 147, 488
Super, C. M. 206, 211, 212, 214, 479, 484
Susman, A. 523
Sutcliffe, J. P. 127
Sutton, S. 444
Switzer, G. E. 525
Symons, D. 157
Szapocznik, J. 479

Tajfel, H. 77, 81, 82, 250, 256
Tanaka, J. 152, 158, 161, 168, 169, 171, 173, 174, 175, 176
Tang, C. S. 168
Tang, M.-L. 368
Tangney, J. P. 521
Tapé, G. 210
Tasdemir, O. 441
Taylor, D. M. 81, 138, 259
Taylor, L. A. 78
Taylor, S. P. 101
Teasdale, G. R. 485
Teasdale, J. D. 445
Teasdale, J. I. 485
Tellegen, A. 118, 127
Templer, G. 13
Tennen, H. 13
Teplov, B. 34, 35, 36
TerKuile, M. M. 118, 120
Terry, R. 527
Teti, D. M. 534
Teti, L. O. 520, 532
Thelen, E. 497, 504
Theorell, T. 307, 308, 310, 311, 312, 313, 327
Thiel, W. 39, 45
Thiessen, D. 157, 167
Thivierge, J. 47
Thomas, A. 34, 35, 36, 37, 38, 46, 47
Thompson, L. A. 10
Thompson, R. A. 520
Thompson, W. W. 517
Thomson, R. 458
Thorndike, R. M. 146
Thornhill, N. W. 158, 159
Thornhill, R. 158, 159
Thurstone, L. L. 7

Thurstone, T. G. 7
Ting-Toomey, S. 141
Tobares, N. 398
Tobin, D. L. 55
Tolman, E. C. 389
Tomada, G. 529
Tomarken, A. J. 444, 449
Tooby, J. 153, 154, 170, 243
Torres, A. 79
Townsend, J. 463
Townsley, R. 437
Trapnell, P. D. 160
Tremblay, P. F. 354
Tremblay, R. E. 515, 528
Triandis, H. 78, 252
Triandis, H. C. 138, 141, 142, 147,
    239, 482
Triandis, H. D. 66
Tripathi, R. C. 241, 336
Trivers, R. L. 162, 167, 525
Troadec, B. 210
Trompenaars, F. 140, 144, 147
Troughton, E. 518
Troutman, B. R. 61
Trumbull, R. 307, 310, 315, 321
Tsai, H. Y. 261
Tshingeji, M. 216
Tukey, J. W. 381
Tulviste, P. 239
Turián, R. 466
Turner, J. 77, 80
Turner, J. C. 75, 79, 80, 81, 82
Turner, S. 437
Turovsky, J. 438
Tyler, R. B. 76, 83

Uhlmann, R. E. 397
Uhrich, J. 439
Ullman, J. 354
Ullwer, U. 45
Umansky, R. 10
Upshaw, H. S. 189
Urbina, S. 9, 10, 11
Usher, B. A. 527, 529

Vache, K. 447
Vágó, P. 119

Valecha, G. 336
Vallone, R. P. 189
Valsiner, J. 222, 236, 478, 479
van der Vijver, F. J. R. 221, 232, 233,
    236, 238, 239, 240
van Geert, P. 503
Van Harrison, R. 310, 311, 318
van Kammen, W. 529
Van Knippenberg, A. 79, 81
Van Lancker, D. 241
van Lieshout, C. F. M. 514
Van Oers, H. 81
Van Oudenhoven, J. P. 86
Vandell, D. L. 515
Vanderlinden, J. 118, 120
Varga, K. 119
Vargas, E. 464
Vargas Trujillo, E. 462
Vasconcelos, J. 255
Vass, J. S. 171
Vazquez, C. 445, 447
Velichkovsky, B. M. 322, 323
Venables, P. H. 529
Venditti, C. P. 10
Venkataraman, R. 336
Verhelst, T. 216
Verney, S. 447
Vernon, P. A. 10
Vernon, R. 463
Viek, P. 435
Vignetti, S. 10
Viguera, S. 398
Villareal, M. J. 78
Virmani, B. R. 336
Vitaro, F. 515, 528
Vivian, J. 85, 86
Volpato, C. 79
von Eye, A. 533
Vondra, J. I. 527
Vouilloz, M.-F. 215
Vuchetich, G. G. 322, 323
Vuchinich, R. A. 536
Vuchinich, S. 536
Vygotsky, L. S. 235, 478

Wachs, T. D. 37
Wagner, A. R. 430

Wagner, E. 524, 532
Wakenhut, R. 257
Walder, L. O. 527, 528
Walker, I. 83
Walker, R. 59
Wallace, B. 121
Waller, N. G. 169
Walschburger, P. 45
Wan, C. W. 278
Wang, X. D. 283
Wang, C. 525
Ward, C. 261
Ward, T. 165
Ware, J. E. 397, 401
Ware, W. B. 56
Wargo, J. B. 515
Warr, P. 309, 310, 312, 313, 318
Wasserstein, S. 519
Wassmann, J. 216, 217
Wasson, J. 398
Watkins, D. 146, 147
Watkins, J. G. 123, 125
Watkins, P. 447
Watson, J. B. 430, 432
Watson, M. W. 526
Watson, S. 146, 147
Watson, W. S. 189, 191, 195
Watts, F. 431, 444, 446, 447
Weber, M. 335, 339
Weber, T. A. 121
Weekes, J. R. 122, 123
Weeks, D. G. 356
Wegener, D. T. 425
Weiner, B. 93, 94, 95, 96, 98, 100,
    103, 104, 107
Weiser, P. C. 324
Weiss, B. 526
Weiss, H. 479
Weiss, J. M. 440, 441
Wells, G. L. 124
Welsh, J. D. 524, 527, 529
Welti, C. 457
Wen, Q. F. 146, 147
Wentzel, K. R. 523
Wenzl, C. 398
West, S. G. 363, 364
Wethrell, M. S. 80

Wheeler, K. G. 56
Wheeler, L. 146, 416
White, B. J. 79
White, G. M. 478
White, J. 56
White, R. W. 187
Whitehouse, W. G. 121, 122
Whiting, B. B. 139, 211, 213, 477, 479
Whiting, J. W. 477
Whiting, J. W. M. 211, 213
Wickless, C. 119
Widiger, T. 6, 9
Wientjes, C. J. E. 310, 320, 325
Wierson, M. 535
Wierwille, W. W. 323, 325
Wierzbicka, A. 141
Wiggins, J. S. 160, 165
Wiklund, I. 390, 396
Wilde, O. 11
Wilder, D. A. 87
Wilkin, D. 401, 403
Willemsen, M. E. 241
Willett, J. A. 153
Williams, E. 102
Williams, J. 397, 401, 441
Williams, J. J. 398
Williams, J. L. 439
Williams, J. M. 445
Williams, M. 431, 444, 446, 447, 529
Williamson, D. A. 447
Willis, E. E. 165
Wilson, A. 534
Wilson, E. O. 525
Wilson, L. 123
Wilson, M. 155, 156
Wilson, M. N. 479
Wilson, P. H. 61
Wilson, S. C. 127
Windelband, W. 395
Windle, M. 39, 40, 47, 536
Winer 418
Wingield, J. C. 160
Winnubst, J. A. M. 325, 327
Wisdom, C. 398
Wisniewksi, N. 152
Wispé, L. 104, 159
Wittenbrink, B. 83

Wober, M. 241
Wolff, Ch. J. de, 303
Wolfson, A. 535
Wolkenstein, B. 433
Wolman, B. B. 9
Wondimu, H. 146, 147
Wong-Rieger, D. 260
Wood, R. 56, 58
Wood, W. L. 199
Wood-Dauphinee, S. L. 398
Woodhead, M. 479
Woody, E. 515
Worell, L. 166
World Bank 457
World Health Organization 391, 393,
    395, 398, 408
Wozniak, P. 515
Wrangham, R. 156, 157
Wright, S. 357, 360
Wright, S. C. 81, 138
Wright, W. P. 255
Wu, E. J. C. 354
Wu, Z. Q. 283, 284
Wynne, L. C. 430

Xu, M. D. 283, 284

Yapko, M. D. 125
Yates, E. 171
Yates, W. 518
Yonas, A. 514
Yoon, G. 66
Young, R. K. 157
Young, S. 525
Yuan, K.-H. 364, 365, 366, 367, 368

Yuille, J. C. 123
Yunes, J. 456
Yung, Y. F. 364

Zahn-Waxler, C. 166, 513, 514, 517,
    521, 523, 524, 525, 526, 527, 528,
    529, 531, 532, 534
Zamansky, H. S. 131
Zamarrón, M. D. 391, 395, 398, 400,
    402
Zanna, M. P. 83, 407, 409, 413, 418,
    420, 426
Zarakovsky, G. M. 310, 312, 313, 321,
    324, 325
Zawadzki, B. 38, 39, 40, 41, 45
Zeichner, A. 409
Zeiss, A. M. 60
Zhang, M. L. 283
Zhang, H. 271
Zhang, J. X. 144
Zhang, Q. 529
Zhang, S. Y. 283, 284
Zhang, X. 281
Zhang, Y. 282
Zhang, Z. G. 284
Zigler, E. 479
Zinbarg, R. 429, 432, 433, 434, 435,
    436, 437, 438, 439, 440, 441, 443,
    449
Zinchenko, V. P. 310, 312, 313, 321,
    322, 323, 324, 325
Zoller, D. 522
Zucker, G. S. 107
Zuckerman, M. 35, 36, 39, 42, 45,
    46

Subject Index

Ability vs. effort 94–95, 97–99
Absolutism 222
Academic achievement 63–65
Acculturation 259–262
Achievement evaluation 94–95
Adolescents
  antisocial behavior 168–169, 173, 517
  effect of marital discord 535–536
  emotional development 522–523
  psychopathology 530, 533
  sexual aggression 168–169, 173
Aggression *see also* Sexual aggression
  against women 152
  in children 102, 517, 526–529
  evolutionary model 155–156
  intergroup 79–80
  retaliation 101–102
AIDS 408, 457–458, 466–467
Alcohol and behavior 407–427
  alcohol myopia 409–411, 422–424
  condom use 418–422
  correlation studies 409
  drinking and driving 411–418, 426
  expectancy effects 414–415,
    424–425
  inhibitory cues 422–424, 425–426
  sexual behavior 409, 418–422

Alcohol myopia 409–411, 422–424
Altruism 525
Ambulatory assessment of personality
  13–20
Amnesia, posthypnotic 121
Analgesia 123
Anthropology 211, 216
Antisocial behavior 168–169, 173, 517,
  526–529
Anxiety
  alcohol 410–411
  cognitive biases 444–448
  conditioning models 431–443
  efficacy beliefs 59–60
  gender differences 519
  intergroup 86–87
  post-traumatic stress disorder
    439–443
  social phobia 437–439
  specific phobias 432–436
Applied research 297, 299
Attentional bias 444–445
Attitudes
  attention 187–188
  bipolar vs. unipolar 194–195
  cogeniality effects 186–187,
    189–190, 192, 193–195

exposure to information 186,
187–188
information processing 186–187,
194, 195–196, 198–199
judgment 188–189
memory 189–199
perception 186, 188–189
selectivity 186–190
strength of 198
Attributions 58–59, 97–99
Autonomous–Relational Orientation 78

Behavior, cognitive/physiological model
499–500
Behavior genetics 518
Behavioral data recording 14–15

Causal attributions 58–59, 97–99
Causal modeling 354–368
EQS 354, 355–362, 363
LISREL 354
Children
academic achievement 63–65
aggression in 102, 517, 526–529
antisocial behavior 168–169, 173,
517, 526–529
of depressed parents 523, 534–535
depression in 520, 527
development niche 206, 210–216
education 280–284, 485–486, 487
emotional development 520–523,
531–532
empathy development 523, 524–525
learning through observation
485–486
marital discord 535–536
obedience in 483–485
only children 278–279
peer relations 515, 519–520
physical punishment 517, 526–527
prosocial development 523–526,
531–532
psychopathology in 530–536
sexual aggression in 168–169, 173
social development 483–486,
500–502, 514–515, 519–520,
532–533

social identity 251
socioeconomic status 63–65, 517
stereotyping by 531
temperament 37, 43, 46, 519
China 271–289
aging population 279
brain drain 282
counterculling effect 278
crime 287–289
cultural revolution 288, 289
culture development 272–276
economic growth 272
education 280–284
family values 275
floating migrant population 272, 288
joy education 284
mental health 284–287
modernization 273–275, 281–282
morality 283–284
one-child family policy 276–280
only children 277, 278–279
Opium war 272
population growth 272, 276–277
poverty 272, 274
psychology 282–283, 284–286
psychotherapy 286–287
Qigong 286
transient population 277–278
Cognition and emotion 431, 444–448
Cognitive biases 444–448
Cognitive models of stress 315–316
Cognitive motivators 58–59
Cognitive processes
culture 209–210, 478
efficacy beliefs 54–55, 57–58
Coherence analysis 21–25
Collective efficacy 65–69
Collectivism vs. individualism 65–67,
78–79, 214
Conditioning models of anxiety 431–443
Condom use
alcohol consumption 418–422
Latin America 458
Confluence model of sexual aggression
159–164, 173–178
Congeniality effects 186–187,
189–190, 192, 193–195

Consciousness of national affiliation 257–258
Constructivism 221
Contact hypothesis 84–86
Contextualism 234–238, 432, 476–483, 487, 506, 517–518
Contrast analysis 380
Control 52
Correlation studies 238–241, 409
Counternull value 376
Crime 287–289
Criterion-referencing 9
Cross-cultural psychology 137–148, 205–223, 482–483 *see also* Cross-cultural research methods
  ecological fallacy 140
  everyday cognition 216–221, 478
  "unpackaging" 139–140, 142
Cross-cultural research methods 229–243
  correlation studies 238–241
  cultural bias 232–234
  culture comparative studies 231–234
  psychological measures 141–142
  qualitative research 236–238
Cross-sectional studies 6–8
Cultural bias 232–234
Culture *see also* Cross-cultural psychology
  changing 259–265
  cognition 209–210, 478
  ecological fallacy 140
  "unpackaging" 139–140, 142

Data analysis *see also* Statistics
  meta-analysis 373, 376–382
  nonnormal data 355, 362–366
  structural equation modeling 354–368
Data sources 5–6
Depression
  in children 520, 527
  cognitive biases 444–448
  efficacy beliefs 60–61
  parental 523, 534–535
Developmental niche 206, 210–216
Developmental science 508–509

Differential psychology
  assessment methods 5–13, 21–25
  history of 2–5
Drinking and driving 411–418, 426

Ecological fallacy 140
Ecological models 206–210, 517–518
Economic status 63–65, 517
Education 280–284, 485–486, 487
Educational psychology 282–283
Effect size 373, 374, 375, 376
Efficacy beliefs 52–53
  benefits of 56–57
  cognitive processing 54–55, 57–58
  collective 65–69
  defining 53
  effects of 57–62
  emotions 54, 59–61
  motivation 58–59
  performance 54–56
  sources of 53–54
Effort vs. ability 94–95, 97–99
Emotions
  and cognition 431, 444–448
  basic vs. higher-order 520–521
  cross-cultural studies 234–235
  development of 520–523, 531–532
  efficacy beliefs 54, 59–61
  measuring 520
  prosocial development 524
  regulating 520
  sexual aggression 169–172
  social motivation 104–105
  understanding 521–522
Empathy development 523, 524–525
Empiricism 230
EQS 354, 355–362, 363
Ethics of hypnosis 125, 128
Everyday cognition 216–221, 478
Evolutionary models 153–155
  aggression 155–156
  sexual aggression 156–164, 172–178
Experimental methods
  coherence analysis 21–25
  correlation 238–241, 409
  criterion-referencing 9
  cross-cultural 229–243

cross-sectional 6–8
field assessment 13
laboratory-based 13
longitudinal 11
nature–nurture 10–11
pattern analysis 504
pilot studies 381–382
qualitative 236–238
questionnaires 12
self-monitoring 14
trans-occasion 12–13
Experimental results *see also* Data
    analysis
  defining 372–373
  replicating 374–376

False memories 122
Family relationships
  antisocial behavior 526
  emotional development 522–523
  marital discord 535–536
  psychopathology 534–536
  social development 515
  socioeconomics 63–65, 517
Fatigue–boredom syndrome 319
Field assessment of personality 13–20
File drawer problem 376–377
Forensic hypnosis 124–125, 129, 131

Gender differences
  antisocial behavior 528–529
  anxiety disorders 519
  effect of marital discord on children
    535–536
  emotions 522, 531–532, 533
  evolutionary theory 155
  mating strategies 167
  prosocial behavior 524, 531–532
  psychopathology 531–534
  self-esteem 533
  social development 532–533
Genetics
  behavior 518
  sexual aggression 169
  temperament 43–46
Group conflict 79–80

Group socialization theory 519–520
Groups *see* Intergroup behavior

Hallucinations 126
Helping 100–101
HIV 408, 457–458, 466–467
Holistic approach 496–499
Hostile masculinity 170–172
Human agency 52, 62, 65
Hypnosis
  amnesia 121
  analgesia 123
  brain mechanisms 126
  collaborative studies 118, 125–126
  defining 129–130
  ethics 125, 128
  false memories 122
  forensic 124–125, 129, 131
  hidden observer 123
  imagination 121, 127
  lying 131
  measuring 119–120
  memory 121–123
  recovered memories 122–123, 125
  research trends 112–117, 125–127,
    130–131
  susceptibility to 120–121, 127
  theories 117–119
  trance logic 123–124

Identity, defining 249 *see also* National
    identity
Imagination and hypnosis 121, 127
Indian work culture 333–348
  aram 335
  exploitation 343, 347
  family ethic 335–336
  health and safety 346
  industrial growth 335
  management styles 336, 339–340,
    341, 344–346
  private sector 338
  public sector 337–338, 339
  small organizations 342–347
  soft vs. synergetic 339–340
  work ethic 336

Individual differences research
   assessment methods 5–13, 21–25
   history of 2–5
Individualism vs. collectivism 65–67,
   78–79, 214
Inductive thinking 238
Infants *see also* Children
   antisocial behavior 527
   attachment 514
   of depressed parents 534
   emotions 520, 521
   temperament 43
Information processing 186–187, 194,
   195–196, 198–199
Ingroup bias 75–76, 77
Ingroup favoritism 74–75, 76–77, 81
Intelligence, cross-cultural 214–216
Intergroup behavior
   affect 82–83
   aggression 79–80
   anxiety 86–87
   bias 75–76, 77
   changing 84–87
   defining 74
   differentiation 74, 80
   discrimination 82
   distinctiveness 77
   favoritism 74–75, 76–77, 81
   outgroup derogation 74, 81–82
   prejudice 83–87
   realistic group conflict 79–80
   self-categorization theory 80
   status 80–81
   stereotyping 80
Invariance studies 238–241, 409

Job modernization 319–320, 325–327
Job stress *see* Occupational stress

Laboratory-based research 13, 377
Language and identity 258–259
Latin America
   abortion 456–457
   AIDS/HIV 457–458, 466–467
   contraceptive use 457
   safe-sex 458
   sex education 459–466

   unplanned pregnancies 456, 457
   vasectomy 467
LISREL 354
Longitudinal research 11

Management styles 341
Marital discord 535–536
Mastery experiences 53–54
Mate deprivation model 158
Mating strategies 166–168
Memories
   false 122
   recovered 122–123, 125
   selective 189–190
Memory
   attitudes 189–199
   hypnosis 121–123
   stress 322, 323
Memory bias 445–448
Mental health 311–313, 316–317,
   530–536
Meta-analysis
   attitude and memory research 191–195
   benefits of 378–382
   criticisms of 376–378
   history of 373
Methodology
   coherence analysis 21–25
   correlation 238–241, 409
   criterion-referencing 9
   cross-cultural 229–243
   cross-sectional 6–8
   field assessment 13
   laboratory-based 13
   longitudinal 11
   nature–nurture 10–11
   pattern analysis 504
   pilot studies 381–382
   qualitative 236–238
   questionnaires 12
   self-monitoring 14
   trans-occasion 12–13
Mood and efficacy judgments 54
Motivation and cognition 58–59
   see also Social motivation
Multitrait-multimethod (MTMM)
   models 6

Naive empiricism 230
National identity
  acculturation 259–262
  changing 259–264
  language 258–259
  self-stereotypes 252–256, 266
  social identity 251, 256–259, 267
  supranationalism 264–265, 267
  theories 248–251
Nationalism 248
Nations, defining 249
Nature–nurture research 10–11
Neurophysiology of temperament
  45–46
Neurosis 430
Number systems 217

Occupational stress 307–328
  fatigue–boredom syndrome 319
  job modernization 319–320, 325–327
  mental health 311–313, 316–317
  output 311
  person-environment-fit models
    310–314, 327
  physical health 311
  state-regulation models 310, 321–327
  stress outcomes 310–311
  transactional models 310, 314–320,
    327
Organizational psychology 302–305
Orientation systems 217–220
Outcome expectations 53
Outgroup derogation 74, 81–82

p values 375, 378, 379
Parent–child relationships
  antisocial behavior 526
  emotional development 522–523,
    533
  obedience expectations 483–485
  prosocial behavior 523
  social development 63, 211,
    483–485, 488, 515, 517, 519,
    532–533
Parental depression 523, 534–535
Pattern analysis 504–506
Peer relations 515, 519–520

Personal distress 524–525
Personality
  culture 251–252, 266
  sexual aggression 164–165
Personality research
  coherence patterns 21–25
  criterion-referencing 9
  cross-sectional 7–8
  data sources 6
  field assessments 13–20
  longitudinal 11
  nature–nurture 10–11
  trans-occasion 12–13
Phobias
  social 437–439
  specific 432–436
Physical punishment 517, 526–527
Physical state and efficacy judgments
  54
Piaget's theory 207–209
Pilot studies 381–382
Positivism 221
Post-traumatic stress disorder 439–443
Prejudice 83–87
Prosocial development 523–526,
  531–532
Pseudomemories 122
Psychological research see also
    Methodology
  applied 297, 299
  diagnosis 297, 300–301
  person approach 504–507
  pilot studies 381–382
  professional use 297, 301–302
  pure 297–298
  strategic 297, 298
  variable approach 503
Psychopathology 311–313, 316–317,
  530–536
Psychotherapy 286–287
Pure research 297–298

Qualitative research 236–238
Quality of life 387–404
  defining 390–393, 395
  measuring 396–403
  subjective vs. objective 393–394

Questionnaires
  problems with 12
  temperament assessment 37–40

Rape 152, 156–157, 165 *see also*
    Sexual aggression
Realistic group conflict 79–80
Recovered memories 122–123, 125
Rejection 172
Relativism 222
Research, types of *see also*
    Methodology
  applied 297, 299
  diagnosis 297, 300–301
  person approach 504–507
  pilot studies 381–382
  professional use 297, 301–302
  pure 297–298
  strategic 297, 298
  variable approach 503
Research results *see also* Data analysis
  defining 372–373
  replicating 374–376
Responsibility 103–105

Selective attention 187–188
Selective exposure 186, 187–188
Selective judgment 188–189
Selective memory 189–190
Selective perception 186, 188–189
Selectivity and attitudes 186–190
Self-categorization theory 80
Self-consciousness 126
Self-efficacy *see* Efficacy beliefs
Self-esteem 533
Self-image 252–256, 266
Self-labeling 256–257
Self-monitoring 14
Self-stereotypes 80, 252–256, 266
Sex differences
  antisocial behavior 528–529
  anxiety disorders 519
  effect of marital discord on children
    535–536
  emotions 522, 531–532, 533
  evolutionary theory 155
  mating strategies 167

prosocial behavior 524, 531–532
psychopathology 531–534
self-esteem 533
social development 532–533
Sex education in Latin America
    459–466
Sexual aggression
  aggressor's characteristics 164–172
  childhood experiences 168–169, 173
  confluence model 159–164, 173–178
  emotions 169–172
  evolutionary model 156–164,
    172–178
  genetics 169
  hostile masculinity 170–172
  mate deprivation model 158
  mating strategies 166–168
  personality 164–165
  rape 152, 156–157, 165
  rejection 172
  socialization 166, 168–169
  theories of 152–153, 164–178
Sexual behavior and alcohol 409,
    418–422
Sexual coercion 156–165, 166–168,
    169–171
Significance tests 373
Social development
  gender differences 532–533
  holistic approach 500–502
  learning through observation
    485–486
  obedience expectations 483–485
  parents 63, 211, 483–485, 488, 515,
    517, 519, 532–533
  peers 515, 519–520
  theories 516–520
Social identity theory
  children 251
  ingroup favoritism 77–78
  national identity 256–259, 267
Social modeling 54
Social motivation
  achievement 94–95
  effort vs. ability 94–95, 97–99
  emotions 104–105
  helping 100–101

responsibility 103–105
retaliation 101–102
stigmas 95–97
theory of 103, 105–107
Social persuasion 54
Social phobia 437–439
Socioeconomic status 63–65, 517
Spatial orientation 217–220
Statistics *see also* Data analysis
  contrast analysis 380
  counternull value 376
  effect size 373, 374, 375, 376
  nonnormal data 355, 362–366
  p values 375, 378, 379
  significance tests 373
  statistical power 375–376
Status 80–81
Stereotyping
  gender-based 531
  intergroup 80
  national identity 250
  self-stereotyping 80, 252–256, 266
Stigmas 95–97
Strategic research 297, 298
Stress *see also* Occupational stress
  cognitive models 315–316
  efficacy beliefs 59–60
  memory 322, 333
  temperament 47
Structural equation modeling 354–368
  EQS 354, 355–362, 363
  LISREL 354
Supranationalism 264–265, 267

Temperament
  assessing 36–40
  defining 34

functional significance 46–47
genetics 43–46
inventories 37–40
neurophysiology 45–46
stress 47
theories 34–36, 519
traits 34, 41–43
Traits
  coherence analysis 25
  temperament 34, 41–43
Trance logic 123–124
Trans-occasion research 12–13
Triadic reciprocal causation 62

Violence *see* Aggression; Sexual
  aggression
Visual illusions, cross-cultural studies
  231
Vitamin model 312–313

Women, aggression towards 152
  see also Sexual aggression
Work culture in India 333–348
  aram 335
  exploitation 343, 347
  family ethic 335–336
  health and safety 346
  industrial growth 335
  management styles 336, 339–340,
    341, 344–346
  private sector 338
  public sector 337–338, 339
  small organizations 342–347
  soft vs. synergetic 339–340
  work ethic 336
Work psychology 302–305
Work stress *see* Occupational stress